TIMELESS CARAVAN
The Story of a Spanish-American Family

TIMELESS CARAVAN

The Story of a Spanish-American Family

Thomas E. Chávez

SUNSTONE
PRESS

SANTA FE

Sunstone books may be purchased for educational, business, or sales promotional use.
For information please write: Special Markets Department, Sunstone Press,
P.O. Box 2321, Santa Fe, New Mexico 87504-2321.

Book and cover design › R. Ahl
Printed on acid-free paper
∞

Library of Congress Cataloging-in-Publication Data

Names: Chavez, Thomas E., author.
Title: Timeless caravan : the story of a Spanish-American family / by
    Thomas E. Chávez.
Description: Santa Fe : Sunstone Press, [2019] | Includes bibliographical
    references.
Identifiers: LCCN 2018054047| ISBN 9781632932518 (softcover : alk. paper) |
    ISBN 9781632932518 (softcover : alk. paper)
Subjects: LCSH: Albuquerque (N.M.)--Biography. | New Mexico--Discovery and
    exploration. | Spanish Americans--Biography. | Ambassadors--United
    States--Biography. | Spain--Biography. | America--Discovery and
    exploration--Spanish. | Romero, Edward L., 1934- | Romero family.
Classification: LCC F795 . C516 2018 | DDC 929.20973--dc23
LC record available at https://lccn.loc.gov/2018054047

WWW.SUNSTONEPRESS.COM
SUNSTONE PRESS / POST OFFICE BOX 2321 / SANTA FE, NM 87504-2321 /USA
(505) 988-4418 / ORDERS ONLY (800) 243-5644 / FAX (505) 988-1025

DEDICATED
to the Memory of
Cayetana (Tanna) García y Gallegos de Romero
(March 7, 1936–January 19, 2013)
Friend, wife and mother who lived her life joyously, positively, and full of meaning
with sensitivity, graciousness and dignity.

Contents

[En] el primer milenio del cristianismo tres conocidas rutas eran consideradas sagradas y que daban una serie de bendiciones e indulgencias a quien hiciese alguna de ellas. La primera ruta conducía hasta la sepultura de San Pedro en Roma: sus caminantes tenían por símbolo una cruz y eran llamados romeros.

In the first millennium of Christianity three known routes were considered sacred that gave various blessings and indulgences to whoever traveled them. The first route went to the tomb of Saint Peter in Rome: its travelers had a small cross as a symbol and were called romeros.

—Paulo Coelho, *The Pilgrim*

Ed Romero's family legacy began in Spain four centuries ago. His ancestor, Bartolomé Romero, left Spain for Mexico, once called Nueva España, and then traveled north to join the first settlement in New Mexico. He arrived in 1598 (before Jamestown or the Mayflower) and made a home for his family in Northern New Mexico in a place named San Juan de los Caballeros across the river from today's San Juan Pueblo. Another ancestor, Baltazar Romero, was one of the founders of Albuquerque. (A street bears the name Romero in "Old Town.") These two men and their families represent the many men and women who forged a living with bravery, confidence, survival, and migration through four centuries. In the process they created a legacy, a heritage that continues today as people continue to migrate and seek improved lives.

This book begins and ends with Ambassador Ed Romero, a thirteenth generation New Mexican, a lineage shared by the book's author, a Chávez, who is also a thirteenth generation New Mexican.

Ed has been a New Mexico icon and one of the leading Americans of Hispanic descent in the last century. While he is proudest of his unique Hispanic heritage, his accomplishments as a political, diplomatic, business and philanthropic leader in the United States only enhance his legacy.

He was instrumental in the establishment of the National Hispanic Cultural Center in Albuquerque, as well as the University of New Mexico's King Felipe VI Endowment that funds a full-time professor and four full scholarships for students from Spain. As a businessman in New Mexico, Romero was one of the pioneers of the solar energy industry through his founding of Solar America. He was also a founder of the Hispano Chamber of Commerce.

Having traveled the diplomatic and political circles myself, I can attest to the fact that many in Spain and the United States have said that Romero has been the best American Ambassador to Spain and Andorra that we have ever had. Appointed by his friend President Bill Clinton, Romero deftly navigated the difficult Spanish political terrain with diplomatic skill and grace. He established solid relationships with the King and Prime Minister, and advanced key U.S. interests in the political, military, and trade arenas. The Spanish people, from billionaires to restaurant servers, loved the Romero touch and humility. But it was, perhaps, in the cultural and educational arenas where

Romero did so much to enhance Spanish and U.S.-Latino ties, especially with New Mexico.

In the political world, very few Governors, U.S. Senators, Congressmen or even County Commissioners in New Mexico have not benefited from Ed Romero's support. And while he has been influential in New Mexico politics, he never turned his back on those modest New Mexicans who would come to him for advice and assistance.

On the national level, many Presidential candidates—from Jimmy Carter to Al Gore, Barack Obama to Hillary Clinton—has sought Romero's help with the national Hispanic community due to his prowess as a fundraiser. Despite being a strong Democrat, Romero is well known as a bipartisan politician with strong ties to prominent Republicans across the nation and in New Mexico. Romero has always been an American first and a partisan Democrat second. Nationally, he was one of the founding members of Hispanic American Democrats (HAD).

Without question, Romero is proudest of his family. His inspiration and great love was Cayetana, the Romero matriarch and his spouse for more than fifty years who passed away on January 19, 2013. At the time of the book's publication, Romero has four children, twelve grandchildren, and one great grandson, Lucas, who is a sixteenth generation Romero. Like many New Mexican families, the Romero name has endured for all these centuries.

Romero was granted his own coat of arms by Spain's King Juan Carlos and its Minister of Justice. A monument was built in Albuquerque on the Camino Real Route, which honors the Romeros who traveled that route. Romero's coat of arms, which reads "Viaje de ida y Vuelta," is displayed on that monument, symbolizing the Romero legacy from Spain to New Mexico and back to Spain again. His ancestor Bartolomé left Spain in the sixteenth century and Ed returned in the twenty-first century, over four hundred years later. In Spain, there is a park and a street named after Ed Romero.

A remarkable family history is chronicled in this book, a journey of appreciation for the Hispanic culture and legacy of a great family and its most famous prodigy, Ambassador Edward Romero.

ACKNOWLEDGMENTS

Any book is a product of many people. The creation of a book is a history in and of itself. Along the way friendships come to the fore and new ones are made. This particular book originated in a lunch meeting that I had with Ed Romero. Together we came up with the idea of creating a book in which we could make a contribution, a statement about the heritage of New Mexico in particular and the United States in general.

Obviously, then, I must thank Ed Romero for his patience, time, and support. I can only proclaim my profound respect and admiration for him. I love him like family, which, of course, he is.

Luther Wilson, retired director of many university presses read early drafts, made constructive criticisms, and always encouraged me to continue. Nasario Garcia, a good friend and colleague as well as an author of over twenty books, did me the great favor of a very critical reading. Every one of his corrections and suggestions were incorporated.

Amaris Feland Ketchum, an associate professor in the Honors College of the University of New Mexico and faculty advisor of the student's *Scribendi Magazine* gave up a lot of her valuable time to give the manuscript a critical reading from her literary point-of-view. We met on more than one occasion to resolve questions.

Albert Gallegos, a superb genealogist whose knowledge and help in formulating the genealogical charts was indispensable. His own work on the Romero Family genealogy is published under a separate title and listed in the bibliography.

LeRoy N. Sanchez, has to be recognized for the use of his wonderful photographs of Ed during and after his diplomatic career and for reproducing all the images from the Edward and Cayetana Romero Collection. He has perfected his art form.

James Clois Smith, Jr., the President of Sunstone Press in Santa Fe, New Mexico gets special gratitude for he, without hesitation, jumped at the opportunity to publish this book.

To my historian wife, Celia López-Chávez, who helped in all facets of the creation of this book I cannot express enough my gratitude. She listened to my ideas and complaints as well as joy and frustrations with complete reserve. Her competence with my computer saved the manuscript and me many times. Truly, this book would not have happened were it not for her.

How to describe the value of Cayetana García Romero, Ed's biggest fan and lifelong love? Words do not do her justice. She had the foresight to create and organize an archive of Ed Romero's life. She also made sure to spend some time with me and introduce me to her archive.

Like all of my publications, this book would not be possible were it not for the support of family, friends, other historians and teachers dating back into memory. Here I would like to single out two such teachers (and coaches), John Kabealo and Richard Goto.

Writing and publishing has become somewhat expensive and this book was no exception. Special appreciation and thanks go to all the following people who helped fund the book you are holding:

Jim Long and the New Mexico Cultural Foundation
Governor Bill Richardson
Dave and Eileen Hillson
Kevin and Leonor Daniels
Beverly Chávez
Ed Lujan
Ruth Sneddon
Carmen Martínez
and
Rob and Patricia Kurz

The story is real and all of these people have verified that truth.

Part I
The Return: Ambassador Romero

A PENSIVE MOMENT
Late June–Early July, 1998, South of Madrid, Spain

The Cadillac purred along as the embassy's chauffeur steered south. Madrid, already a memory, had faded in the distance. Seated in the back seat with his adult son, the newly appointed United States Ambassador had a premonition. Something nostalgic at least, and life changing at most, was about to happen. He felt bad that his wife could not be with him.

How silent the sedan moved at 120 kilometers per hour. Silent, yet with the car's constant hum, the smoothness. "I've been here before," he thought. The passing landscape of well-manicured rolling hills added to the idyllic feeling.

Ed Romero, from Albuquerque, New Mexico, recently appointed to his post in Spain was "coming home," or so he thought to himself. He had been in the country a few days when he decided to take this trip. He watched more landscape bent to the will of human hands. Villages dotted the countryside like islands separated by an interlock of slanting fields and orchards. The unswerving back of the chauffeur's head was an inconsequential companion. No words, only silence, scenery, and his own thoughts. Two more black sedans followed the Cadillac, one for security and the other transporting his niece, her husband, and grandson.

"Here I am," he thought, "the son of a Spanish-American railroad worker who was born and grew up in the rural San Luis Valley in southern Colorado." Work, the lore of New Mexico, and the love of a woman conspired to send him on a career path that culminated with this drive. Even now he had trouble believing it. He had started as a salesman, then became a successful businessman, and apparently had become an even more successful behind-the-scenes politician, and, now, a diplomat. "Here I am in Spain, my ancestral country, waiting to be officially accepted by the King!"

He thought back to his first trip to Spain. President Jimmy Carter had appointed him to a delegation representing the United States at a Helsinki Conference in Madrid. He was flown on a government plane from Washington, DC while his wife Cayetana had to fly on a commercial flight. As the plane landed, Ed looked out the window at Madrid's hills. A wave of emotion and goose bumps came over him. He had a sensation that he had been here before.

The next morning he went to the airport to pick up Cayetana. As the taxi took them to the hotel Cayetana turned to her husband and said, "Ed, I just had the oddest experience, like I have been here before."

Ed and Cayetana had an instant appreciation of Spain. Almost every year after that initial trip they returned. Now, Ed could not help but remember that first feeling, and then a subsequent time when they went to tour the Royal Palace only to find it closed. The doorkeeper directed them to the main gate upon hearing that they heralded from the United States. He thought that they might be interested in seeing the ceremonial entrance into the plaza of the newly appointed U.S. Ambassador Clarence Todman as he entered the Palace to present his credentials to the King. Ed and Cayetana watched as the entourage in carriages, fully decked out horsemen, marching soldiers, and a full band that struck up the *Star Spangled Banner* escorted the ambassador to be. Cayetana grabbed Ed's arm, "Ed, one of these days that is going to be you."

Ed had replied, "You're crazy."

Now, years later, he could nod knowingly. Within a few days, Ed would be featured in the same procession. And Cayetana would watch with pride. He could not know before the event but when the band would strike up the *Star Spangled Banner*, his eyes would moisten and the chief of protocol seated next to him would turn to him and say, "I understand."

Edward L. Romero, a broad shouldered, rotund man of medium height who never looks disheveled although, presumably, he could be, has a happy disposition and this is reflected in his face, especially, his blue eyes that the *viejitos*, old ones of New Mexico would call "smiling eyes." He knew enough of his family's history to want to visit the village that his direct ancestor left to go to the New World at the end of the sixteenth century. And he knew that Bartolomé Romero was his name. He stared at the passing landscape. He felt at home.

Before presenting his credentials as the United States Ambassador to Spain Ed Romero visited the town that his direct ancestor had left to travel to the Indies and, eventually, to New Mexico. There in Corral de Amaguer he is standing in front of a posted copy of the newspaper announcing his appointment and arrival in Spain. Original in the Ed and Cayetana Romero Collection.

Ed could not believe his fate. He was not treated this well at home. He never had a chauffeur or a company car. The car's smoothness had a calming effect. The countryside seemed more open and the large new white metal windmills on a distant ridge caught Ed's attention. They reminded him of Cervantes' windmills, the giants of Quixote's twisted mind. But the old mills where nowhere to be seen. Ed knew that they had travelled into La Mancha, the land of Quixote. Now the driver, Cristóbal Carzola, medium-sized, a blue-eyed dapper man who reminded Cayetana of Paul Newman, pointed to indicate that they were approaching Corral de Almaguer. The village looked like any of the others that they had passed, a small village of houses gathered around the bell tower of the local church. Like its neighbors it was a mixture of old and new.

They arrived in mid-afternoon, which is *siesta* time so the place appeared empty. Ed instructed Cristóbal to take him to the center of town where he climbed out of the car and walked around the town's two plazas. Ed walked up to a public bulletin board outside the church and saw a posting of a copy of a newspaper article in which he was interviewed upon his arrival in Spain.

On the way out of town they stopped at a small tavern with the name of Las Patas. As his eyes slowly adjusted to the interior darkness, a room of empty tables save one came into view. Three men, one a priest, sat at a table in the room's far side. Ed sat down with his family to enjoy a cold drink and snacks as the elderly waiter and three men studied him. Surely the village did not get many strangers to stop by, nor did the place benefit from the abundant tourism the country enjoyed.

Something had caught their attention and one of the men pulled a newspaper clipping out of his coat pocket. Although Ed could not make out their hushed tones as they huddled over the clipping, he could see enough to know that their conversation had become more excited. After some hurried exchanges one of the men rose and rushed out of the tavern. He quickly returned with other people in tow. Before Ed realized it, he was the focus of all the attention. The men at the table had matched him with a photograph in *El Pais*, one of the country's national newspapers. He was not just a stranger. He was a newly appointed ambassador.

One of the men brought back to the bar was Antonio Macheño, the mayor of Corral de Almaguer, and he understood the importance of the occasion. He knew from the newspapers that the new ambassador had a historical connection to the town. The mayor, an ebullient man, seized the opportunity to order wine and cheese and do his best to welcome his important if unannounced guest. Soon introductions progressed into a full-fledged celebration. Ed felt welcomed but the mayor was not through.

ACCEPTANCE
June 1998, Madrid

When Ed first arrived in Spain at Madrid's Barajas airport on June 27, he was met by a large group of reporters who had been waiting for him in a large conference room. Ed stared out confident in what he was about to say, or read, for he had a prepared speech before him on a podium. He started with the proper acknowledgements and continued in Spanish that impressed his audience. He continued with the speech until he arrived to the part that he wanted to stress.

"The excellent relations between the United States and Spain originate with the founding of my nation when Spain aided the colonies, and they won their independence from Great Britain. Without Spanish aid in money, arms, and soldiers, the result of the war for independence could have been different."

"Also, few people know that in the territory that is today the United States the first European settlement occurred nine years before the first permanent English settlement in Jamestown, and twenty-two years before the pilgrims disembarked at Plymouth Rock. This first European settlement took place four hundred years ago in 1598 by valiant Spanish colonists in New Mexico, my state of origin, that in those times formed part of the far northern frontier of the Spanish colonies in the Americas. I am a descendent of one of those first Spaniards among whom my ancestors originated from Corral de Almaguer, located to the south of Madrid and east of Toledo."

The Ambassador never felt prouder and the reaction of the Spanish press pleased him even more. He had no doubt that he was a perfect fit for his position and that he and Spain would have a very good relationship. His subsequent trip to Corral de Almaguer reinforced his feeling.

His only concern was Cayetana, his wife of forty years. The long over-night flight and, probably, the excitement of the move had left her bedridden. They both wanted to enjoy these moments together and in good health but, so far, fate had not been kind. As much as Ed described to her his first visit to Corral de Almaguer, "and before I knew it the mayor, all the town's officials, people...Tanna...you would have been so happy to have seen it all! We had an improvised fiesta!" He could not help but regret that she was not there with him. She, a García and Gallegos as well as a descendent from old New Mexican families enjoyed history as much as him and, in fact, understood the history of the moment, for she made sure that all the press coverage of her and Ed was collected and saved. Both of them knew that they would return to Corral de Almaguer.

THE HISTORIAN
July and August 1998, Cuenca and Madrid

Not long after that chance meeting the mayor met another man who impressed him. This was a priest and historian named Pedro Izquierdo. Antonio Macheño quickly realized that the ambassador and the priest should meet. He mentioned his plan to the ambassador.

Father Pedro Izquierdo Gismero, a smallish stocky man in his late forties with receding, close-cropped gray hair. He loved nothing more than researching the villages and preserving the churches of his region of Spain. His light blue eyes stared out from behind his glasses. It always seemed he was reading old books and photocopied documents.

He had achieved some local fame, not as a priest although there could no doubt of his dedication in that realm, but as a historian and preservationist. He wrote books, appeared on local television and radio, and gave lectures. He deserved more than a little credit for the preservation of many of his region's local churches. People went to him for their historical questions.

And he was above reproach. Aside from the required sacrificial wine at mass, which he gave daily, he did not drink. Nor did he smoke. He spent his whole life in the region in which he was born. More than that, after his ordination he spent the rest of his life living with and caring for his parents in the only house that he ever knew. Now he lived with his elderly father, for his mother passed away ten years earlier.

He kept a study on the bottom floor of the family's two-story home. Anyone who saw his workspace would wonder how he could reconstruct history out of such an apparent disarray of books and piles of photocopies.

Father Izquierdo did not know Mayor Macheño on the day the new United States Ambassador unexpectedly showed up in Corral de Almaguer. Actually, Father Izquierdo lived in Cuenca, some forty kilometers away and rarely visited the town that drew Ed to it. But he did have something in common with the ambassador: a love for history. The mayor had to call him.

R-r-r-ring, r-r-ring.... The telephone startled Father Izquierdo from his thoughts. "Was it the chronicle commissioned by Alfonso X or the sixteenth century one about King Rodrigo? Where is it?" He couldn't be distracted. R-r-r-ring. "Okay, okay! I'm coming," he said to no one in particular.

R-r-r... he picked up the phone, "Yes! Yes. Speak to me."

The voice of his new friend Antonio responded. They had recently met by happenstance. Mayor Antonio Macheño, was a barrel chested, smallish man, with a squared head, blue eyes, and white hair. On the suggestion of the village priest and over glasses of local *vino tinto*, Antonio agreed that a celebration in honor of Ed's "return" to the town of his ancestors should be held in conjunction with "Our Lady of the "Muela," Mary of the Mill Stone. Upon a subsequent meeting with Father Izquierdo, Antonio sensed that the priest and ambassador would hit it off. "Father, something very interesting has happened. You have noticed that the United States has sent to Spain a new ambassador." And he proceeded to tell the priest-historian about Ed Romero.

Antonio's always-excited voice blasted through the earpiece, "You need to be warned."

"Dear God! What...?"

Antonio cut him off. "No, no. This is good. The new Ambassador, Señor Ed Romero, is going to contact you." He didn't wait for an answer. "Remember his name is Edward Romero and he claims that he is a descendent of a man who left Corral in the sixteenth century and is a founder of a place called New Mexico—where he is from...."

"Who is from New Mexico?"

"The Ambassador, Pedro. Pay attention. He is very interested in the history of his family and we have mentioned you as a person who can be of some help."

Father Izquierdo sat down to his customary position of resting his forehead in his left hand. "Me? How? Why?"

"Because you know the history of this entire region better than anyone. You can't deny it. I think his office will contact you. Be ready."

"How? What do you mean 'be ready'?"

"A figure of speech, Father. I mean do not be surprised. *Vale?*"

"*Vale.*"

"And don't be so cross when you pick up the tele."

A month later, Ed greeted guests to a reception at his residence in Madrid. *"Señor alcalde,* mayor! Here you are! Welcome!"

"Señor Ambassador this is an honor. I have never been invited to the embassy before."

"No, Antonio, the honor is mine. I hope that this will be the first of many visits."

"Thank you. Ambassador Romero, may I present to you Father Pedro Izquierdo." Ed and the diminutive priest shook hands both smiling at one another. They had talked briefly on the telephone when Ed invited him to the embassy. Antonio continued, "I think that you will find him of interest. He is the historian that I told you about."

"Father, Antonio has said good things about you."

"Thank you, Your Excellency. I am interested in your history. You have gone and returned!"

"Yes, in a sense, yes. We need to talk. I'm sorry we have not talked before now but, as you can imagine, this has been a busy time for me." Ed meant it. Even the duties of hosting an embassy reception kept them apart. In passing, Ed asked Antonio and Father Izquierdo to remain behind after the reception. They could not refuse. Enamored with the place and the man, they were ecstatic.

The meeting took place with all of them seated in a sumptuous but not pretentious receiving room. Ed further relaxed his guests by undoing his bow tie and asking them if they would like anything to drink. Antonio joined Ed in a glass of red wine, a good *Ribera del Duero*, while Father Izquierdo settled for a glass of water. Pedro, as Ed came to address the priest, impressed him as a good historian.

Antonio helped, for he explained that Pedro had devoted his life to research and the restoration of various churches around the city of Cuenca in the region by Corral de Almaguer. "He has access to church records. You know, baptisms, marriages, deaths, the Inquisition.... And what he doesn't know, he knows where to look to find out."

Pedro interrupted the praise. "Ambassador..."

Antonio, without pause continued, "Also, he is the director of the Diocese Museum in Cuenca."

"Please call me Ed, the night's formalities are over."

Antonio nodded in agreement to Ed's glance. The gesture relaxed Pedro, he asked, "Ed, how is it that you know about your direct ancestor who left Corral de Almaguer and settled New Mexico?"

"We have some good historians in New Mexico. We have pride in our ancestry, so we know our history."

"But have your historians researched in Spain?"

"Of course, that is how we have the accounts of all the early explorations into New Mexico. And, also, who participated in them."

"But you know where your ancestor came from."

"Yes." Ed paused. "At the official inspection of the expedition that settled New Mexico, my ancestor gave his name and claimed that he was from Corral de Almaguer.

Our historians have used this and other information to establish all, or most, of the founding families of New Mexico. Most of this has been published in English and is available to the general public."

"There is that much interest? That is impressive. Until you arrived, I never heard or, maybe, paid attention to New Mexico. Let me ask you one other thing."

"Please ask, Father."

"Pedro."

"Of course."

"What do you know of your family in Corral de Almaguer?"

"Actually, nothing. Just that Bartolomé Romero came from there."

"With your permission, I think I can help. The local parish archives should list your ancestor. I would be very interested in filling out your family's story."

Ed sat forward and leaned toward Pedro his eyes giving away his excitement, "Father, Pedro, I would be overwhelmed for you to do that research."

CORRAL DE ALMAGUER AGAIN
September 1998

A month later, in September, the Cadillac hummed its way south again. This time it had the necessary though pretentious diplomatic flags furiously flapping in the wind. Ed and Cayetana sat in the back seat. The now fully accredited Ambassador wanted to share with his wife the town of his ancestor's birth.

Cayetana's parents and grandparents came from the village of Algodones situated on the banks of the Rio Grande in New Mexico's "rio abajo" area. She also had family living in nearby Bernalillo and heard about some connections to the Cabezón area on the secluded Rio Puerco. She would learn much later that old eighteenth century maps correctly identified an old "ghost town" known as "Guadalupe de los Garcías." Like her animated husband she came from a family with deep frontier roots in New Mexico, at least as early as the seventeenth century.

Ed not only liked sharing with her but he also took pleasure in showing her off. Tanna, as Ed called her, was a beautiful woman with an oval face, expressive eyes, and slender build. She was very intelligent and could be very observant, many times insightful. She also had a quick wit. Her personality radiated with a remarkable ability to transition to warmth and sympathy with someone that she liked. It was as if she had a physical attitude that altered and drew people into her confidence. In fact, Ed often reminded himself how fortunate he was to have such a life's partner.

Now as they drove to Corral de Almaguer where Mayor Macheño waited for them. Macheño wanted to introduce the new American ambassador to more friends. Also, Father Izquierdo had begun his research and had some information to share. Then, the mayor pursued the idea of his town having an official celebration for their new native son. Antonio knew, of course, that such a celebration required Ed's approval. Thus his anxiety built as he and his gathered friends and officials waited for the arrival of Cayetana and Ed.

The reception took place on Corral de Almaguer's main plaza. The throng of locals gathered around the featured couple with Mayor Macheño, in all his glory, introducing them all around. Ed immediately greeted Father Izquierdo with a full bear hug. He and Ed had become fast friends—more so than even Antonio realized.

"Pedro!" Ed beamed. "Did you bring the papers?"

"How could I not. They are here in my pouch," the priest tapped a leather shoulder bag.

"Great! I can't wait."

But he had to wait. The arrangements for Ed's second visit required time and attention. Learning about his family's history was a priority. Plus, he told Father Izquierdo that he is related to Robledos and wants to learn more about them.

"Are they Corraleños too?"

"No. They are from Toledo, I think. They took a statue of Mary to New Mexico that is from there."

Pedro, by nature a reserved man, listened. He knew that he would have some time with Ed later on. Nonetheless, a statue of Mary from Toledo spiked his interest. "What statue? I mean, did she have a name, you know, like Rosario or Remedio?"

"Yes but I can't remember. Her story is in a book written by a priest, Fray Angélico Chávez, in New Mexico. A miracle is attributed to her. She spoke to a little girl, one of my Romero ancestors. She foretold a major Indian rebellion."

"A miracle! Dear God! But this is important! Are you sure she is from Toledo? I need to learn more. The Robledos you say?"

"About the statue I am sure. Her book is titled *The Lady from Toledo*. I am not sure about the Robledos. They are not from here but are from somewhere close by. Maybe Toledo. Here is what I can do. I will send for a copy of the book and have my staff in Madrid or friends back home look up the Robledos. They will have easy access. The same priest who wrote about the statue did a book about New Mexico's original Hispanic families. I know that I am a descendent of the Robledos, either directly or collaterally. I just don't have the details right now."

Antonio broke in with a question, "Maybe her name was Our Lady of the Muela and she is from the region of Toledo."

"No Antonio, I would remember that name. But it is an unusual or, should I say, not one of the more popular names."

"How about Riansares?"

"No, I don't think so." Ed would later learn that the Virgin of the Muela is the patron of Corral de Almaguer while the Virgin of Riansares is the patron of nearby Tarancón.

The conversation continued through a town tour and dinner interlaced with wine, good manchego cheese and other delicacies from the La Mancha region that they were in.

Discussions of many other subjects continued through the meal. The town's people treated Ed and Cayetana royally. The couple delighted in fielding the many questions about New Mexico.

"The largest city is Albuquerque. The capital is Santa Fe." "New Mexico was settled over four hundred years ago in 1598." "It is an open land with plains (llanos), mesas, desert, and mountains. Spain's landscape reminds us of parts of New Mexico." "And many of Spain's cultural traditions still exist there. Yes, we have *Penitente* brotherhoods just like in Spain."

Here Ed interjected that his grandfather was a *hermano mayor*, a leader of a brotherhood in his native southern Colorado. He added that he had his grandfather's book of prayers and alabados, his *Penitente* badge, and *disciplina,* what the Spanish call a whip.

"Disciplina!" A universal reaction as his audience looked at one another.

Ed explained that self-flagellation is a form of penance that existed up to the previous generations and that he would not be surprised if some believers still felt the need to atone for their sins in such a manner.

"But it is not common then?"

"I don't know."

"It is rare if not non-existent here."

"Really? I heard from someone else that it does exist in certain communities." Ed did not want to let on that the information came from Cristóbal, his driver, who not only explained the difference between the *cofradias de luz* and *sangre*, the confraternities of light and blood but even knew when and where flagellation took place. "In the small villages," He stated as a matter of fact.

"Yes. You are aware of our Holy Week activities?"

"Do you mean here in Corral?"

"In Spain."

"Yes, generally. I have been to the Holy Week in Seville. Also, I helped a friend in New Mexico who brought some *hermanos* from Seville to New Mexico." He would save the story of their visit to some penitentes in Taos for another time.

Ed and Cayetana never tired of such conversations. It seemed as though the more information they shared about their home, the more they endeared themselves to their hosts.

Later that day Ed had a chance to sit down with Pedro. The priest emptied his pouch and began separating papers while telling Ed, "This business of the statue and its miracle has my attention."

While watching Pedro arrange his papers, Ed reaffirmed that he would send for the book and get the information.

"Good. This all interests me very much. So, here are copies of documents about your ancestor Bartolomé Romero. Here is the recording of his baptism in 1563 and here is when he registered to leave the country, probably from Seville although there is a small chance that he may have left from Cádiz."

"When did he leave?"

"Apparently in 1596. Also you will see from the first document the names of his parents and that he had a brother and a sister. Finally, I am sorry to say that the Romero name disappears from the record in Corral. I mean to say that after about 1650 there are no Romeros living in Corral de Almaguer."

"I have no distant relatives in Corral?"

"That is another matter that would require much research. There may be distant cousins who through marriage lost the Romero surname."

"This is wonderful information, Pedro. Thank you. I will add this to the family archive."

"Thank you, but we have much more work to do."

The Baptismal record of Bartolomé Romero dated April 6, 1563. He was born in Corral de Almaguer, Spain and became the first Romero in New Mexico and Ed Romero's direct ancestor and progenitor of the large Romero family of New Mexico. Original in the parish archives in Corral de Almaguer, copy in the Ed and Cayetana Romero collection.

Late September 1998, Cuenca, Spain

What Ed knew of his family's history he had in the form of two books and a genealogical treatise that he had commissioned before he left the United States. He thought that the treatise might have more information than the priest needed but that would be for him to decide. Ed explained the history that surrounded the statue of La Macana. "There was a successful Pueblo Indian revolt in 1680. The statue had been broken in the melee. There was a 'wound' on her forehead. The fleeing colonists, actually my ancestors took the statue with them but the Franciscans got possession of her and took her south into Mexico. There the people started calling her La Macana, because they believed that her 'wound' had come from a blow of a war club that the local Natives called a *Macana.*" Two books, *The Lady from Toledo* and *Origins of New Mexico Families* had all the information Ed needed to give to Pedro. At the ambassador's residence they talked before, during, and after dinner. By now Ed made sure that he had bottled water or coffee ready for Pedro. Ed did not feel embarrassed about having a glass of wine in front of him. In fact, they were as comfortable as good friends could be with each other.

Pedro could not wait to get back to his own desk and begin the slow process of translating the English text about a statue known in America as La Macana. What Ed had told him about the statue originating from Toledo fascinated him. The ever-curious Pedro wanted to pore over the book to see how the author concluded that she is actually a copy of Our Lady of the Sagrario, an ancient Madonna that is in Toledo's Cathedral. That New Mexico statue, as he referred to it, now inhabits a side chapel of an old stone church in Mexico City that dates to at least the seventeenth century. That church is what remains of a once grand Franciscan friary and still is called San Francisco del Convento Grande.

As he impatiently but slowly translated the English words he realized that the novel had a footnoted historical article appended to it. Here he found the documented story of the statue's origins, an educated deduction that it was the Robledos who took it to New Mexico, the story of its alleged miracle that involved a Romero-Robledo descendent, and how it ended up in Mexico.

"I will need to take my time with this," he thought as he pushed the book aside to rummage through a sheaf of papers Ed had given him. Pedro, once again, faced English text that Ed had photocopied from a book. Fortunately, Ed had the foresight to save Pedro some trouble by having his staff translate the four pages of text.

"Yes, here it is." Pedro read that the Robledos originated from Maqueda and possibly lived in Toledo. A Pedro Robledo took his family to New Spain. Even some of his children hailed from Maqueda. One of the daughters, Lucía, married Bartolomé Romero, so Ed was right. He is also a descendant of the Robledos and they are from the region of Toledo. Pedro knew then and there that he would add to the Robledo story. First, he also needed to know about this "Oñate" who seems to have everything to do with the story.

A quick telephone call to Ed provided Pedro with some immediate information.

"He was New Mexico's colonizer and first governor in 1598. Bartolomé was with him."

"Yes, Ed, but I need more detail."

"There are many books but they are all in English. Maybe a check in the National Library here in Madrid can help with the Spanish narrative."

After hanging up, Pedro turned to his own extensive notes, which, quite naturally, focused on his own region in Spain. Finding anything dealing with distant and unheard of New Mexico would be a minor miracle. "Maybe I should pray to Sagrario." Then it hit him: this whole story took place in 1596–1598 at the end of the reign of King Felipe II. "Maybe there is where I should look."

He went back to the article about La Macana to survey the footnotes. There was something about Oñate in English, just as Ed had warned, but then he noticed the curious citation. The author cited two seventeenth century New World Spanish Franciscans who wrote about the statue called La Macana. He might have trouble locating those books but he would see.

Two days later he was on the bus for an hour-and-half trip to Madrid and the National Library. Once in the great halls of that neo-classical building, Pedro ambled directly to the indices. Within minutes he was sure that he had found his books. Pedro loved the feeling of old books. There was nothing better in his mind than a priest with an old book in hand, and he had two!

Fray Agustín de Vetancurt's floppy leather-bound 1697 chronicle titled, *Teatro Mexicano* would be read later. Pedro scanned the table of contents and index and, then, meticulously wrote in his notes that the section dealing with La Macana was the 4th part, treatise 3, number 64.

For the moment his priority had to be the 1619 Madrid publication of Luis de Cabrera de Córdoba's *Felipe Segundo Rey de España: El Serenismo* (Serene Highness) *Principe*. Here was a history written about the reign of King Felipe II just two decades after Ed's ancestor left Spain. The large, leather-covered book had been compiled under order of the King's son and successor, Felipe III.

Pedro felt the ribbed spine and the book's weight. The thickness of over two inches of printed pages excited him even more. An arbitrary opening revealed double-columned pages on high quality paper still good after almost four centuries. Pedro pulled out his pencil and note cards and wrote, "1176 pages not including the Table of Contents and Indices." He carefully turned the pages back to the title page and wrote down the book's full title and its author. Then he sought the 1619 publication or printing date, for, at that time in the 17th century, they were synonymous. Pedro smiled with the pleasant discovery that the much-noted Luis Sánchez in Madrid did the job. "The king must have offered a nice subsidy for this work," Pedro surmised.

The Table of Contents directed Pedro to page 1161, Book XIII, chapter XI. He copied the information in his notes and then turned to the page. There it was, printed in old Spanish, a chapter heading that read "The Discovery of New Mexico in New Spain, and what happened there." He read the four-page chapter that described Juan de Oñate's settlement of New Mexico. There was not much detail and no mention of Ed's ancestor, but Pedro had enough to have an idea of what happened. He had a start but he needed more.

Now he turned his attention to the Franciscan Agustín de Ventancurt and Our Lady of the Macana, and where to start his narrative, for he had an idea. But, first, he needed to return to his own office at home.

Days later Pedro paused, scratched the tip of his small nose, took off his glasses, and rubbed his eyes. Seated at his "work table" at home he relished the feeling of working in his familiar environment. A second trip to the National Library left him at his desk faced with a file of notes. The Ambassador, he thought, would appreciate what he had discovered but he wanted to put the information in written form rather than just tell him. Perhaps it was the late evening hour, the accustomed silence after his elderly father went to bed, but Pedro now faced a slight case of writer's fatigue.

He knew the information and, if asked, could explain it verbally without hesitation. Writing it was another matter. All that he needed was a coherent page or two. As he had done many times before, he did what he knew to do. He began to write, the result of which be damned.

Somewhere in the process, he wasn't conscious of when or how, Pedro realized that his relationship with Ed Romero had become more than solely a local historian feeding morsels of information to an ambassador.

Ed's passion for his past and Pedro's enthusiasm for that interest had made them fast friends. Within the parameter of Pedro's initial research and writing, the idea of a book surfaced. Pedro decided that he could write the tome in bits and pieces, which he could share with Ed.

He started with the village. "Almaguer," he wrote is an Arabic word the translation of which is 'irrigation ditch,' a clear reference to water...." Using sources that ranged from the fifteenth century into the nineteenth century, Pedro laid out the various theories of the meaning of Corral de Almaguer.

A sixteenth century Jesuit, Padre Mariana, wrote about a Muslim captain named Magued who drank from a spring on the site and in his language described the good, sweet water with the word "*alma*." "A*lma*" combined with "Magued" became "Almaguer."

Another historian named López de Obexa, who wrote slightly earlier than the Jesuit, claimed that Almaguer was the name of a lord of a castle in that area and that "corral" refers to the Riansares and Albardana rivers that meet to form a "corral" there.

Pedro moved on to Julio González, who wrote much later that Almaguer's origin is Arabic and it means "irrigation ditch or water." Finally, Pedro found in his own files a photocopied handwritten "Brief Description" of Corral de Almaguer. The author, "El Padre Francisco Tercero," pointed to the "*nobilario*" of the parish church that had the date of 1712 and the word "coral" was spelled with one "r" thus concluding that the village is situated between two rivers just as "*coral*," or a coral reef, is between water and the sea. Without questioning the simple possibility of a misspelling, Pedro rejected that argument as he continued to pen that the land of Almaguer is a land of water from the river and various irrigation canals, thus concluding that Corral in the town's name refers to Almaguer being in the corral of, or next to the river.

When he later presented his information to Ed, the priest added, "and there is more," as he handed his two typed pages over, "with the expansion of the Christian conquest, the whole area around Corral de Almaguer was inhabited by Christians because of a combination of its strategic location, the water, and the land's fertility. The locale was a land of abundance."

Ed listened with interest. He knew better than to interrupt his friend at such a moment.

"And because the town sat in a region between the Christians, who moved south from the north and the Muslims who had come from the south.... Understand the area was sparsely populated and exposed. The knights of Santiago put a special emphasis there. Corral became a village under the protection of the Order of Santiago and the inhabitants, for their bravery and situation—and, obviously, to attract and keep them there—received certain privileges. This happened over time, little by little until the Maestro Diego Muñiz issued a community charter in 1315 that said, "those who dwell there now and in the future from now on, will be more secure and protected than they were until now...."

Ed interrupted, "You have done a lot of work, my friend."

Ignoring Ed's praise, Pedro pressed on, "So you, Ed, your ancestor had certain rights and privileges when he left."

"Like what? Was he a member of the Order of Santiago?"

"No, under the protection of the Order. He could own land as his parents did. He could wear a sword, own and ride livestock. These were all important distinctions in their time and before."

Ed smiled as he thought about the information Pedro had thrown at him. He was pleased but the priest did not pause. "Listen, Ed, as you can see I have put this in writing and made some copies of the original documents for you. You know that I will continue with the research. I have questions about your Macana, but that is for later. What I am trying to say is that I would like to compile a book length manuscript about you and your family. I doubt that it would have wide enough appeal for publication but it would be useful to you and your family. I hope that you will agree."

Ed did not expect this, nor was he surprised. "Can you find enough information?"

"I believe so, especially with your genealogy. I want to include your personal information. The fact that your ancestor left and you returned is what is intriguing."

"But I am not unique."

"Well, not that you returned but after so many centuries you knew about your ancestor. Also, you returned as an ambassador. Yours is a special story."

Ed did not reply but the pleasure in his beaming face could not be mistaken.

"Well okay. What do you need from me?"

"Your friendship as well as information. For example, tell me, when did you first become interested in you heritage? Do you remember?"

"Well, I grew up speaking Spanish as my first language. I was even put into a special class to learn English when I started school. When I think about it, my grandfather talked about being Spanish. My other grandfather, on my mother's side, was a *Penitente*. He was very religious, always reading his Bible or other religious books. Both grandfathers loved to read.

"We lived in Alamosa, in southern Colorado just north of the New Mexican border. My paternal grandfather moved there from a place called Abiquiu in New Mexico.

Actually, it is just twenty miles up the Chama River from San Juan Pueblo, the place where Oñate made his first settlement.

"Anyway, my grandfather started out as a shepherd like his father I suppose. He told me that he lost the family land in a card game. So he hired himself out as a shepherd. But he gave it up and moved a few miles north to Alamosa where he became a shoemaker. I can still see him sitting at his bench pounding small nails into shoes. And he had a big sewing machine."

"Did he tell you stories or..."

"He talked to me. He was very quiet and humble. He mentioned his own parents but I don't remember what he said. I was a young boy. Actually, I always had trouble believing the story about losing the land but other members of the family said it was true.

"I always liked the *viejitos*, the old ones. I would help them and listen to them. They always spoke Spanish among themselves and to me. We had a well in our yard and when they came over with their buckets, I helped them get water.

I loved the music. I grew up with *huertas, cuñas, redondos, valces,* and *varselianas.* I think part of what became my interest in my heritage had to do with the music and language. Years later when the Ballet Folklorico performed the old dances, I knew all of them. I still do."

Pedro tried to keep up writing notes. "What was your grandfather's name?"

"Faustín Romero. My grandmother was a Lucero de Godoy. Talpita, Talpa Lucero."

"And your parents?"

"Isaac Romero. He was born in 1901. He worked for the Denver and Rio Grande Railroad for his whole life in the machine shops. My father was one of the most respected men in the community. He became a Grand Knight of the Knights of Columbus. Mom was a member of the Rosary and Altar Society. They were active in the community."

Pedro put down his pen and looked at Ed. "So we have only three centuries to fill in."

"Huh?"

Smiling, Pedro replied, "From your Bartolomé, say from around 1600, until your grandfather or father from around 1900."

"Oh! No. I already have all the names. I am a twelfth generation New Mexican. You have the genealogy."

"You New Mexicans surprise me. Still the names are a beginning. We want to know what they did, *who* they were."

WE ARE BROTHERS
November 21, 1998, Corral de Almaguer, Spain

The town was both abuzz and unsuspecting, for among them their mayor was greeting the arrival of the country's Vice President Francisco Alvarez Cascos and his young wife Gema Ruiz, along with Carlos Moro who was a representative from the

Castile–La Mancha regional government, and Gary Johnson, the governor of New Mexico. Other yet unidentified dignitaries like Earl Salazar, the governor of San Juan Pueblo in New Mexico, stood among them. Mayor Macheño was in a euphoric state. Never had his town received so many important dignitaries in one day.

Despite all the publicity that Macheño had put out, the general populace still had not turned out in great numbers and, it seemed, a good percentage of those who witnessed the moment had been caught off guard. Then the real newsmakers pulled up in a bus. Twelve Native Americans from San Juan Pueblo filed out in full ceremonial regalia, white clothes piped with triangular bright red, green, and black colors. They wore leather mid-shin length moccasins replete with shells, bells, and feathers, and Buffalo headpieces. The assembled public was mesmerized if not startled. The dancers were uncomfortable with the attention. The subsequent word that quickly spread throughout the town did more to assure a huge crowd than all the phone calls, press releases, and advertisements.

A convergence of New Mexico's 400th anniversary since its first Spanish settlement in 1598 and Ed's appointment as ambassador had descended on Corral de Almaguer. Lou Gallegos, a small energetic man who served as New Mexico's Governor Gary Johnson's chief of staff came up with the idea of accepting an invitation from the Spanish government to send a delegation to Spain. Gallegos, also from an old New Mexican Hispanic family, suggested that the governor lead the delegation and that San Juan Pueblo represent the cultural aspect of the group. After all, he knew that a previous visit of Spanish officials, including Vice President Alvarez-Cascos had met with New Mexican and Pueblo representatives. The contacts and friendship already existed, largely on behalf of Alvarez-Cascos.

Now, on a cold, blustery late November day in Corral de Almaguer the Vice President, ambassador, and a crowd of wide-eyed Spaniards, completely entranced by intimidated Pueblo Indians, gathered for what would be a memorable moment. As is normal in Spain, protocol dictated that the assembled dignitaries speak. First Mayor Macheño welcomed everyone with a brief history of his town and region. Then Ed gave a prepared speech, which would be quoted in the next day's newspapers. Dressed in a long dark overcoat that revealed a white shirt and dark tie, Ed began by thanking God for this day and acknowledging Cayetana's presence. He quickly referred to the "grandparents of his great grandparents" and the beauty of being able to return to the town that was the birthplace of his ancestors.

Then Ed turned to Vice President Alvarez-Cascos and explained to the audience that just last April the vice president had gone to New Mexico where he learned first-hand about the culture of the southwest in the United States. Because of his appreciation for what he saw and experienced, he extended an invitation to New Mexico. Ed paused, looked out at the assembled people, and in a clear voice thanked the Vice President "on behalf of the United States and New Mexico. This visit completes a re-encounter between Spain and New Mexico." Ed thanked him a second time for his "hospitality, dedication, and effort."

Obviously enjoying the moment, Ed then announced that he had "brought a gift," which immediately got the attention of everyone. "A gift of your language and culture that has been conserved for four centuries in New Mexico. Because of this New Mexicans feel at home in Spain. We are a part of you. We are brothers."

In reference to the Pueblo dancers, Ed explained that they "are from the Pueblo of San Juan where the first settlers"—he used the word *"pobladores"*—"from Spain settled...and very close from where the Spanish established the first capital of the territory [that] today is a part of the United States." The dancers "offer you the most important thing a Pueblo can offer, a religious sharing between communities. This is the first time... that they have danced away from their pueblo."

Ed then thanked his friend Antonio and "all my relatives of Corral de Almaguer" for hosting this proud moment. Ed explained that the dancers would perform a Buffalo dance but not for entertainment or "color" but for very real and sacred reasons.

Earl Salazar, the governor of San Juan Pueblo, then stepped to the microphone and spoke in serious and hushed tones. "The Pueblo of San Juan has initiated a spiritual trip, a pilgrimage in honor of the people of Spain." The people concentrated on his every word and the brisk weather emphasized the obvious seriousness of the moment. With all the dignitaries seated on a stone and cement bench backed by a large window with wrought iron, Salazar explained the meaning of dancing in harmony with nature, the significance of the dance costumes, the buffalo heads, the eagle and macaw feathers, the bells and shells....

Ed watched with pride and an inward sense of content. He looked upon people for whom he truly felt a strong affection. He leaned forward and winked at Cayetana. She answered with a smile of approval.

As Ambassador, Ed Romero helped arrange for Buffalo dancers from New Mexico's Ohkay Owingeh Pueblo to dance at Corral de Almaguer. Ed is seated at the far left shading his eyes. The dancers also performed in Madrid before the Prince of Asturias who is now King Felipe VI. Original in the Ed and Cayetana Romero Collection.

"The buffalo dance...is a religious ceremony in which we offer prayers, offerings of good intentions, a long healthful life, and peace to the Spanish people and their leaders." The dancers, Salazar explained, are dressed in traditional outfits and performing a serious matter. They cannot talk nor should you touch them, nor take photographs, or ask for autographs, "and we would be very appreciative if you do not applaud at the end of the dance."

Here Salazar paused and looked out at the complete stillness before him. "In all our Pueblo's history, this is the first time that we have done a pilgrimage like this. For San Juan Pueblo this is an occasion of immense historical and religious significance. This also will be a pilgrimage in which a full cycle will be completed when we return to our land of San Juan Pueblo where we will dance the sacred Buffalo dance among ourselves."

He then turned and nodded to the drummers who began a rhythm that Ed's ancestor Bartolomé Romero first heard over four hundred years ago. It was a rhythm that had become familiar to pretty much every one of Bartolomé's descendants, including Ed. The dancers filed into the open space and performed before the gathered and mesmerized citizenry of Corral de Almaguer. No, Ed Romero was not a normal ambassador, at least not to them.

Hardly noticed but seated and comfortable behind the scenes, Father Izquierdo scribbled notes. Afterward he gathered copies of the written speeches. He went with the whole entourage to the Hermitage of the Virgin de la Muela where the Pueblo Indians presented a floral bouquet to the Virgin. The local parish priest led everyone in a prayer for cooperation, peace, and thanks. At lunch afterward, Pedro was able to get a word in with Ed.

"I have more information for you."

"Pedro! What do you think?" Ed saw a confused look come over Pedro's face. "No, about all this." And he motioned to everyone around them.

"It is great! Spectacular! Ed, I have more information for you."

Ed saw Vice President Alvarez-Cascos coming toward him. "Okay, give me a call and we can meet at the embassy for lunch or dinner. Do you have more about my family?"

"Some, not much. I have more about Our Lady of Sagrario." He paused. "Who you call La Macana."

"That's wonderful. We will talk at the embassy."

"Yes, until then."

"Until then."

As Pedro turned away, Alvarez-Cascos congratulated Ed on the day's events but Ed deferred to the Vice President for his invitation and to Governor Johnson for arranging the delegation. He only took credit for suggesting that the dance be held "in my ancestral home town."

"Well, Mr. Ambassador, fate has brought us here and I am sure she has more in store for us. We will have to meet in a less formal setting sometime soon."

Ed's face lit up, his eyes smiled, "This is for sure Mr. Vice President. As you can imagine, I already have some ideas."

"I look forward to hearing them."

Ed could not have been happier when he finally relocated and joined Cayetana. She said, "You did well Ed. The people love you."

"You know something, Tanna. They make me feel completely at home. They are so appreciative...and gracious."

"We have to come back just to visit. Can we do that without all the hoopla?"

Cayetana did not have an answer to her question, and looked at Ed who replied, "I don't know. We'll have to find out."

Back in the limo they put the question to Cristóbal. "Can we visit Corral informally, like normal tourists?"

The chauffer tilted his head sideways to the right, looked into the rear view mirror and answered. "You are not normal tourists. You can go with less formality but never anonymously. Security will not allow it."

"Oh no."

"Yes, but not all is lost. There does not need to be formal speeches or receptions. You can visit people in their homes—even stay—but this has to be arranged beforehand."

Cayetana spoke under her breath but loud enough for Cristóbal to hear, "This will not be easy."

"No ma'am. That is true."

Ensconced in the limo's back seat with Cayetana nestled next to him, Ed Romero looked out upon the evening's landscape completely satisfied. He meant what he said to the people of Corral de Almaguer. Words could not convey his true emotions for the town and country of his ancestors. This was a different feeling for a person in his position, and with what just occurred probably qualified as unique.

Back in Corral de Almaguer, Antonio and the still animated remnants of his friends celebrated a very successful day over wine and leftovers. Pedro, enjoying a *"coca lite"* sat with them as they began plotting their next big day with their new friend.

"He is one of us!" someone said.

"And look what he has done is such a short time!" added another.

The parish priest reminded them of his idea to have a fiesta and mass "before Our Lady," as he referred to the community's Virgin patroness, "to name him a native son."

Pedro immediately agreed. "The Ambassador would like that!"

"And you will co-officiate the mass with me," the parish priest volunteered.

"Wait a minute." Antonio's animated face looked around. "Shouldn't we invite His Excellency José García Casco?" Casco was a native of Corral and had become the Bishop of Valencia.

"Good idea, very good."

"Of course."

"How could we not invite him?"

FURTHER RESEARCH
Late November 1998, Cuenca, Spain

Pedro drove home completely overwhelmed by all that he had seen and heard. He anxiously anticipated the next day's newspapers. He had decided that part of his book about Ed would include the articles and speeches of events like today. Moreover, the day's events had been impressive and drew him back in time to wonder at what Bartolomé Romero must have thought as he encountered the Pueblo Indians in New Mexico four centuries earlier.

He had more work to do and the day's activities reinvigorated him. His keen historical instinct as well as the National Library's search aids had located two copies of the same book that would be of help to him. He still sought historical background about New Mexico and what awaited him among his files and papers on his desk were two copies of Gaspar de Villagrá's 1610 *Historia de Nuevo México*, one published in Astorga in 1991 and the other undated but maybe, Pedro thought, published around 2003. The editor of the second book, Mercedes Junquera, who lived in Málaga and was a friend of a friend. She taught at the University of Toledo in Ohio. He did not know the editors of the other volume. No matter, he would read the frontal matter of both editions before embarking on Villagrá's actual history, which a cursory look surprised him on two scores. The history was written as an epic poem by one of Oñate's captains, and was originally published in 1610 in Spain! He had his hands on a firsthand account.

He started reading that book the same night but the long day caught up and he dozed off within an hour. After the next morning's coffee and obligatory mass, Pedro continued. Just before breaking for a mid-day meal, he came across a most interesting discovery. Villagrá actually mentioned Bartolomé Romero! He first mentioned Bartolomé as an ensign who participated in a tournament, or mock battle, in a vacated Indian village on the feast day of Saint John the Baptist. Even more astonishing to Pedro, was that Villagrá also mentioned "the Robledos," who participated in the same tournament. Further on, Villagrá wrote about an expedition on which captains Quesada and Farfán claimed they had found rich, abundant lands, with "metals" and "pearls." Then Villagrá explained that Oñate made captains of "Romero and Juan Pinero" in celebration of this "splendid news."

Pedro could not believe his good luck. He paused, stood up, and stepped back from his desk. "My God," he thought, "these are the words of someone who knew Ed's ancestor!" He moved a few paces, and then decided to fill his cup with cold coffee and sit down again to read. He never touched the refilled coffee and completely forgot that he worked into his mid-day mealtime. After reading another forty-five minutes or so, he found nothing more of Romero or the Robledos. Then, tired and reminded by his father, he stopped to eat.

Still his mind raced. Bartolomé Romero existed. His history exists hidden in books and documents of the time. He will surface little by little. Rejuvenated by some fresh hot coffee and a full stomach, he decided to forego his usual *siesta*. No, he would check with his father who was watching television upstairs in his room and then continue to read Villagrá's poem.

Within fifteen minutes he came to the end of Canto twenty-seven, where he read that Francisco Robledo was posted to guard one of the four entries into the plaza of San Juan while the women, including Bartolomé's wife guarded a section of the plaza's ramparts. Two chapters further on, and the following chapter, Pedro read that Bartolomé participated in the siege of Acoma Pueblo. Bartolomé and others faced and defeated a fierce charge and "right and left dispatched the Idolaters most swiftly from this life."

The word "idolater" caught Pedro's attention. "A typical Castilian attitude of the time." Then he reconsidered, "No, a zealous attitude, even for then. This Villagrá must have had a biased view." But that was his religious expertise. Villagrá's attitude did not concern him as much as what he wrote about Bartolomé Romero. No, he could not wait to see the Ambassador. He would call.

PART II
THE JOURNEY: BARTOLOMÉ

The First Three Generations in New Mexico
(Ed Romero's direct ancestors are highlighted)

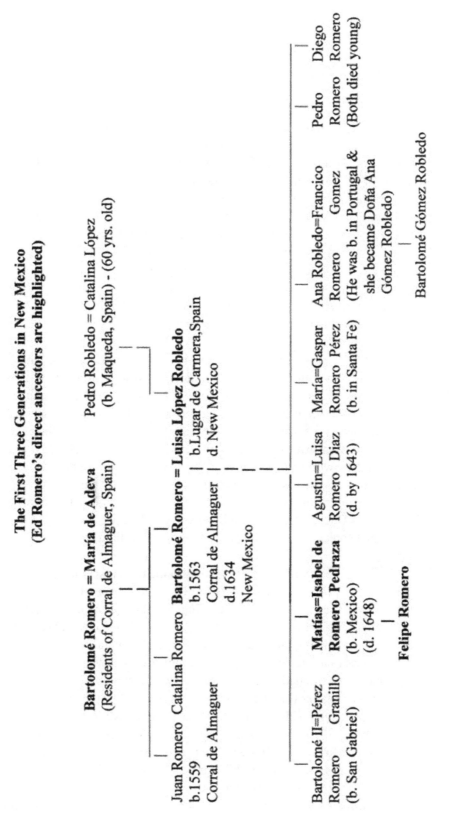

Bartolomé Romero = María de Adeva
(Residents of Corral de Almaguer, Spain)

Pedro Robledo = Catalina López
(b. Maqueda, Spain) - (60 yrs. old)

Juan Romero   Catalina Romero   **Bartolomé Romero = Luisa López Robledo**
b.1559   b.Lugar de Carmera,Spain
Corral de Almaguer   Corral de Almaguer   d. New Mexico
                                                d.1634
                                                New Mexico

Bartolomé II=Pérez   **Matías=Isabel de**   Agustín=Luisa   María=Gaspar   Ana Robledo=Francico   Pedro   Diego
Romero   Granillo   **Romero Pedraza**   Romero Diaz   Romero Pérez   Romero   Gomez   Romero   Romero
(b. San Gabriel)   (b. Mexico)   (d. by 1643)   (b. in Santa Fe)   (He was b. in Portugal &   (Both died young)
                        (d. 1648)   she became Doña Ana
                                                                                        Gómez Robledo)

Felipe Romero   Bartolomé Gómez Robledo

May 1596, Corral de Almaguer, Spain

Perched on the bank of the Riansares River, roughly eighty kilometers or two-and-a-half long days on horseback from Toledo, the nondescript village of Corral de Almaguer boasted more of its distant past than its present. Thanks to the river, its tributaries, and some natural springs the inhabitants were able to live a secure lifestyle raising sheep and some cows on abundant pastures. The town laid claim to special privileges granted to them through the prestigious Order of Santiago from long-ago kings, whose names had been forgotten. The exact nature of the privileges, other than annual fairs and that the men could wear a bladed weapon, was not completely understood. Nonetheless, to be associated with the Order of Santiago was worthy of some note.

Even the origin of the village's name had been lost in time. For sure, everyone agreed it had its origins in Arabic. Whether it referred to an old Muslim leader, or that Almaguer is an Arabic word *"castellanizado"* Castilianized or Hispanicized to mean, "water channel" or "irrigation ditch," or, even, refers to the "water" of a channel—no one really cared.

All this meant little to Bartolomé Romero, a bearded, stout, middle-aged man with black hair. Showing the effects of three decades working outside in the fields tending animals, crops, and stone fences, he was both muscular and dark-skinned. He'd grown tired of life in Corral de Almaguer. Legends and historical arguments aside, perhaps he had succumbed to the many tales of the New World, that place referred to as the Indies, and the realization that his village's male population had noticeably shrunk due to the number of men who had left for an opportunity of a different life in an exotic place. Besides, he had neither wife nor family to hold him back. Everyone knew of someone who had left. Some, they believed, sailed with Columbus although on which, if not all, of his voyages was left unsaid. Over a hundred years had passed since news of those fateful voyages had spread across the land. Yet, people and families talked as if they left only yesterday.

In the last few years, Bartolomé could name friends and neighbors who had decided to go. There was Juan de Acre, Pedro García Redrobán, Francisco de Peria Juárez, another Morales, and another Sánchez, Andrés Hidalgo, and most recently, another Juan de Acre who left eight years after the first person of that name, Gabriel Martínez Raposo, Diego de Resa Saldaza, and María Fernández la Patronera. Now, another friend, Alonso Sánchez Cortés had decided to go. It was unclear who was bending whose ear about going. Bartolomé decided to leave with Sánchez Cortés.

Not even nearby Toledo could attract Bartolomé like the Indies. Life was oppressive enough in the countryside, it would be more oppressive in the city, where government and Church officials had their hands in and eyes on everything. The village of his birth offered him the future of his parents, which was not bad. They owned land and animals. They could afford to give their children the rudiments of an education, maybe three or four years. Still, he wanted a change.

In the Indies, he postulated, a person could succeed and life would be different.

New foods, new peoples, different lands tempted the still young mind of a thirty-five-year-old. There was one other thing. Of all those who left, none returned. Something good must have kept them there, he reasoned. The conquest was complete or so it was said. Yet, there was land and opportunity, and, a new life.

Yes, he would go and like the many before him, nothing could be said to change his mind. "Keep my share of the lands. Split my possessions with Juan and Catalina." His father, also named Bartolomé, and mother, María de Adeva, patiently listened. "I have saved some coin to pay my way and have a start. I will take two of my horses and some clothes. With the money and proceeds from the horses I will survive."

"And how will you survive once you are there?" This question came from a concerned father rather than a critical mother, but Bartolomé could see from her face that the question was his mother's.

"Mamá," Bartolomé winked, "as I always have. With the skill of my hands and the slow wit of my mind." Bartolomé always had a wry sense of humor. It got him through difficult and boring times.

"No, my son," his more practical father now intoned, "You will need more. Your slow wit may be enough for here but there...*quién sabe?* Who knows? We will sell off some cows to assure your safe passage and a chance at a good start in that other world. Okay?"

"But father, this is my decision and it is not meant to be a burden on the family."

"Son, allow me to be a caring father this last time. Your mother and I know that we probably will not see you again. Most likely, like the others, we will not hear from you either. Allow us this parting token. We wish you well and pray that God will grant you the fulfillment of your dreams."

The time for departure arrived. The early morning's crispness felt good. The first hint of a new day's sun had yet to reveal itself. This was not an unusual hour for the townsfolk to be up and to begin the day's chores, especially if the unbearable heat of midday was to be avoided. Yet, this morning was different, for over half of the villagers had gathered in the plaza for a different reason. If the crispness felt good, the adventure facing Bartolomé Romero and his two companions invigorated them. Alonso Sánchez Cortés and his servant, Alonso Corraleño, had five horses to make a total of seven for the three of them. They had come together on the plaza with the village's inhabitants where, in front of the church's main entrance, they could say their goodbyes.

The horses, packed and saddled, stood quietly while pawing at the cobblestone as the village priest gave his benediction. Friends wished them well and their parents offered prolonged hugs. Then they mounted and before sunrise on a day in late May of 1596, they rode out of town on the first leg of a trip that would change their lives. As they did with their usual daily schedule they would travel in the early morning until mid-day, then find a place to rest, thus avoiding the heat and saving the energy of their mounts. At dusk, depending on what lay ahead they would ride a few more hours before stopping for the rest of the night. With few exceptions they slept outdoors. If they happened to come upon an appealing tavern, they considered forgoing their usual cheese and bread lunch to pay for some *chorizo* and sit at a table. Water is plentiful on the road to Seville, and they packed wine to supplement it.

The further south they progressed, the more humid and hot it became. After

Córdoba they would have to travel through the well-known stretch between Córdoba and Seville, that no-man's land, infamous for its thieves and blackguards as well as its oppressive heat.

"We will need to keep guard, for luck has no play in this land. The place festers with people who have no qualms about pillorying people like us."

Alonso Sánchez responded over his shoulder as he rode along, "They even rob each other."

"What? No honor among thieves? Hah." Bartolomé smiled inward at his retort.

They marveled at the city of Córdoba with its architecture so different from what they knew. Here they could clearly see Spain's Moorish influence. The castle is called an *alcázar*, a word somewhat foreign and even regrettable to Castilians from La Mancha who used the word *castillo*.

The travelers agreed on a minor splurge and decided to seek out an inn for a one night's rest. Within a hundred feet after entering the town's gate they were faced with the choice of three establishments. Alonso Sánchez turned to his servant the other Alonso. "You chose Alonso, for you know best how to care for our horses." Their mode of transportation and future income did indeed require more attention than they granted to themselves.

The servant, a gangly man of maybe twenty years, with thick eyebrows, shoulder length hair, and scraggly beard that barely grew, dismounted and entered the first of the inns. He then went into each of the other inns to return with the proclamation that the second one on the right had the best stable and the price was equal to the other two.

With the decision made, Bartolomé and Alonso dismounted and left the horses and equipment with the younger man. They entered the establishment and negotiated a price for the night. Inside the low-ceilinged inn, they could barely see the sweating rustics seated around the tables, partially hidden in the dark and smoke from the oil lamps and beeswax candles, conversing with slurred yet happy words. The travelers had made a good choice.

There is much to recommend in moving from ground or straw to a real bed, even if the mattress is strung rope. With a nice breeze blowing through the windows on either side of their room they laid awake, enjoying the momentary comfort, contrasting it to their all too familiar reality of hard pastures and prickly haylofts.

They benefited, as well, by the camaraderie of the inn, for everyone there was a traveler and, after the usual "where are you going" and "where are you from," they planned a shared trip through the badlands between Córdoba and Seville.

Apparently, luck if not planning did have a play in the land of thieves, for they kept their guard and were not threatened even once. Maybe the fact of five other companions, along for common safety, had something to do with their good fortune.

Aware of the danger in the land, they carried on a banter to unconsciously calm themselves. The road itself was hardly worth the name. A more accurate description would be a single, sometimes two tracked trail—and this was a well-travelled *camino*, the last stage of the royal artery that connected the new capital of Madrid to the rich, and getting richer, region of Andalucía and its capital of Seville.

"You know, Bartolomé, if we had listened to the women in our families and gotten married, we wouldn't be doing this."

"That's true. But that is, as they say, history. What do we do for wives in the Indies if all the women stay here?

"That is a problem. No?"

Alonso, the servant, who was becoming more of an equal chimed in, "It is said that the native women in the Indies are beautiful, but I prefer a good *morena* from Castile."

Bartolomé turned to his companions who were riding on his left, "We three adventurers may not have a choice..."

"Si, Bartolomé," the elder Alonso took his turn, "but can you imagine bringing an Indian back to Corral de Almaguer?"

"Who said anything about coming back?"

This threw everyone into silence and thought. They debated between Perú and New Spain. The unclear, to them, new settlements on the Rio de la Plata, were a fleeting consideration. "What would it be?" they said to each other. Pizarro's land or Cortés's land, the Incas or the Mexticas? They always favored New Spain. The name rang of familiarity but shouted of a new beginning. More information had come to the peninsula from that viceroyalty, where rich mines of silver had been discovered already.

Still they had some anxiety. Not about leaving. They worried about where the officials would allow them to go. A low level bureaucrat to whom they had to declare their intent and pay a fee would answer their concern in Seville. And now they had come to Seville.

The humidity conspired with the heat and waste to create a constant stench, a discomfort to anyone who had not spent time in Seville. Bartolomé grew up around animals. He knew their smell, even liked it. He had suffered the frequent horse fly and occasional mosquito bites. Nothing in his experience—not even his two trips to Toledo— prepared him for the commotion and filth that defined Seville.

The port city, up the Guadalquivir River from the coast, gateway to and from the Indies, a city that had more gold and silver flowing through it than any city in Europe, teemed with people going and coming, loitering, sweating, and scamming. Would be adventurers, thieves, government officials, and country folk from the interior looking for passage to the Indies comingled in the Andalucian capital known for its large cathedral with the Moorish tower called *La Giralda*. The place stank. Rubbish and feces from animals as well as humans mingled everywhere with the city's yellow dirt. Over the Triana Bridge and beside the Guadalquivir River was a dismal scene of hastily put up buildings and dusty streets, and the bugs...the local officials could not keep up. Bartolomé was at once excited and repulsed.

The Royal Family expressed its revulsion for Seville as well. However, the attraction of the riches passing through could not be overlooked. Wealth attracted all classes and, over time, Seville came under serious consideration to be Spain's capital city. The King and his entourage avoided the squalor by sequestering themselves in the royal alcázar that was constructed in Moorish style with forced labor under King Pedro II, the

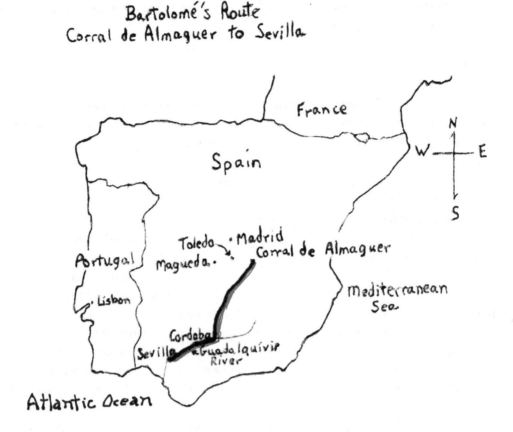

Bartolomé's Route
Corral de Almaguer to Sevilla

Cruel. Bartolomé and his companions heard that a different, almost magical environment existed inside the alcázar, not like "out here" in the streets.

Every street tavern, and there were many, seemed to host a loud-mouthed lout either bragging about his American experience, which usually was a lie, or some great unrewarded former soldier who had risked his life fighting for the King against the Lutherans in other parts of Europe who now sought his fortune in the Indies. This latter person could have been speaking the truth. Then, there was the periodic philosopher who could ramble on in true quixotic style. Mostly, however, the noise of talk rose and fell, bursting out in squabbles then laughter all of which could subside to a universal whisper that ended with the whole cycle beginning again.

Bartolomé and the two Alonsos quickly determined to arrange their business as fast as possible and leave Seville to their collective memories. They needed to get away from this press of chaos. A few inquiries directed them to the newly constructed *Lonja* or money exchange building, situated between the alcázar and cathedral. They entered and found themselves standing inside a great cavernous room, at the center of a wide floor and peering at a scene of irregular and disarranged desks manned by darkly dressed lookalike clerks. A doorman directed them to a grim looking man with a jutting chin who scratched away with a quill in his bony, ink-stained right hand. Nothing but business would take place with this obviously dour man.

After the initial introductions and explanations, the bureaucrat took their fees. He then stated that they would be destined for Cartagena.

"No!" Bartolomé could not help himself from the quick reaction.

"And why not?" Came the rhetorical reply with hands extended out.

"We want to go to New Spain."

"So does everyone else. The King needs bodies in other places."

"Then the choice is not ours?"

This brought a pause and with his brows puckered in consternation the clerk replied, "Technically yes. You can choose."

"We are sorry then, for we will go to New Spain."

"Fine." And he lifted his pen. "Give me your names and where you are from. Beginning with you." He pointed to Alonso Sánchez.

"I am Alonso Sánchez Cortés from Corral de Almaguer and this is my servant Alonso Corraleños from the same place."

"Repeat his name."

"Corrale-ñ-os. With a tilde over the n."

"Good. And you." He nodded to Bartolomé.

Bartolomé dictated the information that the bored man wrote out but forgot to note the date, 16 June 1596 that he had put for the other two men. The bureaucrat's last act was to give them their official papers and directions to an address where they could stay until they had to board a ship, which would sail within a week.

Within five minutes Bartolomé and the two Alonsos had reached their destination, a huge warehouse with chisels, planes, mallets, saws, adzes, and braces-and-bits littered throughout the place. To their relief there was a smell of freshly cut wood, glue, and paint. Even the sawdust, thick on the floor was a welcome relief from the filth outside. Many carpenters worked among the boats of various types and states of repair. Here there was no laughter, arguments, or other frivolity.

A tall man, apparently in charge, directed them to a room in back of the large shop. As an aside he advised them to get their affairs in order, for they would be boarding their ship at any time.

Three days later they were on a ship that, with a slight breeze filling one unfurled sail, the river's current, and two long boats rowed by sweating and straining twelve man teams, slowly made its way down river under a burning sun. As they got close to the river's mouth more sails unfurled and the oarsmen slumped over their oars, relieved as the ship left them behind. Bartolomé and the Alonsos watched the machinations with fascination and relief, for as Seville sank behind them it already was becoming a memory.

Like thousands of others, the three men embarked on a two to three month journey that was anything but normal, uneventful, or easy. They suffered cramped quarters and a lack of privacy. One had to suspend oneself dangerously over the ship's gunwale to relieve oneself. The food and drink became stale as time passed—this was only the beginning. People from La Mancha had to get their "sea legs," which is a euphemism for the two weeks or so it takes to get over seasickness and learn to walk unhindered on a constantly swaying deck.

The crew generally remained separated from the passengers except in emergencies. Without doubt corsairs posed a danger and most Spanish seamen of the time, had heard about the likes of Francis Drake. The whole ship's company, including the passengers, would fight shoulder to shoulder against such an enemy. The threat of attack gave rise to one pastime, trying to keep track of the other four ships in their armada. Safety in numbers worked as well at sea as it did in the badlands.

New terms and use of language resonated throughout the day and night. Words for left and right, horizon, up wind, downwind, names of sails—"top foremast," for example—even what wine was called in the Canary Islands—"*malmsey*" or simply "*canary*" —where they stopped to replenish their water and, of course, stock *canary*. Their new world experience began at sea. They quickly learned to share the crew's exhilaration when they became, as the sailors said, "close-hauled," with every sail they could carry bellowing full and ropes taut, twanging, or as the crew said, "singing." And, then, when not close-hauled, there was the, unnatural to them, flat horizon, the daily routine, and same faces. An unavoidable boredom that morphed into anxiety unavoidably possessed them as they approached the port of Veracruz after almost two months at sea.

To the Far North

January 1598, Near the Mines of Casco by Santa Barbara in Northern New Spain

Bartolomé drank at a brook, splashed some water on his face and hair, which he tied off in back. An owl's hoot came out of the dark. Another early morning start and a new life beyond the north horizon looms but it was not the future that held his attention. No. His mind focused on the last year-and-a-half or so, the time since he left Spain and set foot in Veracruz where he found himself in another port city, different, especially for its mixture of peoples. Negro slaves, Africans in chains or branded. Stripped of their humanity. He did not know what to think. Here he saw his first Indians, mostly miserable, emasculated, downcast souls forced into dock labor or seemingly lost in this new world being pressed upon them. He thought of the journey on horseback, for he had purchased two good stallions, from sea level up through humid scorching jungles and into fresh alpine air eventually to cross a ridge that had two towering volcanoes with unpronounceable native names, Popocatépetl and Iztaccíhuatl. There he got his first panoramic view of Mexico City set in a large valley in the middle of the remnants of a still blue lake. Nothing dampened his enthusiasm for coming to the New World.

He wandered through the already legendary city with its ruined, new, and partially constructed edifices, temples and buildings reminiscent of both conquered and conquering. He marveled at who the Mexticas must have been and, even more, at what the great Hernán Cortés had done. Even three-quarters of a century later, he felt himself a part of a history in which he knew he was destined to play a role.

As happened with all new arrivals, the place of his origins had everyone's interest. New arrivals were a source of recent news from a disconnected past. Naturally enough references to others already in New Spain who originated from the same area followed. Eventually, Bartolomé and the two Alonsos were directed to old Pedro Robledo.

The reference came to them while in a grog hall in the middle of a gaggle of idle soldiers. Calling them "conquistadors" would dishonor the term. They had become roaring drunk. Such a state was not new to Bartolomé, for he had sewn some wild oats, but never to the hoggish chaos of this place. Despite the high din and debauchery, one of the costumers retained some control to explain to Bartolomé where to locate Robledo.

Bartolomé quickly departed determined to meet the man. He left the distracted Alonsos behind and hurriedly walked through the darkening streets of early dusk and came upon the designated doorway under the lee of a lone street lantern. Bartolomé inquired about "Don Pedro Robledo" through a lighted, open door of a medium-sized stone building with shuttered windows.

A young woman directed him to a stout man, completely gray with deep-set eyes under heavy eyebrows. He looked in good health while his gray, well-worn teeth highlighted a dark mouth that punctuated a full square-cut beard. His light blue eyes were of priestly gentleness and Bartolomé guessed that the old man might have been a redhead in youth. His partially redheaded children soon confirmed the guess.

The amiable Don Pedro and his wife hailed from the village of Magueda "near Madrid" and Toledo, where they also lived for a few years. At other times Don Pedro claimed to have come from a place called "El Carnero," or "Carmen" but his wife always corrected him to Magueda, "we lived in Carmen."

"Yes, you are right." He replied softly.

They had been in New Spain for over twenty years, moving from one place to another seeking to fulfill their New World dream and achieving it in partial, short segments but never what they expected. His three oldest children, Ana, Diego, and Lucía, had been born in Spain. Three other sons and a daughter were born in different towns of New Spain. Nonetheless, Don Pedro had accomplished enough to maintain his dignity and that of his family.

The family patriarch, still optimistic and charismatic, took an immediate liking to Bartolomé and the feeling grew mutual. Bartolomé's attraction for Lucía, who was in her middle twenties, proved even stronger, for they married within the month. Nor could Bartolomé find any disagreement with the patriarch's idea that the whole family should sign on to a new venture that had organized in the north to Christianize and settle among sedentary Indians in a land much further north called Another México, or "*La Nueva México*" in reference to Mexico City.

"We cannot live on last year's income forever. Fate beckons. Each adult will receive a salary," with this he pointed with his bearded chin toward his boys, "maybe even a rank." Then drawing on his long experience and a well-stocked memory he recalled an earlier exploit in which he had been involved, at which point his wife prompted him back to the present. "The expedition has been delayed over some political matter, but, so what, it is being financed by some Basque *ricos* who struck silver at Zacatecas. They have the wealth and connections..." While listening, none of the family, now including Bartolomé, neither prompted nor responded. Nothing sufficed beyond an occasional nod, a deprecating look, or an assenting smile. Don Pedro sat back, raised his arms with palms up and proclaimed, as he had many times from before he left Spain, "The great double-eagle of Empire opens to heraldically spread on the shields of men, sails of fleets, and in foreign lands upon which the sun never sets. This is our fortune, our opportunity!"

His children, mostly grown, had heard this proclamation for years and each could repeat the words without a miss-step. Only his oldest daughter, married and settled in Zamora would remain behind.

All this had taken Alonso Sánchez Cortés by surprise, especially the marriage. Nonetheless, he supported his friend and wished Bartolomé well in his northern venture. Rather than succumb to Don Pedro's charisma, he wanted to cast his lot in the new royal city of Mexico. He and his servant would stay. Thus the Natives of Corral de Almaguer parted with a prolonged hug as they wished each other the best of good fortune with complete sympathy.

Within months Bartolomé had travelled north to the mines of Casco near the miserable town of Santa Barbara, some four hundred miles beyond Zacatecas, and stood before the Vice royal officials to proclaim himself and his new wife as well as his property, to be a part of the expedition that would settle the lands of New Mexico. "Where did the time go?" He thought. Along with Pedro Robledo, his sons, and approximately, one hundred fifteen other men, he swore loyalty to God and King. Many others chose not to be officially noted and thus disappeared when the officials arrived. The ranks would balloon to over eight hundred people including relatives and Indian servants after the officials folded up their traveling desk and returned south.

But this was not the whole story, for Bartolomé learned that many had deserted while a new Viceroy delayed the expedition. Even though the expedition's leader, Don Juan de Oñate, used his own resources to keep the people fed, they waited in tents pitched in a desperate land of barren hills and a dismal landscape, and huddled around campfires as winter approached. Not even the bright nights full of stars could undo their misery and uncertainty. Rumors as well as the truth of the situation spread throughout the large encampment that in numbers overwhelmed the nearby town of Santa Barbara with its twenty to thirty families. The expedition had just moved to its current spot, "one miserable place after another. At this rate we should reach New Mexico when our grandchildren reach maturity."

These words came from Bartolomé González, who upon hearing that another person from Corral de Almaguer had signed up, sought out Bartolomé Romero. They both stared at each other in disbelief.

"Bartolomé!"

"*Tocayo!*" Bartolomé used the Spanish term for a person who shared the same first name. "What are you doing here? I thought you went to Toledo or, maybe, Madrid."

As they happily hugged and pounded on each other's back, González answered, "A change in plans. First Andalucía, then America beckoned. Toledo was depressing and Madrid disorganized, full of thieves. Tell me: When did you leave? How are things in Corral? Do you have any news of my family?"

González left Corral de Almaguer six years before Bartolomé Romero. Of course, they knew each other and their respective families. González stood a couple of inches shorter and was six years younger. His questions led to a long conversation of catching up. He had answered the call of the recruiter's drum and fife to sign up for the Oñate enterprise in Mexico City. He had been waiting with the expedition for over two years.

From him Bartolomé learned of the problems, the personalities, and of a recent tirade in which a woman, Eufemia, condemned those who left by questioning their courage.

"Hah! It takes a woman to keep us together? That does not speak well for our future."

"No. The reward of a possible silver or gold strike entices me. Others are attracted with the reward of *hidalguía*, becoming a noble, for five year's service." To be a *hidalgo*, which derived from "*hijo de algo,*" meaning "son of something," meant that a person was a noble albeit at the entry level. "I think that we may already have that privilege because of our place of birth."

González paused, rubbed his right eye and gestured with the same hand, "Actually, I am in it for the adventure."

Bartolomé reacted with, "Adventure, sure but it would not hurt to make sure about the nobility, eh?"

González looked off through the maze of people, wagons, and tents. "It is good. I mean, those that left. They needed to go. We are better off without them. They were braggarts and opportunists. Eufemia was right. They have no honor. We can do without their disruptions but, I fear, some of their ilk remain."

Bartolomé nodded in agreement. He already had witnessed the beheading of a conspirator who tried to convince a small group of men to break loose and head north. Apparently, he felt that, like the famous Hernán Cortés, he would win Royal favor after the fact of his success. Oñate, mostly absent from the encampment, returned to arrest the man and his band. Under the strict military constraints by which they all abided, Oñate decided to make an example and show his resolve by having the poor guy executed.

Oñate, his policies, and whether or not he would be allowed to lead the expedition all became hot topics. No one had clear answers.

For his part, Bartolomé saw no choice but to continue. His initial savings, the sale of his horses in Seville, and the gift of money from his parents had been transformed into a surprisingly large amount in America. In addition, Don Pedro Robledo, so proud of his daughter's new husband made sure that she had a small but helpful dowry. As a result Bartolomé stood before the fiscal to join the expedition. Bartolomé claimed a wagon, oxen to pull it, a plowshare, twenty-six horses, six mules, and armor, including three coats of mail, two pairs of cuirass (armor to protect the upper body), and two pairs of beavers (plates of armor protecting the face and throat). He also had the sword laying at his feet, plus an extra one, two lances, a pistol, and harquebus.

The fiscal's use of the adjective "swarthy" as he dictated Bartolomé's description to his scribe, did not sit well. Bartolomé, flinched and wondered, "What did he mean by that?" I have never been called swarthy before. At least, he had me put down as "of good stature."

That was all past and of no significance now as Bartolomé Romero stood before the brook. Corral de Almaguer seemed so far away. "Yes, another world," he thought as he stretched one last time, picked up and buckled on his scabbard and the used sword that he bought in Mexico City. Now they would be leaving for the distant north, to locate the rumored Strait of Anián that had good ports on both the North and South Seas. "Well, maybe," was his only thought about this rumor. Once again, he set off.

The journey's first challenge came with the current of the fully running Conchos River. Then they had to get the sheep, women, and children across the river. Bartolomé could swim after a fashion. He had bathed more than once in the Riansares River and its canals back home. But the Conchos River in front of him had a stronger current and appeared fairly deep. Even Oñate's bravado in forcing himself and his terrified horse across and back again did not fully convince Bartolomé of his own safety. Nonetheless, he had enlisted and had been rewarded with the junior officer rank of *alferez*. He could not wilt now, at the first problem. He had to follow his commander's lead.

The resulting scene of animals, wagons, men—some stripped and swimming, others, especially the Indians, near panic holding on to and urging their mounts or animals to keep moving—thrashing, struggling, yelling, but making progress—lasted for most of the day as the large and long caravan with its livestock entered and crossed the river. The lead wagons and people exited the river as still more entered and others waited their turn. When on land at times the caravan stretched over two miles. Now it bunched up at either bank, either regrouping or anticipating the crossing.

But those sheep, whose thick wool would drown them, and the women and children...? They could not be expected to cross the river in the same manner. Oñate had a plan all along. He gave orders to dismantle the wagons. The wooden wheels had to be tied in pairs and attached to the wagons, which would be used as rafts when turned upside down. Then Oñate ordered that the makeshift rafts be strung in a line across the river and that bark, branches, and, finally, dirt be spread over them. When complete the women and children walked across in complete safety while the sheep hardly needed direction to follow. Bartolomé could not help but be impressed. The river had been crossed in one day. Not a life was lost, neither man nor animal.

Now the whole mass had to be put back together. Exhaustion set in. The animals needed to be pastured, tents pitched, wagons reassembled, reloaded, and tied down. The encampment spread over several acres as people grouped from around forty to fifty campfires, aligned by friendships, family, or profession. Bartolomé and Lucía naturally camped with the Robledos. González and his servant also joined them.

Their conversation was less about the expedition's leadership or hardship although it could not be avoided this evening, but rather their concern for Don Pedro whose health seemed to be failing. Bartolomé and Lucía kept their own anxieties to themselves. Fortunately, concern for Don Pedro distracted the rest of the family while the others, like González, did not care enough to notice.

At dawn on the second morning, with dew still creating a mist on what little grass that existed, the whole colony received the brusque orders to pack up and make ready to move. The two Bartolomés, as junior ensigns hurriedly rushed to meet with the captains and sergeant major where they learned that the colony had orders to move to a new site two days march away. The reasons could be explained in many ways. They wanted to keep the people from becoming complacent, they had been delayed enough, they needed to

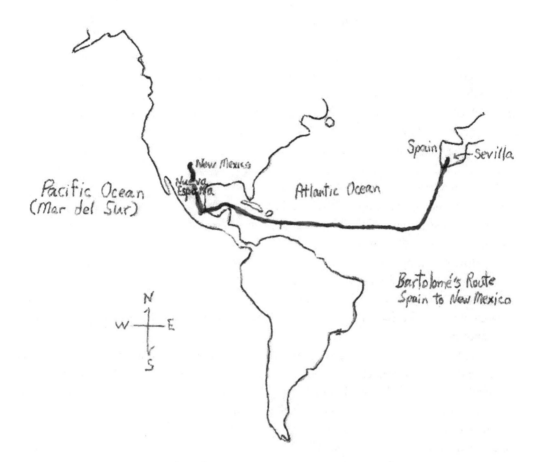

Pacific Ocean
(Mar del Sur)

New Mexico

Nueva
España

Atlantic Ocean

Spain — Sevilla

Bartolomé's Route
Spain to New Mexico

N
W — E
S

move to a place with additional firewood and a new pasturage, etc. They let on that a less but equally serious motivation was to demonstrate to the Viceroy's officials, especially Juan de Frías Salazar, who had completed their inspection that the colony would not wait any longer. Nor could they hold it back. Besides, Captain Juan de Zaldívar, Oñate's nephew, let it be known that Salazar had been hostile to his uncle so, hopefully, if the colony started moving north he would be encouraged to leave. Bartolomé understood perfectly, for the smallish, arrogant and petty Salazar had alienated just about everyone associated with the expedition.

Also, the governor heard that some replacement friars had departed from Mexico City and were on the trail to catch up. The Franciscans had been assigned to the expedition after a majority of the initial group of Franciscans grew impatient and left.

Oñate came to the meeting after it started. He personally wanted to confirm that he now had the royal permission, the resources, and determination to carry on the enterprise to a successful conclusion. The governor produced a copy of a letter from the King of Spain to the Viceroy of New Spain, dating from April 2 of the previous year, 1597, to order the expedition to proceed. Now, with Salazar satisfied, there would be no more delays. Oñate pointed out that other Spaniards had been to New Mexico before them so they were not going to an unknown land. Then he added that he carried an arrest warrant for Bonilla de Leyba, who earlier had led an illegal expedition into New Mexico and presumably was still there.

Two days later, Bartolomé secretly cheered as he watched Salazar and his small entourage leave for the south without fanfare or formality. They happily watched the despicable man bounce away, his thin jutting chin visible from the distances. Almost as if a spell of pessimism had been lifted, and a new positive attitude replaced it the further away Salazar and his group rode.

Oñate did not wait long to call his throng together to take advantage of the moment. There would be no more vice regal interference. Royal permission had been secured and they answered only to themselves, Oñate summed up the situation: "Hardships and misfortunes are the common lot of the brave adventurous men...who knows but what these present trials and tribulations are sent for the express purpose of preparing us for the glorious future that awaits our expedition."

However, they could not move too far or fast, for Oñate made a subsequent decision to wait for the Franciscans. "Just a few weeks" he said, noting the newly downcast postures of his followers. "We should use this time to regroup and rest for the long, arduous journey ahead." The outlook improved only a little more than the surrounding dire landscape.

With Pedro resting in the tent, his wife, sons, daughters, and the two Bartolomés sat around the campfire. The men shifted in their soft buckskin breeches, cotton shirts, and leather jackets with bone buttons. They all wore boots, some knee high. Their more elegant brogues, gray and green laden jackets, and buckled shoes had been packed away. Felt hats covered and warmed their heads. All their armor was stored in an accessible place ready for any emergency. The women sat in cumbersome dresses wrapped in blankets with a kind of bed cap over their hair pulled up on their heads.

Only the men talked and the chaos in crossing the river still elicited some comment.

"If the rest of this journey is like that our luck will run out."

"Give Oñate credit. He led by example and had a solution."

"He was lucky."

"Maybe so. I would rather follow a lucky leader than one who is unlucky. Besides, we have people like Captain Juan de Victoria, who has been to the north showing us the way."

"Really, who showed us that crossing? It wasn't Victoria."

"That is behind us. Maybe the worse is done."

To this Bartolomé observed, "Politics is worse than any river crossing, for that is a hardship from which we are never rid. And that, too, is past with Salazar's departure."

Then the subject switched to where they were going and the people they would encounter. They all clearly noted the differences between the Natives from the central valley to those of the north who they called Chichimecas, a contrast between well-organized city dwellers who farmed and dressed themselves well, to near-naked wanderers.

González offered that he had heard the reports of people farther north who wore clothes, lived in houses in large towns, farmed, and produced cotton clothing. "From what I hear they do not have cities like Tlaxcala or Tenochtitlan, but they are more advanced than those around here."

Diego the oldest of the Robledo boys added, "Anything would be an improvement over these naked barbarians. Look at their poverty. They eat nothing but roots and prickly pears."

Everyone nodded in agreement while staring at the flames and embers of a fire that they had started. Yes, life would be better in New Mexico, if they got there.

"And how is Don Pedro this evening?" González asked.

Here the women spoke, for they were his main caretakers. Lucía responded, "Better. He has been able to rest while we wait for the priests."

"A small gift from God," Bartolomé added laconically.

Lucía's sister, Francisca, somewhat less positively added, "But his mind is wandering more. He still recites the Hapsburg eagle's wings but now to himself. I think he is getting weaker."

Diego then asked his mother how she was doing.

"Oh, I am fine," Catalina replied barely above a whisper. "I worry about father."

"So do we."

They kept busy. After the Franciscans arrived, the colony once again began its movement north. The officer corps alternated on missions searching for campsites, pasturage for the 7,000 head of livestock, watching out for an unlikely Indian attack, and scouting for the best wagon route. Bartolomé and his brothers-in-law, except for Francisco, the youngest, with González alternately joined parties seeking out a more direct northern route through sand dunes to the Rio del Norte. Oñate tried to save time by avoiding the better-known and safer route up the Conchos River to the Rio del Norte that veered off to the northeast. The first party sent into the dunes suffered mightily before arriving at the northern river. The second party sallied out to find the Conchos first, which they did. Between the two of them they located a route that the colony, split in two with double-hitched wagons, could cross in two very hard, stressful days.

In early April they all arrived at the banks of the Rio Grande that they called El Rio del Norte. Exhausted and parched, the men welcomed the cottonwood trees, water, and abundant game. The governor wisely called a halt, while scouts, including Bartolomé, rode up river to find a ford. The people welcomed the week's rest after which the colony moved up the south side of the river to a well-used crossing. Local Indians, who they called Mansos, helped guide them on one of their trails to the river crossing.

After a morning mass on April 30, the whole colony, the soldiers formed up in full armor with all banners flying. Oñate, Governor, Captain-General, and Adelantado of New Mexico wanted to take the formal and legalistic act of possession of the "Kingdom of New Mexico." He began reading, "In the name of the most Christian King our lord, Felipe, second of the name...." After the formal reading the ensigns raised and waved the Royal Standard while trumpets blared and the men, including the two Bartolomés, fired their harquebuses. The rest of the day was spent in celebration.

Bartolomé and Lucía joined in the festivities. After shedding his hot armor,

Bartolomé grabbed Lucía to walk hand-in-hand through the happy camp. They watched a drama put on by Captain Farfán de los Godos that mimicked their own entrance into New Mexico. With uncritical eyes they watched as their brethren portrayed humble Indians with bowed heads and bended knees as they welcomed, almost invited, Franciscan missionaries to teach them the word of God. The rest of the day mostly gave over to celebration and thanks. They could never have guessed that almost four centuries later some people would call their celebration the "First Thanksgiving" in what became the United States of America.

"Bartolomé, we are here," Lucía said as she pushed some of her wind-blown dark hair from her face.

"No, my love. We have more to travel."

"But we just heard Don Juan..."

"We are at the entry, the pass into New Mexico. We will not stop until we move into the land. Oñate has no desire to settle at the southern end, but, like Toledo in Spain, in the center where the Indians who live in houses and their towns are."

"How much longer then?"

"I am not sure but we are told that the road is easier."

"What road? There is no road."

"The route. A route known by some of our soldiers from previous expeditions."

"Bartolomé?"

"Yes Lucía."

"For myself, I am fine. I can feel the change, the hardening of my body as I have become used to this life. I worry about father. As I, he believed that the journey was over."

The boys had dressed Pedro and supported him in the day's formation. Ecstasy filled his face and tears came to his eyes. He, too, wanted to celebrate but he needed to rest, for the ceremony and emotion had drained him. One of the other soldiers would write about this time on the Rio Grande as "Elysian fields of happiness where we could forget our misfortunes." Those around Don Pedro could not forget their misfortunes, for the old man had become weak and feeble. They feared that his time was short.

In three weeks they had crossed the Rio Grande passed through a narrow pass cut by the river that would forever be called El Paso del Norte, and followed the river up its east bank through a beautiful valley to a point where the advance scouts indicated a short cut should take place. Instead of following the river over land that wagons could not traverse in a western u-shaped loop, they should head directly north across a ninety-mile desert to hit the same river again as it curved back.

Initially mistaking the scouts' report for information provided by Captain Victoria and some other veterans of New Mexico, Bartolomé mused sarcastically, "Now they know where they are going. Seeing tracks from their wagons made seven years ago may have jogged their memories. Then they remember that Morlete had some Indians hanged for stealing horses not far from here. I just have no faith in them."

Fortunately, the misadventures of one of Oñate's captains who traveled the direct route to the first of the northern "pueblos," towns of Indians, gave Bartolomé more confidence. "At least, the route has been travelled by one of our own."

Unfortunately, Captain Pablo de Aguilar violated Oñate's orders not to enter a pueblo and thus forewarn the Natives of the colony's pending arrival. The incensed Oñate wanted Aguilar beheaded as another example, but the officer's fellow captains came to his aid and convinced Oñate to be more lenient.

Sixty miles further north, in the third week of May, the expedition's chronicler dipped his quill in ink and wrote, "On the 21st day of the Most Holy Sacrament, we buried Pedro Robledo." Father Cristóbal de Salazar, another Oñate relative, administered the Last Rights and officiated over the burial of Don Pedro. Pedro was the second to die after moving through the pass. A child died and was buried five days earlier.

The women dressed Don Pedro in his best doublet with black breeches, red stockings, a brown three-quarter length coat, buckled shoes, and a felt hat. One of the colonists drew a double-headed Hapsburg eagle that was placed on his chest. The sons lowered him into his grave with complete sympathy. Bartolomé helped them shovel in the dirt and pile the rocks on top to keep animals out. The whole company seemed to melt in a sympathetic sorrow. Don Pedro Robledo's New World quest had come to an end.

"*Así es*, this is how it is. He ended buried in this dry, desperate land with a headstone of those crenulated mountains to the east and this ugly gray-red mound of a large hill across the river to the west."

Bartolomé added to the oldest sons words. "He will not be forgotten, not with all of you to carry on." He nodded toward Pedro's family.

"This was his idea, his dream," Diego shot back.

"Yes," Lucía spoke up, "and quite possibly he will be the first of many generations of Robledos to live and die in this New Mexico."

Diego, still staring at the mound of his father's grave, looked up and around at the stark skyline with distant mountains, desert, and a river valley offset by a bright blue sky with puffs of white clouds. "I'll hold judgment on that thought."

Bartolomé saw the perplexed look that his wife could not hide.

They walked back to their campsite still talking in the silence. "Father will be remembered." The words were almost a plea from Lucía.

"Of course he will. His whole family will see to that." But then, Bartolomé thought, will they stay together without their father? Also, what importance can be attached to a memory in so faraway a land? "At least everyone who stops here will know that he is buried here." Maybe that was not the answer his family expected to hear but before he had a chance to explain, the gruff, short, stocky, sloop-shouldered, bull-necked, and bald Gaspár Pérez de Villagrá rumbled into their circle. The family never interacted with the captain. He was a confidant of Oñate and had a reputation as a religious zealot. Very educated and elitist, he kept to himself. His condescending attitude was more than enough for people to avoid him. Besides, as so many said among themselves, "As the only member of the governor's inner-circle who was not related to him, he could be dangerous." Generally, people avoided him.

Yet, here he was. Everyone figured his presence meant something important, maybe even unpleasant.

He spoke through his downturned walrus moustache and goatee, "You Robledos, all of you are to ready yourselves to travel tomorrow. The Captain-General will include you in a group that he will lead in advance of the main colony. Which one of you is Romero?"

"I am." Bartolomé stepped forward.

"Good. You are married to one of the Robledo sisters, yes?"

"Yes."

"You will go as well, and your wife. We leave at dawn." He looked around. He never seemed to smile. "Be ready. Oñate will not delay. He repeats his condolences for your loss." At this point the captain turned on his heels and retraced his route from wherever he came.

One of the brothers spoke first. "Why us?"

Another answered, poking a stick at a rock, "Maybe this is his way of helping us with our grief. An occupation..."

"No. Someone fears that with our father's death, we will abandon the expedition."

The first brother kicked at some dirt. "That makes no sense. Why would they think that?"

Lucía answered, "We all know that some people are not pleased. Remember before we even left many abandoned us. Then at the river, Oñate had to give a speech to encourage us. Now, he almost executed Aguilar for disobeying his orders."

Bartolomé agreed. "He knows that there are discontented among us but he does not know who. He even thinks that his enemies in Mexico have planted people to disrupt the settlement. He is mistaken with us and this we need to demonstrate."

The family nodded in agreement and began the process of preparing for the next morning's departure.

A New Colony

August 18, 1598, Newly Named San Juan Pueblo in New Mexico

By the time the main caravan reached the pueblo that Oñate chose to make his permanent settlement, Bartolomé had visited every pueblo along the Rio Grande north from the one they called Senecu. He had been to some of those in a region on the east side of the mountains where Natives that they call Jumanos lived. He also went to Cicuyé on the Pecos River and the Tano villages, one recently named San Marcos in the Galisteo Basin. From there they travelled down the Galisteo watershed to a pueblo the governor named Santo Domingo where they met the main caravan now led by Juan de Zaldívar. Bartolomé followed Oñate west to Zia Pueblo and then around the base of the Jemez Mountains to the Towa Villages situated in a beautiful canyon fed by mountain streams.

The memory of the five days "shortcut" they took to cross the desert, a route that his grandchildren would come to call the Dead Man's Journey, paled in his mind when compared to the many new sights and events that he had seen as part of Oñate's advance group. The thinly whitewashed kiva walls at a pueblo that they called Puaray failed to completely hide depictions of the stoning death of two Franciscans. Now they knew what happened to the two Friars who stayed in New Mexico seventeen years earlier.

Bartolomé, like his fellow travelers, was angered but Oñate told everyone to keep calm and ignore the images. "We must look to the future not the past," he proclaimed.

The depictions made an impression on Bartolomé, for after that he paid more attention to some of the veterans who had been to New Mexico before. He learned that Oñate depended heavily on these people, at least five of them as near as Bartolomé could figure. Bartolomé witnessed the moment at a southern pueblo when an Indian came up to them and proudly said in Spanish "Thursday, Friday, Saturday, Sunday." With hand gestures and words that nobody completely understood the native correctly directed the governor to the pueblo where two Mexican Indians resided. Tomás and Cristóbal, who had been left behind by one of those previous expeditions, became invaluable interpreters as well as sources of insightful information.

Bartolomé found Picurís Pueblo the most picturesque for its setting in an alpine-lined mountain valley. The multi-storied buildings of Taos Pueblo impressed him more than San Juan and Cicuyé. After the latter pueblo, Taos seemed to be the largest and richest of the pueblos.

Lucía waited to hear his accounts after each of his forays, for while she bore witness to much of the advance group's march north, neither she nor any other woman was allowed to join their men on special assignments. She enjoyed hearing from her husband and brothers. She saw the meeting of Pueblo leaders that Oñate organized at Santo Domingo. Their demeanor and apparent strength of character impressed her. They had a stoic confidence about them.

On August 18, 1598, the main group of over seven hundred people slowly streamed into the plaza surrounded by a cluster of two-story rock and mud buildings that would be their new home. The Natives called the village Ohke but Oñate renamed it San Juan de los Caballeros. The main group had slowly made their way north for almost three months after the advance contingent left them. Bartolomé and Lucía watched with curiosity main group's arrival. A majority of the new, but worn out, arrivals were on foot with a minority of horsemen, and fewer people rode on the great ponderous wagons pulled by oxen with wooden yokes across their shoulders and tied to their horns with the familiar studded leather harnesses. Hundreds of well-proportioned Indians bore their loads and tasks such as maintaining the herds of livestock with stoic, weathered faces, mute and unsmiling. None of the people showed any happiness or even some relief. Overall, Bartolomé concluded, this was an exhausted group.

Lucía spotted the González first. Pointing she exclaimed, "There he is! Look, my love, over there on the brown horse."

"Where Lucía? There are many brown horses." Bartolomé shaded his eyes from the late afternoon sun that showered the valley.

"Riding toward us. He has spotted us."

"Hey, Bartolomé."

"Tocayo! Lucía!" Their old friend Bartolomé González scurried off his horse and hugged them both.

"How great it is to see you. I was sad that we could not spend more time together at Santo Domingo but the governor was in a hurry."

By this time the rest of the Robledo clan had come over. "And I am glad to see all of you." Then in a lower voice he said, "I see that you have not abandoned the enterprise. And, Lucía you are as beautiful as ever!"

Bartolomé smiled. Lucía laughed. "I think this venture has aged me beyond my years."

"And how is mother?"

One of the brothers answered, "She is okay, very quiet."

A few hours later after they had taken care of his livestock and placed his personal items in his "rooms," González sought out Bartolomé and guided him away from the others. Looking around for eavesdroppers he said under his breath, "We need to talk."

"Now?"

González looked directly into Bartolomé's eyes. "Seriously." They waited for nightfall when they had passed out of the fires' circle of light and now stood under a radiant sky of brilliant stars in a cloudless void. "There are problems, brother." González used the word "brother" as an indication of affection. "You know that Aguilar incurred

Bartolomé's route, Veracruz to San Juan

Oñate's disfavor. Then Captain Gasco started talking against the governor. And, Sosa y Peñalosa, our esteemed Lieutenant Governor, who was left in charge of our group, let them spread their venom. He is spineless. He never disagrees, always agrees, and, then, throws his hands up and does nothing."

"Oñate chose him to be our Lieutenant Governor. He is loyal. Is he not?"

"Loyal, yes. But it is a job for which he is not favorably disposed. Nor does he seem grateful for the appointment. He is not close to Oñate, but I don't believe he has the guts to betray him."

"Listen, my friend. I know that something happened soon after we left you because Oñate had to leave us and return to you."

"Yes, that is what I mean. There was a near mutiny. The evildoers found willing souls. People became despondent. They had been on the trail, enduring hardship, as you know. The majority had no idea how much more they would be required to endure. It is easier to undermine uncertainty than certainty. We were three days on the desert short cut when Oñate arrived. He met with Sosa in a one-sided conversation. Then he gathered the people to tell them what lay ahead. He described the villages and more pleasant climate. Of course it helped that he brought some supplies that, he told us, had been provided by the Pueblo People."

"So, once again, Oñate was able to placate the people." Bartolomé looked at González. "Or maybe not?"

"Certain leaders, including Captains Aguilar and Casco, continue to speak ill of the governor. They say he has become a despot and that he lied about the riches of this area. Why do you think that he finally had to send Juan de Zaldívar with some men to accompany us?"

"Do they expect to find gold and silver bricks put at their feet? They have not been here one day. How would they know? We need to search. Certainly they knew that these Pueblo," Bartolomé gestured at the house blocks and people around him, "Indians do not have the riches of the Mexticas."

"Personally, Bartolomé, I think some of our colleagues never intended to obey their oaths. Tell me, how are the Robledos keeping up?"

"They miss their father but they are fine."

The next day Bartolomé sensed unrest. The new arrivals moved about unhurried as if they had no desire to unload the wagons and settle in. Their suspicious glances and hushed conversations might mean nothing but Bartolomé was not sure.

He still worried the next morning when just as González came up and clapped him on the back they heard a distant thunder over the mountains lining the west side of the valley.

Bartolomé shared his observation that when the clouds formed enough to cause thunder over the mountains this early, for it was still mid-morning, the chance of a thundershower over them was almost certain. "But there is no rush. The rain will come at mid-afternoon."

As the clouds welled up, heralds called all the men to gather outside the governor's quarters. By the time the Robledos and two Bartolomés got there, Oñate, with his two Zaldívar nephews, and Pérez de Villagrá stood before the men. The four of them rested hands on the hilts of their swords as the governor loudly addressed two men in front of him but directed his words to a group immediately behind them.

Bartolomé sized up the scene. He could see two groups of men. The first stood together up front behind two men facing the governor. The second group stood scattered in a half circle behind them. Yesterday's arrivals made up the first gathered group, while the majority of the scattered group consisted of those, like Bartolomé, who had been in Oñate's advance guard.

Oñate was speaking, "You have been a problem from the beginning. I never should have listened to your defenders. You never lived up to your oath...oath," and here the governor raised his voice, "to the king, as all of you have done."

Captain Casco answered instead of Aguilar. "You promised many things. We sold all our possessions, invested, and brought our families through this misery based on your words. All that we have received is hardship. There is no wealth and we are treated as chattels while you play favorites with your family."

Oñate lowered his voice for an evenly stated answer. "You have been here two days. How would you know what is here or not? Your hollow words do not make sense. How is it that Aguilar poisoned you? Don't answer. He is a bad influence who will not stop." Oñate turned to the total group with his blue eyes staring hard at no one. Maybe he saw the irony of the quickly darkening sky. Bartolomé figured that another speech would come.

"These people here arrived only yesterday or the day before and today they want to abandon the colony. I will not allow it. As your governor and captain-general and," he stressed, "by the oath you took to our Catholic Majesty the King and to God, I order you to start unpacking and move into your assigned quarters. If any of you do otherwise or attempt to desert, for that is what it will be, you will be punished accordingly. Now is not the time for division, for we are facing a cold, long winter and preparations must be made beginning immediately."

He then ordered the posted guards to keep an eye out for anyone trying to leave. As an afterthought he added, "The choice is yours. Deport yourselves as true loyal Spaniards or become cowards." Then he announced that until further notice Captains Aguilar and Casco and another soldier were under house arrest.

González leaned to Bartolomé, "I told you."

"Yes, problems. Maybe things will change after they get settled and rested. And here comes the rain."

"I doubt it. Many of these people do not want to labor for food and shelter. They did not grow up like you and I. They seek a quick, easy pay back and that has not happened."

Within hours the announcement came. Everyone would be assigned specific tasks. Some would dig irrigation ditches, others needed to prepare the fields for next spring's planting, corrals for the livestock had to be constructed, and others had to help build their first church.

The livestock and seeds that had been brought north with great care would become important to their survival in future years.

Actual construction on the church began three days after the confrontation. The people worked quickly and completed the primitive mud-brick and rock structure in fifteen days. Of course the roof would come in the following weeks for that required cutting and hauling crossbeams from the nearby mountains. Nonetheless, even though tensions remained on edge, everyone shared in the sense of accomplishment in being able to attend services in a real church that the Friars dedicated on a crisp afternoon on September 8th. Father Salazar gave a sermon in which he reminded the throng that they were on an evangelic mission to convert the Pueblo People.

On the following day Oñate began assigning the missionaries to various pueblos. Once again, Bartolomé sensed a problem. The priests did not seem anxious to leave for their assigned places. Perhaps, he thought, the image of their martyred brethren depicted on the walls of the kiva at Puaray was the reason for their hesitation. He heard that the priests asked the governor to send escorts with them. The governor, at first, scoffed at the idea but then gave them an excuse to linger while he decided to consider the request.

The governor as well as everyone else was soon distracted—again. Oñate decided that idleness was an enemy. Bartolomé knew that he planned to explore the new kingdom but when? There was more than enough work to do. Then things happened quickly. First a ragged looking Indian snuck through the guards and walked into the village. When confronted, he spoke a broken Spanish in a familiar accent. Upon addressing some of the Mexican Indians in excellent Nahuatl, everyone understood.

He volunteered his name as Jusepe and that he had been a servant of Antonio Gutiérrez de Jumano who had gone onto the Plains under the leadership of Francisco Leyba de Bonilla to a place he called Quivira. Bartolomé knew enough of the area's previous history by now to instantly understand that Leyba's journey was unauthorized and illegal. In fact, Oñate had instructions to arrest him and his followers.

Someone was sent to tell the governor about Jusepe. Oñate immediately rushed to the scene. Jusepe told the story of how they travelled among the strange, shaggy brown cows on the plains until they came to some expansive Indian settlements that they supposed were Quivira Indians. Then he related how there was dissent in the ranks, at which point Oñate pulled on his square-cut gray streaked beard in a knowing manner. Gutiérrez stabbed Leyba to death and Jusepe fled and was captured. When he heard that more white men had appeared, he escaped and made his way back to the Rio Grande Valley.

Jusepe's tale of herds of humped-back cows that stretched "as far as he could see" had everyone's attention. To date, they had seen blankets and clothes made from the animal's hide. Jusepe assured them that their meat was as tasty as any found anywhere. Oñate, Bartolomé now knew, had studied the narratives of previous expeditions to New Mexico, a place that, almost sixty years earlier, Vásquez de Coronado had called Cíbola, which, he thought meant land of the buffalo in the language of one of the pueblos.

Bartolomé returned to Lucía with the news. "I fear that the governor will seize on this opportunity to split the settlement by sending a group onto the plains to gather meat. And," he said as an aside, "to keep our minds off of the idea of leaving."

Lucía sighed, "Will you be going?"

"It depends. He can't send everyone and he needs loyalists here as well as there. He will use this expedition to help defuse some attitudes."

Within a few more days, on September 12th, the whole settlement was rocked with even more startling news. Four men had taken provisions, stolen some horses, and left for Mexico. This was a direct affront to the governor and the reaction was quick. He dispatched his trusted captains Pérez de Villagrá and Gerónimo Márquez with three soldiers to capture and "promptly" execute the culprits. Oñate, his eyes flashing and beard bristling, made sure that everyone within hearing range heard the sentence, the intended result of which was accomplished within a minutes.

Bartolomé and his immediate friends all agreed that they were glad they were not assigned that task. "But what does that mean for the three under arrest?" Someone asked. "Surely, the governor sees them as the instigators. I would hate to be in their place."

"Could Oñate lose control?" González addressed the question on everyone's mind. None had an answer. The possibility of a major mutiny lingered. They felt caught between disloyalty and the thought of following a vengeful despot. And Bartolomé had become more concerned for Lucía than himself.

Three days later Oñate's captains selected sixty men, half of the available force, to follow Vicente de Zaldívar onto the Plains to supplement the colony's food supply with buffalo meat. With Jusepe leading the way the excursion was sure to be a success.

Bartolomé was relieved to learn that he had not been selected for the hunt. Two of his brothers-in-law would go. For the first time, the family was split up. "I want to be here with you Lucía."

"I know my love."

"I think Oñate carefully selected who would go. This hunt will give us meat as well as distract people."

"Oh dear, let's talk about something else."

"Like what?"

"Our future." She shrugged her shoulders and permitted herself a half smile.

"I know, but it is fun to speculate." And they hugged in genuine affection.

They had two weeks together arranging things to make the best of their new home. Recent events hovered in Bartolomé's thoughts. He had a new sense of reality. He and Lucía were in a distant land with an uncertain future.

Then he learned that he had been assigned to accompany the governor on a three-fold journey to further explore the kingdom, search for some trace of valuable minerals, and receive the submission of more pueblos. They left on a brisk October 6th morning heading down river. Six days later camped outside the first of a series of villages that they called the Saline Pueblos because of the close proximity of recently discovered briny lake beds. They were east of the Manzano Mountains.

The locals called their Tiqua village Acolocu. Oñate called out the leaders through the interpretation of an interpreter. He then began the formal ceremony of submission. With his squadron in formation and his scribe, the smallish Juan de Velarde seated at a small portable table with an ink dipped quill in hand, and, of course with the head Franciscan, the Father Commissary Alonso Martínez, offering the Church's approval, Oñate took on his best official look to read "the act of obedience and vassalage" to the Pueblo leaders.

He began, "In the name of the holy trinity: Be it known and manifest to all." He named the "chieftains" before him. There was Acilici of Cuzaya Pueblo, Tegualpa of Junetre Pueblo, Ayquian and Aguim from Acolocu. He went on to explain that he "had come to their lands to acquaint them with God and the king...on whom knowledge depended the salvation of their souls." After a lot of such verbiage the governor asked them to consider whether they wished to render obedience and if they did, and then failed to observe the laws and the king's will "they would be punished as transgressors...."

Bartolomé had seen the same act and heard the same words at other pueblos, specifically at Santo Domingo and San Juan. The first act at Santo Domingo was the one that Lucía had watched wide-eyed. Representatives of, at least, twenty-eight villages swore to obedience there. The act at Santo Domingo included representatives from Pecos, Taos, and Picurís, among others.

Despite all the formality Bartolomé had no confidence that any of the Natives understood the meaning of it all, even with interpreters. Nevertheless, he went along and stood ready for any disruption, although that appeared unlikely. He also took his turn along with some other officers, including the governor's teenaged son to sign the written record as a witness.

This procedure would take place, again, at a nearby Jumano Pueblo called Cueloze where Bartolomé, again, signed as a witness.

Then Oñate ordered the men to mount up with the announcement that they would head west to visit the pueblos of that region and, maybe, push on in search of the South Sea. This was startling news. Bartolomé had a foreboding, for winter approached and if it is as severe as they have been led to believe, now was not the time to embark on a journey of uncertain length.

The governor sent a messenger back to San Juan to share the change in plans. He ordered Juan de Zaldívar to follow him with a contingent of thirty reinforcements as soon as his brother, Vicente returned from the Plains. Bartolomé could only reason that the governor believed that the constant movement would keep his men too busy to ponder on the recent events. Besides, they were heading to a place where an earlier expedition had reported evidence of a rich silver vein. If discovered all dissent would vanish.

Intermittent cold rain drove the men into themselves as they rode through a pass in the mountains, crossed the Rio Grande, and headed west. Bartolomé mostly thought of Lucía and her safety. She would worry about him. He had been gone over three weeks. The buffalo hunting expedition had been gone two weeks before they left and a messenger reported that they were still out on the plains.

"The distances are vast, *mi querida,* my darling." Bartolomé mentally replied to the imagined concerns of his wife. "Do not worry. Aside from this miserable weather, I am fine."

Toward the end of October they approached the high mesa village of Acoma. Bartolomé tried to compare the mesa's cliffs to something in his experience. They are not quite as high as the Giralda in Seville but higher than the cathedral. He found the place incredible. He could not believe that anyone could live up there. They had to descend to grow crops and to get water. Living up there, he thought, must be an inconvenience. In answer to spoken words expressing the same sentiment, Bartolomé replied, "They must have some serious enemies to want to live there."

They set up camp at the mesa's base. Bartolomé could see the miniscule shapes of people standing on the cliff's edge watching them. Before long a number of people descended to their camp with gifts of corn, beans, squash, and rabbit meat. They acted very friendly. Bartolomé and his companions noticed that the Indians looked with suspicion at the horses. "How can that be? Some of them have seen us before, even when we played our war games."

A soldier joked, "Maybe they think the horses are talking to each other. Ha, ha"

Bartolomé rolled his eyes and sighed. "These people know the difference between an animal and a human."

After a cold night during which the wind erased any vestige of comfort, Oñate accepted an invitation to visit the village. He selected Bartolomé to join a group of a dozen men to make the difficult climb with him. The rest were left on alert below. The path quickly turned into primitive stairs that gave way to hand and footholds carved in the rock. The climb was awkward, even clumsy, for the men's boots, armor, and weapons worked against them. Aside from the enemy above them they had nothing but space and rock below them. They felt extremely vulnerable as they climbed single file along the only way up.

Once on top Bartolomé looked around to see all the village people peering back at them from rooftops. "We are horribly outnumbered," he thought. Then he observed, "But there are women and children. No, there is nothing to fear."

Oñate disagreed, for he told his men to stay together and be alert. He had been invited to their underground kiva and would go by himself. The underground religious chamber by now was familiar to all the Spaniards. Maybe, thought Bartolomé, the village's leadership would greet him there.

He watched as an Acoma escort took Oñate onto the kiva's roof and to the opening out of which a ladder stretched. Both the escort and governor gestured to one another. The native seemed to indicate that he wanted Oñate to descend into the kiva's dark interior.

Bartolomé could not tell whether Oñate agreed or not. The governor talked and gestured but appeared noncommittal. Bartolomé could not help but notice a hushed silence. The whole community concentrated on the scene on top of the kiva.

"Don't go in there," Bartolomé said under his breath. At the same time his right hand grasped his sword's hilt. For the first time in New Mexico he felt an anxious and immediate fear.

It looked like Oñate smiled. Bartolomé couldn't tell from his angle and distance. He smiled as he threw his hands up, turned on his heels, and walked back to his men.

"Let's go." He said. "We need to get off this rock." No one disagreed.

By dawn the next day every man was booted, spurred and mounted. They waited to see if the Acoma leaders would accept the governor's invitation to descend and agree to the act of obedience and vassalage. They did. Bartolomé had his jaundiced view of the procedure. He was not certain that the Acoma leadership understood all the formality. He also believed that they did not see their agreement binding in any way. Again, Bartolomé and the others formally witnessed the written document.

After the ceremony the squadron rode off on the ancient trail that would take them through the nearby lava beds to a valley that led them to the Zuni Pueblos. They stopped at a natural pond at the base of a high sandstone cliff. They called the place Agua de la Peña for the water and pine trees that surrounded the area. Indeed, even as they filled their water bags they did not bother to notice the scenery of the valley through which they traveled. Yellow sandstone mesas topped with evergreens that matched strands of the same trees in the lush canyon bottom. The land was not rugged or difficult. However, the bitter cold and threatening sky demanded their attention.

Just after they had remounted to continue working their way west toward the mountains that cradled the Zuni villages, gusts of swirling snow began to blur their lines of vision. The whistling wind and snow spooked some of the spare horses. They stampeded and ran away. Bartolomé and his companions were able to get most of them back but a few remained lost.

Even as cold and damp as he was Bartolomé wondered about the events at Acoma. He shared his thoughts with some of the others. No one could agree. One soldier thought he saw a head or two peering down at them at the water hole. But he was not certain. Oñate kept to himself. It seemed that the bite of a lingering winter at over seven thousand feet elevation had obscured all other thought.

The welcome sight of the first of the Zuni Pueblos suddenly came into view through a full-blown blizzard that the men now battled. First they saw a shadow, then more of a silhouette maybe an apparition, and finally they faced the reality of some buildings immediately in front of them.

At roughly the same time back at San Juan, Lucía and Francesca tended to their mother. Compared to what Bartolomé was going through, they were in relative comfort. They were indoors, seated around a newly installed corner fireplace with a chimney. Also, the hunting party finally returned with enough meat jerky to last into next summer.

Still they worried. Word of mouth indicated that the governor had decided to search for the South Sea. Among the women, this decision seemed foolhardy, especially at the inception of the colony's first winter. They thought that the governor must be desperate.

Not even the return of Diego and Francisco with their tales of adventure on the plains distracted the three women from their concern.

"We tried to herd them into a make-shift corral but they nearly killed us. The cows started moving together in a circle that soon became a dervish whirlwind. We barely escaped the mayhem. It was unbelievable!"

"The Natives showed us that if you do not force the issue a person can get very close to the animals and even with a harquebus shot, you can drop an animal without disturbing the others."

Diego smiled and said, "Now we have meat and blankets. But it is nice to be back. I never thought that I would feel this way but this is home. I hope I do not see a saddle for the next week at least."

Their mother, Catalina, spoke very softly and with a halting voice. "Your father would be proud that we are all together. We need to give thanks for this to Our Lady." She directed them to a *nicho*, a small built-in opening in the wall that her son Alonso had carved out for his mother. There, dressed in an elegant Spanish dress, stood the small statue of Our Lady of Sagrario that Catalina had brought from Spain many years before. The statue stood on a wooden pedestal and except the very well-done and cute, doll-like face and two nicely fashioned hands, it has a roughly carved wooden torso. Altogether the statue is almost two feet tall.

IN SEARCH OF SILVER AND A PROMOTION
November 17, 1598, the Hopi Pueblo of Awatobi in northern Arizona

Neither the layers of clothes, armor, or his worn out gloves could keep the bitter cold wind from him. He shivered, even in the sun, which sat low in the southern hemisphere. Bartolomé had just witnessed the last of the acts of obedience that Oñate dictated at the Hopi Pueblos. He could not, nor cared to remember the name of the village beside which he stood peering off the mesa into the distance. Maybe his mind had gone as numb as his body.

Still, as he pulled out his comb to use in a vain attempt to clean his hair, he thought of Lucía and what could be happening in San Juan. He tried to pull the comb through his straggly, almost matted mass that passed for his hair. The thinly toothed comb was designed more for cleaning out lice, chunks of dirt, or any other foreign entity his hair had collected. The comb had met its match.

They had been traveling over a month, survived a major blizzard the likes of which he had never seen, and visited countless pueblos, including the Hopi villages. The four-day ride from Zuni to this place, "as far away from anywhere as can be," had not been pleasant. Now he looked out to a horizon as far as the eyes could see—in every direction. "Why would anyone live here?"

The moment was not made any easier when he thought about Lucía. Captain Pérez de Villagrá, whom everyone simply called "Villagrá," had been found emasculated and nearly frozen to death. Three of the men sent from Zuni to gather runaway horses came upon him lying on the ground by a spring at the bottom of the cliff at Agua de la Peña, which would become known as El Estanque del Peñol and finally as El Morro.

Upon reviving him with food, water, and a warm fire, he told a tale that he would later write. After returning from the south where he had been in pursuit of four deserters, he sought out Oñate to make a report. Upon hearing that the governor had headed west, he decided to hurry after him.

Then he told the startling tale of avoiding an ambush by Acoma Indians only to ride into a disguised spike laden trap that killed his horse. Left on foot and in the same blizzard that had caused the horses to runaway, he stashed his armor, and began to walk. He had no provisions and admitted his luck upon being found by the three men.

Given Villagrá's story, Bartolomé and some of the others could not help but wonder why the governor insisted on moving further away from San Juan. Maybe the governor brushed it off as a mere exaggeration. But, then, where was Juan de Zaldívar? He still had not shown up. None said it aloud, but maybe thought, "The governor should be more concerned."

All these thoughts exacerbated the difficult snow-laden journey to the faraway

Hopi province.

"Hey Bartolomé, Don Juan wants to talk to us." Marcos García, a slender man in his late thirties with a long face and partly gray hair, and native of Sanlucar de Barrameda on the south Atlantic coast in Spain, gestured back toward the village.

"Yah. I'm coming." Bartolomé waived acknowledgement of the summons, tried to run the comb through his hair one last time, gave up, and then ambled back to the men gathered around their leader, Governor Oñate.

"My friends," the governor began, "a previous exploration into this area reported having found evidence of silver. Unfortunately, the report was not detailed and indicates somewhere in that direction," Whereupon he pointed to the vast expanse in the general direction of the southwest. "I have determined to send Captain Farfán with eight others in search of this reputed discovery. Captain Quesada will be second in charge."

He then had Farfán name those who would join him. Bartolomé had no reaction when he heard his name—unless, indifference can be judged a reaction. They would leave immediately under orders not to overextend their supplies, search for two weeks, and return to the Hopi Pueblos. Bartolomé could only concern himself with packing his bags while the wind bit his face and the fleeting question of when would Oñate decide to return to San Juan became more poignant. "We have been away over a month." He thought to himself. "Is there no end to this man's ambition? And what about those, especially Lucía, who that are left behind? With one group on the Plains and the contingent here, the people left behind are exposed. And, where is Zaldívar, who was ordered to catch up with us as soon as his brother returned from the Plains. Now, we depart on another exploration. How long? Two weeks?"

Bartolomé, outwardly indifferent, and internally becoming depressed, saddled up and joined the eight other men chosen to ride with him. No one talked as they headed off in the general direction Oñate had pointed. There was a distant mountain from which to draw a bearing. Mostly, they leaned against the wind, listened to the crunch of frozen ground and snow under their horses' hoofs, and looked down. A silver discovery? None cared at the moment.

For the first day-and-a-half they traveled over sandy semi-barren land. The first night's camp was miserable. The men supposed they slept but were not sure. Nor did the meager fire help. Midway through the second day they started riding through juniper and small pine trees. The trees thickened as they bore witness to the party gaining elevation as they neared the mountain's west flank.

The wind abated and the temperature dropped as they gradually gained elevation. Then, they came to a north flowing river that they had to cross. This was another bitter turn of events, for the men would not stop to dry off, but rode on stoically suffering the cold and wet. They finally set up camp and put flint to steel strike-a-lights, called *chispas* to start a fire. With plentiful wood at hand they set up a blazing and welcomed fire. They woke the next morning to a freshly fallen snow. Captain Farfán ordered that they continue along the mountain's southern slope because, "Under these circumstances, it is better that we move than not." Captain Quesada questioned how they could find anything much less evidence of silver under this thick blanket of snow. Another soldier mused aloud that they should head in the direction from whence they came.

Farfán, a veteran and eternal optimist, or so he seemed, replied with his customary positive outlook. "We are not lost and the horses need sustenance. Let us move on and depend on our guides." They had two Native speakers from Hopi with them. "They will find a good camp spot for tonight and we will have a needed rest. We will pass this mountain and, in doing so, leave the snow."

A day later, the guides indicated that they knew of a source of water nearby. Farfán ordered an escort to go with them. A few hours later they returned to camp with a whole contingent of local Indians. The captain gave them gifts of beads, hugged their leaders, and let them understand that the Spanish meant no harm to them.

These friendly Natives invited the weary group to travel to their village, which was close by. When they got there, the series of huts were mostly abandoned. Bartolomé supposed that the Natives did not completely trust the intruders, "and why not?" he reasoned.

More gifts were given, including brass hawk bells that seemed especially prized. The men were treated to venison and dates. More importantly they moved "indoors" into the primitive makeshift huts that the Natives had left behind.

Bartolomé and his colleagues needed a respite but they knew it would not last, for they noticed that the Natives had pearls and powdered ores. When asked, the Natives volunteered to show the Spaniards the source. Now they had a real sense of purpose and reason for their discomfort.

The local Natives led them south through knee-deep snow and a pine forest. After about fifteen miles they set up camp in a small valley. The next day they came upon another village with columns of smoke rising out of their huts. That meant warmth and food.

They left the mountain beyond the northern horizon. The weather warmed and the snow receded but, still, they negotiated through a thick pine forest. They could not help but notice the abundant wildlife, "Castilian" partridges, deer, hares, and rabbits. Finally they dropped into a large valley and came to a village full of women and children. Apparently word had gone ahead, for these people harbored no suspicions of the strange newcomers. A large river flowed next to the village and on its welcoming flats Bartolomé and his companions camped in a cottonwood grove.

As they sat around their campfire, munching on the venison and corn meal provided by their hosts, they pondered their plight.

"The further we go, the longer our return," one man mumbled.

Bartolomé noted that it seemed as though the locals knew of a silver lode but before he could continue, another interrupted, "And what? This is so far from San Juan. What would happen? Pick up the whole settlement and move here?"

Captain Quesada answered. "The priests would never allow that. They prefer the sedentary Pueblo People for conversion."

Another chimed in with, "Where there is silver or gold, people will move in. Look what happened at Zacatecas."

"Besides," Bartolomé observed, "look at this land. It is fertile with much game and water. People could live here easily." There was no reply, for everyone felt the homesickness that weighed upon him.

Two days later they were led into some hills that hid some small rivers and springs from which warm water enticed some of the men to rinse off. The Natives then showed them "a mine" with a vein "very wide and rich" that extended "over many ridges." Farfán had the men fan out and begin to stake out claims both for themselves and the rest of the colony. They pried samples out of the ground using knives and daggers.

Bartolomé did as everyone else. "Was it possible?" He thought. "Would he become rich?" The samples looked inconspicuous to him. But some of the others, more familiar with ores and mining appeared convinced, in fact, enthusiastically so.

Through interpretation and sign language the Natives gave them the impression that they were thirty days travel to the "salty sea" where the Natives' pearls originated. They also listened as they were told that other richer settlements existed there. The men quickly calculated that the distance to the coast was somewhere between eighty or ninety leagues further on.

With new information and ore samples in hand, Farfán ordered that they begin the journey back to report to Oñate. The allotted time had run out and their provisions were low, even with the aid from the friendly Natives. At once tired and excited the men returned over the same route. They continued to suffer from the cold and deprivation but they were not so depressed, for they were not pushing into unknown territory but traversing a known route and home was the destination. In addition, they had good news to report. Farfán, at least, felt that the rich veins would develop into a major strike of various mines.

By the time they arrived back at the Hopi Pueblos they had travelled a total of over ninety miles into what would someday become known as Arizona, south of a town called Flagstaff to a place now called Jerome. Their total trip was over 180 miles in the dead of winter. One can imagine the disappointment when they discovered that Oñate had not waited for them. A Hopi Indian waited for them at the base of a mesa holding a letter from the governor who had returned to Zuni.

Farfán heaved a sigh, surveyed his motley crew, now dismounted from their jaded horses, and made a quick decision. He and Captain Quesada would take the healthiest horses and immediately leave for Zuni to catch up with the governor.

He gestured toward Bartolomé. "Romero, you are in charge. Stay here to give the mounts a chance to heal. Then catch up with us at Zuni or wherever we may be. Don't take chances or be impatient. Act, as I know you will, with mature judgment. Understand?"

"Completely. We will follow when ready." He, along with the others, was disappointed in the plan but they understood. The horses had suffered more than them. Their horses meant everything in this hostile world. Better to wait than to lose a horse. They had been on the trail for over two weeks. A few days rest would not hurt.

Actually, a few days were all that they could wait. Anxiety won out, for on the third day the men mounted their still tired animals and headed for Zuni. Everyone agreed that it was time. They missed their families and friends, questions about the Zaldívar's disappearance played on their imaginations, and with any luck they could be home for Christmas. They had enough of exploration, of being constantly on horseback, deprivation, cold, snow, and uncertainty. San Juan seemed a luxury. Hopefully, Oñate would agree.

They pressed forward as well as their mounts could take them. Their long-rowel spurs were of no use and the men knew it. Neither desire nor demand concerned them as they steadily rode across the dry cold land, through some deep arroyos (dry river beds) and turned right where an easternmost canyon ran south to the beginning of a juniper and small pine forest that hinted of their proximity to Zuni. Eventually, through the trees they could see smoke rising from the first of the Zuni Pueblos.

But neither Oñate, nor anyone else waited for them. The governor had left another note. "We are off for El Estanque del Peñol. Catch up." That was the place where Villagrá had been found. They were heading back to Acoma and they left two days earlier.

Nourished by the friendly Zunis the seven men remounted and headed out.

"Maybe Don Juan has similar thoughts as us," Bartolomé said to make conversation.

"You mean like what happened to Villagrá." García, a naturally thoughtful man, hesitated and answered his own question. "No, I guess not. The governor would have warned us to be on guard if something was wrong."

"So, he just wants to go back to San Juan," Bartolomé paused and continued, "for Christmas. Why not? The season is late he will have plenty of time for exploration come spring."

They rode on a few minutes in silence when García added, "Don't forget, my friend, he has seen some of the ore samples. He may be anxious to put the quick silver to them."

Bartolomé allowed himself a whimsical smile. "Yes Marcos. That would be the best of all reasons but the samples still look like plain rocks to me."

"Ah, Bartolomé. We have had enough misery. Let us, at least, relish what little hope we have."

"True enough, *compadre*, true enough. We will soon learn the truth anyway. These moments are ours. Too bad we don't have any dragons to slay. Ha, ha."

Tired and bedraggled but in a good mood, the seven men found Oñate and the main force camped at El Tanque. Bartolomé realized that some new people had joined the force. "Unhuh. Zaldívar showed up." But he was soon corrected.

Captain Quesada met the men. "Welcome. I trust that all has gone well."

"Yes sir. No problems." García reined in next to Bartolomé and nodded in agreement.

"Good. And you have the rest of the ore samples. Yes?"

"Of course."

"Good. Take them to Farfán's tent, first thing. It's over there." Quesada pointed out the proper tent. "Also you will hear it but I want to tell you first. Yesterday we received word that the Acoma Indians ambushed Juan de Zaldívar and killed some of his men."

Unnerved by the news Bartolomé asked, "How many? Who? Do you know?"

"Five, six, ten. No, I don't know. The governor has not left his tent since hearing the news. He has been there since yesterday afternoon. As you can imagine, we are all waiting."

Bartolomé nodded in understanding. He and the others no longer felt the fatigue of their bodies. People had been killed. Was it just Acoma or were all the pueblos involved? If so, the people in San Juan might be in jeopardy.

Nor did Bartolomé overlook the thought that one of his friends or brothers-in-law could have been with Zaldívar. Now in the middle of December, a mere six months after their arrival to this land, he had the uneasy feeling that the whole New Mexico experience had come to a crucial moment.

Bartolomé barely had time to unsaddle and pasture his horse before hearing the news spreading through camp. His brother-in-law, young Pedro, only nineteen years old had died at Acoma. Pedro's older brother Francisco survived the attack. In all thirteen men had died, including Zaldívar.

"But how?" Bartolomé asked about Pedro Robledo.

"We were told that the survivors or, at least, those who were in the village on top of the mesa, had no choice but to jump off the side."

"Uh, no, that can't be. No one would survive."

"No. They found a place where a sand dune had piled up to within twenty or thirty feet of the top. That's where they jumped."

"And?"

"Well, Pedro and another, Nuñez de Chaves, I believe, missed the sand and hit the rocks."

"My God. Such desperation."

The adjective "uneasy" did not adequately describe the camp. All the men watched and waited. Oñate was awake. They knew this when Villagrá answered a summons to his tent, a round, red and gray-striped dwelling with crenulated trim. An hour had passed since. The morning's violet light had long since given away to a bright blue sky.

Finally, the tent's entrance was pulled back and the two men stepped out. Villagrá followed his commander and stepped to his side. The men did not need to be summoned. Everyone concentrated on their leader. He stood there, haggard from a sleepless night and his swollen red eyes left no doubt of his grief and worry. Then he spoke, at first barely heard.

"Men, as you undoubtedly know, we have received news of an insufferable event. My nephew, Captain Juan de Zaldívar and twelve others have fallen victim to treachery at Acoma Pueblo."

"My inclination is to march on Acoma and set an example without hesitation. However, Captain Villagrá, here, has reminded me that sometimes it is foolhardy to be bold when prudence and legality dictate otherwise. We have not heard and do not know if other Pueblos likewise are in rebellion."

"Therefore, we will return to San Juan, sending advance notice that we are coming. We will avoid Acoma and, as much as we can, every other Pueblo in route. Nothing will be done until after Christmas, which will give us time to study the matter and make a proper determination about what to do."

The decision relieved Bartolomé. Finally, he would get back to Lucía. She had lost her father and now her brother. He needed to be with her. Others around him grumbled while some questioned, but the majority of the men saw the wisdom in the governor's decision. Just at this moment Bartolomé's thought process was interrupted with the news that the governor wanted to see him.

This perplexed Bartolomé, for he could think of no reason for this first-time summons. Most of his dealings with the governor had been indirectly through his officers nor had he been a part of the factions that wanted to give up the enterprise. He supported the governor pretty much all the time from the advance into New Mexico to the subsequent explorations to all the Pueblos. Why would he be singled out? Bartolomé had no answer.

Another *alferez*, the same rank as Bartolomé met them at the front of the governor's

One of three mentions of Bartolomé Romero in Gaspar Pérez de Villagrá's 1610 epic poem *Historia de la Nueva Mexico* about the settlement of New Mexico titled. Here Bartolomé is being promoted to captain. Original edition of this book is in the Fray Angélico Chávez History Library and Photographic Archives, Santa Fe, New Mexico. Photograph by Blair Clark.

tent. The slender Juan Piñero of medium height, which is to say he was a little shorter than Bartolomé, was five years Bartolomé's junior. He came from Fregenal in the poor Spanish region of Extremadura. He had dark hair and a full chestnut colored beard. Bartolomé knew him only in passing. The fact that Piñero had not been on the recent journey to the silver lodes caught his attention. Anything related to that adventure could not be the reason for the governor's attention.

Farfán entered the tent with a formal "With your permission," and continued to a muffled interior answer, "*Adelante.*" A few seconds later, the captain pulled back the tent's entry flap and signaled the two junior officers to enter.

The two men needed a few seconds to adjust to the light. Oñate stood before them, for he had no furniture with him. "Ah, so here you are. Thank you."

"It's an honor...."

The governor waved them off, hesitated and looked at the ceiling as if someone where there. "Time is short. I will not waste words. One of my captains is dead and another two are untrustworthy. They continue under arrest. The Natives may be in rebellion and there is dissention in our ranks. At times like these, decisions must be made and loyalty is paramount. Our fate is immediately before us."

He stopped and stared into each of the men's eyes in turn. "On recommendation of those who have been at your side and from my personal observation, I have decided and have therefore ordered that each of you be promoted to captain." Here he sighed and raised his hands slightly. "Of course, as if it matters at this moment, I will see to your pay. What—" and he emphasized this last word with a louder intonation and slight nod of his head, "does matter is your loyalty and effectiveness. Understand?"

He looked at Piñero who whispered, "Yes, my commander."

Bartolomé added as the governor turned to him, "Yes sir. Thank you, sir."

WAR AND DISSENT
January 1599, San Juan de los Caballeros, New Mexico

Christmas and New Year's Day had passed. Masses were said on both days. The governor wasted little time conferring with the priests and his captains. He had the survivors of the conflict at Acoma describe what had happened. They did not hold back. The bodies of those left on top of the mesa were stripped, mutilated, and thrown off the side as the Natives jeered and mocked the men below. Oñate sat and listened stoically even though his emotions raged.

After days of testimony, consultations, and meetings, the time came for Oñate's decision. The people debated among themselves. Some of the married men feared for their families if Acoma could not be penalized for its act. Others, like Vincente de Zaldívar and some of the Robledos, wanted revenge for the death of their brothers. Everyone feared that Acoma's example would morph into a total rebellion. Some cautioned against war, arguing that they were vastly outnumbered and needed to live among the Pueblo people. However, no one with the latter attitude spoke out.

Not surprisingly, then, when called together, all eyes alighted simultaneously on their governor to hear what everyone expected. They knew that the priests had granted his desire to make Acoma Pueblo an example. With a determined look, the governor concluded his short speech with his decision, "If they do not agree to surrender and turn over those responsible for their despicable deed, a war of blood and fire will be declared and the Pueblo of Acoma will be brought to its knees." He appointed Vicente de Zaldívar to lead the expected attack.

So it was "war" and it would happen soon, which meant that at any time now, the men would be riding off in the winter's snow and cold once again. This time though Bartolomé and his comrades would ride with a specific goal over a well-traveled route. They would attack and suppress Acoma in punishment for the murders of Juan de

Zaldívar and twelve of his men.

Bartolomé did not relish the idea of leaving again. He had not warred against anyone in his life and really was not a soldier by vocation. He found most of the Pueblo people to be peaceful. Yes, he suspected something at Acoma that with hindsight convinced him that, instead of Juan de Zaldívar it could have been Oñate who could have lost his life. And he understood the governor's logic to make an example of the pueblo. Still, he had been away from his family and livestock long enough. He wished that the whole controversy would go away but that was a wish not to be fulfilled.

Oñate's choices for who would be on Zaldívar's war council for the attack on Acoma, seemed curious coincident in Bartolomé's mind. His friends and family had raised eyebrows even before he left for the battle. "Why would the governor appoint Aquilar and not you to the war council? Aquilar does not like the governor and has led resistance against him. And Piñero? Wasn't he promoted to captain the same time as you?

Lucía, dispassionate, calmly stated. "Remember how we were ordered in the advance group after father's death? Yes, you were promoted but he still suspects. Maybe you are too quiet or perhaps he senses that you are reluctant in some things."

Bartolomé's initial urge to protest his loyalty subsided because he knew that she was right. Lucía also missed him while he was a way. There was other news, of course: The death of her brother, and her mother's now strong desire to leave New Mexico, a place that had come to mean nothing but grief and anxiety to her. Catalina wanted to move back to Zamora and live with her other daughter and son-in-law. "I'm too old for this," she said, and she left it at that.

Lucía left the other news to the men. They would talk to Bartolomé. And they did. Bartolomé, the three remaining Robledo brothers and González, along with a couple of others gathered off to themselves. They wanted to hear about Villagrá's rescue, which one of them expressed as unfortunate.

"He's a religious zealot, a legend in his own mind and, now, he is Oñate's main advisor."

Another person added, "Oñate needs to trust someone besides that son of his who is just a kid."

"How 'bout you Bartolomé? You are a newly appointed captain."

Bartolomé feigned surprise. "Me? He doesn't know me well enough. He circles himself with friends and family. I am like you, a late arrival to this venture."

"The problem is Villagrá. He is humorless and mean spirited if you ask me, " said Bartolomé González.

"He is conceited. Lucky, too. But mean?" Bartolomé settled a glance on his friend González after surveying the others.

González lost no time. "You...don't know?"

"Know what?"

"About what happened when he went south?"

"He caught the four deserters and executed them. I suppose he had orders to do that and he was not alone."

"Yes, Captain Márquez went, too, but Villagrá was in charge. Your account is partially correct, but there remains a part that you do not know."

Bartolomé raised his eyebrow and focused his attention on his friend who continued, "He garroted the two Portuguese and let the two Rodríguez brothers go. He claimed that they escaped but we heard from others who were there that he gave them a nod and wink because they are Castilians and friends."

Bartolomé did not wait to react. "How is a Creole," he said in reference to Villagrá's birth in New Spain, "more different than a Portuguese?" Both New Spain and Portugal, so far as the men knew were a part of their king's empire.

"Heck, Oñate was born in Zacatecas." Bartolomé shook his head in disbelief.

"The man is dangerous and now he is going into battle with you." González, who would stay in San Juan, looked knowingly at Bartolomé and the Robledo brothers. "Watch your backs. Be careful."

Bartolomé did not have much time for long conversations. There is plenty of time for that on the trail. He needed to prepare himself and wanted to spend what little time was left with his wife. He treasured his intimate moments with her.

"I worry about you, us," she whispered.

"Give me your hand." He reached out to her extended hand and stared into her concerned eyes. "I promise to be safe and I promise to come back to you whole."

"Sorry, my man from La Mancha." Here she used the term *"mi Manchego."* "I worry about us, my brothers, mom, and friends. Above all I worry about you." She pushed a few inches away from him to look into his face. "The governor constantly depletes our little village for his explorations and, now, wars. He leaves us with a handful of fighting men and exposed to attack. The Pueblo people we have settled among are not stupid."

"Yes, true. That's why he was careful not to alienate them when we first came. Most of the people I have seen have been friendly. But you are right, they are not ignorant, and we are the foreigners in their land."

By his very nature and background Bartolomé had an interest in the livestock, all of which except the horses, mules, and donkeys had been pooled into a common herd. Cattle, sheep, goats, chickens, and pigs were a key supply of food into the foreseeable future. However, because of the governor's priorities the fate of the herds had been left to the Mexican Indians. Bartolomé did not share Oñate's faith in their allies' expertise. After all, Oñate himself was a rich miner and really did not have much practical experience raising livestock, or, for that matter, raising crops.

Bartolomé spent what time he could sharing his expertise with the Mexican Indians. He helped birth a couple of cows, build a pen for the sheep, and told the herders to let the goats forage at the river bottom where they could feast on the abundant undergrowth. "But," he cautioned them, "Don't leave the goats in any one place for long, for they will overgraze the area and kill any chance for more growth." The pigs, Bartolomé favored the pigs, "They eat garbage so, yes, we need to collect and store it in a place away from our dwellings. The pens need to be strong." Some of the other men showed the Mexican Indians how to build small huts to help the pigs survive through the winter.

Protection from predators, including the Pueblo People was another matter. The latter quickly learned that the animals were a source of food. Sensing that this could be another source of irritation, Bartolomé proposed a solution at an officers meeting. "We have taken from them, including their domestic turkeys. Why can't we initiate some small exchanges, so they can raise their own livestock?" He received minority approval while the majority shook their heads in opposition, the standard rationale being, "We may not get through the winter ourselves."

Riding and camping in the snow had become second nature, but Bartolomé never got used to being away from Lucía. The frustratingly slow nine-day trip to Acoma exacerbated his thoughts of "home," as San Juan had become. Not even the immediate reality of combat diverted him from dwelling upon the safety of his wife.

Upon arriving below the great mesa that held and protected the pueblo of Acoma, Zaldívar designated a base camp, ordered that the two artillery field pieces be left there with a guard, and then had the rest of the contingent join him as they rode around the mesa to look for weaknesses in the pueblo's defense. Meanwhile, the Natives looking over the high cliffs of their mesa felt secure enough to hurl insults, rocks, and pieces of ice at the men on horseback. Out of range from the hurled missiles the men were amused. They especially noted how the ice splintered in puffs of dirt as it hit the ground.

Vicente de Zaldívar's offer of peace on the condition that the Acomans turn over those responsible for the ambush of his brother and his men resulted in more ridicule. Everyone knew that they would not surrender. Even the lowest ranked soldier could see that the Natives felt invincible in their "sky city." The miniscule size of the Spanish force only gave the Acomans more confidence.

Yet these same soldiers, Bartolomé included, looked up at their enemy from a different perspective. Some of the men had fought the Chichimecas around Zacatecas, others like Bartolomé squinted up in the mid-day's winter light to see the silhouettes of his antagonists. The scene prompted thoughts of the Spain of his earlier life. This is what all the romantic tales of knighthood were about and the histories of el Cid, or the more recent exploits of Juan of Austria, or the feats of Sampson of Trujillo as they confronted their enemies who many times stared down at them from the ramparts of crenulated fortresses situated on top of cliffs. Bartolomé thought of the castles like La Mora and Almenasedé de Tolets near his hometown. Yes, he felt an inner ancestral pride. As Zaldívar had encouraged them all, Bartolomé would "fight like a true Spaniard."

Zaldívar shared his "simple" strategy. "It always is simple going in," one of the veterans quietly commented. The Natives think that the only way to gain the top is up the one stairway, which at certain points consists of foot and hand holds. Therefore, Zaldívar ordered that the main force fake an attack at the stairway while he and twelve others scale up the mesa's backside. Once on top, the Acoma warriors would divide their defenses and allow the rest of the force to scale the *peñol* at both the stairway and at Zaldívar's route.

Bartolomé had no opinion on the strategy. He had no battle experience. His brother-in-law, Diego filled with revenge said, "It doesn't matter. One way or the other, these people will pay for my brother's death." Neither Diego nor Bartolomé were battle-hardened veterans but both would do as told. All the men waited with their thoughts as a determined quiet overcame the small army.

The winter's sun, lying low, continued to silhouette the peñol. The main force, prepared to charge at the northwest base where the stairway had been cut. They would occupy a part of a dirt path that ascended through rock and crag until it changed to stairs cut and, finally, the aforementioned hand and foot holds. Bartolomé was in charge of a contingent of harquebusiers, riflemen who would set up behind the charging men and pick off the defenders as they appeared at the cliff's edge. The advancing men had to get to the base of the stairs so that the attack looked authentic and would be close enough to the cliff's bottom to draw the attention and fire of the Acoma Indians.

Bartolomé ordered his men to load and prime their matchlocks and have them supported and ready on their respective metal forks. The trumpets sounded to begin the siege. Fifty some men charged up the stairway's trail. True to form, the Pueblo fighters came to the defense shooting arrows and throwing rocks. The diversion worked: Bartolomé ordered his men to commence firing. He had the men fire in three groups of four, although one group had five. This gave the men time to reload while the fire remained fairly constant and rapid as they picked off defenders. Bartolomé knew that the Indians would be surprised at the range and firepower of their oversized guns. From the distance, he could see darkened figures violently jerk and fall. He assumed that what he was doing was according to plan and was indifferent to the results of his shooting. Nor did he know that the ruse had worked until just as the sky turned a brilliant turquoise against a fiery bright orange of the setting sun's reflection on the clouds. Zaldívar sent word back that he and his men had secured an area on top of the mesa. With the eastern sky already a dark violet at the lower horizon, the fighting stopped.

Orders came to prepare for an all-out assault at daybreak. Meanwhile the men were to rest and prepare to haul a log plus the two field pieces up the mesa's backside. With reinforcements climbing up the mesa's backside, the Pueblo defenders could not afford to concentrate on the stairway.

Bartolomé never really talked about the rest of the battle. The blood, sound, smell of gunpowder and especially burning flesh would stay with him for life. In the telescope of time he would forget the toil of hauling the log and field pieces up the cliff, and his incidental wounds, one from a deflected arrow and the others from thrown rocks. Even the winter's cold and biting wind comforted him little as he struggled to see through beads of sweat. He would never forget the devastation that those field pieces brought to the Indians. Shrapnel tore apart bodies, disfigured faces, splattered blood, and left the ground strewn with dead and withering bodies and body parts.

They used the log to bridge a deep natural crevice, which along with the reinforcements and the two culverins, left no doubt who would be the battle's victors. The cannons belched, deafening everyone. Bartolomé advanced with the others. Some set fires to the buildings, incinerating many of the defenders. Out of the corner of his eye, he saw Diego flaying like a madman, exacting his revenge.

He would not remember how many times he ascended the cliff. Twice? Three times? He also could not recall fear. Instead "ferocity" and its ugly result of burnt, maimed, withering, and lifeless bodies came to mind.

To the relief of everyone the last of the Acomans finally surrendered after a day and a half of fighting. Even Diego had tired of the task. Mostly women, children, and elderly were left. Most veterans of war don't talk of the post battle quietness against the backdrop of what has happened, while everyone has become overcome with an extreme weariness. The sight of the result of their deeds coupled with the sudden silence added an even more sinister tinge that pervaded everything in sight and rendered equal to the gloom of the defeated as well as the elation of the victors.

Bartolomé felt no elation, just relief and disbelief. For the rest of his life he would carry the image of that disparaging atmosphere, the result of fast and ugly deeds that he and the others dutifully and efficiently carried out. A lesson, he knew, had been taught.

"Anxiety" would be an understatement for the people left in San Juan. Left undermanned and under rumor of an attack, the women manned the ramparts. The small male contingent, including Bartolomé González, secured the plaza's entryways while keeping watch on the ramparts. Doña Eufemia, Sosa's wife, once again called the people to task and led the women to the ramparts.

Braced for an attack, the women stayed at their places during the night. Fear and determination broiled in their minds and conflicted with concern for their husbands, brothers, fathers, and sons who had gone to battle at Acoma. Yet, the women persevered.

Lucía later explained while Bartolomé listened. "The governor ordered all the men left to arms but there were not enough."

"We thought so."

"Well, one of the ramparts was left exposed so we women went there."

"With arms?"

"With what we could find. The men had most of the arms. We took what we could. Oñate said that our mere presence would give the attackers pause for thought, for the place would appear to be heavily defended."

Looking down and shaking his head in disbelief, Bartolomé encouraged Lucía to continue. "Yes, and...?"

"Well, I went too."

"To defend the town?"

"Yes. All the women went."

"And your mother?"

"Well, no. She wanted to but, you know, she is old. She and some of the other old ones (*viejitas*) did the cooking and brought us food and warm drink."

"But there was no attack."

"Yes, but we helped prevent it."

"Who was attacking?"

"Pueblos. I don't know. We never saw anyone."

"Not San Juan. People from here?"

"That was the rumor but it was the Natives from here who warned us."

"I doubt that they would do such a thing. These are good people."

Later, González confirmed the whole episode with Bartolomé. "It was just a false rumor but no one knew that. To us the threat was real."

"Oñate should enlist Sosa's wife!"

"Ha, probably true. He accepted her leadership this time."

"He needed all the help he could get."

"Still, thanks to God that there was no attack."

For years later Bartolomé exclaimed with pride and partly in jest how Lucía had manned the walls of San Juan. Bartolomé boasted, "She wasn't given rank but she is my equal!"

Lucía was equally anxious to hear what happened at Acoma but could only get the story of Acoma in hesitant bits and pieces. Bartolomé, she noticed, had returned a changed man, like every veteran of combat. He would only talk to Lucía about it and even then, reluctantly. With others and sometimes with her he would simply reply. "Yes, I was there." He never mentioned his many wounds, most of which were inconsequential and a couple of which left small scars, the only remaining testimony to his presence at the battle of Acoma.

He did not know how many Natives had died. Maybe hundreds or maybe fifty. Too many. Why count? One Spaniard died, mistakenly shot by one of his own men. Bartolomé helped take the survivors, who had become prisoners, to Santo Domingo Pueblo where Oñate would preside in a trial over them. No one doubted the outcome. The governor wanted to continue with his "example." He would hand out a devastating punishment of some kind.

Bartolomé was thankful that he did not have to attend the trial or assist in the subsequent punishment of maiming the males that Oñate meted out. Bartolomé was left at San Juan to help secure the village against possible attack.

He was secretly pleased when many of the "prisoners" escaped before they got to Santo Domingo. When he tried to politely refuse accepting an Acoma man and two women as servants, he was given no choice but to take them. He was pleased and not surprised when he woke up one morning to find that they had disappeared during the night.

"I've no revenge left in my heart. They need to go home and live in their pueblo, if they can. I can imagine that the ruined village holds very unpleasant memories for them."

People began to notice an increasing disdain in Oñate's attitude. He became convinced—how, was anyone's guess—that Taos Pueblo had organized the supposed failed attack on San Juan. Maybe the local Pueblo people told him this information. Perhaps the idea was planted by one of his inner circle. This, of course, got the men to speculate that Oñate would try to make a second example of the northern most Pueblo. Even the Robledo men joined the increased grumbling.

"He's punished the Acomans but his appetite is not satisfied."

"Maybe he sees a profit in the captives."

"No. None of this is true. He wants to create a reputation as a great military leader."

"Sure, on our backs and with our blood. He wasn't even at Acoma."

Oñate surprised everyone at a general meeting when he suggested that it was time to layout and construct a new town, which he named San Francisco. He spoke nary a word of Taos or any other campaign. His mood appeared to have improved. Many correctly speculated that the ore that Bartolomé and the others had brought to him had assayed positive for silver.

Bartolomé accepted the announcement on its face but he remained skeptical. He could not understand how such plain rock could ever contain silver. The fact that some of the others, who had some mining experience, shared his doubt, gave Bartolomé even more pause for thought.

While, Oñate's announcements could have been worse, with declarations of more war for example, the people did not like the thought of building a new town. They hadn't been at San Juan a year and had more than enough to do just to survive. The affair at Acoma and Oñate's trip west still weighed. Virtually no one agreed with the idea, and the unanimity of that feeling permeated the colony enough that even the governor had to acquiesce.

Bartolomé voiced his opposition, diplomatically, of course. When asked by Piñero, he answered that San Juan provided readymade ramparts and a semblance of defense. The colony would be exposed while building a new town or even a presidio. Besides, he added, "Some are unsatisfied and feel that we should wait until the viceroy sends more people." Piñero, a thin man with a pronounced Adams apple, nodded in agreement, hesitated for a moment, thanked Bartolomé, and left.

Oñate did not share another idea with the whole colony. Rather, he chose to be discreet by calling his officers together for a discussion. Bartolomé studied Oñate's surprisingly sparse living quarters while he listened to the governor reveal that royal law and instructions required that a civil government be created.

Every man in the room read in Oñate's humorless face that the time had not come. The embers of dissension glowed enough to render changing the government over to anything but a stern hand would be disastrous. Without hesitation, they concluded that Oñate should continue without change.

Back among family Bartolomé expressed a concern that he dared not reveal to Oñate or his cadre. "I agreed with the decision but worry about the result."

"Why not speak your mind?" One of the more impatient Robledo brothers questioned.

"I wish I could but to do so would be to dip my bread up to my fingers. I need to maintain something to hold on to, to survive. Some of us, including a few in this room, have become frustrated with the man. And with reason."

"You needn't tell us." This came from Francisco, the youngest of the Robledos.

"If Oñate turned the colony over to a civil government the whole project would disintegrate."

Diego, the eldest of the brothers, added with raised eyebrows, "You mean return to New Spain."

Bartolomé continued, seemingly not paying attention to the comments, "Some of us would like to see this through."

"Not many." Francisco wined. "And why? There is nothing here."

The attitudes of his brothers-in-law perplexed Bartolomé and now he showed some emotion. "That is a different argument. Please allow me to continue without your incessant commentary. I feel that the longer Oñate stays in power the more abusive he will become. He is used to dealing from strength and has invested more than all of us combined."

"He is richer than all of us...."

"Yes and his fall, his embarrassment greater. The fear is to what extreme he will go to avoid failure if the negativity among us continues to grow. On the other hand..."

Francisco spoke again. "Bartolomé, you are not painting a rosy picture. So, why support the man?"

Bartolomé continued, "On the other hand, he may succeed and will have to convert the government from military to civil and, then, who wins?" Bartolomé waited for an answer but none came. He answered his own question. "We do. If we stay."

Later in their own privacy Lucía, who with her sister and mother had quietly listened to the discussion, asked Bartolomé if he meant what he said.

Laying on his back and shirtless Bartolomé simply replied, "Yes, *querida.*"

"You know that mamá wants to return and my brothers are debating as to how that should happen."

"What do they say?"

"That coming to New Mexico was a bad idea."

"It was their father's idea."

"Yes, I know. They have overlooked that. I think that they all want to leave but do not want to be a part of a conspiracy."

"And, they do not know how to resolve this problem."

"Yes."

All the speculative conversations ended the next day when word spread that the governor would be sending the assay reports and specimens to Mexico City. He would request more aid from the Viceroy and, hopefully, recruit more settlers. Maybe another three of four hundred people with abundant supplies would replenish the colony.

Bartolomé worried. He did not want to be one of those the chosen to go. The trip to Mexico City meant that he would be away for one or two years. What would Lucía do during that time? No. He wrung his hands, paced, and tried but failed to sleep that night.

They soon learned that captains Piñero and Farfán would join Villagrá on the trip to Mexico City. Fathers Alonso Martínez and Cristóbal Salazar, Oñate's cousin, would go to recruit more priests. Everyone recognized that those five men were Oñate's trusted lieutenants and advisors who would plead the governor's case before the Viceroy and hopefully lead back new recruits. But there was one omission. Everyone wondered, "What about Zaldívar?"

Almost as quickly the answer became obvious. "Of course he is not going. The governor can't send away all his trusted people."

At the same time, Oñate decided to organize a search party to look for silver and gold deposits. He announced a plan to conduct a thorough search all around San Juan and he quickly called upon Bartolomé, telling him that he would be leaving soon and that his experience from the previous trip to the western "silver lodes" would be invaluable. "Zaldívar will be in charge and he will need you."

Diego Robledo could not help but react out loud. "What about Piñero and Farfán? Both of them were with you before."

"You see," Lucía added, "you are trusted but not really. Oñate has divided his most loyal captains with the emphasis on putting on a good face before the Viceroy. You are kept from harm's way by leading his nephew on another pointless expedition."

"It's more than that, I am afraid. As I understand it this expedition is to be one of many. The governor plans to send mining explorations out in all directions. He plans to turn over every rock and look under every tree within a two days ride from here."

Lucía continued, "He plans to keep the men busy and avoid a mutiny."

Bartolomé shrugged and replied, "Yes, *mi querida*. That is exactly correct."

For the rest of that year the colony was kept busy unsuccessfully searching for mineral wealth, improving its new church and compound, and barely surviving. They tended to crops and livestock and renovated and expanded their dwellings and built outdoor adobe beehive-looking ovens that they called *hornos*. They suffered through another harsh winter huddled indoors around their fireplaces when they could. They also suffered the anxiety of expecting the arrival of new settlers and supplies, but that did not happen.

With the first hints of spring in 1600, no one was exactly sure of the dates any more, Oñate decided to send a second expedition to the "silver mines" and further to the South Sea "where the pearls came from." Once again, Bartolomé was determined to be invaluable to Zaldívar because, "of course, Zaldívar has not gone there and you know the way."

Lucía pointed out that he was being sent on another pointless expedition. She knew from him that the rocks brought back were highly doubtful. Then, Zaldívar and Oñate announced that a discovery had been made close to San Marcos Pueblo. As soon as the reinforcements arrived, men would be assigned to begin a mining operation. Zaldívar even produced what looked like a real piece of silver. This surprised Bartolomé because he had been with Zaldívar searching that area and he never saw anything like that.

Bartolomé's brothers-in-law chimed in with their sarcasm and this time Lucía joined them.

"Lucía please! I'm not happy about this either." Privately, Bartolomé hated the idea of going on another winter trek over the same route past the Hopi pueblos. Besides, unknown to the others, Lucía recently informed him that she thought that she might be pregnant.

"How do you feel?"

"Fine."

"Are you sure?" He touched her stomach.

"That I am fine or with child?"

"Both." He stroked her hair.

"Well, yes and not completely."

"What does mother say?"

"She still wants to leave."

"No. About you, your condition. She is experienced in these matters."

Lucía smiled, "She brought some of the other women over. They poked me, asked questions. 'What do you eat?' And I answered, 'What is before me.' They laugh and theorize 'yes' or 'no.'"

"Lucita," Bartolomé rarely used the affectionate diminutive of her name, "this uncertainty is driving me crazy at a time when I least need it. I do not want to leave without knowing."

Nevertheless, when the time came his horse was saddled and he was spurred. He set out with a group of twenty-five men in the last week of a bitterly cold February and he knew that it would not get warmer until a week after they headed south from the Hopi Pueblos. He was in for a long, miserable, and generally tedious journey.

They retraced their way to the largest of the Humano pueblos where they were unsuccessful in getting corn. The band of men moved on to the apparently abandoned Acoma Pueblo and camped at their old site at the peñol's base. Everyone had a sense that they were being watched from above and that maybe some people had moved back to the village. They never saw anyone, nor did they attempt to go up and look around. They only had a feeling.

Bartolomé led the way beyond the Zuni Pueblos. He revisited the route all the way to the quarries where he and the others had gathered the samples. The others, of course, were now on their way to Mexico City. Once again, the local Natives offered assistance and this became a cause of a conflict between Bartolomé and Zaldívar. The governor's nephew did not share Bartolomé's confidence in the Natives. He questioned why they should listen to them. "These barbarians can't be trusted."

Bartolomé tried to be discreet. "But, my captain, they have cooperated on both trips and have shown no hostility."

"Like the Pueblos before they killed my brother. And these are more primitive. I don't trust them."

"We can be both alert and observant. It seems that the further south we go the more pearls we see."

"I don't like this. We are willingly riding into a trap and I will not share my brother's fate."

Thus concerned, Zaldívar led his men into *tierra incognita*, intentionally ignoring the advice of the friendly Natives. Within days they were effectively lost, for they had dropped to the desert where the heat, even in early May, suffocated both men and animals. And, without help from the local guides, finding water became a matter of luck.

The men shed their armor, and stripped off their shirts to tie over their heads. The broad brimmed hats of future generations had not yet become a part of their vital equipment. Finally, it fell to Bartolomé to confront Zaldívar with the futility of the journey, for by then they were aimlessly wandering with no sea, much less pearls, in sight. It was time to make for the soothing climate of the northern alpine forests where they would find water and game to regain their strength. After three months on horseback in a futile search they finally returned to San Juan.

A NEW TOWN AND THE NEXT GENERATION
May 1600, San Juan

An unsatisfied Oñate sullenly reacted to Zaldívar's report. "I'll have to do it myself," he grumbled through his chapped lips and beard. Visibly hurt by his uncle's reaction, Zaldívar threw up his arms, did an about face, and walked out the room.

Bartolomé followed with a formal "With your permission."

"No. Stop. Wait!" Oñate was not through. Both men turned to face their commander. "I have decided to move the colony."

"We will build San Francisco?"

"No nephew. We will move to the village across the river. I have negotiated." here the governor paused with a knowing look, "With the Indians to trade villages."

"W-why across the river?" Given the recent criticism of him, Zaldívar was hesitant.

"Defense. Not only will the river help but it will separate us from all the nearest villages."

Rather than appear puzzled, Bartolomé asked, "When do we move?"

"Yes, Romero, you are the practical one. Preparations have begun. We have thirty to forty good wagons. This will need to be coordinated and quickly. Do you understand?"

"Yes sir," the two men answered in unison.

Bartolomé rushed to Lucía who waited impatiently. She looked beautiful. She did not have to say anything. While rubbing the outside of her forearm and, then, affectionately holding her hand, Bartolomé said, "Ah Lucía, I love you. You are beginning to show!"

Lucía laughed. "It will not be long before I give you a son and my mother a grandson."

"A son! You know that?"

"No, but it is fun to speculate."

They embraced in mutual pleasure of each other. In their child they sensed a future. And Bartolomé could take solace that many experienced women would join Lucía's sister and mother to comfort her through her pregnancy.

The winter's mountain snows had begun to melt, and the Rio Grande's water level and velocity rose accordingly. The move to new quarters would have to be delayed until August when loaded wagons and people could cross safely, for not even the colony's gruff, hardened men and stern women desired to cross the roiling brown river during runoff.

Moreover the priests, who had resisted out of fear, started to openly complain about Oñate's treatment of the Indians. The governor's proposed move and further displacement of their Native hosts was their latest complaint.

Bartolomé's family and friends beseeched him with smug complaints about "Don Juan." They told him the horrifying story of how he went to the largest of the Jumano pueblos, the ruins of which would later be called Gran Quivira, and punished the people for refusing to give corn to Bartolomé's group as they headed west in pursuit of pearls. The enraged Zaldívar had sent back word that instead of corn they were handed rocks.

"But that is not what happened!" Bartolomé pled. "They had no more to give and used rocks in their hands to convey that message."

"Well," González reacted, "that is not what Oñate said." The others nodded in disgusted agreement.

They continued with how they all were ordered to ride to the Jumano pueblos to exact revenge. When the beleaguered Indians could only provide "ten or twelve blankets," Oñate ordered cannon and harquebus shots fired into the crowd. Then he hanged two leaders and when, in his rage, he became suspicious of his own interpreter, Oñate had him hanged as well.

"He has taken all he can from those people. He should have known."

"Yuh, well," Francisco argued, "I can understand that he is bitter. Still, he has been heavy on us too. I don't trust him."

Alonso Robledo picked up the narrative. "Francisco and I went with him to Taos to get more maize and, once again, he decided to set an example."

"Why?"

"I suppose he thought the Indians reluctant to meet his demands. So he ordered one of the house blocks fired upon and destroyed. We burnt it to the ground."

"My God! Exactly what do the priests think?"

"They argue that rather than convert he has alienated them, made enemies of the Indians, and they see no point in living among them asking for certain death."

González took up from Alonso, "And now he wants to displace a whole native village and move the colony. He is insane!"

Bartolomé was speechless. He did not know what to think. Obviously circumstance, unexpected events, acts of God, or bad luck could hinder the settlement. But, what he heard indicated something different: Oñate's impatience had created an atmosphere of fear, anger, and even hopelessness. Bartolomé had no doubt that a majority of the colony had become disgruntled. The only hope, it seemed, would be the quick addition of settlers and supplies from New Spain and he said as much.

That night with Lucía, Bartolomé repeated the day's conversation before he turned to the one topic that interested both of them, the pending birth of their son.

"And what does our son say? Stay?"

"I don't know. I think he is loyal to you. Why don't you listen?"

Bartolomé put his ear against Lucía's stomach. "You are right. He agrees with me!"

But the governor could not wait for relief, so rather than sit still until the runoff abated, he decided to move his colony *en situ.* In other words, he renamed San Juan as San Gabriel and ordered its extensive renovation. He wanted a three-sided plaza with a larger, permanent cruciform church centered in its middle and the open end of the new u-shaped town closed with a rampart and a sturdy gate.

"He's mad!" The Robledos had no doubt.

"Why? What's he thinking?" That was a thought that resonated throughout the colony.

The governor's reasoning slowly surfaced. He needs to demonstrate some progress to the Viceroy. The image of creating a new town was more about politics than convenience.

And it was in the "new," partially complete town of San Gabriel in the summer of 1600 that Bartolomé and Lucía gave birth to their first child. Surrounded by Francisca, her mother, and some of the other women, they named their son Bartolomé after his grandfather and father. Family history notwithstanding, they soon started calling him Barti.

Young Barti's birth brought some joy in stark contrast to the ever-increasing atmosphere of dejection. Oñate's unfailing search for silver or gold in the harsh foothills and wrinkled mountains distracted the people from tending to crops and livestock. Not even an advance arrival of seven men, a priest and a small quantity of emergency supplies relieved the colony of its pessimism. The news that even more supplies and people were on their way north gave momentary relief.

Lucía now questioned their future in New Mexico. Her mother and her brothers all expressed a desire to leave and with a newborn son she could not help but raise the issue. On the other hand, her sister Francisca had married another colonist, Juan de Tapia and he wanted to stay. Bartolomé found a quiet ally in his new brother-in-law.

Dissent ran rampant. Even the priests had begun talking privately to people. Bartolomé could not tell whether Oñate clearly understood what was going on. He seemed to be more interested in taking a major expedition east on to the plains. Jusepe continued to fill the governor's head with tales of "Quivira," large Native settlements close to the North Sea.

Bartolomé resisted the temptation, even pressure to join the growing "mutiny," as he called it. He felt secure enough to approach the governor with his concerns and advise him not to deplete the colony with another expedition. Leaving the colony would embolden his detractors to abandon New Mexico. "Also, the Jumanos are recalcitrant. Rather," he posed, "it would be more prudent to wait for the reinforcements coming north before following Jusepe."

Oñate scratched the side of his face and pensively spoke, "Yes...there are immediate problems. I should deal with them." Then he dismissed Bartolomé with a wave of his hand.

More disappointment came on Christmas Eve when the main caravan arrived. The much-needed supplies were a boon but only eighty new recruits arrived. And the news spread that Pérez de Villagrá had deserted along with Farfán and Piñero when the Viceroy refused to put him in command of the return expedition.

"That zealot didn't return? I thought he was loyal to Oñate?" The Robledo brothers were elated.

"No, I heard that he ran into a church for asylum. And the other two were supposed to be Oñate loyalists, hand-picked to represent him." The brothers could not believe the news. Moreover, they agreed that Villagrá, at least, would not be missed.

New cotton shirts, pleated jackets, pantaloons, boots, buckled shoes, even buttons, needles, and thread, horse gear and much needed tools such as hoes, axes, adzes, and plow shares filled a desperate need for the colony. News and some letters helped lift spirits. Word that King Felipe II had died and that his son Felipe III now reigned gave pause for conversation and relief from their constant dire thoughts.

Despite the disappointing number of new settlers, Oñate seemed reinvigorated. Perhaps he was spurred to action when four more men deserted. They fled south to the Jumano pueblos where the Natives killed them. Word of this enraged Oñate on two scores. First, the audacity of the men to leave and second, the brazen affront of the Jumanos.

Oñate now gathered his captains. There was no conversation. The governor made clear his determination to deal with the desertions as well as the Jumanos. Almost with a sinister chuckle, he addressed his most trusted confidants, Zaldívar at the forefront. Over his shoulder as he walked out of the meeting, he announced, "I am tired of this. I will deal with it now."

Left behind, Bartolomé could only wonder at what Oñate meant. He did not have to wait long, for within an hour, a breathless Alonso Robledo burst through the recently hinged wooden door of Bartolomé's dwelling. "Aguilar has been executed!"

"What? How?"

"Run through with swords and knives. I heard that Oñate himself applied the killing thrust."

Bartolomé tried to digest what he just heard. Aguilar had been a particular thorn in the governor's side and come close to this fate before. But why now?

Not done with his news, Alonso disrupted Bartolomé's thoughts, "Oñate had Aguilar decapitated so that all may see what happens to his detractors. He is calling Aguilar a traitor."

On a cold mid-February day less than a couple of weeks later word spread throughout the colony that the elderly Alonso Sosa Albornez also had been murdered on the governor's orders. This act seemed even more problematic.

Bartolomé openly mused, "He was an old man with his whole family. Who would want to kill him?"

Lucía added, "Honest, too. He had no secrets."

The answer came soon enough. Alonso, who would not desert the colony, instead sought permission to leave with his family. The governor listened with feigned sympathy that masked a twisted disdain for what he heard. "Sure," he replied, "you may take your family. I will be sending some dispatches soon. You can join the couriers when they leave. You can start gathering your possessions."

Sosa bowed his furrowed and bald head as he thanked the governor for his understanding. But, then, the governor asked Sosa to help round up the stray horses that had been let to pasture. Sosa agreed to do so "with pleasure."

While helping with the herd the next day Sosa was surrounded by Oñate's men who stabbed him and left him to bleed to death. This time Zaldívar oversaw the act.

"Oñate wants us to cower." Francisco could not hide his bitterness. "It will not work. Already letters of complaint are being smuggled south. He cannot persist in this manner."

Diego, the oldest of the brothers who tended to agree with Bartolomé, added, "Execution? It's murder! Enough! This has to end."

Bartolomé did not venture an opinion. Even he had come to disdain the governor's acts. Alonso Sosa, he knew, was not one preaching mutiny. Instead, he did the proper thing and sought official permission to leave. Apparently, the governor did not see the difference. Finally, with everyone expecting him to say something he spoke. "Do not follow in old Sosa's footsteps. Be patient and don't let on that you want to leave if that is what you want to do. Maybe the Viceroy will make a change."

"Wait for how long? *Hasta cuándo?* Until when? When we all have perished?"

Francisco had lost what little patience he had.

None of them had long to think of their plight, for Oñate decided to march on the Jumano pueblos. Once again he was determined to set an example. Bartolomé was pleased to hear that he would be left at San Gabriel, while a majority of the men went on to engage in what became a six-day battle that completely leveled the largest of the Jumano pueblos.

Nor were Bartolomé and Lucía displeased to hear that he would not go on the subsequent expedition to Quivira on the plains. Toward the end of June, Oñate led an army of seventy well-chosen men, some of whom the Captain-general wanted to keep a close eye on, plus all their servants, and guides, including Jusepe. The men and animals hauled eight supply-laden wagons, six pulled by mules and two by oxen. Over seven hundred head of livestock served the expedition's needs.

Those who stayed behind listened as Oñate beseeched them to protect San Gabriel and, then, ordered the banners unfurled. The main body of the impressive army slowly made its way out of San Gabriel heading south to their first rendezvous at San Marcos Pueblo. The large army raised a cloud of dust that the residents could see for over half a day after the last of the entourage had passed from their sight.

REBELLION AND ABANDONMENT
Summer 1601, San Gabriel

Left behind, Bartolomé, Francisco Robledo, and González joined the others in preparation for a hot summer and what they knew would be the next long, cold winter. They needed to tend to crops and livestock. They had to haul, split, and stack wood, maintain their dwellings and keep on constant vigilance against attack. Then, another, more immediate problem surfaced.

The indecisive Lieutenant Governor Francisco de Sosa Peñalosa, who Oñate left in charge, allowed the colony to degenerate. First, some of the people refused to help with the necessary work like planting crops, digging ditches, and tending to the livestock. Then the malignant whispers began, "Why work? I'm leaving." Next, the priests gathered from their assigned pueblos to join in the planned "mutiny."

Sosa Peñalosa did nothing and the detractors saw their opportunity to press on audaciously with renewed energy. They fanned out to recruit like-minded individuals. With safety in numbers they would be emboldened to approach the lieutenant governor, which they would not have tried with Oñate.

Bartolomé's turn came when Francisco Robledo brought Captain Luis Gasco de Velasco to meet with him. Bartolomé had little interaction with Gasco but, in anticipation of the forthcoming conversation, sized up the diminutive, balding man with a rough beard and graying hair hanging off the sides and back of his head.

"Captain Romero, I am led to believe that you are an honorable man so I come to you on good recommendations," Gasco said. He tended to mumble through barely moving thick lips, and his small deep-set, dark eyes darted about.

Bartolomé looked at Francisco, who looked away, and replied to Gasco, "Yes, and why do you come to me?"

"Oñate."

"Oñate?"

"Yes, Oñate. He is gone and may he survive this latest of his follies. Many of us cannot bear to stay here longer. He has started unnecessary wars, killed his own. I, myself, witnessed the killing of Aguilar. Look what he did with poor Sosa and what about Sosa's family?"

"Aguilar had caused problems even before we got to New Mexico. Twice his crimes were warranted execution. You probably know better than I the military law under which we have sworn."

"Maybe. Still, that does not answer for Sosa. You know that some of the recently arrived people are confidants of the Viceroy." Gasco paused for emphasis as well as to see Bartolomé's reaction but was disappointed to see none. "That is why Villagrá and the others did not return."

"Then go to them with your complaints."

"We have."

"Then there is no need to talk to me."

"Listen Romero, many of us are going to leave before Oñate returns. I was told that you might join us."

"You were misinformed." He looked at Francisco. "I will not desert."

"Oh no. Nor will we. We have presented a petition to the lieutenant governor and he has agreed to call a general meeting to hear our complaints."

"You expect him to allow you to abandon the colony and leave the remaining few exposed?"

Francisco now spoke. "If we do not act, we will never have another opportunity."

"Listen Romero," Gasco had a grating habit of constantly telling people to listen. "The fact is that we are all depressed. Many of us invested and lost what little wealth we had. Most are intimidated and frightened. With Oñate we have a legitimate fear for our lives. Who knows what he will do at any moment. He is gone and we have an opportunity. You can stay at your own risk."

The meeting left Bartolomé mortified. He knew that the lieutenant governor would give in to the detractors, especially now that the friars added their persuasive influence to the pressure. The general meeting would be a sham.

Nevertheless, he spoke on behalf of a minority. He stressed that abandoning the colony would leave those who stayed in danger. How could they leave the families of the departed men so exposed? He questioned the priests about their motives. How could they turn from their sacred trust to convert the Natives? Had they not baptized some? Would they leave the newly converted to their own devices?

After the meeting he walked with Lucía who was holding their little Barti. "They will leave us. They are concerned only for themselves."

"They have their reasons, Bartolomé. You cannot argue against that. Mother and my brothers all want to leave."

"Well they can't. Alonso and Diego are with Oñate."

Lucía grabbed Bartolomé's hand and stopped to face him. "Francisco will take mother. They have discussed this. They are leaving."

"What about Francisca and Juan?"

"They are staying. Juan is with you."

Bartolomé dropped Lucía's hand and stepped away from her. He felt a press of chaos coming toward them all. He wanted to talk with González who had been surprisingly quiet of late.

Lucía agreed. He should talk with his friend. She knew that González had a reason for his reticence. He had decided to leave with Francisco and Catalina and he knew that Bartolomé would be disappointed.

"Look Bartolomé, I know how you feel and I cannot disagree. Nor can I disagree with some of those who want to leave, like your mother-in-law or Alonso Sosa's family. They have nothing left here, no future, only bad memories."

"And you?" Bartolomé was not critical. He did not want his friend to leave. He would miss him.

"I've no prospects here. I am single, still young. My future is in New Spain, not here. Besides, you and I know that not everyone leaving has good reason. Some are lazy, others dishonest. I will travel with your brother and mother-in-law. Together we will be safe."

Bartolomé had no answer and, if he did, he had lost any ambition to argue. He merely said, "Brother" and hugged his *tocayo*.

Thus on a beautiful warm September day in 1601 Bartolomé and Lucía joined the twenty-five or so remnants of the colony with their servants to watch a larger, less organized group leave San Gabriel. The contingent of over two hundred people headed south with wagons full of supplies and personal possessions. Some of them helped themselves to things and livestock that was not theirs. Their bittersweet departure left the colony depleted of people and livestock.

Those who remained harbored bitterness and had become very critical of Lieutenant Governor Sosa Peñalosa. Unlike his wife Doña Eufemia, he had no fortitude and that was the polite way that the people described him. He granted the "mutineers" permission to leave, which in effect, gave them legal cover for their actions. He even sent them off with a written justification for his decision. He agreed to let them go while lamenting the extreme poverty of the land, claiming that under Oñate's control, they are "on the verge of perishing." Those who remained were incensed by his words.

His report implied a criticism of them. They also knew that some of the people would continue to spread their venom once they arrived in New Spain. Their words needed to be countered. Then the weak Sosa refused to do anything to prevent the thefts.

Bartolomé agreed that something needed to be done and done quickly. Captain Gerónimo Márquez, along with Alonso Gómez, Cristóbal de Baca, and Bartolomé decided to confront "Francisco de Sosa Peñalosa, Royal Alférez, Lieutenant-governor, and Captain General of these kingdoms," as they wrote it. Along with some sixteen other men they presented the timid Sosa with a "petition of the people who chose to remain in New Mexico."

They selected Márquez to be their spokesman. The captain was fair-minded, had longer time in rank, and had been sent south twice and, importantly, returned each time.

Then after some discussion they agreed on a plan. They would counter Sosa's earlier justifications for what he had permitted with an interrogatory of their own. And they would do it with his permission and in front of him. Then Márquez would take the written report of the interrogatory to Mexico City to present to the Viceroy.

Although none of these people realized it at the time, they formed the nucleus of New Mexico's founding Hispanic families. Aside from captains Romero, Gómez, Baca, and Márquez other names like Martín, Varela, Chávez, Luxán, García, Pérez, Salas, among others would resonate throughout New Mexico's history. On occasion they or their ancestors would travel to Mexico for various reasons such as business, escort duty, or under arrest to be tried in Mexico City. It would not be until the twentieth century that a significant number of their ancestors would return to Spain.

Sosa, of course, did not like this latest confrontation. Now he was a minority of one and he had been maneuvered into a corner from which he had no escape. Bartolomé stood next to Márquez as the latter addressed the timid Lieutenant Governor. "You will do for us as you did for them, Señor. You will witness our testimony, authentic it, and grant permission for me to take it to the Viceroy."

"You ask a lot."

"We ask nothing. Your actions, or lack of action, have denigrated those of us who are loyal and authenticated those who fled. Now you will bear witness to the other side of this story."

"But..."

"No. No more words. At least, not from you. It is time that you listen." Márquez turned to the assembled men and ordered that a table and chairs, with quill and paper be prepared for the interrogatory to begin after breakfast on the next day. Over the next three days, nine of the remaining colonial officers answered a prepared list of sixteen questions.

Sosa, who was required to sit through the questioning as the men spoke and their words written down, was obviously uneasy and mostly fidgeted in his seat. Márquez read each of the nine witnesses the same prepared questions. Four people testified the first day, four more two days later, and one on the day after.

Bartolomé was the second person to take an oath, cross himself, and give testimony. He was one of three captains to do so. The other two were Cristóbal Baca and Alonso Gómez Montesinos. The answers varied very little. Some of the men gave more detail depending whether they witnessed or participated in a particular event like, for example, the leveling of the Jumano Pueblo.

Bartolomé began his interrogatory by stating with a certain degree of unavoidable pride that he "had travelled through the pueblos of the entire land more often than anyone else." He always found the Pueblo People, "calm and peaceful."

When asked if he knew whether the holy gospel was preached to the Natives, and how it was accepted by those who understood even a little, Bartolomé answered that, with the exception of Fray Alonso de la Oliva at Santo Domingo Pueblo, the priests did not try to work among the Pueblos or learn their languages "because they do not care very much to stay in the land."

He went on to state that the abandonment of San Gabriel had put the colony in great danger and that he understood that such an act should not occur "without a special order from his majesty." Instead, he witnessed some captains, with the support of the friars plot the desertion and that they tried to force others to join them so their act would appear to be a common agreement of everyone. He named Alonso Quesada and Gasco de Velasco among other conspirators, and added that they even threatened people to join the mutiny.

When asked about the battle with the Jumanos, he replied that he was one of the officers who advised the governor to deal with them before going to the "North Sea." Because he was not at the battle he could only state what he had heard from those who were there.

Bartolomé joined the other witnesses in stating that the crops of wheat and "Castilian vegetables" had increased each year. That in one year the harvest of wheat alone had increased from "two hundred *fanegas* to one thousand five hundred *fanegas*."

After the last person testified, the secretary took three days to write up the fourteen page report, which was then copied, read out loud, and "validated and endorsed" by Sosa Peñalosa. Thus within three weeks from when the majority of the colony left, a new packet of papers was made ready to be taken to the Viceroy.

Lucía worried about the events more than Bartolomé. Among those being accused were her brother and mother and Bartolomé tried to console her. "No, my love, the questions and answers are written in such a way that the blame cannot be put on them."

"But it sounds as if they were part of the plan and..."

"No. We named the leaders and detailed the pressure that they put on the others. It is they who should be arrested. And, don't forget, they also have Sosa's permission to leave. He could be in trouble for that, not them."

"I hope you are right."

"Márquez will make sure that the innocent are not punished. We have discussed this. He and whoever goes with him know that many of the people were not party to a conspiracy."

"Are you going?"

"No, my love. I stay. Márquez will take a few of the unmarried men."

But the plans changed when the remaining colonists received word that Oñate was on his way back. He had just crossed the plains and was approaching the east side of the mountains. Everyone agreed that they should wait for the governor before sending the petition south.

The sight of only twenty-some of his men waiting to greet him did not please the governor. He wanted to know what happened and, avoiding the usual welcome he waved for his officers to meet with him. The briefing did not improve his disposition. He severely criticized Sosa Peñalosa asking him what he was thinking and then, after a pause, he ordered the lieutenant governor's arrest and announced that he would be tried for treason. Then he ordered Zaldívar who had accompanied the governor on the five-month journey across the plains, to prepare for the pursuit and arrest the mutineers. In his rage, he even charged that those who had stayed were plotting to leave and that it was fortunate that he returned when he did.

After a needed rest and reading the report that Márquez had arranged and was going to give to the Viceroy, the governor calmed down. This gave the captains who had given testimony and witnessed the report an opportunity to explain the nuances of what had happened. They posited that not everyone who left should be blamed. Oñate seemed to nod in agreement but not everyone was sure.

Winter set in and it was a cold mid-morning with a slight snow floating to earth when Alonso burst into their living area while they worked around the warmth of their fireplace. He excitedly announced that he would be going to Mexico City with Zaldívar.

Lucía could not contain her surprise. "My God! Oñate trusts you?"

"No, Zaldívar. I was in his command on the plains. He got to like me and we fought side by side when the Escanjaque Indians attacked us."

Bartolomé still had a look of disbelief. "But he knows that your mother and brother left with the others."

"Yes. It seems that he has come to understand. He briefed all of us who will leave."

"Oñate?"

"No, Zaldívar briefed us. Márquez is going and we will be taking the papers. The governor has added his report of the Quivira journey, which will be read to us all this afternoon if the snow lets up. He also has prepared a defense of himself because he knows that he has come under attack. He blames the leaders not the followers, and Sosa."

Lucía looked at Bartolomé and then her brother. "What about arresting everyone?"

"Our instructions say so but they have been gone three months. They are out of our jurisdiction and in New Spain by now. The governor is more interested in defending himself and the colony before the Viceroy. His brother will help in Mexico City."

The snow did not stop until almost dusk when the clouds broke up to allow the sun to give a slight reprieve from the cold before nightfall. A huge fire was lit in the plaza in front of the church where the people gathered to hear the reading of journal of the recently completed expedition. Bartolomé, in acknowledgement to his new trusted status, scribbled his name below the December 14, 1601 date as an official witness to the reading.

SURVIVAL, HARSH REALITIES, AND A STATUE
1602, San Gabriel

The weather grew worse. The shorter days seemed to become increasingly grayer and the snow did not stop. Even the Rio del Norte began to freeze over. As a result, Oñate agreed to postpone Zaldívar's mission until after Christmas and the New Year. The trip would be made easier as they traveled south and the days grew longer and warmer.

The postponement gave rise to another opportunity for Oñate. "Now," Oñate announced, "is the time to create a civil government. The detractors are gone and those who have remained are worthy." What he did not say, but everyone understood, was that the change would play well in Mexico City.

No one was surprised when Oñate had a letter drawn up and he asked his captains to sign.

The "Letter to the King from some Conquerors of New Mexico, Asking Him to Aid Don Juan de Oñate," announced that because "of our large expeditions" while "we sought means of settling land when others were abandoning it...we were unable to transform our military organization to a civilian one until now." The short letter explained that they had come to "these kingdoms of New Mexico" and built a village to create a stable colony. However, its success would not be possible unless they received some aid. The governor had spent all his wealth while enduring "many hardships." Unless, his majesty comes to their aid, New Mexico ("this land") cannot be settled. Bartolomé and six others, not including Oñate's nephew Zaldívar, signed the letter on New Year's Day 1602.

A couple of days later Bartolomé, Lucía, her brother Diego, and sister Francisca with her husband Juan all wrapped in coats and blankets walked with Alonso to his horse and watched him mount and ride off with the others on their important mission to the south. All of them understood that, given the opportunity, he would defend the honor of his mother and brother. They also knew that he would not return.

As they walked back to their rooms, Lucía told Bartolomé that she had something to show him.

"What?" Bartolomé could sense that whatever it was, Lucía was being both coy and serious.

They entered their rooms and peeled off their coats and shawls. Bartolomé stoked the fire while Lucía opened her travel trunk to pull out a small bundle, which she unwrapped to reveal her mother's small statue of María del Sagrario. "Mamá left this to me. She said that I would need her help more than she would. You will have to make a *nicho*, a place in the wall for her."

Bartolomé understood the importance of the statue to his wife and was at loss of words. Finally, he swallowed and spoke. "You tell me where you want her and I will make the *nicho*. May I hold her?"

As Lucía handed the small doll-like figurine to him, he said, "She will be our family patroness in New Mexico. With her, we will never forget our history."

"She is special Bartolomé and we must impress our children and their children about her."

Bartolomé paused, "Are you?"

"No, *mi querida*. Not yet. We've time for that." And she kissed his unshaven cheek. "First, let's get through this winter and you can start by tending to the fire before it goes out."

She became pregnant soon after and both thought the idea of a growing family a pleasant prospect. Other things kept them more than busy so they did not ponder too much about their second child. The governor continued to send Bartolomé on futile mining explorations. Bartolomé rode all over the rock and sand foothills of northern New Mexico. He even explored north of Taos Pueblo into what would become known as the San Luis Valley.

Oñate continued to send messages to Mexico City, pleading for aid from the Viceroy or so he would lead everyone to believe. The couriers and those who went with them knew that the governor was in a battle to save his political life. After being held back from going with Zaldívar, Márquez left the following year in October of 1603. He was put in charge of an official packet and told to take it directly to the Viceroy.

When Bartolomé and others asked Márquez what he thought the packet contained, the captain could not answer for the letters had been sealed shut and placed in his trust under great secrecy. Only upon his return the next year did he reveal what he had learned. Oñate had successfully recommended that both the deserter Villagrá and Zaldívar receive the minor noble rank of *hidalgo* because of their service to the king in settling New Mexico.

"What about the rest of us?" This was a question that had to be asked. Most of them knew the Royal law that granted them *hidalgo* status if they stayed five years with the new settlement. Then, dumbfounded some wanted to know how Villagrá could be so honored after deserting. Of course, they would not confront Oñate with either of these questions.

They were assured that despite what had happened Villagrá and Zaldívar had teamed up with Oñate's brother in a coordinated effort on the governor's behalf. In fact, all three had left for Spain to plead his cause.

While the news provided some deviation from the tasks at hand, Márquez's arrival brought little joy. He returned with a few new settlers, some priests, and a few wagons mostly loaded with supplies for the missions. The Viceroy apparently did not want to invest in their far north venture.

All this created uncertainty about the colony's future. The colonists could do nothing to influence the outcome. They had to concentrate on day-to-day survival all the while waiting for more news.

Apparently hoping to keep people somewhat distracted, Oñate sent another expedition west with the double purpose of leaving priests at a reoccupied Acoma and looking for the elusive sources of silver and gold. Regarding Acoma, Oñate reacted to the news that the place had been re-occupied by saying, "If they want to live there, let them. I trust the lesson has resonated." Only after Márquez returned with those few extra priests did the governor relent and allow the Franciscans to assign a couple of their brethren to the defeated pueblo.

Taos Pueblo proved a different matter, for the people there refused to contribute more corn or blankets. Bartolomé was selected as part of the contingent to accompany Oñate to that northernmost pueblo. Bartolomé hoped that the result would not be another episode like Acoma or the Jumano Pueblos. Lucía agreed with him. Both considered the Pueblo people docile and peaceful. "They do not deserve such violent treatment."

"But the priests have had little success."

Bartolomé answered the thought. "I know. The first priests cared little about their mission to this place. Now they hardly have enough priests to minister to all the Pueblo People. Still, my love, some of our people have moved to live among them. Look at here and at San Marcos."

"Don't forget Santa Clara! I hear that the people there are becoming good shepherds."

Taos was another matter and it narrowly avoided another siege. The governor showed his anger with his usual violent attempt at intimidation. He threw one of the pueblo's spokesmen off the roof of a house-block. Fortunately the first floor roofs were not too high and the dirt at the structure's base was soft. The victim landed awkwardly but managed to gather himself and limp off holding his arm.

Bartolomé returned home relieved. But not more so as he continued to watch several of his friends and comrades head south as Oñate's messengers. Once again, not all of them returned. Those that did return usually brought a few new faces and a couple or three wagons packed with supplies. They never returned with enough of either reinforcements or supplies.

Bartolomé preferred to remain with his wife and young son. It was during this time that Lucía gave premature birth to another son. The tiny baby constantly coughed. They called in a priest to have him baptized and when the blue robed sacristan asked for his name, Bartolomé and Lucía smiled and said together, "Pedro."

"Ah, a good name for a good apostle. The father of our Holy Mother Church. Yes?" He paused and stared at the parents. "But I think there is more to this name than that."

"Yes, Father." Lucía always maintained a formality with priests while Bartolomé generally addressed them by their first names. "It was the name of my father and brother. Both who have perished here in New Mexico."

The priest gathered his hands under his robe and looked down. "I am sorry. Was your father the Pedro Robledo whose burial site is the camping place that bears his name?"

"Yes father. He was an old man and the trip north was too much for him."

Now engaged, the friar commented, "I hear that he was the first of the colonist to die in New Mexico."

"Almost." Here, Bartolomé spoke. "There was an innocent who died at birth a day or two before."

"Baptized I hope."

"We suppose so. The colony was so big and we were on the move when it happened. We only heard about it afterward."

Two days later the family and some friends gathered with the same priest. As the sun shone against a clear, almost turquoise sky, Bartolomé and Lucía buried young Pedro. Walking back to the village Bartolomé could not resist holding his thought. "He is the third Pedro of our family to die in this land."

HOPE AND A GROWING FAMILY
1604–1606, San Gabriel

As the winter snows began to let up and the sun's warmth began to melt the accumulated drifts, Bartolomé received word that he would be going on a prolonged trip. This would not be the local search for traces of silver and gold, nor would he be going south to Mexico City. Oñate chose him to go on another expedition south of the Hopi Pueblos in search of the South Sea. This time, though, would be different, for the governor himself would be going.

Oñate chose thirty-one other men, including Captain Márquez, and a new favorite of his, Fray Francisco de Escobar. Escobar brought along Lay Brother Juan de San Buenaventura. "This time," the governor growled, "we will get to the South Sea!" The men nodded in agreement while the governor gave a glance to Bartolomé who answered with the slightest of acknowledgements. Oñate expected the experienced Bartolomé to lead the way.

As he rode off leaving Lucía again, Bartolomé solaced himself with the memory of the stench and cramped conditions he suffered while crossing the Atlantic Ocean. He and the two Alonsos, as he fondly recalled them, spent the first four or five days retching until they could not retch any more. Bartolomé smiled to himself about the distant memory as he mildly urged on his horse to head on to open land.

Except for the result, the trip proved uneventful to Bartolomé. Oñate followed Bartolomé's directions and advice. Directions were a matter of retracing steps, even camping in the same places. The latter amounted to a deviation from Bartolomé's previous experience with Zaldívar. Oñate listened to the Natives who directed them down a stream to a large river and, then, down it through a succession of heavily populated villages to the ocean, where they arrived on January 26, 1605. They knew the wide expanse of water was an ocean for two reasons. The large river that they named the Buena Esperanza River, emptied there and the water was not sweet but saline.

Oñate, as pleased as Bartolomé or anyone else had seen him, had Brother Juan follow him into the water holding high a cross. There, with water lapping around their thighs, the governor pulled out some papers and read the required legal taking of possession of this sea and all its harbors for His Highness, the King our Lord. And because they had arrived at that place on the day of the Conversion of St. Paul, he named the "port" Conversion. The constant wind blowing across the water and beach prevented anyone besides Brother Juan from hearing him.

The return trip seemed prolonged, both for the anxiety of returning home and the familiarity of the route. As usual supplies ran short and, this time, they ate horsemeat from some of the worn out animals that they put to death. Even conversation ceased. The men simply had nothing more or new to say to each other, this especially included all the early speculation that their discovery would become a harbor and major port.

One of the men had sailed with Sebastian Vizcaíno in the Pacific Ocean and up the Pacific Coast. He was a good swimmer and swam out off shore before diving to get an idea of the depth. He returned to report that the depth is more than enough for a good anchorage. He proclaimed before Oñate that the location was one of the best "locations he had ever seen for a port." Oñate exclaimed, and later added in a report, that the harbor was large enough "for a thousand vessels to anchor."

The men argued among themselves about the new port. They did not share the governor's optimism or the expertise of the sailor, for he had not otherwise distinguished himself and the men did not trust his words given to the governor. They also noted that the source of the pearls still remained a mystery and, as they picked up more rock samples, they were reminded of the previous silver discoveries, which did not seem like real silver.

Bartolomé felt personally satisfied, for he had won favor with the governor. This paid off when, upon reaching the Rio del Norte, Oñate placed Bartolomé in charge of twenty men to continue the journey back to San Gabriel. The governor, Márquez, Escobar, and the rest of the men turned south to go to Mexico City. Oñate wanted to share his great discovery with the Viceroy in person. "Now maybe he will see the value in this effort." Father Escobar confidently assured him that the Viceroy would be pleased, "It will be so."

Meanwhile, back in San Gabriel, Lucía's anxiety surpassed Oñate's, for she was at least seven months pregnant and worried about another premature birth. She could count the months simply from the time Bartolomé had left last October. This circumstance both pleased and worried her. She dreaded the thought of losing another child yet she dearly wanted to provide a brother or sister for her only son. For sure, she did not want to keep her emotions to herself but share them with her husband. More to the point she wanted him with her. So she listened and watched for any hint of his return.

Lucía did not have to say anything to Bartolomé as he dismounted and rushed to her arms. She was swollen and obviously pregnant. He apologized for not being with her, but Lucía waved off his sentiment. "It is the fate of this place."

The pregnancy became their primary concern. She felt strong. So too, apparently, did the unborn baby, for they could feel it moving in Lucía's womb. Little Barti, now over two years old, gleefully laughed when he felt the movement in his mother's stomach.

Not even Oñate's prolonged absence concerned the couple. Inexplicably, or perhaps not, Oñate had left Captain Juan Martínez de Montoya in charge of the depleted colony. Martínez was a decent enough guy and he seemed very competent. He heralded from a Castilian village near Madrid but did not have any pretentions. He never complained and was happy to pitch in whenever needed. He had come to New Mexico with the second group that arrived on Christmas Eve a few years back.

People were surprised that Oñate trusted him. The governor usually took his time warming up to people. Plus, there was a suspicion that he was one of the Viceroy's men. Nonetheless, with Zaldívar gone and with Bartolomé and Márquez traveling with Oñate to the South Sea, Martínez was the only choice left.

Now as nomadic Indians more brazenly attacked the pueblos and stole livestock, everyone hoped that the governor would successfully gather the much needed supplies and additional recruits. The struggling colony, they felt, could not sustain itself much longer. For good reason the result of Oñate's trip to Mexico City became the major source of conversation and speculation.

In the middle of July the birth of the Romeros' second child, a girl, brought some relief from the constant worry and grind of everyday life. No one felt so desperate to forgo the celebration of a new birth. While death was common enough, it was not so prevalent that people completely lost hope. So far as the colony was concerned either it would be supported or they could always leave. More than a few of their friends had done the latter.

Her new daughter brought great pleasure to Lucía. Even in desperate New Mexico Lucía could not help but plan great things for her daughter's future. Little Barti immediately took on the big brother role, which was a reaction that both intrigued and entertained his parents.

Perhaps because they expected another boy neither of the parents had a name ready for their daughter but it did not take long to decide. Bartolomé initially asked, "Would you like to name her after your mother?"

But Lucía had other ideas. "No. We named poor Pedro after my father and brother. May God keep them. She is María after your mother. Maybe this name will bring good luck."

"And with that reminder I wonder if I will ever see your mother again some day."

"Oh Bartolomé! Do you think?"

"Hush, my love. The way things are going there is a good chance all of us will be returning, at least, to Mexico."

"Oh, to see Ana...and maybe mamá is still alive."

"We'll learn more if and when Oñate returns. All we can do is wait."

DISAPPOINTMENT AND RESIGNATION
1605–1609, San Gabriel

After a little more than a year, Oñate returned to San Gabriel. He arrived worn, aged, and only with a couple of wagons of supplies. Everyone immediately knew that he had been unsuccessful. His hair now completely changed to various shades of gray and white with a beard in complete disarray, he looked older than his actual age, which everyone guessed was in the fifties. His dejected weather beaten face and matted hair did nothing to counter the pessimism overcoming everyone who saw him.

Lucía quietly exclaimed under her breath, "My God! He looks like death's companion."

Bartolomé in a whisper reacted to no one in particular. "No worse. He has lost hope. I don't think we are long for this place." Nothing more needed to be said as they watched the governor slowly dismount, look around and walk into his rooms. Notably missing from the returning entourage were Fray Escobar and Captain Márquez.

The end to speculation came soon enough, for Oñate met with his captains within the hour. He recounted his trip. He stopped at Santa Barbara where it became clear that his detractors had the new Viceroy's ear. Father Escobar and Márquez "volunteered" to go on to Mexico City and present the letters and the report of the South Sea discovery to the Viceroy. "Hopefully," here Oñate looked up from his seat behind a small table, "they will succeed there." He unclasped and raised his hands a few inches above the table and added, "It is our only hope." Once again, they would have to wait for news from the south.

Winter came early with the first dusting of snow in September and two major storms in October. Fortunately, Bartolomé had made use of the summer to collect enough wood and food to enjoy the warmth of his growing family. By now, Lucía's sister, Francisca, had given birth to her first child. The time seemed to pass quickly as they daily gathered around the hearth and waited out their eighth winter in New Mexico. Spain and New Spain had become distant memories as they moved through their now familiar routines. A halt of Indian raids and subsequent punitive chases, added to the general tranquility.

As the days lengthened and cottonwood trees began to show signs of leafing with specs of green, the raids began anew. At first the more distant pueblos suffered attacks. Taos Pueblo, already weakened by Oñate, was almost completely destroyed by an Apache raid. Oñate responded with mostly futile punitive counter-attacks. The Spanish had an important advantage over the raiders, for on horseback they pursued an enemy on foot. But the superiority lost some advantage by the time it took to report the attack, organize a strike force, and send it to the stricken pueblo. By the time the force arrived the attackers were long gone.

Bartolomé went on many of these punitive expeditions. Only once did he come upon the culprits and with the advantage of surprise the New Mexican horsemen overran the native encampment killing all but the lucky few who fled to cover in a nearby forest. He had killed before at the battle of Acoma and had felt some remorse. Now, however, he had no pity, for he did not equate these people with the Puebloans. In his mind, these were uncivilized.

Even Oñate's teenaged son led an expedition in pursuit of some raiders. To be sure of his command, Oñate made sure that Cristóbal had a couple of experienced captains to assist him. These included Bartolomé, Márquez, and the ever-present Martínez de Montoya. These mostly futile chases served as a kind of maturation process for "Don Cristóbal."

In the meantime, Oñate showed no concern about the functioning of the civil government. He maintained his standing as governor and captain-general and, as such, kept his authority. He had no qualms about the *cabildo*, or town council holding meetings. He encouraged them to meet on a regular basis, for it brought him relief as "his councilors," most of who were also his captains plus the Father Commissary and Cristóbal, dealt with all the tedious decisions that had heretofore pestered him. As the summer months passed, the leadership had to make sure that the livestock, crops, and hunts were maintained in preparation for coming winter.

Once again, Bartolomé pushed for teaching and aiding the Pueblos in raising livestock. Unofficially, his idea was working in the Pueblos around San Gabriel. One of the settlers had moved his family to Santa Clara and with the Natives there raised his sheep. This time Bartolomé's suggestion received a more favorable reaction. Nothing much came of it, because the colony really did not have enough livestock to disperse.

Bartolomé's greatest pleasure was watching Lucía tend to their two children. He loved to carry his son on his shoulders where he "can see the whole world! Look," he would add and point south, "do you see *abuela* Catalina?" Barti, looked with wonder in the direction his father indicated. In his affectionate youthful talk he always replied with a curt, high-pitched "*sí!*"

Lucía constantly told the children about their grandparents. She obviously emphasized her own parents. She never knew Bartolomé's parents so Bartolomé was never concerned. Moreover, the children were two young to understand what she was saying.

The littlc statue called "Sagrario" stood in a *nicho* close to where the two children slept. Every night they recited their bedtime prayers before Sagrario. Lucía knew that over time the children would grow with the knowledge of her family and its connection to her mother's statue.

In September, two events diverted everyone's attention from their daily routines. The first of these involved a scare when a band of Indians from the plains attacked San Gabriel. Thanks to the alert Mexican Indians who tended the herds an early warning went up. Bartolomé, along with the other men, rushed to man the town's ramparts. However, when they saw that the skirmish focused on the livestock, stoutly being defending by the Mexican Indians, Oñate ordered the men to their horses. Within minutes the spurred mounts charged out to the fields and the rout was on. At the battle's end a majority of the raiders lay dead. Very few escaped while none took any livestock. Oñate would subjectively report that his men had no casualties or serious wounds. He overlooked many wounds, some serious, as well as five mortalities among the Mexican Indians whose quick action and valiance had saved the day.

Bartolomé sent word back to Lucía that he was safe but would stay at the site to help with the wounded. It "was the least he could do for these men." He found one man with an arrow that penetrated his side, with the tip protruding out. Only flesh had been hit and Bartolomé knew that while painful the wound was not fatal. He pushed the arrow through and out of the wound. The man grimaced, took a deep breath, and smiled, "*Gracias compadre.*"

"*Nada, gracias a ti.*" And Bartolomé meant it. He wrapped the wound and moved on to help with the others.

A few weeks after the attack, Captain Márquez returned from Mexico. He showed up with eight carts packed with goods, two new friars, and an escort of twenty-four soldiers, five of which were veterans of New Mexico. Most notable as well, was the appearance of Vicente de Zaldívar who had been gone some four years. Everyone knew that he had gone to Spain. Surely he brought news. He did but it was not positive. The silver ore assayed negative with some traces of copper. The viceroy openly complained about New Mexico's expense. Never mind that he and his predecessor had been miserly toward the colony. Moreover, no official acknowledgement, much less appreciation, of the Oñate family's large expenditures had come forth.

Zaldívar's re-emergence was a pleasant sight for his wearied uncle in spite of the news. The addition of nineteen new soldiers, mostly young and single would be of some help. However, the cargo carried on the wagons did not bring any relief for the existing colony. Four of the huge wagons were packed with supplies for New Mexico's priests and the others basically hauled the supplies and goods in support of the escort. Zaldívar did manage to transport a couple of finely made suits for his uncle. At least Oñate could turn out in the latest fashion, even though he would look oddly out of place in New Mexico.

Overall, the paucity of the small caravan coupled with Zaldívar's reports clearly left an unfavorable impression on the people and its governor. As winter set in, an atmosphere of weariness, if not desperation, overcame the colony.

Oñate tried to overcome the mood when in late February he sent Zaldívar and a small contingent back to the South Sea. "Maybe you can find the famous silver deposits." At the same time Martínez de Montoya asked the governor if he could leave. Oñate would not hear of it. "Stay a while. I need you. Let us see what Zaldívar brings."

To Bartolomé and Lucía, Zaldívar's mission seemed to be a last desperate attempt to garner something positive out of the New Mexico venture. "Nothing. He will find nothing. I have been there three times. Maybe pearls, but where?"

"What will happen?" Lucía's concern was obvious as she cradled young María.

"I don't know. We wait longer or we leave."

"Go? You mean leave here?"

"No, Lucía, not just us. The whole colony will abandon the venture."

Zaldívar verified Bartolomé's forecast when he returned in early June without either silver or pearls. Now the governor hardly talked to anyone, save to issue orders. He spent a lot of time ensconced in his residence or on one or two day searches desperately looking for silver or gold.

Not even his march to the South Sea had impressed the viceroy. Oñate had come to his wit's end.

Toward the end of August he made a decision and called his captains together. He had penned a letter to the viceroy in which he would resign his position if the colony was not reinforced and adequately supplied. If a reply did not arrive by the following June, the governor announced that he would order the abandonment of the whole colony.

The men were astonished. So it had come to this, a long distance confrontation between the governor and viceroy! Those early embers of discontent finally caught. They would wait a few months more, for finally Mexico City would have to send a definitive reply.

Oñate ordered that Márquez and a small party of eight men take his letter of confrontation to the viceroy. He included Diego, the last of Lucía's brothers in New Mexico as part of the escort. This was a bittersweet surprise. Diego was excited. He knew that he would not return.

Diego divided what little possessions he could not take between his two sisters. The whole family and a couple of friends held a farewell dinner the night before his dawn departure. They reminisced about how they started out on this grand adventure, toasted their departed father and brother, and how the others began to leave, almost trickle away. Lucía gave him a lock of her hair to "place on father's grave." They knew that his burial site had become a regular campsite, a *paraje*, on the trail south. They never thought of it as a trail north any more. The place even bore the Robledo name.

Bartolomé handed Diego a letter to forward on to Spain. It was his second attempt to contact his family back in Corral de Almaguer. Because he never received an answer to the first letter, he figured that it never reached its destination. "As you know, we are starved for information. Let us know how the family is doing in Zamora. Have your brothers married? Children?" He paused a moment and looked off to the distance. "And, I want to know what became of my *tocayo.*"

"I'll make sure. You can count on me," Diego responded. In his anxiety to leave he had become a man of little words.

This is when Lucía in all seriousness observed that, "Only the women are left with the Robledo name."

Bartolomé put his arm around her shoulder. "Oh, Lucía. I suspect that we may be told to leave this distant place soon. God willing, we may be back in Mexico with the rest of your family before Diego here can send us his promised report."

So the two Robledo sisters and their respective husbands watched in the cold of dawn as the small contingent with Diego among them began their journey on the now well-worn trail into Mexico.

"Ah, my love, I am beginning to feel weariness in my bones."

"Bartolomé! Don't talk like this. You look younger than you are. Your hair is still black. No white, not even in your beard, and that goes first."

"It's the uncertainty, I suppose, and the lack of support. It is as if Oñate's troubles have left us to suffer the penalty."

The wait for the Viceroy's answer to Oñate's ultimatum weighed on everyone's minds. What would the Viceroy do? How would he react? What could or should they do? Nothing, of course, just wait.

"Prepare for another winter," was all that Bartolomé could say. The reply came unexpectedly fast. The courier and two escorts showed up in San Gabriel a month before Oñate's deadline.

Word of their arrival quickly spread and most of the people turned out to see the three riders dismount in the plaza. Then came their first surprise. The lead man carrying an official looking pouch asked in a loud and clear voice for "Captain Juan Martínez de Montoya" and not Oñate.

"What is this?" They watched the official and Martínez march off from the plaza to the latter's quarters. A few minutes later Martínez came out of his room looking very perplexed. He quick-stepped to Oñate who had witnessed the whole confusing episode. Martínez asked if he could speak to the governor in private. Oñate answered with a gesture guiding Martínez into his own dwelling.

Meanwhile, the people confronted the other two arrivals about any other correspondence that they might have. "Sorry *señores*, the viceroy's priority did not allow us time to collect letters."

The people did not have much time to react to the bad news before Oñate came out of his residence with an embarrassed Martínez at his side. The governor asked those close to him to call his officials together for a closed-door meeting in the church.

With guards posted outside the doors Oñate stood before the altar while the others haphazardly gathered around. "Gentlemen the Viceroy has acted. First and foremost the colony will not be abandoned." Here he paused, for he knew he had everyone's undivided attention. "It will continue, not as a private venture but as a royal colony. I, who invested too much in this," here he stopped, clasped his hands behind his back lowered his head and then looked up as he almost spit out, "fantasy." With his hands now unclasped and at his side and more reserved he silently added, "I will not be your governor."

The haggard governor waved off the expected exclamations of astonishment and denial. Holding up his hands to quiet his audience he astonished them with another bit of news. "Martínez here has been appointed interim governor until my replacement arrives."

Someone blurted out, "Martínez!"

"Quiet! Control yourselves. Let me finish. I cannot leave until that replacement arrives or I am told otherwise. Meanwhile, Captain Martínez swears that he did not seek this responsibility." The men shifted positions as the governor thought about his next words. "Nor does he want the position, and I believe him. In fact, he has asked leave from this appointment."

Would the twists and turns never end? Bartolomé, as enraptured as anyone, wondered where the governor was going with these announcements.

Even his detractors had to admit that the governor could be very convincing and now he tried his best. "You men represent the leadership of this colony. Among you is a majority of the *cabildo*, which has been legally organized and selected to represent the colony. Only the good Father Commissioner is absent. As a matter of procedure the council can vote to accept or deny Martínez's appointment, and also select a replacement."

Later that day Bartolomé took special care to explain to Lucía, Francisca, and her husband Juan how Martínez could be replaced as the interim governor by Cristóbal, Oñate's teenaged son. "Our ex-governor is clever and in this case, very persuasive. He said that he and some of his followers would be charged with malfeasance. Rather than draw someone else into his problems he suggested that he could keep it in the family if Cristóbal was named."

"Meanwhile," Bartolomé continued while seated at a table with a jug of water at his elbow, "because the viceroy favors Martínez and he has asked permission to leave New Mexico...well, you can guess." No one reacted but the faces begged him to continue. "Oñate and Martínez trust each other. The captain has agreed to take Oñate's reports and advocate for him in Mexico City."

Juan noted that the selection of Cristóbal is a clear indication of the people's support for Oñate and Martínez's acquiescence in the matter will help with his defense.

Lucía had a more immediate concern. "So-o-o, we must stay in New Mexico?"

"That appears to be our plight, my love. However, travel back and forth will not be so stringent and the crown will have to invest, which means more support and people. Who knows, maybe one of your brothers will return."

"And we might become civilized!" Francisca blurted her pointed and sarcastic comment with a cocked head and hand on one hip.

Bartolomé looked at Juan, who raised an eyebrow as he put an arm around Francisca's waist and asked. "Who will go south with Martínez?"

"Not any of us. Probably Márquez, again." And so it was.

That night after everyone went to sleep Bartolomé remained seated at the same table watching and listening to the peaceful rhythm of his children as they nestled next to their mother. He was perplexed and in deep thought. The future had not been resolved. Francisca's sarcasm is warranted. Oñate and his favorites would be replaced by...what? And where did that put him?

He undid his ponytail and unconsciously ran his comb through his shoulder length hair. "Maybe we should leave." He thought to himself. "But to what? The Robledos could help. Maybe. I would have to start over at almost fifty years old. He needed more information. He did not even know what his in-laws in Mexico were doing or how they fared. What about the promise of land or an *encomienda* here in New Mexico? Yes. And the entitlement of nobility? I've earned that. We have been here almost ten years! That is double the requirement."

He recalled that Lucía had asked him why he was so concerned about becoming a *hidalgo*. "Because it is nobility. We will be addressed with respect as *don* and *doña*, d-o-n, *de origin noble,* of noble origins." She laughed, "Oh sure, my noble knight and we will be closer to the king, maybe in line for his crown."

"No but we will be free of taxes and prosecution for minor offences."

"As for taxes, it is taxing enough to live here, and there are neither taxes nor money to pay them. And minor offenses here are commonplace."

"This will change some day. Or, what if we move back to Mexico?"

"Uh-huh."

Bartolomé mocked her "'Uh-huh.' But if we did move where is your 'uh-huh' then?"

Now he thought about his family. Even with an unsure future he felt confident. A whimsical if tired smile crossed his face. He would wait again, not for the potential abandonment of the colony but for a change in leadership and what that meant. Hopefully, the new governor would bring supplies and more settlers. With February ending and along with it the expectation of longer days and increasing warmth matched Bartolomé's growing optimism.

Everyone noted that Fathers Ximénez and Ordóñez left with Martínez. Their New Mexican brethren had wanted to give up on New Mexico but had changed their minds. The local community of five Franciscans had decided to send two of their most persuasive brethren south to convince their superiors that New Mexico is fertile ground for further work.

In September of 1608 word was received that Martínez and company had made a safe journey. The viceroy listened to him and read the reports with interest. The Friars Ximénez and Ordóñez argued that the mission in New Mexico had converted thousands of souls and many more waited for the word of God. In New Mexico that news raised a few eyebrows as everyone shook their respective heads in disbelief at such an audacious statement.

Then in the summer of 1609 news arrived naming of Pedro de Peralta as Oñate's replacement. New Mexico would not be abandoned and almost as an afterthought the directive reminded Oñate that he was to stay *en situ* until Peralta arrived.

The people went about their business. Peace had been made with the Pueblos. In fact, more people moved from San Gabriel to live at some of the pueblos. More priests, they heard, were on their way and this, in itself, created a positive feeling among the people.

Aside from daily concerns from crops, livestock, wood, and shelter, everyone watched out for nomadic raids. Oñate no longer sent men out looking for hard specie, instead the men went out only on the rare punitive expeditions, or for defense. Cristóbal followed his father's will that, in turn, let the *cabildo* make all the decisions.

Bartolomé understood the dynamic. Oñate no longer cared to lead. His son's selection was for show of support and the former governor now let the *cabildo* rule because his father needed what was left of the colony on his side.

All this resulted in a routine that everyone followed. A semblance of a normal lifestyle emerged almost unawares. Bartolomé became a community leader and even Lucía seemed at peace as her two children began to grow. They even tried to help her with household chores.

A NEW GOVERNOR
January 1610, San Gabriel

Thus on a brisk but clear January day the people went about their routine much like any other day when a lone rider galloped into the village plaza and, without fanfare, announced that Governor Pedro de Peralta would be arriving "within an hour, more or less." By the time the small entourage arrived, Oñate had arranged his officers with, inappropriately but telling, his son behind his right shoulder. Bartolomé maneuvered close enough to his former governor to hear any conversation between the two men. The whole colony stood around the plaza and watched. No one knew what to expect.

The lead rider reined in before Oñate and dismounted. He pulled off his gloves and used them to beat the dust off of his three-quarter-length coat. Then he deliberately looked around never acknowledging the man waiting to greet him. Only his head turned from side to side as he pensively slapped his gloves into one hand. Bartolomé saw it for what it was, an act. It reminded him of why he did not want to move to Toledo so many years before.

Peralta had a slender face, full chin and a straight narrow nose with a hint of a hook. His black eyes set under full dark brows penetrated whatever or whoever they sighted. There was a shock of juxtaposition between Peralta and Oñate. The latter would be replaced by a mere youth!

As the two sized up one another, everyone could not help but notice the comparisons. They stood at roughly the same height but that was the only similarity. The viceroy's new governor was in his middle twenties and did not have anything close to the experience that Oñate had before he got out of his teens, much less the rest of his life's history. He had straight black shoulder-length hair parted on the right side and sported a well-manicured thin moustache, unattached to a narrow goatee. He reeked of aristocracy. In contrast, Oñate faced him with knotted gray hair and an unkempt semblance of a full-squared beard and moustache that almost hid his mouth. The former stood straight and latter looked worn out.

Still meticulously slapping his gloves in his hand, Peralta spoke, "Ah, don Juan de Oñate...at last."

The older man bowed. "At your service, Señor. And I assume that you are don Pedro de Peralta."

"The same. You look bewildered."

"Yes..., well, no. I expected someone much older."

"That is understandable, I suppose. Well," here Peralta paused and looked around and then up to the sky, "so this is the famous Kingdom of New Mexico. Much has been said about this 'kingdom' in Mexico City."

Not used to being treated in such a condescending manner, Oñate sharply corrected the new governor. "No, this is San Gabriel. A village. New Mexico covers many leagues. From the south alone you have been traveling through New Mexico," and he emphasized the name, "for a week or more."

"Ah, so I see. And what about your new village? Where is it...Santa Fe, I believe you call it?"

"Yes, Santa Fe. It is south of here on the road to Pecos Pueblo."

Peralta raised a well-practiced eyebrow. "Ah, I see. I have much to learn. But then, so do you." Now he stuffed his gloves into his thick belt. "May we speak in private?"

"Yes, of course. As you wish." Oñate stepped aside to escort his young successor into his quarters. The entire colony watched and strained to listen to the exchange. Bartolomé heard it all. He knew that the new village of Santa Fe was nothing more than a marked off plaza with three one room adobe dwellings. He liked the place, for, to him, it seemed peaceful. It was closer to the mountains and next to a nice stream full of trout and a kind of catfish. But to call it a village seemed a bit fanciful.

Despite the cold, none of the people retired. They waited, while helping the rest of the new arrivals to dismount and start the longer process of unloading the wagons. They could not help but notice the awkwardness of Cristóbal who had been left outside. He embarrassingly fidgeted by the door. They had barely unhitched the oxen to take to pasture, when Oñate emerged and requested to see all his officials in the church immediately.

Bartolomé joined the others as Oñate led the way while Peralta took his time in order to be the last one to stroll into the church. He deferred to Oñate with a nod. This would be Oñate's show but performed under the watchful eyes of Peralta, who leaned against a column holding up the choir balcony in back of the church's nave.

Oñate did not waste time but announced that he had been ordered to Mexico City where he would answer the charges made against him. He added that some of his loyal followers also had been charged and that, aside from Villagrá and his nephew Vicente de Zaldívar he did not know who else had been accused of misdeeds.

He commented that he was free to leave, "if 'free' is what you call it" and that Peralta had granted him leave to choose who would be his escort. However, he could not exceed the number of men who had just arrived, and none of the first time arrivals were free to leave.

Without pause and almost in monotone fashion, Oñate announced that Peralta had come with instructions to move New Mexico's capital to a more central location and away from any Indian pueblo. The new governor had talked with Martínez de Montoya in Mexico City and with Captain Márquez during the journey to New Mexico. San Gabriel would be abandoned, and Peralta had selected the site of Santa Fe for the new capital. Oñate revealed that he also agreed with the selection.

Then Oñate announced who he wanted to accompany him south. Naturally, his family members were the first to be mentioned. Then, Bartolomé could not believe he heard his name. It was everything he could do not to run to Lucía and tell her, but he stayed. A good thing, for Oñate soon dismissed everyone but those who would make up his escort. Given the circumstances they had little time to get ready. They would leave in five days, use the same wagons that brought Peralta but with fresh livestock, and, this is what resonated with Bartolomé, "you are free to include your immediate families on this trip."

Oñate anticipated the reaction of those of the men who shared Bartolomé's familial situation. "You are free to travel –with or without your family—but as to the matter of staying in New Spain that would be a matter that you will have to arrange. Remember, you are still royal soldiers and only the Viceroy or our new governor, God protect them, can grant you relief."

Bartolomé suspected that he had another option that was not mentioned. As one of Oñate's captains he could refuse to go. Neither Oñate nor Peralta would countermand him on that score. This proved problematic and led to some serious discussions within the family. Should he go? Should he take Lucía and kids as well? What about Juan and Francisca? They had not been given leave to go.

When they concluded that Bartolomé and his family would go, the conversation turned to other matters. They would leave most of their possessions, including their prized statue of María de Sagrario, with their sister and brother-in-law. They all agreed that the statue had become the spiritual reminder of the Robledo's role in this distant north and that "as long as one Robledo remained here so would Our Lady of Sagrario."

Bartolomé and Lucía promised that they would study the environment in Mexico to make a determination on whether to stay or return. If they stayed, they would prepare the way for Juan's and Francisca's return as well.

Bartolomé proclaimed, "I will come back here myself to escort you!" And he meant it.

Lucía added without hesitation and equal conviction, "and I'll be with him to reclaim mom's statue!"

For his part, Bartolomé wanted to learn more so he sought out Márquez. The captain encouraged him to go. Whether or not he returned, the trip would do him good. He added that Bartolomé take care to put in a good word "for our governor," by which he meant Oñate.

When Bartolomé asked why he was not a part of Oñate's escort, Márquez's face turned sour as he explained that the viceroy explicitly ordered him to stay in New Mexico and help with the transition. "A thankless job," he added.

"But you are second in command," Bartolomé exclaimed.

"No. That is a determination for him to make," Márquez nodded toward the governor's quarters, "and he has brought a couple of favorites with him."

With Bartolomé's encouragement, Márquez shared his distaste for the new governor. Audacious, uppity, condescending, and, above all, inexperienced were a few of the descriptions that flew through Márquez's lips. "He is fresh from Spain, university educated or so he claims, and so far as I can tell, never led anything." The six-week journey that Márquez shared with Peralta as they traveled to New Mexico only deepened the former's low opinion of the latter.

"Yes go. Now is a good time."

"Gerónimo, you have done this journey many times, and returned. Why?"

"I am a soldier, loyal, the crown's man. And I have nothing else. I would get in trouble if I stayed there."

Thus in late January of 1610, eleven-and-a-half years after they arrived, Bartolomé and Lucía began a return journey that they had dreamed about. Lucía and the two children rode on a wagon that also contained their few possessions. Bartolomé rode high on his mount, a veteran officer overseeing his escort duties.

The January departure meant that they would shorten their winter as they progressed into warmer southern climates. The prospect of camping at the "Robledo *paraje*" became the first goal of their journey. They arrived there on the twelfth day. They had a little trouble locating Pedro's gravesite. Identifying the general area proved no problem, but the exact site took some concentration because the wooden cross disappeared long ago and the rocks placed over the burial had been dispersed over time. Enough evidence existed of the site for them eventually to locate and reorganize it. Then Lucía and Bartolomé took the kids to the place to explain who was there, and to recite some prayers for old Pedro's soul. The children, now ten and four years old, politely listened to their mother's history of the family patriarch. Lucía loosely pieced together his often-repeated words about the spreading of the wings of the Hapsburg eagle.

The trail south now showed evidence of use. Wagon ruts had become defined. Certain campsites had become obvious for their constant use. Some had acquired names like the one at Robledo. Scouts had become unnecessary while escort service was a necessity.

Each day the wagons ground on to the next night's campsite where people went about a well repeated routine settling in before gathering around fires and pots cooking a broth made of a little meat, some vegetables, and bread. On occasion a successful day's hunt could liven up the meal. None of the men had the time or patience to fish. That delicacy would wait until they got to civilization further south.

A TRIP SOUTH
March 1610, New Spain

Oñate granted Bartolomé and Lucía permission to leave the group at Zacatecas. As they suspected the old governor would spend time reacquainting himself with his wife and daughter as well as his extensive land holdings. While curious to see all that, Bartolomé and Lucía wanted to go to Zamora and have a family reunion of their own.

Time had telescoped in their memories. They had forgotten how far they would have to travel to their final destination. And they had to do it via Mexico City where Bartolomé would report to the Viceroy's office. Thus they continued their trip on "the Silver Road," El Camino de la Plata, a name that referenced the silver lodes around Zacatecas. Despite the end of the Chichimec Wars, the trip remained dangerous from both bandits and Indians. Roughly speaking Zacatecas represented the half way point between New Mexico and their final destination.

Mexico City seemed much more chaotic than either of them remembered. It was April and the summer heat had not kicked in, but it was warm enough for the flies and bugs to come out, something that New Mexico's higher and dryer climate gave relief from. They found the city intolerable. They were greeted with Indian beggars, the crowded streets, threatening stares from idle adventurers, and especially the rancid smell rising out of the shrinking lake where all the sewage that was not left in the streets was deposited.

Bartolomé reported to the Viceroy's office where he was granted permission to proceed to Zamora. Bartolomé was surprised to hear that he would be receiving back pay for his service in New Mexico. On a monthly basis it did not amount to much but over the years, well, both he and Lucía felt rich. The office issued to him a third of what was owed. He did not question their accounting but was pleased to receive whatever they determined. The payment came for the most part in letters of credit. He was fascinated with the coins they issued to him. The newer coins had an image of Felipe III impressed on them. Bartolomé had known only Felipe II and now the reality of a different king hit him.

The secretary in the Viceroy's office, a youngish, clean shaven man with manicured hands, notified Bartolomé that he would be recalled from Zamora to be interviewed about New Mexico. At that time, he continued, he would receive the balance of his pay.

The relatively new town of Zamora situated about halfway between Mexico City and Guadalajara. It sat in a startling flat, marshy valley lined with mountains on two sides. People from Zamora, Spain established the town in 1574 under the viceroy's orders. The town's promise as an agricultural center was only beginning to be fulfilled. The place had three churches under different phases of construction, the supplies for which competed with the livestock and agricultural wagons on its straight streets, some of which had been cobblestoned. The town centered on a completed and quite handsome plaza out of which radiated a grid pattern. Still it was a town and not a city.

Along one of those streets an old lady in a black dress sat in front of her house next to its only door. Not yet out of her seventies, she was considered ancient in her time. She sat on a stool and leaned back against the wall apparently sleeping, although an occasional wave of the fan that she held hinted otherwise. The movement barely interrupted the insects that she had become used to long ago. This was her daily ritual in April and May and, again, in late September and October, before and after the heavy summer rains. Her home was one of many dwellings that shared common walls and lined both sides of the street.

It was to this lady that Bartolomé led his family and small entourage. "*Discúlpeme,* excuse me, señora. Could you direct me...," and he never finished, for the lady looked up and they instantly recognized one and another.

Catalina Robledo merely exclaimed in a voice silenced by age, "*Dios mío!*" "My God," before her daughter Lucía with tears of joy streaming down her face, hugged her. Lucía's sister, Ana and her husband who never left Zamora, each of her surviving brothers, now married and with children, lived along the same street. One brother had dabbled in mining in Nueva Vizacaya long enough to bring some money with him when he finally moved to Zamora. Bartolomé and Lucía were pleased to present their own two children, one of whom their grandmother helped birth.

Bartolomé's brothers-in-law were interested in what became of Oñate. Lucía shared with her mother that they located and fixed up "father's" burial site that now bore the family name.

"How nice," Catalina whispered with a small pleased smile as she remembered that she too had dressed up the site upon her own journey out of New Mexico. "We have left our name there."

"Yes, mamá. And Francisca and Juan are still there waiting to hear from us."

As the people around them carried on in related conversations Catalina's eyes misted over as she seemed to lose interest. Then she asked, "And the statue of Our Lady?"

"She is in New Mexico mamá. Francisca has her."

The old lady replied with a quiet "yes."

Much of the conversation focused on Bartolomé and Lucía's future plans. Of course they would stay and make a new home for themselves in Zamora or so the family insisted. The land is plentiful, fertile, and well watered. They could live well, and be with the family.

That was all well and true. That, along with the fact that a few weeks later Lucía announced that she was undergoing the familiar indications of another pregnancy lent weight to her family's arguments. Yet, there was something, a feeling that neither Bartolomé nor Lucía could explain. Inexplicably to them, they were drawn to New Mexico. Even Lucía noted the sentiment. Nevertheless, they enjoyed being reunited in Zamora.

An Interrogation
November 1610, Mexico City

The summons for Bartolomé to appear in the vice regal offices arrived in late October. He would appear before the Viceroy's "fiscal," his assistant. The new viceroy had ordered an inquiry into New Mexico and Oñate's leadership. As one of the original colonists and an officer, Bartolomé's perception "would be much valued."

Bartolomé left Lucía with her family. She didn't need to travel and stay in the dirty city during her pregnancy, she was better off with her family, and, moreover, the trip would be a quick, two days travel each way and a couple of days there.

He preferred to travel on his own. The pending interview was daunting, although he was relieved to hear that the fiscal would ask the questions and he would not have to talk with the viceroy. He had seen the viceroy once. Then and there he felt that he wanted nothing to do with him.

While walking in the city looking for some new clothes for his wife and children, the sound of hooves pounding on stone and the rolling grind of rimmed wheels drowned out all thought. His total attention turned to the source of the ear-shattering racket as it passed by. It was a coach drawn by six black horses with tails braided and matching bridles driven by four dressed men in maroon livery. The ornate oversized coach, itself black with maroon and gold highlights—he learned afterward that it was actually gilded—carried an overweight man with a large, round head. Clean shaven with hair cut short in a bowl shape as was the custom of priests, Archbishop García Guerra and recently appointed viceroy stared out at nobody as if he had no concerns. The Dominican had become at once the head of New Spain's Church and the Civil Government and he seemed to enjoy his unbounded status.

Bartolomé went to the large, impressive vice regal Palace at the appointed time. A uniformed page escorted him through the recently completed building. He could not help to be impressed, as was intended, by the large curtained windows, the beautiful finished wood trimming, and walls lined with tapestries and art. With their steps echoing from the highly polished stone floor, he was taken through two large, hand-carved wooden doors into a high ceiling room where he was seated in the middle of a long impressive table. He was invited to sit in one of twelve matching high-backed chairs. Facing him across the table in three of those chairs sat the viceroy's fiscal and two assistants. A scribe with quill in hand and paper ready sat at a separate desk off to their side and behind them.

"Welcome Don Bartolomé." The fiscal nodded toward him.

"Sir, Your Excellency honors me with the title. However..." The Fiscal raised his hand to silent Bartolomé.

"Your papers, as submitted, have been approved. We are pleased to share this news with you. You and your descendants are *hidalgos* with all the rights and privileges incumbent with the title. From what we can discern, you are well worth the accolade."

Obviously pleased, Bartolomé could only answer, "Thank you, Your Excellency, I am honored."

Again the fiscal raised his hand, "As we knew you should be. Now, may we proceed with the business at hand?" He did not wait or need an answer. Rather he delved into the official business of an inquiry.

The questions started off innocuously. Bartolomé was asked to share his personal background and how he came to join "Oñate's enterprise." Then they asked him to recite his participation in the colonial effort. They questioned a few particulars like the "so-called silver" and, then, about the placement of the capital in a native village.

The questioning about Acoma required some effort from Bartolomé. He still did not like talking about it, so he began with a variation of his standard comment, "Yes, I was there. A soldier in charge of the musketeers. It was a siege, a battle, and my first time."

The fiscal had no intent of letting go of the subject so easy. "And? First time?

"In battle. It is a difficult thing for me to discuss."

"Well, Don Bartolomé, obviously this is not a casual conversation." The fiscal looked up from his white stiff collar and lightly placed his fingers together. One assistant stared at Bartolomé while the other looked down. The fiscal continued, "Was it necessary? The battle?"

"I don't know. I was not privy to all the information. I suppose an example needed to be made of them."

"But you found it unpleasant?"

"Yes."

They asked him about some of the other confrontations about which Bartolomé was relieved to say that he was not at the siege of the Jumano pueblos, or Taos. Nor did he go onto the plains so he missed the battle with the Escanjaques.

"Where those battles justified?"

"Sir, I cannot say. I believe that in all cases he sought the consent of the priests."

"What about the so called desertion. The priests 'consented' to that as well."

Here was an unexpected twist in the interview, for Bartolomé realized that the new Dominican viceroy had a zealous reputation. He had to be careful with his reply. "Yes, that happened and it almost ruined the enterprise."

"Do you blame those who left?"

"Not that they wanted to do so and did. It was when they left and how some of them blatantly stole goods and livestock and cared little for the welfare of those left behind."

One of the assistants handed the fiscal a sheaf of papers along with a note. The fiscal looked at the note and turned to Bartolomé. Unconsciously, both men could hear the scribe scratching their words on to paper against the background of a constant drone of street noise wafting through the open windows. "We have here some letters as well as a report in which you give testimony and witness. You seem to believe that the Pueblo People are peaceful and the priests less than enthused for their conversion."

"Your Excellency. That is how I saw it at the time. The priests argued for abandoning the colony. The desertion, letters, and report all occurred early in the settlement."

"Again you...I don't understand how..." The fiscal paused. "You are aware that the colony will not be abandoned and that two Franciscans recently returned from New Mexico have claimed as many as seven thousand conversions?"

Bartolomé interrupted. "Your Excellency, permit me. Juan de Oñate, my governor and commander attempted a nearly impossible task at his own and his family's expense. It seems that people worked against him from the beginning. His requests for aid went unheeded. Left on his own, he made many decisions, some of which did not turn out well in my opinion. However, I, as an enlisted soldier who was promoted, yes, but was never completely one of his inner circle nor privy to his motives. I was always, cognizant of my status as a soldier in His Majesty's service."

"As to the work of the priests I can only state what I saw. I was not aware of the conversion of so many and cannot speak to that. My words in the testimony that I gave those few years ago are what I observed. Those early priests left with the deserters. Only a few remained and a few more were sent to help. Perhaps those friars cared more for the souls of the Indians."

The fiscal smiled at Bartolomé and folded his hands in front of him. "That is obvious from the testimony of others. It seems that most of your *compadres* trusted your judgment and ability."

Bartolomé lowered his head and thanked the fiscal for his observation. Then the viceroy's assistant turned his attention to the "murders" and "Sosa." Not surprised, Bartolomé looked directly at the fiscal as he replied, "No one should have been killed. The two deserters killed by Villagrá should have been arrested and brought to trial. Aquilar was a troublemaker. He was one of those who always caused problems for Oñate. He did everything he could to undermine the governor. He avoided execution once but would not stop. I suppose under the law, the governor had every right to execute him."

"And?"

"I would have kept him in chains."

"Brought here?"

"Not under the circumstances because at that time everything we heard in New Mexico was that the deserters had the viceroy's—His Excellency's predecessors—ear. The governor felt isolated."

"What about Sosa."

"Our lieutenant governor bent to the deserters. He was within his rights, especially when some of the friars wanted to leave, but his decision was based on fear not reason or loyalty. And he put the remaining people in peril."

"Should he have been arrested?"

"I would have made him stay in New Mexico to suffer the consequences of his decision."

Now there was a pause. The fiscal had something on his mind and fidgeted while he tried to frame the question. Finally, he merely stated, "Will you return?"

Bartolomé did not hesitate. "I don't know."

"And why not? You have the knowledge and experience that would benefit the colony."

Bartolomé again bowed his head in acknowledgement to the fiscal's praise. "Thank you, Your Excellency. However, I hear that Oñate has been charged, as have some of his captains. I was one of them and have not yet heard. I assume that this interview..."

"No charges have been brought against you."

Relieved, Bartolomé thanked the fiscal again. Then he added, "After a decade in that desperate place I am not sure."

"Are you discouraged about Peralta?"

"I barely saw him before I left."

"But you have an impression."

"He is young and inexperienced."

The fiscal raised his eyebrows in coordination with both of his hands. "As to his youth, that is obvious. As to his experience, that is all the more reason for people like you to be there." He lowered his hands to the table, relaxed his face, and leaned forward. "Think about it Don Bartolomé. Of course your service merits that the viceroy grant you your decision and I will thus recommend. Nonetheless, our preference and great appreciation would be for you to return."

"Yes, Your Excellency, I will not take your words lightly. May I have some time to consider...?"

"Of course but not too long."

The meeting adjourned. Bartolomé found his way to the first decent looking tavern where he ordered a cup of its best wine to wash down a piece of bread and a chunk of fresh goat cheese. He had much to think about.

He learned that his old friend Bartolomé González was garrisoned in Mexico City as part of the Royal Guard. Their reunion later that day and night proved to be an opportune moment when González, stated the obvious. "You are in the viceroy's favor" and should take advantage of the fact and go back to New Mexico. And, he added, no, he would not return with him. He was planning to go to Guatemala where maybe he could win favor of his own.

When Bartolomé shared the details of his meeting with Lucía, they both had much to consider. The Robledos, of course, had much to say about the matter, for they unabashedly wanted their sister and brother-in-law to stay. But, then, none of them had been made *hidalgos*.

On the 19th of November 1610, Bartolomé sealed and sent the following letter to

112

the Fiscal.

Your Excellent Sir:

Upon consideration of your request that I return to New Mexico and in consultation with my family, I have decided to accede to your request. As such, and with your permission I will continue in the service of His Majesty. However, I beg leave to delay my return, because my wife, Doña Lucía, is currently with child.

Wishing Your Excellency and His Excellency, the Viceroy of New Spain, God Protect Him with the blessings of all that is good.

I kiss Your hand,

Your most Obedient Servant

Don Bartolomé Romero

Bartolomé's letter was an understatement. Bartolomé did not make the decision on his own. The "family consultations" were many prolonged discussions and he would not return to New Mexico without Lucía's concurrence, which she finally gave. But before she acquiesced, she did everything she could to convince him otherwise. When it became obvious to her that her husband deeply wanted to return, she convinced him that she, too, missed New Mexico despite her desire to stay with her mother, sister, and brothers to raise her family in the relative comfort of Zamora.

Lucía gave birth to a second son in early January. Lucía's mother assisted with the birth. In keeping with family tradition of using the names of the Apostles for boys, they named him Matías. Young Barti, now eleven-and-a-half years old could not hide his glee and fascination with his younger brother. His dad gave him even more reason to celebrate when he presented him with his first horse. Now the young man knew that his time spent riding in wagons with women and children was over. He would ride next to his father, or so he hoped.

The viceroy had decided that the Church's work took priority over his civil responsibilities or, rather, the civil government should assist the Church. In his mind the only reason for using treasury funds for distant New Mexico had nothing to do with extending his civil influence so far away. Another city like Mexico did not exist. Nor had a northwest passage, a waterway connecting the North and South Seas, been discovered. The only plausible reason, he concluded, would be the conversion of souls, which was a task already begun.

The Viceroy decided to let the Franciscans continue their work. To make his point, he called on Father Isidro Ordóñez to recruit a new contingent of friars and gave him leave to purchase the necessary supplies and, as advised, the perfect man to lead the escort north waited in Zamora.

With the decision made and his orders delivered, Bartolomé and Lucía said their tearful goodbyes and traveled to Mexico City. With their children in tow they did not look forward to the pending trip.

Bartolomé learned that he would lead a caravan consisting of ten priests led by Ordoñez. In addition there would be around twenty wagons and all the livestock and men necessary. His personal contingent of escorts would amount to fifteen men. In addition, the Fiscal informed him that the Viceroy, out of appreciation for his continued service, had agreed to an increase of annual salary with a two-year advance.

With his past and, now, advanced salary, Bartolomé purchased enough supplies to fill a wagon and part of another. He bought clothes, tools, pistols, knives, horse gear, a desk, shoes, horses, and mules. He reasoned that the value of the horse and mules would buy him more than enough cattle or sheep once in New Mexico. His purchases included items for Francisca and Juan, who, he hoped, had received word of his and Lucía's pending return.

He then took a couple of bottles of good red wine and visited with his *tocayo* once again. They shared one bottle. The other was left for a later date. Bartolomé knew not to attempt to ask his friend to join him. With a pending promotion coming with his commitment to go to Guatemala, González would not change his mind. At dawn he accompanied them out of the city, wishing them God speed as they continued on as he waved from the distance.

Despite this unexpected good news of his advanced salary, the moment was tinged with sadness. They also learned that the viceroy had become ill and could not personally meet Bartolomé. The fiscal shared that he feared for his death and his concern was well founded. After two days out of Mexico City word overcame Bartolomé's caravan that García Guerra had died.

Almost immediately Bartolomé noticed a change in what he remembered of Father Ordóñez. The priest seemed overly serious, maybe even intolerant as he started berating his brethren. He insisted upon officiating over a memorial mass for the recently deceased viceroy and bishop. Bartolomé allowed the service. However, the sermon got his attention, for Ordóñez emphatically stated that they all should dedicate themselves to García Guerra's desire to make New Mexico a model missionary colony. "A colony," he stressed, "that existed solely for the conversion of the Pueblo Indians."

Bartolomé's concern increased as Ordóñez continued to scold his fellow priests and, finally, a lay brother deserted in the dead of night. When asked about going after him, Bartolomé replied that he could neither hinder nor endanger the whole group in pursuit of one person. Ordóñez's hateful look while he turned on his heals was all the answer Bartolomé needed. From then on Bartolomé always described the Franciscan as a man "who smiled with no trace of humor."

Bartolomé commanded an impressive caravan. It consisted of soldiers, muleteers, servants, some additional families who wanted to try their luck in the north, the blue-clad Franciscans, and Indian hunters and herdsmen. In all Bartolomé looked over a parade of over 120 people, twenty full slowly groaning wagons, and over three hundred head of livestock. Bartolomé could not have been prouder and as he rode in his new suit with matching cape and feathered cap, he looked every bit the role of a successful, experienced leader.

The first hundred leagues to Zacatecas wore on everyone. The uninviting land, interrupted with a few scarce and desperate villages struck both Bartolomé and Lucía as completely depressing when compared to the enthusiasm that they had when traveling south from New Mexico.

Fray Isidro and his already disgruntled cadre had one last respite at Zacatecas before they embarked on the exceedingly long journey across a barren stretch to the small village of Santa Barbara, the last outpost before New Mexico. The caravan outnumbered the village's inhabitants. The priests, families, and most of the soldiers had never been on such a journey. They saw little difference between camping on the trail or next to this village that had little to offer. Their consternation continued to grow. The increasing heat as the seasons moved into spring and then summer added to their uncomfortable situation.

Bartolomé knew from experience that the only solution was to keep the caravan moving. He took solace in Lucía and the experienced muleteers and herdsmen, many of who had been in New Mexico before.

How ironic, he thought, that he put more trust in their familiar personages then the priests and new *vecinos*, Spanish settlers. They, like him, had come to accept life on the trail. They acted from habit and intuition without cluttering their minds with motives or methods, and whys and wherefores. They acted out of experience and each day got closer to the destination. "They persist," was how Bartolomé put it.

Lucía and Bartolomé noted the constant complaints. They took especial note when Ordóñez berated his priests. The friars had never been so deprived. The head priest told them that they had not taken on a life of luxury in their service to God and that they should be grateful for the opportunity that awaited them rather than complain.

The whole trip reminded Lucía and Bartolomé of the even greater trials and tribulations that confronted Oñate in that first journey. They easily progressed from those thoughts to reminiscing as they moved through or camped at familiar places. Yet the whole miserable, monotonous, and uneventful journey was exactly as Bartolomé would have it. Not even the constant broken wheels and cracked axles, occasional wagons stuck in mud or sand, nor the river crossings could distract Bartolomé's immense sense of accomplishment as they reached the first pueblos of New Mexico in late August. There, mounted to share the moment, was his son, Barti, proudly riding next to him.

At Sandia Pueblo in the province of Tiquex, Father Alonso Peinedo, the Father Commissary came out to greet the caravan and relieve it of the priests. Peinedo, an elderly, humble man whose bearded weathered face reflected both his age and personality represented everything Ordóñez lacked. He came to New Mexico with Peralta in 1610 and was pretty much respected throughout the colony.

Rather than offer salutations, the slack jawed, humorless Ordóñez surprised everyone when he wasted no time in reaching into the pouch that he carried strapped over his shoulder to produce an official looking document and loudly announce that he had been sent to replace Peinedo. The saintly friar accepted the news with mere bow of his head and without complaint.

Ordóñez had not mentioned this before. Nor had the fiscal in Mexico City told Bartolomé of this appointment. It was an important bit of information to say the least. Even some of the priests asked to see the document. They already were leery of their zealot brother. As it turned out, some of them never believed his claim.

At the moment, however, there was nothing to do but accept the turn of events. Bartolomé knew enough to leave it as a Church matter. He did not ask to see the document although he had his suspicions, and later shared with Lucía that this did not bode well for New Mexico.

He received instructions at Sandia to proceed to the new village of Santa Fe instead of San Gabriel, which had been abandoned. The caravan's Franciscans stayed in Sandia to be dispersed among the missions. Bartolomé ordered the rest of the people to prepare to move out with a new sense of anxiety as well as relief, if not curiosity. He left Ordóñez and the complaining priests behind and was heading for a new capital that was a day's less travel than going to San Gabriel.

A TROUBLESOME COLONY
Fall 1611, Santa Fe

Santa Fe did not appear much more impressive than Santa Barbara. The town did not look like a capital of anything. Of course, Bartolomé had seen the place before Peralta designated it the new capital. Then it was a few scattered hovels of three or four families around an imaginary plaza. Now the plaza, a few years older, was more defined by the construction of buildings going up around it. Thanks to the efforts of the local Franciscan, Fray Esteban de Perea, the church neared completion and the adjoining *convento* was close to done. None of the other official buildings were close to complete. Foundations of stone in various phases hinted at where the royal houses, the governor's residence, offices, and quarters for the soldiers would be located. Meanwhile Peralta had a temporary house constructed off the plaza. The troops had to fend for themselves. Construction was slow. The people concentrated on their own homes and Peralta mostly depended on the mandated labor of Pueblo Indians from various pueblos.

Other buildings, houses and jacals, in various phases of construction dotted the riverbank radiating from the plaza and church. Every edifice was made of adobe, mud bricks, flat roofed, and, except for the church, one story. Through squinted eyes, Bartolomé easily picked out Francisca and Juan who ran up to greet him and his son. He, in turn, walked with them to the rest of the family. He couldn't fully enjoy the family reunion because he had to report to the governor and deliver a parcel of official correspondence before he could allow his emotions to take over.

Peralta's youth still struck Bartolomé. Nor was Bartolomé especially familiar with the advisors surrounding the governor. Not one of them had been an officer under Oñate. They also attentively listened to Bartolomé's report and, then, asked a couple of questions about the new settlers before focusing on Ordóñez. A quick appraisal of the just delivered correspondence did not reveal anything to do with the new father commissioner's appointment. Bartolomé answered the questions honestly and directly but sensed that the contingent really did not respect his words. Finally, Peralta thanked him and observed, "You are one of Oñate's originals, are you not?"

"I came here as an enlisted member of the first settlement."

"Yes. So I heard. Well, enough. Welcome back."

Bartolomé came to attention, formally bowed, and said, "Thank you, Sir." After which he turned and left. He clearly understood that the governor did not favor him. Soon thereafter Márquez sought out Bartolomé. Márquez told him that his suspicions of the governor had proved true. The man showed his inexperience, cared little for the original settlers and had, in fact, relegated all of Oñate's remaining officers to "menial tasks." Márquez used a more colorful term for "menial."

Finally, Bartolomé turned his attention to a joyous meeting with Francisca and Juan, whose family now included a son named Cristóbal. Juan slaughtered a young goat for *cabrito* and with Lucía's enthusiastic insistence opened one of the jugs of wine they brought from Mexico. The rest of the unpacking could wait.

They were startled to hear that Juan and Francisca had secured land next to theirs for Bartolomé and Lucía. "Over there, where I put the post. It begins there and continues to that third big cottonwood. It's yours."

"But how?" Bartolomé and his wife marveled at their future that would be located on the south side of the river.

"First, you are entitled. I was your proxy. We drew sticks, each with a different number of notches. Peralta set it up and officiated with a friar at his side. Each stick corresponded to a numbered lot and each lot has river frontage. Our *suerte,* luck that's what they call it, landed us here. Yours was on a separate location but Francisca and I, with an added sweetener of a couple of goats, traded to get yours next to us."

"Magnificent! Wonderful! Thank you! I will repay your goats."

"But enough of this. Tell us more about the family and New Spain." They shared an afternoon that turned into an evening of raised eyebrows, exaggerated gestures, and laughter before everyone retired for the night.

The next day Juan shared with Bartolomé that both of them had received the right to extract goods and labor from certain pueblos. By virtue of their status as original settlers who had stayed they had received *"encomiendas,"* "but it is not as good as it sounds brother."

"Well, as you know, we are entitled to our *encomiendas.*"

"Yes, I know. What...?" Bartolomé hand gestured for Juan to get to the point.

"Well, Peralta does not favor us first comers but he had to give us our due. So he gave us *encomiendas* from the distant, poorer pueblos. Mine and Francisca's is a little village two leagues south of Isleta." He paused and half said to himself, "If I a get a blanket from them, I will be lucky. And yours is much further south, the pueblo of Senecú."

"My God. That is a minimum of four day's ride from here!" Bartolomé paused and said half in jest, "At least it is on the road south, closer to New Spain."

Months later Bartolomé and Lucía celebrated the completion of the first of two rooms in their new house. Now they had a place of their own and could stop being a burden on their in-laws. Even before working on the house Bartolomé created stables and a corral for his horses and mules. He also built chicken coops and a pen for his three hogs. He traded for some sheep and left them in the care of Juan. Bartolomé loved, even longed for this type of life-style. It reminded him of his formative years in the distant past.

Yet problems persisted, for Father Ordóñez fulfilled Bartolomé's worst fears. In addition, the hardheaded, self-assured inexperience of Peralta did nothing to help. The two men locked horns over control of New Mexico, many times calling on the colonists and soldiers to take sides.

Bartolomé did not trust Ordóñez, which combined with his long-held loyalty to his "Royal duty" as an officer put him in conflict with the priest. That he found Peralta's attitude did not help. Nevertheless, aside from a few assignments to check on some nearby missions, Bartolomé was left to his own devices.

His position was precarious and, lest he forget, Lucía was quick to caution him. Ordóñez had taken to excommunicating those people who could not agree with him. Over the next months the head Franciscan excommunicated the governor twice. He even had the governor's chair thrown out of the parish church. Later, the governor or one of his men accidentally shot at and wounded one of his own men and a lay brother, Fray Pedraza, during a confrontation with Ordóñez.

Finally, Ordóñez invoked the authority of the Inquisition and with the assistance of Márquez, who had given up on the governor to side with the Father Commissioner, arrested and jailed Peralta. In the process, they took possession of his property and proclaimed that anyone who tried to aid the governor "in any way" would be excommunicated.

All this put a heavy pall over the lives of everyone in the colony. Even those who openly took sides in the conflict worried whether they made the right decision. Bartolomé, Lucía, Juan, and Francisca spent endless hours talking about the ramifications of what was happening. They feared Ordóñez and saw him as a dangerous, non-God fearing man.

"He claims the office of the Inquisition," Juan whispered with the light of an oil lamp flickering orange off his worried face.

"We know. We know." Bartolomé nodded.

"What do we do?" Francisca asked with a serious face that showed two deep furrows between her eyebrows.

Bartolomé did not hesitate. "Wait."

"But, Bartolomé, what if he comes to us?" Lucía phrased her question as more of a plea.

"For what? To arrest the governor? He already has done that."

"I mean..."

"No. Listen. He will ask for tribute or for escort duty. I am bound to fulfill the last. As for the first, we will give what we can to buy time."

"Time!" Juan with hands outstretched had a look of disbelief.

"Yes. Time. Look, we are here to stay. Ordóñez, Peralta?" Bartolomé gave them a look of mock disbelief. "People like them and in their positions come and go. In time we will have new governors and father commissioners. They don't know it but people like us are more important to the survival of this colony than them."

Juan pulled out a wooden chair to sit. "That does not help us now."

"Yes it does. The mere knowledge of it gives us hope. We will be patient, tend to our lives, our families and friends, and property. Over time we will prosper, at least, more so than now."

Lucía waved her arms in slow motion. "Oh, my love, how can you be so positive when all this, this...stuff goes on?"

"We came here, we returned, for our future, which does not happen overnight but over time."

Once again, Bartolomé had laid out a scenario that they could not refute. Such conversations occurred on a frequent basis and they had a calming effect. Everyone agreed that they could share their thoughts openly among themselves but not with others. They did not want the attention of Peralta and especially Ordóñez.

"And what about Márquez, Bartolomé? You know him. Why is he with Ordóñez?"

"He hates Peralta but there is more." Everyone looked up with faces that begged for more. "Ordóñez brought word that Márquez has been charged of crimes along with Oñate and the others. He wants to go to Mexico City to defend himself but Ordóñez told him that it would be better if he did not go." Bartolomé paused, to look around, and then continued, "I believe that Ordóñez told Márquez that he will help. After all, Ordóñez was here before during some of the Oñate years so he can bear witness to the events of the time, and he can do it through the Franciscans who, right now, are in favor.

With a slight change in his voice's intonation and speaking to no one in particular, Bartolomé continued, "So Márquez has two reasons to side with Ordóñez, and both are his personal concern. He does this without consideration for the rest of us. His alliance has thrown the balance of power to the priest. He is afraid."

Actually, Bartolomé understood the dangers flitting about him like a poisoned mist. His predicament felt like he had to hold his breath to stay alive but how could he live without breathing? Rivalries between priest and settler or soldier, the church and state, and excommunication or disobedience to the King with the threat of jail no matter which side is taken did not bode well. The governor almost executed one of his own scribes for refusing to witness his defense against Ordóñez's barrage of charges. The alterNatives were too strange and horrible to contemplate. Bartolomé was never a man of strong faith. Although he practiced his religion he preferred the simplicity of motivation and action. Like on the trail, act from experience without having to think about it. He befriended some of the priests and learned that many of them, too, suffered under the heavy hand of Ordóñez. Now life had become unnecessarily complicated because Peralta and Ordóñez, both ambitious men, refused to cooperate. Despite his words to the others, the future was in doubt.

Perhaps acting out of his loyal, patient nature Bartolomé concentrated on his growing family and new homestead. In effect, he successfully managed to avoid the schism that the colony's two leaders had created. An obvious result was that he was not a favorite of either of the feuding men. Until his dying day, Bartolomé could never explain how he did it.

The Romero property began to take shape. The beginnings of crops, planted in rows and the young sprouts of fruit trees, apples, peaches, quince, and apricots gave testimony to his effort and that of young Barti who now worked side by side with his father.

Santa Fe, still a village with scattered mud houses and an incomplete presidio, did not even match some of the native pueblos in grandeur. The new capital did not compare to what Bartolomé remembered of his native Corral de Almaguer.

After two years, the two properties, his and Juan's, had been developed at a faster pace than the village. Between their houses, each of which had expanded to three rooms on a similar floor plan, was a plot of land with two smaller buildings, large shacks that the two families shared. Here they stored tools and housed horses and mules in one building. The other building took in native workers, laborers. On the side opposite of his in-laws' dwelling, a field stretched out from the river bottom that was defined by a row of stately cottonwood trees. Their refreshing shade next to the sandy river bottom was an attraction from the distance. Bartolomé, his son, and Juan spent many a mid-summer's break in the refreshing shade of those trees. Beyond their properties, houses and fields interspersed and spread up and down the river valley.

Bartolomé drew on his familiarity of crops and livestock to maintain his family. Lucía supported him in every way. And they both enjoyed their children. If truth were told, Bartolomé fulfilled his duty with increasingly infrequent mission escort assignments so he could stay home.

Bartolomé and Juan shared the expenses of Indian labor. They were careful not to become fodder for either Ordóñez or Peralta and took care to pay, feed, and house the Indians properly. Lucía and Francisca enjoyed learning of new meals from the Indian women. In all, the two families had come to appreciate the Pueblo people.

As *encomenderos* both Bartolomé and Juan were entitled to a certain tribute from "their" distant southern pueblos. However, as mentioned, the distance and poor state of the two pueblos offered little to the two families. Neither of the men, who visited the two pueblos on occasion, demanded what was due to them. It was hardly worth the effort. More importantly, Lucía gave birth to a second daughter, whom she named Ana. Bartolomé had a growing family, a second generation in New Mexico. His priority had to be them.

A (NOT SO) DISTANT HORIZON
1618, Santa Fe

On a brisk autumn day in early October, Bartolomé reined in his horse on a hill overlooking Santa Fe. He, Juan, and Barti had spent three days hunting in the foothills north of the town. The thick forests provided abundant game and their three extra horses packed three deer and a larger one for which they had no name. In later years the larger deer-like animal would be called an *alce* or elk.

Bartolomé waved the other two on as he lagged behind staring at the western horizon that distantly framed the still developing village that he called home. Now a graying fifty-five year old man, Bartolomé had become more prone to these pensive moments. He thought about Lucía, always supportive but positively expressive. An intelligent woman, still uncommonly handsome who made sure that their children learned

120

to read, write after a fashion, and know their family history. She especially focused on her father and mother, both of whom had passed away. Word of her mother's death was delivered via the previous year's caravan.

The family continued to grow. Barti, the oldest, had grown into a relatively tall, stringy tough man. He did not talk much but was given to a quick, engaging smile. Now sixteen years old, he had enlisted into the royal troop and had begun to see a little of New Mexico while on duty. He, like his father, received a small stipend from the Royal Treasury every couple of years when the caravan arrived. Also, like his father, Bartolomé "el hijo" had a bit of wanderlust in him.

María, the second oldest, now fourteen years old, had begun to attract the attention of some of the colony's single men. She talked all the time, which gave rise to her mother calling her "María of a thousand questions." Like all her siblings she had straight black hair. That came from the Romero side. Her eyes, on the other hand, were hazel, not quite green and that came from the Robledos.

Six-year-old Matías grew up under the tutelage of his mother and older brother. He rode his own horse and pitched in with the chores as best he could. He seemed to take to animals and became fascinated when listening to his parents, aunt and uncle, brother, and friends talk about politics.

Little Ana, born a year after Matías, had become her mother's favorite even though both parents knew they could not show favoritism. None of their children had given them cause for concern. When Lucía became pregnant again, Bartolomé worried that she might be beyond her childbearing years. Lucía laughed and said "no" but secretly had the same thought. She added that, "Nature will tell me."

And Bartolomé replied, "Sometimes nature's messages are hard."

Lucía sighed and said, "Then it is God's will."

She carried the pregnancy with no problems and in 1615 had a third son that they named Agustín.

Bartolomé smiled at the thought of the new born but quickly frowned, for nature or God did speak when the following year Lucía gave birth to a sickly infant that died within days. Fortunately, a priest was available to baptize the baby.

Now, as Bartolomé watched the setting sun turn the clouds above it bright orange and deep red, he turned his thoughts to other matters. He began with the whimsical observation that he had many times explored beyond the western horizon and then turned to his satisfaction that he and his family had survived another year. He marveled, for this would make twenty years! Although he had arrived at San Juan with the advance group in August, he always counted the years from sometime in late September or early October when the main colony including his beloved Lucía arrived. He could not remember the exact date.

As he had predicted, both Father Ordoñez and Governor Peralta were long gone. Both faced charges in Mexico City. The people in New Mexico found out afterward that Peralta had been exonerated while Ordóñez was disciplined for falsely claiming and using the authority of the Inquisition.

The rivalry between the governors and head Franciscans continued but not as acrimonious as before. Bartolomé concentrated on doing his duty while trying not to offend one side or the other. Each caravan arrived with new evidence of the viceroy's commitment to the colony and its missionary pursuit as the caravans brought more priests and wagons loaded with mission supplies all underwritten by the viceroy.

When Fray Esteban de Perea replaced Ordóñez with the title of Father Custodian it was clear to all that the head Franciscan position had been elevated. He did not have the powers of the Inquisition but it was a tacit acknowledgement that his work was important. Perea had come to New Mexico with Peralta and Father Peinado back in 1609. He understood that Mexico City would not tolerate the methods used by Ordóñez. He also knew that the people had wearied of the threats. By the time of his promotion he had a lot of experience in New Mexico, built a church at Sandia Pueblo, and even had confronted Ordóñez.

One of his first acts was to seek out a noncontroversial colonist who could write. He wanted a new Church notary and it was an offer that Juan de Tapia could not refuse. Yet Juan was not so overwhelmed with the new Father Custodian's attentions that he accepted the position without a request. Aside from the salary, which loomed large in the household, Juan asked that the Church help with the education of his and the Romero children. Perea Pedraza to the task.

Fray Jerónimo had been stationed in Santa Fe to assist the parish priest. He was one of the two unfortunates who received a pistol wound during Peralta's confrontation with Ordóñez. His sense of humor, quiet demeanor, and empathy pleased both the Romeros and Tapias. Besides, he had family in New Mexico and they seemed pleasant enough.

Another new governor would arrive sometime soon. Everyone hoped that he would be able to improve the colony. Bartolomé had his doubts, for with age he had become increasingly despondent of any help from a political appointment made in Mexico City. "Maybe," he thought as he urged his horse down the hill toward town, "the third governor will surprise me." Bartolomé remained an optimist after all.

Opposite Page:

Detail of the 1779 map, "Interior Province of New Mexico" by Don Bernardo Miera y Pacheco. Note "Bueltas de Romero" at the bottom just above the Pueblo of Sevilleta and to the right of the Rio Grande. Almost a hundred years after the Romero hacienda was abandoned, the name remained. "Bueltas" or, properly "Vueltas" means 'turn around' and probably is in reference to the two trails that join the Rio Grande and the Camino Real there. Map from *The Missions of New Mexico, 1776*, Translated and Annotated by Eleanor B. Adams and Fray Angelico Chavez, New Edition from Sunstone Press.

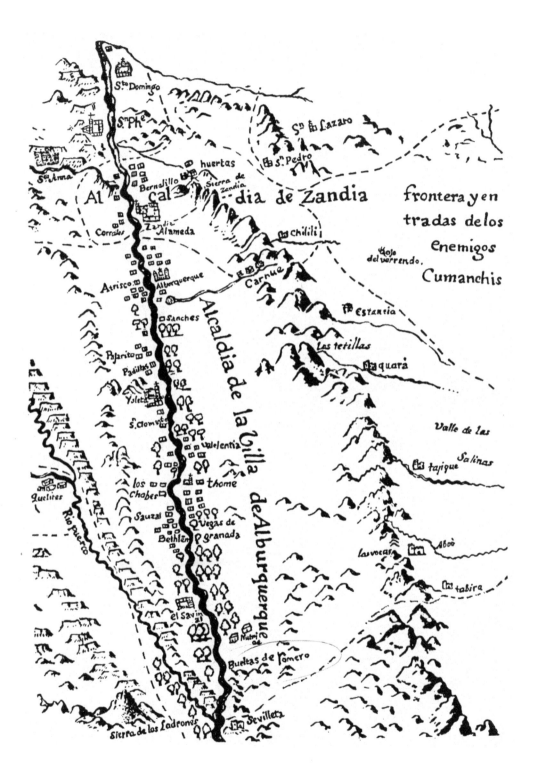

St.º Domingo

S.ⁿ Ph.ᵉ

S.ⁿ el Lazaro

huertas

S.ⁿ s.ⁿ Pedro

Sᵗᵃ Anna

Bernalillo

Sierra de
Zandia

Al cal dia de Zandia

frontera y en
tradas delos
enemigos
Cumanchis

Corrales

Zandia
Alameda

Chilili

ojo
del verrendo.

Atrisco

Alburquerque

Carnue

Sanches

Estantia

Poparito

Las tetillas

Padillas

quara

Ysleta

S.ⁿ Clem.ᵗᵉ

Valentia

los
Chabes

thome

Valle de las

Quelites

Sauzal

Vegas de
granada

tajique

Salinas

Bethlem

Rio puerco

el Savin

Nutri.ªˢ

Aboò

las vocas

Bueltas de Romero

tabira

Sevilleta

Alcaldia de la Villa de Alburquerque

Sierra de los Ladrones

PART III
THE NEXT GENERATION: MATÍAS

The Second and Third Generations in More Detail
(Ed Romero's direct ancestors are highlighted)

Bartolomé II = Pérez Granillo

-Bartolomé III = Josefa de Archuleta
| María (Crippled child)
|-Nicolas (b. in Santa Fe, settled in Sonora)
|-Juana m. Diego Pérez Granillo (settled in Sonora)

Matías = Isabel de Pedraza

[-Pedro = Petrocilla de Salas
[
|-Francisco Romero de Pedraza m. Francisca Ramirez de Salazar
|-Bartolomé m. Luisa Varela
[
⌐ **Felipe m. Jacinta de Guadalajara y Quirós** (sent south to manage the family hacienda)
|-Luisa m. Juan Lucero de Godoy
|-Catalina m. José Telles Jirón

María = Gaspar Pérez

|-Bartolomé Pérez Romero (b.1613/14 d.1633/34) at age 20
|-Gaspar Pérez Romero (d. at age 22)

|-Diego Pérez Romero (m.Catalina de Zamora. He was tried and convicted before the Inquisition)

Ana = Francisco Gómez

|-Francisco Gómez Robledo
|-Bartolomé Gómez Robledo (Sent south to manage Las Barrancas)

-Juan Gómez Robledo
-Andrés m. Juana Ortiz
-José Gómez Robledo
-Francisca m.Pedro Lucero de Godoy
-Ana Gómez Robledo

Note: The family of Agustín and Isabel are omitted as they and their descendants do not play a prominent role in this book narrative.

Matías never grew tired of looking at the building. For long as he could remember he had been fascinated by the construction. He even took advantage of long periods of the construction's delay to play among the piles of broken adobes and adzed beams inside the partially completed rooms. No one cared enough to shoo him or his friends away. It came to New Mexico's fourth governor, the mean spirited, or so it seemed to the children, Juan de Eulate to finally insist that the building be completed.

Now young Matías, already eleven years old, stood in the plaza, which had become the interior courtyard of the nearly finished and mostly two-story structure that would house the governor, his staff, and soldiers. Only the corner towers waited completion.

However, on this day the building did not have his full attention because at any moment a contingent of soldiers, including his brother, now an *alferez,* a lieutenant would be returning from the Jemez Pueblos through the front entrance. The Jemez people had rebelled and forced the priest and the small group of soldiers to flee. The soldiers had gone to punish "those people" for their insubordination, and Governor Eulate personally commanded them.

Matías had no doubt that his big brother would give them a lesson. Sensing his unbridled confidence, his father warned him. "Listen, Mateo," he more times than not affectionately used that name, "these things are not games. Say a prayer for your brother."

"¿*Pero, por qué?*" "Why?" Matías thought. His father, he knew from others, was a hero. He had fought in battles, traveled to Mexico, and been to that seemingly mystical place, the Hopi Mesas and beyond. He is a captain and he served under "*el adelantado,*" the common euphemism for Oñate. His dad had been a member of the colony's council more than once. When he spoke, people paid attention.

Was not his brother cut from the same cloth as dad? Already Barti had achieved rank in the military. He would soon be a captain, no doubt. His brother also travelled to those Hopi Mesas. He told them about a magical place where they camped and where Oñate had left his name many years before.

Barti taught him how to ride, to sit proud in the saddle like dad. Matías grew strong in part because Barti convinced his father that he should water the fruit trees. That meant years of carrying buckets of water to the trees. The irrigation ditches, *acequias*, took a few years to complete and then they had to be adapted to the orchards and some of the trees were missed. Matías did not bemoan the labor. He, in fact, enjoyed it as he watched the trees grow through the seasons and bear fruit.

Matías idolized his older brother and now he waited to welcome him home. What a surprise when the expected triumphant soldiers did not look so victorious. Instead, they looked worn and tired as they filed into the plaza. Matías spotted Barti stooped in his saddle with an arm hanging limp riding next to their cousin Cristóbal. This was not how he was taught to "sit straight and proud." He rushed up to his brother just as Cristóbal helped him dismount.

Barti smiled. Matías, still concerned, could not find words to speak. In fact, he felt his throat tighten and tears well up in his eyes. He could see scratches on Bartolomé's face and a bloodstained cloth wrapped around his upper left arm.

Still smiling, the older brother broke the silence. "Hey Mateo, what's wrong? Look!" Bartolomé held up his wrapped arm. "A badge of honor. It's only a cut from a rock. You know how cuts are, they bleed more than they are worth. I have a small wound so someday I can brag to my kids. Come on Mati. It's okay. Let's go home."

"Can you walk?"

"If I can stand, I can walk. We just rode sixty miles and, right now, I would rather walk than ride. Here take my horse."

Matías took the reins and walked proudly at his brother and cousin's sides. Maybe a prayer would have prevented the wound but then his brother boasted as if it was an accomplishment.

He sought answers in his family's reaction to Barti's wound. Barti's new wife and his mother fussed over him and showed genuine concern as they cleaned and wrapped his wound. Father, on the other hand, more or less confronted Bartolomé and nodded an acknowledgment when he heard, "It's a flesh wound."

"What happened?"

"The Indians took refuge in the cliffs. I was hit by one of their rocks. Cristóbal, here, got a new dent in his breastplate. My blow hit flesh and knocked me off my horse. It looks worse than it is, but it aches."

Cristóbal added that the Indians abandoned their towns for better positions on the mesa close by. "We named the mesa "Santiago" not because the priests already named the pueblo such, but because we were always charging up it with our battle cry to our patron St. James, "Santiago and at them." Left unsaid and, perhaps, not realized was that the Pueblo was not named for St. James the apostle but Santiago de Alcalá.

Matías's brother noted that now the governor would have to decide "what to do with those people. You can bet that it will not be the same solution as Oñate's."

Uncle Juan chimed in, "*Claro que si*. That would be a sure ticket to Manila."

The elder Bartolomé nodded again and barely whispered, "Yes, I know about those rocks." Then he spoke, "Let the women clean you. Then we can talk."

Matías watched his father. His gray hair always pulled back in a tight ponytail that highlighted his weathered features that spoke of respect and wisdom. His dad had a presence. Rather bravely, then, Matías spoke. "Father." His dad looked at him. "May I listen when you talk?"

His father smiled. "Yes, my son. It is time."

Matías counted that day as the beginning of his adulthood. He sat with his father, older brother, Uncle Juan, and Cristóbal. He did not speak. No, not yet. He listened. None of the conversation was directed to him yet it was for him. The men's very actions made him an equal.

He learned that it was Eulate's policies that had caused the Jemez People to destroy their new church and convent. Eulate's open hatred for the priests encouraged Pueblo leaders to live the old ways and ignore the priests. At the same time, the governor felt justified in the taking of what he called orphan children to be servants in settlers' households.

Juan summed it up best. "He thinks he is a military genius and he may have fought in other wars but he is ignorant of the ways of the people here. So he leads us to spill our blood over a mess his policies create."

From that day forward Matías joined the men in their tasks, hunts, and, even, on minor escort duty to the closer and safer pueblos like Pecos, San Marcos, Nambé, Cuyamungue, and San Juan. There he saw the remains of the first town where his brother and sister were born. Now, he took more seriously his mother's history lessons and Father Pedraza's twice a week writing and reading lessons.

Matías grew to appreciate his father and his father seemed to open up to him. Maybe, Matías thought, his father saw that it was time for the boy to become a man. "Be careful of the governors. They don't have your interest at heart. And...be selective of the priests. They care more for the Natives than you. That is their job. Also, they are human, some good, some bad."

Matías listened and questioned. "What about Fray Jerónimo?"

"Pedraza? Your teacher? He is good. He has family here in New Mexico. He is here to stay. He cares. Look, he was wounded during that problem with Peralta yet he carries no grudge."

As time passed only the sons could get their father to talk a little about what happened at Acoma and Taos, or the trips in search of silver to the west "beyond the horizon." Matías did not realize it at the time but his father molded him in his own image in part.

By the time Matías reached his seventeenth year, he had grown into a broad shouldered, sturdy young man who stood an inch taller than his father and older brother. Agustín, his younger brother was still growing but had a few inches to go to catch Matías.

Like his father, Matías tied his straight hair in back. His slightly hazel eyes and the reddish tint of his hair came from his mother's side and although his skin had nice color, he would never be called "*Moreno*" like his dad.

He continued to seek information. Like his sister Ana he constantly asked his mother to illuminate upon what his father had said. He wanted to know more about the first journey north, life under Oñate, and the problems after the *Adelantado* left. After María married and left home, Ana had her mother's full attention and was becoming something of the family's unofficial historian, especially about the Robledos. Matías's older sister and brother both married and had made him an uncle thrice over.

When María moved to live with her husband's family, Barti started talking about leaving as well. Early one spring's Sunday morning as the sun brightly illuminated everything after being washed by a dawn's thunderstorm, Barti explained to his father that the house had become crowded, even with the addition of another room. He had a family of two children and he should strike out on his own. He wanted to start a *hacienda*, a ranch down by Senecú where his dad had been granted another *encomienda*. Barti was proud to note that he, too, had been awarded an *encomienda* at Isleta Pueblo, also to the south. Plus he had a partial grant at the Jemez pueblos.

By moving south, he could more efficiently oversee the family allotments. "Others have moved out of Santa Fe to live closer to their inheritances. Look at them. We can't all stay in Santa Fe." Barti quickly added, "And Fray Jerónimo has been assigned to Senecú. Juan Griego has moved his family to the area."

"That does not make it any less dangerous."

The Pedrazas and the Romeros had become close families. Matías had become enamored with the lay brother's sister, Isabel. Fray Jerónimo's transfer to the distant pueblo had been a topic of conversation. No one could imagine that the affable Jerónimo could offend the Father Custodian. They only could conclude that his superiors had "rotated him" from a relatively easy assignment in Santa Fe to a desperate place like Senecú to test his dedication to "the will of God."

Barti argued, "Father, it is no more dangerous than at many of the pueblos. How safe were you at San Juan or San Gabriel? The danger is exactly another reason for me to be there. I will do double duty, build the family interests, and be in charge of protecting the mission of a friend."

Still his father was not moved and Matías knew it. "Not now Barti. You are needed here. Not by the family but by the colony. You were just named to the council and I have it from those who know that you will be expected to rise to *acalde extraordinario*, Santa Fe's mayor."

This news impressed Matías. His brother was not only an *encomendero* but also becoming an important community leader like his father.

The elder Bartolomé continued, "Look Barti." Stay here and fulfill your term in office. Then go. You are my oldest and I cannot stop you, even now if you insist. But with a little more time you will solidify yourself as one of the kingdom's leaders, Matías and Agustín will take over here and the girls will marry. In the meantime, you can manage the properties from here, even take periodic trips there."

Matías expected his brother's answer. "As you wish father. I am anxious to do something on my own."

"I know how you feel, son. But, I assure you, you are on your own now. When will you make your first visit to the south?"

"We would like to leave in a week."

"María is going with you?"

"I think my wife should see where we will live someday. Ana will watch the babies." Barti's two first born were sons named Bartolomé and Nicolás. The baby Bartolomé was the fourth direct Bartolomé in the Romero lineage beginning with the elder's father in Corral de Almaguer.

"She is with child."

"I know. She will be fine, maybe better. And she is not the first to travel with child, even in this family."

"Bueno. Jerónimo will be glad to see you. Maybe Mateo here can send him a note."

A few weeks later Matías and his father had joined the community to prepare the *acequia madre*, the main irrigation ditch that feeds all the smaller ditches called *venas* or "veins." Matías asked his dad why he left Spain. This gave pause to his father, who at the time had taken a break to snack on a peach, his second favorite fruit after apricots. He stopped chewing, swallowed, thought some more and then said, "I don't know. To be on my own. Do something different. Adventure. Go on a fool's errand. At the time, America beckoned. It was a grand and golden opportunity. Others had left, none returned with tales of broken dreams. We could all stay and do what our parents and parents' parents always did or...I don't know."

Leaning on his hoe, Matías could not help himself. "Like Barti now?"

Again his father paused. "Yes, I suppose so. Remember, though. I was over thirty years old when I left. Also, I gave up my inheritance."

"And your parents? How did they react?"

"They gave me their blessing, a couple of horses, and a little money. Your brother will leave with more."

Matías used this opportunity to bring up his own future by suggesting that it was time for him to present himself to the governor for military service.

"Ah Mateo. Whether or not you are presented to the governor, you will be called upon. No, for now it is enough that your brother, cousin, uncle and father are in the governor's service. Your mother and I need you here tending to the animals and crops. The only advantage of enlisting is the small salary that may or may not show up every few years. It is not worth it anymore."

Barti returned from Senecú even more anxious to leave, for he saw that people were moving down river, the "*Rio Abajo,*" he called it and he feared that before long all the good land would be taken.

Nevertheless, he, like Matías, heeded his father's words. Barti took office and within fourteen months had become an *alcalde ordinario*. Matías continued to take over more of the farm's duties but he had the itch. He hoped that by working with his younger brother, Agustín, he someday would free himself. While he remained in awe of his father he could not help but see in him an old man. In fact, Matías never knew his father as a young man. His father was forty-seven years old at Matías birth. Even then he was one of the older men in the colony.

Things came to a head when Barti and María took another trip to Senecú. While Barti visited Fray Jerónimo, María went to the home of Juan Griego where she visited his wife, Juana de la Cruz, and her mother, Beatriz de los Angeles. Sensing nothing but a friendly reception, María gladly accepted their offer of a mint tea. This was a mistake, for the two women harbored a jealousy for the Romeros. They resented the family's friendly relationship with Pedraza because they felt that he, like all the missionaries had taken the prime land for crops and livestock and then complained when, like them, they used Indian labor for their own subsistence. They also saw the Romeros as a threat to them, for their connections would give them priority for any remaining good land in the area. The Griegos had not been community leaders nor did they have the Romeros' longevity in New Mexico. They had no leverage to prevent the Romeros or anyone else from starting a *hacienda* close by.

María immediately felt discomfort and tried to get to a bed close by, but collapsed before getting there. Informed by one of her servants who rushed from the scene, Barti and Fray Jerónimo hurried back to the two roomed adobe where they found María withering on the floor while Juana and Beatriz sat close by, seemingly unconcerned.

Jerónimo quickly reached into his bag while ordering some water to be heated. Barti's servant did this while the Griegos continued to watch with whimsical faces. The good friar had a lifelong interest in health and healing and quickly made up a concoction that he forced down Maria's throat, which made her vomit. With Barti's help they put her on the bed and propped her up with a pile of clothes they found nearby.

The two men stayed with María as she flushed the poison out of her system and the accompanying fever subsided. After eight hours, Jerónimo sent word to the pueblo to have a wagon brought up to transport María back to the mission. The Griegos obviously disliked the sight of Indians in their house, especially, because they helped the hated Romeros. Between them they knew that they were not done with the Romeros.

Five days later, Barti and Jerónimo decided that his wife was well enough to begin a slow trip north. Pedraza loaned him the mission wagon to transport her. At the little village of Ciénega, a half days ride from Santa Fe they accepted the invitation of Captain Alonso Varela to stay at his *hacienda* where of all of a sudden María had a relapse after Varela's wife gave her a liquid potion.

Fortunately, Barti had the herbs and knew the mix that Jerónimo had used previously. He immediately took María from the house and set up a camp, posting guards with his servants and sending for help in nearby Santa Fe. Matías and his father galloped to Ciénega where they found Barti and María by an early dawn's large campfire. María slept after another rough bout of retching.

Barti could not hide his anger. His father asked what happened. After hearing, he nodded his head. "La señora Varela is an old friend of the Griegos."

Barti was aghast to hear this. "They are witches. Everyone one of them."

His father cut off the conversation and focused on María. "We need to get her back to Santa Fe and away from here. Varela will not attempt anything. Still she will be better off at home."

Through clenched teeth, Barti added, "Of course not. These are men who let their women do their dirty work."

"Even so, we must tend to your wife first. Let's go."

Once in Santa Fe, María healed after a fashion. Her near death experiences had taken a toll and it became obvious that she would never be the same. Barti checked around and discovered that people commonly associated the Griego women contacted mysterious illnesses and that at least two of the people had died. Sensing that his wife had barely avoided death and probably would never completely recover, Barti openly called the three women witches and murderers.

"You really don't believe that?" Matías asked.

"Which? That they are witches? Why not? I'm not alone. There are people who fear them."

"You believe that they cast a spell on María?"

"I don't know but I will tell you one thing. They tried to poison her twice. And that's what happened with the others."

Barti decided to do more than talk and followed the new Father Custodian, Alonso Benavides, to Santa Clara Pueblo north of Santa Fe. Benavides held Inquisitional authority, so maybe he would take action. Barti laid out the whole scenario, including the Griego's hatred for the priests and how enemies of the women had fallen sick and even died. Then he explained what happened to his own wife.

Benavides merely nodded as Barti spoke. When Barti finished, the priest straightened his robe and said, "I don't care to deal with tales of witches and if, as you say, they poison people, well, you should be talking to the governor." Barti left the head Franciscan completely frustrated and, despite his affection for Fray Jerónimo, would never again depend on a priest for justice.

Thus rejected, Barti decided that he would wait no more. He left Santa Fe and moved to Senecú, leaving Matías to take up the family's mantle in the capital. Matías watched as his disappointed father made Barti promise not to take personal revenge while giving him his blessing. With family tradition, if not his father's influence behind him, Matías was appointed Santa Fe's High Sheriff. He had just turned twenty years old.

Dark Clouds on a New Day's Horizon
Summer 1632, Santa Fe

Bartolomé had grown to appreciate, even anticipate, each day's dawn as the night's clouds suspended over Santa Fe's mountains showed the first hint of a new day from an as yet unseen sun's reflections. Then, an hour, later with the sky no longer dark, the sun revealed its brilliance from behind those same mountains. He regularly woke up and began his routine of work before dawn, continuing with his tasks through nature's morning show. Now, at sixty-eight years old, he paused for a much needed rest. Yet, more so, he paused to appreciate the moments. Not even New Mexico's many spectacular sunsets that elicited comment from most of the other people, supplanted his love for sunrise during his early morning ritual. Sunset ended the day, sunrise was a new beginning. As a lifelong optimist as well as by the habit, if not necessity, of an early riser, the latter appealed to him.

Yet, he sensed dark clouds on his horizon. His oldest son had left taking his family with him. María remained weakened. The three grandsons, the oldest of which had been named Bartolomé, had given him great pleasure but now he would have little to do with their upbringing. His son Agustín was still young. He did not concern himself as much for his daughters, for they were close to Lucía and were less troublesome. María had married and had given him two grandsons so far. Ana would be next and Bartolomé approved of her boy friend, Francisco Gómez. While born in Portugal, Gómez would be an important addition to the family. He was raised by Juan de Oñate's brother and educated by Franciscans. While not one of the original colonists he had risen in esteem and to the rank of captain fairly fast and already had commanded escorts of the caravans going south. Also, he was close to Father Benavides.

Bartolomé turned his attention to Matías, who had become sullen. He knew that Matías remained restless and had begun questioning him. He liked politics and openly admired the governors in their never ending struggle to exert control over the priests. Had he learned nothing from his relationship with Jerónimo even now as he courted the friar's sister, Isabel?

Lucía understood Bartolomé's concern and tried to sooth his thoughts. "This is the way of things my love. Just as you left home, our children will find their own way. You must be proud and have faith. You have been a good father. We have been good parents."

Bartolomé felt that he loved Lucía more now than ever before. Like him, she had aged, worn by years, weather, and life. Yet, when he looked at her, he saw the same spry, handsome woman he met many decades before.

"All of our daughters," she continued, "will marry and move to their husbands. Our sons have reached maturity under your shadow. They are the next generation and must make their own story."

"I know but I care. Barti lives in a dangerous place. Mateo is headstrong and aligning himself with the governor...." Bartolomé looked down, chagrined. "Lucía, you know how..."

"Yes, how you feel. I know, I know." She sighed. "You must let go. They know, too. They are adults and must make their own lives."

Bartolomé gave Lucía a look of resignation. "I love you more than anything, even sunrise. You are my life. You are always right."

Bartolomé never knew how or who convinced Matías that working on the side of the governors and helping them gather native slaves for work in their workshops or for trade south was more profitable than ranching and collecting his entitled *encomiendas*. Maybe it was his older brother, who became a captain under Governor Eulate the man who originated the idea of taking "orphans" for his profit. Probably not, because Barti had moved south, far away from the governor's direct influence. It could have been Francisco Gómez who had become a staunch supporter of the governors and an enemy of the priests. All that Bartolomé knew was that Matías had completely ignored his advice to not take sides.

Bartolomé did not fault his son when soon after becoming High Sheriff he refused to testify against his brother-in-law Gaspar Pérez who openly and constantly ranted against the Church. That was family. Bartolomé long before concluded that Gaspar Pérez, an armorer by profession, acted foolishly especially given he was born of a Spanish father and anonymous woman from Brussels. He did not need to bring unnecessary attention to himself, but he did.

It seemed to Bartolomé that the next generation was taking unnecessary risks. He tried to rationalize that maybe it was the sense of risk or a test of manhood. But why tempt the friars or volunteer for slave raids under the thin guise of keeping the peace. "We make war to keep peace" was an old phrase that Bartolomé never understood.

Maybe Matías's recent marriage to Isabel de Pedraza would calm him. At least, get him to reconsider his attitude toward the Franciscans. Yet, Isabel turned out to be just the wife Matías wanted, a docile, quiet, non-opinionated woman. If he couldn't stand other men questioning him, he certainly would not tolerate a wife contradicting him. With Isabel he had no worries. He could politic and soldier while she maintained the household. And when his first child was born in 1632 Matías named him Pedro after his maternal grandfather.

Matías had long since put the family ranch behind him. Thoughts of fruit trees and life giving water running through *acequias* were a thing of the past, a matter of youth.

He was on his way to becoming an important man and he enjoyed the status. Not even the "ramblings" of his colleague and future relative through Ana's pending marriage could convince him otherwise. Francisco Salazar had become a captain and cautioned his friend. "Careful Matías. You can be condemned by the priests."

"Here? In New Mexico? That means nothing to me."

"It does to others. Your parents..."

Matías cut him off. "My dad and my mom, well, they are old."

"Matías, listen to yourself. They are respected and wise...."

Matías cut him off again. "I know my own parents."

"But you favor the governors who upset the Natives with their raids."

"The Indians? They live like animals. Who cares about them? And why? No. Don't answer."

"So, you don't mind creating war instead of maintaining peace? War that has taken many lives already."

"We live in a dangerous place. These people need to know who is in charge. I am a soldier and am not worried about my life."

Salazar smiled sarcastically at that comment. "No, my friend, you have mixed up martyrdom with unnecessary deaths. The dead did not die for anything but the governors' personal gain."

Matías lips quivered. He did not like this confrontation. In fact, he did not like anyone questioning him or telling him what to do, except the governor of course.

But Salazar persisted. "If the governors cared then why don't they prepare defenses? Where are they, huh? What about counter attacks? None. They're not lucrative enough."

"Enough!" Matías's eyes flared, a visible vein on the side of his forehead pulsated, and his face flushed. "Take your dribble elsewhere. I don't need this. You are soft and stupid. You don't understand."

The whole argument brought up thoughts of his father, who he hardly saw anymore. Salazar was old fashioned just like his father. Left standing alone, Matías picked up a stone and ran it through his fingers. He felt something for his mother but, too bad, she sided with his father so he did not visit her either.

The final break came within months after he became High Sheriff, when Bartolomé reported to Governor Mora y Ceballos that the elders of Alameda Pueblo, just south of Sandía Pueblo, appeared to have reverted to their pagan ways.

What business was it of his? Of course they had, thought Matías. Matías was with the governor when he extorted more blankets and corn from the small pueblo. In exchange, he magnanimously granted them permission to practice their old religious ways. This was done to undermine the local friar not to please the Natives. His dad was out of touch and did not understand. Matías rationalized that he and Francisco Gómez are the ones receiving the accolades and *encomiendas*. We have the ambition and are becoming successful. And that Salazar acts like it is a big scandal when each governor pays off his successor or he will not do the required thorough investigation of his activities. Stupid Salazar.

A Hardened Resolve
1636, Santa Fe

Matías could not get Salazar's words out of his mind. Nor could he forget his in-law's look at the funerals, one after the other a year apart. First, his brother-in-law's oldest son, another Bartolomé and just twenty years old was killed on one of Governor Mora y Ceballos's slave raiding jaunts. Then his brother-in-law's namesake Gaspar Pérez took an arrow through the neck on a subsequent mission "to collect orphans." Both were buried with honors in Santa Fe's church. After all, as the governor said with a straight face, they died "in service of their King."

With two sons and an infant daughter being cared for by Isabel and his parents, Matías could have used the deaths of his first cousins to think about what he would do with his own sons when they reached maturity but he didn't. Instead, he hated Salazar for questioning his motives.

After the second funeral, Matías went home where he gave a cursory greeting to the two boys, Pedro now four years old and Francisco, named for Matías's brother-in-law whom he admired, who had just turned three years old. He dumbly stared at little Lucía. Yes, he had pleased his mother with the naming. And this, in turn, pleased him.

Isabel received a hug and was wise enough to have food and some fermented plum juice ready. That night while embraced, Matías told her that he had to leave for a while and think about things. He would go to Senecú and visit his brother. She nodded agreement and said, "Okay. How long will you be gone?"

He sighed as he lay on his back with his hands behind his head. "I don't know. A week, I guess." He left the next morning before daybreak.

The trip proved to be shorter than he thought. Seated at the kitchen table during the first night, the conversation with Barti took a turn. They had been discussing the motives why two of Barti's sons had lit out for Mexico with no intention of returning to New Mexico. Barti thought it was the lure and false romance of seeing so many people go back and forth on the Royal Road. Their *hacienda*, after all, sat right on the trail.

That was when Barti said, "At least their fate is better off than Maria's two sons. Thank God I moved here...away from all that in Santa Fe."

"'All' what, Barti?"

"Politics. Taking sides. Here I have to take care of myself and family."

"And you have these Indians to help you out." Matías let out a short laugh.

"Sure, but not like you think. The differences between tribes run deeper than their names. The Pueblos, this pueblo, and us need each other."

Matías's attention now engaged. "Huh? We don't need them. We can fend for ourselves."

Barti smiled. "Maybe you know something that I don't. Maybe you can fend for yourself but I doubt it. We help each other, especially for defense against marauding tribes. We share the same enemies. We Spanish cannot feed ourselves without partaking in the output of the Pueblos. We don't weave enough of our own blankets to cover ourselves. That's why we have the *encomiendas*."

"Maybe if the priests did not usurp all the good land for the Indians we could raise enough for ourselves."

"Who? You? The governor? His soldiers? A good many of us good people don't want to labor in the land or with livestock. Good. I don't begrudge the choice but, in doing so, realize that it makes all of us dependent on the pueblos." Here he paused for a second and held up his hand to prevent Matías from speaking. "Fray Pedraza originally worked with me to come up with a system that worked for everyone. Here we mix our livestock with the Natives of Senecú and the other pueblos. We also work the same fields. Then we share the production appropriately. We depend on, and work with each other."

Matías could not believe what he had heard. He blurted, "They are sullen thieves. They act like they are better than us. You can't trust them."

"Matías, they are different yes. Who is better than who? Who steals from who? You believe what you want but I am telling you that down here, well, we work together."

"I don't get it." Matías almost plead with his brother. "You fought with Eulate, fought at Jemez Pueblo. I thought that you understood."

"Understood what? That Eulate was the cause of the fight and then miss-managed the result? Come on brother, things are not black and white. That is not the way of the world."

Matías went to bed disturbed and mad. His brother had disappointed him. He left for Santa Fe the next morning. Such discussions only hardened Matías's resolve. And now, with Governor Baeza he was more convinced than ever. Baeza was more efficient than Mora y Ceballos and already had awarded partial *encomiendas* to Matías and Francisco. Ironically, one of those tributes would come from the Jemez Pueblo of Santiago.

He had plenty of time to think while on horseback and he took his time on the trip back. Isabel's warm embrace did not help. Instead, of staying home he ambled over to the governor's residence to be with his like-minded friends. But then, three weeks later on an early November evening he received a message that he needed to go quickly to his parents' house.

"Why?"

"Your father is sick."

"Of course he is sick. He is seventy-three years old!"

Bartolomé had barely made it out of the house for his pre-dawn routine. He felt weak and didn't do any work. Instead he sat on a bench and watched the sun rise. He noted that the November sunrises were not as impressive as those of the summer. Not feeling as good as usual he shuffled back into the house. Immediately concerned, Lucía grabbed his arm and helped him to the bedroom where he lay down and dozed off. She prepared some herb tea but he barely took any, instead fading in and out of sleep.

Sensing the importance or severity of the moment, Lucía sent word to all the children. All save Barti down south had arrived by evening. Bartolomé lay on his bed propped up with pillows. He mostly slept but he spent his waking moments babbling about Corral de Almaguer, the first years in New Mexico, old Pedro his father-in-law, and the Hapsburg Eagle that spread its wings.

At one waking moment, Lucía combed his still long hair and pulled it back into his accustomed ponytail. Awake with eyes closed he whispered, "Gracias, mi amor." Then he opened his eyes and looked at those around his bed. "Maybe someday," he paused for a short breath, "one of you or your children will visit Castile." He stopped to breathe again. "Light a votive in front of Sagrario for me." And he went to sleep.

Agustín stepped forward as Lucía, silently crying, held her husband's hand. He placed his fingers on his father's neck. No pulse. "*Esta muerto.*"

Matías felt some sorrow but saw it as a sign of weakness. His father's death would not change his mind about anything. His mother? Well, his sisters could take care of her. Probably Ana with Francisco, which is what happened. Agustín took over the family property in Santa Fe. He and María were close enough to help out with their mother. Matías felt liberated and did not have conscience enough to question himself. Not even the outpouring of community support at the funeral could influence him. His resolve hardened with the arrival of a new governor.

Luis de Rosas was like no man anyone had encountered before, except for maybe Juan de Oñate. He rode into town riding high on a barely broken, feisty stallion that he had no trouble controlling. He was a broad shouldered but bony man with a thin face, straight lips, a narrow nose and straight raven black hair. His long slender hands added to his image and he intentionally gestured with them theatrically to add to his effect on people. He had an intimating personality, was quick to action, and was focused. Everything about him dictated that he was not a man to be taken lightly. People loved or hated him. If he were alive Matías's father would have despised him. Matías didn't care, for he admired a man who, like himself, did not like to be contradicted.

Rosas's character became clear with three incidents that occurred in rapid succession. The new governor immediately met with his predecessor and let him leave the territory without doing the required investigation of his tenure. Rosas's lackadaisical attitude toward Baeza clearly indicated that they were of like mind and that Rosas intended to carry on with the established policies. He would enrich himself, protect the crown's interests, and damn the Church. Of course, he would use his Royal authority to fulfill the first of his priorities. If the Franciscans or the people had any doubts about his position, his trip to Pecos Pueblo put them to rest.

The recently promoted "Captain" Matías Romero commanded a contingent led by the governor. Battling the late spring gusting winds and biting cold with capes wrapped around them up to their eyes, the men followed the well-worn trail to New Mexico's largest pueblo.

The governor already sent word that he wanted dried meat, blankets, and hides either from the pueblo itself and/or their Apache trading partners who happened to be camped nearby.

Fray Antonio Jiménez greeted the new governor with open arms. With his blue habit blowing in the wind he lowered his hood to reveal a recently tonsured head and a smiling, clean shaven face. "Welcome! May God bless you. The People of Cicuyé, Pecos are anxious to meet you."

"They do not need to meet with me to trade with me. I came here because I heard they did not want to trade."

The priest's arms went down and his smile was replaced with a puzzled look. "But governor, surely you have been advised that this is not the season..."

"Father, Father! I've no time for this." Rosas impressed Matías with his confident staccato speech. He spoke with no inflection at all and rarely looked at the person he addressed, such as now. "You will convey to your neophytes and their friends camped over there, what I want." Without changing his nonchalant look, he held out a hand to his personal secretary who handed him a rolled paper that Rosas pointed at the friar and handed back to the secretary. Without a word being said the secretary nudged his horse ahead to the standing Jiménez and handed the scroll to him. "Now, where do I go to get out of this wind? No. Don't speak." He said these last words slowly. "The convent, your quarters will do. You have three hours to gather the goods."

"But governor..."

"I said no words."

"We have not even met!"

Rosas raised a black eyebrow that made his narrow face look sinister. He smiled, showing uncommonly white teeth. "We don't need to meet. Do we?" He looked up sternly. "Romero! Take some men and post them around the buildings. Three hours Father."

Nothing happened during the first hour. A few blankets along with some squash trickled in during the second hour. Rosas became impatient half way through the third hour, for it became obvious that nothing more was coming. The Apaches camped close by left. In a rage he called out for Fray Antonio who received a vile tongue lashing upon arrival. Then Rosas threatened to take him back to Santa Fe under arrest, and ordered that he consume the hosts that represent the Blessed Sacrament now. Fray Antonio protested that he could not do as ordered because he had just eaten and therefore had broken the required fast. The priest's plea resulted in a rush of ugly words from Rosas's mouth.

At this point Fray Antonio's assistant, a seventy-year old lay brother came to his aid questioning the governor's treatment of his friend and colleague. This enraged Rosas even more and he turned on the old man and threatened him with arrest. Rosas then turned back to Fray Antonio, "Well, Father, you want introductions. Allow me to introduce Captain Romero." He nodded in Matías's direction with that telltale sinister smile or was it a silent snicker? "I trust, Captain, that you know the good friar."

"Yes sir."

"Good. Be so kind as to assist the good Friar in gathering all the Natives before the church."

Father Antonio was aghast. "But Governor! The weather!"

"Yes exactly. Get them here or Captain Romero will have it done for you. Do you understand?"

"No. I mean yes. But why?"

"There is no 'why.' Do as I say."

The elderly lay brother had recovered his wit enough to insert himself again. "The women and children too?"

Matías sensed that Rosas had lost his patience and sure enough, the volatile governor answered by calling both clergy "sons of the devil," and then bellowed out, "Enough. Captain arrest these men and place them under guard. Then have your men round up everyone and bring them before the church."

Matías grabbed the elderly Friar by the arm. The old man offered a weak initial resistance but then went limp. Also restrained, Fray Antonio spoke to Matías. "I am a servant of the Lord."

"I am the servant of the King," Matías replied.

"Of that you are mistaken."

"We'll see. Now, shut up."

Both priests were taken to their quarters and guards were posted. Matías left to oversee the roundup. The men seemed to enjoy the bullying. When everyone was gathered before the church, Rosas came out and ordered all the protective blankets and cloaks taken off the people.

He had the goods packed on some mules to be taken back to Santa Fe. Then, through an interpreter he announced, "I am your governor. I am the law. Maybe now you will understand and obey when I ask for something. I have been harsh because your priest has misled you. I am a fair man. I brought many knives to trade but you did not trade. Nevertheless, I am leaving these knives for you. Also, henceforth I grant you permission to practice your old religion and ignore the priests."

Rosas, Matías, and the men left the people of Pecos terrified and shivering in nightfall's freezing cold temperatures. The horrified priests were speechless as they slowly emerged from their quarters.

The next telltale incident also involved Matías and came when the *cabildo* refused to go along with Rosas's policies. The governor directly acted by abolishing the council then personally choosing new members who would be friendly to him. One of these, of course, was Matías, now in favor with Rosas and a *regidor,* just like his father and older brother had been.

Look at me now, thought Matías. Rosas chose me to be on his council because of who I am, not because of my father. I am a *regidor*, in the governor's favor, and becoming wealthy in the process.

A WARRIOR FOR ROSAS
June 1639, Santa Fe

During the rush of Rosas's arrival and Matías's rapid rise to grace, the latter hardly acknowledged that Isabel gave birth to another son, their fourth child. Matías, perhaps to assure himself of his righteousness, showed his chauvinism by insisting that the child be named Felipe, after the current and previous two kings of Spain.

Nor did he notice that Lucía, his mother, never really recovered from the loss of her Bartolomé. Ana cared for her as best as she could but Lucía had lost her will to live. Toughened by forty years in New Mexico, six births, witness to deaths, and travels on the Camino Real, Lucía could not shed her grief any more than she could stay her advancing years. Her family and friends tried in vain to fill the void.

Matias simply felt uncomfortable around his mother. He saw a wrinkled, shrunken, shaking and sometimes salivating old lady. She made him nervous. He felt that they had nothing to share therefore he looked at her in awkward silence. He was incapable of seeing the embarrassment in her eyes and looked for the first opportunity to leave.

In early 1638, a mere eight months after her Bartolomé had died she quietly joined him. Matías was away on the governor's business.

In the process Matías was not told nor cared to know that his mother quietly passed his grandmother's little statue to his sister María, the oldest daughter. He had no time for such trivialities. His service to Rosas occupied all his attention and time.

Meanwhile, as a man of action, Governor Rosas did not waste time. He followed up his disappointment at Pecos by sending a contingent of men onto the Plains to "show those savages who was in charge."

Matías overcame the disappointment of not being chosen to lead that mission when Rosas immediately announced, "you are staying with me. I understand that there are pueblos far west called Moqui, or Hopi, who have never acquiesced to His Majesty. We need to correct this oversight."

Matías was about travel the route his father had forged four decades earlier. Now he would see for himself where his father and older brother had gone and, oh yes, complete the mission. Matías never quite grasped or no longer cared to grasp the details of his father's history.

The Governor and Matías left Santa Fe leading twenty handpicked soldiers. Matías was surprised to see that the pueblos of Sandía and Santa Ana had been abandoned, including the priests. He and the others with him noticed that the Natives had started fortifying their villages. This included Santo Domingo Pueblo where the Franciscans maintained their New Mexican headquarters.

The ever-suspicious Rosas reacted the only way he knew. He ordered his men, led by Matías, to ransack the abandoned *conventos* attached to the churches in the abandoned pueblos. He shouted out that "those infernal priests need to learn who is in charge." Matías led his men in an efficient operation as they went through the priest's dwelling. They fortified their vigor when they found the sacramental wine.

By the time they sighted the high mesas upon which the Hopi Villages sat, Matías and his men were of the same sinister mind as their leader Rosas. There would be no pleading, negotiating, or questioning. The Natives better submit immediately. The governor did not care or even consider if the Natives did not understand his demands. A siege ensued.

Matías reacted to the governor's attitude with enthusiasm. He joined in the fight with pleasure. Now he relived his father's attack on Acoma. "Ha! This is not so difficult. These people are not worthy of being called warriors." They had faced little resistance.

Rosas had a retort, "But they make good chattel." And he proceeded to separate out about forty young, healthy captives for his workshop in Santa Fe and for trade down south.

"Now," he asked through his interpreters, "Who are your trading partners?" The reply came back that the Utes or Utahs who live close by in the mountains to the northeast trade with them on a regular basis.

We must go meet these people. Romero, organize a contingent to take our captives back to Santa Fe, then we will see about these trading partners."

It just happened that Matías's cousin Cristóbal had been selected for this journey. Now an *alferez*, his disposition for a military career had become less of a concern when compared to family and farm. Matías suspected that Cristóbal had not been completely won over by Rosas and that his cousin did not have an appetite for slaving.

It was not surprising then when Cristóbal found a rare idle moment with Matías and asked, "What is the plan?" When told, Cristóbal observed that everyone knows that the Utes are peaceful and willing traders. They trade on a regular basis at Taos.

"Good. Then they will trade with us."

"I hope that is all. The governor cannot be looking for more slaves. He will make enemies of them."

Matías gave his cousin a stern look. "Be careful what you say. The governor knows what he is doing."

Cristóbal answered with an unconvinced look and nod of his head.

Understanding the gist of the conversation, Matías decided to send Cristóbal back with the escort of captured Hopis. "He's too weak for this. He doesn't understand," he said to Diego de Guadalajara, a relatively recent arrival from Mexico and native of Oaxaca. Diego had become a favorite of Rosas's and confidant of Matías. They had like minds.

Nor would Cristóbal have understood what happened with the Utes. They had been warned by their Hopi friends, so did not come out to greet the mounted intruders. Instead they sequestered their women and children in the mountains and prepared to fight.

The whole conflict exhilarated Matías, he led the charge up the hillside and into the rocks where the enemy hid firing arrows. Matías felt a sharp burning sensation and then throbbing ache when an arrow pierced his thigh. He fired both of his pistols, missing each time. But he didn't care. With an adrenalin rush at a lifetime high he felt invincible. He unsheathed his sword and urged his horse forward. Now the real fighting would begin. He slashed and stabbed, elbowed someone, was knocked off his horse by someone else, rolled over to his feet in time to meet his attacker with a thrust of his weapon almost to the hilt. Now exposed, he used his foot for leverage to free the sword. He saw the shooter before he shot and ducked as the arrow swished by.

Then the commotion suddenly stopped. An uncommon silence ensued, broken by human groans. A victory had been won and Rosas rode up to bask in its glory. He had watched from a distance, and now for the first time unsheathed his sword in a show of bravado.

He used the weapon for effect as he gestured, directing his men in gathering together the last of the defeated Ute warriors. "We'll take the healthy ones with us. They'll bring a fair price in Mexico." He pointed his blade toward Matías, whose throbbing thigh caused no little discomfort, "And you, Romero, will be rewarded handsomely."

Everything about the venture to the Hopi Pueblos and, then, into Ute territory conspired to make the return trip long and tiresome. They left five colleagues in shallow graves, many of the survivors had wounds. All were exhausted, edgy for their vigilance over the captives, on top of which Matías was concerned over his own wound. All this prolonged an already long trip. Not even a refreshing dip in the cold, clear waters at "el tanque," where Barti, Eulate, and Oñate left their names carved in the sandstone walls, improved things.

Matías inwardly gloated over his experience even while aggravated over the immediacy of the journey. In his mind, he had made his own reputation. And, in his biased view, his accomplishments stacked up to anything that his father had done or, for that matter, his older brother. Everyone with him agreed on one thing, Matías Romero did not lack for courage.

As they entered the capitol, the people came out to meet them. No priests appeared. Nor was there a sense of celebration, only curiosity and a sense of relief for loved ones who returned. Isabel stood waiting for Matías with the three oldest children at her side. Little Lucía held her hand. Felipe, the baby, stared out of his bundle of blankets nestled in his mother's other arm. Isabel and Matías barely had time to greet one another. Matías had not dismounted when Rosas summoned Matías and Captain Gómez to a meeting.

His brother-in-law had been left in charge of the foray onto the Plains. Matías learned that Francisco had led an attack on an unsuspecting Apache village thus garnering more captives for Rosas. "Now they are well-punished and will obey us." Rosas self-assurance was so convincing.

In acknowledging Francisco's exploits the governor added that, "It seems that military prowess is a family trait."

Francisco answered, "We serve at your liege, sir."

"We serve the King." Rosas spoke with a hint of sarcasm. "However, our work is incomplete. The Franciscans have been inciting the Natives to rebel. Their pueblos are being fortified, and worse, I have heard that they have sent written complaints to Mexico City."

Matías spoke up. "The priests have complained and opposed every governor since the beginning."

Francisco cut Matías off. "They have affected and exhausted this land and leave us, who protect them, in despair."

"Yes, obviously so." Rosas stared at a wall. "Romero, how is your wound?"

"Superficial. It is fine."

"Can you ride, travel? Yes, of course you can. Can you be ready at tomorrow's dusk for a prolonged trip?"

"As you wish. Where am I going?"

"To Mexico City. I need to counter those nefarious friars. I will entrust you with my written reports to the Viceroy. Silence would work against me."

Matías returned home where he explained his latest assignment while spooning mutton stew with pieces of bread. After dinner he cleaned and dressed his wound, arranged his equipment, rearranged his bedroll, watered, fed, bedded down his horses, and lay with his wife. He never bothered to review what she might need or have to do during his absence. She and her family can take care of that. Besides, she had become used to living without him.

Early the next morning Francisco and Ana came over to see him off. Francisco praised the luck of his assignment, openly gloating at Matías's recently gained importance. Matías soaked it in and looked at Isabel as if to say, "See? You should be proud."

After the two brothers-in-law left to meet with the governor and receive his packet of letters, Ana followed Isabel into the kitchen were the hot water was ready for tea. Isabel arranged the herbs and poured while Ana consoled her. "My Francisco is the same. We are single, married women and they are wed to the governor."

"I suppose it is necessary."

"Maybe but I remember my father. He always cared for us children. He held all the same high positions. He was a captain. I don't know. It just seems that he preferred to be at home with the family and working on the land or with the animals."

Isabel finished pouring and set down the kettle. "Matías barely knows his children. He has been around the baby only a few days."

Ana sighed, "Well, times have changed. We must be patient."

Meanwhile, Agustín waited for Matías outside the governor's residence. "Eh, Matías. Going south, I hear."

"Word travels fast."

"Of course. There are no secrets. You know that."

"I suppose."

Agustín paused and then handed an envelope to Matías. "Here. No doubt you will spend a night with Barti."

"Yes, of course."

"Give him this letter. Its just catch up news. Nothing more. He can read it in front of you."

"Sure. Should I tell him anything?"

Agustín thought for a second. "Just to take care and that we miss him and the family up here." He hesitated and added, "Also, brother, there is a paper for you. Barti can add to it. His son and daughter with her husband have moved south to New Spain. They are probably living with mom's family in Zamora. Maybe in Mexico City. If you see them, and I hope so, say hello for us and bring back some news about them."

Matías looked into the doorway and distracted with other thoughts replied, "I don't know. I will be on important, official business for the governor. We'll see."

Agustín acquiesced. "Yes, yes, I understand. Well, just in case, yes?"

"Of course. What do you think? Of course."

The brothers hugged. Agustín wished his brother a safe trip and acknowledged Francisco, who was standing close by, with a tip of his hat.

URGENT BUSINESS SOUTH
1639, On the Camino Real

Governor Rosas gave Matías command of twelve soldiers with fifteen mules packed with the governor's trade goods. "Sell them wherever you get a good price."

They spent their fourth night on the trail at Senecú where Matías delivered Agustín's letters. In exchange, Bartí and María handed over letters for their son and daughter in Mexico. Matías could not help but notice that both his brother and sister-in-law had aged beyond their years. Bartí aged because of his choice of where he settled, and María as a result of her long battle to overcome the poisoning she suffered. In addition, they had lost touch with their two children in Mexico. The parents supposed that brother and sister were together somewhere. Hopefully, the Robledo relatives would know.

The next camping spot had the name of Fray Cristóbal. One of the men told a story that the name came from a Franciscan who was a relative of Oñate's. While on his way south he died and was buried at this spot, the northern point of the trail where it begins the desert crossing. "*The Jornada*," the crossing could take up to three or four days.

Unburdened with wagons, women, or children Matías and his men traveled the *Jornada* non-stop. They left Fray Cristóbal mid-day, traveled through the night and arrived at Robledo at the southern end of the crossing a little after midnight the next day. In the process, they barely paused at the two *parajes*, the second of which the men called Perrillo Springs, where one of Oñate's dogs found water.

None of the men knew where the name Robledo came from except for the fact that the large hills across the river had the same name. Matías remembered that the name had something to do with his mother's family, maybe her father. His mother, and now Ana, repeated the story but Matías never cared enough to register the details. He thought that maybe his Robledo grandfather did something or possibly died here. Nevertheless, he did not let on that he knew anything about the name. No one would believe him anyway. Matías had no interest in these references to history.

The group moved through "The Pass" and left New Mexico behind. The journey through the Chihuahua desert and into the hill country to Santa Barbara seemed interminable. Matías was anxious to see New Spain proper.

Santa Barbara had grown to a town twice the size of Santa Fe. Still, with around eleven hundred residents it did not impress anyone. The next major stop at Zacatecas was a different story. The area's mines continued to produce silver and the town's buildings, especially the cathedral and its sister churches, reflected the wealth being extracted from the ground.

Here, for the first time in his life, Matías visited a real tavern and slept in a real inn. This, he thought to himself, is what his father gave up to go to New Mexico and farm. Could it be better? Even the wine had a sweeter taste. He would make his own judgment. Nor would he tarry in Zacatecas. Only the successful sale of most of Rosas's merchandize kept him there for two days and nights.

Unencumbered of Rosas's goods, he and the men travelled at a more rapid rate. The invaluable mules were left under the care of a trusted stable and would be picked up on the return trip.

South of Zacatecas, Matías made the decision to avoid the most travelled branch of the trail that passed through the cities of Guanajuato and Queretaro, the last of which is a Franciscan seat of power with some influence over New Mexico's missionaries. Instead, he took the less travelled route through San Miguel.

The population became dense and the towns larger the further south they travelled. The larger cities grew like giants among many smaller villages, many of which were larger than Santa Fe. Matías noted the enormous majority of Native and African people and the apparent paucity of Spanish people. The Natives and some Blacks, *"Negros,"* walked the streets as if they belonged.

Mexico City overwhelmed Matías. Had there not have been someone with him who had been in the city before, he would have been lost. Matías could almost feel the smells of human and animal waste drying in the sweltering heat on the streets while waiting to be washed into the receding lake. He could not help but put his hand up to his mouth. The resultant insects helped to give the New Mexicans a sensory experience heretofore unknown. Odor, insects, noise, and commotion all conspired to oppress them.

Then it slowly became obvious to Matías that their livery, their clothes, weapons, and horse gear, identified them as *extranjeros,* foreigners. "Uncomfortable" understated their feelings by the time they entered the great entryway and dismounted on the cobblestone courtyard of the viceroy's palace. Impeccably uniformed soldiers stood guard and moved about their duties. They could not help but notice the oddly dressed and travel worn strangers. Some openly had a look on their faces that said, "God, what have you brought us now?"

Matías stated his business to a rather stiff, dour, even effeminate acting man who walked up to them. He escorted Matías into the chambered building passing through a series of twelve foot high, wooden, double doors to a large open office the back end of which housed a large ornate wooden desk manned by a pink, small man in a well-coiffured white wig.

No one offered a chair so Matías stood waiting where indicated. When man looked up with a bored, curious expression Matías stated his business, handed over the packet of reports and letters from Rosas, and waited for further instructions. None came. The wigged man merely dismissed him with a wave of his manicured hand.

Matías did not find or hear anything about his niece and nephew. Actually, Matías could not wait to put Mexico City behind him. Moreover, he would not make any diversions on his return trip. A visit with his Zamora relatives and possible encounter with Barti's kids only crossed his mind, nothing more. Instead, he added his own letter to Agustín's letter and sent them to Zamora. He asked about Nicolas and Juana, and requested that a return post be sent to Zacatecas where he would receive it on his way north.

He did receive an answer. The Robledos were still centered in Zamora and doing reasonably well. They were happy for the news from their New Mexican cousins, but saddened to hear about the deaths of Matías's father and mother, their aunt Lucía. Nicolas, Juana, and her husband spent a month in Zamora. They decided to strike out north to Pimería Alta, called Sonora where rumors of rich silver lodes persisted at a place called Arizonac. They asked, "Are these the same, that our uncle, your father had seen?"

The question jumped out at Matías. How would he know? Nor did he care to think about it but could not avoid it. Aside from Castile, the so-called silver lodes were the only other place where his father had been that he hadn't. Whether he recognized it or not his father's exploits haunted him.

El Paso was under consideration to become a new mission and when the group arrived there on their return trip, they found the Franciscans' reception completely indifferent. The priests greeted them in a subdued even resentful manner. And it did not take long for Matías to find out why. Rosas had come there to escort the friars west into the Sierra Madre Mountains to create a new mission. Instead of assisting, Rosas ignored the priests and effectively pushed them aside, as he demanded trade goods and then forcibly subjugated the Natives. Most of the Indians fled into the rugged canyons and hidden valleys of the mountains. Any chance at conversion was lost so the priests returned to El Paso in complete disgust. Like their brethren further north the Franciscans put their writing skills to use sending south scathing reports about Rosas.

As one of Rosas's captains, Matías came under immediate suspicion. Fortunately, Matías only sought a restful night for himself and his men. He assured the priests that they would not inconvenience them more than one night and this placated the blue robed Franciscans. Still, the friars kept their distance.

Four days later the small band had made it to Barti's hacienda. Barti could not wait to hear what news Matías brought back. Over cups of his locally made wine, the taste of which became the first topic of conversation, Matías gave a detailed account of the trip and his impressions of New Spain and its capital. The news of their two children satisfied Barti and María, although Matías was unable to help them out with news of a grandchild. Barti did not think that the silver lodes in Pimería Alta were the same place visited by their father, "although it is possible."

Ever cognizant of his duty, Matías left for Santa Fe the next day. Barti tried to convince him to send the men on and stay a while, but Matías sensed that he needed to report personally to Rosas.

The governor's attention confirmed his belief, for Rosas eagerly listened to Matías's account. He puzzled over the bureaucrat's reception of Matías, his emissary. "What is the significance of that?" He asked no one in particular. He mulled over the question and concluded that the Franciscans had gotten to the Viceroy first. However, he reflected, that was not necessarily bad.

Rosas stood up and cut off Matías as he began relating the bitterness encountered in El Paso. With a wave of his hand he dismissed the El Paso missionaries, "They are small minds and would not have converted those primitives under any circumstance. I did those religious a favor of sorts. Those people, if you want to call them that, now understand the reach of our power. Had I done nothing and left the friars there, no doubt they would now be passing through Peter's gate as fine martyrs all. They should be pleased that they can still preach, even complain. To hell with them!"

Matías listened and nodded in agreement, for he knew, that Rosas had collected more trade items and captives. Rosas's nearby workshop could not be missed and left no doubt of that.

"Prepare yourself, Romero," Matías never questioned the normal way that Rosas always addressed him in military fashion, either by rank or last name, "we're going to pay a visit to that mystical Quivira."

"When?"

"In two days. We should not waste time."

"Yes sir, gladly sir. How many men do we take?"

"Forty. Get together with Gómez and chose them. He is waiting for you. Also, no wagons, just mules. I don't want to be encumbered."

"If I may ask, is Captain Gómez going as well?"

"No. Gómez will be left in charge here."

"I see. At your leave, sir. I've work to do."

"Yes you do."

He returned home to begin a by now well-known routine. None of the children knew how to react to the weather-beaten, busy man that their mother told them was their father. He did not react to them any better. His youngest was starting to walk and the older ones had developed personalities. To them he had become a man who came and went.

When the time came, Matías was mounted and ready. Now he would go to a place that his father had not been. Travel on the Plains had become fairly common. When Matías was young he heard of a person who led an expedition past Quivira to a great river that he named Espiritu Santu. Some priests unsuccessfully tried to take the word of God to the Quivirans. Of course these same people were well known in New Mexico as trading partners to Pecos and Taos Pueblos. Now, Rosas wanted to make direct contact and subjugate them to his business empire. He also would be looking for the Pueblo people who had moved to the Plains to avoid him.

Although known to others, the route onto the Plains was new to Matías. They followed a route to the northeast crossing rivers at various stages until they came upon the first of the Quivira villages. The journey took them over three weeks.

They had no desire to learn anything of these people nor understand that Quivira was not one tribe, rather than many tribes some of which rivaled each other. Among New Mexicans all the people of this region were Quivirans.

Rosas even shunned the representatives of one tribe who brought word that they had traded at Pecos and were friends with the Spanish. Instead, he sought out what he considered the largest and most important village and ordered a summary attack "to set an example."

The element of surprise assured victory, if not a slaughter but it also brought resistance and more casualties and, of course, it made enemies.

Once again Matías acquitted himself well in battle. The advantage of being on horseback suited him. This time he exhibited more patience before firing his pistols. The almost point blank shots found their marks. He took an arrow through his vest, sweeping across his chest and sticking out under his arm. The missile did not break skin. Unlike his father, Matías liked war.

The return to the Rio Grande Valley and home passed in a flash, for Matías reveled in his warrior status. He revisited and relished his battle exploits. He had become a legend in his own mind. Rosas did nothing to lessen Matías's self-esteem when he made him an *alcalde ordinario* and awarded him parts of two more *encomiendas,* at Santa Ana and Sandía Pueblos.

Matías spent the rest of 1640 doing Rosas's bidding. The tactics became more desperate as a severe epidemic swept the land and took a hard toll on the Pueblo people. Thousands died. No pueblo was left untouched. The Native leaders blamed the mysterious affliction on the anger of their old Gods for following the priests. Rosas's open opposition to the Franciscans did nothing to counter their belief and, in fact, encouraged them to turn from the missionaries.

Death and disease depleted the Native work force and its production. Trade decreased and nomadic trading partners were hesitant to get close to the pueblos. Yet, Rosas only saw his sources of revenue decreasing so he pressured the pueblos even more. As the Pueblo people found it more difficult to produce, his frustration grew. With Matías and Francisco in the forefront, Rosas's men took to raiding missions and sacking the convents.

All this created severe resentment among the Pueblo people. Rebellion had become a possibility and the hints were obvious. The pueblos of Jemez and Taos killed their priests. This prompted Rosas to take revenge. In Taos he found an empty village. The people had fled into the mountains and onto the plains. The latter group chose to live among the Apaches rather than return.

Rosas's greed blinded him to the growing resistance among the settlers. He concentrated on the pueblos, for they were his main source of income. The Spanish people would fall in line. He had no fear of them or the priests. Yet, he did not notice that society had split to extremes and his detractors openly had come to the defense of the priests. His iron grip had weakened but he and his followers seemed oblivious to the fact.

REALITY COMES HOME
1641, Santa Fe

Change came in the form of an elderly new governor sent to replace Rosas. Juan Flores de Sierra y Valdés arrived to take office and to begin the review of Rosas's administration. However, he suddenly became ill. His advanced age and the toll of the trip north left him susceptible to the epidemic still rampant in New Mexico.

Flores quickly ordered the election of a new *cabildo* that replaced Matías, Diego de Guadalajara, and the other Rosas men. Apparently misunderstanding the deep divisions Rosas had created, the terminally ill governor named Matías's brother-in-law, Francisco Gómez to take his place upon his death. He died after a couple of days in bed. Even before he was buried the *cabildo* rejected Rosas's right hand man as governor and then voted against Rosas who tried to get himself named.

The emboldened *cabildo* then arrested the ex-governor and placed him under lock and key. In quick fashion some men entered Rosas's cell and killed him. The *cabildo* conducted a quick investigation and concluded that a jealous husband had killed the governor. At any rate they did not express any remorse and refused to allow his burial in the church.

The good fortune that Matías had enjoyed had turned sour. Now he and Francisco worried about their own fate. They had enemies, dangerous enemies. If they could kill Rosas, they surely could take revenge on them.

Matías had not seen this coming. For the first time in his life his clear vision of who he was and intended to be was replaced with surprise, confusion, and consternation. But, he retained his desire to survive. Both he and Francisco focused on the immediate future as they lived in fear. They watched out for each other and learned to appreciate the protection of their extended family. Nevertheless, they slept lightly.

At one point, they decided to take their families to the distant safety of Senecú for an extended stay. Now, Matías understood what his brother Barti meant when he talked about being away "from all that." But Barti was not well. He had visibly aged even more and slowed down. His hands shook enough to be noticed and he constantly coughed, especially when he tried to laugh.

When an entourage bringing a new governor, Alonso Pacheco de Heredia, came out of the south, Matías and Francisco joined them for the final leg to Santa Fe. The governor had questions about what had happened and hinted that he brought general amnesty for all concerned. This welcome news was a great relief.

The *cabildo* arranged a nice reception for the new governor. Everyone was pleased to see an energetic, apparently fair-minded man take over the colony. His announcement of forgiveness brought on a calm not witnessed in years. As was his prerogative he organized a new *cabildo* and not even the reinstatement of many of Rosas's old cronies alerted the people. Both Francisco and Matías received their old military ranks. Matías became a *regidor* once again and his brother, Agustín, was named Secretary of War.

Meanwhile, Matías and Isabel produced another son. Isabel suggested that he be named Bartolomé. Matías hesitated. Isabel responded with an unusual show of bravado. "Not for your father but your brother. He is sick and he helped us." Matías was too distracted with his political career to bother an answer. Isabel won her point.

Matías quickly learned that the new governor had an agenda. Apparently, he had an interest in Rosas and his fate. His constant questions, especially about who opposed him and why, did not raise eyebrows. It was a natural curiosity for a man in his position. He had surrounded himself with Rosas people and those were the ones who fed him information.

The outcome of the governor's curiosity came to a head when Matías, Francisco, and some other officers received explicit instructions to arrest eight men, all of whom had opposed Rosas. Some had served on the very *cabildo* that had welcomed Pacheco. Others, like Diego Márquez, had been New Mexico's treasurer. Most were from founding families and prominent men, especially Antonio Baca, Diego Márquez, and Juan de Archuleta. Even more disconcerting is that through marriage Archuleta and Captain Francisco Salazar was a relative of both Matías and Francisco.

Despite suspicions, the men were efficiently arrested and taken to the jail in the royal houses. Matías and Francisco did not feel remorse. After all, these were the people who "did not understand." They would be tried and most likely fined or punished in some nondescript way. The worse that could happen would be a civil trial in Mexico City. They could be banned from New Mexico or assigned to mandatory duty somewhere else in the empire. If acquitted they could return to New Mexico, but the ordeal would leave them financially destroyed.

Everyone soon realized that all that was speculation, for the governor revealed secret instructions from the viceroy. He had orders to punish those responsible for the death of Rosas, "the King's official." The royal instructions mandated that the governor use his own indiscretion and mete out the punishment in New Mexico.

"Well," Francisco sarcastically noted, "they made their own bed."

Matías was not so sure. His father's warnings resonated, "We are here and will stay but the governors come and go and do not care about us." Yet, he could do nothing but let the scenario play out. He was helpless and without influence. Nor could he escape being a part of the events. Unlike his father, Matías could not avoid being called to duty on behalf of the governor. While not realizing it Matías had lost his taste for being so close to power.

A few days later, on a partially cloudy mid-July afternoon a messenger came from the governor. His presence was requested at the Royal Houses. Matías had a foreboding feeling and it was not alleviated when he found Francisco and twenty other soldiers waiting on the governor's presence. His old colleague, Diego de Guadalajara looked as if he were about to enjoy a repast. He had some advanced knowledge. A majority of the men had come to New Mexico with the governor. Neither Matías nor Francisco had learned the names of all the men. Both figured that their loyalty had everything to do with the governor and not them. The two were pawns in the governor's plans.

The governor and his secretary came out and signaled everyone into a room. Behind a closed door the expressionless governor had the secretary read from a paper that he held.

I, the Lord and Governor of New Mexico, Alonso Pacheco de Heredía in accordance with instructions from His Excellency, Juan de Palafox, Bishop of Puebla and Viceroy of New Spain, say and hereby order it, the execution of [here he named the eight men] whom I investigated and found culpable for the murder of His Majesty's governor, Don Luis de Rosas.

The secretary stopped and looked at the governor. Still expressionless, Pacheco said, "Gentlemen, you will fulfill this order immediately."

A stunned Matías looked at Francisco whose temple muscles visibly tightened. Francisco stared beyond the governor at nothing. "No," thought Matías. "This can't be true." He continued in shock as the secretary and one of the governor's men explained how the prisoners would be blindfolded and beheaded.

Matías knew those men. He disagreed with them but never hated them. Nor was he convinced that all the victims were directly involved in Rosas's murder.

Someone had the audacity to ask if the condemned knew?

"No."

"Do they see a priest?"

"No. That would alert them to their fate and make things messy. They are murderers and should die with the mortal sin on their souls if they have not confessed by now."

As officers, Matías and Francisco did not do the actual killing. They oversaw the acts. The blindfolded men were taken out to a dirt courtyard two at a time. One soldier per prisoner had the assignment of slitting the throat and severing the head. They passed two well-sharpened *belduques* between them as the condemned were brought out. Wide-eyed and scared themselves the executioners tried their best for clean kills but most needed second and third attempts. Their clothes and nearby walls became splattered with blood as bodies dropped and withered far too long for anyone's taste.

Half of the soldiers, including Matías, vomited in the process. This was something to which not even battle experience could harden them.

After the executions Matías felt as if he were in some kind of bubble. Nothing was real. Disposing of the bodies was left to the soldiers. A town herald announced the deed and the governor went to the plaza to announce that henceforth all would be forgiven if those who had been part of "the rebellion" came forth and begged forgiveness.

Matías did not stay to hear the herald or governor. He snuck off to the ditch running through the Royal Courtyard. He didn't speak, just cleaned as best he could. He had to get rid of the blood. Then he aimlessly wandered about town in a daze. He crossed the river, walking through it, to the Barrio de Analco on the town's south side. There he entered the San Miguel church and stood on the dirt floor staring at the altar screen. He didn't pray. "Why bother?" He thought. "God would not forgive this. What have I done?"

Time passed. Matías did not notice. The sun had set but its rays still played off the clouds in the western sky. Unconsciously he walked home where he entered an empty house, nabbed a change of clothes, and just as a thunderstorm opened up, he bathed in the river.

He felt shame, not guilt. Reality had become illusive. He wanted the day's events to be a dream. How could he go from that blood bath to his family, the children? And, then he realized that no one was home when he arrived.

He buried his bloody clothes at the river's edge and started for home again. From the distance he saw light in the house. Someone was there. He was exhausted, not physically but mentally.

Isabel saw him coming and rushed out to meet him. She looked concerned. "Oh, Mati, here you are. Thank God!"

"Yes Isa. It has been a trying day."

"Did you hear? Do you know?"

"What?" Matías had a look of resignation as he entered the house and sat at the kitchen table.

"The governor executed the eight for the Rosas affair. Archuleta, Márquez, Baca and the others. Word and fear are spreading all over town."

Matías lied in an attempt to avoid more talk about it. "No, I didn't know. Lock the door. There will be trouble."

Death is hard to forget, particularly when a person senses that the unfortunates were wrongfully killed. The families of the executed along with the priests pledged loyalty to the governor, mostly out of fear. At the same time rumor spread that they will write reports to Mexico City charging the governor with abuse of power and murder. The environment reeked of tension.

Matías realized that his and the others' association with Rosas and the "revengeful governor" did not bode well for him. The governor's assurances of forgiveness fell on doubtful ears. Hadn't he already granted amnesty and broken it with "secret instructions." He could do it again. Even though he issued certificates of amnesty the overbearing feeling of grief and bitterness could not be erased. His plea to forget the past and tend to the future struck Matías as something harder to do than it sounds.

The sad news that his brother Barti had died at home was an additional and unwelcome distraction. Barti outlived his namesake father by a mere seven years. He was still in his forties. Everyone knew that he had been sick. Still his death was a surprise.

Now Matías resented the call to duty, nor did he care anymore about accolades. Life for him had turned cruel. His brother's only child in New Mexico, also named Bartolomé, the third direct generation of that name and sometimes called "El Hijo," decided to abandon the southern *hacienda* and move back to Santa Fe. He left the place in the hands of hired help.

Time started to move slowly for Matías. He remained depressed. Everyone knew that he had been involved in the executions, but only Isabel had a full understanding of its effect on him. He felt shame for the first time in his life. Not even the news that the governor had decided to send Agustín to Mexico City shook Matías from his doldrums.

Agustín sought Matías's advice about the trail and what to expect in New Spain. Matías did his best, but could not help to add, "I hope that you have a more favorable reception than I did." Then he remembered. "By the way, ask our sister Ana about the Robledos and why the paraje at the southern end of the Jornada has that name." When he heard that Diego de Guadalajara was part of the escort, Matías instructed Agustín to be wary of him. "He is experienced on the trail. Good. However, he is mean-spirited. Do not get too close to him."

As the winter's cold spell lifted and trees began to develop their leaves, Matías slowly began to heal. He would never forget or be the same. His days of warring were over. He lost his taste for it. Fortunately, the current governor did not share Rosas's greed, so Matías was not called to a duty for which he no longer cared.

Isabel enjoyed having her husband at home. He tried to help with the children but decided that Isabel's experience and relationship with them worked better. He never became comfortable with the children, now totaling six with the birth of Catalina. Life's habits could not be completely reversed.

Then came a reminder that people had not forgotten the past. In the spring of 1644, the arrival of another governor apparently emboldened the still embittered folk to anonymously accuse Matías of mistreating the Indians in Quivira. The arresting officers came to his house and allowed him to prepare himself. He kissed Isabel, waved to the children, said that he would be back soon, and left without protest.

That same day, the governor released him. He was given a couple of weeks to prepare his defense and he used the time to line up his family and friends to influence the governor. They easily convinced the governor that Matías's missteps were a matter of being a loyal officer who followed orders. As such he still is a loyal and valuable officer. The governor quickly realized that he came from an influential family, and was the type of person who could be valuable to him. Conversely, the governor would create more problems than necessary if he alienated the family and its allies.

While relieved at the governor's judgment, Matías realized that he would have to be careful. Yes, he had made his bed and he accepted the burden. He had enemies.

He concentrated on working with his immediate family, taking short trips to collect the tribute from his encomiendas. He had not changed his attitude toward the Natives. They were something like chattel, and he sometimes still puzzled over Barti's sentimental attitude that he needed them to survive. That was a bias that would not change.

On the other hand, practicality dictated that using force or threats of force did not work anymore. As such, he had come to expect something less than the entitled amount from the encomiendas and to leave well enough alone. So he, his brother, in-laws, and nephews worked together, pooling resources to extract a decent lifestyle in a desperate place. For the next four years he fell into a regular routine while avoiding the political fighting that never ended.

A Mysterious Ailment
Spring 1648, Santa Ana Pueblo

While on a trip to collect tribute at Santa Ana Pueblo, Matías doubled over in excruciating pain. His stomach burned and the people around him immediately took him into the convent next to the mission and put him in bed. Ironically, he had ransacked this very building a years before. He lay in a sweat and slipped in and out of delirium as his men quickly transported him back to Santa Fe.

As night fell the pain came and went. "My God," he thought as he struggled to sit up, knocking over a water jug and oil lamp on the table next to the bed. "What is wrong?" He tried to retch but that only exacerbated the pain.

The noise from the broken pitcher and fallen lamp attracted the attention of others in an adjoining room. They rushed in to find Matías on the floor doubled in a fetal position struggling to breathe.

"Get him up. Put him in bed. Someone get a damp towel."

Back in bed the pain became constant. His stomach was on fire. He had never felt anything like this before. Delirium set in for long periods. He groaned in pain. The blankets became drenched in his sweat. His breathing became heavier. In different moments he thought to himself, "Good God this hurts. Was I poisoned? Is this how María felt when she was poisoned?" Minutes passed. He moaned and whispered, "No."

Someone asked for a priest.

Alone in his world Matías wondered, "Could one of the families in nearby Bernalillo have arranged for the poisoning? The families around there hated Rosas, and then, Pacheco. Was this their revenge?"

Matías never had an answer to his questions, for he died that night. He was young, only thirty-six years old and he left behind a family with six young children. Of his brothers only Agustín still lived. His sister María died a few months later, leaving Ana with the family statue as the only survivor among the girls.

PART IV
THE END OF AN EPOCH: FELIPE

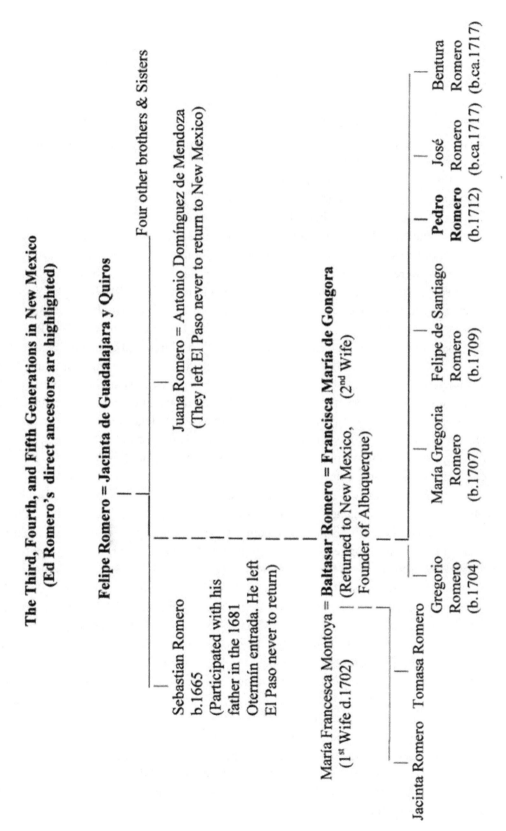

The Third, Fourth, and Fifth Generations in New Mexico
(Ed Romero's direct ancestors are highlighted)

Felipe Romero = Jacinta de Guadalajara y Quiros

Four other brothers & Sisters

Sebastian Romero
b.1665
(Participated with his
father in the 1681
Otermín entrada. He left
El Paso never to return)

Juana Romero = Antonio Domínguez de Mendoza
(They left El Paso never to return to New Mexico)

María Francesca Montoya = Baltasar Romero = Francisca María de Gongora
(1st Wife d.1702)   (Returned to New Mexico,   (2nd Wife)
                            Founder of Albuquerque)

Jacinta Romero Tomasa Romero

Gregorio
Romero
(b.1704)

María Gregoria
Romero
(b.1707)

Felipe de Santiago
Romero
(b.1709)

Pedro
Romero
(b.1712)

José
Romero
(b.ca.1717)

Bentura
Romero
(b.ca.1717)

155

A FAMILY *MATANZA*
September 1653, Santa Fe

Felipe had not reached his tenth birthday when his father died. His last image of the man was an already stiff, odd-colored body in a wooden casket. Then they nailed the lid over him and proceeded to Santa Fe's church for the funeral mass.

Five years later Felipe stood staring at the crowd, all of them relatives. Many of them he knew, others he had only heard about. Some he knew but never realized that they were relatives, while others about whom he knew nothing milled about. His Uncle Francisco and aunt Ana had organized this reunion. They called it a family *matanza* with pig and *cabrito* so as not to attract too much attention, or so young Felipe was told.

Here were the Romeros or what was left of them. His uncle Faustín was "the last of the sons." Bartolomé, El Hijo, whom they sometimes called El Mozo (the Younger), Felipe's favorite cousin nine years older had some status already. He shared his Bartolomé name with at least four other cousins, including Felipe's younger brother. The Robledos, including all of Uncle Francisco's and Aunt Ana's children and grandchildren, had the largest contingent. Then, there was that crazy Diego Pérez, a cousin from aunt María and uncle Gaspar Pérez, who had died when Felipe was eight years old. Diego could be heard above the din of the noise, always laughing and boasting with his long curly black hair highlighting his hilarity. Felipe met Montoyas, Archuletas, and Lucero de Godoys, all family members, in-laws, through marriages too many for Felipe to remember. Aunt Ana kept track of that stuff. Felipe tried to count but gave up. Surely, he thought in his exaggerated view, they numbered over eighty.

Felipe, like his two brothers, had his share of fame mostly because of his father. Many of the relatives came up to him. "So you're Matías's son." And they would size him up and continue with something about the exploits and bravery of his father. He had heard this in great, exaggerated detail from aunt Ana and in odd, short moments from Uncle Francisco.

He learned that his father and uncle Francisco had been great friends as well as brothers-in-law. They had shared many adventures together and, Felipe knew from others that they somehow had been involved with the Rosas affair. But, no one ever spoke about the cause of his death as anything but a sickness. He also knew that uncle Francisco's importance and fame exceeded even that of the governor. This influence extended to aunt Ana, for he could not help but notice that most people addressed her with the very formal "Doña" as if she were a noble. She even had the demeanor of a duchess or at least as Felipe imagined such a person.

That his aunt and uncle could demand the attention of so many people did not surprise him. He watched his uncle as he supervised the slaughter of three pigs and five lambs. He noted that his uncle would not test the chili while everyone in the younger generation had come to crave it, with the red pods ground up and mixed with corn, beans, and squash and eaten with meat.

Uncle Francisco, in his late seventies, remained a stout man. To Felipe he always appeared bigger than life. He stood about five feet nine or ten inches tall, which made him taller than average but not unusual. Perhaps it was his large head with hair pulled back but not tied. His receding hairline exposed a prominent forehead and a broad face. His full mouth of straight teeth, now yellowing and ground smaller from years of use, only showed through his tight-lipped smile as it penetrated a wide jaw with a full, well-manicured beard. Unlike most of the other people at the gathering, Felipe had seen his uncle's many battle scars, testimony to his many exploits. This added to his grandiose impression of the man who with his wife and nephew, Bartolomé El Hijo, had taken young Felipe under their wings.

After everyone ate, Aunt Ana ushered the women and children away. Francisco led the men and teenaged boys, including Felipe to sit around a blazing fire. He signaled his indigenous servants to pour chokecherry juice out of the big clay olive jars in which he allowed the juice to ferment. The men eagerly held out their cups and bowls, some made by the Pueblo Indians.

Felipe watched with curiosity. Dusk had come and the fire's flickering light began to take effect. His uncle drank from his cup, wiped his mouth and looked up.

"How do you like this juice?"

"It is good!"

The answers came back in unison.

"But would you rather have some real wine? Say, like is used at mass?"

The question caught everyone off guard. They looked at each other in askance. Francisco gave his rare smile. "No, we will not attack the convents. Just answer. What is your preference? This swill or the real thing?"

Still his questioning was met with dumbfounded looks. So, he nodded to his servants who knew beforehand what he wanted. They went into the shed and brought out a small keg and uncorked it.

Felipe's uncle took another drink from his cup but this time he did not swallow, he spit the mouthful on to the ground. "So tell me...," as he poured the cup's remnants out and held it out for a servant to fill with real wine from the keg, "Aaah, *mucho mejor.* Much better. Have some."

Most of the men immediately emptied their cups while a few of the frugal types drank the last of the liquid in their vessels. All held out their empty cups and bowls for a refill from the keg.

"Now, what say you? Do you agree with me? This is better. No, don't answer. I can see. So why not drink real wine?"

Again, no answer.

"Look at us. Here together we represent a majority of the most influential and propertied people in this kingdom. Because of our continued service to the king we, each of us, have been rewarded with *encomiendas* and *haciendas.* The first comes to us as tribute and the second in land, from which we extract a living. I, most likely, am the wealthiest man in the kingdom. I know that I have that status among you.

"So here is my proposal." At this point Felipe felt the air became unusually still.

Coyotes barked in the distance and an owl periodically hooted ensconced in one of the silhouetted cotton wood trees across the river. It seemed that even sound of the mountain stream rushing downward over rocks became subdued.

Felipe stood enraptured as his uncle laid out a plan that proposed that the family and all its branches pool their resources. "Together we have property that stretches from the Taos Valley almost to the beginning of the Jornada. Why struggle individually when we can prosper together?"

Francisco proposed that the family's properties be reoccupied to create satellite warehouses with a central warehouse in Santa Fe. All their trade and goods would run through Santa Fe and then be transferred south along the Camino Real through their *haciendas*. "In that way we can better control and move our merchandise."

"Yes," he offered that this system would take some planning and coordination. He and Ana had the most to lose. He turned that information to his argument's advantage by observing that their relative wealth amounted to collateral for the venture.

Moreover, and here he paused in all seriousness, "together we present a stronger, united defense against the machinations of the priests as well as the comings and goings of the governors."

The men nodded and asked questions. Only Diego Pérez dissented. "I'm not afraid of the Franciscans. No, why should I share the fruits of my labor? My property is mine and for my children."

He had no children except for a rumored child that he fathered by an Apache wife. No one dared to make a comment on that score. Diego, like his father Gaspar, was an adventurer. He followed his father onto the Plains where both men maintained good relations with the Apaches. It was claimed that each of them had been made honorary chiefs and he had a half-brother or sister on the plains. Diego, a free spirit, cared little for the politics of Church and state. He could not be convinced that he had the most to gain because he had the least amount to lose. In fact, he had little to contribute to the venture.

Francisco did his best to parry Diego's loud barbs. He continued to present his plan by noting that the families have relations and friends in Mexico, some living on the Camino. He added that many family members had traveled south and would continue to do so.

"This is not new." He raised his eyebrows and opened his mouth in mock disbelief. "Some of us have cooperated in joint ventures. We have made efforts to protect each other's property and our *encomiendas*. We have learned from various governors how the trade works. But, rather than copy the governors' attempts for quick profits, we have the opportunity to work for ourselves and gain constant profits over time."

The Move South

1655, San Antonio de Sevilleta

Uncle Francisco's speech and arguments was the beginning of an expanded family business that two years later dictated that Felipe and his cousin, Bartolomé Gómez Robledo, one of Francisco's and Ana's sons, move to the distant south to run the *haciendas* of Las Barrancas and San Antonio de Sevilleta by the pueblos of Sevilleta and Alamillo.

Felipe was assigned the old *hacienda* at Sevilleta that his Uncle Barti had started and where his son, Bartolomé, El Hijo was raised. The latter spent a lot of time with Felipe

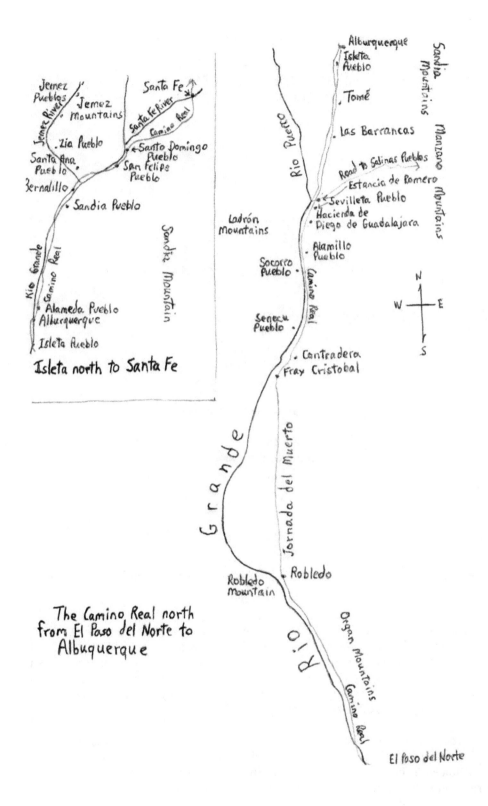

Isleta north to Santa Fe

The Camino Real north from El Paso del Norte to Albuquerque

Chart on next page gives the distances from Albuquerque to Fray Cristóbal.

The Camino Real
Alburquerque South to Fray Cristóbal in the Seventeenth Century
With the Distance Between Them

Alburquerque
5 miles
to
Isleta Pueblo
9 miles
to
Hacienda Tomé Domínguez de Mendoza
13 miles
to
Las Barrancas (Bartolomé Gomez's estancia)*
7.5 miles
to
Felipe Romero's estancia (Vuelto de los Romeros)*
6 miles
to
Sevilleta Pueblo
4 miles
to
Diego de Guadalajara's estancia*
5 miles
to
Alamillo Pueblo
13 miles
to
Socorro Pueblo
31 miles
to
Senecú Pueblo
13 miles
to
Fray Cristóbal

Note: The distances are rounded-off estimates based on the distances and place names noted by various travelers and maps beginning with Oñate and carrying into the nineteenth century. The Spanish measured distance by leagues, which varies depending on who is using the measure. Generally, and for purposes of the above the figure of 2.3 miles for a league was used. Also, the Camino cannot be measured in a linear line as it wound and had branches.

*The three southernmost haciendas belonged to members of an extended family. Bartolomé Gómez and Felipe Romero were first cousins. Diego de Guadalajara was Felipe Romero's father-in-law. In 1681, after the exodus, Felipe's sister, Juana, married Antonio Domínguez de Mendoza, the son of Tomé II.

sharing his knowledge of the place and its operation. Felipe had a sense of excitement to take up where his famous Uncle Barti had been. He knew that Uncle Barti's son recommended him. El Hijo promised to visit. "Actually, Felipe, I miss the place." But he had to stay in Santa Fe. The family decided that his good relations with the Franciscans were needed. He had inherited his father's attitude down south and befriended the Franciscans on an individual basis. He tried to prepare Felipe by going over tasks, schedules, and working with the local Pueblo people. He described the flat lands, great pasturage, and plenty of water from the river if the *acequias* were maintained. "But watch out for serpents!" Both Felipe and Bartolomé Gómez Robledo reviewed plans for corrals and storage buildings. Outside of actual experience there was nothing more Felipe and Bartolomé could do to prepare them for this life-changing venture.

Bartolomé Gómez Robledo, a year younger than Felipe, inherited his dad's height and more. He stood almost six feet tall and had red hair and a full beard. His slender build made him appear to tower over Felipe's lithe, broad shouldered average of five feet two inches with straight black hair and hazel eyes. Felipe and Bartolomé now rode south with cadre of servants and two wagons full of all their worldly possessions. Now considered adults at seventeen and sixteen years old respectively, they both faced daunting challenges.

They understood the plan. Goods from the north would be transported to their care to be prepared for the longer trip south. They needed to build structures to handle a larger capacity of livestock and wagons, some of which would come from the south. Worn livestock would be replaced with fresh animals. Wagons in need of repair would be replaced and fixed. At first, neither of the cousins understood the reality of what was expected on paper or by word of mouth, but they each quickly learned from experience.

Felipe's *hacienda* had belonged to his uncle Barti. The hired help left behind had kept it operational. It was strategically located on the Rio del Norte, above the junction of the Rio Puerco that offered a route to the western pueblos, and where the trail from the eastern Tompiro Pueblos and nearby salt beds also converges. Moreover, the ranch hands maintained normal relations with the local priests and pueblos. The closest pueblos were Sevilleta and Alamillo. Sevilleta had been named because one of the old settlers, they didn't remember who, exclaimed that the Rio Grande and surrounding landscape reminded him of the Guadalquivir River at Seville, Spain.

Cousin Bartolomé had the task of starting up and managing the *hacienda* that belonged to his father. It was just three leagues, about eight miles, upriver at a place the Gómez's named Las Barrancas, because of the nearby gorges and cliffs that cut through the soft terrain.

The two cousins' lives completely changed. They left the kingdom's capital, pitiful and small as it was, to live in a desperate place among a series of small pueblos. Their hired workers became their immediate companions, a group of men some, married, who were mixed-bloods and full-blooded Indians from both Mexico and New Mexico. One of these workers, Alonso Cadimo, a descendant of one of Oñate's soldiers in 1598, would become a trusted foreman. He would come to appreciate Felipe so much that he changed his surname to Romero and started a whole new Romero clan in New Mexico.

At first, Felipe missed the high altitude climate of Santa Fe but resigned himself to the Rio Abajo's, "Lower River's" hotter and drier weather. Only cottonwoods and no pines grew along the river bottom. The rest of the land was sandy, rocky, exceedingly dry and dotted with sage and junnipers. In time, he noticed that the hotter weather suited him well. He lost some bodily aches caused by Santa Fe's change in seasons. He discovered the pleasure of a mild winter. And, quite naturally, he and his cousin worked together to fix up their respective homes. They saw a lot of each other.

Both cousins enjoyed the company of people travelling on the Camino. The travelers brought news from both directions and usually spent the night at one or the other's place. The two young men also looked forward to an annual trip back to Santa Fe where they visited family and friends, and also sat with Aunt Ana and her maiden daughter of the same name who did the family's bookkeeping.

Unfortunately, Felipe and Bartolomé's first trip north had an unexpected purpose, for Bartolomé's father fell prey to the beginning of another epidemic. After a brief sickness, Francisco's eighty-year-old body gave out. The family patriarch died in bed surrounded by most of his family. Felipe and Bartolomé arrived the next day in time for the funeral.

Francisco's solemn mass and burial was the largest, most elaborate funeral Felipe would ever see. The church overflowed with mourners and, despite his uncle's notorious opposition to the priests, his connection to the famous Father Benavides and the statue of Our Lady of the Rosary (Rosario), affectionately called La Conquistadora, assured that he would be buried properly. Aunt Ana made sure that La Conquistadora's confraternity turned out in full regalia.

Felipe approached his aunt with a renewed interest in the family's history. He knew that his interest would please Aunt Ana, for, by then, she had a well-earned reputation of being the family historian. "Listen, *mi hijo*," she used that term, "my child" for all of her children, nieces, nephews, and grand progeny, just like the priests used it for everyone. "Your uncle, as you know, was very prominent. Many times the governor entrusted him to lead the caravans to New Spain. On one of those trips, my Francisco brought back Governor Sotelo Ossorio and Fray Alonso Benavides, who for a while became a family friend. Along with building the San Miguel Chapel, he is remembered for bringing a statue of the Blessed Virgin. She was called Assumption, but that name was quickly changed to Rosario. Father Benavides nicknamed her La Conquista or Conquistadora, for he said that Mother Mary conquers all with love. Uncle Francisco and the good padre formed a confraternity in her honor and ever since then he has been either the *mayordomo* or, if not the leader, in an influential position of that confraternity. And, I have cared for her wardrobe."

She paused to take a deep breath, looked directly at Felipe and smiled. "And now our son, Bartolomé's brother, Francisco will take his father's place."

Felipe nodded in understanding. Aunt Ana continued. "But don't forget, *hijo*, there is another statue of the Blessed Virgin that belongs to the family."

Felipe knew nothing of this and his reaction signaled Ana to continue with her account of how her Robledo grandparents brought a copy of the famous Our Lady of the Sagrario, "who sits on her throne in the great cathedral of Toledo." She continued with

Nuestra Señora del Rosario, La Conquistadora. Brought to New Mexico by Fray Alonso Benevides in 1626, saved during the Pueblo Revolt in 1680, and returned by Diego de Vargas in 1693. The Romeros were members and leaders of her confraternity. Photograph by LeRoy N. Sánchez.

the story of how a copy of the statue came to New Spain and then to New Mexico. "... and, so, now she is in the care of Bartolomé, El Hijo, the third first-born Bartolomé here in Santa Fe. Your grandfather, God keep his soul, was the second of that name."

"I know that statue!" Felipe now realized that the old statue that he had seen forever in the house of his Aunt María was the very one.

Ana smiled again. "Of course you do."

"She is small."

"Yes, *hijo*, but her importance is great."

Felipe enjoyed his visits with Aunt Ana. Her open, friendly nature had a calming effect from every day survival. He appreciated her insights and knowledge. But he had to put aside his interest in historical matters as the reality of politics and business came to the fore. Nevertheless, now he understood that the two could not be separated.

Uncle Francisco was right. Business boomed. The family had become a force. Even the governors paid them to take advantage of their warehouses and transport system. Their caravans were getting close to rivaling even the tri-annual Church supply trains.

THE BEGINNING OF A COMPLICATED STORY
1656, San Antonio de Sevilleta

Within a year after the two cousins took their positions at their respective *haciendas*, New Mexico underwent a couple of important changes. Juan Manso, the twenty years or so younger brother of long-time Father Custodian Tomás Manso, was named the new governor. Father Manso had been laboring in New Mexico for many years. Because of his efficient management of the Franciscan's supply caravans he was promoted to Provincial of the Province of the Holy Evangelist in New Spain. As head of most of the Franciscans in New Spain, his new position required that he leave New Mexico. Within the year of taking office he used his influence to have Juan named governor of New Mexico.

Felipe concentrated on his new challenge at Sevilleta and actually paid little attention to politics. He knew of Juan Manso and, as a child, had met Father Manso. The new governor was the first of many governors to pass by Felipe's *hacienda* on their way to and from New Mexico. Felipe greeted the new governor pleasantly. He appreciated Manso's familiarity with the Camino Real. Juan Manso had grown into adulthood assisting his brother with the mission supply trains. He informed Felipe that this trip was his eighth or ninth trip on the trail. Felipe was impressed.

For his part, Governor Manso was pleased to see that Felipe and Bartolomé had re-occupied the southern *haciendas*. "I knew your uncle. My brother respected him. His son Bartolomé is my age. We entertained each together the many times we passed through here with the mission caravan." Their presence, he expressed, would expedite trade along the road. He also shared the thought that he wanted to fulfill his brother's dream of creating a permanent mission among the Indians at El Paso. Not only would the new mission succeed in making travel safer in that area but also the pass is a strategic location for a new "warehouse."

Felipe readily agreed with the governor's vision. He knew that the family business would benefit as well. As an added incentive Manso, only six or seven years older than Felipe, alluded to additional business coming his and Bartolomé's way via contracts with both church and state. Felipe made sure that this news preceded the governor to Santa Fe.

Almost immediately, both Felipe and Bartolomé increased their revenues by taking small percentages off of the eventual sale of goods that both the missionaries and governor put in their care. They added other revenues from the exchange or purchase of livestock, maintenance of wagons and, on occasion, the construction of new wagons. Felipe and Bartolomé's successful ventures benefited from their attention to the local environment. They maintained good relations with the local people and the two priests who administered to them. Both of the friars had been there for over thirty years. The farthest reaches of what was then the Rio Abajo had become a model of cooperation. Their uncle Francisco's model proved correct.

Governor Manso's effort to help the Franciscans create a mission at El Paso del Norte impacted Felipe in two ways. First, the elderly priests of the nearby pueblos were put in charge of the effort and, second, in an effort to simplify things, Manso ordered that all the inhabitants of Sevilleta Pueblo move to nearby Alamillo Pueblo. While the abandonment of Sevilleta Pueblo seemed unnecessary, Felipe had no sense of urgency over the matter. Most of his income came from the *hacienda* and greater family business. Until then, the family received the total *encomienda* tribute from both Sevilleta and Alamillo Pueblos. Given their exchange of tribute for labor and their mutual cooperation, what little was left of the tribute did not matter. Besides, the larger idea of a way station at El Paso outweighed any criticism he might have.

His northern cousins agreed. Both Francisco and Bartolomé, expressed confidence in Manso. His reign had brought a sense of calm to the kingdom. Of course rumors spread. There was talk of the governor's trysts. Then there was the news of two of the governor's Indian servants who were caught stealing from the Royal House.

Cousin Diego had been named captain as well as Protector and Defender of the Christian Indians, those who had converted to Christianity. He ended up defending the two servants. This defense became his first official task but the preponderance of evidence against his clients could not be overcome. Both received the normal corporal punishment of a public whipping.

On the other hand, Diego continued with his boisterous and carefree ways. He openly carried on affairs, which, as a married man who was not the governor, drew attention. He openly criticized the clergy and questioned why the family "catered to the Church." He directed this last expression to some in his own family, whose open faith and kindness to the friars was well known. To a lesser extent, Diego's criticism also focused on Aunt Ana and Francisco's devotion to the Conquistadora confraternity. Diego found inexplicable Felipe's and Barti's relationship with the pueblos down south. Felipe understood that the family tolerated Diego and that only its efforts kept him from being arrested.

Felipe realized that the halcyon days might be undergoing a change when a large caravan with both a new governor and father custodian arrived at his doorstep. Word came in advance from Senecú and again from Socorro, that Diego López de Mendizábal was a haughty, arrogant, abusive man. The news was not misleading. When he arrived at

Sevilleta neither the new governor nor the father custodian cared to talk to each other. In fact, Felipe learned that ten of the original twenty-four priests who set out with the new governor had deserted the trip north before it reached Santa Barbara.

Felipe and Bartolomé avoided upsetting the new governor. They knew enough not to take a position one way or another. Their family in Santa Fe could take care of the politics. However, both of them immediately found the man to be an unpleasant person. His extravagant entourage along with his insistence that he spend the night in his own, ornate tent and eats off of his silver place setting by himself, was more than enough for both of the cousins to dislike him.

Another visitor, travelling in the opposite direction, stopped by a month later. The surprising arrival of now ex-governor Manso with Bartolomé riding alongside him attracted Felipe's full attention. Manso rested for a few hours but could not delay longer. Manso explained that he fled the capital and that there would be pursuit. "That man," as he referred to the new governor, "is overly ambitious and he likes no one. He threatened me with a negative *residencia* unless I paid him off. I refused so he put me under house arrest and started taking possession of my property. I left."

"But governor...."

"No. Listen. If asked, you know nothing. I passed by, watered the animals and kept on going. That is innocent enough. Understand?"

Bartolomé and Felipe nodded "yes" in unison. However, Felipe pressed. "What will you do?"

"Defend myself. Can you get me a basin of water?"

Felipe ordered a servant to do so.

Manso continued, "With my brother's help and the reports of Father Ramírez, the man's false charges will be meaningless."

"Do you know the charges?"

The basin was placed on a table. "No," he walked up to the basin and with both hands scooped water out, twice splashing his face and running his wet fingers through his hair, "but they will come. Listen friends. Be aware. López cares for nothing but himself. The priests already are alienated. Ask yourself how he treated Fathers García and Navidad at Senecú and Socorro. You do not have to believe me, but I know you will believe them."

While Manso used his untucked shirt to dry his face and hands, Felipe whispered a profanity under his breath. Bartolomé nodded in agreement. Manso, slapped both hands on the table and added, "You will learn soon enough from up north. The man is a scoundrel. Be careful."

FAMILY AND POLITICS
1659, Santa Fe

Reasons other than politics beckoned Felipe to Santa Fe. While on his the annual trips north Felipe continued to nourish a special relationship with his childhood friend, Jacinta. Of course, Felipe knew about her father, Diego de Guadalajara, now in his sixties. He had been a Rosas man and remained in favor of the Governors.

In 1654 Guadalajara led an expedition southeast across the Llano Estado to the Nueces River in Texas where they set up a camp among the Jumano Indians. Guadalajara's army joined the Jumanos in a successful battle against their enemies. They returned to Santa Fe with booty from the battle plus two hundred prisoners, which endeared him to the governor. Ever since then, his reputation preceded him.

Felipe grew up afraid of him because of his family's warnings. His father had fought with Guadalajara against the Indians but something that Felipe did not understand had come between them. Nevertheless, Felipe grew up around the old man's son and daughter. The former was a couple of years older and was mostly remembered for a constantly running nose, a spiteful laugh, and as a bully. Jacinta was quite the opposite and became part of the close-knit cadre of kids who ran around village's streets.

Now, in the brilliance of a mid-summer's day they wedded. Jacinta de Guadalajara shared Felipe's love of life in the fields. Not adverse to work, she had grown up healthy and physically strong. She was not the town's beauty nor was she unsightly. She had chestnut brown fiery eyes, dark brown hair, a small chin and a ready smile. Her personality dominated her looks and enhanced her beauty.

Felipe and Jacinta's companionship had never been a matter of doubt. Felipe's long absences south brought him to the realization that he authentically loved her. He dreamed of her being with him.

His choice of Jacinta pleased both families. As expected, her mother bemoaned the loss of her daughter and her father was glad to see her off. The mother openly praised Felipe, who she liked very much. Felipe's mother gladly accepted her new daughter-in-law and was relieved that her son would have companionship at his distant *hacienda*.

The wedding took place in the parish church. Even Governor López begrudgingly attended. As a wedding present, the governor made Felipe a captain. Felipe had no doubt that his cousin Francisco had made the arrangement for his appointment. So far, Francisco had successfully endeared himself to the difficult governor.

Aware of Jacinta's father's long-standing desire to get out of Santa Fe, the family agreed to give Diego de Guadalajara a partial *encomienda* of the re-established Sevilleta Pueblo. The governor also granted him permission to establish *a hacienda* six leagues from Alamillo Pueblo and one league from Sevilleta Pueblo. Felipe's in-laws would be close by in the southernmost of the estancias.

Felipe continued to hear stories about the governor. In Santa Fe, a cousin, who sat on the *cabildo*, sent word that confirmed what Manso had warned. López cared little for New Mexico and only sought to benefit himself. Moreover, unlike Manso, he had little concern for the missionaries. Further evidence of this came to Felipe with the news that López reversed Manso's policy and ordered the reoccupation of Sevilleta Pueblo. In addition, he offered no support for the new missionary effort in El Paso. "Let them do it themselves," was how the cousin paraphrased him.

Cousin Diego was another matter. The family was astounded to watch how their wayward Diego had become one of the governor's favorites, if not trusted. The governor trusted no one. Maybe it was Aunt Ana who commented that the governor and Diego "think alike."

Perhaps, but it was Francisco who approached Felipe and Bartolomé as they prepared to return to their *haciendas*. With hitched mules waiting patiently and horses pawing at the dirt, the family had organized a caravan of eight wagons to be transported to the southern warehouses. Some of the load included Jacinta's small dowry and, of course, she commanded a prominent position in the lead wagon.

Looking up at his younger, mounted cousin and brother, Francisco said, "Be aware of the governor. Leave him to us here in Santa Fe. You tend to the business and keep a low profile. You do not want to be noticed by him." The two nodded in acknowledgement and spurred their horses. Felipe heard and understood Francisco's advice.

But Francisco was not finished, for he grabbed his brother Bartolomé's reigns and stopped them. He looked straight at Felipe. "Take care of your in-laws. Diego has had a long checkered career. He is old now. Still tough."

Felipe looked puzzled. "Listen, Francisco. He is part of the family. That is why you gave up part of our *encomienda* to him. I know. I remember my father's warnings. I am told that people change. *Vamos a ver*, we will see." And with that Francisco slapped the rump of his brother's horse. "Go with God."

Felipe was happy to be heading home, all the more so because Jacinta was going with him. He rode next to her wagon pointing out landmarks and describing her new home. "You can decorate it any way that you want." He delighted in answering her questions. "Yes, we have servants and they are good people. Some of them have even taken the Romero surname."

"What? I should have realized. You have never seen the Rio Del Norte. Yes. It is much larger than the stream that runs through Santa Fe. Some say it resembles the grand Guadalquivir River that runs through Seville. But you have not seen that either."

Jacinta teasingly remarked, "You have?"

Felipe laughed. "You got me. No I haven't."

The newlyweds settled down to a tranquil life, or so it seemed. At times, Felipe wondered how he ever survived without Jacinta. Her companionship, her conversation, merely her presence had a calming effect on him. While he did not realize it at the time, his goals could be summed up as managing the *hacienda* and pleasing her.

Then in quick succession Governor López mandated an increase in the wages to be paid to native laborers while prohibiting any volunteer labor for the priests. This included serving at Mass. Next he sent out a proclamation prohibiting the movement of any livestock south to New Spain. He, in effect, froze a major portion of New Mexico's trade. A good portion of that trade was used to maintain the missions. Each of his policies affected the revenues of the extended Romero family but, except for Diego, they said nothing openly.

Word rapidly spread of López's next gambit. This time he got everyone's attention when he ordered the massacre of Navajo Indians who had been invited to parlay at Jemez Pueblo. After summarily killing the men, he took prisoner their women and children to be sold in New Spain. This news left Felipe aghast, for now he had no doubt that López was on a path that would be the ruin of New Mexico. Within days, Felipe became further agitated when he heard that Diego had participated in the Jemez affair and as López's trusted captain had been ordered to lead an expedition onto the Plains. Felipe joined his cousins in wondering what havoc that might bring. He told Jacinta that they should prepare—"brace ourselves."

"Why? My love."

"I fear the governor's greed will be the death of us. He is leading us into war."

"But not here."

"Jacinta, look. Revenge has no limits. The Apaches range far. They could attack anywhere."

López's tactics along with his abusive personality quickly alienated almost everyone in New Mexico. Felipe could only watch the awful site of López's captured Indians herded south. And he silently received the many messengers sent south carrying reports and letters of complaint. He hoped that change could come before López created irreparable damage.

Meanwhile, cousin Bartolomé impregnated a young girl who worked at Las Barrancas. As he explained it, the act was not a matter of love, but physical. Nevertheless, he acknowledged his deed, took the young lady under his care, and, when the child was born, had him baptized with a name that all should know and understand. Bartolomé gave him the name of Bartolomé. He would raise him as his legitimate son. Henceforth, the boy was called Bartilito or Bartillo. Later in life he would be known as *Barti.*

Bartolomé's son was a small distraction and pleasant source of happiness. After all, Bartolomé was not the only man to father a child out-of-wedlock in New Mexico's male dominant society. The birth did give hope and rejuvenated enthusiasm to Felipe and Jacinta who were childless.

It did not take long before Felipe's favorite cousin, the other Bartolomé in Santa Fe, incurred the wrath of Governor López. Animosity had built up and the governor knew that word of his corrupt deeds was getting out. At the very least, the Franciscans and ex-governor Manso had submitted charges against him. To protect himself, López dictated a written defense that everyone knew was a complete fabrication. Barti el hijo was one of two councilmen who refused to add their signatures as witnesses to the document.

Bartolomé and the other councilman took a brave stand in their refusal to cooperate with the governor. They knew that López would make them pay, and he did. Both were exiled, sent on missions under false pretenses. This time Francisco could not help and Diego refused, for he sided with the governor.

Soon enough, in the dead of winter cousin Bartolomé and his pregnant wife, Josefa de Archuleta, were ordered to go to the high mountain pueblo of Pircurís. Forced to leave in the winter, the two had to travel on horseback through the cold and snow. Josefa suffered considerably and soon after their arrival at the pueblo, she had a miscarriage. López had his revenge.

Word of this episode spread through the family. With the possible exception of Diego who, for once, wisely kept quiet, everyone turned on the governor. Francisco kept his disgust to himself. He hoped that things would improve with a quick replacement. Josefa never quite recovered from the severe chills she incurred on that trip and later would give birth to a sickly daughter, which she and her husband easily blamed on the ill-fated exile.

Mexico City acted quickly in the spring of 1661, within two years of López's appointment, a new governor was sent to New Mexico. Felipe received the caravan bringing Don Diego Dionisio Peñalosa and a new Father Custodian and Commissary, Fr. Alonso Posada. The rugged man who was introduced as the governor surprised Felipe. This was especially so when he spoke, for he sprinkled his delivery with any number of rude comments and foul words. He had a hard body and his manner verged on a swagger. His shoulder-length straight black hair, a well-manicured goatee, and his ready, but false smile created an image that did not bode well. As near as Felipe could tell he was in his middle forties. In some inexplicable way, Felipe pegged him to be an adventurer, not unlike his own wayward cousin Diego.

Felipe wondered how this new governor and the ex-governor would react to each other. Both men were pretentious and, Felipe suspected, corrupt. They were the same. He sent his impressions to his brothers and, especially to his Santa Fe cousin Bartolomé. However, word came back that one of Peñalosa's first acts was to appoint Bartolomé the mayor of Santa Fe. Then, he put ex-governor López under house arrest pending the results of the required inspection that he would be conducting.

Even as Peñalosa attempted to endear himself to the populace, everyone realized that he shared his predecessor's same bad qualities. Even Bartolomé, who hated López and had been rewarded by Peñalosa, realized that the latter sought to endear himself by using the rampant hatred for his predecessor to his advantage. Nor did he show any sympathy to the Church. He made it clear that he represented the supreme law of the land. His apparent initial cordial relations with Father Posada quickly dissipated into a severe rivalry.

Felipe heard all the news with a curious interest that amused him. His work required his attention and that was fine with him. Nor could he be distracted from family business by an incident in 1661 when Felipe and Bartolomé were accused of killing cattle that belonged to Alamillo Pueblo.

Francisco prevailed upon Diego to approach the governor about the incident. Peñalosa only laughed. "So what if they killed some cattle? Who is complaining? The priests or the Indians? I don't care for either."

The governor knew that the complaint came from some of the newly arrived priests. "Hot heads," he called them. Francisco turned to his mother, "La Doña Anna," to successfully appeal to the Father Custodian. The two men, she pointed out, have been very cooperative with the missionaries and Natives "down there." "Surely, Your Eminence can understand that they did not intend any harm."

The matter was a distraction, but not serious. The Felipe and Bartolomé adequately proved that the cattle in question had strayed far away from the pueblo's land. Nevertheless, they agreed to diminish the Pueblo's annual tribute for that year as a means of compensation. The shrinking and impoverished pueblo readily agreed to the arrangement.

The incident passed without repercussions but trouble with this governor could not be contained. Many people wondered if the Rosas regime was like this. Only a generation removed, that episode was still fresh in many a mind. Aunt Anna insisted that things had changed because "except for Diego, the family has maintained a more neutral approach."

Felipe continued to concentrate on his *hacienda*. Jacinta put him and some of his laborers to work laying cobblestone in some of the rooms in their house. She even borrowed an idea from the pueblo to have a sauna built next to their *horno*, the outdoor oven. While this was unplanned work, Felipe enjoyed it because it pleased Jacinta and, in truth, he liked the improvements.

As a result of the troublesome and cantankerous governors in Santa Fe, Felipe's brothers tended to visit more often. To them the southern *hacienda* was a welcome refuge. Their wives provided a welcomed respite for Jacinta as well, as her mother suddenly died within two years after moving to her husband's new *hacienda*. Having no sisters Jacinta's Romero female in-laws were more than welcome in her home. Felipe enjoyed the banter and laughter of the women as they fussed about the house.

Then Felipe's sister, Catalina married Captain José Telles Jirón. After conferring with the family and then with Felipe and Jacinta, they successfully received the governor's permission to move south by Socorro Pueblo. Now, Jacinta had another woman relatively close by.

Felipe's older brother, Pedro, shared the information about cousin Diego's escapade on his latest trip to trade with the Apaches. Diego participated in a ritual of some kind, "that made him a captain among the tribe, just like his father." And then Pedro added, "Moreover the ritual required that he take an Apache wife!"

"But he is married!"

"Yep. Diego claims that the ceremony was a formality and that he went along with it for better relations...."

Felipe winced and cut off Pedro. "Brother, 'relations' is not a good choice of words."

Yah, well. 'Word' of this has gotten to Posada. Diego may be in trouble and no one in New Mexico will be able to help."

THE RETURN OF MANSO
Fall 1662, San Antonio de Sevilleta

Yes, Felipe thought, his Uncle Barti was right. Life was much better away from the capital. Distance had its value but he was not completely devoid of New Mexico's political machinations. His tranquility was interrupted again the following autumn when, while cleaning ditches that water his orchard, two riders galloped up to him with the surprising news that Juan Manso would be arriving within a few hours.

Fall in the Rio Abajo region, the down river area, is a time of contrasts. While winter comes much earlier in the colder climate of northern New Mexico, the Rio Abajo days seem to remain longer and warmer. For Felipe, fall was his favorite season because traffic on the trail would pick up from virtually nothing to almost weekly visitations.

Spring also has its differences, for it is interspersed with a periodic winter storm that usually drops more moisture than anything during winter. Then winds with strong gusts pick up and fill the air with blowing sand and dust. This is a period of time when people become depressed. Yet it is spring and a time of anticipation, the end of a long cold, dry winter and the beginning of a warm, bright summer. The *acequias*, irrigation ditches, are cleaned and the corn is planted.

Trail activity, too, was seasonal. The caravans left the north in the fall while those from the south timed their journeys to arrive in late summer and autumn. Why? To avoid the spring run-off that made the Rio del Norte impossible to cross.

So, it was a fall day nice enough to enjoy the sun's warmth but feel uncomfortably cold in the shade that Felipe and some of his ranch hands were working on the upper *acequia* or, as they called it, the "mother ditch," cleaning it of unwanted growth, excessive sediment, and loose debris. The royal road snaked by within one hundred yards so a rider or wagon could not be missed.

Everyone at once noticed the dust being kicked up in the south through the partially barren cottonwoods. With the fact acknowledged by a glance or nod, the men continued with their work. The travelers would arrive soon enough. No sense wasting time speculating. They would know soon enough. Obviously, the men realized that the ex-governor had a reason for returning to New Mexico. When an official came at this time he came with important news and usually wanted to get to New Mexico before the first caravans embarked for the south. All of the men had been in New Mexico long enough to realize that Manso's arrival had some importance.

Adding to their sense of the obvious, Manso did not travel with a caravan. He came with a group of what looked like a dozen or so riders, traveling lightly with around twenty pack mules in tow. These men were coming from New Spain in advance of a caravan that would follow days, maybe weeks behind. They had urgent business.

Upon seeing Felipe and his workers, the riders reined up. Two of the men dismounted and walked toward the ditch. Almost immediately Felipe recognized Juan Manso. "Ah, governor Manso! Juan! It's been a while. ?Cómo le va?"

"Felipe! My old friend. I hoped it was you." They hugged and happily slapped each other's backs. Both men, equally sweaty and dirty, sized up each other. Manso spoke first. "No, I am not a governor, but I have come on important business."

Felipe gave an experienced smile. "I've no doubt of that. Is it so urgent, or will you stay the night?"

"No, we have ridden enough today. Besides, I need to catch up. That is more urgent and pertinent than time."

Felipe left his men to continue with the *acequias*. He mounted his own horse and noticed that Manso rode a mule. "But, Juan, a mule? Why?"

"Chinita, here," he patted the animal's neck, "is more sure footed and a smoother ride. We are old friends and she is easier on my bones, especially on a long journey."

"Ah, makes sense. I might have to try one sometime."

Ten minutes later Jacinta greeted them from the portal of their five-room house. They had a rather large, fenced and cleared yard with a closed front gate. Felipe explained that they kept the pigs in the yard around the house because they killed snakes. "I would rather tolerate the pigs, than worry about serpents."

"And you question my preference for a mule? Ha!"

Manso returned Jacinta's greeting and then joked about her poor choice of a husband. She, somewhat star struck, remembered him as the governor when she lived in Santa Fe. She kept silent and shyly smiled at his jest.

Manso surprised Felipe with his constant questioning about local news, rumors, and politics. Obviously, he was searching for something. Manso pretended to laugh and feigned indifference, but he could not hide his underlying interest. Felipe understood that Manso was not making small talk.

Manso seemed to put a lot of credence in Felipe and this caught the latter's attention. When he told the story of his cousin Bartolomé and his wife, Manso leaned forward with raised eyebrows and interrupted. "López sent them because he refused to sign the report? Why?"

"Well, Juan, you were right about López."

"No. Not him. Why did Bartolomé resist him?"

"I was told that the report was false, full of lies. Bartolomé is an honorable man."

Manso sat back. "And brave."

"Yes, that too. But it cost him. He lost a child and Josefa remains sickly."

At this point, Manso sent word to his camped entourage for a jug of wine. While waiting, he continued, "I will have to visit with him."

"I'm sure he will enjoy seeing you. But, Juan, if I may, what is going on?"

The ex-governor paused just as his aid entered the room with the jug. Felipe kept his eyes on Manso as he uncorked the brown clay jug and filled two cups. The question had made Manso uneasy. "Listen, friend, there is not much that I can say. Do not worry about Bartolomé or for yourself. You will learn soon enough. Yes, it is obvious, I have returned with some urgency. Unfortunately, I cannot divulge my instructions."

Felipe took a stab. "Are you replacing López?"

"No! No. Ha! Nothing so drastic. By God, you do have a good imagination." He took a drink, wiped his mouth with the back of his hand, and sighed. "Ah good, I needed that. For now, I must be informed. Tell me about your cousins the Gómez's, Francisco and Doña Ana. Has Diego calmed down?"

Felipe laughed. "I doubt it. I suspect he is as crazy as ever. A true frontiersman. For some reason, the governor favors him."

Manso sat up. "Really! Is he in Santa Fe?"

"No. He is with the governor on an inspection tour of the western pueblos. By now, they should be among the Hopi Pueblos."

"I hear that my old friend López is under house arrest. Is that still true?"

"As of last week, yes. Peñalosa ordered it."

"Unhuh. Between you and me that is one snake biting the tail of another. What is your opinion of Peñalosa?"

"Listen, Juan, I am distant from the politics of Santa Fe. I can tell you how he treated my cousin and his family. Also, I wonder about his favoritism of Diego. Aside from that, any opinion would be cause for trouble."

Manso took another drink and smiled. "You are wise, Felipe. I sense in you the same attitude as your uncle, a good man."

"Juan, I can say that the governor is not trusted and I hear people talk. They say that he is, as you have said, 'the same as López.' But, you will learn more up north."

Manso left Felipe anxious and he could not exactly explain why. He could not be certain but he knew that something profound, some news would be coming his way. This time he told Jacinta to beware not from Indian raids but from politics, something far beyond their control.

The expected news came back quickly. Armed with instructions from the Office of the Inquisition, Manso had authority to arrest three people and to investigate a fourth. Manso did not hesitate. By the middle of May he arrested all four men. First, Manso met Peñalosa at Isleta Pueblo on the governor's return from his western inspection. There he arrested the governor's main henchman, Nicolas de Aquilar and, then, Diego. Felipe heard that Diego created a ruckus and had to be physically restrained. The next two men were arrested almost two weeks later in Santa Fe. A man named Cristóbal de Anaya, who Felipe could not recall, turned himself in upon hearing that he was wanted. The last person fulfilled Felipe's worse fears, for it was an unexpected act. Manso arrested Francisco. At first, Felipe did not see the connection of the four men. Then, upon hindsight he realized that, yes, all of them were seen as staunch royalists and were relatively well-off *encomenderos*.

He would learn later that the young, recently arrived priests had made many of the charges, especially those against Francisco. The antics and activities of Aguilar and Diego helped build the cases against all of them. For Francisco and Anaya it seemed as though they were guilty by association. How they overlooked Felipe's father-in-law was beyond comprehension, except for his advanced age, maybe. The new Father Custodian, Fray Alonso Posada had no choice but to put the accused in shackles and under close arrest pending their transfer to Mexico City for trial.

Messages came to Felipe almost daily. His brothers kept him informed. First and foremost they did not want him to take sides. Do not criticize Manso. Appear neutral. *The governor is powerless in this matter.*

In regard to family business, "keep on." They told how Francisco learned of his pending arrest with enough time to disburse all his significant properties and possessions among the family. Many years later, Felipe would learn that his suspicion about how that happened was correct. Manso warned his Santa Fe cousin Bartolomé who, in turn, got word to Francisco.

At the time, though, everyone, including Felipe's relatives denied knowledge of Manso's involvement. Instead the official line was that the previous arrests of Diego and Aguilar tipped off Francisco. No matter how it happened Francisco's quick action prevented the governor or the Church from taking possession of his property. Diego, however, lost everything he owned. He paid for his refusal to cooperate with the family.

Finally, Felipe received word that no more arrests were expected. The relatives in Santa Fe were doing all that they could to help Francisco. No one could learn what he had been charged with. Everyone expected that he, along with the others, would have to resolve the matter in Mexico City.

A few months passed without any new incidents. The prisoners were kept at Santo Domingo Pueblo, but there seemed to be little movement toward transporting them south. Everyone wondered, "What could be the delay?"

174

Although it was not clear at the time the answer came that summer when, in August, another official messenger hurried through Felipe's *hacienda*. Felipe felt positive that the man could be carrying orders for Francisco's release or, at least, to put him under house arrest. But, he was wrong. Word quickly spread throughout New Mexico that Manso, who had been newly appointed the Inquisition's High Sherriff, arrested ex-governor López and his wife, Doña Theresa. As such, López was taken from Peñalosa's control. As everyone understood, this meant that Peñalosa could not benefit from López's arrest, as he surely intended, for he wanted to take possession of López's properties and wealth. Not only was this bad news for the ex-governor but also it was a blow against the current governor. It appeared that the Franciscans had taken control. How this would fall out for the regular people, much less the Christian Indians was anybody's guess. In a matter of days, Felipe was summoned to Las Barrancas for a family meeting.

Felipe learned that while López's arrest created concern throughout the territory, the act brought with it an answer to another question. The ex-governor, his wife, and the four men already sequestered would be transferred south in the same caravan but in separate wagons. Because of the necessity to gather evidence and take depositions, they would not be transferred until after the following spring's runoff.

Then, the conversation turned to business. First of all, López had arranged for a load of salt to be stored at Las Barrancas before sending it south. They agreed not to move it, because Posada and Peñalosa were engaged in a legal battle over who should be in control of López's property. Moreover, the governor had placed an embargo on it.

"Let them fight it out. We do not need to bring attention to ourselves by taking sides or even appearing so in this matter." No one objected.

Bartolomé confirmed that Peñalosa has a shipment of piñon nuts coming in from various Pueblo tributes and he wants it stored either at Las Barrancas or Sevilleta. Felipe and his cousin agreed to cooperate and expedite the matter as soon as possible. Send it south. The governor is not under arrest and this is perfectly legal.

When asked why cooperate with the governor when he is in a serious conflict with the priests, the Santa Feans quietly explained that they had a plan to help Francisco. Along with the governor's legal shipment, a herd of livestock will also go along. This herd will be placed in the care of Bartolomé at Las Barrancas. His brothers, Andres and Juan, will come to Las Barrancas to help out. Juan will take over management of the *hacienda* while Bartolomé accompanies the herd south. The money made from the livestock's sale will pay for Francisco's legal expenses. With the help of family connections in Mexico, Bartolomé will locate the best legal representation for both Francisco and Diego. "Yes, we will do what we can for Diego. It might not be much. From what I have heard and know from experience, he is his own worst enemy. The priority is Francisco. Understand?"

Felipe returned home very concerned. The idyllic life of the Rio Abajo had come to an end. Both he and Bartolomé had been sucked into the politics of church and state. Jacinta reacted in her usual understated manner saying, "Maybe we should put more pigs out to keep the snakes at bay."

"Ah, Jacinta, in this case we don't have enough pigs."

Felipe changed the subject to one that had been of growing personal concern for both of them. After over two years of marriage Jacinta remained barren. They tried. Both wanted children. Out of habit, Felipe had begun asking, "How are you feeling?"

This time he got the same answer. "Sorry, darling. No change."

Felipe asked, "Maybe we should talk with Isabel." Isabel was the local *curandera*, a healer and mid-wife.

"I have and she just shrugged and said, 'In such matters it is God's will.' Maybe all this concern about Santa Fe and the family is the problem."

"Maybe."

Political Chaos, A Distant Trial, and A New Generation
1663, San Antonio de Sevilleta

Winter came and the heavy snows could not dampen Felipe's anxiety. He spent time helping Bartolomé, Juan, and Andrés, select and feed the stock that would be sent south. Aside, from the work at hand and the weather, they speculated on the fates of Francisco and Diego. The latter, they now knew, had been heard condemning the priests. He was charged with immorality. He had fathered two children out of wedlock. He acknowledged one and the other came as a result of an Apache ceremony.

The men were at a loss for words as to why Francisco had been arrested. Yes he was a staunch royalist, an officer in the governor's corps. But, unlike the reputation of his father he performed his duties with moderation. Moreover, he welcomed Franciscans into his house and was the *mayordormo* of La Conquistadora's confraternity. They could only guess the motives for his arrest, jealousy, rumor, imagined connections to López or Diego. Nothing made sense. Of necessity, too, Francisco's brothers cared more about their big brother than the wayward cousin Diego.

Even before travelers began arriving from the south, Peñalosa ordered the first caravan to leave the north. Felipe and his cousins loaded the governor's salt into wagons and gathered their herd. They would use this opportunity to get a head start on Francisco's defense. All of them, including Felipe, escorted the herd and wagons to the San Cristobal rest stop and the beginning of the Jornada. There they said their goodbyes to Bartolomé and returned to their respective *haciendas*. Their mission was accomplished.

Felipe did not realize it but he had aged beyond his twenty-four years. His slender, well-muscled body belied the hard work that had become part of his daily routine. Yet, the political machinations, and constant threat of an Apache attack added some wrinkles and the hint of gray hair in his beard.

There was something else that worried him even more. He became possessed over his and Jacinta'a futile efforts to produce a child. Everyone, his family, his cousins, aunts, and uncles had been blessed with many children. He could not keep up with the names of the children of his first cousins and had even lost track of how many children his brother Pedro had up in Pojoaque. Another brother, Francisco had four children, or so he thought, and had moved to Santo Domingo where he was the assistant mayor, whatever that meant. Even his cousin Francisco, recently arrested, had started a family. And his brothers... Well they were still young. Bartolomé remained single, which Felipe did not understand. Oh well.

It seemed that half of the males in the family had the name of Bartolomé. Even the recalcitrant Diego had produced children that only now Felipe heard about. Was the Lord punishing him and Jacinta? Why? Maybe, like Job in the Bible, this was their test. But, why? He asked himself that timeworn question that every human being has asked under trying circumstances.

Felipe worried even more when he saw his wife's concern and shame. He loved her so much and to see her suffer troubled him deeply. He cared more about shielding her from blame than whether or not they produced a child. He pretty much had given up. It would have happened by now.

The ride back to the *hacienda* gave Felipe the solitude to ponder over all these problems. So it was that when he rode through the gate that now enclosed solid rock walls, he smiled his best and greeted Jacinta joyfully.

"Well, Bartolomé is on his way."

"And we are here." For some unexplained reason, Felipe loved the way Jacinta always had a short rejoinder.

"Yes, *querida*. In our happy home at the end of another winter."

They ate dinner as they usually do with many of the ranch hands and their families. These were their closest friends. Besides, they had very quickly learned that communal eating was very efficient.

Not long after another caravan camped on the now well-used area between the *hacienda* and the river. This caravan originated in Santa Fe and had many wagons plus an armed guard and two priests. Finally, after many months the four accused men and governor López de Mendizábal and his wife were being transported to stand trial in Mexico City. Each prisoner was carried in a separate wagon. They could not interact or even see each other. Nor could they communicate with anyone except the priests and guards.

An anxious Felipe questioned the group's commander, for he wanted to speak with his uncle Francisco. The commander merely rolled his lazy brown eyes. "Come on, Señor Romero, you know why. For the very reason that you are related."

Felipe sized up the man. Here was a dedicated, obedient soldier who would not flinch from carrying out the letters of his orders. "May I inquire as to his health? Is he in shackles? What about the governor?"

The officer feigned a deep unconcerned sigh. "All are fine. Francisco is calm but alert. The governor, well he is defeated, and his wife hates everyone. She curses us and then pleads with us. We watch Diego carefully. The others are fine."

"Can I send a message to Francisco?"

The commander answered with a wry smile, and looked to the sky. Then he looked around. "Walk with me señor." They turned and walked away from the encampment. The commander put his right arm around Felipe's shoulder, and with his left hand pulled a folded paper from under his belt. "Not until you read this."

Felipe did not noticeably react. "From Francisco?"

"Yes, careful."

"Will you and the friars join us for dinner?"

"I will be pleased to do so. However, I doubt that the priests will join us. They must maintain their vigilance over the prisoners."

They stopped walking and faced each other. Felipe replied, "Perfect. We will meet again in a few hours. I will send a man."

The note revealed nothing important. Instead, it instructed Felipe to be confident and maintain the family business. Francisco gave assurances that he would be acquitted and would return soon. As to Diego, "he is his own biggest problem and beyond help, although we try."

At dinner that evening the commander refused to accept a note from Felipe explaining that it is best to convey any message verbally. Felipe had no choice but to acquiesce. He trusted the officer to an extent. He did not know him personally and could not pass full judgment on his character. Nevertheless, he asked that Francisco be told that he and Jacinta where well, that the family business continued and the last shipment had been sent. Also, they would pray for his speedy acquittal and return to New Mexico.

Felipe hoped that Francisco would understand the hidden meaning of the innocent message that, as planned, Bartolomé had departed with the necessary goods to pay for his defense. Felipe then handed the commander a couple of coins that were rare in New Mexico. "These are yours and will be of some use to you in Mexico. Take care of my cousin." They both knew that he referred to Francisco.

Many more arrests had been made that summer. Even a member of the Chávez clan, which had always managed to avoid the political infighting, had suffered the increasingly long reach of the governor's paranoia. Then Felipe heard the news that the Father Custodian had been put in shackles. It seemed that governor Peñalosa had declared war on the Church. Word spread that he openly proclaimed something to the effect that not even the Pope had authority over him!

Felipe knew that none of this boded well. He departed on his annual trip to Santa Fe with trepidation. He would learn more but he feared none of the news would be good. As expected, he was correct. Peñalosa was out of control. Bartolomé advised him to cut his visit short and return to the *hacienda* before the governor noticed his presence, for "no good will come of that."

Felipe and Jacinta spent two nights in Santa Fe. They stayed with Doña Ana and her daughter because each of his three brothers lived out of town. They had a family dinner at the old family homestead, where Felipe regaled his cousin's infirm little daughter, María. He could not help but think that even a child like her was better than nothing. Her parents brought him up to date on the family business and politics. He understood the former while the later seemed more distant than before, as if they talked about another, strange world.

Then came September, his favorite month. He and the men spent a satisfying day, counting cattle. His herd had not been depleted by any raids and the local pueblo had not taken more than usual.

As Felipe rode into the yard, Jacinta waited for him under the veranda. He noticed something different about her. She had a pleased yet concerned look. Felipe immediately realized that she was anxious. Maybe he knew it because she was wringing her hands, which was something she rarely did. "What could be the problem?" he thought to himself as he hopped off his horse.

Jacinta did not move. Rather she waited for him to walk to her. Felipe could not wait, because he worried about her. "What is it, Jacinta?" And he put his hands on both of her shoulders and stared directly into her chestnut eyes.

"Felipe, I have waited to make sure. I am with child."

Felipe did not even blink. "With child. Are you sure? Oh my God!"

Jacinta stared back into his face while she broke into a shy smile. "Yes, my love. It has been two months. All the signs are there. I have consulted with María," referring to the *curandera*, healer, mid-wife, and wife of Jola, Felipe's favorite ranch hand, "She was the first to recognize..."

"Holy Mary!" Felipe could not contain himself. "Thank you, Lord! My God! A baby!"

Felipe could never remember a better spring. There was nothing that he could not do for Jacinta. She, in turn, quietly noted the change going on within her while she parried much of Felipe's attention. After all, she was in robust health and confidant. She never doubted at any time that her first child would be anything but healthy.

In late February 1664 Felipe and Jacinta had a son who they quickly baptized with the name of Sebastián. Their son brought such happiness to the household that Felipe hardly noted the rush of news swirling around him. Within a month of Sebastián's birth a contingent of riders escorted two partly filled wagons heading south that included Governor Peñalosa. They came to the front gate requesting entry. This time Peñalosa wanted a bed and food. He had lost his pretentious attitude and hardly acknowledged his hosts. They didn't care. His evil looks now exacerbated by worry and, they surmised, fear, was satisfactory enough for them. They learned that Peñalosa was abandoning New Mexico before his replacement arrived. He did not want to undergo the required *visita* that his successor had to conduct. Also, he knew that the Inquisition had decided to proceed against him. He would not wait to be arrested and sent to Mexico in chains like he had done with López. No, he would beat them to the punch and plead his case before charges could be brought. He left without a word before daybreak. From Felipe's point-of-view he could not have left soon enough.

Within a week another entourage came to the *hacienda*. A dozen men with no wagons in tow rode up. They carried papers from the Father Custodian and Juan Manso. Moreover, Manso, obviously in favor with the Franciscans, had been appointed to his older brother's old position as the person in charge of the missionary supply trains.

Manso and the friars had built a case against Peñalosa. The mean-spirited governor would suffer more than the required *visita*. He was facing some serious charges. Now Felipe understood why Peñalosa left in a hurry.

While digesting this news, Felipe and Jacinta turned toward their baby and uniformly gave out a sigh of relief. Neither of them liked Peñalosa. For the time being, at least, they were satisfied to know that their friend Juan Manso was in charge.

A few days later Felipe's father-in-law and his son rode by the *hacienda* to announce their decision to follow their old friend Peñalosa south. Among Diego de Guadalajara's earlier bad traits, he had one that he never lost. He was lazy and depended on the governor's favoritism. Part of his profits came from working with the governor in extorting salt from the saline pueblos on the other side of the eastern mountains. Without official protection, working land or animals proved too daunting to him. Besides, he could be the next person to be arrested.

Then, in August, cousin Bartolomé returned from Mexico City. His news had their full attention. "The charges against my brother are political. Some jealous merchants and young priests teamed up against him. They thought that by destroying him, the family business would no longer compete with the missions."

Felipe answered. "Huh? We work with them!"

"I know, I know. Anyway they used my grandfather's birth in Portugal against him. Then they claimed that he had a little tail. Well, two of my brothers were born with a deformity at the base of their back but not tails. Anyway, this is the evidence used to accuse him."

"Of being a Jew?"

"Yes."

Felipe stood up speechless and walked in a small circle. Bartolomé continued, "We hired the best legal representation, wrote out answers to all the charges. We also noted Francisco's devotion to La Conquistadora and that he has been the leader of her confraternity for years. We rendered the charges as ridiculous. He should be free by now. At least, that is what the lawyers expect."

"Thank God. He is missed."

Bartolomé sighed. "I can imagine. What about you? Bring me up to date."

"First, what of the others?"

"Well Diego refused our help and is representing himself. You can guess how that is going. When I left he came to some semblance of reason and threw himself on the mercy of the tribunal. He is in trouble.

"The Governor, López, I mean, and his wife wait under lock and key. The tribunal is taking its time with them. They may be distracted with the Mendizábal charges. I don't know. That Anaya fellow is charged with being outspoken against the Church. Do you remember him? He had an *hacienda* up by San Felipe Pueblo at La Angostura, the Narrows."

Felipe thought for a moment. "Yah, kind of a simple person but harmless."

"That's the one. Well, he made no attempt at defense but admitted and apologized for his crimes. The Inquisitors liked his attitude so it is expected that he will receive a light sentence. Aguilar is a different matter. His fate is not so good."

Bartolomé left Felipe with a good feeling. Peñalosa was gone and Francisco would return. The news could not be better. Still standing, Felipe called to Jacinta and raised his arms with the proclamation, "Come Bartolomé we must break out some recently minted wine. Not only to celebrate your return and the good news but...," he turned to nod at Jacinta as she entered the room, "share the news of our new son."

Bartolomé's face lit up. "A son! We should exchange news more often. What have you named this *macho?*"

Felipe let Jacinta answer. "Sebastián."

Bartolomé smiled at them and repeated the name. "I like it! Thank God you didn't name him Bartolomé. We have enough of them. Ha, ha. Where's the wine. We definitely should drink to this. Now our boys can grow up together, like we did."

A month later, the new governor arrived. The pleasant spring of 1664 and following year belied what lay ahead. Manso kept his position and, by all indications cooperated with the governor. Things settled into a normal routine. Felipe and his family visited Santa Fe where his family doted over little Sebastián. Felipe made it a point to visit Manso who was as friendly as ever. He, too, was sure that Francisco would return soon.

Then in the following August when another caravan pulled up to his *hacienda's* gate, Felipe sensed that something important came with it. A blue robbed friar walked up to him and introduced himself as Fray Juan de Paz, the new Father custodian and commissary. Perhaps Felipe should have noted that the violet eyed, thick-lipped priest carried that second title, for that made him much more influential than a custodian, he had Inquisitional powers.

Without thinking about it, Felipe instinctively took the priest's hand and kissed its ring. "Welcome Father. Welcome to...," here he stopped for he saw over the priest's shoulder walking toward him a vaguely familiar figure. He continued his phrase without meaning, "...New Mexico."

It was Francisco! Francisco, much thinner but his hair still that telltale red, had returned. "Pardon me Father." The priest nodded as Felipe brushed by him. "Thanks be to God. You have returned!"

BODINGS OF DIRE STRAITS
1675, San Antonio de Sevilleta

At the time Felipe could not have known that events around him would turn his euphoria into despair. And now, eleven years later, he sat under his veranda staring at the green stately cottonwood trees that shaded the banks of the Rio el Norte. He was preoccupied at what the future would be. Jacinta had given birth to four more children and was pregnant with their sixth child, which was due in another month or so. The household bustled with three sons. Sebastián celebrated his eleventh birthday and had started helping with chores. Young Baltasar, now two years old, had just started stringing sentences together. The two girls followed their mother everywhere. Nine-year-old Juana had become quite the homemaker and the seven-year-old shy Isabel looked like her mother. God blessed them with their latest child, a boy named Juan José.

The family's growth should have pleased Felipe but he couldn't help but think that the family's increasing size would become a handicap. The reality of his world pressed upon him. Try as he may, he could not see a positive future. Instead, he saw a foreboding darkness with no definition. Life had become more complicated than before, and he worried for his family. He also worried for some of his loyal workers, like Jola's family. He was the godfather of Jola's two children, Ana María and Diego. He wished, yes prayed, that the future could be as azure as the sky above him.

He was troubled about the severe drought that resulted in famine and pestilence that led to human frustration that brought New Mexico to the brink of collapse. People, including some of his own family had begun deserting New Mexico. Bartolomé's brother, Juan, had started a *hacienda* above Isleta Pueblo but the hardship proved too much and he, too, gave up and went to Mexico. He was not alone.

181

The Pueblo people suffered horribly. Felipe saw some of the emaciated bodies himself, left at the sides of roads or acequias to rot because the living feared contact with them. The Pueblo population had shrunk so much that whole villages had been abandoned. Some of Felipe's closest trading partners located on the other side of the eastern mountains through a canyon directly east of his *hacienda*, had abandoned their pueblo.

The oppressive tactics of Father de la Cruz, who recklessly wielded his Inquisitional powers and spread fear throughout the communities, ended with his replacement. On one hand, the governors had become cooperative with the priests and that ended the incessant political fighting. However, the emboldened priests became even more zealous and oppressive with their neophytes. This came at a time of extreme privation among the Native people.

Felipe never had trouble with the Pueblo People. In his mind, he and they survived and suffered together. He witnessed and understood their plight.

He survived a bout of infestation that left him pockmarked. Jacinta kept him secluded in an outbuilding to protect the children. Her care and the potions given him by the *curandera* brought him back to good health. Many people were not so lucky, especially in the Pueblos. Some of Felipe's fellow workers did not survive, and others disappeared, presumably latching on to a caravan or group heading south.

Reality especially and literally hit home in February of 1668 while Felipe and his family had gone to Las Barrancas to visit Bartolomé. A large contingent of Apaches raided Felipe's *hacienda*. His workers, including some Pueblo Indians from nearby Alamillo Pueblo, put up a stout but vain defense. Many were killed, including Jola, who bravely led the defense. The raiders ransacked the buildings and ran off with what horses and cattle they could find. Jola's wife and children and some others hid out by the river and survived

News of the raid reached Santa Fe within days. The governor organized a *junta de guerra* in preparation for a punitive expedition against the Apaches. Felipe received orders to take his family and people to Sevilleta Pueblo where he heard that his brother-in-law José and his sister survived a raid by the same band. They were ordered to seek refuge in Socorro Pueblo.

Both families were lucky despite their property losses. Felipe thanked God every time he thought about it. At least they hadn't suffered the fate of Senecú where just a few months before the Apaches overran it and killed the priest plus a good portion of the inhabitants. The survivors fled in a horrifying journey of around thirty miles to Socorro Pueblo. Senecú no longer existed as a living community. Although Felipe had restored the *hacienda*, he feared that he and his family were not out of danger.

With no empathy coming from the friars or the governor's men, Felipe instinctively knew that some among the Pueblos called for rebellion. And he was shocked when even his own cousins and brothers seemed to shrug at the idea. Even Bartolomé, in Santa Fe, chimed in with Felipe's brothers, "We can protect ourselves."

Exasperated, Felipe answered with a question. "What? Punish them? More than they already suffer?" He believed to his marrow that suppressing an already suffering people was not a defense but a recipe for something that would require a defense. He thought to himself that maybe if Manso were still here things would be different. But he wasn't. Manso had a fatal fall from his mule two years ago. There is something about that town....

He thought about the conspiracy that had been uncovered at the Saline Pueblos. The leaders were publicly whipped and some hanged. Given all that had befallen them Felipe understood why those native villages were abandoned.

Then just last year an event occurred that seemed to reinforce the spiral of events. Bartolomé's sickly daughter in Santa Fe, bed-ridden these last few years, suddenly rose and walked to Santa Fe's parish church to tell the priest that the statue of Our Lady of the Sagrario had come alive and gave her a message for him. "A message! The old family statue talked to her!" Felipe did not know what to think. The message as conveyed by the priest was that the people had better follow the priests or suffer dire consequences.

"What more could be done? Execute more desperate Indians?" Felipe's mind raced. The governor, he knew, just called on everyone to pool their resources to help feed the refugees gathering at the Galisteo and the abandoned Senecú Pueblos. What resources?

Even Jacinta parroted Felipe's question. "What resources?"

Felipe's cousin in Santa Fe, Bartolomé, had become the High Sheriff and fully endorsed the new policies. Neither he nor anyone else paid attention to the family business. Why? The drought, which included three years of absolutely no crops plus the complete depletion of the herds, rendered the business obsolete.

Naturally enough the weakened communities became prey to increased Apache raids not to mention thievery among the settlers. At Barrancas, Felipe's other cousin received a severe wound on his forehead when he and some ranch hands surprised a group of Navajos trying to make off with a couple of head of cattle.

Felipe stopped taking his annual trip to Santa Fe. The trip became too dangerous, and, outside of pleasantries, there was no reason. The family business had failed. Only the opportunity to visit family gave him cause to go to the capital.

However, when Felipe heard about the alleged miracle attributed to Bartolomé's daughter and the family statue, he decided to go to Santa Fe. The statue had spoken and warned people to listen to the priests. He wanted to hear from his family members what had happened.

"But cousin, such repression causes more resentment."

Bartolomé tried to explain, "You don't understand. The friars and God are on our side. The governor does what he must."

Felipe surveyed his brothers who sat by with no intention of joining in. He thought how estranged they had become. "God is on our side? I thought God wanted to convert the Natives, not kill them."

His cousin postured. "Listen, Felipe, you have been away."

"No. I have never left New Mexico and my life has been next to the Pueblos. I have worked shoulder to shoulder with the Natives. They are suffering."

Bartolomé spread out his hands and pled. "So are we."

"So you believe the priests. Did you believe de la Paz when he falsely accused the

German merchant who escaped and died on the Jornada? You chased after him. What about the others? What does Francisco say about this? We are not Gods, but men."

Bartolomé pointed a finger toward Felipe. "Careful cousin. It is not only the clergy. The miracle..."

"Ah yes," Felipe interrupted, "the miracle. Do you believe it?"

With his answer to this question it became clear that Bartolomé would not consider any argument. "Everyone believes it. You should. You know my María. You have seen her. She was left for dead, received the Last Rites. Now, now she can walk and is healthy. Do you think that we are stupid? That we would ignore all the complaints against the priests for nothing?"

Felipe would not quit. When he was alone with his brother Francisco he brought up the subject. "María talked to the priest."

"No. She went to the priest."

"Her mom took her?"

"No. She went on her own."

"But, she..."

Francisco interrupted. "Yes. A miracle. There is another if you want to believe."

Resigned, Felipe replied. "Go ahead."

"María told the priest that her mother's statue, you know the one..."

"Yes, yes. I know it well. The family statue."

"Well it, she came to life and told little María to go and warn the priest..."

Felipe's face had a curious mixture of astonishment and doubt. Francisco continued, "...that if the people did not quit their ways against the priests, there will be serious consequences."

"Consequences?" Felipe waved an arm. "This drought is enough." He gave out a sarcastic laugh. "Ha, God has punished us these last years. We are desperate."

Francisco pointed at Felipe as if he had taken the conversation's high ground. "Yes, and the Natives are reverting to their old ways. They blame us and complain that they never should have listened to us. In their minds we are the reason for the drought."

"But surely little María did not say all this."

"No. Of course not. She talked about many deaths." He looked askance at Felipe. "Well, Father Juan called his congregation together and proclaimed María's miracle, or miracles, as a message from God through his 'Blessed mother' and..."

"And now the people are panicked over something that should be obvious. The Pueblo people are restless. They suffer more than us. The message is not a miracle but a statement of the obvious. We are in danger for lack of food, and no lack of disease. And not surprisingly, there is unrest among the Natives. If this continues, well...you know. And it has nothing to do with the treatment of the priests. They, too, share some blame."

"Felipe. I agree. I am only telling the tale."

"What do her parents say?"

"They point to her sudden good health, which cannot be denied. Also, because of the press of people they have moved the statue into the front *sala.* Their home has become a virtual chapel. Oh, Bartolomé denied the priest's request to move the statue to the church. He was insistent. She belongs to the family. Our ancestors brought her from Spain."

Nuestra Señora del Sagrario de Toledo, later nicknamed La Macana, the statue presumably brought from Spain to New Mexico by the Robledo and Romero families. The statue to which is attributed a miracle forecasting the Pueblo Revolt. From *The Lady From Toledo* by Fray Angélico Chávez.

Felipe, of course, knew the story. "I agree."

All this passed through Felipe's mind as he sat under the veranda of his house. He could only shake his head at such memories. He had aged. He felt alone, alone with his

Jacinta and children. And it was not long before the reality of his foreboding began to take shape.

Later that same summer's month, a rider arrived with depressing news. As the man mounted and turned to begin his return trip, Jacinta, with young Baltasar on her hip and the two girls trailing her, came out to hear the news. "Ah, my love, what now? I can tell. It is not good. What has happened?"

"A group of armed Pueblo Indians, Tewas from the north rode into Santa Fe and broke into the governor's house where they confronted the governor. They demanded the release of their brethren who had been jailed. The poor governor, who was left without protection, had to acquiesce."

"No protection?" Jacinta sat down on a wood bench next to Felipe and handed him Baltasar.

"All the governor's men had left to chase Apaches who had raided Galisteo." He put his son on his knee and bounced him softly. "All the prisoners had been arrested and punished as conspirators. Under the governor's orders three of them were hanged. One hanged himself. The rest were taken in the raid."

Felipe and Jacinta sat side by side. The gravity of the moment was obvious to even the three young children around them. They, too, fell into silence and waited. Their father spoke. "Jacinta, I fear a rebellion has started. I fear for us, for our children. I see no future in New Mexico."

"We can't leave."

"No love, we can't. Nor will. But we should prepare."

"For what, Felipe?"

"I am not sure. Perhaps an uprising."

"Not our neighbors? Our friends at the pueblo?"

"No. No. The northern Pueblos are the emboldened ones. Look at what they just did. Besides the Jumano villages are abandoned. Our neighbors are very weak and few. Already, many have gone to Isleta to live. Or Senecú. We should worry about the nomads...and pray."

BAD NEWS FROM THE NORTH
August 1680, Isleta Pueblo

An uneasy quiet came over the kingdom. Felipe and Jacinta had two more daughters. Ana María and Antonia were born in 1678 and 1680 respectively. Now they had a total of eight healthy children. They had become whimsical about their early concerns. Sebastián and Juana had become strong young adults. Both grew taller than their parents and appeared even more so because of their thin bodies. They had their mother's broad shoulders and long straight hair. Sebastián had slightly thick lips and a long face.

They both knew how to fire the family *harquebus* and two pistols. Under the guidance of his father and the help of the ranch hands Sebastián had become fairly adept with the short sword. In fact, now he had taken it upon himself to teach his eight-year-old younger brother, Baltasar, how to use weapons and ride a horse.

The thought of someone teaching the children how to read and write did not cross Felipe's mind. The necessities of survival took precedent. In fact it preoccupied him. Governor Antonio de Otermín's decision to divide New Mexico administratively into the lower and upper river regions with the dividing mark at La Bajada pleased Felipe. La Bajada, that lava escarpment through which the Rio Grande flowed southwest of Santa Fe delineated the Rio Arriba from the Rio Abajo. Its name, La Bajada or the Lowering, demonstrated certain haughtiness of the Santa Feans. Naturally, Felipe sarcastically thought, they could not stand naming the escarpment La Arriba. From their point of view everyone had to lower themselves when they left Santa Fe, the New Jerusalem.

The announcement that the governor had appointed *Maestre de Campo* Alonso García Noriega to be his Lieutenant Governor and captain-general in charge of the Rio Abajo surprised Felipe. García had settled on land along the Royal Road halfway between Isleta and Alameda pueblos. Both Felipe and Bartolomé knew him well. They had stayed at his *hacienda* on occasion. That the governor acknowledged an obligation to the south satisfied all the Rio Abajo folk, for it meant that a small contingent of ten soldiers would be stationed in the area. "At least," Felipe openly expressed, "the governor has recognized our peril."

Also worthy of some note was that the drought appeared to have ended in the last three years, the moisture increased each successive year. It still was not enough but it was a start. The crops had started to come back and the livestock started to reproduce.

The talk of abandoning their southern *haciendas* had stopped. Not as many people sought to leave. Population slightly increased in the central Rio Grande Valley from Isleta north to La Angostura, near San Felipe Pueblo.

But the hardship was not over. The Pueblos suffered worse than the settlers and rumors of rebellion persisted, especially in the north. Governor Otermín, who had taken office three years earlier, had spies out but found it hard to believe that the Pueblos could rebel as a whole.

Nothing that August day, no dark clouds, pending thunderstorms, or other unusual natural events hinted at the news that a sweaty, dust-blown, and hurried rider brought to the *hacienda*. He dismounted before his equally fraught horse came to a full stop. "García wants everyone to gather at Isleta. Do not wait. There has been a major revolt in the north. Everyone is in danger."

Felipe tried to digest the words. "Danger?"

"Yes, a rebellion. Word is that everything north of Santa Fe is destroyed. The capital itself may be lost. There has been no word of survivors."

"Not everyone. Surely there is resistance...in Santa Fe."

"We don't know. No word has come to us."

"I have family there."

"Sorry, I can't help you. I am a messenger sent from Isleta. I only know what I was told. You should concentrate on your immediate family. García sent me. Is there anyone further south?"

"Don't worry. A few. I will get word to them."

"Thanks. Can I trade my *macho* for a fresh ride?"

"More. Have some food and drink. Give yourself a rest. My people will take care of you."

"Thanks, *patrón*."

"Call me Felipe."

"Yes. Thank you, señor Felipe."

Felipe waived him off. He had to prepare for a quick trip north while sending some men south, especially to warn José and Catalina. Everyone had questions but the answers were few. "We will take what we need for a week. The men should prepare for a campaign." Felipe thought that there was a chance that they might head to Santa Fe. Felipe could not imagine what had happened in the north. He still knew little as he led his contingent to Isleta Pueblo. Not even the few men Bartolomé had left at La Barrancas to join Felipe's group had any new information.

When he arrived at Isleta he saw that García had gathered the people from all over the Rio Abajo. He also learned that this rebellion was different from the others. Unlike in the past when individual pueblos or a few of them got together, this revolt involved a coordinated effort of most of the Pueblo world. Only the southern pueblos, from Isleta down past where Felipe lived and on to Senecú remained calm. A few survivors from Jemez and Zia came to the camp. Still, no word came out of the Rio Arriba.

García and his grown sons had gone back to their *hacienda* to see if they could learn anything. The lieutenant governor was a good man. People thought of him not so much as a politician but as a farmer. In fact, he was born in Zacatecas and was not one of the founding families. As an adult, he had taught himself how to read. Most people figured that he had been appointed the governor's man in the south because of his preference to live at his *hacienda* and not burden the governor with his presence in Santa Fe. *Quién sabe?* Who knew?

García really had never commanded anything. Now, if the governor had been killed, García would become responsible for the whole kingdom's survival. The people at Isleta looked to him to make decisions. And their number had grown to around fifteen hundred people.

García rose to the occasion. So far, he showed no hesitancy in his actions. As he rode back from his foray, his patchy beard and robust round face suddenly looked like a leader. The people anxiously gathered around him so García thought it best to speak while mounted. With a firm face that revealed neither sadness nor anger, rather than determination, the lieutenant governor reported that everything north between Isleta Pueblo to Santo Domingo Pueblo and including the Jemez area had been devastated. He and his sons could not get to Santa Fe but felt, indeed, heard that all their brethren in the Rio Arriba had been killed. The naked, mutilated bodies and burnt and ransacked *haciendas* that they had seen confirmed this dire belief.

Felipe had heard enough from many of the people gathered at Isleta who talked of their narrow escapes and what they had witnessed to believe that García had given a true report. Like many of the people around him, García's words disheartened him, for that meant that his brothers, cousins, nieces and nephews had died violently.

García called for a *junta de guerra*, a war council, to discuss a plan of action.

Felipe, Bartolomé, and José attended. The first order of business in the outdoor meeting was to conduct a survey of the men in arms. They tallied one hundred twenty men, two thirds of whom had a firearm and not quite that many had a mount. The elderly, the infirm, women, and children made up the majority of the refugees.

Garcia's body language bespoke of the seriousness of the situation. Now was not the time to mince words. He wanted officers and officials around him to give honest advice. He led the discussion with his deliberate speech in which he assumed that he now had charge of "the kingdom."

He presented the men with three possibilities. First, they should fortify themselves in Isleta Pueblo and hope that some survivors from the north show up. Second, they should send an armed contingent north to search for survivors. Finally, they abandon New Mexico and take the refugees to the safer confines of El Paso.

The first, emotional reaction of everyone, including Felipe and Bartolomé, was "never, never. We will not abandon the Kingdom." But, then, they calmed down. They heard that Father Francisco de Ayeta was bringing a caravan north, which would have much needed supplies plus a contingent of thirty returning soldiers that Governor Otermín had sent to escort the wagons. This could not be overlooked and, in fact, loomed important to everyone. A majority agreed with García who believed that the caravan should have arrived in El Paso by now.

Felipe looked around at the twenty some men and seven friars. He had never been in a *junta de guerra*. Rather than speak, he decided to listen and watch. Isleta's plaza with the cottonwood tree under which they met was pleasant enough on that hot August day. The people, Spanish and Indians alike ringed the plaza against the buildings and on the roofs. They watched with interest and unsuccessfully tried to listen. Given the circumstance, Felipe marveled over the curious mixture of people and place.

The discussion progressed almost with a life of its own. Many of the senior officials pointed out that García, as titular head, had a primary responsibility for the refugees gathered around them. They also noted that they only had a few days' supplies at most. In addition, the Native inhabitants of Isleta and the southern Tanos, who had taken refuge with them, were becoming restless. Eventually, the general sentiment moved from the initial emotional output to the more reasoned idea that the colony, or what is left of it, needed to move south.

Felipe was one of many in the contingent who had family in the Rio Arriba. He, Bartolomé, and José, while saddened by the possibility of abandoning the area, nodded in agreement to the prevailing sentiment. Felipe and Bartolomé had sons now counted among the men in arms. Felipe's son Sebastián was now seventeen years old and Bartolomé's son had passed his twentieth birthday.

Felipe looked at his cousin who returned the look with a resigned shrug. With an unspoken knowledge born from years of working together, they both wanted to do something but did not know what. They knew that the consensus was correct but still doubted such a decision.

Felipe stepped in no general direction and took the opportunity. In a loud voice so all could hear he spoke. "How can we leave, abandon this place when our friends, our families, may be fighting for their lives? We can't leave without knowing."

Another person answered, "We have tried. There is no news. We need to save ourselves."

Bartolomé stepped next to Felipe. "I would rather die trying to save another, then run to save myself."

Felipe chimed in, "We must..."

But the lieutenant governor cut him off with a wave of his hand. "We are not arguing about saving ourselves. We are talking about the women and children, the old ones." He paused, heaved a sigh of resignation. "Listen, my friends, I agree with you. We should send a rescue contingent. But, how many men? At least fifty or sixty. And, where does that leave the rest?" He paused again, looked around, and extended his arms in front of him. "Exposed to attack and elimination."

García made sense. Felipe and Bartolomé looked at each other while García continued. "No my friends, we must deal with what we know and have. I can tell you with certainty that there are no survivors from here to La Bajada. Only death. And, if the Rio Arriba is anything like what I saw..." He stopped and in lowered voice stated, "... there is no chance."

The lieutenant governor won the day. A vast majority of his officers agreed.

After the meeting Felipe and Bartolomé made a private appeal to García. Let them lead a stealth operation of twenty or thirty men. García took them seriously and appreciated their gesture. He thanked them for their zeal and bravery but added that their value resided in protecting what was left of the colony.

The Exodus
August 1680, Isleta Pueblo

That same day, August 13, the whole colony started a meticulous, slow, and dangerous march down the *camino* toward El Paso. García organized the exodus with the utmost care for its protection. He realized that the movement would be slow, only as fast as the slowest person on foot. They passed abandoned *haciendas* one by one. The people had salvaged a few wagons and some horses and mules. More importantly, they had collected a few head of sheep and cattle left behind by others or scattered during the rebellion. Still, the colony did not have enough of anything, especially food.

Felipe, Bartolomé, and José received assignments to join a small contingent of men who would fan out in front of the migration. The advance guard was made up of men, like them, who had some familiarity with the trail going south out of New Mexico. They had an intimate knowledge of the land, especially to Senecú. They knew the danger spots, safe river crossings, good pasturage, and the most favorable route for a desperate people.

At least the guards where mounted. They did not suffer like the majority who had to navigate the dusty, rock strewn road on foot. The extra horses carried the supplies left over from the wagons. The elderly and infirm and very young children, when possible, were put in the wagons. Otherwise, people walked always alert for a call that an attack was

190

coming. Guards circling the main body of people constantly reported seeing "hostiles" watching from the distance.

As they trudged along in the summer's heat praying for some cloud cover, the men stripped their shirts off. Even the women rolled up their sleeves and tied their skirts up from their lower legs. García noted in his official report that the people left New Mexico on foot and almost naked.

While nighttime brought a welcome rest, there was never enough food to satisfy their hunger. The vast majority of people slept on the ground. If they were lucky they found a place under a tree or under one of the wagons. They used their scarce bags or horse gear to create small barriers to protect them from the constant wind that seemed to menace them intentionally.

Quite naturally people tended to group among other family members, friends, or familiar faces. The Romeros and Gómez Robledos along with their ranch hands, gathered together each night. They had a relatively larger number of horses, plus they had a wagon. In total there were nine adult males in the group, including José, Felipe, and Bartolomé, with their two grown sons. On clear nights Jacinta and the younger children slept in the wagon. Others, as many as could fit, slept under it. The younger boys, those too old to be coddled but not old enough to be counted among the adults, pretended to guard the wagon. Those boys, including Baltasar and Jola's son José found nighttime more exciting than the day's walk or the bone-jarring ride in a wagon. Jacinta, stern as ever with her brood, did her best to keep control of her children.

As part of the advanced guard Felipe saw the place first, a full hour before the main body with Jacinta arrived. More focused, he did not let the ruined state of his home distract him from the more import task of searching for anything that might be of use to the struggling colony. He and Sebastián, who happened to be riding with him that day, gathered some of the clothes that were strewn about. They located a few pigs running loose, and the raiders had overlooked spare axles and wagon wheels stored in one of the buildings. These last items would be invaluable.

Jacinta showed emotion for the first time when they approached their abandoned *hacienda*. They had left six days earlier, and the place had been ransacked. She looked away and silently cried. Their gates had been removed, a partial roof remained in place, while her sauna room had been torn down. The other buildings, stables, and pens had been torn apart. It looked like someone had tried to set one of the buildings on fire, but the rock and adobe did not burn. What little furniture they had, either had been taken or smashed beyond use.

The main party camped on the well-known river bottom site next to Felipe's *hacienda*. Two days later, now south of his father-in-law's long ago abandoned *hacienda*, Felipe rode across a rise lost in thought, but alert to the two riders coming up behind him. They attracted his attention a full hour before, and Felipe was astute enough to know that they were his own people and not a threat.

Felipe intentionally tarried. The day was too hot for a rider to push his mount hard. They must be bringing important news. Felipe had signaled to the other scouts on either side of him with hand gestures. Now they, too, rode toward Felipe to hear what news the riders brought.

Both men and their horses were winded when they pulled up. "Two men and a boy have escaped the north! From Taos. They got to Santa Fe but saw that it was under siege and outnumbered so..."

"Wait!" Felipe blurted out. "There are more survivors."

"No, my *capitán*. Only the three. They thought it best not to tarry but to save themselves but keep moving south. Then, they saw evidence of other survivors, us, which gave them hope. They caught up with the rear guard who escorted them to García and the main body."

Felipe looked incredulous. "But what about the people in Santa Fe? It was under siege, you say. There are others still alive?"

The rider gave an askance look. "I am sorry. I cannot speak to that. Maybe we can learn more tonight in camp. At any rate, García has ordered a halt."

Felipe, Bartolomé, and José had quit talking or thinking about their kin in the north. Now, like a miracle, there was the possibility that some of them were alive, desperately defending themselves in Santa Fe. The three of them regretted losing the vote to go north. Maybe they could have helped. And what about now? Had time run out? Maybe not. Three people had survived.

The camp buzzed with the news of the siege at Santa Fe. Sebastián de Herrera Corrales and Fernando Durán y Chaves had become household names. These two men and Chaves's young son Cristóbal had escaped from the far north and eluded capture and sure death for over two hundred miles. Because of them, speculation about other survivors ran rampant throughout the retreating colony.

The people halted and gathered on a rise that García called El Alto. Roughly twelve miles south of the abandoned Alamillo Pueblo, the people almost could see the Pueblo of Socorro. For sure, they could see smoke rising from the pueblo's location at the foot of a mountain that the bore the name of the pueblo.

Felipe worried even more over his family. In his mind Jacinta was a miracle worker. The children remained in fine spirits and in apparent good health. She remained steadfast in her care for them, and she constantly told Felipe not to worry.

But he had his doubts, for he noticed something else. Jacinta appeared more worn and aged every time he saw her. Felipe could see that the journey and her concentration on the children were taking its toll. Of course it would, for she had the care of seven children ranging from fourteen-year-old Juana to the baby, Antonia, merely three months old.

Baltasar, the second oldest son after Sebastián, had celebrated his seventh birthday a few months before. To him the whole exodus was an adventure that bestowed upon him certain grownup responsibilities. Although he longed to be with his older brother and his father in the advance guard, his age relegated him to his mother and siblings. He and José, a couple of years older than him assumed the position of being their personal escort, and they kept an alert eye in search of any breach of the mounted guard fanned out around the main body of people. What Baltasar did not know, nor would ever realize, was that he had become closer to his mother than his father. As he grew through this experience during his formative years his mother would have a greater influence on his personality than his father.

He loved and admired his father, but he had developed a jealousy toward his brother. He anticipated the moments when his father and brother returned to camp. His father always made sure to greet him and ask if all was well. Thus reassured of his important position, Baltasar proudly replied, "Yes, *papá*," and sometimes added, "All is in order," like a true soldier.

And this afternoon was no different. Baltasar hurried over to his brother where he became a kid of a thousand questions. "How was it?"

"Boring."

"Don't you talk?"

"No, we ride separately and quietly."

"Oh. What if you see something?"

"We signal with our arms."

"Oh." Here Baltasar paused, then continued, "Why don't I go with you and papá?"

Sebastián had fielded this question many times. He merely sighed and smiled at his little brother. "Because Mamá needs you with her."

Baltasar did not know if he believed his brother, but he accepted it and dutifully carried on with his responsibility like a true soldier.

Four days later, when they arrived at Socorro, García decided to hold a second *junta de guerra*. Herrera and Chaves, now a part of the exodus, had fielded a mountain of questions. They could not believe that anyone could survive the siege at Santa Fe. They had seen two thousand or more Indians attacking the presidio. How could anyone survive? Nevertheless, they had to admit that they saw someone who was alive and offering resistance.

García wanted a consensus on what to do. The anticipated approach from the south of Father Ayeta's supply caravan and the extra soldiers weighed heavily on everyone's minds. By their calculation, the relief now should be far north of El Paso, maybe a few days away. Until they met up with the caravan and replenished their numbers, refilled their ammunition pouches, and nourished themselves, they could not think of sending a rescue mission north.

The lieutenant governor made an initial proposal that he lead a contingent south to meet the caravan with its escort of thirty soldiers. Reinforced with the extra firepower, he would turn north in search of survivors. Then he turned to his *maestre de campo*, Thomé Domínguez de Mendoza who gave a long review of what they had witnessed, of the group's current desperate state, and of the uncertain whereabouts of Ayeta's caravan. He concluded that dividing the miniscule under-armed group of men able to fight would invite an attack. He reiterated that the enemy was not only the Pueblo Indians but Apaches and others, for word had spread, and the Apaches were now armed and on horseback from what they had collected during the revolt.

This time all of the men agreed that the colony should keep moving south. Felipe and the other lookouts reported that Apache scouts watched them almost daily. Foodstuffs were dangerously low. They could not risk waiting to see if there were more survivors. The large occupied pueblo of Socorro seemed friendly enough, but who knew if it might turn on them, too.

Felipe was one of the twenty officials who spoke and agreed with the sentiment.

He could see the desperation in his own family. The scribe recorded his words for the record. Felipe spoke with conviction: "In as much as this small camp lacks sufficient forces and is entirely surrounded by enemies who can communicate by smoke signals over great distances and can surround us, this camp...should not delay, but should march on until we meet the wagons and the men who are escorting them, and then decide what is the most appropriate action."

No one objected nor was surprised when García announced, "Okay, then. Good. We will proceed to San Cristóbal and rest for two days. We hope the relief will arrive while we are there. If not, we will embark across the desert. Meanwhile, our security guard trailing us will keep an eye out for sign of anyone else escaping from the north. While at San Cristóbal we will also send scouts back up the trail. Above all, though, we must continue to care for ourselves."

So the colony continued south past Senecú Pueblo, the southernmost of the pueblos. The people worried less about the rebellious Pueblo people and more about the nomadic Manso Indians who had replaced the Apaches and Navajos as they moved south. Still, Felipe, Bartolomé, and José could not help but look over their shoulders in anticipation of more news. None came before the refugees made it to San Cristóbal where they set up camp at a place where their brethren and ancestors had rested many times since Oñate led the first settlers north.

STARTLING NEWS
September 4, 1680, San Cristóbal

"Riders! Riders! Riders coming!" Felipe heard the shouts. The mere fact that shouts boomed out indicated that this was not the normal changing of the guard but something important. Although some of the enemy fighters had become mounted, Felipe and those around him quickly recognized the riders as some of their own.

As they became more identifiable, Felipe could see that the riders included more than the rear guard. One of the riders wore the distinct Franciscan blue robe. More survivors for sure!

The news aroused the whole camp. Even the children, now too hungry and worn to play, gathered around their parents as the riders approached. Not even the thunder from a storm washing over the western mountains on the distant horizon could divert their attention.

As the riders approached, the people could see that two of the soldiers and the priest were new to the colony. The priest dismounted, walked up to García and introduced himself as Father Francisco Farfán. The friar spoke formally. "Señor García, we are sent to you by our Lord Governor and Captain General of this Kingdom of New Mexico, Don Antonio de Otermín who we left at Isleta Pueblo with a thousand refugees, survivors of the siege of Santa Fe. Our governor commands and does order that you halt your exodus, and that you, with an escort return north with us immediately to confer with him." Then, Farfán handed García an envelope.

García immediately ordered an aide to organize the small escort and prepare it to leave within the hour. Then riders came in from the south with more good news. Upon receiving news of the revolt, Father Ayeta had released Captain Leyva and his soldiers from their escort duty to lead a relief column north. They had departed El Paso on August 30th and had been on the trail fifteen days. The refugees were only a few days apart from much needed support.

Young Baltasar, standing next to his older brother, noticed the look on his father's face when he came to his mother and said, "Oh Jacinta! Thank God." Then he told the news that a large contingent of people had survived from the north. "Surely, some of our brothers and sisters are alive."

Ten days later Otermín and another thousand refugees plus an uncounted number of Piro Natives caught up with them at Fray Cristóbal. Felipe's outlook brightened when he learned that his cousin, Francisco Gómez Robledo, had become Otermín's *Maestre del Campo* as well as one of his main advisors. He also learned that many of his cousins had survived, and he cried at the sight of both Bartolomé and Aunt Ana.

Not all the news was good, for the joy of the union was diminished by the news of the devastation. Felipe learned that his brother and sister-in-law, Pedro and Petronila, and their nine children were killed at Pojoaque. Also, his cousin, Bartolomé's brother, Andrés was the only officer, and one of five casualties suffered at the siege of Santa Fe.

Finally, nourished by the aid brought by Ayeta, the whole reinforced colony of over twenty-five hundred people stretched out over three miles as it struggled across the perilous ninety mile Jornada del Muerto to the welcome riverside resting place still called Robledo. The desert crossing took over two weeks, which was too much for Aunt Ana.

Aunt Ana's advanced age, generally thought to be over eighty years old, left her very vulnerable to the harsh realities of the retreat. She was not alone among the old and infirm. More than a few did not survive the journey. Not even the care of placing her in a wagon seemed to help. She groaned with every bump and couldn't stand on her own anymore.

Her only solace, it seemed, was the little statue, Sagrario, that had healed her grandniece and predicted the revolt. Broken in the siege and returned by an attacker who tossed her over the presidio wall, the little statue had been saved. María, now a healthy juvenile, had a special fondness for Ana. María made sure that both her great aunt and her miraculous statue received good care.

Ana had the telltale signs of death. The people around her had become experienced in the sad matter. With the family watching over her at the campsite of Robledo, her breathing became prolonged and seemed to rattle. She turned her head with closed eyes and seemed to reach for Sagrario. At that moment she exhaled her last breath. Her daughter Ana, who was rubbing her forehead, handed the statue to María who laid it next to her while she whispered, "take care of my *tía.*"

The irony of Ana's death was not lost even on young Baltasar. Her daughter made sure that everyone knew why the place where she died was called Robledo. This was the spot were the family's Robledo forefather, Pedro, had died and was buried. Now his granddaughter would be buried in the same place. None of them could foresee that the names of Robledo and Doña Ana would be attached to that locale for centuries to come.

Baltasar's parents made sure that he and his siblings knew about Aunt Ana, and that she was a great woman. Her story involved "María's statue." Perhaps because of his youth, and maybe because of all the events swirling around him, Baltasar never really appreciated the value of the statue. He was surprised when, after arriving in El Paso, the mission priests, led by father Ayeta, paid a visit to the family camp. They asked to talk to María and then to see the statue. Ayeta then turned toward Maria's parents and told them that he had to take the statue with him to the Franciscan motherhouse in the far south. The story of the miracle would be of invaluable help when they petition the authorities in Mexico City to save the colony. How could they refuse as Father Ayeta and his priests looked on? Not even a replacement statue of Mary could prevent María from crying. To her, the loss of her statue was as tragic as the loss of her great aunt.

Baltasar felt for his cousin but then reasoned that she would see the statue again when her father announced that he and his family would leave El Paso and move south.

A FORLORN COLONY
October 1680, El Paso del Norte

The departure of María's family did not upset Baltasar as much as some of the others in the family. Bartolomé and his brothers all left as well. Baltasar could see the hurt in his father. Bartolomé had been his best friend, a lifelong companion. What hurt Baltasar more was when his father and brother signed up with governor Otermín to return north. They hadn't even settled in their partially built *jacal* when they had to leave.

Not even the impressive sight of all the departing men on horseback snapped Baltasar out of his depression. "What's so special about New Mexico? Stay. Why do you have to go back?" Baltasar had decided that everything in the north contained nothing but bad memories. Baltasar would rather stay in El Paso. "Why," he thought, "couldn't father feel the same?"

Felipe had no way of realizing that his son's observations were true in another, unfortunate way. From the first colonists whom had deserted Oñate to those who continued to desert the refugee colony as it moved south, or to those who now abandoned El Paso and to those who now made excuses not enroll in Otermín's projected reconquest, Felipe never realized the historical irony. He agonized over the lack of support and even outright denigration of Otermín. Just like the first colony with Oñate, Felipe's colony three generations later had become disconcertingly divided.

He could not understand those who left. They seemed concerned for themselves and not anyone else. This was an attitude foreign to everything he understood. In short, in his mind, they were dishonorable.

Thus, Felipe stepped forward with great pride and stood shoulder to shoulder with Sebastián to proclaim that both of them were fit and ready to serve his majesty with Captain General and Governor of New Mexico, Otermín. Sebastián, slender like his father, stood a half-foot taller with the same straight black hair. Felipe declared what arms they had along with five horses and a mule. Both he and Sebastián received the prescribed 250 pesos worth of supplies and equipment, plus four iron hoes, a plowshare, and an axe.

The moment's euphoria came to an abrupt halt after Felipe signed the ledger. The scribe then motioned to Sebastián to follow suit, and gave a surprised expression when Sebastián signaled that he did not know how. Felipe shared the obvious embarrassment as he signed for his son, after which the scribe added a notation, "He did not sign because of not knowing how." The scribe laid down the quill and looked up, stating, "That's it. Next."

Felipe felt a deep emotional pain for his son. The incident reminded him that none of his children could read or write, much less sign their names. So far as he knew, they were the first generation of his family to be illiterate. He had neglected them. He could only look up at his son's long, thick-lipped face and say, "I'm sorry son. I should have taught you years ago."

Sebastián put his hand on his father's shoulder and replied, "Papá, *no me molesta,* it does not bother me."

"Yes, but it bothers me. I will teach you to sign your name. It is as important as wielding that lance you carry. I will teach you." "And," he thought to himself, "your brothers as well."

"Ah, Sebastián, when we return, we will be able to do what we do best. We can plant crops, corn and fruit trees. We will see if we can get a few head of cattle and, yes, some pigs."

As he always did, Sebastián nodded in agreement with his father. Yet, he was not convinced. Felipe could see in his son a simple-minded approach to life. If left to his own devices he had survival skills equal to any man. He could be left in the desert and live to talk of the adventure. The reality of actual military duty had captured his imagination.

Felipe did his duty as he saw it but he had his reservations about the current expedition. As an *alcalde mayor* in his earlier years, he led a couple of forays after some Indian rustlers. Life in the saddle in pursuit of an enemy was not novel to him.

Yet, this was different. With no women, children, or the infirm, but with wagons loaded with supplies and munitions, including tents and fifty new carbines sent from Mexico City, this group of over two hundred men had a different purpose.

As a captain, Felipe expected to get one of the new carbines. His decades' old harquebus barely functioned. A swath of leather, wrapped around the weapon and tied in place with dried pig sinew, held the wood stock attached to the rest of the weapon. The new carbines had a lighter, more efficient firing mechanism. It weighed about half as much, and Felipe heard that it fired with a deadly force superior to his old firearm.

Despite his sense of honor, Felipe had his doubts. "Why," he wondered to himself, "are we leaving in November at the onset of winter? And, did Otermín really believe a force of a hundred plus soldiers plus another hundred or so Indian allies could defeat an enemy that numbered in the thousands?" Felipe knew better.

But there was another reason why he enlisted on the expedition. He had an unusual conversation with his cousin Francisco Gómez Robledo, who had become Otermín's second in command, but who would be left in charge of the garrison at El Paso. Felipe first volunteered to serve with him but he thundered, "No. You go with the governor. I don't need you here."

197

The words took Felipe aback. "Hey, Francisco, why so abrupt? I am willing to serve wherever I am needed, and Sebastián too."

"Good. You need to."

"What is the problem? Why are you so mad?"

Francisco opened his shirt to expose an ugly scar on his shoulder. "Look at this. Otermín has two of these, one on his face and the other on his chest. So do many others. We received these defending ourselves. And, my brother was killed while you and the others fled."

Felipe stood face to face with his more famous cousin. He had heard enough. "Is that why your brother deserted? Go ahead, hit me if that is your inclination. Otermín reviewed all that with Gallegos. Otermín understands and agrees with why we did not try to go north. I have explained it to you before. If you refuse to understand, so be it. Under the circumstances, we did the right thing. *Bueno,* fine. I can't help how you feel. Too bad. Given where I have lived most of my life, I have nothing to prove."

The Indian rebellion had caused more than a societal division. It had broken the Romero's extensive landholdings and sources of wealth that had withstood New Mexico's politics for seven decades.

ADJUSTMENT

August 1682, El Paso del Norte

Felipe fixed his plowshare to the bottom of a new wood hand-adzed vertical plow. The iron share would outlast its wooden parts. When he could, Felipe worked on a plot of river bottomland that had been assigned to he and Sebastián. The family grew, indeed survived on beans and corn. However, his preferred work seemed to be constantly interrupted by the call to arms.

After the Otermín expedition, Felipe determined never to go north again. As miserable as the El Paso district was with its less fertile land and greater heat, New Mexico held bad memories and less possibility.

His lasting memory of the 1681 expedition was the bitter cold, constant snow, and burning pueblos. Only Isleta Pueblo welcomed them and did so after an initial show of arms. All the other pueblos were vacated. Their inhabitants, armed and resentful, gathered in the nearby mountains preparing for an opportunity to attack. Upon interrogating the few people who they did encounter, the army learned that the combined Pueblo forces planned to attack and destroy the horse herd, then wipe out the army. This affected Felipe, for he was put in charge of a ten-man contingent responsible for guarding a part the herd.

Otermín ordered each of the vacant pueblos to be burned, including Isleta after he gathered its inhabitants to march south, under close guard. Felipe knew that Otermín's policies would alienate the Indians even more. In addition, the lack of forage caused by the extreme winter weather weakened the horses thus achieving a heightened possibility to an attack. By the time that they decided to abandon New Mexico, Felipe's guard had only two able horses at their disposal.

That was why Felipe joined the debate that became an argument during another *junta de guerra*. The *maestre de campo*, Juan Domínguez de Mendoza, a man Felipe knew more by reputation, argued for immediate military action. He led a vociferous contingent that boasted that they should spend the winter in Isleta, or close by, and make war to punish the recalcitrant Natives.

By then Felipe had developed a deep, guttural cough. Coughing and hacking with his poncho wrapped around him he stood up and countered the military officer. He had heard enough. "I have twenty-eight years of experience in New Mexico. I was an *alcalde mayor*. In all honesty, I must state that the defeat of the Pueblos at present is impossible." He watched Domínguez de Mendoza mock him with a self-satisfied look, and continued, "With this meager force and lack of strong mounts: impossible," He stopped for a second and looked at the governor, "unless we have reinforcements."

Domínguez de Mendoza, scowled as only he could with his round, high boned cheeks and beady-eyed face. Otermín waived him off before he could say anything. Felipe continued, "we must deal with reality. Only two soldiers of my squadron are mounted, the rest are left on foot. The horses are weak and dying. In this season, with this weather, we cannot stay in one place long enough to find forage to feed what is left of the herd, much less ourselves." To this many of the men openly agreed with nods and understated words of agreement.

Felipe took advantage of the moment. "Besides, we have an obligation to the people of Isleta. If we abandon them, the others will overrun them. We must take them with us for their own protection."

Felipe's argument, along with those who echoed his sentiment convinced Otermín. Yet, the debate and decision caused hard feelings. Domínguez de Mendoza led a powerful group that included most of the colony's civil leadership. He did not suffer contrary opinions well. He became very critical of "that coward Otermín."

After his return to his new, but poor home next to the river crossing south of the El Paso mission, Felipe concentrated on his field and, in particular, his plow. Reminded of the distance that he had kept from the politics of Santa Fe, Felipe did the same in El Paso by concentrating on growing food for survival.

Felipe worried for Sebastián and Jacinta. His oldest cared little for farming. Felipe hardly saw him anymore. Sebastián spent his time at the presidio a few leagues away.

His concern for Jacinta was more immediate. Her hair had turned grey and she permanently stooped as if she had the weight of the world pressed upon her. She never smiled, even when she tried. Felipe knew that he was part of the problem. His nagging cough never seemed to go away. She, too, could see the change in him, the disappointment. She did not consider their future. In truth, she did not see one.

Young Baltasar, Felipe's next oldest son, now nine years old, began to follow his dad everywhere he could and help with the chores. Indeed, he seemed fascinated with his father's tales of the *hacienda*, the business, and even the mechanics of fixing a plow. Baltasar asked about his grandparents, but learned little beyond that his grandfather had died while his father was young.

It fell to Baltasar to become the first of his siblings to learn how to sign his name.

His father also taught him the rudiments of mathematics. With Sebastián's absence Felipe concentrated on teaching Baltasar.

"Now son, I want you to pass this on to your other brothers. I want all of them to know how to sign their name and maybe to read. Perhaps someday you and they, and your sisters if they marry good men, will have your own land and even have an *hacienda*."

Baltasar raised his eyebrows over his expressive dark eyes. "Like before, papá? In New Mexico?"

"I doubt like before. Maybe better. And for New Mexico...who knows. Someplace." Felipe stopped with a short cough after which he cleared his throat and spit.

Later that year Domingo Jironza Pétriz de Cruzate replaced Otermín. The new governor was a career man who was much more decisive. Although everyone openly supported the new governor the colony remained politically divided.

Felipe managed to convince the governor's people that his age precluded him from making the difficult trip into New Mexico. How he did it mystified even him. He impressed upon the officials that his loyalty did not waiver but, because of his age, he could not always be available. He would join in the defense of the El Paso villages and mission and even go on some punitive expeditions in the area. Perhaps because Sebastián volunteered for all the military forays, including a minor scouting expedition that met Apache resistance at the old *hacienda* of Las Barrancas, Felipe succeeded in his desire not to return to New Mexico.

His rather obvious clogged throat and constant cough did not preclude him from all military duty. This was especially true when the various native tribes in the El Paso district became brazenly resistant to Spanish authority. As a result, Felipe was called to arms as the third in command of a major expedition that took him east, riding over four hundred miles down the Rio Grande across the Nueces River, past where his father-in-law had gone, to a place where they stopped and built a two story adobe tower to help defend themselves.

Governor Jironza put Juan Domínguez de Mendoza in charge and assigned the officer's son-in-law, Diego Lucero de Godoy, to second in command. Felipe, whose health continued to decline, was ignored in any command decisions. Domínguez de Mendoza remembered their earlier disagreement and Felipe had become distrustful of the man as well as his relatives.

They were on the trail for seven months and would not return until July 17, 1683. The trip was brutal at times, pressed for food and water. They suffered hostile attacks and an internal schism that resulted in a major desertion. During the battles, Felipe exerted himself, firing his carbine, then, charging into the chaos. He blindly swung his sword from one side to the other. Sometimes the weapon hit something, a human being left gasping for air or holding back entrails. He and his mount survived the conflict completely exhausted.

He returned a defeated man. Jacinta recognized the decline in his health. She took hold of him while ordering her two grown daughters to bring pails of water to be heated over the fire.

"Felipe, my love, calm down. You are safe." She could not hide her concern. She propped Felipe up on a bench. He could breathe better. Still, after a calm moment, his chest heaved as he gasped for air and coughed.

Beside herself, Jacinta shouted at one of Felipe's companions who brought him to her, "What did you do? How could you bring him back like this? Couldn't you see that he was sick?"

"Señora, we put him on his horse and rode with him, helping him every step of the way. At night we fed him and provided blankets, even our own..."

"Yes, yes. Good. You did what you could."

"We could not leave him there."

She turned back to Felipe as he tried to speak but caused another coughing fit. The water came and she took him inside and sat him down as they waited for the fire to warm the water.

Jacinta bathed him with a warm cloth, all the while calming him. Baltasar stood at her side, assisting at her every order. "Bring more towels, more pillows...." He helped dry him and found his brandy, which she warmed to sooth his throat. "Hurry, *hijito*!"

Felipe survived the night and next day. Then, he lasted through the week after which he was able to walk again and seemed to gain strength. Jacinta, though, had an intuition, for she could see that he lost weight and the cough persisted. With Baltasar at his side, Felipe insisted on tending to the chores. He progressively worked less time, as he needed to sit and rest to catch his breath.

Then, another call to arms for another expedition came. They would be going back to the same area as the last time. Only, they would be a much larger force.

Jacinta saw the officer approaching on horseback, at first as an illusion lost in the heat waves rising from the ground, then in focus. She rushed out to meet the man. "No. He cannot go. Can't you see? He is sick! My God!"

"*Señora, lo siento*, I am sorry. I can convey that to the governor and captain Madrid."

"No!" Felipe staggered out the door behind Jacinta. "When do I report?"

"Felipe, no!" Jacinta stomped her foot. She had never done that before. "You will die from the trip. You can't."

"Jacinta! Woman. Please. You know..."

She cut him off. "No I don't. I don't."

The officer held up his hand. He had heard enough. "With your permission. You report the day after tomorrow. In the meantime, I am witness to your condition and will support such in case you do not report." He bowed his head, tipped the brim of his hat and politely said, "With your leave," and left. With Jacinta's care, Felipe recovered after a fashion.

PART V
A New Beginning, Less Glory: Baltasar

A Plowshare and Survival
August 1683, San Lorenzo del Paso

Life in El Paso never seemed the same. It felt temporary. Felipe's extended family worked together. In his quiet way, Francisco, the oldest, worked with Bartolomé to combine the family lots and divide tasks. They worried about Felipe's health. He had become weak for his age. One of the first things they did was to rush Juana into a marriage so they would not have to care for her. Now ten years old, that was how Baltasar saw it. His younger sisters were sent to live with her and her new husband, at least for the first year or so. That left Isabel, his other older sister, to watch after his mother. Baltasar stayed with Isabel to help around the house and continue with his chores there.

Then, one spring day Baltasar decided to detach his father's old plowshare from the worn plow. He did this because that very morning his older brother-in-law, Antonio Domínguez de Mendoza, showed up and started collecting tools, anything with iron. When Antonio turned the plow over to inspect the share, Baltasar spoke up, "That's mine!"

Antonio smirked as he continued to finger the share.

"You can't have it. Its mine." Baltasar never felt so invested.

Antonio was not impressed. "Listen, kid, what is yours is mine. Beat it."

"No. Its mine," Baltasar shouted.

"Shut up you little pest." Now Antonio was looking for something, which he found. A file. He started prying the share from the plow.

Baltasar was livid. Perhaps overwrought for the state of his parents, words did not come to him. Instead he picked up a rock and threw it as hard as he could while shouting, "No!"

The rock hit Antonio direct on his left shoulder. Shocked by the sudden and unexpected pain, Antonio immediately dropped the plow. He cursed and yelled at Baltasar, "You son of a..." but stopped short. "I am going to teach you a lesson you will never forget." He started at Baltasar.

Baltasar anticipated his move and took off running. He was a fast runner and with his calloused bare feet he easily got away from the boot-laden Antonio. He ran around the house, through a gate and hid behind a manure pile. It would be a matter of time before he was discovered.

"Where are you? You little piece of...ah, there you are. Come here."

"No." Baltasar got ready to run again but, just then, Felipe rode up, returning from some business in the presidio. "Hey, what's going on? We've too much work to be playing around."

Antonio answered with an angry red face, "Your son hit me with a rock. He needs to be taught a lesson."

Still mounted Felipe answered, "That would be my task, not yours. Baltasar come here. Is it true?"

Baltasar felt helplessly outnumbered. He knew he was in trouble. He could only reply, "Yes, father."

Felipe sighed and dismounted. He walked up to Baltasar and stood over him. For some inexplicable reason the chirping of some birds had Baltasar's attention. "Why?"

The question snapped Baltasar out of his stupor and he repeated his father's question. "Why?"

"Yes, why?"

Antonio seized the opportunity. "Because he needs discipline. He is a punk."

Felipe ignored Antonio as he concentrated on Baltasar. "Tell me. Why?"

Baltasar looked up at his father, "Because he wanted to take my your, my plowshare."

"He wanted? Is that all?"

"No. I mean..." Baltasar could feel the rapid beat of his heart. His lips quivered, and if ever his close-set eyes looked like those of a scared rabbit, this was the moment, "...he was taking it from the plow. I don't care about the other stuff but that..."

His father cut him off with a calming motion of his hands and asked, "What other stuff?"

"That stuff." Baltasar pointed to a pile of iron implements.

Felipe looked at the iron implements, dismounted, handed the reins to Baltasar, leaned on one leg, hitched a thumb in his thick black belt, and looked askance at Antonio. "It seems that my son caught you in the act. You are lucky it wasn't me who caught you."

Antonio looked defiant.

Felipe continued, "Don't even think of standing up to me. Nor are you permitted on this land again. Your wife may visit her mother but without you. Now leave."

Antonio shuffled, and then scowled at Baltasar. He began to speak but he was cut off.

"Don't even try. Leave." Felipe had a deadly serious look.

Antonio turned on his heels and defiantly strode off to his wagon and lashed the two mules pulling it. As he left, Felipe turned to Baltasar. "I am proud of you. I, too, would never give up a plowshare. You did good." Then he paused and smiled. "Look son, that plow is of no use but the share is. Take it off and build a new plow for it. Understand?"

"Yes. I will do it now."

"And put all those tools back where they belong."

"Yes, I will."

With a sense of euphoria, Baltasar quickly cleaned up the area and started on extracting the two nails that held the share to the old plow.

He enjoyed working with livestock and nourishing the fruit trees. Except for José who was not really related, his cousins did the work out of necessity. Baltasar found joy in the labor. Probably because he worked harder and longer, he grew into a strong but slender man. Like generations before him, he pulled his straight black hair back into a ponytail to keep it out of his face.

Baltasar's uncles shared the information that the *cabildo*, maybe fueled more by ambition than dismay, twice sent unauthorized word to Mexico City petitioning the removal of a governor. Domingo de Mendoza unabashedly twice put himself forward as the ideal replacement for the removed governors. The cabildo also complained that Father

Ayeta sided with Otermín. The petitions for removal as well as Domingo de Mendoza's campaign fell on deaf ears. The latter not only was rejected but also discredited. As a result most of the Domínguez de Mendoza family abandoned the El Paso area to Janos, two days ride southwest of El Paso.

Baltasar's family agreed with one of Jironza's actions. The governor turned his attention to survival of the colony and ordered the consolidation of its villages that ranged almost thirty miles down river from the El Paso de Guadalupe mission. The most obvious move was the relocation of the military headquarters of San Lorenzo de la Toma that was the most distant of the Spanish establishments. He ordered the new headquarters to be established next to the mission by the river crossing and kept the name San Lorenzo in reference to the saint's day on which the 1680 rebellion in New Mexico began. Everyone in the colony knew and, in some way, commemorated the date of August 10th. They would not forget. The New Mexicans, as they began to call themselves identified with San Lorenzo.

The move made sense for defensive reasons. The local Indians had become belligerent. Seeing the example of their brethren to the north they had reason to resist the settlers and their soldiers. As a result a series of punitive expeditions sallied out of the El Paso area. Baltasar's father and brother had gone on some of the earlier ones. Sebastián continued with his military life. Eventually, he transferred out of El Paso. Baltasar received periodic reports about Sebastián, he was at this presidio or that presidio and over time he had received a number of minor wounds but was okay. The family thought that he might be a *cabo*, a corporal but were not certain.

The consolidation itself did not affect the family because they did not have to move. Felipe had established himself and his family in the village nearest to the Mission, therefore next to the new *plaza de armas*. On the other hand, the limited river bottomland and the sandy hills provided little succor. Now with people moving in under the governor's orders, the area became crowded and tempers shorter. Felipe and his two brothers, Bartolomé and Francisco, one of whom suffered from allergies, bound together to protect their land and small possessions.

While his uncles discussed the various attempts to resettle New Mexico, Baltasar heeded his father's warnings about ever returning. His uncles appeared to be gaining influence as governors came and went. That may have been the result of attrition. Almost two-thirds of the original colony had left. With the exception of a couple of linear cousins, all of the Gomez Robledos had left, and those who remained carried a different name from marriage. For that matter the Domínguez de Mendoza clan had abandoned the valley after their failed power grab. Uncle Bartolomé told him that the Domínguez de Mendozas had a reputation for thievery and confirmed that they hoarded iron. "*Ya se fueron,* now they are gone. It is best."

Baltasar, like his brother before him, grew taller than his father and uncles. He was athletic and strong. He became proficient with the bow and arrow. Even though the family elders taught him about firearms and he had his own horse, the family understood his value with, as they said, "those sticks and bare feet." Why waste valuable powder and balls on small game, when Baltasar's talent for bringing back rabbits and birds, especially ducks and geese, was more efficient. His reputation in this matter spread beyond the family. People talked about how well he supplemented the meager family tables to the point where his uncles counted on him. Baltasar had earned their respect. He was a hard, dependable worker who put food on the table.

One afternoon, as Baltasar, with his shirt off, poured water over his head to cool off, Felipe came to him to announce that Uncles Bartolomé and Francisco wanted to see him inside the house.

Uncle Francisco was not necessarily imposing but he did command respect. He was a thoughtful man who, while solidly built, looked his age, which was, in Baltasar's mind somewhere in his late fifties. He had a full head of wavy black and white hair, heavy eyebrows of the same color over deep-set eyes, an upturned nose, and a full beard of snarly gray hair. Normally a quiet man, the family listened when he spoke. His best friend and confidant was his brother Bartolomé who returned the sentiment. The two men worked in tandem and they appreciated Baltasar.

Now fifteen years old, Baltasar no longer felt like a child. In fact, that feeling ended with the episode over the plowshare. Yet, like all his cousins he deferred to his uncles, Bartolomé who he liked and Francisco who he respected.

He walked with his father to the house. He suspected nothing special. Maybe he would be asked to ride over to the mission on some errand. Felipe's small talk offered no hint. All his uncles and sisters, many of his cousins, and his two aunts greeted them as they entered the house. The old man stepped forward and held up a hand for quiet. "Ah, here he is. Because of him we eat less corn and mutton but more bird, including the chickens he raises. Because of him our stomachs are fuller than our neighbors," he stopped and looked around with raised eyebrows and smiled, "some too full." Small laughter filled the room.

"Here, Baltasar. Take these." Francisco held out what looked like rolled up cloth.

"What is it?"

His uncle handed it to him and replied, "Socks."

"Socks?"

"Yes, socks."

"But why? I don't have shoes."

"Yes, yes. We know. And we can't nail that plowshare to your foot and leave the other bare."

Baltasar had no words in reply. He merely looked at the bundle in his hands, then noted his father's approval.

"Listen, nephew. You and I are going to see Fernando Calderon, the leather worker. He is going to make you a fine pair of shoes, the kind that take spurs. He will also make you a pair of *botas*, leggings so that you don't cut yourself while riding. It is time. Besides, both will protect you from a surprised snake. How you have avoided them until now is beyond me."

Francisco was correct about the snakes. There were many at the river bottom. Nevertheless, the barefooted Baltasar never had a bad experience with them. He had developed an innate sense about the reptiles. In fact, his Piro friends had taught him that snakes were a deity as well as a source of food. Baltasar startled his family when he brought his first pair of snakes in to be skinned and cooked. The times had become so desperate they could not deny another source of food.

Baltasar's two younger brothers admired him. They saw Sebastián, the oldest brother, once or twice a year. He had become a distant, almost estranged family member.

Isabel, his other older sister had married Diego del Rio. They stayed with the family. She helped to raise the younger daughters, one of them living with her. In all, Baltasar felt comfortable and, tough times aside, happy.

A Funeral
August 1685, San Lorenzo del Paso

Another attack overtook Felipe. Jacinta depended on her sons to put him to bed. She could tell that he had caught the all-to-familiar disease, the flu, or *gripa* as they called it in New Mexico that was sweeping through the colony. She was not feeling too well herself. Late that night he awoke and asked for his weapons. Intuitively, Jacinta told him to get them himself. She watched as he rolled to one side, coughed, and turned his legs over the side of the bed, and tried to push himself upright. Instead, he coughed again and fell on the floor.

Jacinta shouted for help. All her children in the house came running. Together they lifted Felipe's dead weight back on to the bed. The next morning he stayed in bed struggling to breathe between guttural coughs and, then, spitting up some blood.

Using wet cloth to give him moisture, Jacinta stayed at his side. The children kept close by for any request. At nightfall, his breathing became slow but constant, the coughing less violent. As they lit candles for light, Felipe's breathing became more spaced. Twice it seemed to stop. The third time it did. Jacinta held his hand, waited, and then placed it on his chest as tears welled up in her eyes. Left with memories, she felt as if life had left her as well. She had no memory of the next few hours before the burial of her Felipe.

Jacinta could hear the wind howling outside as she squirmed in a new pair of shoes. Someone had sent them to her for the occasion. They were uncomfortable both because they did not fit and because she had become used to sandals or going bare-footed. Thoughts of her feet aside, she stared at the elongated lump laid out before the altar. Her husband lay there under a tightly wrapped blanket. The priest intoned, blessed, and looked solemn. Soldiers, dressed for an upcoming campaign, tolerated the proceedings. The crowd easily overflowed the small chapel.

None of that distracted Jacinta. The lump that vaguely silhouetted her husband, and the weakness overcoming her own body, had her attention. Jacinta cried as her children tried to console her. In fact, she hadn't stopped crying since Felipe's death earlier in day. The cause of his death necessitated that he be buried as quick as possible.

Then four pallbearers lifted him on a wooden litter and led by the priest, accompanied by a screeching violin and never-tuned guitar, they took the body out of the chapel to the *campo santo*, a distance of a hundred and twenty feet. They were accompanied by the women singing a high-pitched song that was grating to Jacinta.

Por las ánimas benditas (For the blessed souls)
Que en el purgatorio están... (who are in purgatory...)

207

Then,

Los ángeles en el cielo (The angels in heaven)
Alaban con alegría, (sing joyous praises,)
Y los hombres en la tierra (and men on earth)
Responden: !Ave María! (Reply, "Hail, Mary!")

The family men lowered Felipe into his grave. Everyone left except Jacinta, her grown children, and the men who filled the hole.

Just as they finished, small gusts of dry wind started up again. One of the heavily sweating men came up to Jacinta. "Your husband was a good man," he said. There was finality about his words. The burial work was finished and Felipe was consigned to history.

Jacinta stopped crying but she hardly spoke. For the next couple of weeks she mostly stayed in bed. She had no sisters or brothers, and Felipe's brothers and their wives were not close enough to help.

Outside of her small compound Baltasar's younger brother Juan was lost in his sorrow, concentrating so hard that his uncle Francisco startled him when he came up to him and spoke.

"Juan. Huh, oh sorry. Take my horse and go to my house to bring our wives here. Then go find the friar and bring him."

Juan's disposition changed to an open mouth and troubled look. His uncle's serious demeanor did not help.

"Your mother, Jacinta has gone to your father. Don't cry. Be a man. She died in her bed, peacefully. I found her. Your sister was in the next room, preparing food. She heard nothing and had just checked in on her. Your mother went to sleep. It was a *buen retiro*, that's it. Now go."

The family buried Jacinta beside Felipe.

ANOTHER NEW GOVERNOR
1691, San Lorenzo del Paso

Like his predecessors, the new governor arrived amidst a lot of local fanfare. He came with a lot of confidence and grand ideas. Baltasar had seen this before but this man was different. Now newly enlisted in the El Paso garrison, he sized up his new commander.

Diego de Vargas arrived in style, dressed in fashionable clothes, with lace and a three-quarter maroon overcoat lined with gold lace and matching tasseled pantaloons. Clearly, he was a propertied man, and, as the locals would learn, from a minor noble family in Madrid. The governor had served some posts in New Spain and had some experience in mining. His demeanor spoke of his status. Yet, he was not above acknowledging and speaking to the poor, desperate folk that he had come to govern. He was a little shorter than average height, maybe five feet, two inches tall, which made him seven inches shorter than Baltasar. He wore his hair long and parted on the side, had a clean-shaven face set off by a well-manicured thin moustache to match a small tuft under his mouth. He spoke with a lisp because of a small deformity on his upper lip, a lifelong handicap. The affliction added to his well-born aura.

Aside from his now distant memory of his father's *hacienda*, Baltasar knew no other life than the day-to-day existence in El Paso. He did what he could and had proved his worth. He witnessed the many departures of military expeditions under different governors. The first of these was the one his father and brother joined. The winter campaign. Then, how many more? Under governor Jironza, Baltasar could count at least four *entradas* into New Mexico, some of which, he heard, progressed as far as the first one under Otermín. None made it to Santa Fe. All met resistance, one result of which was the sacking and burning of various pueblos, some abandoned and others defended. The last two of these destroyed pueblos came under siege. The first by governor Reneros, who leveled Zia Pueblo and then, most recently, Santa Ana Pueblo that resisted Jironza's force from dusk to evening before submitting to annihilation.

The remaining New Mexicans whispered among themselves their concerns about these violent actions. Nor did the public executions of some of the Native leaders calm resistance.

Now, Diego de Vargas, the new governor, came to revive the colony's expectations. But more than that, he talked to people. First he asked about silver mines in New Mexico, and then talked about recruiting all the exiled New Mexicans. He noted the extreme poverty in which everyone lived and called them "deplorable conditions." They had no cattle and hardly any sheep. He boasted that he would improve things.

However, like his predecessors, the local Indians distracted him. He led two expeditions against the Suma and Manso tribes. In the first one he went west where he joined forces with troops from Parral to defeat a band of defiant Sumas. The second expedition went up river, through the pass to the Organ Mountains where he caught up with a band of Apaches and had a minor skirmish. He served notice that he would take war to the enemy.

Baltasar found the charismatic governor appealing. He was at the point of his life where subconsciously he sought a change. He never really thought it through. He just knew. Enlistment into the presidio corps was the solution.

His uncles reacted to his decision with approval. They knew he was not like his older brother. "Yes," they agreed, "it is time." So in the spring of 1691, Baltasar became a soldier under the command of Governor and Captain General Diego de Vargas. Now Baltasar had a salary and food, a horse, new weapons, and a new pair of boots. Of course, the boots and some of his other equipment were credited to his pay. No matter, he had a sense of excitement that he had not felt since his fantasized guard duty during the exodus. The routine of military life did little to abate it. He wondered what his brother would think, or if he knew.

The governor's request for fifty reinforcements from Janos and Parral had been accepted. The needed troops were on their way. Word spread through the ranks rapidly. Everyone figured out that the troops were supplied to help the governor retake New

Mexico. Then came the bugle call. Time to form up. An announcement was coming. Sebastián Rodríquez, the African crier who came with Vargas, announced that they would be leaving to retake New Mexico on Saturday, August 16. The men were to be ready and in formation at eight in the morning.

Because of the close proximity of the Romero homes, Baltasar breathlessly ran home, where he found the women but none of the men. Of course! The men had work to do in the middle of the day.

"Where's everyone?" He asked no one in particular but rather excitedly.

"Both of your *tíos* are down by the big cottonwood. They are planning for a new *acequia*, irrigation ditch."

Baltasar didn't wait for an explanation but ran the two hundred or so yards to the tree where, at first glance, he found everyone along with José, Diego, and a couple of elderly neighbors using sticks to draw in the dirt. Baltasar's rushed demeanor caught their attention.

"We are going to New Mexico! In a week. Reinforcements are coming."

The men, not nearly as excited, looked at one another then at Baltasar. One of the neighbors shrugged. Another spat, "So, another fruitless chase."

The immediate realization that he needed to curb his excitement overtook Baltasar. Given that he was sweating profusely and out-of-breath didn't help. His uncle Francisco, who had become hard of hearing, repeated Baltasar's words in the form of two questions.

Still excited, Baltasar answered, "Yes! That's right!"

"Good. Maybe this time..." Francisco did not finish.

Uncle Bartolomé reacted to the gleam in Baltasar's eyes. "So, finally, you will see New Mexico. The home of your father, our home, and our grandparents'. God willing, you will see the capital."

"You too! You can volunteer."

Bartolomé lit up and laughed. "Good one Baltasar. This will be a mission for the soldiers...plus some necessary volunteers, muleteers and carpenters." He nodded at the others, "We are more valuable here."

"But..."

"No, *hijo*, we will go after the army does its work. Our military campaigns are behind us."

The next few days dragged for Baltasar. He could not contain his anxiety. The expedition would be his first one. He prepared, checked, and rechecked his equipment. Dinner the night before the departure was glorious, not for the food that, as always, was sparse, but for the attention his family heaped on him. And the elders, his uncles and aunts told one story after the next about New Mexico.

"Oh, you will learn about the *jornada* soon enough. It begins at a place called Robledo and ends at a camping spot called Cristóbal or Fray Cristóbal. Both places are named for someone who died there. Aunt Ana is buried there, at Robledo."

"Yeah, even the *jornada* is called *'jornada del muerto,'* for a man who died on the trail. Uhuh," with raised eyebrows and an impish grin Bartolomé continued, "You are not a man until you have survived the..." he paused and lowered his voice... "*Jornada del mueeerto*. Right Francisco?" This was followed by some "Oooohs" and, then, laughter.

210

Francisco wiped his mouth with the back of his hand and continued. "Look for the pueblos with the same names as the ones here."

"Senecú, Socorro, Isleta...don't forget. And then you will come to the ruins of your father's old place. I wonder if it will bring back memories in you."

Baltasar smiled and listened. "How will I know?"

"It is after the Pueblo of Alamillo as I recall." Bartolomé looked at his brothers for help but they just stared at him while José nodded in agreement. He did not hear the comment. Francisco continued, "Some of the veteran officers will know. Roque Madrid and others who are New Mexicans. They will remember."

Francisco added. "And, oh, after your place is Las Barrancas that belonged to our cousin, Bartolomé Gómez Robledo. He was your father's best friend, the same age more or less. You remember him."

Bartolomé waved his hand for emphasis, "And, that is where the name Robledo comes from. Our common ancestor."

One of the women spoke up. "And, don't forget Tia Ana. Wasn't she a Gómez Robledo as well? *Que no?*"

"Yes, yes," the men answered in unison.

One thing led to the next. His relatives reminded him of the statue from Toledo and how their uncle and his family followed it south after the Franciscans took it. They talked more about the uprising and returned to various landmarks on the trail. "Once you get to Las Barrancas look up river to the right side for mountains. You will see the beginning of them at you father's place, plus the trail through the pass to the pueblos that harvested salt, Los Humanos. From Las Barrancas follow the mountains north and you will see Sandía Mountain for the first time. Santa Fe is north and just behind it."

Baltasar could not help but ask. "Sandía? That's an odd name for a mountain."

"Why? I don't know. Maybe 'cause it looks like a slice a watermelon. I don't know."

"Come on Francisco." Bartolomé chided his brother. "Because it looks like a slice of watermelon at some sunsets when its face turns red."

Francisco tisked. "Old wives tales." Then he continued, "Beyond the Sandía you will pass a mountain to your left. Follow the river to a rise of lava rock. Once you get on top, you will see more mountains. Santa Fe is at their base. Or, that is where it was."

"It probably still is."

"Not without us. And, who knows, it probably has been destroyed and abandoned."

Baltasar had a restless night. He and the family rose early and walked to the parade grounds. He let his younger brothers take turns leading his saddled horse. A festive atmosphere gave levity to an otherwise gloomy existence.

Baltasar and the other soldiers milled about talking until Vargas strode out of his quarters followed by a covey of officers. The governor stood before them and in a clear voice handicapped by his harelip, announced that a contingent of fifty presidio troops from the Parral district that included Janos, inexplicably had not arrived. "Nonetheless, we have waited long enough. I have ordered that an advance group under the command of Captain Roque de Madrid to advance with the wagons as far as the place called Thalenita, north of the pass into New Mexico." Then he announced: "I will wait here for the extra troops."

With this he ordered his officers to take over and see to it. They read out the names of fifty soldiers and ten civilian volunteers. Baltasar's name was not listed. Then, he was assigned to spend the rest of the day leading double-teamed wagons filled with supplies onto rafts, and manning the ropes that pulled them across the river. The work did not finish until after dusk and it was all that the exhausted, slightly disappointed Baltasar could do but to walk to his bed and collapse.

Baltasar's anxiety faded. He kept himself ready to leave at a moment's notice. He learned that he would be part of the governor's contingent but nothing was mentioned about a departure date. They waited for the reinforcements but he could tell that they were not anywhere close because word of their whereabouts would precede them by days. How long would they wait? That was the question on everyone's minds.

The time gave Baltasar a chance to question his uncles for more details, which, after a while, became repetitive. Only a few short-lived morsels of new information surfaced from their distant memories, the mountain streams up there yield tasty trout, even in the Rio del Norte! Or, the ground is more fertile and the climate better for fruit.

Baltasar asked about the Natives. The answer came quickly, *"Quién sabe.* A lot has happened since we left. The Apaches won't change—that's for sure."

Then Baltasar openly wondered about Sebastián. No one had heard from him in over a year, or was it two? "Maybe he'll be with the reinforcements. The governor has offered special rewards for returning New Mexicans. Maybe we will go north together."

The men shrugged and nodded. "That would be nice," they seemed to say.

Like most days in El Paso, the fifth day dawned hot and cloudless. It was Thursday, August 21. Word came. Time to form up in the *plaza de armas.* Be there at mid-afternoon. The whole community woke up. Activity buzzed and, like a current, slowly and then more rapidly moved toward the parade grounds. There, at the appointed time, Baltasar and the remnants of the Presidio troop waited mounted on fresh horses provided by the governor. With pack animals milling around behind them the noise most noticeable to Baltasar was the quiet flap, flap of the banners, as the three of them mildly waved in the light breeze. They watched as the bugler put his horn to his lips and blew a fanfare to the roll of the drum.

Vargas, dressed for a campaign, except for a telltale oversized plume feather in his hat, strode up to his horse and mounted without breaking stride. He turned toward the troops and spoke. "Men, companions. Destiny is at hand...and cannot be lost. We can wait for reinforcements who already are three weeks late and loose the opportunity of good weather and a goodly amount of supplies, which, God willing, are approaching the *paraje* called Robledo. Or," he stressed the "or" with a pause and visual survey of his men, "we can call upon the grace of God to fulfill the will of Our Majesty, May God keep him, and achieve what has been illusive these last dozen years."

Baltasar had no doubt that the mounted men around him had the same surge of confidence. One of the captains yelled out, *"Si, señor. Vámonos! A Nuevo México!"*

And the troops answered in unison, *"Si señor!"*

Vargas stood in his saddle and with clenched fist in the air yelled, *"Entonces, adelante valientes,"* "Then, forward valiant ones!" With that he nodded to the bugler and drummer who started up again. Vargas led the column of men into the river for their first

212

crossing on the way north. The notes of the bugle and roll of the drum gave way to the clopping and whinnying of the horses. They rode north along the river's east bank for five leagues, around thirteen miles, where after nightfall they set up camp at a place north of the pass called Ancón de Fray García.

It had been twelve years since Baltasar had seen anything north of the pass. Then he was a seven-year-old youth traveling south with a large band somewhat in disarray. He didn't remember much of the panorama through which he passed. Maybe the landscape looked different because he was a foot-and-a-half taller and perched on a horse. This time he studied the north as he moved into it.

As the sun rose the next morning he stared at the Organ Mountains, gray and black silhouetted against the morning's sun. With the jagged peaks, over twenty of them he thought, reaching for heaven, Baltasar easily understood why they were named for the instrument.

After a full day's ride they caught up with Roque Madrid's advance wagons just as the sun dropped behind a lone cloud on the western horizon. They were at Robledo and, now a full contingent of fifty soldiers, their officers, ten armed civilians, and a hundred Indian allies, Vargas was ready to lead the re-conquest of New Mexico. The men talked very little of reinforcements as they all concentrated on where they planned to go. Their immediate task would be to complete the ninety-mile Jornada that waited just over a northern rise.

A large rainstorm struck their first night out. The water drenched them and filled all the otherwise paltry waterholes along the way. Then on their third day in the desert an overcast sky and a nice cool breeze out of the north greeted them. They crossed the Jornada in a leisurely four days, or an average of a little more than twenty-two miles per day.

Baltasar marveled at their rapid progress. He tried to reach back in his memory to reacquaint himself with each site along the way. The vagueness of the abandoned and charred southern pueblos of Senecú, Socorro, Sevilleta, and Alamillo stirred his curiosity. However, it was not until they rode past the last of those pueblos onto a vast flat river bottom and then a clearing that a nerve was struck. Baltasar immediately recognized the place of his birth and youth. The pasture, the ruins of the buildings brought his memories to life.

Like many expeditions and caravans before him, Vargas ordered a halt on the good pasturelands. Here was a place to camp and rest the livestock. Vargas announced to no one in particular that, "it is said that this place belonged to Felipe Romero." He didn't know that the very man's son was among his contingent.

Baltasar knew. When word of Vargas's comment came to him, he could not contain himself. "That's my father!" But he got little reaction. Everyone was busy with his or her routine. "No, sí! Felipe Romero is my father! This was our home!"

At this, an older soldier looked up and squinted at him. "Married to Jacinta? You're his son. *No es posible.* You are too young. His son was a man when we left this place."

Now some others had started listening. They anticipated the possibility of a good argument or even an opportunity for some good-natured hazing as some of them knew Baltasar. But Baltasar was serious and knew what he was talking about. "You are thinking of my brother Sebastián. I was born here. My mother had pigs. I tell you what...I will give you a tour later."

Four of them took him up on the offer and an hour later they walked through the ruins. Baltasar talked. "We had a rock wall and there is the main house with three rooms. Over there is where Diego Romero and his family lived." Baltasar turned to the elderly man who had challenged him earlier. "You may remember him. He worked for my father. His father was called Jola but his real name was Alonso. Jolá changed his last name to Romero because he liked my father so much. I think he was a Cadimo or Colina originally. The old man died a few years before the revolt. Look! This is where the bathhouse was."

Bathhouse?" This got everyone's attention.

"Yeah. My mother poured water over hot rocks to make us sweat. Then she had us wipe ourselves with a damp towel. She said it cleansed our skin. Who knows? See? Right here this was it." He pointed at a depression for the fire pit inside base of what would have been a small square enclosure.

The rest of the trip was somewhat of a blur. Like all youth he wanted to test if not prove his manhood. But Vargas had other ideas. The governor negotiated. Baltasar didn't know what to think about not engaging the rebellious Pueblo Indians in battle.

Rather than tease or harass the first-timers like Baltasar, the veterans tried to share their experiences. At one time a sergeant warmed up to Baltasar because both had survived the revolt. Time had blurred the significance, if any, of whether the person was in the Rio Abajo or Rio Arriba when hostilities broke out.

The sergeant began to explain the importance of horses saying, "Without them we are dead." He went on to state that the enemy always wants to destroy or scatter the horse herd during the night while everyone slept. He concluded that a soldier's most important assignment was to protect and guard the horses. To this admonition Baltasar reacted without hesitation, "My father did that for Otermín..."

"Otermín?" The sarcastic question shot back at Baltasar. The sergeant spit. "Who is your father?"

"I thought you knew."

"No."

"Felipe Romero."

"Yes, you have his narrow face. I knew him. He was good. We were together that winter, bitter winter. Otermín..." the sergeant stopped and looked at the ground and then turned his ruddy, full-bearded face toward Baltasar, "Never mind. Just say it wasn't like this. Thanks be to God." No it wasn't the same. Otermín's foray into the winter snows did not compare to this current expedition of the late summer. Baltasar especially enjoyed sleeping under the open sided tents. He felt more comfortable than in his house in El Paso.

Baltasar could not figure out Vargas. The aloof governor nonetheless shared a connection with his men. He seemed to have some kind of power, an appealing self-confidence. He depended more on words than war. At times Baltasar joined with his comrades in their impatience with the man as he talked and waited, talked and waited. Then he would make some gesture like he did at Santa Fe. As if with some preconceived notion, he dressed up in his finest formal suits and walked unarmed into the enemy's midst to secure peace. He first did this at the fortress of Santa Fe then proceeded to follow suit with variations at one pueblo after the next.

The reinforcements from Jano and Parral finally caught up with the main body at Santa Fe. Baltasar thought that the sight of so many new soldiers helped Vargas in his negotiations, for now water into the fortress was cut off and the place was surrounded. The reinforcements and Vargas's patient negotiations gave Baltasar time to visit the ranks of the recent arrivals. He asked about his brother and learned that he was not among them. In fact, only a couple men claimed that they even heard of him. They proffered theories that he might have gone to Sonora or gravitated south into New Spain. No one could say for sure that they really knew him.

Sebastián had disappeared, apparently forsaking his family. Baltasar would carry the effect of this mystery with him for the rest of his life.

Baltasar followed Vargas throughout New Mexico. He visited every pueblo of any significance. Vargas led his men from Pecos to Taos and back south again to visit Jemez then west to Zuni and the Hopi Pueblos. Baltasar saw the whole kingdom.

While traveling to and from western Pueblos the trail took them by El Tanque where they camped by the permanent pond at the base of a cliff. The place had become a much used and popular camping stop and the inscriptions carved in the cliff's side fascinated the men. Vargas became impressed enough that he decided to carve his own name into the rock for posterity. Yet, it took another person to draw Baltasar's attention to one carving. "Hey, Baltasar, look! Here's a Romero! Is he one of yours?"

Baltasar shrugged. "I don't know. What does it say?"

The other person ignored him as he studied the name and slowly made out "Bartolomé López Romero." He turned to Baltasar and asked, "Sound familiar?"

"No. A little." Baltasar had no way of knowing that the man's name in the rock belonged to the brother of his grandfather, his great uncle. While he never forgot the name, he never learned more about him.

An Anxious Interlude
Summer of 1693, San Lorenzo del Paso

After four months in the saddle, Baltasar returned home with a greater geographical knowledge of New Mexico than anyone in his family. He regaled them with stories and descriptions. Uncle Francisco thought that there was a López somewhere among their distant *antepasados* but could not be sure. José was curious about Socorro Pueblo wondering, "Does it still exist?"

His uncles had purpose behind their questions. Everyone knew that Vargas had made it to Santa Fe, and then visited all the pueblos. Miraculously, it seemed, he had secured a peace and negotiated a resettlement of New Mexico. The governor announced to everyone that they should be ready to leave for the north the following summer. Then he headed south to arrange for supplies and recruit more settlers. The community buzzed with the often-repeated question, "Hey, are you going?"

Baltasar's uncles did not take long to volunteer themselves and their families.

Baltasar did not have the same luxury. As a presidio soldier he had to do as told. Given his experience with Vargas the previous year, Baltasar assumed that he would be going north again. After all, Vargas asked for volunteers both to go and to stay. This time Baltasar would travel with his family.

Fate, though, had a surprise for Baltasar. It began with his uncles, who in their enthusiasm for the upcoming venture observed that someone should stay in El Paso to maintain their properties, "just in case." José noted that he did not plan to leave Isleta but the uncles insisted on someone else staying. Baltasar had no doubt about whom that would be. "Staying can be a good thing," Francisco said, as he tried to encourage Baltasar. "No. Listen. You are young with life ahead of you. You will get our properties. Remember, everything we own here will become yours. What was originally for three families is now yours as one."

Not convinced, Baltasar began to protest, "I am a soldier. I have no time..."

"You will. You will figure it out."

Francisco had been favoring his best ear to hear the conversation, added, "Your father was sent to the southern *hacienda* when he was younger than you. Do you know why?"

Baltasar meekly answered, "The land?"

"Huh? The land? No! He was part of grand plan for family business. Trading on the *Camino*! Farming was necessary, yes, but it complemented the business."

Baltasar had never heard this before, nor had he thought about it. Francisco continued, "and one of our last plans, was to place someone in El Paso. Yes! Here! Another warehouse to transport goods and exchange livestock. Your father went off on his own and learned. You will too. Think about it. Fate has brought you here."

"Are you telling me that you want to set up the same system?" Baltasar had to ask.

Francisco quickly answered. "No! No. Who knows? Things have changed but we must keep our options open. We cannot predict. We may even be back here." He threw up his hands and dropped them palms down on the table. "Only God knows. Say we stay in New Mexico but life is so different that trade is out of the question. Still we stay."

Less animated, Baltasar's uncle Bartolomé added, "What's so bad for you? Huh?"

"That I'm here." Baltasar stuck his chin on his chest.

"Come on!" Francisco had not been so animated in a long time. "You are young. Not even married. You have a soldier's salary, three houses, such as they are, and property."

"Plus family," Bartolomé added.

Bartolomé added, "Baltasar, you have a life changing opportunity here and, who knows, you still can decide to move north. Soldiering does not have to be a lifetime proposition."

This was an odd moment for Baltasar. He remembered his father's recriminations about returning to New Mexico. Now, he took a walk to clear his mind. He never felt this way before, a kind of dejection. This was a life-changing moment. Yet, he would do as they wanted.

The next morning he went to the headquarters office and explained the situation. There was no objection. A squadron was needed to man the presidio in El Paso. Then, he was told that he would have to assist in the preparations, and help get the wagons across the river. The thought of it depressed Baltasar.

Everyone expected the governor to return from his recruiting trip in Zacatecas before summer or at the latest in July. They remembered the previous year when Vargas wanted to leave in July and was badly delayed waiting for reinforcements. When June passed into July and Vargas still hadn't shown up, people began to doubt whether there would be an expedition at all. People started to question the validity of his "peaceful conquest," and doubted that the Indians really wanted them to return, much less welcome them. Baltasar worried about a late departure. A colony with women and children could not move as fast as a well-mounted army. They needed to leave soon to avoid the winter weather up north. Many of the people knew from bitter experience how that could be.

Baltasar assured his family and friends that he had witnessed the peaceful conquest. It was true that Vargas met with Pueblo leaders and that many had accepted baptism. Vargas, himself, stood as godfather for hundreds of the converts. Baltasar granted that he was not experienced enough to judge whether the Natives would be true to their word or whether they were buying time to mount a resistance.

July turned into August that, in turn, gave way to September. Still no Vargas. An occasional arrival of livestock and wagons loaded with supplies gave evidence of his activities in the south. Still, time was of the essence. September was perilously late to begin the *entrada*. Many of the people became discouraged.

Then in the middle of September Vargas arrived leading a caravan of wagons, supplies, and families. He immediately sent word out for the volunteers in the El Paso region to get themselves ready quickly for the trip north. After a two-day rest, he ordered the southern contingent to continue their journey north, and to wait at the vacated pueblo of Socorro. They left on September 20th. Baltasar helped with the river crossing with a heavy heart. He held a distant hope that his brother, Sebastian, might be with the people Vargas brought but no one even heard of him. Exactly two weeks later the El Paso contingent began its venture north.

A PARTING OF WAYS
October 4, 1693, San Lorenzo del Paso

Over fifty families, another one hundred soldiers, a hundred plus Indian allies, thirteen blue-clad Franciscans, a dozen or so wagons, plus two cannons and a mortar, began the difficult task of crossing the river to head north.

Baltasar reported to duty to help get everything and everyone safely across the river. He worked three days driving livestock, escorting double-teamed wagons, assisting people, and transporting supplies through and over the current. All of his family had crossed by mid afternoon on the first day. He gave them all hugs, even the little ones and especially his younger brothers and sisters who were not so little any more. He also said goodbye to Diego and his family, who had made their decision to go.

Uncle Bartolomé said, "Take care of the property Baltasar, we may be back."

"Of course. I will."

"We'll see you soon."

"I know, I know."

They parted and Baltasar returned across the river to continue helping others. By the time he climbed up the far bank he could not make his family out through the dust, afternoon's glare, and movement.

By the end of the third day the work was complete. The last vestiges of the colony had crossed the river and headed north. Those who remained behind hardly spoke. Not since the exodus thirteen years earlier had so many people congregated in El Paso. Now, not since before the exodus had there been so few in the area. The many empty small adobe structures added their silence to the barren land.

They would fend for themselves. With fewer people they had a better chance to feed themselves. Yet, there would be adjustments, and who knew what news would come out of the north. This was a time that tried one's patience.

Baltasar immediately confronted his situation. He had a home and two empty houses with their respective fields. The harvest was in and he was by himself. Still, there was work to do and he needed help. First he asked an elderly widow if she would cook and clean for him. Then, because he knew her family, he invited her son and his family to move into one of the empty houses. They had the place rent-free if the widow's son, his brother, and oldest son worked the land. In addition, Baltasar agreed that they would receive a percentage of the harvest, beginning with the one in storage. All newborn chickens, goats, and pigs would be divided equally.

Next, he sought out a second family and offered them the same terms for the last house. The two families amounted to six healthy adult men, all capable workers. The two wives worked with the widow and some of the older daughters to share their tasks. Baltasar, in effect, had a new family. More importantly, he was becoming an *empresario*, running what amounted to a small *hacienda*. He never felt closer to his father.

He enjoyed being with the men. Their lifestyle and conversation was pretty much what he grew up with his whole life, especially with Jola's family. But they were gone too. At some point before the spring planting he would choose a foreman to help run things when military duties called him away from home.

Yet, at every opportunity he worked on the lands. It turned out one February day, when the men where sharpening and preparing tools, that Baltasar told them the story of his confrontation over his father's plowshare. The guys enjoyed the tale but marveled over the risk he had taken. He explained that his father had given him that particular share. He looked around and spotted it. Pointing, he exclaimed, "There it is! That one. I can spot it anytime."

The plowshare lay on a bench so Baltasar walked over to it and picked it up. "Look at this. It is worth its weight in gold, maybe more. Gold is too soft to cut the earth or pretty much anything else." He held up the plowshare. "This, this makes ready the earth to receive the seeds that bring us food."

The men listened attentively as Baltasar pulled a coin from his pocket. At this, many of guys stared harder, for they had never seen one, rare as they were. "Yes, a coin. Can you eat it? No. Can you make a tool out of it? Perhaps. Yes, you can trade it for a tool or seed. But, when you have the plowshare already...?" He left the question unanswered. "We grow what we can to feed ourselves. Next to water and seed, nothing is more valuable than a plowshare."

He knew that he had given a myopic view, but he wanted to impress upon the men the value of their work. He wanted to give them a sense of pride in working the fields. He felt that his father had done the same for him.

SURVIVAL AND A FAMILY
1694, San Lorenzo del Paso

The winter of 1693–1694 was especially cold, so Baltasar was not surprised to see the return of some of people who went to north. They complained that the colony had left too late, and that the further north they went, the colder it became. They then conveyed even more discouraging news. The pueblos were abandoned except for the very one they expected to occupy. Instead, Santa Fe had been fortified and the occupants showed no signs of leaving.

The official reports painted a dire picture. The Natives in Santa Fe were in defiance of the colony. True to form, Vargas had set up camp outside the town and once again sought to negotiate a solution.

Like everyone else in El Paso, Baltasar anxiously waited for every report. Initially, he heard nothing about his family. No messages had been sent. He was pleased that none of his relatives had deserted. Then came the bittersweet news that Santa Fe had not been abandoned and was attacked after twenty-two youths had succumbed to exposure while the governor negotiated. After a two-day battle, the town was occupied. Then, Vargas ordered the execution of many of the male defenders. What this news meant was anyone's guess in El Paso.

The weather then took its toll. Aside from the deaths of the youth, news came that Baltasar's uncle Bartolomé caught an infection that lingered and, finally, in late February, turned to pneumonia, which killed him as he struggled to breathe.

As the weather warmed and spring matured, Baltasar focused on his lands. He worked shoulder to shoulder with his workers, cleaning the irrigation ditches, cutting minor waterways into the fields, plowing, planting, the work never ended. Everyone pitched in, because they had to be self-sufficient. They truly provided for themselves.

Eventually, the stream of deserters returning from the north stopped. Baltasar thought that he might be called upon to escort additional supplies to the new colony. Instead, he was kept on call for the defense of the El Paso communities. The people kept on edge for fear of a surprise attack because of their reduced numbers. Fortunately, even the local Natives seemed mesmerized by the attempted resettlement. Despite the obvious anxiety, calm prevailed.

Perhaps sensing that he needed someone around him, or maybe because the environment dictated it, Baltasar became infatuated with, and quickly married María Francisca Montoya, who was a fellow refugee from New Mexico. He appreciated her broad shoulders, ready smile, and determined looks. Baltasar welcomed her into the household and she more than fulfilled his expectations. She took charge. Her youth and energy enlivened the whole place. Baltasar affectionately called her Marifran, combining her two names. When formal he called her Francisca. In the spring of 1694 she gave birth to their first child, a girl who they named Jacinta after Baltasar's mother.

Now, Baltasar really felt a renewed sense of responsibility that he likened, as he always did, to what it must have been like for his own parents. He could now concentrate on his life and that of his family. He continued in the military for its regular pay, which, after all, nicely supplemented what his properties could produce. It seemed that as long as the weather cooperated, an uncertain proposition at best, his properties had a chance of improving their production each year.

In the following year, 1695, Vargas's officer in charge, Juan Paez Hurtado, passed through El Paso on his way to Zacatecas and Mexico City to recruit more colonists for New Mexico. He retraced Vargas's earlier recruitment efforts, and returned with a modest and not very promising number of people. Baltasar was not surprised at the result because Vargas's so-called peaceful resettlement had devolved into a continuous war. Hearing some of the details made even Baltasar hesitant to volunteer, especially with a young family. He worried for his northern brethren. He constantly sent word north asking about their wellbeing. He would not have been surprised to hear of some untimely deaths or even that they planned to move back to El Paso.

His concern about the colony heightened when he heard that they suffered another bitter winter followed by a pestilence. Many had died. Then, word came that a second revolt erupted in June. Again, people were killed, including some friars.

Continued Vigilance
1696, El Paso del Norte

During this time Baltasar participated on a couple of minor expeditions, but saw no military action. He spent most of his military time helping to construct a true presidio and improving the *plaza de armas*. His labor continued at home where he and his workers continued to improve and expand their homes. In fact, the whole El Paso area had begun to change from a haphazard, unplanned village to a permanent town. In comparison to the north, El Paso was doing well.

In 1697, Baltasar formed up with his fellow soldiers to give a proper military welcome to Vargas's replacement, a big-boned, crimsoned-faced man who had nothing good to say about his predecessor. In fact, he sought to belittle Vargas and, as it turned out, successfully put him under house arrest, and then prohibited any correspondence with him. It would not be long, Baltasar thought, before Vargas's friends in Madrid would put an end to the ex-governor's shabby treatment.

He was mistaken in one respect because Vargas remained under arrest in Santa Fe for almost three years before officials in Mexico City ordered that he be allowed to answer the charges brought against him in Mexico City. So, in July of 1700, Baltasar and most everyone else living in the El Paso area silently received Vargas's entourage as it crossed the river. The fanfare that El Paso gave Vargas many years before was a distant memory.

No one really spent much time pondering the significance of Vargas's arrest. The immediate task of day to day living had priority. In late 1698, Marifran announced that she was pregnant with a second child. It had been five years since the birth of Jacinta and the news overwhelmed Baltasar. In his mind, and probably Francisca's as well, another child was overdue. He thanked God and marveled, "Another child!" He secretly fantasized that it would be a boy. His son. However, it was not to be. Eight months later in the late spring of 1699, María Francisca gave birth to another girl who they named Tomasa Ignacia.

Presidio responsibilities cut short Baltasar's time with his new daughter. He received verbal orders to prepare himself to escort a supply caravan to the northern settlements. This gave him pause for thought. He was infinitely curious about those settlements, but he had also become comfortable with his home routine. He had no choice but to go, so he said his goodbyes, sadly leaving Francisca with a five-year-old girl and an infant. He assured them that he would be back before Christmas, "God willing."

Naturally enough, he was anxious but, in truth, did not resent the assignment. He would see his siblings. And, for once, he would see for himself the progress of the colony.

The trip was tedious, much slower than the military expeditions he had been on. At its best, escort duty was boring. Traveling over terrain that barely qualified as a road with heavily laden wagons pulled by oxen, hardly qualified as exciting. Yet, the much-needed supplies were crucial for the desperate people up north.

Fortunately, the trip's monotony was not disrupted by an Apache attack, an over-abundance of broken axles, broken wheels, or any number of impediments. Despite the dry heat they crossed the dreaded Jornada del Muerto under cloudless skies and without incident.

While on the Jornada, Baltasar gladly accepted the assignment to join five men, each with an extra horse, to ride through a gap in the western mountain ridge, where they reached the Rio del Norte and filled up leather water bags to take back to the thirsty caravan. Further north, he found that the ruins of his childhood home and then Las Barrancas virtually disappeared. Only the remnants of some fruit trees and odd ground cover over the pastures marked the places.

Santa Fe had changed. First, he reunited with his family members as well as uncle Francisco, who had been appointed to his old post as Santa Fe's alcalde. They traded family stories, the birth of children, marriages and deaths, and who had or had not changed. While they wanted to hear more about El Paso, Baltasar continuously directed the conversations to Santa Fe and their lives.

Everyone agreed that for the first three or four years they had been virtual prisoners in the capital. It took that long to quell the hostile Indian resistance. With the violence apparently under control, they talked among themselves about moving out of Santa Fe where they could settle on some good land and fend for their families.

This gave rise to Baltasar's inquiry about re-establishing the old family business, which was met with a resounding "no." "That was then, things have changed and are not given to such a venture now." Instead they all needed to survive, become farmers and ranchers.

Baltasar, naturally enough, then asked why they did not return to El Paso. They uniformly answered that returning would be the same, "starting over." "And," old, deaf, but wise Francisco nodded, "the land is more abundant and rich here." They then turned the question on its head by suggesting that Baltasar move north. They pointed to the land below San Felipe Pueblo, or maybe near the abandoned Sandia or Alameda Pueblos. "Study the area upon your return to El Paso. The Duran y Chaves clan already claimed some land and has begun an 'operation.' He calls his place Bernalillo."

In the minds of Baltasar's uncles they would either move there or go to a little river valley about twenty miles north of Santa Fe. Francisco reminded Baltasar that it was the place where his brother Pedro was killed.

Thus informed, Baltasar made a point of talking with the people who had settled by the abandoned Sandía Pueblo. He introduced himself to Don Fernando Duran y Chaves and was surprised to learn that they had moved there three years earlier, over the governor's objections. Don Fernando, a rather gruff man, treated Baltasar with courtesy. He appeared older than his age and asked Baltasar who were his uncles and his father. The older man realized that the relatively tall, slender soldier with the inquiring mind came from an old, respected New Mexican family. "In fact," he growled with a slight twinkle in his eye, "if we dig deep enough we are probably related." That was a thought that never crossed Baltasar's mind. Don Fernando smiled and coughed out a laugh showing some well-worn, yellowed teeth. "So, El Paso, huh? You didn't come back. Why? I know. Duty. But now...well, *bien*, good. I can tell from your interest. If you should decide to come back, look for me, that is if I am still upright. I know your uncle Francisco well," he gave a knowing nod, "kindred spirits you know."

Baltasar left Bernalillo pleased. His mind spun with many old thoughts colliding with the new information he heard. Should he continue with his relatively good life in El Paso or move north? What about his property? Or, how would Marifran react to such a change? No, he made up his mind. El Paso was his future, not the north. As promised, he was home by Christmas.

A Turn of Events and Grief
1702, El Paso del Norte

Baltasar could not refrain from bringing up the idea of moving. Much to his surprise, Marifran enthusiastically thought it was a good idea. She almost could not contain herself in support of the move. "But, Marifran, there is much to do and discuss. The property. Our employees."

"Oh, Balti, don't make it sound so difficult. My family is in Santa Fe. I will see them again. As for the rest, well, you will handle that. You are good at that."

They agreed that the time had come to leave El Paso. They had a settled future but they wanted to seek a new life up north. The certainty of an improved life exhilarated Baltasar. He felt reborn. The move's process proved to be no challenge. He met with the families who had moved into the Romero houses and worked the land. These were his friends and, of course, they accepted the news without hesitation. Their acceptance turned into undiminished gratitude when he announced, with a self-pleased smile, that he wanted to give them all the property in exchange for two things. He would take some but not all of the livestock with him, and that they agree to send him a percentage of the annual harvest in the annual caravan. This last request ensured him of a quantity of foodstuff that would be beneficial to him for the first few years, or until he could get established.

The caravan had formed, and Baltasar, like his ancestors before him sat upright and proud on his mount. Almost simultaneous with the order to move out, whips snapped along with the colorful language of the oxen drivers that woke up the doleful animals to begin their labor. Baltasar had the usual task of ferrying the wagons across the river and helping the few women and children who accompanied their men for the move north to New Mexico. Only this time, Baltasar did not return to El Paso when his work was finished. This time, he turned his mount toward the barren pass up river to join his family for the journey north.

He had no doubts or trepidations, only a sense of exhilaration. The past, with its turmoil, struggles, and death, faded behind him both figuratively and literally as he rode away. And while the past became distant, Baltasar faced an unclear future with renewed confidence, and even delight.

At night he regaled his wife and daughters with stories of his experiences on the trail. As best he could, he recalled the tales behind the place names: Robledo, El Alemán, Perrillo Spring, Fray Cristóbal. "See," he told them as they approached the mesa called Contadera, the place where livestock was counted, "look back and you will see the good friar Cristóbal lying in repose." He pointed to the outline of the northern edge of the ridge that they had passed the day before.

Baltasar had travelled the road more than once and the fact of its familiarity shortened the journey. There were no fresh sights to distract him. His own conversation borne out of his desire to share what he knew of the trail, while not particularly engrossing, shrunk the trip even more for him.

They came upon the old hacienda, now called "*La vuelta de los Romeros*." Why *La vuelta*? No one knew, but it initiated a pro-longed discussion about his earliest memories and his parents.

The trip ended for Baltasar and his family at Bernalillo. Don Fernando greeted him with the same yellow-toothed smile, and said, "So you decided to return home." He watched as a couple of wagons, some horses, and about twenty head of trail-lean cattle were separated from the caravan. "And you come with a dowry. Good. Welcome to Bernalillo. Are your cows branded?"

"Yes, with a stylized 's' over a 'b.'"

"Good, mix them with ours. You will find an abandoned house up river a half a league. Go ahead and move in. Improve it, as you will. As for the horses, they are invaluable and prime targets for the raiders. Watch them carefully."

Later that afternoon, after they had been nourished with mint tea and bread, everyone stood as Baltasar and his family took their leave. "Oh, by the way." Don Fernando noted, "take care of your wife. She is *en camino*."

Not thinking Baltasar answered. "To Santa Fe? No, she is staying with me." Baltasar thought that the old man was suggesting that she would continue to the capital to reunite with her mother, sister, and brother.

Don Fernando broke into a wry smile. "No, Don Baltasar, she is with child."

An astounded Baltasar quickly reacted. "What? How do you know?"

"I am old and have been around. People tell me things. Take care. We need more Nuevo Mexicanos."

When confronted, Francisca demurely answered, "But, Balti, I did not want to concern you. Now, we are here and we can make a home."

Baltasar heeded the old man's words. He wasted no time moving into the abandoned two-room adobe house. He went to work, putting a new roof and a wooden hinged doorway on the place. He butchered one of his cattle, dried the meat, and covered the windows with its hide. Constructing his horse corral took a little longer. Thanks to Don Fernando who invited him to stable the horses in his corral, Baltasar did not have to hobble his stock to keep them from strolling away.

Maybe it was the trip, or the pregnancy, or, perhaps, the anxiety of it all. Most likely, the combination of everything. There were no words. Just shock. And the high winds added to the despair. Marifran just collapsed, fell on to the dirt floor. She shivered and stopped with her mouth open as if gasping for air with her eyes half shut staring into nothing. It happened in a matter of seconds, even before anyone around her could get to her. Marifran and her unborn child had died.

Baltasar didn't witness María Francisca's death but was close by working on the corral. He heard the yells and rushed to the house too late. The women and children cried as they aimlessly stood around. Baltasar went to her and rolled her on her back. He closed her mouth and silently called to her. He knew she heard as well as he realized there would be no answer. He lifted her up and took her to their bed, where he said a prayer. Then, he came out and calmly issued instructions to some of Fernando's workers who had been loaned to him. "Consuelo, fetch the priest. Rosa, take charge of the body." And, gesturing to another, "You get some of the elders to help. Put her best dress on her, the baby blue one. No, not the yellow. Blue is the blessed Virgin's color and she is with her now."

Baltasar never remembered that he picked her up and laid her in bed, nor did he remember much of anything else he did at that moment. He recalls that he left the house, going his own way, silently, without reference to anyone, to the river where he found a spot and sat on his haunches staring at the sun's reflection off the current's ripples. Little Jacinta followed him and watched until she could stand it no more. She walked up to her father and hugged him, which he gladly received and returned.

For the next couple of months he seemed to be going through the motions. He withdrew into himself, and all the people around him watched for any hint of normality. His personality had changed, became subdued. In reality, María Francisca's death resurrected his past years' thoughts about moving north. He felt at fault for her death. The passing of his parents and now Maria Francisca's death faded one into the other. He internally cursed his plight.

A parade of people offered condolences, a ritual of sorts that he thought would never end. They continued to stop by with pastries, tortillas, and pots of beans with chile.

As he tried to distance himself from his wife's death, survival dominated his thoughts. Once again, he needed a change. Place and time dictated a change, for aside from his daughters he had no other familial obligations.

As a still young and vibrant man, albeit a single father, he realized that he needed some immediate help with the household. Unlike his earlier experience and that of his siblings, he could not count on his aunts and uncles. They either lived in Santa Fe or distant El Paso. Nor did Baltasar think it proper to burden his cousins, for they had their own children.

He recruited a few people to help with his property. Their children became friends with his. "Still," he thought and felt, "something more is needed." It did not take long for him to find an answer. One woman in particular always asked for the children and seemed less concerned about him. Even at mass on Sunday she sought him out.

"*Hola, como está?*" "Hello, how are you?"

"Fine, thank you. And you?"

"Good. And Jacinta and Tomasa? How are they?"

"They are good but very active."

"Where are they?"

"At home." Baltasar knew this was not the right answer and pawed the ground.

"But Don Baltasar, they should be here."

He knew that she would say that and still did not have an answer. He had not given a thought about bringing the children to mass. Why would he? When he was their age, mass every Sunday was out of the question. The closest church was at the pueblo and, even then, the priest was only there some of the time. Baltasar thought that going to church was something done when his parents took him and his siblings on a trip to visit relatives.

These small chance exchanges grew on Baltasar. Francisca Góngora, whether intentionally or not, had grabbed his attention. She was younger then him by about ten years. Her looks did not particularly appeal to him. Nor did they offend him. She was a small but muscular woman, not stocky or soft. She had beautiful long black hair, an aquiline face, with a thick nose that her large chestnut eyes overwhelmed. Her vibrant, caring personality appealed to him. As she and Baltasar saw more of each other, she brought him out of his lethargy and he made a decision.

He visited Francisca and asked to see her brother Juan José. She blushed but answered, "*Que sí, por supuesto.*" "But of course." As was proper and because her father had passed away many years before, Baltasar asked Francisca's brother for permission to marry her. Juan's eyes lit up, but before he could answer Baltasar added that he planned to settle in Bernalillo.

Juan hesitated but only for a moment. Juan had returned from Santa Fe after going there with his widowed mother and family. His sister came with him and he was giving serious consideration to returning to El Paso. He didn't like the politics in Santa Fe or its cold climate. But he added, "However, my sister needs a husband and she is used to the cold. You have my blessing." Happy again, Baltasar married Francisca in Bernalillo's new church on January 22, 1703.

A New Life in a Distant Land
1704, Bernalillo, New Mexico

Not much time passed before Baltasar witnessed the truth of Chaves's warnings, for in the spring of 1704, a band of Faraon Apaches came around the north edge of the nearby Sandía Mountain and raided a ranch upriver at Ciénega. Then they overran Don Fernando's place and made away with a good portion of his livestock, including some of Baltasar's cows. Baltasar immediately wondered if El Paso wasn't a safer place. As in

225

El Paso, he knew that he would be required to join the punitive expeditions against the marauding Indians.

Governor Vargas, now in his sixties, and exonerated of all the charges against him, had returned to New Mexico for a second term as governor. He reacted quickly and sent a contingent of fifty soldiers and one hundred eighteen Pueblo Indian allies to Bernalillo along with instructions to Don Fernando to recruit a local militia to add to the force. Anxious to demonstrate his willingness to take a full role in his new community, Baltasar was one of the first to volunteer.

The governor joined them with a small, depleted guard. Heralding further trouble, a couple of his men had become ill and were returned to Santa Fe. Following the advice of his advance scouts, the army moved south along the Camino Real hoping to catch up to and surprise the Faraones. They had enough men all of them on horseback to give them the option to split up if required. With evidence of fresh track they were confident that the culprits would suffer the consequence of their raids.

However, the pursuit was cut short at camp after the third day. Vargas fell ill with a severe stomach pain. His officers recognized the reason and seriousness of his condition, the pestilence. They rushed him back to Bernalillo on a litter carried by the Pueblo Indian allies. Vargas suffered horribly. They travelled through the night and next day, and then put him to bed in Don Fernando's house, where after a few days, he expired.

Baltasar and Francisca watched with clasped hands and bowed heads as the governor's soldiers passed by transporting his body to Santa Fe where he would be buried.

A little more than a month later a son was born. Baltasar turned to Francisca for a name. Without hesitation she said, "Gregorio," after one of her sisters. Baltasar liked the name. It was different, at least, from the usual names in his family.

The death of Vargas gave rise to a change in administrative styles and, it seemed, a dawning of a different governmental attitude. Vargas's successor, Francisco Cuervo y Valdés granted permission for settlement in the central valley south of Bernalillo. He issued a summons for families who wished to take the risk to create a new village, claim some land, and move onto some of the pre-rebellion haciendas. Priority would be given to descendants of those families who had lived in the area before. The governor wanted twenty-one families.

Baltasar learned from his uncles that a Romero had settled just north of Isleta Pueblo, and that one of his Gomez cousins had settled south of Alameda Pueblo. He felt that his father's *hacienda*, the place of his birth was enough to qualify him for one of the properties. He preferred to settle on land somewhere around the ruins of Alameda Pueblo, maybe on the old Gomez ranch. Baltasar knew from personal inspection that those lands were fertile and had prime pasturage. This was an opportunity that Baltasar could not resist and Francisca agreed. They needed to be on their own and not ingratiated to Don Fernando or anyone else. Besides, the move would mean more and better land. They needed more space if they intended to expand their herds.

To make sure of the move, Baltasar spent a couple of days scouting the area to get a clearer understanding of the lay of the land. He rode off with a couple of other potential settlers. They walked through the ruins at the abandoned and destroyed Alameda Pueblo and then rode through the ruins of one hacienda after another but did not go as far south as Isleta Pueblo. At the old property of Doña Luisa de Montoya, a person they knew only by name, they gazed on the place where the governor wanted to locate the *plaza de armas* and his new village.

"Sure," one of the men sneered, "right across the river from the property that old Don Fernando has claimed."

"Of course, that makes sense," another nodded and then added, "He already has tenants."

"And...?" Baltasar left the question open.

"And, we can claim the rest."

"Yes, exactly. It is clear. There is plenty of good land and we will not be under anyone's thumb."

"*Claro!* Exactly." This was a sentiment that they all shared and Baltasar was now convinced that he wanted the old Gomez land. That land was not as swampy nor, he figured, as prone to flooding. If the Indians survived there, then he would follow their lead. He would build on a rise and farm the river bottom. Unfortunately, Baltasar found out that shortly before his death, Governor Vargas, had granted the land to someone else. Left with no choice, Baltasar claimed the next available land south of the grant.

When they returned to Bernalillo, they were shocked with the news of the death of Don Fernando's son Bernardo, from whom the name Bernalillo came. Little Bernardo or "Bernalillo," was Bernardo's nickname before the rebellion and the name stuck to the place. Baltasar met him in El Paso and knew him enough to know that they were around the same age. Bernardo had served in the El Paso presidio for a short time. While there he married the daughter of the procurator, a self-styled legal representative, of New Mexico. However, because of Baltasar's relationship with his father, Baltasar and Bernardo never became close friends even though they remained on a first name basis.

The death of a man in his prime is news enough. Everyone in New Mexico lived in danger of death. They lived in peril their whole lives, but Bernardo's fatality was worthy of note because of his family's stature and because it was accidental, in part the result of the very danger in which they lived.

With his curiosity piqued and wide-eyed with surprise Baltasar asked, "What? What do you mean?"

"Bernardo followed his female cousins to the river where he pretended to be an Apache and jumped out of the bushes to scare them. Their guard shot him. One shot through the heart!"

"My God!" That was all Baltasar could say. But he thought to himself, first Vargas and now this. Now he really questioned moving his family from El Paso.

The new governor had agreed to his petition to occupy the land next to and south of an earlier grant given to the Montoya family by Vargas. The land was the property that belonged to his Gomez ancestors! Baltasar could not believe his good luck. He and Francisca hugged in delight over the news. Francisca's second pregnancy added to their joy.

In 1706, Baltasar and his family joined twenty other families, or so it was said, escorted by a ten-soldier contingent commanded by Captain Martín Hurtado to establish the new "*villa.*" They travelled south out of Bernalillo toward the designated location. In reality, the move was not as orderly as it appeared on paper. The families dropped out as they arrived at their assigned *haciendas*. The Romero family was the first to separate as their land was on the far north end of the area, a few miles south of Alameda Pueblo and a league (2.7 miles) north of new village's plaza.

With their land claimed Baltasar decided to delay the move until Francisca gave birth. Baltasar did not want to risk her health. The wait gave him twice the joy, for both the mother and the baby girl that they named María Gregoria, come through healthy. Their son and daughter would share a name.

Now they could plan their move. Once the crops were harvested and María Gregoria had a few months to gain her strength they would move in late summer. But after they packed up and moved to their future home with two wagons full of household goods, supplies, and their children, reality set in. They stared at the abandoned, partially melted, roofless adobe walls of the building they would call home. Not even the welcoming sound of birds cheered their thoughts. They needed to get organized in a hurry. Settling in would not be so simple. They would need to work out of a campsite for the immediate future. At an opportune time, Baltasar would go back to Bernalillo for their livestock.

As required, Baltasar attended the formality of founding the new village. The village's first mayor, Captain Hurtado, followed all the proper legal procedures. He read the formal documents and laid out the plaza as well as all the official structures, barracks for the troops, government offices, and the church. Aware that very few of the families chose to live in the village thus calling into question its status as such, the captain ordered all the families to keep a house by the plaza where they could attend mass on Sundays. During the proceedings he announced that the place would be named San Felipe de Alburquerque for King Felipe V and for the current viceroy in Mexico City, the Duke of Alburquerque.

Baltasar was always aware of the not-to-distant ruins of Alameda Pueblo. He used some of its cut stone and logs to incorporate into his house and corral. In Baltasar's mind, the ruins, while not necessarily prominent anymore stood like the last outpost of a bygone era. They represented a place and time in which he did not participate.

Of necessity he lived in the present and the routine of the household, much helped by the unchanging ritual of the surrounding landscape otherwise disputed by the threat or reality of a thunderstorm, did not give him pause for historical considerations. This was his life. Sixteen months after moving to the valley another son was born, now he had three daughters and two sons. They named him Felipe de Santiago. Jacinta, the oldest, now fourteen, had become very helpful to her stepmother. Already there was no mistaking her for a woman.

DANGEROUS PURSUITS
1707, Alburquerque

Another day dawned and, as usual, Baltasar, Juan, who decided to stay, and a worker named Manuel with his son in tow, set off to the task of making adobes. The sun rose over the crest of the Sandía Mountain. For a while, the steep western face remained in shadow while the sun's light became brilliant and the sky bright blue.

The work was hard. First they needed to fill a pre-dug hole with water carried in buckets from the river. Then they mixed the water with the dirt and dried grass to a certain consistency, which they then placed into square wooden forms. Then, they let the sun dry the mud to create a mud brick, which they gathered in sufficient quantity for building another wall in the house. This day Manuel and Juan continued bringing the water while Baltasar was bent over the hole, working his hoe mixing the dirt, straw, and water. Manuel assisted by frolicking bare-footed in the adobe mud.

Well into their second hour of work, Baltasar stopped twice and looked around, stroking his beard, listening. He never spoke, but held out his hand for silence, sometimes turning his head. He started working again, stopped and moved his army-issue *escopeta* closer to him. Then he broke off, his head raised and intent like an animal that had caught a scent. "Did you hear that?" he asked.

Baltasar heard sounds foreign to the normal polyphony of his new domain. Sounds came to him from the distant, from the very distant and, then, from unusual movements up close. The faraway gunshots did not concern him as much as the closer movements. With *escopeta* in hand, Baltasar pointed to a small bush-laden inland rise about thirty feet beyond a mature cottonwood tree. Sure enough, one and then two other Apaches revealed themselves. Within seconds Baltasar, Manuel, and Juan fired two shots and two arrows into their midst. A yelp was heard. Then silence.

Baltasar realized that they had encountered a scouting party, indeed had discouraged them. Most of Baltasar's livestock remained pooled with Don Fernando's herds. The pickings for the Apaches were not worth the risk of confronting a prepared defense. Instead, the main body of Apaches had swept south.

An hour later, word came from the high pitched sound of hoofs of a horse in a hurry that carried a brown-faced man in a suit of drab, worn, clothes. Both man and animal were drenched in sweat. "We have been attacked. Most of the Indians are on foot. We leave in two days." By that he meant in the early morning. "Meet at the plaza, such as it is, before sunrise." The Apaches successfully attacked Don Fernando's place, making off with a great deal of livestock, almost a hundred head.

Thus, Baltasar left on the second of what would be many punitive expeditions from his new home. This would become recurring part of his life. He and Juan rode from his unfinished house, looking back on a melancholy group standing under the still framed, open portal, some indeed in tears. This was a scene that he knew would be repeated. It reminded him of the times his father and older brother left the family in El Paso.

In the following dawn with stars still visible in the western sky, a group of over fifty settlers, including thirty soldiers sent from Santa Fe, and around one hundred Pueblo auxiliaries set out. They headed south down the old Camino. Don Fernando rode next to Baltasar. Don Fernando had something on his mind, and as the early mists along the Rio Bravo evaporated, he asked Baltasar about the Indians that he saw. The old man looked around to take notice of who was within hearing range, then went on in a low voice, "There is some talk that the raiding party was not Navajos or Apaches but Pueblos disguised to place the blame on them."

Baltasar broke out in a self-confident smile. "I don't think so. First, our stock has brands and we would notice soon enough if they ended up on Pueblo lands. Second, I've no doubt what I saw. As you, I have lived next to and among Pueblo people my whole life. Then, look where they are leading us: to the south, away from the Pueblos. My guess: to the Ladrón Mountains. No Pueblo would go there on his own."

The mounted brigade rode at a constant, rapid rate. Within ten hours they had left Isleta behind them and were within sight of the hills and flat lands around Las Barrancas. The evidence there indicated that the raiding party had turned away from the Camino and headed directly to the Ladrón Mountains. There was no time to waste. The Indians were trying to reach what they considered their safe lair. This was land vaguely familiar to Baltasar. After all, from familiar landmarks and a pass in the distant eastern mountains he could discern where his father's ranch had been. He also remembered some of his father's and others' tales about leaving on a similar chase into the same nearby mountains. Usually, they came back empty-handed, but not always.

This time, however, the pursuers surprised the Apache's, who apparently did not expect to be followed into the rough, barren mountains. There was no hesitation when word came back from the scouts. Everyone was silenced as they approached. Then, they attacked. They killed a majority of the camp. Only those who fled survived. The attackers had no desire to chase after individuals. The commotion had scattered the stolen stock and recouping their source of food took priority.

Baltasar participated in the battle. He knew that he had effectively fired his musket and pistol, had ridden over some of the enemy leaving them exposed to his comrades following him, and had severely wounded, if not killed, at least two of the enemy with his short sword. Aside from a scratch, a sword arm drenched in blood, and some blood spatters on his leather vest, he emerged from the struggle unscathed. The whole encounter did not last more than fifteen minutes. The rest of Baltasar's effort was spent helping round up their stolen livestock.

They gathered the enemy bodies together and left them to be tended to by their own people. Then, they began the return trip north, this time camping at the end of the day. The camp was jovial for the success of their journey. In a celebratory mood, they even slaughtered a couple of the recaptured livestock to enjoy the moment. They knew from bitter experience in pursuing the nomadic Indians into their territory that the success of this expedition was an exception to the rule.

Apparently, influenced by the good news of the Ladrón campaign, or because he felt that the region would be better off if all the royal troops were concentrated in Santa Fe, the new governor recalled Alburquerque's small ten-man garrison. Maybe he felt that the battle-hardened settlers could fend for themselves. Not everyone thought so because within months the Navajos and Apaches started raiding with impunity. They came in small stealth parties, usually to skim off exposed livestock. They were not above taking hostages, so people had to be on constant alert.

By the fall of 1708, the settlers had suffered enough, and they blamed the governor's decision to transfer the soldiers away from Alburquerque. People grumbled, Baltasar among them. An already perilous life had become more so. Thefts increased and the much riskier pursuits became more fruitless. The humdrum routine of daily life had a strong underlining of anxiety.

At their wit's end, the settlers decided to make an appeal to the governor. He had been in office almost a year, and they felt that he had enough time to realize that he had

Muy Iluestre Cabildo Justicia i regimiento

Los Capitanes Dn Phernando Durani Chades i Balthasar
Romero vesinos dela villa de Alburquerque en nombre i Con poder
i fa Cultad de todos los vesinos de ella paresemos ante V
en la mejor via i forma que aia lugar que mas nos Conbeng
i desimos que por Cuanto el señor Genl Dn franco Cue
Boi Baldes Gobernador que era deste dho Reino quien
en su tiempo por pareserle mas Conbeniente mando poblar
dha villa de Alburquerque el año demil setesientos
para cuio efecto i debido Cumplimiento nos mando assen
no torio la intencion que tenia deque fuera mas este Rei
noia delantasemos nuestras asiendas i no esperimentara
mos en lo de adelante las epidemias de los años pasa
nos asistio por Causa deno tener donde sembrar ni Criar
estros ganados aunque es berdad que lo ai amplio en ellu
gar dondea ssi tienen no nos determinamos assentender
por la Copia i irriesgo delos enemigos que nos ircunbalan
por todos Cuatro bientos motibos que obligaron adho se
ñor Genl a darnos para nuestra guarda i defensa una es
Cuadra de señores soldados para que estando depie i nde
esemos adelantas en alguna manera motibo quenos oblig
a desamparar el puesto de Bernalillo donde estabamos
abe indades; llebados del interes i nuestra bien Conbeni
encia por lo que nos allamos prestado a durasi poblar dha
Villa i Conseguido assi Luego eso in forme el los señor Genl
Dn fran Cuerdo a el exelentisimo señor duque de Albur
querque a quien se de Claro i dio en tender es estado de
La fundasion de la nueba Villa a dia poblado i que
para ello nos abia dado dha es motibos que al dho
señor Vi Reio bligaron a dar [...] una a eleccion Con[...]
Costa de su mandamiento [...] questro fa [...]

The 1708 petition on behalf of the people of Albuquerque compiled and signed by Baltasar Romero and Fernando Duran y Chaves. Courtesy of the Spanish Archives of New Mexico, New Mexico State Records Center and Archives.

made a mistake when he pulled the troops. The people turned to Don Fernando and Baltasar to compile their petition.

"Why me?" A surprised Baltasar asked. He never learned to read and barely knew how to sign his name. Don Fernando was an obvious choice. Now showing his age, Chaves furled his forehead and gave Baltasar a knowing look. "You are experienced, respected, and...and your family in Santa Fe has kept a good reputation." He stopped for a reply and seeing that none was forthcoming, he continued, "Come. I will draft the letter and read it to you. If I omit something, together we will make it right. *De acuerdo?* Agreed?"

"*Bueno.*" "Okay." The answer was not said with confidence.

They labored on a wood table in the coolness of Don Fernando's main living room. The two men worked through the late afternoon and into the early evening before they felt they had a draft worthy enough to present to the community. They made their grammatical changes based on how their syntax sounded when spoken.

The next morning they made a couple more minor changes before they read it to the gathered community leaders. Few who gathered to hear the petition could read or write. Even fewer of them felt the need to criticize what Don Fernando and Baltasar had compiled.

"The Captains Fernando Duran y Chaves and Baltasar Romero, residents of the Villa of Alburquerque in the name and authority of all of the citizens of the same..."

As Don Fernando read, Baltasar looked out over their nods in agreement and pleased looks. Fernando continued,

"The governor has been pleased to take away our squad, which for reasons the enemy, seeing our weakness, has dared commit barbarous robberies, daily running off stock.... Now...they may be planning to surprise and destroy us and our wives and children."

Don Fernando read how this was not possible before "because of the presence of the soldiers." The petition concluded with the request that the governor "grant the return of our squad."

With everyone in agreement, the petition was copied, signed, and sealed. Then Don Fernando and Baltasar, along with a small escort mounted up and began a two-day ride to Santa Fe where, on April 14th, 1708 they presented the petition to the governor's Council of Justice and Order. The petition got the governor's attention and, after some delay, he reinstated Alburquerque's ten-man contingent.

While not necessarily prominent anymore, for others had helped themselves to the site as well, the ruins of Alameda Pueblo stood like the last outpost of a bygone era. They represented a place and time in which he did not participate.

Of necessity, he lived in the present. He had become accustomed to the routine of the household, helped by the unchanging ritual of the surrounding landscape unless disrupted by the threat or reality of a raid. This was his life. In 1709, a second son was born. Now they had two boys and a daughter plus two girls from Baltasar's first wife. They named him Felipe de Santiago. Jacinta, the oldest, now fourteen, had become very helpful to her stepmother.

Now a bona fide community leader, Baltasar tried to ignore the fact by concentrating on his fields of squash, corn, beans, chili and grapes. He worked with his neighbors up and down the river to improve upon the pre-rebellion irrigation system, so everyone could be assured of their fair share of water.

Aided by the river runoff that annually overflowed the banks and left the lands covered with a new coat of mucky, rich sediment, Baltasar marveled at the rapid and lush growth of his fields, especially when compared to his struggles in El Paso. He no longer needed a percentage of his former workers' product and gladly informed them that the lands and produce were all theirs. "After all," he wrote them, "my lands provide enough excess crops for me to trade. And, added, that he hoped their lands would prove as beneficial.

His children had not grown enough to help, but this was alleviated, first with Juan and then with Manuel who eventually built his own house politely distant but within sight of Baltasar's. Baltasar's family in Santa Fe sent him a "gift" of a group of "Panana" or Pawnee Indians captured by the Navajos. This group included three mature women in their teens and seven youths ranging from around seven years old. Baltasar and Francisca could only guess that the women were sixteen or seventeen years old.

If treated well, the Pawnees could be great assets to the growth of his hacienda. Again, drawing on his experience in El Paso, Baltasar concentrated on including the Pawnees into his household. He set about constructing their own dwellings and made sure not to overwork them, especially at first. The younger ones did not work but played with his children. The women partnered with Francisca and Jacinta, now fifteen years old. Both the maturity of his daughter and the addition of female help proved to be a big relief to Francisca, who, once again was pregnant.

Baltasar's believed that Pawnee help was not unlike the Pueblo Indians or other people who his father hired to work on his lands in El Paso. He did not care to understand that his Pawnee captives were not hired help. Harkening back to his youth, Baltasar, like his father, appreciated and even was sometimes fascinated by the Pueblo people. Now, these people captured by the Navajos, a common enemy captivated his curiosity.

That common enemy had become more audacious. They nearly wiped out Jemez Pueblo and in quick succession they attacked Santa Clara Pueblo north of Santa Fe. The governor declared war on them, and, in 1709, he sent a huge army that swept northwest out of Santa Fe up the Chama River Valley and into western New Mexico. The expedition inflicted some major damage on the Navajos, the result of which brought a couple of years' relief to the Rio Grande Valley, at least from that quarter.

The governor's attention shifted to the east to deal with the Faraon Apaches. Like their Navajo cousins, they had become more than a nuisance. Carnue Canyon that cuts through the Sandía Mountains had become one of their favorite routes into the valley and to the village of Alburquerque. Successive punitive expeditions went east onto the Plains to deal with the Apaches. Though not as successful as the western sweep, most people felt that the mere effort would send a message to the recalcitrant raiders.

During the relative calm, Baltasar joined on a couple of innocuous and short expeditions. Such activity was a necessary evil. He preferred to concentrate on his lands and livestock. He preferred staying at home enjoying his growing family. In 1712, three years after Felipe de Santiago was born Francisca gave birth to another son. They named him Pedro after Baltasar's uncle who was killed in the Pueblo Revolt. Baltasar insisted on the names of his last two sons in an attempt to retain some family memory.

Then in the spring of 1713, Baltasar's relatively tranquil, if uneventful life changed. First, his friend and *"patron"* succumbed to old age. Baltasar, especially, would miss Don Fernando. Somehow, he felt as if Don Fernando's mantle had passed to him.

More obviously, the western expeditions along with the establishment of a permanent troop, however small, and the obvious fertility of the place, encouraged a new influx of settlers into the Alburquerque area. The land immediately to the north of his was the large Montoya grant that had been conveyed to Elena Gallegos just after the first of the year. Elena and her brother Felipe, along with many of their family, moved into the area. As the higher and best land was at the southern extreme of the grant, just north of Baltasar's land, he suffered an unwelcomed sudden influx of nearby neighbors.

The Gallegos family, their friends and the many workers they brought with them made up a whole new community. They needed assistance as well as advice. Besides that, they would need to cooperate with the existing settlers, most of whom lived down river and, more importantly, on the irrigation system.

Naturally, they sought out Baltasar, their closest established neighbor, who patiently explained the irrigation system, how everyone must pitch in, how the water would be distributed, and the role of the *mayordormo*, the ditch boss. "Without this we would all be fighting over the water and nothing would grow. Together, everything grows." Then he explained to them the obvious, to build on high ground because "as you can see, the northern part of your land has some swamps, which are the result of this year's rains but more often from the river."

"From the river?"

"*Claro.* The river floods every spring. And this is good." Baltasar playfully left it at that.

"Good! Did you say it is good for the river to flood?"

"*Claro,*" and he smiled and leaned forward, "because the waters leave a fine, rich silt. That is what makes our land so fertile. It is God's gift." He watched the wonderment on everyone's faces with pleasure. He had become their Don Fernando, and Francisca who sat quietly beside him looked at him with pride.

Baltasar walked with them to show them the prime planting areas and others that would be better for fruit trees. "Here is another area subject to flooding. See? You can tell from the soil." He helped plan their *acequias* and staked them with some beginning seeds. He profited from selling them some of his excess harvests, which he exchanged for land as they did not have money. Thus, Baltasar acquired property in the Gallegos grant. Eventually the new community of people would be the first to form a small plaza north of Alburquerque. Other plazas soon followed. Beginning with the closest land north of Baltasar's place these plazas strung along the Camino and became known as San Antonio de los Poblanos, Nuestra Señora de Guadalupe de los Griegos, Plaza del Señor de los Gallegos, San José de los Ranchos, and El Rancho. Off to the east and closer to a lateral road to Santa Fe, a plaza named for the Martínez family emerged.

Baltasar understood that the majority of his property abutted the Gallegos grant, but as the new plazas gradually came about, he never objected. Opportunity came with the influx of people so he started acquiring and selling properties. Nor would he realize that some day he would be associated with both Alburquerque and the plaza of Los Poblanos as a founder. More importantly and realistically, Francisca sensed a safety in numbers. On the other hand, Baltasar began to feel the press of their dependency.

With people moving in all around him and tired of dealing with quarrels over water issues along with other minor squabbles, Baltasar started to disperse some of his land. First he arranged to convey property to his workers, including Manuel. Then, to his advantage, he bargained with newcomers. "My God!" He exclaimed to Francisca on more than one occasion. "There is more than enough water for everyone." He just could not understand how these people constantly squabbled.

Throughout this initial flurry of transactions, Baltasar made sure that each of his children would have land. Aside from survival, he had an abiding ideal that he needed to look out for his children. That, and his desire to live without the entanglements of society, led him to Don Fernando's family, who had abandoned their lands in Bernalillo. Would they work a deal with him? Could he purchase or trade for some land? He and Francisca found the less populated and, perhaps, more exposed Bernalillo desirable. Perhaps they would move there. He wanted to concentrate on farming, raising crops, and he sought untapped rich river bottomlands. Thus, by the fall of 1715 he acquired land in Bernalillo. He had, in effect, left his community responsibilities behind him, or so it seemed.

In 1716, he volunteered for duty on an expedition that the governor was sending to the Hopi Pueblos. At forty-three years old, he could not deny, even to Francisca, that a sense of adventure, if not curiosity, had overcome him as well.

The large force travelled over a well-worn trail past Laguna and Acoma Pueblos, then through the lava flows that some of the soldiers called Malpaís, "badlands," and on to the watering hole and camping place with all the names carved into the rock wall. Baltasar had a vague memory that his father had gone on the same route to the Hopi country. He had no other familial memory about traveling there. The history was lost. Nor did anyone bring to his attention the Romero inscription at the place that would become known as "Inscription Rock." He tended to the business of the expedition and to readiness for conflict. He was relieved when they rode up to the Hopi mesas without any problems. They had successfully traversed hostile territory.

Baltasar wondered about the western pueblos, for, unlike those in the valley, these villages were placed on top of almost inaccessible mesas. He puzzled over why these Pueblo Indians would live in such a desperate place in the middle of Navajo territory instead of living in the friendlier confines of the Rio del Norte Valley. Some of the Tiquex Indians, who had fled during and after the Pueblo Revolt to live among the Hopis, were asked to move back but they refused. Baltasar did not understand. Oh, he understood that their villages had been sacked and burnt but, in his mind, that was then and now was different. He could not help but think that some of the unconvinced people before him were descendants of Alameda and Sandía Pueblos. Thus, the expedition returned, its only achievement being a show of force. Nevertheless, Baltasar took great pleasure in describing the western pueblos to his wide-eyed family.

AD INFINITUM
June 1724, Alburquerque

Baltasar leaned on his hoe, as he, his sons, and some other members of the community watched the entourage barley acknowledge them as they rode by. Without a word, everyone agreed that someone in Santa Fe was in trouble. The king would not send an inspector without reason and this rigid, high-cheeked, square-jawed, unsmiling man looked the type who did not trouble himself with trifling matters. "So what," thought Baltasar; he had seen it all before.

At fifty-one years old, the gray-bearded and bald Baltasar allowed himself a moment's pause before he went back to work with the official cadre still within sight. Politicos and politicians were not Baltasar's concern. In fact, he had become pretty adept at avoiding the turbulence of New Mexico's politics. Relatively speaking he had prospered in anonymity. From his move to Alburquerque and subsequent land acquisitions, Baltasar had turned his excess crops into a comfortable lifestyle. He left the sheep and cattle trade to others. Living off the land along with property and its conveyance had become the source of his relatively good standard of living, good at least, for New Mexico. Besides, he did not care to interact with the new *empresarios* from Mexico who were beginning to monopolize the sheep trade.

He worked his fields. He could never rid himself of his youthful enjoyment of creating something of substance from the earth. He did so in the confidence that he would always have land enough for his family to be self-sustaining. He also learned that raising a couple of pigs as well as a few sheep for food and a few for sale to the *empresarios* was much more lucrative than raising cattle.

He felt that life had been good, and Francisca joined him in this appraisal. They now had eight children, the last born in 1717. His daughters born to his first wife had married well and remained close by in Alburquerque. His oldest son, Gregorio, recently married, almost matched his dad's height and had his slender body. He stood out with his blue eyes, a physical attribute that periodically surfaced among the Romeros. He lived on his own. Importantly, though, Baltasar and his sons shared the labor and management of the family lands.

Felipe de Santiago now fifteen years old and three years older than Pedro, still lived at home and had begun to take on the full responsibilities of adulthood. Yet, he had a rebellious nature so often associated with his age group. At twelve years old, Pedro was growing into a mature man with his mother's stout body. He was not nearly his father's height but had his father's image when it came to personality. All the sons, like their father, had become fairly adept with a bow and arrow. Now Baltasar started teaching Pedro how to fire the *escopeta*. But, willing and as adaptable as he was, the kid still was not mature or strong enough to be of much help with many of the tasks.

The royal entourage raised more questions than not. When Baltasar, his sons, and workers sat down under the welcome shade of an aged cottonwood tree for their mid-day meal of mutton, chili, and corn tortillas, the conversation morphed from the haughty inspector to Baltasar's apparent lack of awe, then to the many such officials he had seen in his lifetime and, finally, to what motivated him to leave El Paso. "Not only that, but to Bernalillo, then to Alburquerque."

As Baltasar cupped a piece of tortilla to scoop some mutton and chile, he hesitated and said, "My dad, your grandfather took risks. I never understood how or why he would live so secluded by the Ladrón Mountains. Although I have childhood memories of the place and people, I don't remember the danger, not even when we left during the revolt."

Felipe enthusiastically interrupted, "He must have been brave!"

"Yes. And that is why your mother and I gave you his name. My older brother, your uncle Sebastián was also brave." Actually, Baltasar worried that the impetuous Felipe was more like Sebastián.

Pedro gulped down some food, cleared his throat and asked, "What happened to him?"

"He disappeared." Baltasar continued with a brief history of his long-lost brother. The boys had heard the story before but they encouraged their father to repeat it in case he might relay something he had overlooked before. "My father did not want to come back here. That was certain."

"But you did."

"Yes." Baltasar paused and stared at the tree leaves flickering in the sunlight over a slight breeze then nodded to Pedro. "The fate of my wife's death." Everyone knew he referred to his first wife, María Francisca, "Had I known, I never would have moved. We, I would still be in El Paso. Maybe rich. But let us not talk about what isn't."

Sensing his father's wistfulness, Pedro spoke. "We are here and I am glad for it. This is home. Maybe we are not rich but neither are we poor."

"Thanks be to God. Yes, this is home." Baltasar paused, "And where I want to die."

The boys looked at one another at a loss for words. Felipe spoke, "Father, you are like grandfather. You moved like him. You came back to New Mexico. Why?"

Baltasar answered with a sigh. "Land, better pasture, rich soil. And, don't forget, your aunts and uncles moved up north."

"But, father, what about the Indians? The danger?"

"It is everywhere the same. El Paso, Santa Fe, Taos, here. The same." He finished his tortilla and cut off another piece to scoop, so Pedro continued.

"We have always been here. I guess we will break the tradition."

Baltasar choked as he swallowed and tried to laugh at the same time. "Don't be too sure." Cough. "Pass me some water." He wiped his mouth with the back of his hand and grabbed the water jar passed to him. "You are young and have plenty of time. Right now, you've no reason to move. You and your families will have enough land, plus our investments." He paused and took a drink, licking his lips after. "The time will come for your children or their children to find new land, new opportunities when the land we have cannot support them all. This is not a bad or good thing. It is how life is here."

Then he pointed to the empty irrigation ditches that they were clearing for the life-giving water that would run into the waiting and carefully tended fields lined by shimmering green leafed cottonwoods. "That is life. That is what I live for. I, you, we are all part of life's cycles, God's design."

A FAMILY GATHERING
October 1736, Alburquerque's North Valley

Baltasar could not keep track of all of his grandchildren or the growing brood of great-grandchildren. This lapse of memory began somewhere in his late fifties, four or five years ago. Francisca, of course, remembered all of their names and who belonged to whom. Maybe it was no coincidence that her sudden passing a few years earlier coincided with his loss of family memory. He lost his second wife to another stroke.

Nor, when he thought about it, was he surprised to date his many physical problems from her death. His hips started to decline almost ten years ago, the last two years of which he used a cane, then canes. Also, he had lost most of his teeth. They just loosened and then came out almost unnoticed. He had become an old man, ancient by the standards of the day, past his sixtieth birthday. "*Ay de mí*," he exclaimed almost every morning, when he hobbled with short steps, his stiff hips and legs barely allowing him to arrange himself to use the chamber pot in his room. "Why has God burdened me with this long life?" He wandered through this ultimate unhappiness, a desolation made tolerable by living so customary a daily life, and by his memories. How he longed to run barefoot along the riverbank with a bow and arrow.

But his mind remained sharp, matched only by his appetite and pleasure in a nightly cup of wine. And conversation, he loved conversation. The rest, well, he preferred not to dwell on it. "I am useless," he would say only to himself. Whether he knew it or not, he was a proud man. His only personal solace was sleep, which put him in a perfect state, where even the high winds or inconsistent howling of the coyotes could not disturb him. The fact that he was completely deaf in one ear and getting close to it in the other helped.

So it was on a late autumn's day, sunny and beautifully clear, that his family gathered around him in his home. His youngest son, Felipe and his wife helped prepare the anxious old man for the big day. They, too, shared his anxiety, for the family enjoyed these reunions as much as their father. They fed off his joy. They reveled in his often-repeated stories. They loved him and rued the rapidly approaching day when he no longer would be with them. Baltasar, for his part, many times reminisced about the irony of how his rebellious youngest son grew to become the one who would care for him.

Pedro and his family of three young children—two boys and a girl—were the first to arrive. Pedro rode a horse while helping his wife manage a double team pulling a wagon with the excited kids. The rest of the family arrived a mid-day. Strewn up the valley north from Alburquerque's main plaza, they had left their respective homes in the cold morning dark, already in route before the sun's first light showed over the Sandía Mountain.

Everyone participated in the gathering, the *matanza*. Today they would butcher a pig as well as a sheep. At dawn, Felipe prepared with the help of a couple of his ranch hands. Before some of the wide-eyed children, they hoisted the pig and then the lamb by their back feet and slit their throats. The women collected the pig's blood as it drained into a bowl. They would make *morcilla*, an onion-based blood sausage out of it. Pedro took charge of dividing up the pig and slicing off the roasts to be cooked over an open fire.

Felipe concentrated on the preparation of the sheep's meat, including many of its internal organs. Even the intestines, cleaned by the women, would be roasted in the sheep's fat to create a delicacy called *burroñates* that would become a family staple for the next two centuries.

Baltasar watched the proceedings from a specially prepared seat. He noted the rising sun, its light and its welcoming heat seemingly bringing life to the still valley, rising in a clear, deep blue sky that promised a perfect day. Baltasar would not be disappointed.

The afternoon meal, eaten outdoors, lasted almost three hours. The *sobre mesa,* table talk ranged from humor to serious. Here is where everyone caught up with family news, reacquainted, conversed, and solved real as well as superficial problems. As the family patriarch, Baltasar had precedence.

They laughed at the memory of Baltasar's attempt to sell the Bernalillo land to the nearby Santa Ana Pueblo. "And why not?" They agreed. But the governor did not approve the sale. "Too bad. It was a good idea."

Smiling in self-satisfaction over the memory, Baltasar's gray-bearded brown face lit up with a toothless mirth. "Maybe," he replied.

They talked about their cousins. Baltasar was the last of his brothers and sisters. His sons and daughters admitted with some embarrassment that they had lost contact with the cousins. Yes, they believed that, most of them still live in Santa Fe and Santa Cruz. No, they could not remember all the names of their children or even how many there might be.

Over the years, Baltasar had taken his family to visit his brothers and sisters in Santa Fe and Santa Cruz more than a few times. Then, ten years ago, Baltasar, with the acquiescence of his two surviving sons, purchased some prime land in Taos and sold it to their "cousins" the descendants Diego Romero, Jola's son who kept on the Romero surname. Baltasar always remembered his friendship with Diego and the loyalty of Jola to his father and that the old man had died in defense of the hacienda. The gift of land allowed the Cadimo Romeros to move to the far north.

Time and distance had conspired to limit the visits of Baltasar's siblings. Now, all four had died. Baltasar was the last of his generation. Gregorio's fate was not brought up. His unexpected death, the family knew, had been hard on Baltasar. Nevertheless, Baltasar, as always, lifted his cup to toast the memory of his oldest son, and enough said.

Nor would they forget the story of uncle Domingo, Baltasar's youngest brother who had participated in the ill-fated Pedro de Villasur expedition sent across the plains looking for a French army. Initially thought to be one of the many casualties in the disastrous battle that ensued, he miraculously made it back to New Mexico on his own.

They reminded their dad about the times he petitioned the governors. First, to get the troops back, and then, more recently, when he printed out his signature on a petition protesting the governor's restriction of sheep and wool exports from New Mexico. The embargo, they protested, cut much-needed income to maintain their families. The governor ignored them.

Baltasar did not like to devote much time on war stories and politics. He had a few of his own, but had long since quit talking about them. He always recalled an old family warning about getting caught is such romanticism. Reality was very different.

He sat up and lifted his hand a few inches from the table, his sign that everyone recognized. He had something to say. "War, violence is not our survival. Those are..." he paused for some kind of response as he pointed to the cultivated fields. Then, he signaled for one of Felipe's daughters and whispered in her ear. She nodded and ran into house. "...And," he continued in a low voice, "while we must protect ourselves, we also must eat. I once...Ah, here it is," as his granddaughter returned with a flat, boat-shaped iron plowshare, "an old friend. A plowshare, a tool, very old, like me. We share a history." He hung his head, fully aware of the undivided attention upon him. "This tool does not kill. No. It makes possible life, sustenance." He gave a slight cough and whispered, "This plowshare has more romance in it than any *escopeta*."

Silence answered him, for all the men of his family had heard a variation of this talk many times before. Although not completely convinced, they knew enough of their father and grandfather to realize that he spoke from the heart. This was not small talk, their respect and love for him emanated in the silence.

Four months later, his children had gathered around him again. Except possibly for Baltasar, the occasion was not as joyous, actually reflecting the gray, gloomy, freezing weather. Baltasar had grown very weak. Now bedridden and semi-conscious, his breathing had become labored. Fray Pedro Montaño, who had become a family friend, stationed at nearby Santa Ana Pueblo, administered the last rights. He warned that the time was near on his last visit and that the family should be called together.

Pedro arrived just as Felipe and his wife had propped Baltasar up in a chair with a towel tied around his chest and attached to the chair to keep him stable. They were spoon-feeding him some corn mush. Baltasar had not spoken in days. He only nodded. Pedro looked into his blank eyes and love welled up for his father. "Dad. Dad! Can you see me? Do you know who this is?"

Baltasar acknowledged the words, for he slowly turned his head to look into his son's face. Under his breath he barely whispered a guttural "Ped" then swallowed and took in some air, "dro."

Simultaneous smiles and tears broke out around the room.

Father Montaño visited that night. "I think I will need to return tomorrow. Stay with him. God will call him soon."

They laid him on his side and cleaned him with a damp towel. He spoke twice. The first time he reached out his arms and said, "Francisca, si!" A little later he again reached out exclaiming, "Soy yo, soy yo!" "It is me, it is me." He died lying on his side, achieving death, the ultimate relief from a long life.

By the time the priest returned the next morning Baltasar's body had been cleaned and dressed, not in a formal suit, but in a clean set of his work clothes. The family buried him in the family chapel next to his beloved Francisca.

PART VI
PEDRO, TWO FAMILIES, JUAN JOSEPH, AND ABIQUIU

The Fifth, Sixth, and Seventh Generation in New Mexico
The Sixth generation (Juan Joseph Tomás) moved to Abiquiu
(Ed Romero's direct ancestors are highlighted)

Gregoria Baca Luna (m. 1728) = **Pedro Romero** = Josefa Varela Jaramillo (m. 1751)
(1st Wife. 1711-1746)   (b.1712)   (2nd Wife. 1731 - 1780)

Pedro Romero II (1732-1784)

María Antonia Romero (b.1733)

Juan Antonio Romero (b.1735)

Cristobal José Romero (b.ca.1736)

Miguel Severiano Romero (b.1741)

José Antonio Romero (b.ca.1744)

Juan Joseph Tomás Romero (b.1757. m.1781 in Abiquiu) = **María Lucía Martín**

Lucia Guadalupe Romero (b.1753)

María Petrona Romero (b.1754)

Raphael Antonio Romero (b.1774)

María Manuela Romero (b.1782 in Abiquiu)

Salvador Antonio Romero (b.1786 in Abiquiu)

María Concepción Romero (b.1788 in Abiquiu)

Ygnacia Diega Romero (b.1794 in Abiquiu)

Francisco Antonio Romero (b.Nov.1795 in Abiquiu)

Manuel Tomas Romero (b.1797 in Abiquiu)

A Sedentary Inheritance
March 1737, Alburquerque's North Valley

Pedro and Felipe worked in unison. Each silent in his own thoughts as they shoveled dirt on to their father's casket to the sound of their sisters' mumbled drone reciting the rosary. As prearranged, everyone else left, including Father Montaño. Baltasar asked to be buried on his property by the small chapel he and his sons had built many years before. He would be with his second wife. The sons silently shoveled dirt into their father's grave. Pedro could not rid himself of the obvious and ominous thought that his time would come soon enough and he, like his father, would lie lifeless as, maybe, his own sons buried him.

They finished by tamping down the earth and covering the site with rocks. Then they placed a temporary wood cross that would be replaced with a stone marker as soon as it was ready.

The brothers walked back to the house together. "Now what?" Pedro asked to no one in particular.

Felipe shrugged. "I know, life without Dad. It seems strange."

Pedro nodded. At first appearance the two men would never be taken for brothers. Pedro, three years senior, now twenty-five years old, had more of his mother's features. His stringy hair came from his mother. He had his father's eyes and lighter skin. Felipe inherited his mother's broad face and big-boned body as well as her dark complexion. He had his father's straight black hair that he kept pulled in a ponytail.

Unlike Felipe, Pedro had begun to show premature signs of aging. The weather had furled his face and his full beard showed signs of premature grey, presaging the process underway with his full head of black hair that hung to just above his shoulders.

Pedro clucked loud enough for Felipe to hear. "You know. Dad was the last of his generation. Now it is us. He was lucky to live so long."

They continued to walk but Felipe could not help himself. "Lucky, yes but unlucky, too. Our mother," he paused and looked off searching for words to match his thoughts, "and then Gregorio..."

Pedro cut him off. "Felipe, this is true. But not unlike everyone we know. Everyone has lost someone."

Pedro considered himself lucky. Yes, his life had not been near as adventurous as his father's. Thank God. A day did not pass when his mind settled on some point of his father's advice or example. It was almost as if he were there with him, which, in reality, was Pedro's feeling. He acknowledged that a good part of his lucky life had to do with his father. For most of his adult life, his father had treated him as an equal and, then, depended on him and his brothers to keep things in order. They had cultivated lands, cared for and expanded their livestock. In fact, they personally had become successful farmers. Yes, fate and inheritance pointed to a relatively tranquil future.

The journey home ended with a brilliant sunset as the rays cast a bright, almost red sheen across the clouds in the western sky. Pedro's low-lying adobe home, expanded since his father first built it, looked dark in the early evening shadows under cover of the cottonwood trees. He stretched from the ride. His wife, holding the baby, carefully lowered herself from the wagon and scurried inside with the other two children hurrying in after her. She lit some candles, started a fire in the fireplace and, left unsaid, availed herself of the bedpan, in reality, a large part of what once was an olive jar imported from down south.

Without speaking, Pedro unbridled and unhitched the horses and led them to some water at the *acequia*. Then, he prepared feed before the worn animals were corralled. Unloading the wagon could wait until morning. That is, except for the foodstuff. There was no sense in inviting unwanted creatures to the hearth.

Actually, Pedro deferred unloading the wagon less from fatigue than from a subconscious desire to avoid the task, because a good part of the cargo belonged to his departed parents. He had convinced himself that he could stoically carry on but even a good nights rest could not relieve him of his grief.

With the dawning of another clear fall day, Pedro started unloading the smaller items from the back end of the wagon. Here were his father's clothes, his saddle, some tools, a buckskin coat, two hats, and an old *escopeta* that, Pedro knew, still worked. Then came the small plowshare.

"Ah, yes," he thought, "the share. How dad liked this useless share." It had been retired over twenty, maybe thirty years and Pedro's father kept it on his *repisa*, wall shelf, as if it had become an important icon. Pedro knew the story, for he had heard it many times.

Pedro dispersed the wagon's load. Most went into temporary storage, divided between what would become one of the children's rooms in the house and the small barn. Pedro saved the plowshare and took it into the main *sala*, the living room, where he began to make space on a *repisa*.

Before he could finish, his wife saw him. "*Que estás haciendo?* What are you doing?" Her high-pitched voice offered no hint of condemnation, instead curiosity. Pedro had long ago acquiesced to the reality that her domain was the house's interior. So, now, an explanation was in order.

He turned to face her. He never took her for granted. She was a smallish, gentle, sweet-looking woman who, in her middle twenties, after two children and pregnant with a third, she retained her youth in a contented face. "Ah, Gregita, this plowshare..."

As he held it up, Gregoria Baca calmly and without expression cut him off, "So ugly!"

Although she had seen the plowshare and heard her father-in-law talk about it, Pedro intuitively realized that, by happenstance, the full story of the plowshare had been kept among the men. Instantly and without compunction Pedro decided that he would repeat for his wife the story, and he did so enthusiastically.

Pedro would never forget the winter of 1737–1738. This first winter without his father was especially different, maybe empty, given the last years of helping to care for his father. Well stocked with food and more than enough wood to burn, that winter was the first that Pedro could devote himself full-time to his own family, most especially to Gregoria who gave birth to their fourth child, another son. Sitting in front of their hearth, stirring ashes, being mesmerized as the fire warmed them, reminded him how deeply he felt for her. They didn't talk much. They merely enjoyed each other's presence. Even the children sensed a renewed family bond.

Pedro's brother made a quick decision to vacate and, then, sell the property in Bernalillo. Pedro encouraged him and told him to keep the proceeds. Felipe deserved it, for living and caring for dad all those last years could never be repaid. "Interesting," Pedro thought, "how after dad's death Felipe and I see less of each other." In part, this was due to their agreement to divide equally the estate among the brothers, and the priority of caring for their respective families separately.

Pedro was satisfied with life. As he lay in bed, he many times looked over at Gregoria as she slept, her even breathing, so peaceful, somewhat like his life. He reminisced, "...a good natural, not unusual life, with its certain regularity whatever the weather or Indian threat might bring. Thanks to God." And he meant it.

Teaching his children, especially the older boys gave him special pleasure. He did not want them to forget who their grandfather was. By 1744, Gregoria had given birth to two more sons. The family had grown to six children, with the oldest now pitching in with chores. Junior had reached his twelfth year and started taking up adult chores. Juan and Cristóbal, at eleven and ten were not far behind. All of them had their own knives and knew how to fire an *escopeta*.

Pedro tried to share what little family history he knew. Like many people, he realized how much he did not know after his parents' death. "If only I had paid attention," he thought. There was one legacy that was clear in his mind, and the memory came when he ambled up to the shelf and removed the old piece of rusted iron.

"Enough, *basta*!" He signaled to the boys. Actually, he had no idea what they were doing at the moment. "*Vengan*, come here. I have something to show you." With that he hunched down and held the plowshare before his face. He asked as they gathered around him, "Do you know what this is?"

His sons looked at him, and then at one another. The eldest spoke. "Of course, that is grandpa's plowshare."

Pedro, with furrowed eyebrows to make his point, replied, "And do you remember anything about it?" There was no answer, which, of course, Pedro expected from his young sons. "Well, let me tell you," and he proceeded to repeat his father's story, a *cuento* that began in El Paso. In the telling, Pedro had a new sense of being. He knew that he wanted his sons Pedro, Juan, Miguel, and Cristóbal to share that feeling.

The spring of 1746, that usually positive season that bespoke of the future, proved contrary, for Gregoria caught a cold with a nagging but persistent cough that lasted through the month of May, and then morphed into something worse. The changing weather and seasonal high winds, carrying all the newly sprung pollen, touched off her allergies and sent her to bed.

There, with his Gregita's contorted face, hacking, coughing, spitting blood, and gasping for air, Pedro watched helplessly and forever lost any feeling of good luck. He could not help but realize what his father must have felt with the loss of his wives. On a windy evening, Gregoria died. It was June 23, 1746 and she was only thirty-five years old. She left Pedro with six children, none older than fourteen years old.

Pedro became despondent and would never be the same. As an aggrieved single father, Pedro's stupor lasted more than a few years. Was this how his father felt when he lost his first wife? Aside from private subconscious conversations with his father, he could not bring himself to share his thoughts with anyone. Only his father would understand his feelings. He mouthed what needed to be said, smiled when called upon, and forged ahead with life. He left his children to the guidance of Gregoria's *genízaro*, thus growing distant from his own sons and daughter.

A TIME OF TRANSITION AND INTROSPECTION
April 1750, Alburquerque

Pedro the son always loved his father, and as time passed from his mother's death, he began to realize that his love would not be returned equally. His exasperation with his father grew. He felt for his father, he could remember, indeed witnessed, his father's close bond with his grandfather and his love for his mother.

Now eighteen years old, Pedro wanted to, indeed needed to confide in his father. His father had stopped confiding in him or anyone else. It seemed as though a part of him had died with Gregoria. But the son knew better. There were signs. Four years had passed since his mother's death. In his mind, his father had started to act oddly, not exactly the same but not so depressed. For this reason, Pedro always remembered his father's improvised talk about the plowshare. But there was something else. People talked and Pedro could not remain silent.

The younger Pedro thought about this moment for a few months and then took more than a few days to finally act. He walked up to his father who was seated under the veranda. He wasn't noticed. "Father."

"What." It wasn't a question but an acknowledgment of his presence. To him, his father appeared distant and beyond his age. He had become a quiet man.

Pedro leaned down toward his father and looked earnestly into his face, cleared his throat, and continued, "I've two things, father. I have volunteered to leave tomorrow for Laguna and Zuni. Juan and Cristóbal know, and have agreed that they can take care of things while I am gone." He repeated. "I have volunteered. I cannot stay here anymore."

The old man chewed on nothing as he thought about his eldest son joining the militia. He looked up at his son through his permanently misty eyes, "Yes, I suppose. I was younger than you when I first left. Good. It is time." He paused as the slight look of approval that had risen in his face faded. He became old and remote once again. Still, he stared at his son who returned the look with concern, "And the other?"

Pedro shifted his weight and then squatted down in front of his father. "I come to you, to say that it is okay with me and the others. You don't need our blessing. We know that you are interested in that Varela Jaramillo girl. Its. Just..."

The old man looked at his son a little embarrassed and irritated. He knew she was a year older than him. The son continued, "Josefa is pretty. People talk."

An enigmatic smile crossed the old man's face. "Son, if you are in love, then she is pretty. But," he raised a finger in front of his face, "looks are not everything and can change." Then he leaned forward and in a plaintive voice volunteered, "She comes from a good family. She is a descendent of the Jaramillos, Hurtados, and Varelas, and we are distantly related." He avoided talking about her age. At nineteen years old, Josefa Jaramillo was twenty years younger than him. His daughter and second son respectively were two and three years younger.

His father's infatuation with such girl at his age bothered Pedro. He was frustrated that he could not be more direct with his father. He replied with the only, safe words that came to mind, "Father, I am glad for you and happy that you are thinking about it. I only make one request."

"And what might that be?"

"Wait a few months. See how this military stuff works out. Yes."

"I promise. There is no rush." Pedro leaned to his father and kissed his check and hugged his grey head. "Thank you father." There was nothing Pedro could do to change his father, who answered, "No. You are a man now. I share your mother's love for you." And he meant it. He just felt distant from everything. Josefa offered him a companionship that his family lacked.

As they separated more words surfaced. "You know, son, my aunt Lucía, whom you never knew, was a Varela Jaramillo." His eyes smiled as his face remained stoic. "Good family."

The subject of his father's pending marriage to a girl who was two years younger than Pedro, came up more than once as he rode west with the militia. His friend, Cisco, merely laughed and shrugged at Pedro's concern about close-knit family ties. "Come on, Pedro, here in New Mexico we are all cousins."

"Except you and me."

"Don't be so sure. Besides, I am not the one betrothed to you."

"God help me. This conversation is going nowhere."

Cisco, a good-natured man, twenty years old or a few months older than Pedro, laughed again. "Maybe we should ask for God's help for your father. And he will have to get permission from the priests. Too bad old Father Otero is not around."

Pedro sighed. "Maybe not. He knew everything. Who is the new friar? You know, the one with the ugly beard? Fray José..."

Cisco at once corrected and finished the name. "José Irigoyen. He has been around and knows everyone."

Pedro already knew that he would not return to live at home, not with such a young stepmother. She would be like a sister and the idea of seeing her with his father made him very uneasy. No. If his father had not figured it out, this journey would be the first in the making of a career that, he hoped, would take him away from this *vergüenza,* this embarrassment.

The business at hand helped a little. Upon returning from a relatively uneventful trip to Zuni the contingent camped at Inscription Rock. The barely literate Pedro tagged along with a small group of soldiers who looked at the inscriptions carved in the cliff's face. He could make out the numbers for years and dates as well as some of the simpler names. One of the more literate men did the reading and as they progressed and came to the name Lopez Romero, Pedro decided that his name had to be added to the outdoor archive.

Pedro Romero's inscription at El Morro, "Inscription Rock" in western New Mexico. It reads, "Por aqui pasa Pedro Romero a 22 de Agto, año 1751," ("By here passed Pedro Romero on the 22nd of August, year of 1751.") Photograph courtesy of the National Park Service.

He had heard enough to know that most of the inscriptions said something to the effect, "I passed by here" with a date and name. He had the literate soldier trace the words out and then carved the letters in the soft rock with his knife, "Passed by here Pedro Romero on the 22nd of August of 1751."

Within two years he had secured a permanent transfer to El Paso that took him away from Alburquerque, his father, and the life that he wanted to put behind him. His marriage in 1755, and his quick promotion up through the ranks to Captain by his twenty-eighth birthday helped.

His father did not seem to care. Yet, something about his eldest son's escapades diverted his attention enough to let his mind focus more on the future rather than stumble through the past. He rationalized that his oldest son had an independent streak in him. He was a good son but Pedro understood or thought he did, these last few years had been hard on him. On occasion, Pedro checked and heard nothing but praise for his son as a soldier.

Although not as drastic or certain as death, Pedro could not avoid the sense that his oldest son's departure was another loss. Pedro tried to focus on the future, for he had four other boys and a daughter to raise. Others whispered behind his back that he would have two daughters with the addition of his young wife, all around the same age. He did not care.

He vowed not to ignore the children as he had with his departed son, and he would start by officially arranging for them to inherit his property. Yes, he and Felipe had divided their father's lands between him and all his brothers. Now, he would start partitioning his own property. He and his brother already took care of Manuel and his family, many of whom still worked for one brother or the other. Something about it all exhilarated him. It was what his father would have wanted. Such is life, and a new generation was on the horizon.

Just from the reaction of his new in-laws, he should have known that his marriage would be a source of problems. Pedro forced his will on Josefa's family. He was better off than they, and her father was the first to agree to the marriage. "She will be well off and not a burden on us. Besides, she in nineteen. If not now, when?" To him, love had nothing to do with the match. Her mother, like all mothers, cared for her daughter and saw it for what it was, an old man having his way with a defenseless young woman. Courtship and formality had no role in this arrangement. Everyone knew that Pedro and Josefa would become a source of gossip.

Because winter already had set in, Pedro agreed to have a discreet wedding as soon as possible after Easter. Along with his son's departure, Pedro's new married status really meant change. He fooled himself, because his personal exhilaration would turn to exasperation within hours. How he could not see the effects of introducing his young Josefa into his household with children, basically her age, spoke to his twisted mind.

"Mother" was an impossible concept for his teenaged children. Nor could they adapt to her being a "head of household." Any attempt by Pedro to insist on her place or to favor her, was met with resistance and over time, dislike, if not hatred for her and him. Through no fault of her own Josefa was miserable. The children, especially, María, Juan, and Miguel, could not accept her. The two younger ones followed their other siblings' lead. After all, their father had been absent through their formative years. Maids and their older brothers and sisters had raised them.

Pedro had a dysfunctional family and rather than correct it, he ignored it. Josefa's constant complaints and tears upset him. The bickering of his children distanced him from them. Nor was he stable enough to make sense of the situation. Instead, he ignored the family and obviously was pleased when María and Juan married before they reached their twentieth birthdays. This turn of events emptied the household, for María and Juan each took one of the younger siblings, and Miguel moved in with Juan and his new bride.

The boys still shared and worked the family lands with their father. The labor before them limited thoughts or conversations about what had divided them. For himself, Pedro was relieved to return home with only Josefa in the house. No more fights and complaints. Although some crying fits continued.

Nevertheless, almost a year after everyone moved out, Josefa gave birth to a daughter. Lucía Guadalupe was born and baptized in June of 1753. Her name reflected the growing New Mexican veneration for the Virgin of Guadalupe in Mexico. Neither Pedro nor his still teenaged wife knew enough to realize that the first name heralded back to one of the Romero founders in New Mexico, or that a Virgin of Guadalupe existed in Spain. A second daughter was born a year later, and, on January 2, 1757, their first boy was born whom they named after his twenty-two year old half-brother and his mother. It did not hurt that one of his other half-brothers had the name of Cristóbal Joseph. They added a third name, "Tomás, "because" Pedro joked, "having another boy was in doubt." Not understanding the humor, Josepha merely stared at his laughing face in silence. The baby was named Juan Joseph Tomás Romero.

Our Prayers Go Unanswered
1760s, Alburquerque

Juan Joseph Tomás Romero grew up under the guidance of his mother. His father did not bother with him or his siblings. Pedro chose to spend most of his time out of the house, basically ignoring his new family. He was a sick, unhappy man who had no desire to impart to anyone what little positive feelings that remained in him, and that included his wife. Essentially, Josefa was a kept woman who was left to fend for her children.

Juan Joseph grew up without a father. His two sisters, Lucía and María Petrona shared his plight. Needless to say, they grew up illiterate like their mother. What little they learned of their father's family, they picked up from the hearsay of distant relatives who were everywhere. On the rare occasions that their much older half-brothers were around they learned practically nothing, and from their mother even less.

They pieced together that their Romero grandfather had two wives just like their father. And this explained the plethora of Romero relatives, the exact relationships of whom they had long since given up on figuring out. That was their father's family, and from birth they returned his lack of affection. They were closer to their mother's Jaramillo family. In fact, they knew more about them than the Romeros.

When Juan Joseph was old enough, his father put him to work with myriad chores. As he grew older, he worked like any other day labor on his father's land. "You have to earn your keep. We are not *ricos*," was the stern and often repeated reasoning of Pedro, who, by Juan Joseph's fifteenth year, was an old, permanently frowning old man of sixty years. There was never any conversation between them. At least, not that Juan Joseph could remember. He feared his father, or the repercussions of his half-brothers, and merely did as he was told.

What a surprise, then, that two years later Pedro sired another son. As near as Juan Joseph could tell, the birth of his brother, Raphael Antonio, was not a source of joy so much as the subject of laughter between his older half brothers and their friends. "See, another uncle who is younger then his nephews."

If Juan Joseph was estranged from his father, what could be said for Rafael? His father died before his fourth birthday. He would have no memory of the man, which, in Juan Joseph's mind, was best under the circumstances.

The death of Pedro, of course, raised some problems, for the land and the house in which Josefa and her children lived belonged to the boys of Pedro's first wife. They graciously agreed to allow Josefa to continue living there, but made it clear that the property and house were theirs. When the time came, her children, and this especially meant Juan Joseph, would have to leave.

By this time, Juan Joseph had become accustomed to the head-of-household role. He was going on twenty-one years old. Over the years he naturally started filling the void left by his father, and now, with the old man's death, Juan Joseph continued without disruption. While his upbringing, or lack thereof, had its influence, he maintained empathy for his mother and did all that he could to make her happy.

He accompanied her to Pedro's funeral. If not for her, he would not have attended. The only emotion she showed was when she was shown the place of honor as the wife of the deceased. Juan Joseph watched as she proudly held up her head. This caused him to gaze at his half-brother Romeros and their families to really appreciate his mother's sentiment.

Juan Joseph's immediate concern was not the problems of an estranged family. Alburquerque had become a perilous place to live. At the time of Rafael's birth and his father's subsequent death, New Mexico was undergoing a prolonged drought. In places like Alburquerque, sixty to seventy days passed without a drop of moisture. It seemed that each year became dryer than the previous one. The drought peaked the year after Raphael's birth.

Crops became scarce. Livestock went barely fed, or in some cases, unfed. The Romeros fared a little better than some because they did not have large herds to worry over. They carefully tended their fields, solely concerned with raising enough food for their own sustenance. But even this had become problematic.

Invariably Indian raiding accompanied drought because they, too, suffered. No one in the settlements was surprised when the raiding started. They had braced for the inevitable and did not have to wait long. First, the Gila Apaches hit Alburquerque, then, the Navajos came with their smaller stealth operations. Not even the valley's dried up pastures, and dry, non-irrigated lands discouraged them. Then, in 1773, the Comanches rampaged through the valley. Each succeeding raid took livestock and hostages. Juan Joseph heard that a cousin was missing. He knew of other people who had been killed. Nor was he beyond the danger. He joined neighbors and family in their common defense.

Fortunately, the large Romero clan only had lands to protect. Because they had no livestock to speak of, the raiders bypassed them. Still, they lived on constant alert and were quick to run to the defense of their neighbors.

Pursuit of the raiders was beyond question. The people and what was left of their horses and mules were too weak for such ventures.

Thus, with no father, no hope of an inheritance, and the desperate times, Juan Joseph began to ponder his future. A new governor had given him more reason to think. The battle-hardened man from Sonora quickly showed his mettle. Early in the fall of 1779, word spread through the settlements that Governor Juan Bautista de Anza had surprised and defeated the Comanches on the eastern plains.

Juan Joseph could enlist in the royal army, become a *presidio* soldier. It could be perilous but danger existed everywhere for everyone. This governor seemed to know what he was doing. However, rumors circulated that the people in Santa Fe had come into conflict with him. The Franciscan friars began to claim that he was trying to run the Church.

Juan Joseph knew that the government wanted to settle lands on the periphery of the Rio Grande to set up buffers against the raiders. That was an ongoing idea since before Juan Joseph was born. Now as the former colony's centers became over-populated, especially with younger men whose skills in farming could not be utilized, people as well as the government talked about the concept. They questioned what the chance for survival would be if an individual accepted being a part of this first line of defense?

If the settlements of the Rio Puerco west of the Rio Grande were an example, the answer was, "not much." That area had to be abandoned. However, a place called Las Trampas in the mountains north of Santa Fe, survived even though its name, "The Traps," referred to the situation in which the settlers found themselves.

So long as his mother lived he would do nothing. He cared for her and his little brother. His sisters had married and moved out with their husbands. His mother knew and encouraged his planning, for she had initiated the idea of leaving Alburquerque. More than a mother, she had become his confidant. "Hijo, you need to think about what you will do."

"Yes, *mam*á. I will be with you."

"Yes hijo, I know. But, I am getting old. We can't stay here."

"Yes we can."

"I feel old. When I am called..."

"*Mamá*!"

"No, we must be open and plan for you. I want to know that you and Rafael will be well."

They continued to talk and plan when, in the spring of 1780, a smallpox epidemic swept the Rio Grande Valley. Josefa fell ill. She was forty-five years old and had lived a hard, unhappy life. Disease of any kind would have found a perfect target in her.

Juan Joseph could do nothing but try to comfort her with cold damp towels and soothing words. He sat at her bedside tending to her any need and prayed. "Dear God, she is a good woman. Please, spare her." But they both knew from the many deaths occurring around them that God had other plans.

They had agreed that Rafael would stay with his sisters, if they survived the pox. Juan Joseph would leave to try his luck in a place called Abiquiu on the Chama River in northern New Mexico. Josefa gave her approval with a weak smile and nod.

Juan Joseph accompanied her in her last hours. At one moment she regained consciousness and spoke slowly in a low whisper. "Listen, *hijito*, I don't know if there is a church where you are going."

Juan Joseph, with his eyes misting up, tried to talk, "I, I think...."

She continued. This was her moment. "We went to church when we could. It is not important." She paused to breathe. "Remember, if you pray and are good. If you are sincere, you believe. God will come to you. You do not need to go to him. Understand?"

"Yes, *mamá*. I promise." He looked at her second smile of approval.

Josepha Varela Jaramillo died in her sleep before daybreak of May 14, 1780. She would later be counted as one of the almost five thousand New Mexicans who died in the smallpox epidemic of that year. As planned, within a month her oldest son rode north out of Alburquerque.

WITH HIS OWN CONFIDENCE AND DETERMINATION
1780, Abiquiu

Abiquiu was another New Mexican locale where incessant Indian raids had dictated the pace of settlement. After a couple of false starts, and after Governor Anza forged a peace with the Comanches, people started moving back up the Chama River Valley. The village of Abiquiu sat on top of a small rise above the Chama River, a tributary of the Rio Grande. Built around a plaza as a defensive bastion, the town's appearance spoke of danger. However, the people needed to farm and the rich river bottom was where they worked, so a number of other smaller villages grew up along the river valley.

As Juan Joseph approached Abiquiu from down river he rode through a series of sandy, dry arroyos and, then, passed some of the smaller settlements of people who chose to challenge fate and live closer to their fields. First, he rode through the semi-deserted village of Santa Rosa de Lima, a place that locals claimed was the original settlement in the area. Now, it was a reminder of the area's vulnerability with most of the small plaza's buildings destroyed. A small adobe church with a burnt-out, collapsed roof gave testimony to harsh times. The place had been overrun and sacked. God would have to come to them, they could not go to God.

He noticed the prevalence of *torreones,* defensive towers, associated with a majority of the dwellings. These were not new to him. Perhaps a half a dozen such bastions sprinkled the Rio Grande Valley from Bernalillo south to Alburquerque. The presidio in Santa Fe had the vestige of at least one tower, and the area around La Ciénega sported a couple. These distinct defensive features continued to be evident up through Santa Cruz, but nowhere were the *torreones* as prevalent as around Abiquiu.

A few miles on he came upon a few houses and barns at a place the locals called Sierra Azul. The people in these places did not see Juan Joseph as an oddity, but rather as another of many new arrivals moving into the area. He would be welcomed as another able body for their common defense, while he also would be seen as another person who would claim some of the limited land that already seemed overpopulated.

He continued on, trailing a second horse packed with what little he possessed, an extra set of clothes, some utensils, a coffee pot, a blanket, some jerky, and one keep sake, his father's plowshare. He had taken the rusty brown piece of iron from the shelf where it had been his whole life. He never heard the story about it and did not take it as an heirloom, but for its value as a piece of iron, which was a rare and valuable commodity in New Mexico. He planned to have it forged into a short sword.

He carried an old army issue *escopeta* and fine knife that he had tucked into his belt at his back. A lance tied on the pack was his only other weapon. He tied his locally made *serape* behind his saddle. His pants, shoes, and leggings, the last tied below his knees, were all leather. Fully bearded under a well-used, wide-brimmed hat, Juan Joseph approached the small terraced, rocky rise that harbored the village of Abiquiu as a well-proportioned, average-sized man in his middle twenties.

He was starting over with nothing to lose and everything to gain. He had chosen to begin his new life in a place where its history indicated that the clash of arms was a

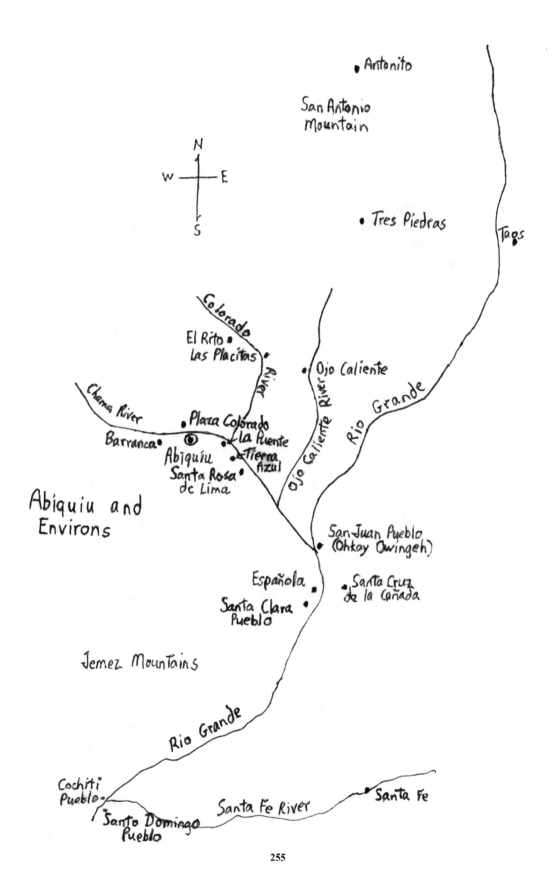

• Antonito

San Antonio
Mountain

N
W ─┼─ E
S

• Tres Piedras

Taos

Colorado

El Rito •
Las Placitas

River

• Ojo Caliente

Chama River

Ojo Caliente River

Rio Grande

• Plaza Colorado

Barranca •

◉ la Puente

Abiquiu

Tierra
Azul

Santa Rosa
de Lima •

Abiquiu and
Environs

San Juan Pueblo
(Ohkay Owingeh)
•

Española
•

• Santa Cruz
de la Cañada

Santa Clara
Pueblo

Jemez Mountains

Rio Grande

Cochiti
Pueblo •

Santa Fe River

• Santa Fe

Santo Domingo
Pueblo

necessary evil. For this he was prepared. As he approached the mesa with its fortified plaza he was a man schooled on the means of survival in an environment of want, which was perfect for Abiquiu.

At the base of the mesa, Juan Joseph rode up to a man who was leaning with one foot up against a wall of what would best be called an adobe *jacal*. At first, he appeared to be a lean, middle-aged man of Plains Indian, Hispano-Mexican origin. At closer view his aged, hollow face bespoke an old man unremarkable of mind. His discontented expression, forecast a querulous person ready to find fault with everything including life itself.

Juan Joseph stopped his horse and tipped his hat. "Good day, *señor*." The old man spit in reply, so Juan Joseph continued. "Is there a priest in the village?" He thought that a priest, if one existed, would be his most informative source.

The reply came in the form of a growl. "*Por que?* Why? Do you need to confess?"

"In truth we all do, no? Ha, ha."

Leaning heavier into the wall, the old man spit again. But Juan Joseph would not be discouraged, "A priest?"

"Sure," The old man made an almost imperceptible nod toward the mesa, "where he should be. At the church."

Following his direction, Juan Joseph saw low-lying adobe walls and a couple a small steeples.

"Sebastián Fernández."

"What?"

"That's his name. Sebastián Fernández. He has been here as long as me. And has more need to confess."

"Thank you friend." Juan Joseph gave his horse a nudge and tipped his hat again.

"Yah, sure." The old man spit again.

Juan Joseph rode up the dusty mesa and entered the fortified plaza of Abiquiu from a corner entrance. The plaza was ringed with continuous structures, including the small church, with no windows or doors facing out. He rode directly to the church where he found the priest seated in front of the attached residence. As Juan Joseph dismounted, the old priest invited him to sit at a table next to him. He poured a drink liquid from a pitcher.

Fray Fernández was a mostly bald, thin-faced man with patches of stringy, dirty gray hair hanging from his lower head, and a failed attempt at a goatee. Juan Joseph introduced himself with the information that he had come from Alburquerque.

The friar revealed badly yellowed and worn teeth as he smiled. "Ah, another Romero. There are a few here. Not like the Valdez or Martín clans mind you. But enough."

"Father, is there a place where I can spend a couple of nights before I figure out what to do?"

Apparently not used to Juan Joseph's show of respect, the priest wanted to talk. After a couple of minutes' diatribe, Juan Joseph cut him off by repeating his first question and added a second. "Do you know of a Miguel Romero?"

The priest would not be hurried. "Sit down son. Drink. I know it is not brandy. I've barely enough for the Holy Sacrament. Still there is no reason to rush. Not here."

Juan Joseph clearly realized that patience would be the best of strategies. As a result he learned that he could temporarily occupy one of the empty buildings along the west side of the plaza. Fray Sebastián pointed them out. He could truthfully say that he knew of a Miguel Romero from Albuquerque. He named a few, "Juan Pablo, a Tomás, and Juana whose husband was killed in an Indian raid. "But, they are all from Santa Cruz de la Cañada, I believe. Maybe Santa Fe."

"I heard that the Comanches had agreed to a peace?" Juan Joseph wanted to elicit some information about the all too familiar danger of raids.

"Yes, but the Utes still linger. Things are better now than before. The truth is that at one time not long ago, we were all depressed, cowed, and frightened. Death could come at any moment."

Juan Joseph thanked the old priest for the drink and led his horses across the plaza to one of the empty residences. Save for an empty room off another of similar size, not much larger than a common stable, only a door and one window covered with hide hinted that the place was constructed for human habitation. Juan Joseph did not care. He was too tired and dirty. Plus, he still faced the task of taking care of his horses, his most valuable possessions. He relieved them of their burdens, storing the saddle and baggage in the first room. Then he brushed them down and led them off the mesa to the river below. There the animals drank and foraged while Juan Joseph rinsed himself from the waist up. The fresh cold water felt good and the sun's heat drying him off re-energized him. He was thinking again as he took his horses back to the plaza. He hobbled them and, then, used some of his supplies to create an outside seat next to the wall at the side of his door.

"Dear God!" He thought as he sat down and executed a piercing search of the near landscape and distant mountaintops. "Where do I begin?" The increasing darkness would give him time to look for answers after a night's rest.

A loud but distinct, bang followed by lighter sounds of metal on metal woke him. That had to be a *herrero*, a blacksmith! Juan Joseph threw off his blanket, stretched, and cursed when he realized that he did not bring up any water to his room last night. "Oh well, back to the river." But, first, he wanted to find the source of the sounds that woke him.

The smith worked in one of the plaza's buildings with an open front. Juan Joseph found him surrounded by smoke, flying sparks, and the wheeze of his black double bellows, the force of which sent out the smell of well-heated coal. The man at work appeared not quite as tall as Juan Joseph. He had receding, close-cropped gray hair and a large round face set on powerful shoulders, a stocky body with hands larger than any Juan Joseph had ever seen.

Juan Joseph introduced himself and found the smithy to be friendly, perhaps an attitude he assumed when Juan Joseph held out his plowshare and asked if it could be turned into a short sword blade.

The smith gave an initial quizzical look and, then, smiled. "You want me to beat a plowshare into a sword? Perfect for here. But shouldn't we check with the *padre*? Doesn't the Bible say we should be doing the opposite?" He laughed at his question.

Juan Joseph smiled in acknowledgement of the moment. The smith continued, "Sure, I will do it while the coals are hot. I'm Chaco Ramírez." His handshake was as strong as his hands indicated.

They talked as Chaco worked with his hammer banging away on an anvil. The most important families in the valley are three, Valdez, Montoya, and Martín. "None of them are rich, understand. They have been here longest and have the most land. Their influence does not extend beyond the valley."

"As for the Romeros," he continued between strokes on the red-hot piece of iron, "yes, there are some. But I do not place a Miguel, which means little. I am bad with names, especially first names. I probably know him, but would have to see him."

They agreed that any description from Juan Joseph would be futile, for he hadn't seen Miguel for many years and that when he was a child. Chaco assured Juan Joseph that if Miguel existed in the valley, he would find him. Then he stuck into a tub of water the newly formed, glowing red piece of iron that he had been hammering, the steam rising and hissing. "Here *amigo*. A fine blade for a short sword."

"How much?"

"Nothing. I would rather tend to your horses. Here defense is mutual." Then he shared where to look for some Romeros, "Working in the fields back toward Tierra Azul."

Juan Joseph retraced his route down river for not quite four miles. The first person he asked pointed out a man working in one of the field's furrows. His name? Pedro Romero, the name of his father and a half-brother who he never met! Upon being hailed by a stranger on horseback, Pedro stopped working and waited for the man, now on foot, to approach. Pedro had the unmistakable look of hard outdoor labor. He nodded in the affirmative when asked if he was Pedro Romero.

Juan Joseph introduced himself with a brief history of his move from Alburquerque, and his search for his half-brother, Miguel. With this information, Pedro dropped his defenses and proposed that they meet at sunset at a small adobe that he pointed out.

"Bueno. 'ta pronto. Good, see you soon."

Later the two Romeros conversed over cups of mint tea. "Yes, Miguel Romero is here. And, there are others, some from Taos but mostly from Santa Cruz. Some of us are related 'cause we moved here together. The others, well, who knows? Maybe somewhere with our *antepasados*, our ancestors." They commented on the coincidence over the Pedro first names.

Miguel worked for the Martín family. At the moment, Pedro did not know where Juan Joseph would find him. "His work takes him many places in the valley. You should go ask Los Martínes. They have the long house there in Tierra Azul, but they have land throughout the valley."

Pedro gave good advice, for not only did Juan Joseph locate Miguel but also the Martín family also sized him up and immediately offered him work and a place to stay. Moreover, something far more important occurred at that fateful first encounter.

Nothing about her appeared pretentious, just a young woman husking corn with members of the household. Her long and not quite straight hair did not stand out, nor would her rather normal almost black eyes. Maybe it was the barely perceptible acknowledgement that she noticed him. How could he know? Was he sure? Whatever it was he noticed her and time would tell.

Miguel, his long-lost half-brother who he barely knew in Alburquerque, filled him in, "She is Lucía, María Lucía. A Martín." He also informed him that she was single, then ended with an exclamation, "Good luck!" His emphasis dealt more with reality than wistfulness. Juan Joseph had never courted a woman before. He would be the problem not her. He was shy.

Miguel had married and had a growing family. He introduced Juan Joseph to everyone he knew. They became brothers, not distant half-brothers. Sixteen years older than Juan Joseph, Miguel had passed his fortieth birthday. He had been in Abiquiu for around ten years, "*más o menos*." He was not sure. He was a slender upright man with broad shoulders, a narrow face with a concerned look and ready smile. Juan Joseph liked him but not as much as he came to like Lucía.

He soon learned that most of the so-called wealthy Martín family lived in a house that, with the exception of an impressive *torreón*, was not much larger or well appointed than the one in which he grew up. As he got to know his employers, which came easy because they worked in the fields or with the sheep along with everyone else, he learned of two advantages that they had over him. First, all the men could sign their names and, after a fashion, some could write. Second, he learned from Lucía that the family had a sense of history about itself, which Juan Joseph lacked. She knew about a governor named Vargas and that her great, great grandfather, his brother Luis, and Pedro Martín Serrano came to New Mexico with him. No one used the Serrano surname anymore. She was told that they advised their grandchildren to move to the Abiquiu area where today they have lands from Santa Rosa de Lima to Abiquiu.

The Martín men were sure that the Romeros also came to New Mexico with Vargas, "and probably were here before the great revolt." They also heard enough from other Romeros to convince them of this point. Juan Joseph shared that he thought his grandfather had survived the revolt. From this conclusion, it was an easy step to speculate that both families were related. They even speculated that the families originated in Spain.

Juan Joseph had no problem being accepted by the Martín family. He was a hard worker, obviously experienced with work in the fields. He quickly learned how to work sheep. Moreover, he had his own weapons and did not cost the Martíns when Governor Anza mandated that every *pobre* had to be armed with at least a bow and twenty-five arrows, or be fined. Nor did Juan Joseph flinch at the potential of Indian raids.

He won over Lucía who came to know him as an unusually sensitive, shy man. His apparent empathy attracted her. His mother's influence remained a strong aspect of his personality. Love came naturally to them both but Father Fernández's demand that they attend his regularly scheduled catechism for the unmarried every morning and evening for two weeks delayed their wedding. Fray Fernández married them during the height of summer on August 1, 1781.

NOT HEROES OR VILLAINS, JUST COMMON FOLK
Fall 1798, Abiquiu

Three boys and three girls. Equal. Six children spread over fifteen years. Perfect. Now, against the morning backdrop of a cacophony of singing birds, Juan Joseph wished he could look over to the other side of his bed and watch Lucía in a soft sleep. Maybe another day, but not now. As usual she was up early preparing the household for the day ahead.

She silently left Juan Joseph to his semi-conscious thoughts because he had returned from a trip to Alburquerque to visit his sisters and younger brother. He had gone there twice before. He tried to convince Rafael to join him in Abiquiu, but his brother could not leave his sister, María Petrona who had raised him. Juan Joseph understood.

The Rio Abajo family survived and that was all that could be asked. Juan Joseph shared with them his small success in Abiquiu. He continued to share his labor with his wife's family. He occupied and then successfully put in a legal claim for some abandoned land. He explained to his siblings that the land became his, "Because some people could not stick it out, he was able to become a land owner."

After a pleasant visit of a week, Juan Joseph was pleased to return to his almost completed three room home. He arrived with a new, commercially made short sword along with a bag of seed, a water bowl, and, for Lucía and the girls, a porcelain chamber pot. The last was more expensive than all the other items put together.

As expected, Lucía's pleasure, indeed glee, upon seeing the chamber pot more than offset the cost. Besides, Juan Joseph had decided that Lucía and the girls should not have to go out to the *pozo*, the outhouse, basically a hole he had dug and enclosed on three sides with wood and tree branches. Modesty was not the issue so much as the snakes that seemed to be attracted to the *pozo*'s warmth. "An irony," in his mind, "for the two deserved each other." Now, armed with an old lance to clear and kill the snakes, only he and the boys, when they came of age, would go there, or else do as guys could do and use the great outdoors.

Of course, the newly purchased sword had more immediate value. The old sword made from a plowshare eighteen years ago would go to twelve-year-old Salvador, his oldest boy. The old sword's greatest use would be as a tool, cutting crops and collecting kindling. A weapon when necessary, the reshaped iron still primarily worked in the fields. Juan Joseph's two other sons would have to wait a few years before they could handle a sword, much less deal with a snake. Neither Francisco Antonio nor Manuel Tomás had reached their third birthday.

Reminiscing reminded Juan Joseph of the time Lucía encountered a snake close to the house. Rather than panic, she moved the children out of harm's way, had the older ones collect some dry brush while she lit a stick from the fire in the fireplace. Then she went back outside to confront the defiant snake. She threw the brush on top of the coiled snake, then, tossed the lit stick on top of the mass, which lit it, and killed the snake.

Her action with the snake astounded Juan Joseph. He looked at the charred dead snake and looked at her askance. Lucía shrugged and said, "It came to me." And that was yet another reason why he admired her.

As required, Juan Joseph participated with the local militia. The people of Abiquiu were expected to protect themselves as a matter of fact. Juan Joseph never knew anything different. Acceptance of his plight worked to his advantage. Those who stayed and survived ended up with the land vacated by those who left, This reality, combined with his familial connection worked in favor for Juan Joseph. He had some land of his own.

He participated in a few punitive expeditions. Other than a minor skirmish just outside of Santa Rosa, he had not participated in any actual fighting. At the same time, while on the expeditions he learned about the surrounding territory, especially up the

Chama River to a place called Las Nutrias and beyond. He also had gone north up the small Vallecitos River, a branch of the Chama River. He had traveled past some hot springs as far as the cone shaped San Antonio Mountain where those with him agreed that the area was perfect for tending to sheep. On a later trip, he heard from some of the older men that the valley beyond San Antonio Mountain was the headwaters of the Rio Grande, and that it had plenty of irrigable land. They predicted that once the Indian menace could be solved, the place would be settled quickly.

Juan Joseph stood and stretched. In his mind, the San Luis Valley would not be settled in his lifetime. A settlement around the Vallecitos hot springs had failed more than once. That was not even half way to San Antonio Mountain, much less beyond. Besides, he had wasted enough time in his own thoughts. Winter approached and he wanted to lay the final *adobes* for the last wall of his third room. With luck and a little help from his neighbors, he could get the roof up and layered before the first snowfall. Today, he needed to make the *adobes* so the rest of the day's sun could dry them out and have them ready in the next few days. He could hear Salvador priming the fire to make tea. They had a hard couple of day's work ahead of them.

Working alongside his son brought joy to Juan Joseph. The distant memory of his father, his long absences, and lack of attention rested heavy on his mind. That was not the model he would follow. Beyond being the oldest son, Salvador became his father's best friend. Juan Joseph shared everything with him. A good part of that included Juan Joseph's vision of fatherhood, which, in turn, brought up his mother's influence and a profound respect for women. The two of them shared the task of fathering with the rest of the children and, especially, paying attention to anything Lucía needed.

With the room completed and the first light snow changing the landscape's color, Juan Joseph and Salvador had another task to complete. On that crisp late October morning they mounted and pointed their horses south into the Jemez Mountains to look for bear. Now was the time when bears started to slow down as they prepared for their winter's hibernation. The success of their hunt meant the winter's major portion of meat plus the much-desired warmth of a new blanket or coat.

However, their success did not come without some degree of danger. Finding their prey was not difficult and it did not take long. Bear were plentiful in the Jemez Mountains that defined the southern ridge of their valley. They had two shots from their primed *escopetas* and neither of them expected to be so lucky as to bring down the animal with those shots alone, and they didn't. So, while Salvador, hurriedly reset his powder and rammed another ball down his weapon's barrel, Juan Joseph, with lance held firmly in his arm charged on horseback at the angry, withering beast.

Salvador marveled at his father's dexterity, as he crept up to the still bear and shot it again to make sure that it was dead. Juan Joseph leaned down to his son and clapped him on the shoulder. "It will be your turn with the lance soon enough."

They returned home with their butchered prize packed on a third horse. Rather than celebrate, a concerned Lucía met them with questions about the details of their hunt. The other children watched and listened with wide-eyed wonderment. The event was something that little Francisco Antonio, or "Cisco" for short, as he approached his ninth birthday, would always remember. His mother surprised his father and older brother

261

by telling them that they would have to fast until they went to church and received communion the next day, or when Father agrees to say mass.

Juan Joseph's opened mouth expression elicited an explanation from her. This was not their first bear. She did not hesitate but rather calmly said, "All animals are God's creation put here to feed and clothe us. He permits us...for our survival. You know..." Here she gave a knowing look at Juan Joseph, "...how much this bear means to us. We must give thanks and not take it for granted." She stopped in silence, looked at her husband and oldest son and continued. "We don't know what he meant in the wild. How many other bears did he sire so that the forest is full, so that others may partake?" Silence abounded. "God deemed that his time in the wild would end. Not you. We, you, must show your appreciation."

Juan Joseph and Salvador had no choice but to rise hungry early the next morning, dress against the cold, and ride up to the mesa to attend mass. Life was too precious not to give thanks, nor to disagree with Lucía.

In the following May the village became abuzz with news that the governor had authorized a trade fair at Abiquiu. The children listened as the adults, especially the menfolk, talked about past trade fairs and told how trade fairs have been held in Taos. One of their mother's uncles talked about a relative who had attended a trade fair at a pueblo called Pecos. Cisco especially started paying attention when his father shared with him that he could accompany him to the upcoming fair.

On the appointed day, Abiquiu filled with outsiders, including government soldiers who looked wondrous in their almost matching leather jackets and wide-brimmed hats. At a designated field north of the mesa, the *vecinos,* or Hispanos, set up their campsites on the side closest to the mesa, while the far side was left for the Indians, who arrived in sudden fashion. As smoke began to rise from newly started campfires, the beat of drums and the sound of chanting voices permeated the air. It was the first time that any of Juan Joseph's children had heard Indian music, much less had seen them dance.

Juan Joseph had nothing to trade. He watched as other wealthier merchants, including his Martín in-laws, bartered. Cisco watched, as captive Indians and settlers seemed to be the objects of exchange. He could not be sure. It seemed that humans were the major trade item that the Indians used to purchase horses, blankets, foodstuff, and, especially, steel weapons. Juan Joseph quickly explained that trading weapons to the Indians was strictly forbidden, even though it went on.

Cisco could not help but overhear a conversation that his father and Salvador had with a man who dressed like the Indians, but who did not look like them. The man talked in a heavily accented, broken Spanish and kept saying, "Yo Diné, Diné," while pounding his chest. An interpreter came up to them and explained that their suspicions were correct. The man was not a full-blooded Indian. Rather, he was captured in the Rio Puerco near Cabezón Peak when he was a young child. He had lived with the Navajos ever since. Diné was not his name but his way of saying that he was Navajo and did not want to return to Spanish society. The interpreter casually continued, "There are many like him. Enough to form a clan, their own extended group, that the Navajo tribe calls the Mexican clan."

With their curiosity piqued to unimagined heights back at home, Juan Joseph answered his children's rapid-fire questions by holding up his hands. "It is very complicated. I will tell you when you are older." The children clearly understood that their father had no taste for the subject.

A Small Inheritance, A Caring Gesture, Francisco
Spring 1807, Abiquiu

Juan Joseph naturally favored his oldest son, Salvador. Francisco, the second son was his mother's favorite. Yet, none of the children ever felt slighted by either parent. Cisco remembered the day his father gave him the wrought iron short sword. He was 15½ years old. The sword did not measure longer than from his hand to his elbow. Cisco had witnessed everything from the return from the bear hunts to the trade fairs. He had only heard of the past Indian raids and subsequent punitive expeditions. Everyone knew about the miracle when Santiago had appeared in the form of a great cloud to save the women and children of Ojo Caliente from an eminent Comanche attack. The adults made sure to awe their children with this proof of God's favor. Many people credited that miracle, rather than governor Anza's defeat of the Comanches and their terrifying leader, Cuerno Verde, for the current relative peace.

The moment began with his father talking about inheritance. "You are a Romero and a Martín. Like me, you will not have an inheritance of land or much else. But, you will be better off than I was, for you have a father who cares for you." Juan Joseph then proceeded to relate the story of why and how he left Alburquerque to start a new life on the Chama River, "and to meet your mother."

"I had two horses, some pots and pans, a few clothes, the escopeta, a knife, and this." He held out the short sword for emphasis. "Only it wasn't what it is." Here, he paused to watch his son's quizzical reaction to this small riddle.

"This, Cisco, was an old plowshare that belonged to my father, to his father, and, maybe, before. *Quién sabe?* Who knows?" He paused again, looking pensive with one eye open staring out into the past. "The first thing I did when I got here was to have the blacksmith, change it into this. At the time and for a while after, this, yes, this," he held out the sword again, "was important to me. Now it is yours. Use it. It is a fine tool and, God willing, you will not have to use it as a weapon."

Cisco held up the sword. It was nothing but a hand-carved wood handle and a pockmarked dull blade held together with dried rawhide strands. It was truly a weapon or tool unique to the place, but Cisco understood. It was something special that his father now shared with him. The sword represented more, his father's love and concern for his second son. In Cisco's mind, he had come of age. The household had added another man. It was time for him to transition from mother to father and Salvador.

Juan Joseph's act was intentional. He cared for all his children. In June of 1797, he and Lucía had the last of their six children, three girls and three boys. He was forty years old. That was ten years ago and now he had turned fifty, an age when he needed to think about his family and his own mortality.

He expected the girls to marry, and, God willing, have good husbands. The small parcel of his land would, by custom, go to Salvador. This was especially so because Juan Joseph expected his much younger Lucía to outlive him, and she would stay in the house under Salvador's care.

That left Francisco and Manuel, the two younger boys. Cisco was no longer a child and Manuel was about to pass his tenth birthday. Juan Joseph had seen and knew enough. He was a subsistence farmer, a poor landowner. He had spent these last years trying to raise enough squash, beans, corn, wheat, and chile along with some chickens, a pig or two, and, in good times, up to five head of cattle to support his growing family. From around the age of seven, the children had chores such as fetching pails of water from the river or carrying in logs for the fireplace. As the boys matured, their labor increased and lightened his workload. However, he understood that his small parcel had been producing at its maximum. Additional labor would not help increase its production.

Moreover, the population in and around Abiquiu had more than doubled from the time he moved to the place. These newcomers wanted land and needed work. Frankly, Juan Joseph worried. The world around Abiquiu never matched the lifestyle he knew in the Rio Abajo. Now, the future had no positive answers for his children.

Along with these direct and personal concerns in 1806, the men in the community had come to life over the news that a group of foreigners had been captured on the headwaters of the Rio Grande north of San Antonio Mountain. These men called themselves "*Americanos,*" and came from the east. It seems that another country, another civilization, neither Catholic nor Spanish-speaking, so they heard, existed to the east beyond the mountains and the *llanos*, the plains. Over the last three decades a few of these people came to New Mexico, mostly, to Santa Fe. Then, this recent episode caught everyone's attention, because the captured men belonged to the military and were found camped in New Mexico territory.

Such information slowly filtered out of Santa Fe then down the societal ranks to the workers and *peones.* By then, reality had been clouded in the telling and retelling of the news. Although the news did not have an immediate effect on Juan Joseph or his friends, it was of concern and cause for some thought. If fact, when the men got together to talk, the topic, such as they knew it, served as a perfect foil for speculation.

Up until now Juan Joseph's world was the lower Chama River valley. Albuquerque hovered in the distant south. His hunting and militia duty had taken him into the local mountains, up river through a succession of valleys, and north past San Antonio Mountain to a trout rich river they called the *Conejos*, because of all the rabbits in the area.

The idea of another people other than Indians never entered his head. In fact, even the vague mention that he had heard early in his life about a place called Spain had been lost from memory. Then, there were some people who recently moved into the Abiquiu area. They were not New Mexicans rather they claimed to come from a place in the faraway south that they called Mexico.

While concerned over what the arrival of these "*Americanos*" meant, Juan Joseph tried not to agonize over the future. He did this by turning to his work, steadfastly doing each year what he did in past years. When spring came and the snows let up he plowed until called to work with the community to clear out and repair the area's *acequias*. Then he finished plowing and started planting each crop in its turn. His life had come to this. Someway, somehow he and his family would survive.

He felt blessed with Salvador. His first-born learned quickly and worked hard. And, recently married, he would be starting his own family. Compared to Salvador, Francisco seemed a little soft. Juan Joseph attributed this to Cisco, as everyone still called him, being the second son and not the oldest. He did not work as hard as his older brother. He was not lazy rather he had his own pace for doing things.

To Juan Joseph's pleasure, Cisco matured with the years. As Salvador and the girls married, Cisco replaced his older brother as his father's consistent companion. As age continued to creep up on Juan Joseph, Cisco compensated for his father's decreasing physical abilities.

Then, in February of 1816, Cisco, who was twenty-five years old, asked his parents if they would go to the house of Miguel Lopes and his wife María Josefa Martín and ask if they would allow their fourteen-year-old daughter to marry him. The fact that the bride was young, or that her mother and Lucía were related, did not give them pause for thought. After all, Juan Joseph married Lucía when she was slightly younger. Such matches had become normal. As for the family connection, well, that was for the priest to decide. When the time came, the good Father mumbled something about "first cousin once or twice removed" or "second cousin." No one understood him except that the padre approved the match.

With the wedding date set for April, Juan Joseph, now approaching sixty years old, sat down with Lucía. He had decided on a plan. "My love, after the wedding only Manuel will be left." Manuel, their youngest, was eighteen years old. "And, he, not for long. The boys continue to work our land but it cannot support all the families."

The always patient Lucía waited, seated with her hands folded on the table in front of her. She looked directly into her husband's dark, misty eyes. He continued, "I have been thinking but I cannot be sure. We were going to leave the land to Salvador." He hesitated and ran a finger under his nose, which was a nervous habit of his. "The others will have to go off on their own."

Lucía uncoupled her hands. "Juan, that is the way. They will go like you did. They are good, healthy. You have taught them."

"Yes, yes." Juan Joseph sighed. "I know. They will find a way."

"With the help of God, they will be fine." Lucía gave her husband a reassuring smile. "They are ready. We can do no more."

"Ah Lucía, my love, but there is. That is why I want to talk to you."

Lucía gave Juan Joseph a doubtful look. She did not need to ask for clarity. He continued, "Our land. I want to trade it, sell it."

"But why?" Lucía was puzzled.

"To your brothers. They can add it to the other family lands. In exchange, they will let us and Salvador stay in this house and we will receive two good horses, some tools, a good lance, and three used, but good, short swords. We can add this to what we have before dividing it among the boys."

"How do you know this?" It dawned on Lucía that Juan Joseph had planned and arranged everything.

"And your family wants to help out. The boys will be hired to work their lands and livestock. This gives them a future better than I had."

A now submissive Lucía could only react with, "And?"

"And I need your blessing." With these words he grabbed hold of Lucía's hands.

Lucía looked at the loving grip and straightened herself. "You and the family are my life. God put us here for our family. How can I say no to this. Of course you have my blessing."

A great deal of emotion overwhelmed Juan Joseph, who stood up and leaned over the table and kissed Lucía on her forehead.

Another Wedding, Francisco
29 April 1816, Abiquiu

Pleased, he leaned on his staff. So far as weddings go this was not different. He had witnessed his children's four previous weddings. The youngest, Manuel, had a girlfriend that Juan Joseph was sure would become his wife.

But, for now, Cisco and Dolores stood at the altar before the aging priest. Today was theirs and, really, the beginning of their adult lives. Juan Joseph still wondered what would become of their lives even with the small stake he gave them. Before the wedding, Cisco made arrangements to leave the household and take up residence in nearby Tierra Azul where, with his father's help, he had secured work.

As he walked out of the adobe church with Dolores on his arm, Cisco spotted his father bent over his staff in the building's shade that had a backdrop of low-standing brown residences set off by the deep green of the towering cottonwood trees behind them. He saw his father as he always saw him a strong, upright, proud man, not the white haired, old man who actually stood there.

Cisco was determined not to be a burden on his father and had told him not to worry about him. Now he was anxious to go to his new home to start his own independent life. Work needed to be done and he wanted to make his father proud.

Cisco became one of many who worked for the Martín family. The family's extensive holdings extended throughout the valley from Abiquiu, south through the many plazas or *puestos,* like Tierra Azul and Santa Rosa de Lima that were within walking distance of each other.

When Antonio Severino Martín moved his immediate family to Taos in 1804, the family's influence grew to extend throughout northern New Mexico. Cisco, a Martín Serrano through his mother and by marriage, was too far removed to enjoy the family's prominence. Rather he worked for them as a laborer. Among the workers, he was at the top of the social pecking order, which included many mixed-bloods and ransomed Native Americans from the surrounding tribes.

Still, clad in his buckskins with his long dark hair tied up in two braids, as was the fashion, it was hard to tell Cisco apart from the others. That Cisco, or his brothers and sisters for that matter, could neither read nor write also separated them from the Martín family. The more immediate boys in the Martín family took advantage of the one teacher in the area. Old Severino's oldest son, Antonio José, two years younger and a distant relative of Cisco's, became so enraptured with education that the family sent him south to Mexico, Durango to become a priest.

Cisco's father never gave a thought to sending his boys to school. He had his reasons, none of which had anything to do with a dislike of education. First, he could not afford it. Time was too precious to be spent away from the tasks at hand. He could not take the time to transport them up to the plaza when they were young, and when they matured he needed them in the fields. Such is the reality of subsistence living.

Juan Joseph had other concerns. He realized that the valley had become too crowded, which meant more people trying to survive off the limited land. Also, after four decades of intensive farming and constant grazing, the land produced less. Juan Joseph did not know the reason but he noticed the result of too many people on limited, tired land. By 1800, only Santa Fe boasted a larger population than the Rio Chama Valley.

Leaving the valley was not limited to the Martíns, los Martines. Even some of Juan Joseph's Romero cousins joined in a petition for a land grant up river at Las Nutrias, later to be known as Tierra Amarilla.

Cisco did not have a sense of adventure in him. He focused on his abundant daily tasks and the maintenance of his new, young wife. Their two-room house qualified more as a *jacal*, the saving grace of which was the large fireplace that heated up the whole place.

Cisco's youthful time spent with his mother in the kitchen proved to be of value in helping Dolores. She was willing, but had not quite acquired all the knowledge that her mother was in the process of teaching when the marriage interrupted. Nevertheless, they did come to appreciate and even love each other. They spent many an evening in their modest "palacio" as the fireplace's golden light reflected off the beams and branches of a ceiling not more than two inches above their heads as they stood. They walked over a floor of packed earth, made hard by a good dose of ox-blood.

Possibly because of her youth, their first child did not come so quickly. They were not bothered by that. God would bless them with a child when the time was right. Meanwhile, life continued with their daily tasks and the year's passing, punctuated by the seasons and religious holidays.

Some of history's larger events became known to them and seemed to have little or no effect on their lives. They were more excited with the birth and development of their son, Juan de Jesús who was born in 1820 four years into their marriage. Within a year later a neighbor told them that Mexico had won its independence from Spain, and, "we are a part of the new country of Mexico."

Cisco shrugged his shoulders. "How can that be? Mexico is far away."

"Come on Cisco, you cannot be so dumb," teased a friend, "We were a part of Spain and it is further away, across an ocean."

"Yah, but..."

"The king in Spain ruled over us."

And Cisco added, "So now we have the king of Mexico to rule us."

"No! Mexico, which was New Spain when ruled by Spain, does not have a king. So I hear."

To this Cisco's face lit up. "Ah hah! Now I know. We are part of a new country without a king to rule us." Then he reverted to a puzzled look. "How can that be? With no king?"

His friend gave an almost imperceptible shake of the head. "*Ay*, Cisco. You are so difficult. Sometimes I do not know whether you are kidding or serious. We are part of a new country called Mexico and without a king. That is how it is."

With a knowing smile Cisco said, "I guess Mexico has come to us. It is no longer so far away to the south. It is here."

This resulted in a sigh, "Exactly, Cisco."

So life continued. Cisco learned to grow *punche,* a local, potent tobacco. Although illegal, nobody ever questioned them. Besides it was a highly desirable trade item. The

267

new country allowed trade with the Americanos. A new trail across the plains connected two countries. As a result, these foreigners became more commonplace, even around Abiquiu. In fact, Cisco saw one of these people for the first time, when a group of three of them and some New Mexicans rode up the valley to go trap beaver. Except for their accouterments, they looked pretty much the same as anyone.

At this time Cisco visited his father, now wholly incapacitated except for his brain. "Yes, Cisco. I understand. Spain is the reason we are here. We are descendants of the Spanish who came to this place many years ago. I guess the people down south wanted to rule themselves. They got tired of the king. As for New Mexico, we have no choice but to be a part of Mexico. We have been connected to that place for forever."

Lucía, Cisco's mother, who, Cisco noticed, looked very frail, overheard her husband's explanation. She could not help but add, "Spain, Mexico, king or not, we will not change nor will they...," She waved her hand as if there were some unseen mystical existence in the air, and continued, "...do anything for us. We will continue as we are."

Cisco nodded in agreement. All he ever wanted is to continue as he is. Now was not the time for change in his life. He had more pressing concerns. With the help of the other women in the village, Dolores gave birth to a second son in their house on May 30, 1822. They named him José Tomás, using Cisco's father's two middle names. And as they would do with all their children, they baptized him in Abiquiu's San Tomás Church.

Cisco and Dolores followed a custom of naming their boys José, for Saint Joseph, the father of Christ, just as the locals tended to name their girls María, for Mary, the mother of Christ. Because everyone had the names of José and María they became known by their second name, like Cisco's mother who was María Dolores, but known as Dolores. Thus Cisco and Dolores had five boys. Three of them were named José with a different second name, Tomás, Vicente, and Albino. They named their only girl, born in 1832, Maria Manuela.

Also, Lucía's words proved prophetic. In 1825, the Mexican government made an attempt to forestall an increasing unrest over the area's crowded conditions. The governor ordered that a survey be taken of the land and land ownerships. Subsequently, he ordered a redistribution of land that did not include anything for Juan Joseph and his family, nor did it quell the unrest. Rather, the policy created even more animosity. For the Romeros, nothing changed.

Lucía did not have long to complain or even express an "I told you so." In that same year she unexpectedly saddened Juan Joseph by preceding him in death. María Lucía's frail appearance told of the result of a life in which she gave six births while living in harsh conditions. Her death was quick and relatively painless. She caught a cold that within a day left her bedridden. Juan Joseph, with the help Salvador's wife, his daughter-in-law, did what he could to make her comfortable. He sent for a priest who arrived in time to administer the Church's Last Rights. That was Juan Joseph's last act as the family patriarch. She died on the third day.

The sorrow that Juan Joseph felt carried over into guilt, for he was the one who she and his daughter-in-law cared for. They cleaned him, fed him, and helped him to get around when needed. How was it, he thought, that he never noticed her plight until the end? Only then, he got himself up to help her. Had he learned nothing from caring for his mother? Now, with Lucía not there to help him, there was no purpose. He watched Cisco openly cry at her bedside. Salvador merely turned away to hide his emotions. The girls all wept and Manuel stood staring at his mother in stark silence.

Juan Joseph mustered all his strength to attend the funeral and to keep a stern face as, he thought, was expected. He could not explain his inward hurt. He felt as if he cried internally. He lost any desire to live. Almost as if he willed it, he died six weeks later and was buried next to his Lucía. He was sixty-six years old.

Cisco and his brothers kept in touch. They helped each other when needed and, in season, pooled their livestock. They stood as godparents for one another's children, the baptisms for which mostly took place in Abiquiu. The Martíns let Salvador keep his father's house while the rest of them continued as hired laborers, mostly working for the Martín family.

More activity came to the Abiquiu area by the middle of the second decade. People became interested in a route to another land called California, also a part of the new country called Mexico. Most of the locals knew the terrain up river from them and beyond. They had hunted and, on occasion, sought out marauding Indians in the area. The elders vaguely remembered an expedition led by two priests who came to Abiquiu on their way to California. No one remembered whether they made it, although the locals reasoned that they must have been successful, for, in 1828, an official from Santa Fe named Juan María de Rivera led his third contingent following the same route. Although Rivera failed to reach California and returned through Abiquiu, he and his men added to the knowledge of the area beyond the headwaters of the Chama River.

In the following year, a merchant who introduced himself as Antonio Armijo showed up with thirty men and three times that number of mules laden with locally woven blankets. He bragged about how he and those with him would get rich by selling the blankets in California. He actually convinced some of Abiquiu's men into joining him. One of those volunteers was Cisco's youngest brother, Manuel.

Like his ancestors many times before Manuel embarked on a long and dangerous journey. The trip would take six months. His family, especially his brothers anxiously waited for his return.

Manuel finally returned with a string of four horses and two mules. The family gathered at Salvador's place where they buried over hot coals and rocks a side of beef to cook overnight. This would be a rare *fiesta* for the family. Even the sisters and their families came, each contributing something to the meal: chili, beans, tortillas, corn, etc. The men contributed a locally fermented brew that barely qualified as brandy.

Salvador, the more direct of them asked, "How did you come across the horses and mules?"

"Pay." Manuel gave his older brother a false serious look.

"Pay?"

"Yep. We traded two serapes for one horse and two blankets for one mule. Armijo and his partners are rich in horses and mules. You saw the herd when we returned."

Cisco chimed in and asked, "But what will they do with so many animals?"

"They will trade them to the Americanos for tools, cloth, furniture, weapons, anything."

Still curious but not convinced, Salvador continued, "So you worked for half a year and received six animals? Nothing more?"

Manuel smiled again. "Well yes. In California I traded a mule for a pair of boots."

"Boots!" Cisco could not help himself. No one in the family had boots. They always made their own foot wear out of animal skin. "Where are they?"

At home, brother. They are not for everyday.

"Are they like those that the officials from Santa Fe wear?"

"Yes, exactly."

"My God! Be careful. They will resent this." This warning came from Salvador.

Manuel sighed. "Soon everyone will wear boots and, if not, I can always barter with them. Yes?" He answered himself. "Why not. They wear their boots all the time. They will need a new pair. Maybe I can get a new *escopeta* or a dress for my wife Pepita. *Qué se yo*?" What do I know?

Salvador bellowed forth. "It appears that our brother has become a merchant!" Everyone, including the women, laughed at the exaggeration.

One of the brothers-in-law, who had spoken with Manuel earlier, spoke, "Hey Manuelito, tell them what you brought for your wife." This quieted everyone with renewed interest. They waited to hear his answer.

And Manuel did not disappoint them. "A blouse. Made in Mexico, down south."

This impressed everyone, and, because the men started weighing the possibilities of going to California themselves, the conversation turned to the journey, the task of getting there. They listened and questioned as Manuel described traveling through the mountains, then dry lands, and along the great canyon that they entered and crossed, and, finally, the desert that seemed to go on forever before they went through a high mountainous pass to the mission of San Gabriel.

Cisco started the walk home in deep thought. Dolores knew what troubled him. "Cisco, I am happy with what we have." She paused to look at the infant in her arms. "Manuelito, well, he and Pepita have no children. Her family took care of her while he was gone. It is harder with children." Juan de Jesús, now going on ten years old, listened enraptured at the family gathering. Now he listened to his parents as they reacted to the conversation.

Still pensive, Cisco answered slowly. "Wouldn't you like a new blouse? A dress?"

"Or an *escopeta*?" She looked knowingly into his eyes. "No, we can find another way. I do not want to be left for six months or longer."

"But, Dolores, my love...." Cisco knew enough to let the discussion die. Besides, he was not adventurous at heart. Such a journey or venture truly did not appeal to him. He only wanted to show that he thought about it.

Yet, in each of the subsequent years, Cisco watched as men left Abiquiu, or others passed through Abiquiu to enrich themselves in California. In truth, they came back slightly different from the experience, and maybe better off. Some of these men included Romero cousins. After a few years, some of the married men heeded their wives' complaints and packed up the whole family for the journey. Some never returned. They died from deprivation or Indian attack, or some chose to remain in California. The stories of those who did return permeated throughout New Mexico.

Cisco brought up the idea of taking the family, but Dolores, more of a realist, staunchly opposed that idea. Instead, Cisco resigned himself to the routines that he learned from childhood, the only interruptions being the two occasions that he was called out on militia duty.

On one of those occasions he rode into Navajo country along the first part of the trail to California. They pursued a band of that tribe that had stolen some horses. After Mexican Independence, the Navajos became the first of the native groups to violate the peace. They began by stealing livestock, a task that eventually expanded into taking and sometimes killing captives.

Some in the valley thought that this new wave of violence came about because the Indians realized that the New Mexicans no longer had a king to protect them. Others, more reasonably believed that the Indians reacted to the new incursions through their lands by these new efforts to get to California. Cisco only knew that life had become more dangerous, and did not bother to look for a reason why. He tended to the task before him, which, in his case was to protect his family that, by 1837, had grown to five boys and one girl.

Cisco needed to raise his children as he had been raised. In this effort, Dolores was a welcomed asset. She not only matured into a good keeper of the household, but also liked to pitch in with other chores. On many an occasion the whole family could be seen working together in the fields. Cisco enjoyed these moments of family unity. Thanks to their love for one another they were happy. Cisco's work and family seemed to him an essential happiness, a form of fulfillment. As such their lives continued without concern for the troubles brewing in Santa Fe, a mere forty miles away.

PART VII
MIGRATION NORTH, JUAN DE JESÚS, ABRÁN, FAUSTINO, ISAAC

The Seventh Through the Tenth Generations
Showing the migration north into Colorado

Miguel Lópes = María Josefa Martín

Francisco Antonio Romero = María Dolores Lópes (m.April 1816)
(b. Nov. 1795 in Abiquiu) | (b.1801 in Abiquiu)

Juan de Jesús=María Ysabel Martín
Romero
(b.Tierra Azul)

José Tomás
Romero
(b.1822. m.
María Margarita
Martín)

Manuel Lorenzo
Romero
(b.1827)

María Manuela
Romero
(b.1832)

José Vicente
Romero
(b.1835)

José Albino
Romero
(b.1837)

María Tomasa
Romero
(b.1846 in Abiquiu)

José Abran de Jesús = María Cleofa de Refugio Casillas
Romero (b. Dec. 1849 in Tierra Azul, m. Jan. 1875 in Conejos, Colorado)
(Killed as a lawman ca.1885)

Luis
Romero
(b.1852 in Abiquiu)

Faustino Romero = *Talpa (Talpita) Lucero de Godoy
(b. Feb.1877 in   (b. March 1885 d. April 1948)
Abiquiu)
(d.1962 in Alamosa,
Colorado)

Martín Romero = *Ciria Lucero de Godoy
(b. ca.1882)

Terecita Romero=Apolorario
Duran

* The brothers Faustin and Martín named the young Lucero de Godoy sisters in a double ceremoony in the spring of 1897
in Conejos, Colorado.

273

CHANGE

Summer 1846, Tierra Azul (Abiquiu)

War

Neither the influx of caravans and people over the Santa Fe Trail, nor the 1837 rebellion in Taos that moved south to assassinate the governor and give rise to Manuel Armijo as New Mexico's governor, nor the failed invasion of an army from Texas in 1841, gave Cisco reason for concern. His family had grown united. Unknown to them those events would shape New Mexico's history but in Abiquiu, life continued as before. Now, his two oldest sons, Juan de Jesús and José Tomás had married Martín sisters, both young women distantly related to Dolores and to his mother. When Juan de Jesús's wife, María Isabel Martín, gave birth to a daughter at the end of February in 1846, Cisco could not help but wonder if she were more Martín than Romero.

Juan de Jesús, or Juan as he was called, had no such thoughts. Now in his mid-twenties, he shared his father's joy for family and work. However, his experience gained from his militia duty had touched a nerve. As a result he could not hear enough from the various men who returned from California. He was familiar with the first part of the trail. However, the land to the north past the hot springs to San Antonio Mountain appealed to him. Actually, the land past the mountain had captured his imagination. Even before his marriage, he thought about moving to the north to try his hand at raising livestock, first for a *patrón*, then on his own.

Maybe, he thought, the seed for the idea of leaving the valley came from his father's stories about his grandfather. Juan was five years old when his *abuelo*, Juan Joseph, died. Juan had a vague memory of an old man with a face and head full of white hair. He had heard how that man left Alburquerque to start a new life in Abiquiu.

Then, there was something about an old short sword that the *abuelo* had given Juan's father. That sword, now lost, Cisco's dad noted, "means more to me today than it did then. But it is too late. *Bueno.* We move on." Yes, Juan thought, the time for moving on was close.

Juan was mulling over those same thoughts while working a field with his father and some other men. The day was nice. A warm breeze rustled off the nearby cottonwood trees and chased away any hint of mist from the night before and initiated a typically bright day with a deep blue, almost turquoise sky from horizon to horizon. It was a day that Juan appreciated for its transparent air that allowed for small details to be seen a great distance off. But, before the details of a hurried mounted rider could be seen, the stillness exaggerated the unnatural sounds of a lone-mounted man coming towards them.

The men squinted to see the source of those sounds and they were not disappointed. A man dressed in a well-worn presidio soldier's blue and red uniform came into focus. His black boots could not be missed.

The soldier reined in his lathered horse to announce that war had broken out between Mexico and "the *Yanquis*." All the men must gather at the plaza of Abiquiu or before the church at Santa Rosa de Lima.

The Romeros gathered with most of the Martíns and their workers at the latter location. They were told that an enemy army approached New Mexico from the eastern plains and the governor had called up all men of fighting age to gather in Santa Fe with weapons. They would defend "this land for God and Country." With this statement the soldier plunged his right fist into the air while the gathered men less enthusiastically repeated his words and gesture.

Because of his age Juan had no choice. His father did. After all, Cisco was fifty-five years old. But he was a young and very strong fifty-five. The years of work had enhanced rather than depleted his health. So, Cisco joined his three older sons to ride off to war, but not before attending a special mass for all the men and boys who would heed the call of their governor. The valley's women insisted on the mass.

Dolores instructed the boys to look out for one another and especially for their father. Her arguments that he not leave fell on deaf ears. So, she was left with her fourteen year old daughter and two younger sons, all of whom gathered close to her as they followed her lead when the second tear gravitated down her cheek.

None of the men had gone to war, at least not this kind. All had experienced forays into Indian territories and some even had participated in some minor skirmishes. It seemed that they always chased the enemy. Now, the enemy was coming to them. Speculation over "the Americanos" dominated the conversation as they rode toward Santa Fe. They stopped at Santa Cruz and bivouacked for two days as their ranks grew from volunteers coming in from Taos and other northern villages. When they started up again for the one-day journey into Santa Fe, they could not help but to be impressed as the trail into the capital was filled with men. Some, like Cisco and one of Juan's cousins, had old *escopetas*. Most carried short swords, lances, and even bows and arrows. With the self-effacing confidence built from the sight of so many men with a single purpose, the men trailed into Santa Fe primed for an assured victory. "How dare those Protestant foreigners think they could take over our beloved New Mexico?" Beloved New Mexico? This was a new concept for Cisco and his sons. Nevertheless the enthusiasm for their forthcoming successful defense obscured any such thoughts. Even the news that the foreign army was uniformed, had artillery, and was outfitted with an advanced type of rifle that did not require flint to be fired, could not temper their spirits.

Juan de Jesús felt no different, but he was curious, as he entered the capital city for the first time. With its streets full of men called to arms, the place seemed to bustle with activity. The parish church, *La Parroquia*, was larger than any church he had seen. Others pointed out some *yanqui* foreigners who, for some reason beyond his comprehension, freely walked the streets. Maybe because they are merchants, or Catholics, or had married local women. Who knew? Juan found the situation a little weird and, then, wondered, "Where is the governor?"

Presidio troops obviously feeling superior sprinkled throughout the throng. Their officers barked out orders to create what little order existed. When they felt secure enough, the lesser soldiers tried to enforce their officer's commands.

After waiting for about a week, they received word that everyone should march south of town to a place called Apache Pass. A long day's march brought them to a place where the trail funneled through the base of a mountain and a large mesa. The Santa Fe Trail came through this narrow pass and it was expected that the American army would do the same. The governor decided that this place would be the perfect location for defending New Mexico. The governor ordered that his artillery be located on a small hill immediately facing the canyon.

Meanwhile, the men kept busy building up breastworks. The military process of preparing for battle intrigued Juan. He wandered over to the small hill some fifty yards from the canyon's opening. There he saw the first cannons of his life. He could not help himself but to slowly scurry up the hill for a closer look. As he reached the top and began to walk toward a cannon, a voice rang out. "Hey, *compadre,* what are you doing here? Huh?"

"I..."

"Interested in cannons?

"I don't know."

The officer seemed kinder than the other uniformed soldiers. He embarked on an explanation of the cannons and what they can do. This encounter was an opportunity to burn off some boring time. The officer kept on talking. "...and even if we miss and hit the walls, the explosion will shower broken rocks upon them below. And because of the surprise, they will not have time to move their cannon into place."

Juan listened and became intrigued with the process. The officer, who was a New Mexican, went to artillery school in Mexico. He added that he still was a cadet waiting to hear about his promotion. Juan innocently asked if all the soldiers with the cannons went to the military school.

"Oh, no. No. These patriots are New Mexicans. I trained them. Why? Do you want to be one of them?"

Until then the idea had not crossed Juan's mind. He hesitated, "I had not...no, yes. I would like that."

"Ha, ha." The Cadet gave a friendly laugh. "We do not have enough time to train you now but if we survive this *lucha,* this struggle, come and see me. Remember my name, I am Rafael Chacón, at your service." He paused and gave a knowing look at Juan. Then he added, "*paisano,*" fellow countryman. "But you are needed more with your group. You should return."

"Yes. You are right. I should return. Thank you." Juan turned to descend the hill but he stopped and faced the officer, "I am Juan de Jesús Romero from Tierra Azul, near Abiquiu."

Chacón saluted him and said, "Let us pray that your namesake favors us in this battle."

Juan walked back to his contingent. An unconscious seed had been planted in his mind. He had not forgotten the cadet's words: "if we survive" and "pray" that we are "favored." This friendly, educated man knew more. He was confident, yet not as enthused as everyone else. The invitation to become an artilleryman resonated. Did Juan really want that? The idea of it appealed to him. One thing was certain, Juan envied the man for his education and experience.

One more night camped behind breastworks, nothing unusual happened. The men sat around campfires mesmerized by the dancing flames and avoiding the smoke. They slept in the open under a clear night sky with stars beyond counting. Only the regular soldiers had tents. But they were unneeded, as the days were warm and the nights comfortable.

Sunrise brought a new day with heightened anticipation. Warm water and mint leaves that the men called *yerba Buena,* made a nice tea. The drink and a tortilla with some beans, assuming anyone took the time to warm them, made breakfast. After that, they waited, not at the ready, but anxious.

At mid-day, Juan saw the governor for the first time. In fact, this was the only time he would see any governor.

Governor Manuel Armijo, a charismatic man among his own people, had a presence that he used to his advantage. He was a big-boned man who stood over six feet tall, some seven inches taller than the average height for the time. He rode in an impressive powder blue uniform with highly polished boots on a fine mule. A feathered hat, folded up on both sides, sat on his head. A voice that demanded attention emanated from a handsome well-proportioned face. Moreover, Juan and everyone else had "been told how the governor had saved New Mexico from the Texans back in 1841."

Certainly, this great leader arrived with his personal contingent to lead them to another victory. Now, things would begin to happen. Surely, the enemy approached.

Everyone watched as Armijo gathered the officers around him. Juan easily picked out his new friend among them. The meeting lasted about fifteen minutes after which some confusion broke out. Some of the militia contingents, including Juan's, were ordered to take up arms—against the governor. The militia officers were calling him a coward and traitor. They challenged him "to fight like a man."

Juan followed orders. He, his brothers, and father formed up behind their officer, but Juan was confused. Why this confrontation? Why were some of the officers shouting at the governor? Now, even more to Juan's surprise, the governor ordered his *presidio* troops to face the militia contingents. Juan watched his friend Chacón order the artillery turned on them as well. What was going on?

Then, the governor spoke. "You want me to stay and lead a hopeless defense. Look at yourselves. You are farmers and ranchers. You are not soldiers. An army of trained soldiers, many more than us, is coming." Here he paused for a second, "Moreover, everyone of them is armed with a rifle. You would have me send all of you into a sure death for the dignity of having taken a stand?" His voice rose to a high, resonant pitch with that last sentence, then he boomed out in his best baritone, "No! You will not die today but live to raise your families. Go home to your fields, your animals. Go!" He stopped and stared out over the men, his mule under him frozen for the moment.

Now there was no confusion. "What?" That was a common but quiet reaction. "We will not fight?" And Juan asked himself, "But what about our cannons." The men were dumbfounded. The governor had given up! And the words resonated. They had no choice but to disperse and begin the journey home. All agreed that the governor was a coward and not a patriot. When they heard that the governor had fled south out of New Mexico, they were confirmed in the belief. None of them noticed or realized that not one of them was sacrificed for a lost cause.

The reasons for the return of their husbands and sons did not matter to the women of Abiquiu. They cried again at the sight of the men. Juan hugged both Ysabel and their baby, María Tomasa who she held. His mind raced and he wanted to share with her his thoughts that had nothing to do with war. He wanted to talk about life and the future.

The one thing he did share with his father and brothers was his encounter with cadet Chacón. They listened and really did not have a comment about him becoming an artilleryman. They really did not need an answer because the U.S. Army had occupied Santa Fe. Governor Armijo and many of his troops fled south. For Juan to join the artillery now, he would have to move south and hope that something was available after the war. Reality aside, Juan already figured out that a regimented life in the army did not appeal to him. He posed the issue only for discussion's sake, already knowing he would stay and make his own life close to the people he knew.

He continued to talk, some would say jabber as he carried on without a point to be made. He talked about education, about the world at large as he knew it, "and there is more, much more that we don't know." Ysabel paid more attention than the men. She realized that her husband's call to arms had created a restlessness that ate at him. He spent the winter thinking and talking about a wider world. She kept her patience. Besides, there was another matter to consider.

Isabel was three months pregnant with their second child. She did not show, and Juan did not notice. Had he not been so wrapped up in his own thoughts, he could have noticed a change in her eating habits. Finally, she had to tell him.

Juan used the news as an opening, "The child will be born this winter. Yes?"

"Yes that is true."

"Well, we need to consider our future."

"About what? Our future is now. Like it always is."

"No. It does not have to be. My great grandfather changed his future. So did yours."

"How do you know?"

"Well, someone did, because the Martins, just like everyone, came here from someplace else."

Ysabel took a deep breath. "Juan, my husband, what are you saying? This is too much. You are like a dancer who cannot stop."

"No, Ysa. Listen. I am thinking that we should move to a new place with fewer people so we can maybe have a better life and lives for our children."

"Where? When? No wait. And do what?" Ysabel had become truly exasperated.

But Juan continued. "For now, nowhere. As to when, well at least after the birth. And I can always trade my labor for a living. But, I understand. This is too much to think about right now."

The topic overwhelmed their thoughts. They couldn't stop thinking and talking about it all through Ysabel's pregnancy. And, Ysabel came around to agreeing with Juan. The daunting idea of starting a new life somewhere else started to intrigue her. The only question that remained was, "Where?"

The birth of Juan Abrán, their first son, gave them more incentive for a change. He was born during the Holy Days of 1849. They decided to forestall any move to give the infant time to grow a little. Everyone at that time was familiar with infant mortality. Better to make sure.

Life continued pretty much as normal in 1850. They shared their idea for change with other family members. All agreed that the notion of moving was not such a bad idea. Their father said little. At least he did not disagree. He, too, saw that the valley would offer less and less opportunity for a constantly growing family. Juan represented the third generation of Romeros to live in the valley. "Maybe," he thought, "the time has come." After all, he would not be the first of the Romeros to leave. Many of the cousins already had done so, to places like Las Nutrias and Tres Piedras.

Then, not unexpectedly, Francisco expired in his sleep one night. Dolores, who was lying at his side, did not realize he had died until the morning when she woke up.

The death and burial of his father put an exclamation point on Juan's decision to relocate. He had hit upon a place. El Rito, a new community next to a small stream that gave meaning to the locale's name. It was north of Abiquiu, a direction that for some unknown reason intrigued Juan. It was out of the valley and not one of the *puestos* and plazas of the general Abiquiu area. Still, the distance to El Rito of sixteen to seventeen miles was a one-day ride. In fact, on a good day, the smoke from the valley could be seen in El Rito.

Juan began to prepare for the move. He talked with friends who knew the place and had ridden by the site over the years as part of the local militia. He found out that the sheep owners always needed men to care for their flocks. The market had become very profitable. After the initial rush to California, the influx of *Americanos* created a large local market not only for themselves, but to ship wool across the Santa Fe Trail to markets back east. The new markets also replaced a barter system with hard specie. American money filtered through the New Mexican sheep *patróns* who paid in coin as well as barter. They also continued to offer a percentage of the flock's winter offspring to the shepherds. Moreover, in places like El Rito, the land was free. It belonged to no one and was a perfect place to raise sheep. Juan did not wrestle with the idea of becoming a shepherd. He already had some experience tending to the Martins' flocks.

He and his brother, Vicente, scouted El Rito. Juan loved the site. The stream ran year around. Only a few families had moved there. Significantly, the surrounding forests had an abundance of game and the Indians no longer raided. Juan returned to Tierra Azul convinced that he had chosen the right place. He announced that he would move in the spring of 1851.

Perhaps with the advantage of separation, Juan realized that something else was happening in the Abiquiu area. Now under the administration of the United States, "outsiders" that included those new "*Americanos*" and their rich New Mexican partners, began buying up the land. The time was perfect. At the same time he moved to El Rito, two large groups abandoned their land and migrated from the valley to move even further north to the Conejos River. The "outsiders" bought up the abandoned land.

Already suspicious of the Americanos, Juan became very critical. They not only took over abandoned land, but also started forcing the small landowners out. Juan saw the vicious cycle and called it for what it is. People like him and his family were of little value to these greedy folk.

Yet, he would work for one of those *ricos*, beginning with Pedro Gonzales—Juan refused to use the honorific "Don" before his name—who had built a sheep empire by the middle 1850s. Eventually, this patrón would maintain fifteen sheep camps and around 150,000 sheep on his land that ranged from the Chama River valley at Abiquiu to the north. Juan maintained a constant but level detestation for what these rich men meant to him and his lifestyle. He complained. "See, there is another example. Even the Martíns are becoming poor." Or, "and now Protestant ministers! What next?" Without verbalizing it, Juan agonized over a vanishing lifestyle. He was glad to be in the mountains tending a flock or at home in relatively forgotten El Rito.

Juan felt a special connection to the area. His siblings continued to struggle in

Abiquiu. He maintained ties to his family and friends in the valley. His parents and grandparents were buried there.

When Ysabel gave birth to their second son in El Rito, they took the infant to Abiquiu to be baptized. Two years later, in 1855, they had their last child and did the same thing. They baptized David in Abiquiu in front of his four uncles and aunt. The birth was difficult, and Ysabel could not have more children. Three boys and a girl fit Juan's plans just fine. He wanted all of them to learn how to read and write. He even hoped that one would teach him how to sign his name.

He arranged for the children to spend time attending class in Abiquiu during a few winter weeks. They stayed with their uncles and aunts, sometimes rotating from house to house. Then, he helped arrange for a teacher to spend time in El Rito. After a few years, Juan joined his neighbors to pool enough money to pay for a part-time seasonal teacher. Abrán, in particular, took advantage of the teacher, Mr. Griego, to learn more than the alphabet and how to spell out his name. Eventually, Abrán and Mr. Griego helped to fulfill Juan's dream. They taught him how to sign his name. He did not know it but he developed a clearer more confident signature than that of his ancestor in Alburquerque a century-and-a-half past.

Juan loved the mountains. They were his sanctuary. Many a day he sat on his horse looking over a flock of sheep to the deep green pine forests and interspersed meadows in the distant horizon. As soon as the boys were old enough to ride, he took them with him. The boys came to appreciate the outdoors as well. Moreover, they became good shots as they had more than a few opportunities to fire at the wolves stalking their sheep. Tomasa stayed with her mother but Juan did not overlook her. She, too, went to Abiquiu to be schooled and grew up literate.

Overall, Juan was pleased with the move to El Rito. It did not work out as planned in that he never raised his own flock of sheep through the *al partido*, a system in which he received some of the flock's newborn. When the time came to divide the offspring sheep, Juan chose to sell them back to his patron, receiving both trade goods and cash, American money. He kept one or two of the animals for himself. When they fattened up enough, he traded their wool to a local weaver and slaughtered the animal to provide for his family. When possible, he sought out young goats because he loved their meat. He had become locally famous for his the *cabrito*, young goat meat that he marinated and barbecued.

By necessity Juan learned the rudiments of math. He had to agree to a price for each animal he sold, then total the amount as he and the patrón's manager settled accounts. Juan never met his patróns but he knew their managers. They were the ones who did the local negotiations.

The system allowed Juan to pay for household items such as, tools, cloth, and updated firearms. The old *escopeta* had been long lost. He expanded his one room *jacal* into a three-room L-shaped adobe house with a small porch. Ysabel and Tomasa mostly looked after the chickens and ever-present pig or two. As an outgrowth of his good cabrito, Juan became known for overseeing the community's annual *matanza* in the fall when the pigs were slaughtered and butchered. The event had become an annual fiesta. One pig provided enough meat and fat to last through the winter and into the summer.

The *matanza* signified to the community that they had survived another year and needed to prepare for the upcoming year. The small community came together with their pigs and a few lambs. Everyone had a job. Juan had become expert in a clean and quick kill. He used a sharp knife to cut the neck so that the blood could be drained, dried, and mixed with the area's wild onions to make *morcilla,* blood sausage. The men did the butchering. The women cleaned the tripe that would become sausage skin. They separated the fat for soap or to be used as a kind of butter spread over a warm tortilla. Of course the fat or lard became a prominent ingredient for cooking, not the least of which would be the *bizcochito* cookies made for Christmas a month later.

On those occasions when a priest happened to be making his round in El Rito during the *matanza*, he blessed the whole proceeding. El Rito did not have a permanent priest. Actually, it was a rarity when he showed up, which is one reason Juan and Ysabel had their children baptized in Abiquiu. Juan criticized the newcomers because, in his mind, he felt the influx of Protestants had chased the priests away. He overlooked the reality that El Rito never had a permanent priest.

Mexican educated priests like Juan's distant cousin Father Antonio José Martínez, who returned to serve briefly at Abiquiu but had become the permanent priest in Taos, never really numbered enough to serve all the people of New Mexico. So, the people had to fend for their spiritual needs themselves. This gave rise to the *Penitentes,* formerly called the *Fraternidad Piadosa de Nuestro Padre Jesús Nazareno,* the Pius or Compassionate Fraternity of Our Father Jesus the Nazarene, a lay religious confraternity with roots in Spain that arose throughout northern New Mexico and southern Colorado. The Penitentes, as they are popularly called, led the community in prayers, buried the dead, and generally became community leaders. They even constructed their own places of worship called *moradas.* They did not want to be confused with the official functions of the Catholic Church. Some of the Mexican trained priests quietly supported them for the devote people they were.

Two *cofradias* organized in Abiquiu. Juan knew many of its members. Initially, some of Juan's El Rito neighbors joined the Abiquiu brotherhoods, but time and distance took its toll. Eventually, they formed their own brotherhood in El Rito.

Juan appreciated the Penitentes. He never said a bad word against them. He saw them as allies in his undeclared struggle to maintain his Hispanic identity against the incursions of the newcomers. Yet, he never became a member. When asked, he replied, "I am not a joiner."

"But you are a Catholic and one of us."

"Yes, but I did not join the Church, my parents took care of that. It is enough for me. And by the same token...."

"You never joined anything?"

"Never formally, except when called to the militia. And that did not work out so well thanks to Armijo who ran away."

Still, Juan took his family to Penitente observances, especially the processions. The boys learned their prayers, awe for God, and were prepared for their First Communion by the members. As they grew older, their ability to read proved invaluable to the brotherhood, for they asked the boys to read passages from the Bible for their members, most of whom remained illiterate.

Still, the idea that something was wrong and that the blame lay with "the gringos," a new word that he picked up, remained latent in Juan's subconscious. And, now, those people ran the government.

Juan did not speak or understand English so he never heard an overt racial slur. His children picked up a few words in Abiquiu and this worried Juan. Their influence spread in nefarious ways. The four children grew up with a profound respect for their father. They relished his discipline and honesty. They listened, indeed inherited his words, his fears, and his fierce love of his heritage and of the outdoors. More than anything, his love for them was obvious.

The oldest son, Abrán, took on more of his father's personality than the other three. Abrán did not feel consigned to a place and had a hint of wanderlust in him. More noticeably, he also inherited his father's distrust of the gringos and their allies. Abrán could not help but be influenced from the many nights he sat with his father by a campfire in the high alpine forests listening to him pontificate about the ills of society. He had a customary closing.

"Be careful my sons. You are young but growing into a different world. The gringo influence has not reached here yet. But it will." His sons stared at the fire's dancing flames, and the old man would continue. "They cannot be avoided. You must learn to adapt without losing yourself."

The replies were predictable. "Sí, papá."

A Mysterious Death, Abrán
Spring 1884, in the Mountains by the Conejos River

The ride was so peaceful. Abrán, a deputy sheriff in his middle thirties, had just crested onto a rolling mountain meadow. All around him, front and back, the beautiful day spread all its grandeur over the green scenery that Abrán loved as much as his father. Under that huge cloudless sky and perfectly calm day, he paused to savor the moment, taking conscious pleasure in the moment when....

Somewhere in the forest, possibly from behind a rock outcrop to steady the rifle, a shot fired and the echo rolled over the meadow. Just as the sound registered with Abrán, he felt as if his chest had exploded and with no strength slid out of his saddle and crumpled to the ground where he lay in a fetal position. He felt the warm moisture of his blood as it permeated his shirt and covered his hands. Within thirty seconds he was dead.

He did not hear the riders who rode up to his body, paused and rode on, one saying in English something to the effect, "Dirty Mexican, let's see how the law protects you now."

If Abrán's recently freed spirit hovered above, it would have agreed with those words in part, for Abrán had bought into the new system of laws that he felt would protect his people from the voracious appetites of the newcomers. He proudly wore his deputy sheriff's badge. He should have paid more attention to the many times his father told him and his brothers to be careful.

Silence followed the murder. At first, no one knew it had happened. After a week or so, Abrán's family felt that something was wrong. Such an unannounced absence was not like Abrán. A month later another rider discovered his remains, unidentifiable, and badly picked over by the mountain animals. Only his badge, prized six-shooter, and the still spurred boots led to his identity, but not to how he died.

The family and its community knew. He was too experienced to just fall off his horse. Here was another atrocity brought on by the newcomers. The racist cowboy who shot him got away with murder, a killing never reported in the local newspapers.

Abrán had been the image of his father. He and his brothers were most at home outdoors. They lived most their early lives in the saddle tending to flocks of sheep, protecting them from wolves and mountain lions. The sheep provided the family with a relatively good, but modest life. With the changing markets—California lost its attraction by the early 1850s—the animals became more valuable for their wool than their meat. The boys thus became adept at working the sheep from the lambing bin to shearing.

They stuffed the wool into large sacks provided to them by their *patrón* or by the merchants in Abiquiu then shipped them via wagon to the valley from whence the wool continued to various parts of New Mexico and on to the eastern United States. The business, along with family ties and those early educational opportunities, kept the boys tied to Abiquiu and their extended family.

Then, Abrán did something that on the face of it his family had not done for three generations. On a cold winter day with snow covering their village of Conejos, just north of the recently surveyed northern border of New Mexico, he married María Cleofa del Refugio Casilla. Everyone one who showed up on that January 16, 1875 day, knew that his bride's mother, Guadalupe, was a Martín and a close cousin to Abrán's mother.

All that, of course, did not cross Abrán's mind. As an independent soul, he went through the process of getting the required permissions. Above all, Abrán felt ready to begin his own life. No longer did he want to be one of the children. As a sheep man, Abrán, of necessity had to cover a lot of territory. Again, because of his father's influence, Abrán probed the northern country at every opportunity. It was while in Conejos on just such a trip that he met Cleofa. Despite the fact that she was "family," she had a kind of fragile dignity that Abrán admired. She was small, not quite five feet tall and slight, a wisp of a woman and no more. Abrán never saw her without the thought of gentleness coming to his mind.

Yet, like most women of the area she had a mind of her own. Call it a sense of independence that was perfect because Abrán's work required that he spend long periods of time away from home. Ironically, it was not she, but he, who grew tired of the absences.

Initially, Cleofa made time to join him on those occasions when he needed to take the three or four day trip to Abiquiu. Their first child, a son, was born to them on February 19, 1877 in Conejos. Unlike three generations before him, little Faustino was not born in Abiquiu. He was baptized in St. Augustine Catholic Church in Antonito, Colorado. In the next four years Cleofa would give birth to another son and a daughter. Not ironically, the boy was named Martín Epifanio. The girl was named Teresita.

His young family and his aging parents gave Abrán pause for thought. As the oldest son, he gladly accepted the responsibility of caring for his parents. For the moment they were more of a pleasure than a burden. He delighted in watching them interact with his children. Juan had passed his sixtieth birthday and Ysabel had turned fifty. Both appeared in good health despite the fact that Juan had started to lose teeth. One of the advantages of the recently arrived railroad was the availability of good whisky, a bottle of which was always on hand when another of Juan's teeth started acting up. He did not question this new influence. The ongoing joke was that Juan willed his dental problems as an excuse to get to the whisky.

The whole countryside was abuzz with the railroad's arrival. Two separate companies laid track that converged on Santa Fe. One of them, the Denver and Rio Grande, entered the San Luis Valley and gave rise to a town called Alamosa, which started in 1878 as a tent town. From there the tracks headed south to another new town called Antonito, near Conejos, from whence the rail route split to head south to Santa Fe, and west, along the Pinos River through southern Colorado, to Salt Lake City.

Within a couple of years both Alamosa and Antonito replaced their tents with real buildings, at first wooden sideboard affairs, that was replaced by the brick brought in by train. Antonito's buildings gave some definition to the often very muddy streets, which gave rise to a constant and unavoidable stench when mixed with animal and human waste.

Neither the buildings nor the train caught Abrán's attention. He focused on what came with them: opportunity, jobs, and people, outsiders, many of them hucksters and scam artists looking to turn a quick buck. Other people simply came with the railroad, laying track. Stores, banks, cheap hotels, and saloons tended to the needs of this influx of people. They also needed a sense of order, but this would come later. For now, a sense of lawlessness prevailed, and a bad aspect of that was prejudice toward Hispanics. Never was there a greater time for Abrán to heed his father's words to be wary.

Abrán understood the situation, but he also felt the unavoidable pull of opportunity. Here was a chance to plug into the excitement of these new communities. Even the wool could be moved north to a closer railhead and more efficiently sent to larger markets.

Abrán's father and brothers agreed. They should move their operations to the northern slope of San Antonio Mountain. They knew the area, for they had taken their flocks there. They could take advantage of the free range, and stake a claim of their own before the place became inundated with people.

Abrán volunteered to go north and make preparations. In the process, he heard stories and, then witnessed that the "newcomer gringos" had started claiming land as well. They preferred to run cattle and to fence their property. Fencing off land ran counter to the centuries' old open range customs of the Hispanic community. The practice added to the already rampant racial tensions, as the area grew ripe for conflict.

No one knew how, and Abrán could not explain it, even to himself, but he let a total stranger talk him into taking a job as deputy sheriff. Michael Connel, an Irishman and veteran of the western Indian wars, had become a friend of Cleofa's immediate family. He was a verbose, decent man who, oddly enough for the place and time, thought that having a Hispanic lawman as one of his deputies would be an asset. Connel already knew from Cleofa's family that Abrán spent a lot of time in the saddle and was a decent shot. Moreover, Abrán had come to town looking for work.

Connel told Abrán that he could look after his own people, and he would take care of the *gringos*. It sounded so clear and simple. And, in truth, Abrán learned that Connel believed in what he said. Abrán saw this as a new adventure, a change. What neither of them realized was that neither the time nor the place was ready or conducive to such an arrangement.

Abrán soon learned that a "Mexican" lawman was incomprehensible to most of the newcomers. Actually, most of the Hispanic community took the concept with a jaundiced attitude. They could only shrug and say that, "Abrán is very brave," and "God help him."

Word filtered to the people from Abiquiu north, that in other parts of New Mexico, especially in the Mora Valley on the other side of the Santa Fe Mountains to the east, the locals had started fighting back. An anonymous group of Hispanic men, who called themselves Las Gorras Blancas, "the White Hats," for the white hoods they wore, had started cutting fences and burning stables. The local people quietly supported, indeed, encouraged the Gorras Blancas while the newcomers and their representatives proclaimed them to be outlaws.

Maybe Abrán felt that his presence negated the need for such activity. He sympathized with what the Gorras Blancas were doing, but hoped for a different outcome in his jurisdiction.

Cleofa had another concern. Already some fences had been destroyed. She worried. Every time her husband left their modest home, she prayed for his safety. She knew that the Americanos would have their way. They did not value life. A man like Connel was not enough to protect her husband.

Abrán's deaf ears to her words aggravated her. And his words did not help. "But Refujita," as he called Cleofa, "we have enough money to buy land so the family can start to build our own flock."

"Yes, Abrán. *Y qué*? We will have land. You can quit and work with our sheep. Your brothers need you."

"And the others?" Abrán waved his arms as if he meant the world. "They need me, too."

Cleofa did not cry often but here she could not stop her eyes from watering. "*Abrán, por favor*, please let Miguel handle it. It is not your fight. The children...."

"Well, I will think about it." And with that he was off to work, a part of which required that he accompany shepherds while moving their sheep from the highlands or back. On occasion, they met resistance but with deputy sheriff Romero at their side the shepherds felt safe. At least, that is what Abrán had come to believe. He had become invaluable to his people. Cleofa did not understand. He would make his family proud.

On one of these occasions, Abrán rode alongside some shepherds when a group of cowboys confronted them.

"Hey, Pancho, you need turn your animals back."

The shepherds turned to Abrán, who rode up to confront the cowboys. With his badge obvious, Abrán spoke in his best, broken English. "No. *Pueden pasar*, pass," and he motioned with his arm, "...eets the *ley*, law."

The ringleader stood in his stirrups and waved out. "This property belongs to my boss."

Abrán stared at the man who was sizing him up. He had the cold gray eyes of a bird of prey, patient and calculating. But Abrán had experience with animals of prey. "No fence, *pueden* pass." Abrán stared into the calculating eyes. "Eeets the law."

Just then Abrán surprised everyone, when in one smooth quick and exact motion he pulled his rifle out of its scabbard and fired through the cowboys. The smoke rose from Abrán's rifle that he still held in firing position. He made a head motion for the cowboys to look behind them. He had noticed that the sheep had started scattering, and some had ambled behind the cowboys where another pair of cold eyes prepared to move. Now, some thirty yards away lay a dead coyote that moments before had been a part of a pack that thought it would have some easy pickings. "*Que raro*. Those dogs never get so close." He kept his rifle frozen in firing position. The cowboys could do nothing.

"Okay," and here the ringleader emphasized the next word, "*señor*. You can pass this time."

For obvious reasons, Abrán did not talk about such episodes with Cleofa. He preferred to tell her about his boring day or days and that he was happy to be back in her arms. Still, he knew that he had developed an inward pride and, maybe a sense of invincibility. And that did nothing but heighten his frustration every time Cleofa brought up the subject of him quitting his job.

She and everybody else knew that racism ran rampant throughout the area. The Anglos tried to exert what they considered their cultural superiority over an inferior Mexican race. After all, the territory had been conquered outright in war. To the victors go the spoils. The idea of a Mexican sheriff ran counter to everything they believed. An inferior man cannot enforce the law over them. Thus it was inevitable that Abrán had developed a reputation, especially among the Anglo cowboys. While they understood that he could be dangerous, they still regarded him as an upstart. As Cleofa feared, Abrán's reputation made him a marked man. He went missing within a year.

As was customary, his mutilated remains were buried on the spot. Abrán never had a Christian funeral, much less a burial mass. His family and the community had more than a few memorial masses said, and his brothers, a couple of uncles, and some other men accompanied Cleofa to the site on the mountain meadow where they left a small, crude, wooden cross. Even that marker shared the fate of Abrán's remains that dissolved back into the earth.

With the definite belief that the Anglos killed him, Cleofa and her brothers-in-law made sure that her children knew that Abrán, their father, had died, killed defending his people. The details would be lost but the family would always know that Abrán had died trying to protect his people. The legend, as such, would survive for generations.

NEVER AN ORPHAN
Faustino, 1890, Conejos, Colorado

When Abrán was killed Faustino was seven years old, Martín was five, and Teresita not quite four. They had a basic understanding of what had happened to their father. The younger two would maintain a vague memory of their father. Faustino, however, would always remember how he looked, how he talked, and his mannerisms. A qualifier for all of them was his reputation, for the Hispanic community called him a hero. He was a martyr to be sure, but a hero, too, who sacrificed his life for them. Early on, the children felt like heroes because of their father. Even their friends treated them with wide-eyed awe.

"You're Abrán's son or daughter!"

The children would think to themselves "yes, we are Abrán's," but they did not understand the admiration. What good is admiration when he is dead? They would rather he be with them. Cleofa's worst nightmare came true. Now a relatively young widow with three children, her and Abrán's families immediately surrounded her and the children with love and compassion. The boys had their two Romero uncles and even some great-uncles. Teresita grew closer to her mother and both grandmothers who still lived.

Uncles Luis and David made sure that the boys would grow up in their father's image. They helped tend to sheep and learned to live under the open sky. Their uncles taught them as they had been taught.

After Abrán's death Cleofa returned to nearby Conejos where her family had settled. And after a year of mourning, Cleofa agreed to marry another man. José Benito García appreciated her for her past. He too had lost his spouse. In the previous April, now over a year past, his wife of eleven years died while giving birth to their seventh child. He was a kindly man, a person with whom Cleofa could commiserate. Both had children, were alone, and had suffered the loss of a loved one. After a short period, they married on September 18, 1885. Abrán's children would not be overlooked. They suddenly had become part of a family of ten children that would continue to grow.

The children went to school in a two-room building heated by an iron wooden stove. For the first time they had a female teacher. She was fun. The kids especially liked how she came up with odd information.

When one of the students wiped his snotty nose on his shirtsleeve, she pointed out why the newer shirts and suit coats had buttons on the sleeves. "And do you know why?" She would look at the class in mock askance.

Knowing that the answer was forthcoming, none of the students dared to venture an answer.

"To keep men and young boys from doing what you just did," as she looked at the guilty, now penitent boy.

On another occasion she let everyone know that the great Benjamin Franklin invented the wood stove. Then she launched into a lesson explaining why an inventor of a wood stove was so great.

Because all her students spoke Spanish and very few, if any, had any knowledge of English, she taught in Spanish, which was fine with the students, especially Faustino, Martín, and Teresita, for they did not care to learn the language of their father's killers.

The boys especially delighted in listening to their grandfather Juan. They reveled in his toothless tales about Abiquiu, Governor Armijo and the artillery captain, El Rito, and how he always dreamed that the land north of the San Antonio Mountain was a mythical paradise. "Now here we are. Conejos is fine but maybe too far north." Then the still sharp old man would nod toward the town of Antonito, the buildings of which they could see from Conejos. "It is not so small and is full of gringos."

Juan told the boys about the family that had settled in Abiquiu. "My grandfather was the first Romero in the valley. He came from down south, Albuquerque, I think." He paused to spit tobacco into a spittoon. He never missed and the habit made his tales more fascinating. Then, he would continue relating how he had heard that his grandfather's grandparents, or, maybe, great grandparents survived the great rebellion.

They even learned silly things—or so they thought—about how the straightedge razor had ended the time when all men wore beards. Now most men were clean-shaven with, at most, a moustache. He also talked about how coffee came with the trail from the United States. "Now everyone has to have coffee."

What the boys really liked was when he waxed poetic about the mountains, the open spaces and how he and their father rode side-by-side for hours in the "open space, God's greatest cathedral." "Oh, how your father loved it out there."

Even though Cleofa would have ten more children, all of Abrán's three children grew up together. Faustín and Martín remained close. As they grew into their teens, it seemed that one was never around without the other close by. Maybe this was an unconscious reaction to their father's solitary death.

Teresita was the first of Abrán's children to leave the household. She was fifteen years old when she married. The family had arranged the marriage. She barely knew the man who became her husband, a local man named Apolorario Durán.

Her brothers were sixteen and eighteen years old, respectively. Neither Faustín nor Martín paid much attention to their sister's plight. That was the way of things. They had no reaction but to wish her well.

However, two years later, in 1897, they should have paid more attention when the Lucero de Godoys dropped in for a weekend meal. They had two middle-teen boys and two younger girls with them. Faustín and Martín hardly paid attention to the girls, who seemed to entertain themselves and play with their half-brothers and sisters. Faustín and Martín were more interested in listening to the adults talk but became bored when the conversation turned to how and why the Luceros no longer used the de Godoy part of their name. One name was easier.

Uncle Luis asked Faustín and Martín to show the Lucero children around. Faustín thought that request odd. He was sure that he could not show them anything they hadn't seen at their own home. Besides, he had become accustomed to being included among the adults, treated as an equal. Still, he would do as told.

The food was good and the camaraderie fine. Nonetheless, Faustín was happy to see the Luceros leave. He had chores to do and things to get ready for the next day's work. But he was not given a chance to revert to his accustomed habits when he and Martín were asked to wait a moment because their uncles and mother had something to say to them. They gathered in the patio formed by the "L" shape of their house. In the summer this was where the family did most of its socializing and now it was convenient because this was where they were cleaning up after the Lucero's visit.

Faustín could see that his uncles, Luis and David, would do the talking. His mother had a serious look, so something was up. The older uncle began, "What did you think of the Luceros?"

Faustín usually did the talking for himself and his brother. "Okay, I guess."

Uncle David took a turn. "What about the girls?"

Faustín gave his brother a puzzled look, and received a dumb, unknowing look in reply. "The little girls. Why? Okay, I guess."

Martín broke his stupefied silence and chimed in, "They stayed to themselves, mostly telling secrets to each other and giggling. Kid stuff."

Luis turned to David and Cleofa. "I think we had better stop here. This is going nowhere. Let's finish cleaning up. We all have a long day ahead of us." The meeting broke up as each person went back to whatever they were doing before.

The whole conversation was not lost on Faustín and Martín. They left the confab with more questions than not. "Stop here? What did that mean? Is there more?" They did not have to wait long to get answers.

Their uncles had another plan. A couple of days later they approached the brothers. "Boys, David and I are going to head up into the hills," their euphemism for the mountains, "maybe get lucky and bring some meat back."

Luis knew what he was doing, for Faustín and Martín loved to hunt. Of course, they accepted the implied question. The next day they left at sunrise and headed west. About an hour out, just as they approached the foothills and could hear the first sounds of a distant thunderstorm, uncles Luis, with David riding at his side and staring off into the distance, straight out told the boys what was on their minds. "Your mother and us have agreed with the Luceros that you should marry their daughters."

Both Faustín and Martín reined in their horses. "What?" One said.

"The little girls, the ones with the secrets?" The other asked.

"Yes."

"They have not reached puberty!"

"How do you know?"

"The little one for sure. She probably plays with dolls."

Uncle Luis turned in his saddle. "Listen to me. How old was your father when he married? Around twenty-five. And your mother? Do you know?" He paused for effect, then answered his own question. "Yes. That's right. A little girl as you put it."

Faustín had no answer for his uncle's argument. His only counter was a stubborn "What about you?" He referred to both uncles.

Luis answered. "You know. The same. Look at your sister..."

Faustín cut him off. "She is older than those two."

"What a year? Two years? What's the difference?"

The hunt ended with the conversation. Everyone turned back for a silent ride home.

Cleofa, of course, knew what was happening. She expected the boys to come to her. She knew them. They loved her and never in their lives said a cross word to her or in front of her. She would be the one to convince them. Not their uncles.

She appeared even slighter than usual with her grown sons next to her. At times, her demeanor demanded attention and, now, she came to one of those moments. "The girls are young. That is true. They come from a good family, like ours."

Faustín and Martín sat silently as she spoke.

"The girls will come and live with us or, specifically with me. When the time comes, they will go with you." She stopped and with no emotion stared at her sons. "You are good. I know you will be good to them."

Then she told them that Luis and David had arranged for Faustín, as the oldest, to inherit five acres of land along the Los Pinos River near San Antonio. "It was something your father dreamed about." She gave a whimsical smile and continued to tell them that Faustín and Martín could move there when their wives were ready. Although Faustín inherited the land she knew that the boys would not be separated. Both of them would settle there.

Faustín was taken aback. He did not want the proposed marriages or this inheritance to come between him and Martín. They would talk.

First, there was the matter of who would marry which sister. Martín solved that problem. While he was the quiet one, he also tended to act quicker than Faustín, who was more pensive. Martín claimed Ciria, the older girl who he found out was fifteen years old. Faustin would marry Talpa, the younger girl now in her twelfth year.

In the spring of 1897 in Conejos, Colorado, Faustino and Martín Romero married Talpa and Ciria Lucero de Godoy in a single ceremony. Both families celebrated that day. It was a grand festive day, and when it was over Faustín went home to find his new bride and some of his half-sisters playing with dolls. He left it to his mother to explain to her what had happened.

TAKE THIS LAND
1925, Ortiz, Colorado

Thirteen years later something was wrong. Faustín could no longer hide it. Talpita, of course knew. His left side had been giving him trouble. He had not slept on his left side in months. And, now...well, now there was a growth large enough to be noticeable.

He and his brother had raised sheep on his spread. They managed to avoid the cowmen, stayed out of Antonito. They were glad to have left it. Now they lived in a place called Ortiz, not a town nor really even a village, just a place, a place where they could raise a family relatively peacefully.

For the first few years of their marriage he pretty much left his wife to his mother, who because of her marriage had the Romero García surnames but still was affectionately called Refujita. She helped Cleofa with Faustín's very young half brothers and sisters, all the while growing and learning. Talpita slept with the children. Initially she cried and wanted to go home. But, then, her own family's periodic visits along with Cleofa's loving patience made her feel at home. Ciria did not require such attention. She moved in with Martín from the start. Faustín and Cleofa counted Ciria a blessing, for her presence and, no doubt, her company helped with Talpita.

In the meantime, Faustín and Martín devoted what little extra time that they had to building two houses, stables, lambing bins, and the all-important outhouses on Faustín's land. When Talpita reached her fifteenth birthday all of them packed up and moved onto the land and into the new houses.

Faustín's and Talpita's first child, a son who they named Alfonso, was born in the late fall of 1900, three-and-a-half years after their marriage. Ten months later, on September 24, 1901, Talpita gave birth to a second son, who they named Isaac, pronounced in the Spanish way. Then, for almost every other year it seemed, Talpita gave birth to four more sons and a daughter who were born in the village of Ortiz. They named these four sons in order of their births, Horacio, Rudolfo, Bernabé, and Alberto. They named their daughter Martina, after Faustín's brother. Eventually, after they moved to Alamosa a daughter, Margarita, and a son, Faustino, were born.

Faustín gave his boys chores almost as soon as they walked. Like his father and grandfather, he made sure they learned to read, write, and do arithmetic. Grandfather Juan and grandmother Ysabel lived into their eighties and got to see all the children born in Ortiz, including the four born to Martín and Ciria. The children from Cleofa's second marriage grew up with them as well. The grandparents spent their last years surrounded with children. When they thought about it, children had been a part of their lives all along. Some of the older grandchildren enjoyed listening to the same stories that enraptured Faustín and Martín when grandpa Juan waxed on.

While Cleofa's children from her second husband were half brothers and sisters to Faustín and Martín, they were also aunts and uncles to their first cousins, the offspring of Faustin and his brother. The children had fun with the relationships, sometimes playfully asking, "Which should we be today? A cousin or uncle or aunt?" They actually asked their parents to draw a chart that showed how the relationships worked. And, because everyone lived in Ortiz, they all became very familiar with each other.

Faustín followed another family tradition by introducing his boys to the hard but gratifying work of shepherding. Isaac, in particular, shared one of his father's traits. They both had a fascination for machines or, for that matter anything mechanical. For example, they both could take apart and put together the Singer sewing machine that Faustín had purchased for Talpita in Antonito.

Their inclination toward mechanical things had a practical side, for they lived in a relatively isolated place. They had to maintain everything themselves. This included sewing their clothes. The women did this. The buckskins of earlier years had long since given way to store bought shirts, pants, shoes, and newly popular suspenders. Still, such things cost money and needed to be maintained because every cent mattered.

Faustín had fallen into a pleasing life pattern in a place that he enjoyed. With his brother still close by, Faustín had a positive outlook on life. The only concern was the growth on his hip that slowly but assuredly kept growing and it had begun to inhibit his movement. He was finding it exceedingly more difficult to mount his horse.

Faustín looked forward to the occasional moments when the men in Ortiz got together. Seated around a table, they played a card game called, *cuncán*, a betting game that probably originated from on old Spanish game of cards called *cuca y matacán*. Although none of them could play for high stakes, the play could be intense and so competitive that it often stopped them from conversation. They joked, caught up on rumors and gossip, and speculated on politics. Eventually, Faustín's hip garnered their attention. He had to share that it was becoming more cumbersome. "Why not go see a doctor?" They asked. He always answered that the closest doctor was too far away and, besides, he did not have the time.

One of the guys opined that Alamosa was the place to go because they have better doctors. In fact, Alamosa, chosen to be the home of the railroad's workshops, had surpassed Antonito in size. Alamosa had become the political and commercial center of the San Luis Valley. There was some truth to the idea that Faustín could get better medical care there.

For his part, Faustín let on that he might have to give up the sheep as he found himself increasingly limited. He started hinting to both Talpita and his brother that he might have to move to a town where he could find work. Over a few months the hints morphed into serious discussions. The logic was simple. His physical condition had become a hindrance to working sheep. Alamosa had jobs. Then, there was the additional reality that they did not have enough land to support the future families of all his sons.

Martín was privy to all of Faustín's reasoning. He never raised an objection, which implied to everyone that he would leave with his brother. That meant that the land had to be sold or, at the very least, abandoned.

This was just the kind of news that would liven up the card game, which it did to the point that the game paused for the conversation.

One of the players, Romauldo Guillén, showed an interest in Faustín's plight. He listened and asked a few innocuous questions. Then, with a fake throat-clearing cough, stated that he had an idea. The conversation already revealed that the pending move and sale would happen soon. Faustin guessed that he could hold out a few more years.

"How 'bout you sell to me?"

Faustín, along with others, thought that he was joking. "Oh, okay. Show me the money before the next hand."

Romauldo was serious. "In truth, my friend. The dwelling would have more value than the land for me. My two boys could move in."

Now Faustín sensed the seriousness of his friend's comments. "Do you have the money?"

No one played cards now. The others had become an audience to a real life-changing moment.

Romauldo answered, "A little." He didn't need the place right away and that fit Faustín's plans. Then he laid out his idea, "I can buy the place now for an agreeable sum. Or make payments. Meanwhile, you can stay there and manage your operation like you have always done. You can leave when you are ready. That is, assuming you don't stay too long."

Faustín needed to think about the offer. He trusted the man. All the men in Ortega or any of the other communities from the region were honest. He had a natural inclination to hesitate because the offer came to him unexpectedly. Also, it seemed too good to be true. Neither he nor Martín could find fault with the offer. They reviewed it in every way they could.

Faustín accepted the offer. He would pocket some money that he could help with the move and transition to the city, which only he and his brother knew was Alamosa. This gave him time to plan his move north on his schedule.

Martín and Faustín thought that maybe they would move in three or four years. The kids would be older. The older boys would be grown enough to help with the move. Also, this would give them time to go to Alamosa to scout out the lay of the land. Who knew, maybe they could run sheep there.

Thus, at one of the card games, Faustín brought up the issue. The agreement was made and Faustín, playing on words waived his hands across the table and said, "Take this land," as if he were throwing in his cards and giving up the pot. That became a running commentary among the friends. "Old Faustín lost his land playing cards."

The inside joke spread among friends and family. Faustín's children paid no attention, nor were they privy to the joke. In their world life continued as usual. Life revolved around chores, sheep, and education. Even more than his father and mother, Faustín stressed the importance of education to his children. His second son, in particular, took to his admonitions and developed a lifetime passion for reading.

Talk among the adults became clearer to the older children. As the summer of 1915 approached, Faustín's two older boys approached sixteen and seventeen years old respectively. The other children were not far behind.

The two older boys noticed their father's increasing uneasiness with a visible growth on his hip. They could not help but notice his increasing incapacity to do certain things. He depended upon them to help him.

They also paid more attention to the conversations about a pending move. At first, they wondered where and when. As they listened, the move came into focus. Eventually, they put their father's health together with what they realized were not rumors. The move was for real.

Finally, Faustín and Talpita, called the family together, including Martín's family. A family confab! This was unusual, not the weekend gathering of food and talk, or a *matanza* when they slaughtered and prepared the meat for the winter. No. This was diferent and the sons and daughters reacted appropriately. They waited in quiet seriousness.

Faustín, now in his late forties, stood around five feet, seven inches tall. He seemed larger. He looked over the family, puckered his lips in a clean-shaven face, and began. "For some time Martín and I, and our wives of course," he gave an ever-ready smile, "have been talking about a move to Alamosa." He paused for a second as if giving himself time to think. "That is a town on the railroad north of Antonito." Then he focused on the smaller children, most of who had clustered together. "You will like the schools there. And you will have more children of your age to play with."

Faustín then turned toward his older sons who were seated next to each other. "We will try to run sheep out of Alamosa. We will be closer to the market."

"Your uncle and I have purchased some property there and we have hired some cousins to help us build our new homes, parts of which are good enough for us to move into. They will be complete soon."

No one said a word. Caught up in the news they stared open-mouthed at their family patriarch. Finally, Isaac spoke. "*Papá*," he waited for his father's acknowledgement. "When? When will we move?"

"Yes, *mi hijo*, in two weeks. So we must all work together to get ready. Not everything will be packed. We will leave some things." Then he explained that many of the implements and tools for the planting fields could stay. They were heavy, cumbersome, and, moreover, would not be needed. Even some of the furniture would stay.

Faustín then admitted that the times when he and Martín went north on business they really had gone to Alamosa to work on the houses and arrange for the move.

Now the preparations began. They loaded essentials into the two wagons, one for each family. And they had to make room for the little ones and mother. Right on schedule the little caravan started its journey north. Isaac was excited. This was an adventure. He did not mind the expected tasks. After all, he was fourteen years old, a young adult. Besides, Faustín knew that Isaac liked the horses so he gave his son the responsibility of caring for them. At the end of the day he had to unhitch, feed and water them, and rub them down, before he tied or hobbled them for the night. As they traveled Isaac walked most of the way. He took short turns on horseback, and on one occasion they let him ride on the wagon for a short distance.

The first day was an easy, well-known jaunt down river and, then directly north, to the town of Antonito. The town had a couple of hotels but Faustín and Martín felt that their money would be better spent elsewhere. They moved past the town to the nearby village of Conejos where they set up camp. Here, advance preparations had been made for a family get-together. Conejos was where Faustín and Martín married, and both sides had relatives, including their mother Cleofa and her family in both Conejos and Antonito. The caravan would spend an extra day to enjoy the festivities. Faustín and Martín were offered beds indoors but chose not to be separated from their families.

The daylong family *fiesta* could not have been a better morale booster. Cousins, aunts, and uncles, not to mention the half-brothers and sisters, revisited each other. They shared old memories, recalled names and events, and traded jokes, most of which they all knew. Naturally, Abrán's history came up. He remained a family hero.

After a full night's rest, the family and its two-wagon caravan continued north for the two-day trip. As they approached the town they heard the rail yard noise and saw smoke rising in the sky, then they smelled the burning coal and saw the workshops as they moved closer to town. Except for Faustín and Martín, none of them had seen a town this large with so many houses interspersed along dirt paths that passed for streets. The five or six two-story buildings lining a main street located the town's center. But nothing was more impressive than the dominating large wooden structure where all the noise and smell came from. They stared wide-eyed at the railroad's workshop and roundhouse. They had no idea at the time, but they would become very familiar with the forbidding place with its huge doors and dark wood. They could see a couple of train engines, one bellowing smoke and steam, the other idle. The engines sat on a plethora of tracks headed into the building that housed many unhitched train cars. Faustín sensed the curiosity running rampant in his family, so he explained, "that is the place where they fix the trains." The ever-serious Isaac replied, "Oh." What else could he say?

They stopped short of entering the main part of town. Instead, Faustín directed them to veer left on what barely looked like a road. They passed a couple of houses then angled to the right around another house. Isaac could not help but notice all the faces, frozen in the moment, staring at them. Both Faustín and Martín waved and spoke an occasional greeting to some of the people. In turn, they received obviously familiar reactions that heartened Isaac. He could see that these people were not complete strangers. At least *Papá* and uncle Martín knew these people.

Then, they stopped in front of two almost complete, identical small adobe houses. They were home. Life would never be the same.

Faustín's idea that they could run sheep out of Alamosa never worked out. That niche already was over-filled. Faustín immediately recognized that shepherding in

Alamosa did not have a bright future. Besides the work would take him and his boys out of town and they clearly preferred to stay with the family. Instead, they looked for work in Alamosa.

At first the boys did odd jobs, tasks for other people. They learned to navigate the streets, especially dodging the fascinating "honk-honk machines," as the new horseless carriages were called. Both Isaac and Alfonso got up-close looks at the carriages as they cleaned them for a nickel. In addition to taking odd jobs, they helped around the house, especially helping their father and uncle finish the two dwellings.

Then, one day Faustín came home followed by a wagon that had an oversized sewing machine in its bed. As two men, started unloading it, Talpita had to ask, "We have a Singer. What is this? Its too big."

Faustín was busy directing the men where to put it, but he could not ignore his wife. "Its not for you, *mamá*. Its for me."

Talpita's usually happy face looked puzzled. "You?"

Faustín did not react as the machine had been placed in a corner, and he handed the two men a quarter each and thanked them. They tipped their hats and walked back to the wagon that they turned around to head back into town. Faustín watched them mount the wagon, then turned to his family's curious faces. He explained that the machine was for making and repairing shoes. An old *zapatero*, shoemaker, had decided to give up the trade. The business was not doing well enough for him. Faustín figured that he could repair shoes at home. Eventually, he would learn how to make them.

He reasoned that he grew up making primitive shoes, something more akin to moccasins, for the family. He knew how to work a sewing machine. He would get the hang of this one. Then he turned and picked up a gunnysack that no one noticed he had brought in. "Look at this!" He overturned the bag and dumped the contents on the floor creating a pile of partial shoes, foot silhouettes, leather strips, and rawhide strings. He pointed to the silhouettes, "That's where you start, with the size. I can do this. I watched the shoemaker. He mostly worked sitting down. This is for me."

THE IMPETUOUS AND STERN MECHANIC, ISAAC
November 1915, Alamosa, Colorado

Light had come though the sun was still hidden by the eastern mountain range and there was a mist over the valley, and just enough frost to whiten the valley's low growth. It was cold and as Isaac stepped outside he saw his breath in a glorious cloud.

His father, of course, was already up and working. Faustín loved to use his hands, not in an idle way but for some purpose, and, Isaac, his second son shared the sentiment.

During the first months after their move Isaac worked at his father's side. He helped his father and his uncle finish their houses. He packed the dirt floors. They used animal blood to mix in the mud so when it dried, it dried hard. Ox blood was preferred but no one wanted to sacrifice that preferred beast of burden. They used the blood of sheep and cattle instead. "Blood is blood," Faustín reasoned. He drew the line with pig blood, though. "I don't want the house smelling like *morcilla*." His father's reasoning made sense to Isaac.

Faustín found more than one use for milled-lumber, an item that became available relatively recently. He plopped three or four boards on the damp floor and, then, stomped on them to pack the floor. He claimed that his technique resulted in the hardest, best-packed floors he had ever seen.

Isaac watched as his father played with the new sewing machine and check the result. Then he started again.

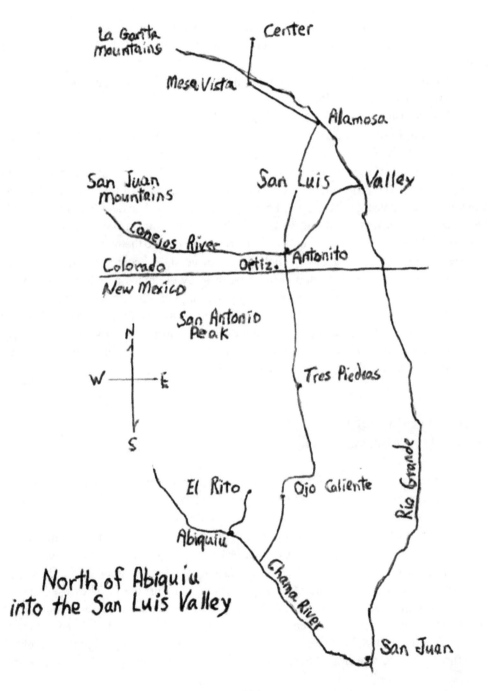

North of Abiquiu into the San Luis Valley

Faustín had an initial problem that he quickly resolved. It had to do with the silhouettes. The shoe invariably came out smaller than the print. Faustín rubbed his chin, scratched the back of his head, and then brightened up. "Of course! I need to accommodate for the space needed to sew the shoe onto the sole."

Isaac watched, perplexed with the explanation until his father demonstrated his discovery. He needed to make the shoe slightly smaller than the sole.

One problem required drastic action. The machine was too loud and big to be inside the house. It and its accessories caused too much wear on the floor. Besides, Talpita dreaded the day he would open for business if the machine was in the house. She could not imagine her household being constantly disrupted by customers parading through her house. Faustín would have to take his new toy and business outside of the house.

So, here they were, father and son on a sunny but cold November morning. They needed to build a work shed, a place were Faustín could conduct his shoe repair business unmolested while not molesting Talpita. They worked fast to get the shed up before the next snow came. They had learned that it is the second storm that initiates the long cold, gray winter.

Alfonso and Horacio, Isaac's two closest brothers age-wise, had become pals. They both had independent souls, while sharing the trait of keeping to themselves. Neither cared that much about mechanical stuff, so both accepted the obvious bond that Isaac

ALAMOSA PROPERTY

SHALL BE OWNED AND OCCUPIED BY WHITE PEOPLE ONLY
(Information acquired from archives, deeds and records)

According to Alamosa County records certain real property near Adams State College in Alamosa Colorado was transferred by Warranty Deed from "The Groening Realty Company" to Frank and Irene A. Cox on February 28, 1936 (entry No.18). County records show that the Groening Realty Company was incorporated in 1931 by Fritz A. Nagel, Mathilde Groening and Harry W. Zacheis.

The Warranty Deed, recorded in book 75 page 454 (pages 105, 106 and 107) of Alamosa County on March 4, 1936, contains the following wording, referred as Restrictions contained in City Zoning Ordinance: "This property shall now and hereafter be owned and occupied by white people only".

All or parts of this real estate were subsequently transferred to various other unrelated parties over the years. On March 1, 1954, descendents of the W. E. Welden estate filed a "Release" to clear up the "white people only" restriction. W.E. Welden, the last known owner of the real estate bearing the restriction, had been dead for many years and the descendents had no further interest in that property.

On August 14, 1954, Mildred Lyman Day and Roy J. Day on behalf of themselves and others filed Civil Action No 2663 in District Court of Alamosa and State of Colorado against a large number of individuals and corporate entities. The Plaintiffs' attempt was to overturn the "Release" which had been filed earlier that year by the Welden descendents. The court (Judge George H. Blickhahn) ruled in favor of the defendants.

Evidence of racism in Alamosa, Colorado. Copy is in the Ed and Cayetana Romero Collection.

and his father developed. They worked odd jobs, obeyed their parents and, basically, separated themselves from the other family members.

Talpita's announcement that she was with child added to the family dynamics. She figured that they would have their sixth child sometime in the summer of 1916.

The boys had become young adults. Faustín and Talpita could see that. They wondered what would become of them. Alfonso and Horacio helped the family out with their odd jobs. Faustín insisted that they keep some of their money for themselves. Isaac did not make as much because of the time he spent helping out in the house. That would change because Isaac and his father agreed that once the shop was up and running, Isaac would look for work in town.

Maybe it came from his father or uncle, or, possibly, his brothers. Around this time he realized that racism existed in Alamosa. Neighborhoods existed for one race or the other. No Anglos, those gringos, lived in their neighborhood. Isaac had been warned not to go to certain places in another part of town, that, in fact, "Mexicans" could not live there. Still, the main street was a mixture of people.

As Isaac approached his sixteenth birthday he walked to the rail yard. The rail yard with its huge roundhouse impressed him. Here were machines. Big machines. And tools, some of them actually smaller machines. Here, too, he did not see prejudice. Rather he saw men, different men working together with a familiarity heretofore unknown to Isaac.

By now, some of the workers had grown used to the boy nosing around. Without being told, he stayed out of the way and avoided dangerous areas. He did not interfere, but obviously had a curiosity about the place. But on this day one of the workers called out to him.

"Hey, kid. *Habla* English?"

"No. Yes, I sure do," he replied in Spanish.

The man walked up to him. He was covered in so much soot Isaac could barely tell where his overalls ended and the rest of him began. Yet, behind the dirty, sweat-streaked face Isaac could see a pleasant person. He stuck his hand in the overall's front pockets and said in Spanish, "Well, if you want to work here, you will have to speak English."

"Isaac nodded affirmatively. He did not even think about his reply. He would learn the language to keep his job.

"Well, good. Can you start next month? By the way, how old are you?"

"Yes, I can start?" Isaac was in another world at this moment.

"How old?"

"I will be sixteen in two weeks."

Ecstatic is an understatement for how Isaac felt. He had a job, a steady job. Moreover, his beginning salary was more than the total of everyone else's pay in the family. He began as an apprentice but that did not last long because he was a fast learner. Plus, he could read! He took to the blue prints and instructions given to him with pleasure.

He regaled his father and whoever would listen to his descriptions of work. "You think dad's sewing machine is big. You should see the nuts and bolts that we use. We have a monkey wrench this big!" With that, he held his hand out three feet from the ground.

"*Verdad,* really?"

If there ever was any doubt, Isaac had definitely become his father's favorite. Each day he came home covered with soot. He had to rotate his clothes. Merely cleaning them kept Talpita busy. His closest brothers thought that it took a special type of personality to work in the rail yard, and Isaac was perfect.

But he was young, still in his teens. Pleasure could not be overlooked. The nearby town of Monte Vista waited. On this particular summer weekend it had its annual rodeo days with a parade, carnival, and dance. Isaac, cleaned, and dressed for the occasion, stepped into the kitchen. Sitting there with a newspaper tilted toward the kerosene lamp and what little morning light seeped into the room, Faustín mouthed the words as he tried to read them then sighed when he recognized Isaac's presence.

"It is terribly sad," he observed, almost to himself.

"Qué, what *papá*?" Isaac thought his father referred to an article he just read.

Faustín put down the paper. "Your brothers, Alfonso and Horacio, they told your mother and me that they will leave Alamosa. Go find work."

"When?"

"Last night. Your mother cried all night. Now she does not want to get out of bed."

"No *papá*. When will they leave?" Isaac knew about their plans for some time. They always talked about the idea of leaving Alamosa. Now, the talk had ended. Isaac also knew that they were unhappy in Alamosa.

Faustín answered, "Today, tomorrow. Soon. I don't know."

Isaac tried to make light of the matter. "It won't be today or tomorrow. I know that they are going up to Monte Vista."

Faustín gave a grim nod and grabbed his newspaper again. Isaac continued forcing out the only words he could think of. "Maybe it will be better for them. They will have more opportunities. Anyway, I'm staying here. And the others, too."

He barely heard his father whisper, "Maybe."

Isaac knew his father well. He took his half-filled cup of coffee and warmed it from the hot pot on the stove. "Here, *papá*. It will be fine. Alfonso and Horacio can take care of themselves." Then, the normally reserved Isaac leaned down and kissed his father on top of his head.

Monte Vista was another railroad town and a stop on a line primarily used to haul lumber from the mountains that define the western edge of the San Luis Valley. Smaller than Alamosa, the town became the focal point of the valley during its rodeo weekend. People from the whole region flocked to Monte Vista for the festivities called The Sky High Stampede. The town was only fourteen miles from Alamosa. The festivities were not limited to the citizens of Monte Vista. The rodeo showed off the talents of people from all over the valley.

Still slightly preoccupied with his morning conversation with his father, Isaac drove in a new Chevrolet that he was purchasing and arrived in Monte Vista in time to watch the Stampede Parade. The parade consisted of decked out wagons, people dressed in their finest while riding well-groomed horses, and the always popular auto cars that regaled the audience while honking their horns, "Aaauuugha." The parade moved up Grande Avenue between the one- and two-story storefronts that made up the small downtown. Isaac watched with a smile on his normally placid face. Then, a young lady riding a horse in the parade caught his eye. He had never seen her before. For sure she wasn't from Alamosa. She had auburn hair defining a roundish face with the happiest smile Isaac had ever seen. "Who is she?" Isaac needed to know. She rode past, keeping pace with the parade, and waved.

Fighting his way through the crowd, Isaac kept up with her as the parade progressed. He never felt like this before. She was beautiful. He had to meet her. But when she got to the parade's end, her parents greeted her and helped her dismount. Now was not the time to approach her.

Isaac thought that she might be at the Stampede dance later that night. That would be a good opportunity to meet. That was all that Isaac could think about as he milled about the carnival grounds drinking root beer and eating booth food. If she came to the dance he would have his only chance to meet her.

Fortunately he had a new Chevrolet automobile. He had learned to drive with his co-workers. He loved machines and worked around engines much larger and more complicated than any automobile. Now it came in handy. He hopped into his car and drove home to clean up and change clothes. Then, he drove back to Monte Vista, but he had a slight problem. A flat tire. Fortunately, he had a set of coveralls in the car, so he put them on over his clothes and replaced the flat with the spare tire. Then he jumped in the car and finished the short drive.

He had not counted on the throng of people who attended the dance. He would be lucky to find her and if he did, would she be with her parents? Then, as if fate were on his side he spotted her standing next to a partially empty table. Her parents were not there. Isaac thought they might be dancing.

True to his personality, Isaac did not hesitate. He forced his way through the crowd, dodging some inattentive children on the way. He came up to her and spoke Spanish. "Hi. My name is Isaac, Isaac Romero, from Alamosa." He paused for a reaction. "I saw you in the parade today and I want to meet you." This time the reaction was a muted giggle. She looked embarrassed.

Isaac continued, "What's your name?"

To his now biased sensibilities, she spoke with a voice that could not have been more pleasingly melodic. "My name is Ramona."

"Ah, Ramona. Such a pretty name. And your last name?"

"Pacheco." With this she slightly blushed. Her eyes darted around as if looking for help.

"Well, Ramona Pacheco, would you like to dance?" This was a daring move on two scores. First, she could say no, and, second, Isaac didn't know how to dance. He figured it was easy enough. He could copy the others. At the moment, necessity took priority.

"I can't." That was an answer Isaac had not foreseen. He looked at her dumbfounded. She saw his confusion and added. "First, I will not dance with anyone in coveralls. Also, you will have to ask my father."

Isaac looked down at his clothes. He had forgotten to change out of his coveralls. They didn't look so good, soiled as they were. He looked up embarrassed. "I had a flat tire. I'll be back." With those words he rushed back to his car, took off the coveralls, threw them into the back seat, and returned in his clean clothes. Ramona watched him approach, and he did not spare words. "Your father. Okay. Where is he?"

"Dancing with my mother." Just about then the music stopped and the dance floor began to clear. Ramona's parents strolled over toward them. They sized up the situation before Isaac could speak. Maybe he wasn't the first to ask.

"Señor Pacheco, I am Isaac Romero. I live in Alamosa with my parents. Your daughter, Ramona, who I just met." Here Isaac got formal, " She informed me, as is proper, that I must ask your permission to dance with her. That is, if she agrees as well."

Mr. Pacheco, a well-groomed man, dark and handsome, a little shorter than Isaac, had a solemn look on his mustached face that at once seemed amused. "Alamosa, eh. Who is your father?"

Isaac answered.

"And do you have a job?"

"Yes sir. I work for the railroad. I am a mechanic."

"I am a shepherd. Does that bother you?"

"Oh, no sir." Then Isaac used the opportunity to explain a little of his and his family's history with sheep.

Pacheco turned to his daughter. "Do you want to dance with this mechanic?"

She looked at the floor and nodded her head affirmatively.

Pacheco turned to his wife. "Hey, Juanita. What do you say? Should we let your daughter risk it?" Juanita stood less than five feet tall and did not weigh more than ninety pounds. She gave her husband a questioning look and answered, "Sí, está bien."

"Well, okay. Go ahead."

That dance was the beginning of a secret, long-distance relationship between Isaac and Ramona. She was fifteen when they met and, he learned, she was born in La Garita in the northwest extreme of the valley at the base of the mountains. She warned him that her father was very strict and religious. He is a Penitente, his first name is Lucas, and her mother is Juanita from Taos. He reads the Bible all the time and has named her and all brothers with names from the Old Testament. Ramona was sure that he would like Isaac's name.

They met when they could through the next few months. On occasion Ramona came to Alamosa with her parents. Isaac tried to in fill the separation between actual meetings with letters. One thing became clear to both of them. They fell in love.

How it happened only Isaac and Ramona, and a complacent priest knew, for on July 3, 1921, they secretly married while Ramona was on another of those trips to Alamosa. Isaac's aunt Millie and her husband Steve Medina were let in on the secret so they could stand as best man and matron of honor. Neither Isaac nor Ramona ever shared how they managed to do it without the permission of their parents. Isaac was nineteen years old, and mature beyond his years. No one expected such a rash act from him. Ramona had turned sixteen years old.

Still they kept their secret, each living with their parents, he in Alamosa and she with her family in Center, north of Monte Vista. They continued as before, seeing each other when they could, and he writing to her. That was their downfall, for his letters gave them away. After their marriage Isaac started addressing the letters to his "Dear Wife." Moises, one of Ramona's brothers found one of her letters and the secret was out.

Word of their clandestine relationship and union enraged Ramona's father. Their act also embarrassed Faustín who had no answers when approached by Lucas. What Isaac and Ramona had done was almost unheard of. The secret marriage was contrary to every tradition known to their respective families. It showed disrespect to both sets of parents.

Ramona Pacheco, seventeen years old. The young wife of Isaac Romero. Ed and Cayetana Romero Collection.

Isaac had his work cut out for him. He apologized to both parents while professing his love for Ramona. Both had to answer for their actions. Their love for one another became clear to the parents and, besides, once the deed was done it was for life. There was no turning back.

Isaac Romero, around twenty years old. Ed and Cayetana Romero Collection.

In addition, Lucas clearly saw that Isaac came from good stock. Both Faustín and Talpita were good Catholics. Isaac had a job and spoke English, although Lucas could not tell how well. He had a certain something about him that bespoke stability. In short, Lucas quickly started liking his new son-in-law. His darling daughter had found a good husband. Moreover, Lucas and Faustín had a lot in common. What more could he ask? "*Bueno*," he and Juanita gave the couple their blessings.

Alfonso and Horacio left Alamosa soon after Rodeo days. They saved enough money to help them while they looked for new opportunities. Horacio moved to Glenwood Springs and Alfonso, or Nick as he was called moved to Denver. They missed the opportunity to witness their parent's reaction to their brother's marriage and they would have felt for Isaac and Ramoncita when a year later in early 1922, their first child died at birth.

The women dressed their precious Ernesto in white, watched as the priest sprinkled holy water on him, and placed him in a small white coffin made by Faustín and Isaac. A large procession followed the coffin and the young grieving parents to the Spanish cemetery, where their baby was buried.

Every person at the funeral had been witness to infant mortality. Faustín knew of people who had suffered similarly. Isaac remembered attending an infant's funeral for a neighbor who, at the time, he barely knew. Isaac was seven years old at the time.

Now, Isaac understood the sorrow he had witnessed before, for it became real to him. But, he tried to keep his grief to himself. No matter how he really felt, he knew that he could not begin to realize the pain Ramoncita suffered. "A mother's loss," he thought to himself, "is only known by the mother." He had to be strong for her.

His job helped divert his attention. He thanked God for his mother, who kept company with Ramoncita and kept her occupied. Isaac's younger brothers and sisters helped, too. And that was critical. The youngest, three year old Faustino was a reminder of what Ernesto might have been.

Then, there was the construction of their new house. It helped because it hinted of the future. As they had before, Isaac and his father worked together to slowly build the adobe home. Construction was different as Isaac drew on his knowledge gained from his job. Just as new technology periodically introduced newer larger and more powerful locomotives that they maintained, the same kinds of processes came to home construction.

With this new knowledge Faustín had found a niche for himself building adobe homes. The idea of becoming a cobbler gave way to his greater skills. With the examples of the two homes that he and Martín had built, then his shed, Faustín turned his attention to carpentry. At times, he would hire a team of men to help him with various aspects of construction, especially the production of adobes.

Faustin had long since accepted the qualities of glass windows. But he could not help but comment on wood floors. "You can see the dirt." Of course, he said that while overlooking the dirt floors in his house. Then, he added, "Packed earth does not warp and is easily replaced."

Indoor plumbing proved a greater challenge to Faustín. One of Isaac's work friends knew plumbing. When they explained to Faustín that the bathroom would go in the house, he exclaimed, "You mean you put the shitter in the house? No. No! How filthy. How can you stand it?"

Isaac and his friend tried to explain the concept of plumbing. "We don't have to pump water anymore. The toilet flushes to a central system. Remember all the pipe that the city buried under the street?" Faustín could not be convinced. He would wait to see how these innovations worked in Isaac's house.

Isaac took his father's comments in good humor. He knew his father would study and ponder the innovations. Eventually, Faustin acquiesced on both scores. When they

Isaac Romero and his father Faustino Romero. They are standing in front of the house that they built in Alamosa. Note the bulge on Faustino's left hip. Ed and Cayetana Romero Collection.

finally put a wood floor in his house, they used boards that had knotholes in them. Naturally enough, Faustín and, especially Talpita, utilized the knotholes. They swept the dirt through them onto the dirt floor below.

Within months after Isaac and Ramoncita moved into their new house they had a baby girl. This "gift from God" was born on November 23, 1925. She was a perfect elixir for Ramoncita. They named the girl Vivian Elizabeth and called her "Betsy." As her mother's favorite, she became her mother's daughter in many ways. A grateful Isaac could not be thankful enough.

The three of them lived happily for the next three years. Isaac continued with his job and Ramoncita busied herself with Betsy. Faustín and Talpita lived about a hundred yards away. There were plenty of children in the neighborhood and, along with Betsy's cousins, she had more than enough playmates to occupy her time. For the first five years of her life, little Betsy grew up as a pampered child.

Now, Isaac and Ramoncita had some time to devote to their community. They became involved with their parish church that Isaac helped build and maintain. Isaac joined the Knights of Columbus and eventually to become a Grand Knight. He and Ramoncita joined the Alianza Hispana Americana, an organization that advocated education and civil rights for all Hispanic surnamed people. Although Isaac had fun teasing her for marching in the parades down 6th street, he knew that she had taken up Abrán's cause.

Isaac was becoming a very respected man in the community. His brothers and sisters looked up to him. They called him "brother." Only his closest friends informally called him by his first name.

Following her husband's lead and the example of her father who was an active member of The Society for the Mutual Protection of United Trade Workers (SPMTDU), an organization that actively fought for the rights of Hispanic workers, Ramoncita started attending democratic ward meetings. The depression did not hit the faraway San Luis Valley as hard as the rest of the country. Still, she appreciated the progressive ideas of the Democratic Party. She liked President Franklin Roosevelt because he wanted to help the poor. He was creating jobs. She would do what she could at her level.

Then, on April 15, 1930, almost five years after Betsy's birth, Isaac and Ramoncita had a son. Ramoncita insisted that they name him Isaac. Isaac, the father, was not so sure about the name but did not argue. Betsy welcomed her young brother and had no trouble sharing attention with him. To avoid confusion the family started calling the baby boy, "Buddy," a name that quickly morphed into the more acceptable "Bud." By the time he was three, Bud assumed the big brother role.

The children grew up speaking Spanish at home and surrounded by cousins, for Martín and Ciria had a growing family that would reach ten children. It seemed like the whole world was made up of Romeros. English came to them on the streets and in school. Both Isaac and Ramoncita spoke an English that improved over time. Nevertheless, Spanish was the language of choice spoken at home.

Official portrait of Ambassador Edward L. Romero. Ed and Cayetana Romero Collection.

Ed Romero and his immediate family in Washington, DC before being sworn in as United States Ambassador to Spain and Andorra. From left to right, Steven, Anna, Cayetana, Ed, Ruth, and Christina. Photograph by LeRoy N. Sanchez.

Ed Romero departing to present his credentials to the King. The Rolls Royce once belonged to Francisco Franco. Photograph by LeRoy N. Sanchez.

Ed Romero arriving in procession at the Royal Palace, Madrid, Spain. Photograph by LeRoy N. Sanchez.

Ed Romero presenting his credentials to Spain's King Juan Carlos. Photograph by LeRoy N. Sanchez.

Cayetana Romero in the ambassador's residence before a Thanksgiving dinner given for the Marines who provided the embassy's security. Ed and Cayetana Romero Collection.

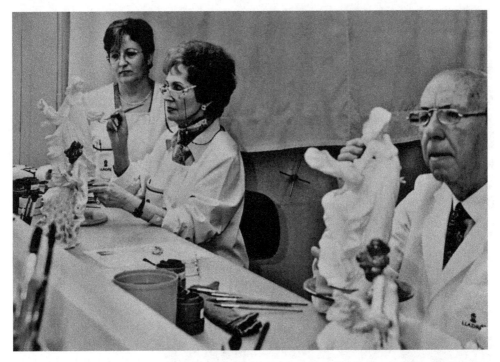

Cayetana Romero visiting the Lladró factory. She was invited to paint a figurine by José "Pepe" Llardo on the rght. Ed and Cayetana Romero Collection.

Cayetana and Ambassador Ed Romero dressed for a formal reception in Spain.
Ed and Cayetana Romero Collection.

Ed Romero with President Bill Clinton and President Barack Obama. Ed and Cayetana Romero Collection.

A monument in a park on the Camino Real named and dedicated to Ed Romero in Albuquerque's Martinez Town. The monument includes his coat of arms and a brief history of his ancestry beginning with Bartolomé Romero. Photograph by LeRoy N. Sanchez.

The lobby of the Roy E. Disney Center for Performing Arts at the National Hispanic Cultural Center that is named in honor of Cayetana Romero. Photograph by LeRoy N. Sanchez.

Part VIII
The Twelfth Generation, Ed Romero

The Tenth, Eleventh, and Twelfth Generations

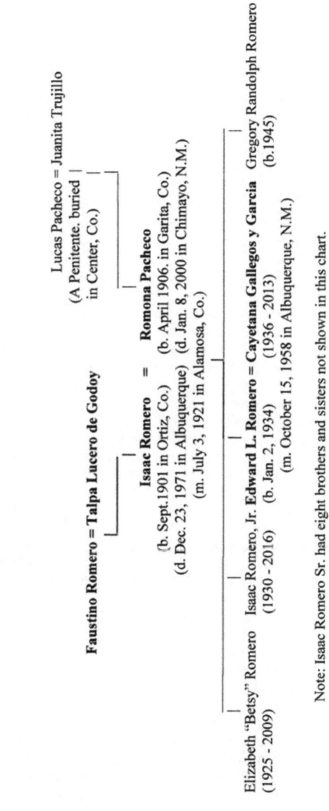

Lucas Pacheco = Juanita Trujillo
(A Penitente. buried
in Center, Co.)

Faustino Romero = Talpa Lucero de Godoy

Isaac Romero =
(b. Sept.1901 in Ortiz, Co.)
(d. Dec. 23, 1971 in Albuquerque)
(m. July 3, 1921 in Alamosa, Co.)

Romona Pacheco
(b. April 1906. in Garita, Co.)
(d. Jan. 8, 2000 in Chimayo, N.M.)

Elizabeth "Betsy" Romero
(1925 - 2009)

Isaac Romero, Jr.
(1930 - 2016)

Edward L. Romero = Cayetana Gallegos y Garcia
(b. Jan. 2, 1934)   (1936 - 2013)
(m. October 15, 1958 in Albuquerque, N.M.)

Gregory Randolph Romero
(b.1945)

Note: Isaac Romero Sr. had eight brothers and sisters not shown in this chart.

"El Huevo Hediondo," "Pique," and Childhood
1934, Alamosa

The January 2nd birth of Isaac and Ramoncita's fourth child was nothing unusual except for the hospital administrator who marked the "other" box as the place where the mother gave birth. The parents named the soon to be precocious child after the good Father Edward McCarthy, who, everyone agreed, personified everything positive about being a priest. Nevertheless, Ramoncita would spend the rest of her life insisting the Edward Leroy was born in the hospital, which, in fact, he was, even though her labor began while she was in route.

Betsy quickly adopted the cute round-headed newborn. What eight-year-old girl needs dolls when her parents present her with the real thing? Older brothers can be a different matter. At least, until they reach maturity. Bud saw the new addition as competition for attention and this became more poignant as young Edward learned to walk, talk, and function in general. They called him by his middle name and he hardly missed a moment to create problems. So it seemed to Bud, who, in his early years, chose to ignore his minor sibling, Leroy.

Now with three children, Isaac hardly skipped a beat in his daily, now life-long, routine. He returned to the shop the day after Edward's birth. His colleagues congratulated him. He nodded acknowledgement while doing his best to avoid discussion. With his cap partially covering his neatly trimmed dark hair that he combed straight back, Isaac concentrated on his work. Even during the moments of his children's birth, he maintained a dignity that commanded respect from everyone around him. Now in his middle thirties, he had become a pillar in his *barrio*, if not the community in general, and was respected at work. It was around this time—no one remembers exactly when—that people started to call him Don Isaque.

Not even the evidence of a full page spread in Alamosa's *The Daily Courier* for Thursday, January 11th that announced that a "boy, son of Mr. and Mrs. Isaac Romero" was the first baby born in Alamosa County in 1934, added to Isaac's stature. Prizes for this feat included "an order for...$1.00 worth of milk tickets and an order...for a Wamba Crib blanket valued at $3.00." Another store offered a "pink blanket," and others provided "baby rings," a savings account in the local bank with a credit for $1.00 and "a bank book." The Optimists Club kicked in another $1.00 with the caveat in their printed announcement that this year's babies should be congratulated for "arriving under the New Deal. We believe they are more fortunate than those of 1933." Other prizes included two cans of Gerber's strained vegetables, $2.00 worth of whole milk, another blanket, and a canvas baby jumper worth $1.25.

Ramoncita, as beautiful and bright as ever, did nothing to detract from Isaac's image. While he continued to be active in the Knights of Columbus and in the Hispanic community with the Alianza Hispana Americana, she crossed ethnic lines to work in the Rosary and Altar Society and had become a Democratic Party precinct chairman. These activities added to the respect that came from their friends and family.

Isaac and Ramoncita maintained a deep reverence for their heritage and for their

Isaac Romero, train mechanic posing in the Alamosa rail yard. Ed and Cayetana Romero Collection.

respective families. They grew up in a time of change. Their youthful experiences of a bygone lifestyle had relevance for them and their children. The influence of their own parents, from Faustín, Lucas, and their wives could not be overvalued. They continued to visit aunts and uncles. On one occasion they took the train to Santa Fe to visit some aunts, who were Faustín's half-sisters.

Obviously, the world was changing. Isaac's job with the railroad and his fondness for Chevrolet cars could not be ignored. "Yes," he and Ramoncita agreed, "our children must be prepared for what is ahead." The plowshare had ceased to be relevant and was lost in memory many years past. They had a new emphasis. "Education. Yes, education. That is the key." If they did nothing else they would stress the value of education to their children.

"Así es." They repeated to each other. "And not just in the school. It is our responsibility too. We, our parents, and family have lessons to share." Father Mac, a close family friend, agreed, for he promoted the positive influence of families. Such an impact made formal education much easier. Under his care, the Romero children would be taught their catechism and receive the Church's sacraments.

Nor could the *Penitentes* be ignored. Grandpa Lucas was the *hermano mayor*, leader, of the brotherhood in Center, Colorado. Although no one realized it at the time, Center was one of the most important and concentrated places of the semi-secretive, religious brotherhood in the southwest. Lucas was an important man. Before he moved in with Isaac's family in his last years, Lucas regularly attended and led prayer sessions. As the *hermano mayor* of the Brotherhood of Our Father Jesus the Nazarene, the local *Penitente* group, he participated in all the group's activities.

Isaac's refusal to join the brotherhood disappointed him at first. Years had passed, eleven to be exact, and Lucas had come to accept the fact. He knew that his son-in-law was a solid and good Catholic. It was enough. Besides, Isaac allowed for his family to attend certain of the brotherhood's processions and functions. There was no disrespect. No, only a show of the opposite.

A steady job, a growing family, a nice adobe home in a safe neighborhood with both sets of parents close-by, many relatives, and good neighbors made for a wonderful environment in which to raise a family. The neighborhood consisted of many houses like Isaac's and the people spoke Spanish. Depending on the season and the weather, the streets could be dirt, dust, or mud and ice. The relatively new highway heralded the future paving of many of Alamosa's streets—another change. But for the moment, the town had to suffer the Rio Grande's annual spring runoff that turned Main Street into a quagmire. During such times, the railroad remained the most expedient connection to the rest of the world. And Isaac was proud to be charged with maintaining that vital source of transportation.

He worked five days a week, eight hours a day, and welcomed overtime. Ramoncita took care of the children and the house. This included the chickens and a few pigs. On weekends, if they were not off for a summer's picnic so Isaac could fish, Isaac worked in the yard and with the animals. Usually with his father beside him, he fixed all the small problems that cropped up around the house, including the plumbing and whatever carpentry needed to be done. He and his father finished the kitchen during the spring after Edward's birth.

Occasionally Isaac purchased a sheep from his brother-in-law, Moises. He took it home where he had a shed set up for the butchering. He hoisted the animal by its back legs and slit its throat. As was traditional, the women took the cuts of meat and other parts to prepare or preserve the food. One tradition out of the past, the *burroñates*, made from the animal's fat and entrails, killed young Ed's taste for lamb or anything related to it for life.

Ramoncita continued her political work as a precinct chairwoman. She kept that position for over three decades. She was invited to many statewide party conventions as well as to some Democratic National Conventions, one of which she attended in Denver. Isaac had no interest in politics, but knew enough about his wife to support her in her endeavors. Because of his job he could not travel with her. They saved his vacation time for family outings and periodic train trips to California to visit his sister, Martina, who moved there with her husband.

They loved to sit around the radio and listen to programs and, especially, news of the war. Isaac, now forty-three years old, was too old to be drafted. Besides, keeping the railroads running was a national priority, which gave him another source of pride. Nevertheless, he looked at his oldest son thankful that he was not old enough for soldiering, or even to "get the itch" and secretly enlist by lying about his age. Stories of such acts ran rampant. He wanted his children to go to college. He would say, "We will need educated people to run this county after the war."

Ed was too young to really appreciate the history being made in those days. His world revolved around the dirt streets of south Alamosa, the halls and classrooms of the public school, the summer parochial school with the Benedictine nuns, summer family excursions, and cold winter nights huddled around a wood-burning stove. He loved the excursions watching his father, mother, and uncles cast for elusive trout that inhabited all the waters around Alamosa.

On special occasions dad used his company privilege to load the family on the narrow-gauge train and head south to Antonito, then west toward Chama and into the mountains where he, his father, and uncle Martín used to shepherd sheep with grandpa Faustín. As prearranged, the engineer stopped the train in the canyon along the Pinos River to let the family off. The return train picked them up in the late afternoon. By then, they had enough fish in their creels for at least two dinners. The children frolicked and napped all day. Isaac tried to interest his children in fishing, but, outside of Bud, they did not have the patience. They preferred to play and eat.

None of the children realized until later in life that they grew up bilingual. Although both sets of their grandparents spoke Spanish and very little English, Isaac and Ramoncita spoke English as a second language that they sometimes sprinkled with Spanish words. They gave their children English names, the first generation of Romeros to have done so. The two boys also grew up with English nicknames. "Bud," or "Buddy," had no connection to anything and Bud hated it. Ed was called "Leroy," his middle name given to him by his godparents. He, too, hated the name. Isaac and Ramona intentionally made sure that their children learned to speak either language without a trace of an accent. This, to them, was very important. Spanish was the primary language in the house as well as in the streets, although English surfaced frequently. To make sure that Ed spoke English well he was put into a special first grade class that emphasized English.

It was the traditions, though, the way of life, that most impressed the children. Ed's earliest memory would be of his father hoisting him onto his shoulders and loudly saying for everyone to hear, "*Aquí vienen*! Here they come. See, look! Can you see them?" A wide-eyed Ed, all of five years old, had the perfect view from his perch, but he was not sure what he was looking at. A group of bundled-up people trudged toward them through the gray cold and morning snow trailing the vapor from their breathing. Sensing that something exciting was about to happen, Ed did not feel the bitter cold at all. It was New Year's Day and, as he found out, anybody born from Christmas through the Epiphany, Three Kings Day on January 6th, officially or unofficially received the name of Manuel or Manuela and became the annual recipient of songs called *Los Días* sung to them by the local group. That included Ed. His earliest memory would be that moment when they played guitars and sang to him, while he looked on from his father's shoulders. Throughout his formative years, this music born of centuries old traditions would be the seed that grew into Ed's lifelong appreciation for his Hispanic heritage.

As a child he loved the camaraderie of it all. Of course, the *bizcochitos* had something to do with it, for after the singing his parents invited everyone into the house for those cookies and wine, of the Mogen David, a sweet, fortified variety. While adults clamored about talking, Ed took advantage of the situation to help himself to the defenseless cookies.

At the same age, Ed learned that he could sneak out of the house. His first stealth adventure took him around the block to his Romero grandparents' house. This was a winter gambit, when he would scoot to his grandparents welcoming kitchen, and the warmth of their wood-burning stove. Then, he curled up in a blanket with his *abuelos* Faustín and Talpita next to the stove, and waited for the inevitable knock at the kitchen door.

Usually, grandpa Romero reacted to the knock. "*Si-i-i?*" He answered with an exaggerated knowledge that Ed was too young to notice.

Isaac answered from outside, "*Padre, está* Leroy? Father is Leroy here?"

"*No hijo. No le he visto.* No son, I have not seen him." Faustín all the while winked to Isaac through the partially open door. "*No está aquí*. He is not here. *Vete*. Go."

"*Bueno,*" came the reply. The door shut and the unsuspecting, self-satisfied Ed remained snuggled with his grandparents next to the warm stove. Usually, he fell asleep and then somehow magically woke up in his own bed the next morning.

Back at the house, Isaac nodded to the inquiring look of Ramoncita. "He's there." She knew. Isaac added: "That kid. He has his own ideas, maybe a wanderlust, but, at least, he keeps his exploits within the family."

"Sure Isaac. It is good. He loves our parents and they tell him stories. But someday? I wonder."

Ramoncita did not have to wonder for long. Ed soon figured out that his neighbors, who in his youthful order of things he considered his aunt and uncle, hosted monthly dances. *Tío* Manuel played the violin and his two sons played guitar while his daughter played the mandolin. *Tía* María taught the dances.

Young Ed could hear the music from his room and curiosity got the best of him. Why not use his practiced and successful stealth skills to steal away to the dances? Thus, he climbed out of his bedroom window to journey next door on a whole new adventure.

Ed knew the house. He had been in it many times with his parents. It was a two-room adobe structure. Nothing fancy except that the rooms were big. The long front porch opened into a large living room with at least six beds and that room opened into a large kitchen. Manuel and María were close family friends, as good as relatives, but not quite.

When Ed scurried over to the house to see the dances and hear the music, the large living room was transposed into a large open dance hall full of twenty to thirty happy people. And the smell! Tía María prepared tortillas smeared with bacon fat and sprinkled with salt and pepper, which she cut into quarters and passed out to the guests.

The music and dancing brought the people together. To young Edward it was magical. He could not resist. At first, Manuel and María thought that Ed had his parents' permission to be there. They welcomed him. And even more so when they saw that Ed immersed himself in the music and dance. *Tía* María took special pleasure in teaching the young man all the dances. No evening passed without the *marcha*. People lined up in pairs behind *tía* María and a chosen partner. Her husband and children struck up the music and she led the way as the paired couples wound about the room then turned on themselves and did a serpentine move into separate lines to return to their original positions. The dance was very intricate and everyone participated. Later in life, Ed would claim that a major reason for his appreciation for his heritage came from the music and dances next door, at the time, the unimagined influence of *tía* María and *tío* Manuel.

A child with Ed's disposition needed to be outdoors and that is exactly where Ed spent most of his early years. With one exception, all of the neighborhood kids were Hispanic. The one difference was Ronnie Gardenswartz, who became one of Ed's best friends. Ronnie did not speak Spanish but at times it seemed that he understood. Otherwise, how could he play *el huevo hediondo* (the stinking egg)?

One person would be chosen to be the first *huevo hediondo*. That person stood on one side of a line drawn in the dirt and faced all the others on the other side of the line. He would knock and the others would reply with the question, "*A quien buscas*? Who are you looking for?"

"*El huevo hediondo.*"

"*De qué color*? What color?" Each of the other players had a selected color of his choice and the *huevo hediondo* now had to run off a litany of colors until he guessed or named one correctly. Of course, the kids chose colors that were not so obvious. However, once chartreuse was used, it was sure to be called the next time. If the correct color was called that person took off running, for if the *huevo hediondo* tagged him, he became the new stinking egg.

Fighting was prevalent, and Ed had to prove himself. When a usually pre-arranged fight broke out, the others gathered and cheered until one or the other of the participants gave up. Ronnie tried but he was not very big or athletic. Ed, however, was above average size for his age, athletically prone, and took pride in what for a while was an undefeated streak.

Ed's run to glory ended when he matched up with his cousin, Fred Koury. Fred's father was Lebanese whose family, like many of his ethnicity, had migrated from the Middle East to the American southwest, quickly intermingled, and became an integral part of society. At the time, Ed had a sense of invincibility about him. Fred, however, was a year or two older, slightly bigger, and, as it turned out, a little quicker and stronger. "Fred beat the heck out of me," was the only thing Ed could say of his first defeat. Young Ed needed a helping of humility at the time. It was part of the maturing process. If nothing else, Ed learned from experience even if it was a bloodied and beaten one.

Aside from fighting, the other favorite game was marbles. That game crossed language barriers as well. The kids called small marbles, "peewees" and large marbles, "jumbos." They played the universal game of placing a certain number of marbles inside a ring drawn in the dirt, then taking turns trying to knock them out of the ring by shooting a single marble from the ring's perimeter. At times, the shooter could call out *"pique,* or peaks*"* which entitled him to place his target on a small, built up mound so he could have a better shot.

Generally, Alamosa was a quiet town. Situated next to the Rio Grande in the middle of the San Luis Valley, the limits of which are defined by different ridges of the Rocky Mountains, the town's very setting lent itself to a sense of tranquility. Only the sound of the trains' whistles, bells, and engines broke the silence. The trains seemed to be a natural and not intrusive part of the landscape.

Isaac was especially cognizant of Alamosa's tranquility, because he ended each workday making the transition from the pounding, hissing, banging, clanking racket of the railroad's machine shop to the calmness of Alamosa's high altitude peacefulness. It was a change that he noted almost every day when he left the shop.

Thus on one spring day in 1945 shortly after the end of World War II, he left work as usual to walk home lost in his own thoughts. The walk did not take long and was even shorter when he did not think about it. Suddenly, he looked up to realize that he had come up to his front yard. He hardly recalled what was on his mind as he walked into the yard but something was different.

Ramoncita waited for him on the front porch. Usually, she busied herself preparing dinner, but not this time. Isaac could tell from her body language and her concerned look that something was on her mind. Betsy, now twenty years old, peered over her shoulder from inside the screen door. Ramoncita initiated the Spanish conversation with her hands clasped in front of her.

"Hi. How was your day?"

"Normal. The same as always," Isaac said, impatient to get by the required greetings.

Ramoncita continued, "Father Mac came by today."

By now Isaac had walked up to Ramoncita. "What for? A problem at the church?"

"No dear. He left a baby."

"A what?"

"A baby. A boy. He was left with Father to take to the orphanage. He said, "It was a gift from heaven."

"Okay. So, why is he here?"

"He said that he needs two weeks to make arrangements in Pueblo, and asked if we could care for the child in the meantime. I said, 'yes.'" Ramoncita unclasped her hands and rubbed them on her apron. She hung her head, which was an unconscious submission to her husband.

"Two weeks! What is Father Mac thinking? Is heaven going to take it back? I should have been consulted, Ramona," he used her proper name when he was irritated, "we have a family and enough to do. Now we have a baby. My God."

Ramoncita did not like to see Isaac in such a mood. He was a stern man but also loving. Instinctively, she knew how to react. She straightened up and stared directly into his face. "It did not cross Father's mind that you would do anything but agree. And so I did."

This reply left Isaac wordless except for a mild, "humph," and silent, "I'm hungry. Let's eat." He walked past her and into the house where he almost bumped into Betsy, who was holding the baby. He paused, looked at the child, took a breath, and continued on to the bathroom to clean up. Dinner that night was relatively silent. About the only exchange occurred when Isaac asked what was the baby's name, and Ramoncita answered, "Gregory Randolph."

The baby won over the family within days. Even Isaac proved to be a soft touch, although no one would dare point that out to him. He had to admit, "He is a cute little fellow." Then Isaac did something unusual. During the second week he called the family together and told them that they had a choice. They could let Father Mac take the child to the orphanage, which would mean an uncertain future for the boy, or they could keep him, adopt the child themselves. Everyone understood that the mere act of calling the family together to decide what to do about Gregory was an implicit admission that Isaac was willing to keep the child. "But," he warned with a most serious look, "all of us, everyone of us, have to make a commitment to love him and treat him as one of our own." Of course there was no debate.

PIANO LESSONS, FOOTBALL, AND FAMILY
1946, Alamosa

Ed's proclivity for music would draw him to his sister. Betsy was a proficient piano player by the time Ed was five years old. When Ed was around eleven years old, she started teaching him.

In 1947, Betsy graduated from Adams State College with a degree in education and took a teaching position down south in Española, New Mexico. While there, she worked on her Masters degree from New Mexico Highlands University. With Betsy gone, Ed's parents arranged for him to continue his piano lessons from Pauline Martínez, who lived close by and was confined to a wheel chair. Ed continued his lessons while attending high school and never lost his affection for the instrument.

Betsy's decision to become a teacher pleased Isaac and Ramoncita. Isaac considered teaching to be one of the noblest professions. Betsy was the first in the family to receive a degree, and Bud, recently graduated from high school followed suit. He enrolled in Adams State College. Now, with the examples of his older sister and brother before him, Ed, the somewhat rebellious son, seemed to have fallen into the desired pattern.

School was a year-round schedule for Ed. When the spring semester ended and summer vacation was supposed to begin, Ed was sent back to the same school building for catechism. Father Mac rented the building and brought in Benedictine nuns to teach the faith. Ed, along with around one hundred other kids, attended daily mass at Sacred Heart Church then went to class. The summer school lasted a month. Each year, at the end of the month, Father Mac took all of the students on the narrow gauge train to Los Pinos for a picnic. Each student, the nuns, and the parents who went along took sack lunches. Father Mac provided them with peanuts and watermelon.

During the summer of his twelfth year, Ed's independence surfaced in another way. When the catechism classes ended, Ed received permission from his father to go work in the fields, cutting lettuce and harvesting potatoes, or whatever crop needed to be loaded into crates or bags. Ed had to get up before sunrise to climb onto the back of an old truck with other adult workers. The driver was Felipe Naranjo, a friend of Isaac's. Naranjo left them in the fields at twilight and picked them up at dusk. The work was backbreaking and the pay was small, but it was enough for Ed. Now he had his own money and did not feel so dependent on his parents. The pocket change gave him a sense of independence. Ed's only question about the arrangement was why the clutch in Naranjo's old truck always seemed to break on the way home, not while going to work. It was as if the clutch had a mind of its own.

In sports, Ed had a great example in his older brother. Bud excelled as a lineman in football, first in high school and then at Adams State College right there in Alamosa. But Ed's interest in the gridiron began earlier as a direct result of his constant sense of adventure and curiosity. If his grandparents' warm stove, or the excitement of a neighboring dance could entice him from home, the attraction of the high school football games played a block away could not be resisted.

There was no question but that young Ed would take off to find out what all the commotion was about. Once there, he did not settle for sitting in the stands with the rest of the fans. Just like he used to settle in a blanket with his grandparents, or take to the dance floor with Tia María, Ed needed to be close to the action. He figured out which was the home team and sat on their bench. And like before, he was found irresistible and was not only allowed to sit on the bench but was welcomed. Ed could not avoid being impressed watching his brother play in high school. The maroon and white uniforms, the crowds, and, yes, the cheerleaders, it was exciting. Then, there was the competition. Football naturally attracted the fairly successful street fighter and Bud, who had become closer to Ed over time, shared his football expertise.

Ed took to the sport and excelled. He had no problem making his high school team. In his sophomore year, he started as a lineman for Alamosa High School. What a year it was. In 1949 Ed's team won the state championship. Alamosa had never won a championship and it would remain a unique achievement for at least the next six decades.

Bud played at Adams State for the 1947 season. Perhaps influenced by the influx of veterans who returned home and played on the team, he decided to enlist in the Navy Reserve, which took him away for a year. He returned home in time to witness the championship season, and was especially proud of Ed, for his younger brother also was named to the all-state team. Ed and his team became the pride of the community.

"Yes," thought Isaac, "maybe he will follow Bud. Perhaps college really is in his future." Yet, some contrary signs worried both Isaac and Ramoncita. Ed's grades were far from good, due in part to his propensity to skip classes. Ed did not like to study or attend class. It seemed that only sports and family kept his attention.

His maternal grandmother Juanita, a Trujillo but not related to the neighbors, shared her husband's religious faith. Because she was the wife of a *Penitente*, she was called a "Carmelita." She died when Ed was very young, so he never had a memory of her. Ed's mother once told him about a Carmelita tradition that, when death approached, the Carmelitas had the soles of their feet rubbed with dirt or sand. Ed's mother performed this task for her mother.

While Ed had no memory of his grandmother Juanita, he did remember the visit of her two brothers. They wore braids and were thin and tall. Ed heard that they and his grandmother were part Native American. It seemed that no one knew exactly which tribe they came from. "Maybe Taos Pueblo or possibly from the plains, perhaps Cheyenne, or Ute," was the standard reply.

Not long after Juanita's death Lucas moved in with Ed's family. He and Bud shared a *"casita"* that Isaac built in the backyard. Lucas already was old, but Ed and Bud grew close to him over the next ten or so years.

Lucas spent most of his time reading the Bible. In the warmer weather he liked to read seated on a small bench under a tree in the front yard. Ed was fascinated by the old man's concentration as he read with a thumb pressed up against his mouth. One time he looked up and caught Ed looking at him.

"You know, *hijo*, I have read this Bible cover to cover eleven times and sometimes I think it is not so clear."

Ed helped bathe the old man and aside from the life-changing experience of caring for an elder, Ed learned another lesson. He saw the scars on Lucas's back, like ancient scratches but permanent. Ed could not help but ask. First he went to his parents, but they wisely suggested that this was a question his grandfather should answer.

This is when Ed learned of true penance, self-flagellation administered by a short multi-headed whip called a *disciplina*. Lucas explained to his subdued grandson. "This is why I read the Bible. Christ suffered many times more for you and me than what the *disciplina* could do to me."

Ed did not doubt his grandfather's sincerity. Nor would he pester him with more questions. He had learned enough for now. He would learn more over time.

Sensing Ed's curiosity, Lucas taught Ed about the brotherhood and as he got older Ed attended many of their functions. Some of their processions illustrated Lucas's importance to the organization, for after the *"dolorosa"* at the *Morada*, their place of worship, they marched in a procession to Lucas's house. There the women, including Ramoncita, set up tables full of food outside. They had *torta huevo* (chile with egg pancakes)*, frijoles, quelites* (a spinach based concoction), *verdolagas,* and *pasteles. Verdolagas* was a low growing weed that Ed ate but did not like

In 1947, while Ed was in junior high school, Lucas's health began to decline. Everyone knew that death was approaching, and Ed was old enough to be conscious of the fact. All of a sudden, though, Ramoncita became very ill. Disease, of any kind, is dangerous and not to be messed with, especially with old ones around. Isaac made the decision that Lucas would have to spend his last days with one of his brothers.

The last time Ed saw Lucas alive was when his mother's two brothers, *tíos* Moisés and Sotario carried him out of the house to take him to their home in Center, north of Alamosa.

Lucas passed away ten days later in Center. The whole family went to attend funeral ceremonies, first at the Morada, then at the church. The *velorio*, or wake, was held at the *morada*. The following morning his brother Penitentes took him to the nearby church. Saddened, Ed was pleasantly surprised when he heard the bells in both buildings begin to ring. Grandfather Lucas many times repeated, "*Ahí llevan a Pacheco, las campanas están doblando.* Now, they are taking Pacheco, the bells are tolling." Now, on the day of the funeral the bells rang for him. A slow paced dong, dong, dong, dong at the church and a similar high-pitched cacophony from the *morada's* smaller bell.

Within the year, Talpita, still a relatively young woman, became very sick. She was moved into Isaac's house but she continued to falter. Finally, the family agreed to take her to the hospital, but before she would go she asked that all the family, everyone, to come to her. When they all came, she asked them to kneel. Then she gave all of them blessing. She was careful to note that the blessing extended to the family members who could not be there. When she was done, she allowed herself to be taken to the hospital where she died. As can be imagined, this whole episode left and impression on the youth.

Ed's Romero's paternal grandfather, Faustín, was not a *Penitente*. As a shepherd for most of his early life he had a very personal relationship with his God. "That is why the *lucero*, the star over Bethlehem appeared to shepherds." A life alone in the outdoors, especially under the spectacular skies of northern New Mexico's high country, would bring any man to his knees. Faustín reflected that quiet understanding. In some ways, he seemed to invoke a life of hardship, of a man whose fate had taken him in an unexpected and not necessarily desired direction, which he accepted. It was his cross to bear. In him one could see where his son, Isaac, inherited his quiet dignity.

Faustín continued to work hard as a carpenter and shoemaker. He loved his family and was proud of the status that Isaac had achieved. Part of his misfortune was a physical deformity of a basketball-sized tumor on his left hip that left him deformed and in constant pain. The growth was ugly and the girdle that Faustín wore to support the growth helped only a little. Finally, late in life, he had the non-malignant tumor surgically removed.

Faustín read a lot. He was a man who tried to keep up with things. He knew all the Kings of Spain. Ed understood that Faustín shared his father Isaac's value for education. Ed naturally approached him with a question about heritage.

Ed waited until after he could hear his grandfather's huge sewing machine stop clacking in the shop. Soon enough, Faustín came out of the shed, locked the door, and ambled into the back door of his house. Ed followed him in, knowing that he would find him seated at the kitchen table waiting for Grandma Talpita to hand him a hot cup of coffee. As soon as Ed sat at the table the old man asked, "Well, *hijo*, what brings you here?" He thanked Talpita for the coffee as she handed it to him.

"Grandfather, why do we call ourselves Spanish?" Faustín could see from Ed's demeanor that this was a heartfelt question, but, before he could answer, Ed followed with a second question after which he folded his hands on the table and waited. "If we are Spanish, yes? Then, what about those people from Mexico, the *surumatos*? They speak Spanish, aren't they Spanish too?"

Faustín had not expected either question, so he bought some time savoring his coffee. He fingered his cup looking for words as Talpita busied herself at the kitchen sink. "*Dios mío!* One question at a time Leroy. We are not them, and they are not us."

"I know. That is clear. But we share..."

"Yes, yes. Language and religion. That is obvious. Somewhere back in time, maybe in Spain, I don't know. Perhaps in Spain."

"*Y México?*"

Faustín sighed. "Yes, we all passed through Mexico, except for the Indians who were here already and the Anglos who have come later. These people,"—he referred to the Mexican workers who started coming into the San Luis Valley to work in the potato fields under a federal government worker program,—"their families stayed in Mexico and mixed with the people there. Maybe that is the difference. They mixed there and we mixed here, like your *abuela* Pacheco."

"But grandfather, how do you know about Spain?"

"I only know what my father told me that his father told him. We are from Spain and that is why we use the term Spanish. Maybe someday you will find out for sure, eh?"

Now there was a thought. Maybe? But it was enough that his grandfather knew from his father that the Romeros were from Spain. At a later date Ed learned from his grandfather Romero that the recent arrivals from Mexico were called *Braceros* for the program under which they worked. They were also called *surumatos* for a poor region in Mexico around Jalisco where many of them originated. At the time, Ed could only imagine about Spain and Mexico. What were those distant places like, and why have they had such on influence on his identity? "Maybe someday?"

Ed and everyone else at the time realized that the *surumato* term came to signify any poor, mixed-blood *Mexicano* relatively recently arrived from Mexico. Lost on them all was the historical irony of how wealthy *Mexicanos*, including many *criollos*, incurred the envy and criticism of their distant ancestors in Albuquerque almost two centuries earlier. Their eighteenth century ancestors in Albuquerque were jealous, then envious of the Mexican merchants who came to New Mexico, arbitrarily fixed prices for New Mexican goods in Mexico, and garnered much of the trade going south.

A DIFFERENT DECISION, THE ARMY AND CALIFORNIA
June 1951, Pueblo, Colorado

Ed graduated from high school—finally, it seemed. He knew all along that he would not go to college. Instead he answered a newspaper advertisement that offered a six-month course to become an agent telegrapher. The ad said that there was a huge need for telegraphers, people who knew Morse code, all over the country. The ad promised many good jobs. The course was being offered at Midwest Business College in nearby Pueblo. Ed could move out but not far. He left ten days after graduating from high school.

The last few weeks had been hard. Ed did not hesitate when he heard the knock. He saw his father park and walk up to the door.

Isaac was not pleased. Now, he knew what he suspected but hoped was not true. The hints existed. Ed never earned good grades and, then, there were the pranks. How many such incidents there had been was a question Isaac could not answer. He remembered one in particular when Ed was in high school.

After a year away in the Navy, Bud had returned to Alamosa to serve the rest of his commitment in the reserve. He enrolled in Adams State College and lied about his age to land a job as a policeman. He also married Imelda Chávez, a local descendent of New Mexican Chávezes, and started a family, which was of great consolation to his parents. Isaac could not forget the morning before work when Bud drove up in his police car to tell him what Ed had done. Along with some cousins and a friend, they stole a keg of beer from in back of the local pool hall. After draining the keg, the boys decided to head back to town, and along the way, started throwing rocks at streetlights and breaking them. Before long they heard a siren and they ran. The siren belonged to Bud's police car, and he caught the friend, who, scared, confessed. "Well, Bud, it was your cousins and Leroy."

The next morning Bud told his parents what had happened, and that the boys would have to go to court. On the scheduled day, the kids appeared before Judge Pasqual Lee, who everyone knew. The Judge looked down at them, and threatened that they would have to go to jail as well as pay a large fine. Then he gave them a lecture to make sure that they were scared before he let them go. Needless to say, Isaac was livid with his son. Ed had outgrown spankings, but not a scolding and Isaac did not hold back. More than anything, Isaac wanted Ed to know why his behavior was wrong, and to make sure it wouldn't be repeated, which with Ed was becoming problematic.

No, Ed would not follow his brother and sister. When Ed told his father of his plans to go to business school in Pueblo, Isaac could only reply, "Fine, you're on your own." Without his father's help, Ed had to borrow some money from an uncle.

Here he was, still settling in his new one room apartment. He had not been there two weeks, and dad was at the front door. "Okay," he thought to himself. "Time to face the music." He opened the door and expressed a mild surprise, inviting his father in, giving him the traditional *abrazo,* a familiar hug. Isaac, always direct, did not hesitate. He didn't look around. He just asked, or was it a statement? "Okay, what do you need?" When he saw that Ed was at a loss of words, Isaac added, "I paid back your uncle. Do you need anything else?"

After that, Ed never felt that he had disappointed his father by not enrolling in college. He knew what his father thought, but beyond that he knew that his father cared for each of his children and wanted them to be happy. Ed had made his choice and his father not only accepted it, but also was willing to support it. Beyond that knowledge, Ed did not need anything else.

Leaving home gave Ed an opportunity for one other important change. From the day he left Alamosa, he made sure that everyone he met knew him as Ed or Edward. He rid himself of "Leroy" pretty much forever. Only the occasional reminders from family or boyhood friends ever brought the name up again.

Reinforced with his father's approval, Ed concentrated on his courses. Not surprisingly, for this was something he had chosen to do, he excelled. He finished the six-month course in two months. Telegraphy was a snap.

Then he applied and immediately was accepted for a job with the Denver and Rio Grande Railroad Company, his father's employer. The newspaper advertisement was correct, jobs abounded. Now Ed was completely independent and on his own. He was an adult with a full-time job.

At first, Ed found the work satisfying. Morse code was how the railroad company ran its system. He was an important cog in the operation. Moreover, he enjoyed his newly found independence. He started in Denver, but quickly found himself farmed out to different stations along the line.

However, after four or five months the novelty began to wear off. Ed's sense of change and independence combined with his patriotism. He began to realize that he did not want to spend the rest of his life being transferred from place to place on short notice. The lifestyle ran against his nature because he would be beholden to unseen bosses. No matter the enjoyment of seeing new places and living on his own, he did not feel independent.

After about five months of moving up and down the rail lines in Colorado, he started thinking of a new priority. Ever since the summer between his junior and senior years in high school, the United States had been at war, officially called a "police action," in Korea. Some of Ed's high school classmates had enlisted for the cause. Bud had gone away for the Navy. The idea of doing his patriotic duty played on his mind. Thus, he once again changed his life's direction. Ed acted while in Grand Junction, Colorado. After only nine months on the job as a telegrapher, he volunteered for the draft.

By June of 1953, he had received his induction papers, and was looking out a bus window at the passing countryside on his way to basic training at Fort Ord, California. If he did not realize it before, he felt it now. He had left Alamosa forever. His father was pleased with his decision. Isaac told him that joining the military was good, saying that it was, the right thing to do. Ed recognized that his father was happier about this latest move than he had been about the earlier one to attend business school. Ed had made his father proud.

Basic training took two months, and toward the end of it, news broke out that an armistice had been signed ending the hostilities in Korea. Probably as a result of the peace, Ed remained at Fort Ord through Christmas. Life at the time was pretty boring. Ed made friends with Ralph Rojas who hailed from Kansas City. The two soldiers liked each other's company. They talked about the war and, then, peace, girls, and their respective and different lives. It helped, as well, that they saw in each other similarities, not the least of which was the Spanish language. They mostly spoke English, and were very much circumspect about speaking a language that their fellow soldiers did not understand.

On Christmas day of that year, Ed and Ralph decided to dress up in their military finest and attend mass in town. After mass they walked around. They had nothing to do but to waste time. The town was abandoned. Every store was closed and the streets were vacant. Unlike some of their friends, the two of them did not have family homes nearby. They bided time on Monterrey's downtown streets.

Then a car that pulled up next to them. The driver rolled down his window and spoke, "Merry Christmas! I see you're in the army."

"Yeah. We've finished basic and are waiting for orders to ship out."

"Do you have any plans for today?"

"No. Not really. Just hanging out."

"How 'bout a nice Christmas dinner with me and my family?" The stranger could tell the answer from the expressions on their faces. "Come on! Hop in!"

Ed and Ralph got into the car, and the man introduced himself as he drove them to his house where an extended family of around twenty people had begun to arrive. The man introduced Ed and Ralph to each person. Of course, the two of them could not

Ed Romero in the United States Army Signal Corp. Ed and Cayetana Romero Collection.

remember everyone's name. The whole dinner became a blur of very friendly people. They were treated royally. They had not eaten so well since joining the army. Thanks to the generosity of that stranger in Monterrey, they had a Christmas that they would never forget.

Ed's civilian skills played into the army's needs. From Fort Ord, he was sent to hone his knowledge in radio communications at Camp Gordon in Georgia and then for a short stint to Fort Lewis in Washington. Finally, he received a permanent assignment to the Signal Corp Headquarters at Fort Huachuca in the southern Arizona desert next to the Mexican border. He spent the rest of his two-year obligation there.

Meanwhile, Bud, with a young family of two children, a boy and a girl, both under four years old, completed his Bachelors degree at Adams State. Bud's future was in education, so he decided to leave his job as a policeman to continue his education in southern California, a place that played on his mind beginning with those earlier visits with his aunt, his experience there with the navy, and, then, a short vacation he had just taken.

Isaac and Ramoncita took the news of Bud's plans in stride. True to form, Isaac, commented that he would have to see Bud's advanced degree before he believed it. Personally, he had no doubt that Bud would do what he said. Of course, they were saddened, for Bud was the last of their natural children to leave Alamosa. Ramoncita especially would miss her two grandchildren. They were left with nine-year-old Gregory Randolph who would grow up on his own in Alamosa before leaving as well. He would become a Navy medic in the Vietnam War before settling in Albuquerque.

As Ed came to the end of his military service, news of Bud's move played into his plans. He knew that he would not extend in the army. He looked forward to a new start in civilian life. He even thought about taking up his father's advice and enrolling in school. Bud, now in California, used every opportunity to convince Ed that California with its free education was great place. Ed decided that his future lay there. So, upon his release from the army at Fort Huachuca, he went directly to the Golden State and moved in with Bud in the Los Angeles suburban community of Duarte.

A NEW LIFE: EDUCATION AND SALES
1954, Los Angeles, California

Even though Bud had a very small house, Ed was welcomed. Bud had started teaching High School for the Citrus Union High School District. At the time, the District operated the public school system including Citrus Junior College, which was the oldest public community college in Los Angeles County. About, twenty-two miles east of downtown Los Angeles, nestled in the foothills of the San Gabriel Mountains in the suburban community of Glendora, the school couldn't be in a more beautiful setting. Distant from the hustle and bustle of Los Angeles in a place that offered open space and quiet, Ed found the junior college attractive and decided to take Bud's advice and enroll. In far away, Alamosa, his father was pleased.

The Los Angeles area was booming and had been since before World War II. Opportunity abounded. Still, the hills, the nearby mountains, the acres of citrus orchards and vineyards, and the nearby Pacific Ocean gave the place a semblance of tranquility found in the countryside, not in a rushed urban setting. Unlike Alamosa or southern Arizona, southern California was green all year around. Everything, it seemed, grew there. And the demographic makeup of the place equaled the botanical diversity.

After almost a year, Ed decided to move out of Bud's house and live with a couple of his friends. He had a job and felt the need to be on his own. Ed sped through the first two years of classes at Citrus Community College, where he received an Associate of Arts degree. Then, he transferred to California State College, Los Angeles, which was called "L.A. State" for short. Bud was finishing up his Masters program at the same school.

Hoping to raise some money, Ed landed a job as a machinist in a company that manufactured parts for factories. He knew nothing about machines, but took the job because he would be working the swing shift in nearby Pasadena. This, he reasoned, fit perfectly with his daytime schedule of classes.

He was wrong. His grades at L. A. State began to fall, if not plummet. Rather than help, the swing shift became a deterrent to Ed's education. Ed left work at midnight and was too wired to go home to bed. He did not get home before two a.m. Then, after a few hours of sleep, he dragged himself to school where he dozed off in class. After a year at L.A. State, Ed quit school.

The decision to leave school was not definite, for Ed realized that it was the job that was the problem. He needed to change jobs. Then, maybe, he could continue his education. He was only a year short of his bachelor's degree.

He combed the newspaper advertisements and, once again, one posting caught his attention. It read, "How to make a thousand dollars a month working three hours a day." "Heck," he thought, "that is more money than I am making working full-time!"

The job was selling *Colliers Encyclopedias*, knocking on doors. Sales. The concept was completely new to him, and he believed it all. He trained for three days. He learned his pitch to tell a perspective customer that the books were free, and when that got their attention, share with them that there would be a fee for "research services," which covered ten years, but must be paid within a year. It sounded workable to Ed. Why not give it a try?

He was sent out with a seasoned manager named John Heflan who drove a pink Cadillac. The car if not the man impressed Ed. "Wow!" he thought. "This is what sales gets you?" Heflan had a crippled left hand that he used to his advantage. Ed watched as one person after the next answered the door, looked at him as he began, "Hello! We have a free gift for you!" They looked at him, then at his hand and invariably let him into their homes. Once in, he made the pitch and more times than not sold a set of books. Ed reacted. "Okay! This is for me."

After spending a couple of days with Heflan, Ed was ready to go solo. Ed, with three or four other salesmen met at the office and was driven to different neighborhoods where they were dropped off. True to the advertisement they had three hours to make their sales, from six pm until nine pm, after which they would be picked up to be taken back to the office to report their sales. The time of day was crucial because it was after work and their potential customers were home.

Anxious and confident, Ed walked up to his first house and knocked. The door opened and Ed barely got out a "Hello!" before the man told him in very unfriendly terms to "get the hell out of here," and slammed the door. This shocked Ed. "Now what?" Ed suddenly lost his confidence. He found a curb to sit down and think about his situation and what to do. He still had almost three hours before pickup.

He worked up the courage to try again. Perhaps that first experience was an aberration. The second person was polite but quickly said, "No." This time the door was shut, not slammed. The third person let Ed into the house where he listened to Ed's presentation, and then said, "no."

Ed survived that first evening without making a sale. Nonetheless, he came out of the experience ready for the next evening when he made his first sale and that changed his life forever. He found his life's calling. School, his parents desire, was never considered again. Sales was where he belonged. He continued working for Colliers Encyclopedias for the next year, and made more money than either his brother or sister who were teaching. On a trip back to Alamosa to visit his parents he showed his father his check stubs. Isaac stoically looked at his them and said, "So what." He was not impressed. Education was more valuable to him.

ALBUQUERQUE AGAIN
1958, Los Angeles

Ed found a more appealing job with a company called Family Record Plan. The company sold a package in which the customer received two portraits of their children for each of eight years. In addition, they received one family group photograph. Also, the customer really did get something free, a card or sign that said, "Shhh! Baby Sleeping."

The company contracted as many as two thousand photographic studios across the country. If people wanted to pay extra, the company could make as many extra photographs as people wanted. Ed found the whole idea an improvement over selling encyclopedias. He still went door to door. Only now when the door opened he held up the card, "Shhh! Baby Sleeping." If the reply came back that the potential customer had no babies, Ed quickly reacted, "Congratulations on your marriage! This is something for your future." He had no problem making his pitch and, more importantly, sales.

Ed's success resulted in a fairly quick promotion to district manager. He now had charge of salesmen in the San Diego and Oceanside area of southern California. His income now came from an override, a percentage of the sales made by his salesmen. Now, Ed was making more money, enough, in fact, to buy a diamond ring that he wore on his pinky finger. He also bought a white '58 Chevrolet convertible with red interior with the spare wheel stored over the back of the trunk. The ever-successful bachelor naturally had a good-looking girlfriend. Nena turned heads with her red hair and green eyes. Ed was doing quite well for himself. He proclaimed himself "a cool cat."

Within two years Ed was doing so well that the company offered him another promotion that was another life changing moment. He accepted the regional manager position for New Mexico, Texas, Oklahoma, Colorado, and Kansas. Not only would he be getting overrides from his district managers, which meant more money, but he also would be moving to Albuquerque where the regional office would be located. He would be closer to home.

Despite the success and excitement of his time in Los Angeles, Ed felt comfortable in Albuquerque. The New Mexican city did not compare to Los Angeles in size. Albuquerque's population might have reached three hundred thousand people. At the time, Los Angeles had a larger population than the whole state of New Mexico. Yet, New Mexicans were Ed's people and he made friends easily. One of these was Mercedes Candelaria, who owned a photo studio that was doing business with Ed and his company. She was an older single woman from an old New Mexican family. She lived with her much older Tia Lupe. Her sister and brother-in-law, Ophelia and Carlos Montoya owned and operated a New Mexican cuisine restaurant that Ed frequented. Neither Mercedes nor Ed realized that each of them were descended from ancestors who were members of the founding families of Albuquerque, which, incidentally, had lost the first "r" in "Alburquerque" in its spelling when the railroad came to the town in the 1880s.

CAYETANA GALLEGOS Y GARCÍA
1957, Albuquerque

Ed had become friends with Mercedes and her family. Occasionally Mercedes invited Ed to her house for dinner, and on one of these early evenings they had just finished and were sitting at the kitchen table when there was a knock at the front door. Mercedes opened the door. Ed heard a woman explain that she was on her way home from work and needed to borrow some curlers. Ever polite, Mercedes invited the woman in to meet Ed. "This is my friend Cayetana." Standing before Ed was the most beautiful woman he had ever seen. She was a lithe, dark-haired woman, with deep-set, round-almond colored eyes. Her ready smile was, at once ironic and affectionate. So engaging, so beautiful, she lit up the room.

Ed found out that Cayetana was a neighbor, lived with her parents, was single, and that her last name of Gallegos-García. Her family came from the Rio Grande Valley, Algodones just north of Bernalillo. Then, another knock on the door interrupted them. It was Mercedes' sister and brother-in-law. They just bought a new station wagon and wanted to take everyone for a spin. Ed followed Cayetana to the car and jumped into the back seat next to her. Cayetana wondered about this guy with a diamond on his pinky. Why is he sitting next to her and not next to Mercedes?

Later that night, Mercedes gave Ed Cayetana's telephone number. He hardly slept. He could not get her out of his mind. This was a new feeling for Ed. He telephoned her at work right after eight am.

She answered and Ed spoke, he was used to making pitches. "Hello, this is Ed. I met you last night."

"Yes."

"I would like to invite you to dinner."

"No." Click. The line went dead. She hung up. Cayetana could not believe this man's audacity. Wasn't he seeing her friend Mercedes? How dare he?

As a salesman, Ed had become used to rejection and appreciated the value of persistence. He figured that he might have telephoned too early, so he would try again at a later hour the next day. This time he asked, "Cayetana, maybe at least you will meet me for a cup of coffee or cocktail."

"No thanks." She hung up again. Ed waited two days before trying again. She answered the phone again and Ed started, "I am calling you back..." but she cut him off and said, "Ed, let me apologize to you. The reason I was so abrupt is that I thought you were dating my friend, Mercedes. I talked to her after work and found out that you were business friends." Ed was surprised at this. He could not believe how anyone would think that he was dating Mercedes. He recovered enough to ask, "Would you meet me for a drink?"

"Sure. Yes, I will."

"Can you suggest a place?" Ed wanted her to feel comfortable for the first meeting.

"Mori's on Fourth Street."

After work the next day, a cold November Friday, they had their first date. Mori's was perfect. It was on her way home and had a fireplace. They met a second and a third time at the same place. Ed drank scotch and she drank grasshoppers. On the third date, they left Mori's for dinner and dancing at Sundowners, which was on Central Avenue at the eastern end of town. Sundowners would become their favorite place.

Christmas approached, and with the season came opportunity. Ed invited Cayetana to a full performance of Handel's *Messiah* that would be given in Albuquerque's convention center, a building that looked like a giant flying saucer had landed next to the Pan American Freeway, a modern version the old Camino Real. By intermission, Ed realized that he had become overwhelmingly in love with Cayetana, with her mannerisms; with the way she tilted her head as if listening with a sympathetic ear. He had succumbed to her charm and needed to tell her, but there were complications.

He took her for a nightcap after the concert, but his timing was off. First, he shared with her that he would be leaving for Los Angeles the next morning to spend the Holidays with Bud. Then, without thinking, or perhaps because his feelings had become so strong and, as a result, muddled, he blurted out, "...and I have a girl friend." Oh, oh. Now he could hear the forceful chords of the *Messiah*'s "amen" fading away. He was in unchartered waters now. Nor could he tell her that he loved her. Not now.

Cayetana calmly looked at him. "Well, Ed. That's nice. Have a nice trip."

Ed knew he wasn't thinking straight. He messed up.

Cayetana thought that Ed planned to marry his girlfriend. Ed didn't know it, but she had her own boyfriend, who was in the military service in Florida and who was coming to Albuquerque for Christmas. Besides, Ed was fun and a gentleman, even if he was so pretentious with his red and white convertible, with his stylish dark suits, and most of all, his diamond pinky ring.

Ed drove back to Los Angeles. The fourteen to fifteen-hour trip along U.S. 66 that seemed longer than it took. He kept thinking about Cayetana. What had he done? Would she really see him when he got back? He missed her even before he left Albuquerque's city limits. He pulled up to Bud's house around ten o'clock in the evening where he found a sympathetic and learned listener in his brother. Bud had completed his masters, and now was teaching at Citrus Junior College.

Bud smiled and as he listened to his little brother prattle on about Cayetana and how beautiful and fun she is. Finally, Bud held his hand up to stop Ed, "Man, you really have it bad." Ed knew he was right. Bud wondered out loud why Ed was in California when a woman in New Mexico possessed him. Ed had to admit that he was in love. His mind raced as he finally went to bed.

Bud had nailed it. Ed woke up the next morning with a plan that he was determined to see through. By the end of the day he had met with Nena for lunch where, they mutually agreed to break up since neither one was serious about the other.

Before sun up, Ed was well on his way back to Albuquerque. The now-familiar towns of Barstow, Kingman, Needles, Williams, Flagstaff, Winslow, Gallup, and Grants blew by unnoticed. Ed's stops for gas faded in a hazy memory. His mind focused on Cayetana.

West of Albuquerque, the highway rises up out of the Rio Puerco Valley and crests at the top of what is locally called "nine mile hill." For a traveler driving east that is the place where Albuquerque can be seen for the first time. The city spreads out along the Rio Grande and at the base of the Sandia Mountains, but Ed was not concerned about the view. He pulled into the rest stop and Hitching Post Bar at the crest to find a public telephone. He wanted to call Cayetana.

To his relief she, and not one of her parents, answered the phone. "Cayetana, this is Ed. I would like to see you right away."

Ed's voice surprised her. "You're in California."

"No, I am back in Albuquerque." Ed did not want to lose the moment. He needed to stay focused.

Still surprised, or perhaps caught off guard, Cayetana replied, "You've only been gone two or three days."

"I know but I am back and I have to see you immediately."

This was too much. Cayetana did not hesitate. "Well, I can't."

"Cayetana, you don't understand. This is an emergency!"

"What does an emergency have to do with me?"

"It is something I have to talk to you about. It's really an emergency."

Still not convinced about this emergency, Cayetana insisted, "I can't anyhow because I'm helping my mother clean house. Call me tomorrow."

Ed persisted, "Cayetana, please. It will just take five, maybe ten minutes." How could she say "no" now?

"Oka-a-y."

"I will be there in fifteen minutes."

"Fifteen minutes! Where are you?"

"Nine mile hill. I will be there, okay?"

"Okay."

Ed pulled up to Cayetana's house. By now it was getting dark. He climbed out of the car and walked up to the front door that was on a converted porch off the driveway. He knocked and Cayetana answered. She was dressed for house cleaning with a scarf wrapped around her head. Ed could not help but notice that she was irritated. There was no "Welcome back" or other such pleasantry. Instead she mouthed a brusque, "Well, come in."

Ed knew her parents were inside so he countered. "Please come out. I only need five or ten minutes. I want to talk to you personally."

Cayetana frowned. "What do you want?" She walked out looking angry and her arms folded across her chest. Ed walked her to the car and convinced her to get in. Then he went around to the driver's side and got in. When he started the engine, Cayetana startled if not worried, exclaimed, "What are you doing?"

"We're going around the corner." True to his word Ed drove around the corner and pulled into a vacant lot on Second Street.

Cayetana had become exasperated and when Ed turned off the ignition she pointedly asked, "Okay, what's going on?"

The moment had come. Ed turned to her. "Tanna, I'm helplessly in love with you and as soon as you fall in love with me, we'll get married."

Cayetana could not believe what she had heard. "What?" she thought to herself. She could not help but to burst out laughing, interspersed with exasperated gasps. She barely managed to say, "Take me home. You're crazy."

Ed did not expect her reaction. Now what? He felt helpless, and silently drove her back to the house. She continued to laugh and shake her head. When she opened her front door to enter the house she turned to Ed, and shook her head in disbelief still laughing. Ed watched completely depressed.

But he would not give up. Even though things had not gone as planned, he had confidence in himself. He called the next day. "Tanna, you know my feelings. Can we go have a drink this evening?"

"Sorry, Ed," she replied, "I can't tonight. Tomorrow night."

Ed did not know it but Cayetana had other plans for that evening. Her boyfriend, Joe Beall, had returned and had a date with her. Ed's return had complicated her night. If Ed had surprised her, she faced an even more serious shock that night, for, as might be expected, Ed was not the only man to fall in love with Cayetana. At dinner, Joe pulled out an engagement ring and asked her to marry him.

This was too much. First Ed's awkward actions and now this, but this time she did not burst out laughing. A decent man had seriously made an actual proposal. Cayetana gathered herself and told him that she liked him but was not ready for engagement, much less marriage. She offered the lame excuse that she was working and going to college. Joe was crestfallen, but Cayetana held firm.

Meanwhile, Ed was encouraged when she agreed to have a drink. Apparently, he had not made a complete fool of himself. Moreover, she had not shut him out.

Ed and Cayetana started dating. Cayetana told Ed about Joe, and that he had returned to Florida. And, no, she was not ready to proclaim her love for Ed. Ed explained his feelings in more detail but, more importantly, he was patient. He would wait. As for now, they continued to date.

Ed got to know Cayetana's family and learned that she was real close to her mother, Felipita. Ed could see why. They mirrored each other. He could see where she inherited her vibrancy, her zest for life, and dignity. Ed admired Cayetana's father, Manuel, a quiet, gentle man, who worked at the Sandia Laboratories.

Just before Christmas, Cayetana invited Ed to her house to meet her brother Bob.

He had been away at a seminary and had come home for Christmas break. Of course, Ed would go to meet him. But he was not prepared for the reception.

When he arrived, Cayetana introduced him to Bob and three other seminarians there with him. One of them was Robert Sánchez, who would become the Archbishop of Santa Fe, and another, Arthur Tafoya, who would become a Bishop in Pueblo, Colorado. They had planned a special joke for Ed and Cayetana.

All the young men stood up and showered him with, "Hi Walter!" "Hey Walter, it sure is good to see you!" "Nice to meet you Walter!"

Taken aback, Ed tried to correct them. "My name isn't Walter. It's Ed." He looked at Cayetana for some assurance but she looked as perplexed as he. Her brother stepped forward and said, "Ah, I know that Walter. It sure is good seeing you." Pranksters all, the rest of them kept calling him Walter.

This reception made Ed nervous and he was beginning to get mad, so he decided to make his excuses and leave. As he turned toward the door, the seminarians stood in unison and said, "We'll see you again Walter."

As they walked away from the house, Ed turned toward her and asked, "Who the heck is Walter?" She had no idea, had never heard of a Walter and, no, she was not part of whatever it was the seminarians thought that they were doing.

Ed was pleasantly surprised to hear that Father Mac had transferred from Alamosa to Albuquerque. Ed immediately went to visit him. They were authentically pleased to see each other and had much to talk about. Father Mac especially wanted to hear everything about Ed's life since he left Alamosa. They sat down facing each other, and Father Mac leaned back, crossing his legs and waited to hear Ed's story. The elderly priest had on black shoes with white socks, and Ed immediately noticed a huge hole in the sole of one of his shoes. Father Mac brushed off Ed's concern by showing him a matching hole in his other shoe. Ed knew that Father Mac did not accept charity for himself very well. Ed remembered when Father Mac's Alamosa parishioners took up a collection to purchase a new car for him. Father Mac thanked everyone for their generosity and good intentions and then turned around and gave the car to a poor family. When questioned about it, he merely shrugged and justified himself, "I can always get a ride."

But Ed would not be distracted so easily, and finally succeeded in getting Father Mac's shoe size. After the meeting Ed went and bought Father Mac a new pair of black shoes.

Meanwhile, Ed's job had him on the road traveling around his region to meet with his district managers. He was away from Albuquerque for the majority of his workweek days. He did manage periodic weekend road trips up the Rio Grande Valley to Alamosa, a three-and-a-half hour trip. On the way, he usually stopped to visit Betsy who lived in Chimayó outside of Española.

Ed and Cayetana kept dating into the spring of 1958. Finally, during one of their dinner-dates, Ed confronted her again. "Tanna, I can't go on like this. I have to know how you feel."

Cayetana looked at her drink sitting on the table and, then, looked at Ed. "I haven't quite figured it out." The answer disappointed and confused Ed. What did that mean? "Figure out what?" But he was smart enough not to say anything. He merely nodded his understanding and changed the subject.

On the other hand, Cayetana understood that Ed could not be kept in the dark much longer. She enjoyed him and liked their current arrangement. Nevertheless, she needed to think seriously about her relationship with him.

Two days later, she asked Ed out to dinner. After they received their drinks and ordered their food, she grabbed Ed's hand and pronounced, "I am in love with you, too."

Euphoria overcame Ed as his face lit up. "Okay, set the date." He did not propose but merely followed up on his earlier promise that when she pronounced her love for him, they would get married.

Soon after, Ed combined business with pleasure and went to California with Cayetana and her family. He used the opportunity to check in with his bosses while enjoying the family vacation. He took Tanna to a jeweler to have her engagement ring fitted and made. Ed kept the ring until they returned to New Mexico. Ed and Cayetana had not officially announced their engagement, because Ed wanted to do it properly. Ed waited to properly ask Cayetana's father for permission to marry her, and he did it in her parents' house. Once the permission was granted Ed presented Cayetana with the ring.

Ed then took Cayetana to Alamosa to meet his parents, who immediately liked her. Poor Cayetana went through a whirlwind of introductions the three days that they stayed at Ed's old house. She met friends, many cousins, aunts and uncles, and grandfather Faustín. Ed's mother, Ramoncita, threw a wedding shower for Cayetana. The whole experience was an eye opener for her. Now she realized that Ed's formative years were not so different than hers. They both grew up in small rural communities, she in Algodones, New Mexico, he in Alamosa, Colorado.

Isaac, of course, had to follow tradition even more so than his son. Soon after Ed and Cayetana left, he and Ramoncita drove down to Albuquerque to informally go through the procedure of representing their son to his future in-laws. The meeting was a genial, wonderful event. Everyone liked everyone, and they all would remain good friends the rest of their lives, as *consuegros* should be.

With all the formalities completed, Ed and Cayetana set the date of their wedding for October 15th. Again, according to Hispanic custom, Ed insisted that he pay for everything.

Aside, from the expenses and normal details of planning a wedding, Ed had some other matters that he wanted to clear up. First, he agreed that his newly ordained future brother-in-law would marry them. That was fine, but Ed made sure to get Bob aside and tell him that if he mentioned "Walter" at the wedding, "he would knock his block off." They both laughed but Ed was not so sure that Father Bob, a prankster at heart, would not somehow insert the name.

Next, Ed asked if Father Mac, the priest who had baptized and confirmed him, could participate in the ceremony. "Of course!" Everyone agreed. Now, all that was left was naming participants, determining where, and what kind of wedding. All went smoothly. Cayetana had her friend, Virginia Kidd, stand as her maid of honor, and Ed had Lino Aguirre as the best man. Ed met Aguirre in Azusa, California where they roomed together. They scheduled the wedding's high mass at Cayetana's parish church, St. Therese.

A major storm hit Albuquerque the day before the wedding. As the rain poured, Cayetana became worried. Her mother soothed her. "Don't worry. God will make it stop

Ed Romero and Cayetana García at their wedding reception, October 15, 1960. Ed and Cayetana Romero Collection.

for your wedding. Besides, rain means good luck!" She was right. The storm passed and the wedding was held on a beautiful day.

Cayetana would later write that the wedding was beautiful and "the start of the happiest years of my life." Ed agreed, yet there were some nuances that made the ceremony unique. The first occurred when Ed went up to the altar to wait for Cayetana's entrance. Father Mac, with a wink and nod directed Ed to his new shoes, which he exposed under his robe. Then, during the actual ceremony when Bob came to the point where he asked the groom if he "takes this woman to be his wife," he started off with "Will you Wa, Wa, uh, Ed take Cayetana to be your wife?" The inside joke did not go unnoticed. And, no, Bob did not get his block knocked off. Then there was Ed's friend the photographer who somehow "goofed," in Cayetana's words, and did not get many photographs. Naturally, at the reception Ed proudly and happily took his new bride to lead everyone in the traditional "*marcha.*"

Then, the rain came again. It was as if God had cleared the skies for the wedding, but for nothing else. Ed and Cayetana had planned to spend their honeymoon at the Broadmoor Hotel in Colorado Springs, but the weather prohibited travel north. Instead, they spent their first night in Albuquerque at the Western Skies Motel on east Central Avenue. The next day they traveled south to El Paso, and spent three days in the historic Hotel Paso del Norte with its impressive two-story high Tiffany dome ceiling with walls of cherry stone and gold trim. Whether Ed knew it or not, or even cared, between Alamosa, Albuquerque, and El Paso he missed only Abiquiu in retracing the steps of his ancestors, nor could he realize that eventually he would retrace those steps back to where four centuries ago a long multi-generational family pilgrimage had begun.

A FAMILY AND NEW DESTINIES
1964, Albuquerque

"Tanna's right." Ed laid his head back against his upright seat as the airliner gained altitude and gently veered to the left. He closed his eyes. "She's right. I need to be home with the family."

This would mean a major change in lifestyle that both worried and excited him. The weekly trips with only weekends at home had become tiresome. "Ah, the countless times Tanna has dropped me off and picked me up at the airport. Every Monday, sometimes Sunday evenings, and Fridays...."

Ed knew that he would lose his good salary. Fortunately, he and Cayetana had saved some money to help. They, he reminded himself, would replace it. Cayetana made that clear. She wanted him home so bad that she insisted that the two of them working together would make out. Still, he made enough money to purchase a nice new house and had started looking. He thought of his life with her.

During the search Ed learned that Albuquerque suffered some of the same problems as Alamosa. His real estate broker had to tell him that a certain subdivision did not admit people of color. The broker was Jewish and assured Ed with the perplexed look that he was not welcomed as well. Ed was reminded of his boyhood friend, Ronnie Gardenswartz who had moved with his family to Albuquerque. His father had purchased the Pepsi Cola distributorship for the city, so Ed and Ronnie got together again. When Ed asked Ronnie why he hung out with the Hispanics when they were kids, Ronnie replied, "You guys accepted me. I felt comfortable with you guys." Now, the broker had expressed a variation of that theme.

Cayetana had given birth to a beautiful girl, Christina Marie. Upon seeing that beautiful baby, Ed, the "cool cat," morphed into a new Ed, a husband and father. He wondered how anything could be more beautiful than Cayetana holding her infant daughter in her arms. "What limit is there to love?" And he soon found out. On June 23, 1961, they had a newborn son. Cayetana insisted that he be named Edward and they both liked Steven for the second name. "We'll call him Steven, not Junior." Ed could not help but reminisce that the name was a vast improvement over Leroy.

As Ed jetted toward Kansas, his mind wandered back to Cayetana. The real issue was the children. Cayetana made this very clear, as well. "She is such a good mother!" He smiled to himself. Cayetana and the children always made him smile. He really never imagined the joy that his family gave him. First, was his profound and unabashed love for Cayetana, and then came the kids. "How fast life passes." Only yesterday he was playing marbles or running to his grandparents house. "Now I am in my father's place. Can I be as good a father?" Cayetana had shown him the way. He had to be home, not traveling all the time. "She's right."

The plane's bell, followed by the beginning of the standard announcement about putting his seat upright, etc., momentarily interrupted his thoughts. Only his thoughts diverted him from another otherwise endless plane ride. One flight faded into another with what seemed to be nondescript flight crews, passengers, and fuselage interiors, a jet-propelled tube. How many times had he looked down the aisle lost in thought?

If the birth of children brightened the future, the death of his grandfather, Faustín, reminded him of the past. Faustín outlived his beloved Talpita by almost fourteen years and was buried with her. Now, with Faustín's passing, all of his grandparents were gone. What memories! "Would his own children have the same experience? Cayetana's parents live close by. Thank God." They are a great help to her, especially given his long absences but now that would change.

How his mother's face brightened when she held little Christina the first time. Dad let the child girl wrap her baby fingers around his burly little finger. Then, when Ed and Cayetana presented Steven to him, well it was a scene that Ed would never forget. Isaac was tinkering with something in his backyard. Looking up, he saw Ramoncita acknowledging a bundle in her arms. "*Isaac, aquí está otro nieto. Isaac, here is another grandson.*" By then, Bud had four children, two boys and two girls. As Isaac slipped off his work gloves, he smiled absently, his eyes, twinkling with a deep pleasure, a look that only momentous moments could bring out of him. How Ed loved his father! He realized it again with the immense pleasure he felt from his father's reaction to his newborn son.

Ed did not realize it, but this theme of connecting the past through the present into the future would grow in his mind for the rest of his life. Now, with the addition of Ruth Elizabeth and Anna Lucía, Cayetana needed a change. "Tanna's right!" Ed smiled again as he pictured her telling him, "Ed, we can't continue like this. The kids need you. I need you."

Ed agreed to the inevitable change. But how? And to what? Almost immediately,

Ed ruled out taking a lesser position as district manager in Albuquerque. He had a good man in the position and did not want to replace him. As he thought about the drudgery of a job search, filling out applications, and being interviewed, he migrated to the idea of self-employment. The idea might have been a product of over confidence but it was a solution. He would work for himself, he would consult with clients about business matters.

Cayetana initially gave him her doubtful look. "What? A consultant? About what?"

"Anything. Businesses and clients. Put them together. It's like sales."

She snickered then paused, obviously in thought. "Okay, why not? I can help."

"No. You...." She stopped him with a raised right hand.

"No Ed. Not with you. I will start my own business. An employment and collection agency. I have experience working in the business, why not run one?"

Now it was Ed's turn to be incredulous. She was as brazen as he. He could not say, no. That would have been futile. He waited a couple of days, at which point he was surprised to conclude that Cayetana could pull it off. She could start immediately. He would need a few months to give notice to his company and help with the transition. He didn't see any sense in burning bridges with people who had treated him so well.

Cayetana began her company and eventually closed the collection section to concentrate on "The Romero Employment Agency." She more than helped out and Ed could only admire how her dignified confidence translated into success.

Ed hustled. He still sold, but now he sold himself, his talent, and his intelligence. "This consulting is different but natural to me," he thought. Now he was home with his family. Things were working out. Then he met Tom Fatjo, a man who had travelled the road Ed had begun. Fatjo came up with an idea to start a garbage pick-up company while attending Rice University. He invested in a truck and starting picking up garbage.

By the time Fatjo called upon Ed, he owned the Browing-Ferris Industries (BFI), one of the largest waste management companies in the United States. Fatjo hired Ed because Ed spoke Spanish, and Fatjo wanted to expand into Latin America. BFI became Ed's first big contract. Beginning with a trip to Columbia with the company's executives, the experience expanded Ed's horizons in many ways. Tom Fatjo inspired Ed. Ed saw him as a mentor, gentleman, gifted salesman, and model.

Ed now had no doubt that he and Cayetana made the right decision in forming their own companies. The future looked good, and the outlook improved one day when a Dr. Smith came to Ed's office and asked Ed to go outside to see a solar panel that the doctor had set up. The studious man looked at Ed and said, "Ed, I want to build these. I built this one." And without hesitation so as not to lose the moment, he stated, "With your investment of five thousand dollars we will be millionaires within two years." Ed thought that this was his kind of deal.

Ed could not resist the idea so he hired Smith and together they formed a new company that at first was called ELR Enterprises, which soon became Solar America. Ed believed that he had made a clever business decision even though further investments were required.

He took advantage of President Jimmy Carter's emphasis on solar energy. The Carter administration had enacted renewable energy credits to businesses as well as to customers. The President even had solar panels put on the White House. Beginning in

1981, Carter's replacement, Ronald Reagan, embarked on a policy of eliminating every tax incentive available to the development of solar energy. The solar panel idea would need a lot more money invested. After $80,000 had been invested, the ever-practical Cayetana asked, "How much more are you going to invest before you're going to become a millionaire?" She didn't need to say more. Ed had no choice. He already had come to realize that he needed to switch away from manufacturing and to concentrate on research and development. As graciously as he could, Ed ended the project. Ed always believed that had Reagan left Carter's credits alone, the United States would have been decades ahead of any other nation in the field of solar energy.

Not all was lost because the solar panel experience introduced Ed to environmental issues. He still consulted. More importantly he had gained a wealth of experience in garnering government contracts.

Politics Calling
1967, Albuquerque

The subsequent change to running their businesses awakened something in Ed that had been germinating over time. The remote motifs of his childhood, or the framework of his family's heritage, happenstance, and coincidence led him to this place in life. He was ready for new challenges. Sometimes the cause of change is inconspicuous. For Ed, that moment came with an innocuous invitation to attend a Democratic Party ward meeting. Maybe it was the experience of his mother, latent in Ed's mental makeup—she would claim credit for his involvement in politics—but Ed immediately took to the give and take, the strategies, and can-do attitudes of politics.

War in Vietnam headlined the news each evening. The fact that Ed's younger brother, Randy, was a medic in Vietnam sharpened Ed's attention to the war. Perhaps, too, Ed's growing opposition to the war led to an invitation to attend a Democratic Party ward meeting. He accepted and went to a meeting where two wards met together. Ed met and listened to the ward chairs, Bert and Imogene Lindsay, who, like him, opposed the war.

The Lindsays had gravitated to a new anti-war organization and invited Ed to join them. Ed found the people there exciting and even influential. Their leader was Henry Kiker, a successful Albuquerque attorney, and, more importantly, the Bernalillo County Democratic Chairman. Bernalillo County included the City of Albuquerque. It also represented the largest block of votes in the state.

Called the "Grass-rooters," the group ran up against the Democratic Party's old guard led by U.S. Senators Joseph Montoya and Clinton Anderson. The Grass-rooters showed up at party meetings with signs protesting the war, and usually were escorted out, as happened at a party convention. At the time, anti-war advocates were seen as communist sympathizers, but the grass rooters, many of whom were veterans saw their opposition as a manifestation of their patriotism.

The upstarts had thrown a major scare into the entrenched old guard, for they used their influence in Bernalillo County to run Fabián Chávez in the 1964 primary for United States Congress. Dapper, wide-eyed, and articulate, the liberal Chávez had made a name

346

for himself before being attracted to the grass rooters. When Ed met him, Fabián had co-chaired the state campaign for John F. Kennedy's presidential campaign, and had been the State Senate Majority Leader with an established record as a reformer. He had fought the liquor industry, led the reformation of the state's corrupt justice of the peace system, and led the movement to establish a medical school at the University of New Mexico. Fabián's articulate manner of speaking and his resonant voice enhanced his political image. He had demonstrated the courage and intelligence to stand up to the entrenched party power brokers, and they openly saw him as a threat. He and the Grass-rooters barely missed defeating the party's choice for Congress.

Ed and Fabián became fast friends. Besides their political beliefs, they shared a sense of humor, the Spanish language, and love of family. Cayetana and Fabián's wife, Corral Jean, also liked each other. Fabián bragged about being a twelfth generation New Mexican. He loved to talk about his older brother, Fray Angélico Chávez, a historian and Franciscan priest who had written about New Mexico's first families and its rich Hispanic heritage. Ed could only reply that he believed that his ancestors came from Spain as well. "Hell," Fabián said with a wink, "we're probably *primos*, Ed."

Eventually, a quick look into one of Fray Angélico's books lent credence to Fabián's words. "Look, here is the first Romero, Bartolomé. He came with Oñate!" Ed took off his glasses to check the lenses and clear his eyes. This was exciting. Ed, too, could claim to be a descendent of one of New Mexico's founding Hispanic families. And if that were true, they realized that they shared common ancestors through the daughters of Pedro Robledo and the Gómez family. They actually were distant cousins. All this information was spelled out in Fray Angélico's books. This love of heritage, not to mention Ed's desire to establish a direct connection between him and that Bartolomé of long ago, was another common bond that made the two men fast friends for life. Not until much later would Ed realize that he and Fabián had another historical connection to Albuquerque's early years. Both of their direct ancestors were founders of the village. Then, too, he could not overlook the story of that statue La Macana, a family heirloom that now existed in a church in Mexico City.

Ed's appetite for the history of New Mexico and his family could never be satisfied. He continued to seek more information, first from Fabián and his brother, Fray Angélico, then from Miguel Encinas, a retired Air Force pilot, veteran of three wars beginning with World War II, and historian, with whom he became acquainted. Over time, Miguel became a major source of historical information for Ed.

Not the least of his colleagues in the appreciation of his heritage was Cayetana. Nothing about her surprised Ed. Cayetana shared Ed's pride in her heritage. She, too, came from a New Mexican family with deep roots in the past. Ed would learn that she was related to that lieutenant governor García, who led the exodus south during the 1680 Indian rebellion. She and her family came from the Rio Grande community of Algodones, roughly the area where that García of yesteryear called home.

While always quick to claim her New Mexican heritage, Cayetana had an even stronger feeling that she and Ed would add to the pages of New Mexico's history. As Ed became more involved in politics and the community, she built an archive of their activities. She kept and organized correspondence and printed matter with the confidence that one day it would be pertinent.

By the time of the 1967 gubernatorial campaign, the Grass-rooters, now called the "grasshoppers" by their opponents, had demonstrated a real strength. This time they challenged for the office of governor and Fabián Chávez surfaced as the Democratic candidate to run against the incumbent governor, David Cargo. Not even the sudden, tragic death of Henry Kiker in a traffic accident could derail their growing strength. Rudy Ortiz was elected chair of the Bernalillo County Democratic Party. He was more moderate than most of the Grass-rooters, but joined them in opposition to the power-grabbing monopoly of the old guard.

Fabián turned to Ed to be the treasurer of his campaign, and this is where Ed really encountered the reality of hard-nosed, behind the scenes politics. Joe Montoya, who derisively called the Democratic ticket of Chávez and Michael Alarid the "tortilla ticket," did everything he could to cut off large support. Clinton Anderson refused to come out in support of the Democratic ticket. Ed was convinced that the two Democratic senators would rather share the spotlight with a Republican than risk giving up a more permanent piece of their influence to a promising upstart Democrat. Montoya and his allies reminded Ed and Fabián of a popular New Mexican saying. Hispanics are like crabs in a bucket. As soon as one gets close to crawling out the others latch on to it and bring it back.

As a result Ed oversaw one of the most frugal gubernatorial campaigns in the state's history. Fabián joked that they sold Coca-Cola bottle caps to make money. Ed sarcastically added that, "the enchilada dinners at a dollar a plate worked out pretty well."

Despite their enthusiastic if frugal efforts, David Cargo narrowly defeated Fabián. The margin of victory was 2,910 votes. Ironically, activist Reis Tejerina garnered almost as much write-in votes and may have cost Fabián the election. Cargo, an incumbent whose campaign grossly out spent his opponent, also had something to do with the outcome and the national politics of the time dammed Fabián's campaign even more so. The Democratic convention in Chicago broke out in riots, then nominated Hubert Humphrey who was pro-war. Richard Nixon defeated Hubert Humphrey in New Mexico by forty thousand votes, and both incumbent Democratic United States Representatives in New Mexico lost to upstart Republicans. That the Grass-rooters kept the gubernatorial election so close was a major accomplishment in itself. In the process, Ed established himself as a player in New Mexico Democrat Party.

As well as serving as treasurer for Fabián's campaign, Ed had become a precinct chairman. Then, a year or so later, Bruce King, who had lost to Fabián, in the previous primary for governor, decided to try again. He and his wife, Alice, came to Ed's house with an important question for him. With Fabián stepping aside, King was a certainty for being the Democratic candidate for governor. King wanted someone to run for lieutenant governor who would make a good running mate in the general election. He asked Ed, "Would you consider running for lieutenant governor?"

The question did not surprise Ed, for he quickly parried with, "Would you publically support me?" Ed knew that King could not do such a thing in the primary election against other Democrats. Moreover, standing behind the Kings, the ever-present Cayetana kept vehemently shaking her head, "no."

Rather than wait for either of the Kings to make their plea, Ed continued, "No, I

Cayetana Romero. A portrait. Ed and Cayetana Romero Collection.

probably won't run." But he would think about it and give them a call in a couple of days. All along, Ed agreed with Cayetana. He did not want to run but wanted a graceful way out. After all, the Kings had paid him a compliment.

Ed's graceful exit came quickly when he found out that Roberto Mondragón, a northern New Mexico liberal, politician who Ed respected, planned to run for lieutenant governor. That news was exactly what Ed needed. Another Hispanic was running, and he would not interfere. As it turned out, Mondragón won the Democratic nomination for lieutenant governor and the King/Mondragón ticket won the general election.

Soon after the election, Rudy Ortiz and some of the other grass rooters asked Ed to run for Bernalillo County Chairman. Ed agreed and travelled up to Santa Fe to meet with the governor and tell him that he was running for the county chair.

While Ed waited in the governor's outer office, State Senator Tony Lucero spotted him. Known as "the *Patrón* of Old Town" in Albuquerque, Lucero was a powerhouse who sided with the old guard. The ever-smug Senator could not hold back and walked up to Ed. "I hear you're running for county chair."

Ed replied, "Yes, that's why I am here. To tell the governor."

To which Lucero rather snidely commented, "You're not going to win. Do you know why?"

"No, why."

This was just the answer the Senator wanted. He self assuredly stuck out his chin with a slight smirk. "Cause I am running against you and I already have twenty thousand dollars to spend on the campaign."

Ed could not help himself. His face brightened up with a mock friendly smile and sarcastically said, "Well, Tony, why don't you give me half of it and I will drop out."

Lucero did not expect nor appreciate Ed sarcasm, or was it lack of awe? Stone-faced and without another word, he left. Nor did Lucero run against him.

With the overwhelming backing of the whole Democratic Party in Albuquerque, Ed unanimously won the election for county chair.

Over a decade later, when both Fabián and Ed had careers beyond reproach, the two of them sat at lunch with a young nephew of Fabián's in a restaurant on top of a Washington, DC hotel. The two long-time friends talked with a self-satisfied pleasure as they explained to the nephew the imagined power of politicians.

"So, you see," Fabián gestured with his fork, "everyone calls me wanting me to do something for them. They think that I have more power than I have. And that is the basis of political power."

Enjoying the moment, Ed joined in. "The art of politics is creating an illusion that you are more influential than you are." He nodded toward Fabián.

Fabián continued. "You see, son, it's arranging the mirrors to create a larger image than you are."

"And," Ed could not wait, "as soon as someone throws a rock, the whole thing crashes back to reality."

The nephew listened with fascination. He had no way of connecting their imagery to the stones that they threw at Joe Montoya's and Clinton Anderson's glass menagerie more than ten years before.

In Ed's case, he would always value more highly a shepherd's son than he would a silver spoon fed and born political icon.

1971, Albuquerque

Had Tony Lucero known—had he realized—the kind of person he was dealing with, Lucero would never have tried to intimidate him. Sometimes people in positions of influence are blinded by their own sense of importance. Lucero did not see, nor cared to see the complicated man seated in front of him. He did not expect the flippant reply. Ed brushed him aside without a second thought.

Lucero's political astuteness was no better than his people skills. The first hint came with the Democratic losses of both Congressional seats. Then, Senator Anderson, at the end of a long career, retired within the year. Albuquerque Republican, Pete Domenici, won the subsequent election to take Anderson's place in the U.S. Senate. Joe Montoya

Isaac Romero, a proud man at age sixty-three. Ed and Cayetano Romero Collection.

had made as many enemies inside his party as he had outside. In 1976, his arrogance caught up with him. He lost in a landslide election to Harrison Schmidt, an astronaut who had moved to New Mexico. In June of 1978, Montoya died at the relatively young age of sixty-two years old.

Ed Romero had found his role, even more so than in politics. Consulting for mostly Hispanic start up businesses appealed to him. He could see the positive effects of his work, and, he was making friends.

His continued relationship with Tom Fatjo gave him an entry into international businesses. Plus, Cayetana worked at his side. Along with her engaging manner—her inexhaustible faculty of placing herself, without compromise, at the level of the person she talked to—she had an impeccable sense of organization. She was a perfect fit with Ed's salesmanship.

Ed's father, Isaac retired at the end of November 1966. He was sixty-five years old and had worked for the railroad for forty-nine years. His colleagues gave him a nice fly-fishing rod and reel with other fishing equipment in anticipation that he would be able to spend more time testing the trout waters of southern Colorado and northern New Mexico. The local newspaper reported on his last day and included a photograph of him receiving the fly rod.

"To Isaac Romero the sounds of a locomotive, the clank of a tank car, and the growl of the drawbar as it couples into a train, have...been a part of his life for almost 50 years."

Now, he would begin his retirement with a month long vacation in Glendora, California with Bud and his family. All of Isaac's children had left Alamosa. Isaac, Jr., "Bud," had a successful career in California, Ed lived in Albuquerque, and Betsy had made a good home for herself in New Mexico's Española Valley, roughly one hundred twenty miles away. Randy enlisted in the Navy and went to Vietnam. They understood when he returned that he would not stay in Alamosa. His childhood had been rough because he was not Hispanic, but was raised in a Hispanic household. He dealt with a lot of teasing in the neighborhood. Besides, while in the service, he had been exposed to a larger world.

Then, there was the war. This became real to Ed and Cayetana as they adjusted their own routines as well as that of their growing family to welcome Randy into their home. After his discharge and return from Vietnam and Okinawa, Randy went through an adjustment as he converted back into civilian life. Some things could be trying, but necessary. In Ed's mind family was necessary. After some months, Randy moved out to live on his own.

Isaac's retirement did not last long before he became ill. Always strong and robust, Isaac seemed to lose his energy. He needed to sleep more than usual and his stomach bothered him. The doctors in Alamosa could not be sure what to make of his malady but they did not rule out cancer.

The children kept aware of their father's plight. Ed felt that he needed to see better doctors to get a more accurate diagnosis. Bud and Betsy agreed. More importantly, so did

Isaac and Ramoncita. In late November of 1971, Ed drove up to Alamosa and transported his father to Albuquerque. Bud and Betsy travelled to Albuquerque as well.

Bud packed his family into their car and started driving east along Route 66 from Southern California. Then, outside Seligman, Arizona he was surprised to be staring at a car coming at him on the wrong side of the highway. He only had a moment to react, a slight turn of the wheel and to throw himself across one of his children who sat between him and his wife in the front seat.

The two cars collided head on. Bud's car was totaled. A young man in the front passenger seat in the other car was killed. By some miracle, no one in Bud's car was seriously hurt. For the rest of his life Bud would marvel at "how very fortunate" they were.

Upon his arrival in Albuquerque, Bud immediately went to the hospital to see his father, who was alert. Isaac perked up upon seeing his oldest son. "Hey, here you are!" And, feigning disappointment, said, "You were supposed to be here two days ago."

Bud sensed the humor. "I know Dad, but we had a little problem."

Isaac let down his façade. "I know."

The diagnosis did not take long. Nor was anyone surprised. Isaac had pancreatic cancer and the doctors gave him a thirty to forty percent chance of survival if they could operate. Ramona, Betsy, Bud, and Ed talked over the options. They did not have much of a choice. Surgery, with an outside chance of survival, or let the cancer run its deadly course. They went to Isaac who agreed to go ahead with the operation.

Isaac came out of the operation worse than when he went in. He was drugged, semi-conscious, and had all kinds of tubes in him. Obviously, he was in pain. The doctors could not say whether he would survive, so they waited. Only after the surgery did the family learn that the survival rate was very low.

Then, one night, Isaac woke up. "Ah," he thought to himself, "this is not right. I need to get control." He looked around and saw all his family including Randy sitting in the room. He motioned for their attention. They had been watching their father intently. What a man he had been. Such memories. They loved him. One of them spoke, "Yes, Dad. We are here."

Isaac spoke in reference to the tubes stuck in him. "*Son brutos. Quitenme estas cosas.*" "They are brutal (or "Damn it!"). Get me out of these things." He took a breath and added. "This is not for me."

Not quite shocked, the family knew their father, they had no need to reply save for doing what was asked. They found a doctor who admitted that Isaac was terminal.

Isaac stoically lay there as the doctor separated him from the hospital. When the doctor completed the procedure, Isaac crossed himself while mentally reciting the words. "*En el nombre del Padre, del Hijo, y del Espíritu Santo.*" Isaac felt whole again. He was at peace with himself. And so, with the help of his family, and with the dignity with which he had conducted his life, Don Isaque, smiled, put his hands behind his head, and lay back to accept the everlasting peace that overcame him a few minutes later. The family watched as their father joined the fate of ten direct New Mexican Romero ancestors before him. Isaac died two days before Christmas in 1971. He was seventy years old.

In His Mother's Image
1972, Albuquerque

Ramoncita would have nothing of it. After Isaac's death the family retired to Ed's house in grief. They barely talked as they sat in the living room. Then, Ramona, her round, normally jovial face aflame, exclaimed, "Stop it! Now! We all go sometime. I will go. So will you." She would not have such sadness permeate her family. "Grief will not honor your father. What you do with your lives will." Her children were shocked. At that moment they realized that the veteran of almost three decades as a Democratic precinct chair had assumed the mantle of family matriarch. She then took the lead to have Isaac buried in Alamosa. She organized the services.

The family could not help but follow her example. Isaac, Jr. (Bud) went back to southern California and continued teaching at Citrus Community College. In 1981, he received his Ph. D. from Brigham Young University. Eventually he would retire as the Executive Vice President of Citrus Community College.

Betsy continued teaching at Española High Schools. It would be the only job she would hold. After marrying a local, Benjamin Martínez, who was no doubt related to the Martins of Abiquiu, she had four children, three sons and daughter. The youngest, named Isaac after his grandfather became a sheriff's deputy and was shot and killed while on a domestic violence case at Pojoaque Pueblo. His mother never got over his death. Whether she knew it or not, her son was the second Romero lawman to be shot in the line of duty. Betsy welcomed her mother, who, after stays in Albuquerque and Denver moved in with her. Betsy would care for her mother—or was it the other way around—for the last ten years of Ramoncita's life.

Ed became the new Bernalillo County Democratic Party Chairman. He went into it knowing that he had a lot to learn and would need help. Then, the perfect person came to his aid. Joe Montoya's insecurity got the best of him again when he fired the party's state executive director. In arguably the best decision of his political career, Ed seized the opportunity and hired Tim Kraft to be his political advisor. Kraft, who had served in the Peace Corps in Guatemala, was flamboyant, energetic, astute, and fearless. He knew politics and was a master strategist. He was just what Ed needed.

The party's hierarchy did not take long to react. One of Montoya's aides telephoned Ed to tell him that the Senator did not want Kraft working for the party in any capacity. Too late. Joe Montoya would not intimidate Ed any more than a state senator could, especially so with Montoya. Ed shot off a quick reply to the messenger, "If that is what he wants, I can resign and he can run for county chairman." Kraft stayed.

Ed served two terms, each for two years. He resigned his position early in his third term. With Kraft at his side, the Democrats won every elective seat in Bernalillo County, from county commissioner to clerk. Ed would later say that his experience as county chair really turned his attention and appreciation toward politics.

Kraft resigned before Ed left his position. Ed was sad to see him go but understood. Kraft decided to take a position with the Jimmy Carter presidential campaign. Kraft could not resist the opportunity.

Ed never heard of Carter until he received a telephone call from Kraft, who told Ed that Jimmy Carter was flying to Albuquerque. He asked, "Can you pick him up at the airport?" Caught off guard, Ed could only ask, "Jimmy who?" After an explanation, Ed agreed to meet the unknown candidate at the airport.

Ed thought that the whole idea of picking up an unknown Democratic presidential candidate at the Albuquerque airport seemed unusual. He decided to ask his friend, Les Houston, at the time one of Ed's precinct chairmen, to go with him. "Les," he asked, "could you go with me to pick up this guy who is running for President? His name is Jimmy Carter."

"Jimmy who?" Les had not heard of him either.

Nevertheless, the two of them met the candidate. Jimmy Carter came by himself carrying a suit bag over his shoulder and wheeling a carry-on behind him. This initial

From left to right, President Jimmy Carter, Cayetana, First Lady Roselyn Carter, and Ed Romero. Ed and Cayetana Romero Collection.

encounter between Ed and Jimmy Carter would be the beginning of a relationship that rocketed Ed into national politics. Kraft had become Carter's field coordinator and, after Carter won the election in 1976, he became Carter's trusted "gate keeper," the appointment secretary and, then, Assistant to the President for Personnel and Political Coordination. His wife, Molly, equally as astute as Kraft, secured a key position in the White House's personnel office.

Kraft's influence solidified Ed's political future. On various occasions, Kraft or his wife recommended Ed to the President to serve in advisory positions as well as on committees. Ed travelled to Washington, DC to meet and advise on Mexican affairs, the Panama Treaty, as well as other Latino/Hispanic relations.

In 1980, again because of Kraft's influence, Carter appointed Ed to a special delegation to travel to Madrid, Spain to attend a conference on security and cooperation in Europe. This was Ed's first trip to Spain.

Griffin Bell, the former U.S. Attorney General, led the delegation. Specifically, the delegation was tasked to review the Helsinki Accord, a 1975 agreement between the Soviet Union and the Warsaw Pact. Carter was especially keen on clause seven that upheld human rights, a major concern and constant theme of his. Many subsequent historians credit the success of the Helsinki Accord, especially clause seven, to adroit United States' negotiation strategies beginning with Carter. His stand opened the way for his successor, Ronald Reagan, and Mikhail Gorbachev to embrace the treaty's humanity, which had a significant role in eventually breaking up communism in Eastern Europe.

In the process of Ed's work for the administration, as well as his business, Ed met and left an impression on Anastasio Somoza, the President of Nicaragua. The United States-educated Somoza had become a heavy-handed leader. He was corrupt and intolerant of opposition of any kind. This especially became clear as a result of the relief efforts after the Nicaraguan earthquake in December 1972. Much of the aid was diverted to offshore bank accounts and was never used for its intended purpose. Jimmy Carter decided to make Somoza an example of his determination to make human rights the cornerstone of his foreign policy. The United States withdrew all American support for Somoza.

Conservatives in the United States strongly disagreed with Carter's stand because they felt that Somoza's armed opposition, the Sandinistas, was supported by communists, if they were not themselves communists. Clearly, Somoza's tactics had cost him popular support. His own people had turned against him, and it became clear that without United States support he would be deposed.

As the Sandinistas gained power, Somoza became desperate. He wanted to talk with Carter but the United States President ignored him. Apparently, in a desperate ploy, Somoza telephoned a surprised Ed Romero.

The call came to Ed on his home phone. He could not believe that the controversial President of Nicaragua had some urgent business for him. Somoza explained that he has some "important information," and wanted to meet with Ed "down here immediately. It will be a quick meeting. In and out."

An exasperated Ed replied, "Me? What do I have to do with important information?"

They talked some more before Ed hung up in disbelief.

When told what happened, Cayetana said to him, "No, don't go." She knew the danger. She could see it every evening on the nightly news. The Sandinistas were closing in on Managua, Nicaragua's capital city and it was just a matter of time.

But Ed could not resist the temptation. He knew Somoza. The least he could do was to go meet with him. What harm in that? Outside of the danger of being in Nicaragua at the time—a danger that Cayetana clearly understood—there was no harm.

Ed flew to Managua. Soldiers in three armed military jeeps met him on the tarmac and took him to the hotel. Then, he was escorted to Somoza where he heard that Carter refused to communicate with the Nicaraguan President and that the Sandinistas could take over the country. It was a matter of time if the United States did not help. Then Somoza presented Ed with a bunch of documents and photographs, "Proof," he insisted, "that the Sandinistas are receiving aid from Cuba and Russia."

Then, he came to the point of the meeting. Somoza wanted to know if Ed would use his connections with the White House to get that information to the President. Ed agreed to try even though Somoza kept the documentary proof.

Once again escorted with military jeeps, Ed was taken to the Managua airport and put on the largest plane that he had ever seen. Ed had made arrangements to go to neighboring Honduras where he would spend the night with Mari-Luci Jaramillo, the United States Ambassador to Honduras. Ambassador Jaramillo, a fellow New Mexican and a former professor at the University of New Mexico, was a friend.

She waited at the airport, and when she saw Ed disembark from a large Nicaraguan military plane, she became very suspicious. Before even greeting Ed she asked, "Ed, what are you doing? What's going on? Where are you coming from?" Obviously, she could see that he was coming from Nicaragua, but she did not want answers immediately. The two of them agreed to save their serious conversation for the Ambassador's residence.

Ed sat down to dinner with Jaramillo and her husband. He started to explain his mission, but the Ambassador cut him off. "No." Then she asked her husband to leave the room. Once he left, she asked Ed to proceed.

After he finished, Ed asked Jaramillo not to tell anyone until he contacted the White House through Tim Kraft. He knew that he was asking her to compromise herself with her government. Nevertheless, she assured him that she would keep the secret.

That night, a couple of hours after everyone had gone to bed, Ed heard the garage door opening and then watched the embassy's official car leaving the grounds. Duty bound, Ed suspected that Mari-Luci Jaramillo was going to her embassy office to report to her superiors.

The response came the next day. As Ed walked in the door to his home, Cayetana immediately said that Tim is trying to reach him. Just then, the telephone rang. It was Kraft. Without any preliminary, Kraft loudly asked, "What are you doing with Somoza?" He broke Ed off when Ed tried to explain. "No. We will not deal with Somoza." Nevertheless, the request went to Bob Pasteur who was in charge of Carter's human rights policies. The answer came back quickly, "They will never meet with him." True to his word, Ed had tried.

Ed knew that Somoza had become desperate to meet with Carter, and Ed, again, agreed to help. This time Ed went to New Mexico's Governor Jerry Apodaca who was at the end of his term. Ed asked the governor if he could invite Somoza to New Mexico. Perhaps such a meeting would give cover for Carter's representatives to meet covertly with Somoza. Somoza's interest in converting volcanic energy into electricity, which was true, would be the official reason for the invitation. The governor politely listened, hesitated, and then agreed. But, again, the White House let them know that they would not meet with Somoza clandestinely or not.

Once again Somoza had been rebuffed. Still, the persistent Somoza traveled to New Mexico where Ed hosted a dinner with the Nicaraguan President. The trip was in vain. Not long after, on July 17, 1979, Somoza fled from his country. In September of the following year Somoza was assassinated in Paraguay. In his posthumously published memoirs, *Nicaragua Betrayed*, Somoza blamed Carter for his downfall.

In September of 1979, an unexpected but exceedingly pleasant opportunity came to Ed with another request from the White House. He was informed that Pope John Paul II would be coming to the United States to visit a number of cities in October. He would visit Washington, DC, where His Holiness had accepted Jimmy Carter's invitation to visit the White House. The Pope and the President would meet in private after which there would be a brief ceremony.

The Krafts had arranged for Ed to select a delegation to represent New Mexico. Ed could not believe what he heard. Along with some New Mexico notables, Ed made sure that Cayetana and her mother Felipita and father Manuel would be included. The reception turned out to be a concert given by the Washington Symphony Orchestra accompanying the famous soprano, Leontyne Price. Dignitaries abounded, ranging from the Kennedys to actor Gregory Peck and, even Colonel Saunders of fried chicken fame. The New Mexico delegation had seats four rows from the Pope. When the music stopped, His Holiness and President Carter gave short speeches. Then it was time to leave. Ed sat on the aisle and, when he realized that the Pope would pass by him, he moved his mother-in-law to his place. As fate would have it John Paul II grabbed her hand and patted her cheek. This was a defining moment for Ed because of the joy he brought to wife's mother, but this would not be his last encounter with John Paul II.

While on a vacation to Europe, Ed and Cayetana happened to be in Rome at a time that coincided with an international convention of *Cursillos*. *Cursillos de Cristiandad* (short courses of Christianity) started in Majorca, Spain in 1944 and spread to the United States in 1961.

Gallup, New Mexico was one of the first cities to hold the three-day weekend courses. By 1981, almost all of the Catholic dioceses in the United States had introduced *cursillos* designed to teach Christianity through the uniqueness, originality, and creativity of each individual to train pilgrimage Christian leaders. Ed and Cayetana were *Cursillisitas*, members, and when they heard that the Pope would be giving a private mass for the convention, they went.

They had befriended a Black Baptist Minister and invited him to join them. Fortunately, they thought they remembered the code word for being admitted into the mass. When asked at the entry, Ed with his patented half-smile replied with a guess, "*de colores.*" All three of them were admitted and seated ten rows back at the side of the altar. When it came time for communion, the Minister asked Ed if he could partake. Ed did not have an immediate reply and the Minister continued that in his religion a true act of contrition was all that was needed. At that moment he kneeled and said an Act of Contrition, rose and went to receive communion. He returned to his seat in tears. Ed could not help but be pleased as the minister became overwhelmed. Once again, Ed had taken an opportunity presented to him and shared the moment.

Ed's third encounter with the same Pope came years later in the summer of 1993, when Vice President Al Gore telephoned. John Paul II was hosting the World Youth Conference in Denver, Colorado. Gore was tasked to head up a delegation to send the Pope off. Would Ed agree to be a part of a ten-person delegation along with Gore and the President? Ed wasted no time, and asked if he could include his mother. Gore said, "Yes."

This time, they met with the Pope and his entourage as they headed toward their plane at Denver's airport. Ed shook the Pope's hand and Ramoncita, standing next to Ed was overcome with emotion and started crying. His Holiness reacted by kissing her on the forehead but she grabbed him and would not let go. Then he blessed her and kissed her again. That was a moment Ed would treasure forever. Fortunately, someone took a photograph of the episode.

In 1980, Kraft left his government position to coordinate Carter's re-election campaign, and Ed became involved. Along with some others, the two of them organized a group that they called "the Hispanic American Demos." They wanted to corner the Hispanic vote and tap into its growing cadre of business people for funds. They worked closely with the national Democratic Party headed by Robert Strauss, a long-time political insider. Ed proved his value. By the end of May in 1980, he was able to send a report to Strauss in which he summarized his "actions and those of the Hispanic community in fundraising for the re-election of Jimmy Carter and Walter Mondale." To date, he continued, a minimum of $640,000 had been raised "through our community." Ed then broke down sources and named the donors ranging from Texas to California. Ed finished his summary with the confidence that more money would be raised.

One of Ed's gambits was to call on some of his old California friends who had become successful. At one point, Ed requested the presence of First Lady Roselyn Carter for two fundraisers. First, she flew to Albuquerque for an event that Ed and Cayetana organized and hosted. Then, Ed and Cayetana flew with her to Encino, California where Mr. and Mrs. Andy Camacho hosted a one thousand dollar per person fundraiser in their house. The Camachos helped Ed raise $86,000 in California. Roselyn Carter thanked Ed for her "enjoyable" time in New Mexico and California. She noted in a newspaper article that New Mexico, "has raised more money *per capita* for the Carter-Mondale campaign than any other state." She singled out Ed Romero as the key figure, adding, "he has helped us all over the country."

Despite Ed's efforts, Ronald Reagan defeated Carter. There would be no second term.

"I HAVE TO RESPOND TO THE PEOPLE WHO ARE MY FRIENDS"
May 1980, Albuquerque

Befriending someone like Anastasio Somoza might have been surprising to some of Ed's colleagues. Still, that relationship was not like Ed's ties in New Mexico. After

Fabián Chávez's 1968 loss to David Cargo, he agreed to run for U.S. Congress against freshman incumbent, Republican Manuel Lujan. Manuel and Fabián had gone to high school together. They were friends. Their fathers had been friends. Fabián went through the campaign motions and lost again.

Manuel's younger brother, Ed ran his campaign. Then, he became the State Republican Party Chairman. Naturally, Ed Lujan and Ed Romero would meet. They sought each other out and met in a restaurant where they sat at a not-too-obvious table. They immediately hit it off. There was something about people like them, prodigies of old New Mexican families. Ed Romero and Ed Lujan connected and their first decision was that they did not have to hide their friendship.

Nonetheless, it wasn't until December 14, 1981 that the newspapers learned of their relationship. On that day *The Albuquerque Tribune* reported "GOP Congressman, Democratic leader partners," and "Land Venture makes strange bedfellows." Ed Lujan explained that he was looking for land upon which to build an office building for his insurance company. "By chance" last year he bought in on property owned by Ed Romero and a close friend, Harold Albert. Apparently reacting to the journalist's disbelief, Ed Lujan nonchalantly added, "Ed's a good friend of mine," and that he had known Ed "for several years."

Now that Ed Romero had lost his White House contacts, he had more time to devote his attention to his family, business, local politics, and his community. Were it not for Cayetana, things would have been difficult and different. As was his disposition, Ed was busy. He always claimed that Cayetana was the family's moral compass. Aside from advising him, or helping to manage the business, or organizing a fundraiser, she focused on the children.

Ed loved his business world as he loved politics, or forging new friendships. He noted how everything seemed to overlap and, like the members of his family, affect one another. He had no explanation for his good life. He travelled extensively and delighted in what he could give back. He pondered this many times. Usually, during these moments in his thought process he paused to reflect then, smiling to himself, continued. He felt in awe of the richness of his life. As a religious man, the one sure answer to it all was to thank God, which he did daily.

Cayetana made sure that the children stayed in touch with their living grandparents. She organized extended family events, especially when it came to Christmas. At times, Cayetana went beyond the ordinary, even getting notice in the local newspaper as she did during Christmas season in 1975. Cayetana, the paper noted, made six hundred and ten tamales. She had the help of her children, Ed, and her parents. Her father collected and saved the necessary cornhusks. Cayetana understood the labor and necessary organizational skills needed to coordinate a family to make six hundred plus tamales. The same skills would support Ed for receptions or fundraisers.

By 1980, Christina and Steven, the oldest two children, had graduated from high school and were enrolled in college. Christina finished her first two years at New Mexico State University. Ed arranged for her to spend the summer in Washington, DC as an intern with New Mexico's U.S. Representative, Harold Runnels. Steven attended the private Christian Brothers' Catholic College of Santa Fe. Ruth and Anna attended high school at Albuquerque's Eldorado High School. Cayetana made certain that each of the children attended catechism to make their first communions and confirmations in the Catholic Church.

Unlike their ancestors, Ed and Cayetana had not settled down to a perfectly regular, self-effacing existence. No, their way of life had become many-faceted with many twists and turns. Ed helped establish the Albuquerque Hispano Chamber of Commerce, and with Ed Lujan and Albuquerque attorney, Arturo Ortega, along with other leading Hispanics in the community, founded the Hispanic Culture Foundation. Ortega had the original idea and called on Ed and then Lujan to join him in the effort. After the terms of Arturo Ortega and Ed Lujan, Ed would become that organization's third President. Under their leadership, the Hispanic Culture Foundation would go on to acquire land and raise over seventy million dollars to establish the National Hispanic Cultural Center on sixty river-front acres in Albuquerque's south valley.

Ed got to know and like the ever-popular Pete Domenici, a Republican who became a multi-term U.S. Senator from New Mexico. For Ed, friendship cut through political parties. When the press questioned why he and Cayetana would hold a one thousand dollar per couple fundraiser for Domenici, Ed matter-of-factly and truthfully answered: "I definitely do not adhere to Republican philosophy and I never will. But I have to respond to the people who are my friends and who are good for our state."

Besides his active support, Ed also financially contributed to various organizations and causes. Ed's contribution to the United Farmworkers was sufficient to warrant a personal letter of thanks from Cesar Chávez who addressed it to "My Dear Brother Romero."

On another occasion, Ed, without hesitation, gave funds to help bring two "*Hermano Penitentes*" from Seville, Spain to New Mexico. Ed liked the idea of sharing and comparing the activities and histories of the *Penitentes* in Spain and in New Mexico. He was intrigued that there could be a connection, and could not help but share his family's historical connection with the *Penitentes*.

Ed made many friends through business. He learned how the government bureaucracy worked. Like friendship, Ed felt that business had nothing to do with party lines. He would take advantage of the happy convergence of government and business. Paul Weick, a Washington, DC correspondent wrote in a syndicated column, "Ed is a decent and generous man. That's why he's where he is." His connections enabled him to turn Solar America into a prosperous business during the Carter years. The column continued to explain his experience and connections "kept the door open when Ronald Reagan moved into the White House."

Ed constantly observed and studied the trends that would affect his business. Ed still had his contacts with the various Federal government departments and agencies. When oil prices bottomed out and Reagan eliminated every tax incentive that the solar industry had, he knew enough to change his business model. Even his friend and mentor Tom Fatjo talked about transferring waste to energy.

Ed and Cayetana morphed their respective companies into one new company that they named Advanced Sciences Inc. (ASI). Over time they would grow that company into over six hundred employees spread over twelve states, the District of Columbia, and two countries. In February 1988, the Albuquerque Hispano Chamber of Commerce reported that ASI had contracted a, "wide range of environmental and engineering opportunities," with projects like the space shuttle and the Strategic Defense Initiative (SDI). Ed's

UNITED FARM WORKERS of AMERICA AFL-CIO

P.O. BOX 62   KEENE, CALIFORNIA 93531   (805) 822-5571

March 29, 1974

E.L. Romero
37 Camino Don Diego N.E.
Albuquerque, N.M. 87111

Dear Brother Romero:

We deeply appreciate your generous donation to our Union. Your
gift is an expression of your love and solidarity which will help
us continue the struggle for justice and dignity for farm workers.

As you may realize, this year is the msot crucial in the history
of our Union. We are engaged in a struggle with the grower-Teamster
conspiracy to destroy our Union. Only recently in the Imperial
Valley of Southern California, thousands of workers walked out of
the fields to demonstrate their resentment because the growers had
signed back-door contracts against their wishes. Farm workers
simply want their own Union and to be recognized as such by their
employers.

Please continue to boycott Gallo wines, table grapes and iceberg
lettuce.

Viva la Causa!

Cesar E. Chavez,
President

CEC:jln
Encl.

A letter from Cesar Chávez thanking Ed Romero for his support. March 29, 1974. Ed and Cayetana Romero Collection.

contacts ranged beyond the government to companies like Frito Lay, Gulf Oil, Coors, the Boeing Company, and Southern California Edison. By 1987, ASI's sales exceeded 10 million dollars and Ed added, "we expect 100% growth this year." In 1997, when his company merged with Commodore, Inc., a public company, he reported 68 million dollars in revenues. In reality, Ed had become more known for his business success than his politics. Many national journals started including him in their "most influential or most important people" lists.

During all of the activity surrounding Ed and Cayetana, they found time to select and purchase some property at the eastern edge of the city at the base of Sandia Mountain. In 1987 Cayetana designed and contracted the construction of their dream

362

home. The spacious multi-bedroom and multi-bathroom house featured a large kitchen and impressive high ceiling living area with spectacular views of the mountain through large windows. A pool and barbeque veranda drew attention to the backyard, and after moving in they installed an "Argentinian barbeque." All in all, the house would become a showcase for Cayetana's beginning Lladró collection, as well as for the artworks they were accumulating.

Beginning with Lyndon B. Johnson in 1965, Ed received an invitation to every Democratic Presidential inauguration. He was either invited or attended every National Democratic Convention since Chicago in 1968. Like his mother before him, Ed had become a regular party operative.

While not a king maker, his work and integrity had some influence. One of the more poignant examples of his influence occurred during the 1984 convention in San Francisco. Ed could not go. At least, he would not be there for the whole convention. Cayetana's father, who had been sick, went to California for an operation that did not help. Ed needed to be with Cayetana and her family. They took turns being with him and Ed was there until a half hour before his passing. José Manuel García, a silent, decent man lived for his family. As he faded, the only word he repeated was "Lipa," his nickname for his wife, Felipita. At that moment Ed had no thoughts about politics.

As Ed tended to his family, the convention moved along. As expected, the convention chose Walter Mondale to be their Democratic candidate. New Mexico's governor, Toney Anaya, had aspirations for the vice presidential position. At the time, New Mexico's governors served one four-year term with no opportunity for a second term. Anaya felt that one logical avenue for his career path would be as Mondale's running mate. The governor had his people try to get an interview, but Mondale had other plans. Finally, Mondale's people acquiesced, but as one newspaper reported, when the opportunity came to Anaya for an interview, he was in Europe, "on one of those magical mystery tours." Anaya lost out and was never interviewed nor considered for the Vice President position.

Nevertheless, Anaya still sought some national recognition. He turned to Ed, who arrived in San Francisco midway through the convention. The governor's poll numbers were down and showed no sign of rising. Ed knew this, but he felt that Anaya had been a good governor and that New Mexico should not be slighted. Before he left the convention early to attend his father-in-law's funeral back in New Mexico, Ed talked to Mondale and by virtue of his good reputation he was able to secure a role for Anaya on the podium. Anaya seconded the nomination of Geraldine Ferraro, Mondale's choice for his running mate.

REALITY, AN OPPORTUNITY DELAYED, AND SPAIN
1993, Albuquerque

It would be twelve years after Carter's defeat before a Democrat would win the presidency. Bill Clinton took office in January 1993. Al Gore became the new Vice President, and Ed Romero, who continued to work for all the candidates during the hard times, once again had friends in the White House. Almost immediately a telephone call came. One of the President's appointment secretaries spoke, "We are going to put your name on a list for potential ambassadorships." Then he heard that Costa Rica was a possibility. Initially pleased, Ed quickly came to reality. His business had tailed off and needed his attention. Sadly, he wrote a letter to the White House's personnel department, who dealt with the ambassador appointments. He asked them to take his name out of consideration. It was, he felt, an opportunity lost, but a correct decision nonetheless.

Then, four years later Clinton won re-election. This time a Marsha Scott called. "Mr. Romero," she said, "I just took out our list of potential ambassador appointments and was asked by the Vice President "where is Ed Romero?"" She apologized for the mistake.

No apology was needed and Ed explained, "Marsha there is a letter in your files that I previously wrote."

Somewhat relieved, Scott asked, "How do you feel now?"

"I don't know." Ed authentically had mixed emotions. His business had revived. He did not want to go to Costa Rica. "Actually," he thought to himself and shared to those close to him, "Spain probably is the only country I would accept," but that position was taken, or so he understood. He heard through the grapevine that Paul L. Cejas an influential Cuban-American was going to be appointed to Spain. Ed did not want to compete for the position, and felt it a better idea to stay home.

Then, a telephone call came from New Mexico's former Democratic Representative to Congress, who Clinton had appointed Ambassador to the United Nations. Bill Richardson had moved to New Mexico, and had a successful political career. In the process he came to know and appreciate Ed. "Ed, they want you to be an ambassador. You have a lot of support. You always push for hiring Hispanos. I don't understand why you don't accept the appointment." Then he suggested that they have breakfast to talk about it.

Ed agreed to talk, so he and Richardson met at the old Classic Hotel in downtown Albuquerque. Ed reiterated that he was not interested in being an ambassador unless it might be Spain, but he understood that someone else was being considered. He did not want to compete nor take the appointment away from someone, so he was fine with the staying home. No problem.

Richardson tried to convince Ed to be open to an appointment, but understood Ed's position. Ed left the meeting pleased at the support he had received, which impressed him because, at the time Ed did not really know the President as well as he knew Carter, Mondale, or Gore. At the moment, his friends Gore and Richardson were pushing hard on his behalf. How could he not be pleased with such support?

A couple of days after his meeting with Richardson, Marsha Scott contacted him. This time she confronted him with a direct statement. "Mr. Romero, congratulations, the President will be calling and asking you to be the Ambassador to Spain."

Ed was stunned. "That's impossible. It has been given to someone else."

"No, he has accepted the nomination for Brussels. The position to Spain is open."

Ed gathered his thoughts. This would be a big change for him and his family. He went to Cayetana then called his son and daughters together. All of them were now adults, graduated from college, and married. They had given him and Cayetana six grandchildren. Ed did not want to admit what even his full head of white hair indicated. This would be life-changing move. What did the family think?

Think? What was there to think about? They wanted to celebrate! What an opportunity. Their father a United States Ambassador? What an honor! And to Spain! The answer was a resounding, "Yes, accept the nomination."

Ed waited for President Clinton's call, and when it came the President officially asked Ed to be his appointment as ambassador to Spain. Ed thanked the President and quickly gave him an affirmative answer. Now, Ed had nothing to do but prepare.

However, fate held up his preparation as well as his appointment. In March, Cayetana started having trouble breathing. At moments, her shortness of breath alarmed her and Ed. Her doctor immediately had her hospitalized, where she was diagnosed with Acute Respiratory Distress Syndrome, a serious disease that caused a sudden failure of the respiratory system that could result in permanent lung damage and potential death.

Ed's total concentration turned to, and focused on Cayetana. He had no thought of his ambassadorship or anything else. He watched and prayed as she was put on oxygen. She needed rest. At one point she lapsed into a coma. She was dying in a room strewn with equipment. Ed helplessly watched as his grandson Adam softly sang a lullaby that she had sung to him as a child. Ed could only pray and beseech her, "Please don't go. Don't leave me."

Cayetana later told how she heard Ed and Adam and knew, then, that she needed to "come back." Ed kept the White House informed about her state of health. He asked that his name be withdrawn from consideration since he did not know what her health would be like after her recovery. President Clinton said, "No, he would not do that. Ed was informed that the announcement of his appointment could wait, "until you find out about her health."

Then, while on a trip to the West Coast, the President stopped in Albuquerque. He wanted to meet with Ed and see Cayetana. This was indeed special but Cayetana asked Ed to give the President her apologies but she did not want to be seen in her current state.

Nonplussed, the President met with Ed over lunch in the Hacienda Restaurant in Albuquerque's Old Town. No, he would not consider withdrawing Ed's nomination. Ed could only answer that he would be ready as soon as Cayetana was well enough to travel. The President nodded in agreement, and expressing genuine concern for her health added, "Once you know, we'll talk."

Meanwhile Cayetana suffered a slow recovery. It was one thing to be out of danger and another for her to be well enough to travel. As she improved Ed began to prepare. He kept the administration informed of her progress, and they, in turn, prepared for a quick transition.

When informed that he was entitled to name one person as a personal aid, he asked for and received a second, secretarial position. Ed selected Daniel Ortega to be his personal aid. The son of Arturo Ortega, Ed's long-time friend, Ed felt an obligation to choose one of Ortega's sons. Arturo, who had been Spain's honorary consul to New Mexico, passed away not long before, and in Daniel, Ed had an eminently qualified

Vice President Al Gore swearing in Ed Romero as United States Ambassador to Spain and Andorra in a private ceremony in the White House. Photograph by LeRoy N. Sanchez.

person. Like his father, Daniel practiced law. He also could speak fluently in English, Spanish, and Catalan. Moreover, Daniel shared his father's and Ed's appreciation for his Hispanic American heritage.

Ed appreciated the symmetry of his appointment and selection of Daniel. Now, Ed seriously sought information about his ancestors. He hired Albert Gallegos to research the Romero genealogy—and Ed wanted the information fast. "Albert, this is between you and me. I will be appointed ambassador to Spain. I need this information before I go."

"When?"

"Soon."

Gallegos went to work. He tried to ignore Ed's constant calls. He liked and admired Ed, and understood the value of Ed going to Spain with an accurate family history. Albert delivered on time. Ed learned for the first time that he definitely was a direct descendant of Bartolomé Romero who originated from a village near Toledo called Corral de Almaguer. Now Ed could hardly wait to go to Spain and share his story.

Almost six months had passed when Ed telephoned the White House. Cayetana finished rehab and received permission to travel. The President's staff fast-tracked his

Bill Richardson swearing in Ed Romero in a public ceremony in the U. S. Department of State. Photograph by LeRoy N. Sanchez.

Ed and Cayetana at his first news conference in Barajas Airport upon his arrival in Madrid as the United State's newly appointed ambassador. Photograph by LeRoy N. Sanchez.

nomination on the Senate's confirmation calendar. The family flew to Washington, DC where Ed attended the required meetings and briefings. He visited Senators and quickly received their approval for his appointment. Senator Joe Biden, who chaired the Senate Foreign Relations Committee, backed him. On June 23, 1998, the Senate moved and confirmed his appointment. With his family present, Al Gore gave him the oath of office in a private ceremony on June 24th in the White House. He took a second oath in a public ceremony in the State Department the next day. Two days later, Ed and Cayetana landed in Madrid.

Ed's appointment was a first of its kind, for it was actually two appointments in one. First, he was named the first U.S. Ambassador to the Principality of Andorra, a microstate located in the eastern Pyrenees Mountains on the Spanish and French border. At the same time, he was named Ambassador to Spain.

Ed flew to Spain from New York with an entourage of twenty-five people that included Cayetana, Steven, his grandson Adam, and the historian Miguel Encinias. Encinias helped Ed craft the speech that he was expected to give upon his arrival at Madrid's Barajas Airport. Ed had a message to give, and he wanted to make sure that it would be the first impression the Spanish would have of him. As they got close to landing, Ed changed into a blue suit with a red and blue striped tie, and waited. A Spanish Press Corp of thirty to forty people waited for him. He had returned.

Ed and Cayetana were taken to a pressroom and given seats at a table facing the cameras and microphones. Cayetana wore an elegant white trimmed in black outfit. After introducing his family members, Ed pulled out his notes and in Spanish went directly to the point. "Our arrival in Madrid and Spain is a very special moment for us. We have admired and known this country that has been connected to us for four centuries." He, then, told how his ancestor, Bartolomé Romero, left Corral de Almaguer and, in 1598, helped establish a colony what is today the State of New Mexico, and that Cayetana's ancestors also left Spain in the same epoch.

Ed continued mentioning the necessary things like the United States and Spain are good friends, good allies, and have had excellent relations and cooperation. He wants to promote and fortify the good relations that already exist. At the end of his short, six-hundred-word speech, he returned to the theme he considered most important.

> "For my President and my country, the United States, I want to serve to the best of my ability and honor. And to my historical mother country, Spain, I want to be received with the same appreciation and the same pride that I have for it."

This would be a theme repeated many times in word and deed during Ed's three-year ambassadorship, "...walking on the lands of the grandfathers of my great-grandfathers as Ambassador of the United States of America in Spain."

Lucas Pacheco and Juanita Trujillo, Isaac Romero's in-laws and Ed Romero's maternal grandparents.
Lucas lived the last ten years of his life with Isaac and Ramona Pacheco.
Ed and Cayetana Romero Collection.

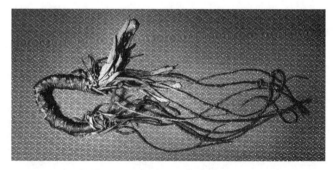

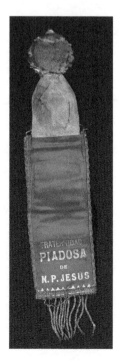

The *disciplina* or whip (above) and badge (right) that belonged
to Lucas Pacheco, Ed Romero's maternal grandfather. He was a
Hermano Mayor, leader of the *penitente* brotherhood in Center,
Colorado.
Ed and Cayetano Romero Collection.

PART IX
THE RETURN CONTINUED, AMBASSADOR ROMERO

June 2000, Madrid, Spain

Ed and the people advising him could not have made a better impression on the Spanish press. He inherited a tricky situation in Spain. His predecessor, Richard N. Gardner, decided to take a teaching position at Columbia University, and announced his resignation in March of 1999. He finally left the post on July 5th. Then the position remained vacant. The Spanish press learned that Ed Romero was a possibility for the assignment as early as October. *ABC* and *El Mundo*, both national newspapers, speculated that Ed would be the next ambassador to Spain.

Then, the holidays passed and February came. The position remained vacant. No news came from the United States. Spain's major opposition party, PSOE, openly questioned if this was some kind of international slight, a diplomatic message that Washington was upset with Spain. Then the government, through the *ABC* daily newspaper, openly wondered why the position had not been filled. Seven months passed. An *ABC* editorial hoped that Clinton would fill the prolonged vacancy to remedy, "a situation inappropriate to existing good relations."

The Clinton administration noted that Spain's was not the only prolonged vacancy and, moreover, the governmental bureaucracy took time in naming a new ambassador. Not until April when the announcement was made did the government let on that Ed Romero, indeed, was the choice. The White House never disclosed that Cayetana's illness was the reason for the delay.

The airport speech, Ed's obvious desire to learn and compare Spain to his native New Mexico and his early activities of going to Corral de Almaguer—the Spanish loved the concept of him going *incognito* to the birth place of his ancestors—where he was made an honorary citizen (*hijo predilecto*) and had a plaza named for him, all played into a true image of a man who really appreciated Spain. He successfully parried any Spanish concern about his delayed appointment.

Ed Romero was never awed by the appointment or what lay before him. Pleased and honored, yes. Anxiety about his ability as an ambassador to Spain? Never.

In Albuquerque he met with people to discuss what he could do for his home state. They discussed various ideas and concluded that the best idea would be an endowed chair to be named for the Prince of Asturias, the heir apparent to the throne. Ed also decided that once in Spain, in addition to being caught up in high society, he wanted to attend the festivals and visit the small "pueblos and towns."

In Spain Ed, as a Catholic, felt that he needed to take the initiative and visit Spain's Catholic leaders. After receiving his credentials and making the necessary visits to the government officials he set up appointments with the Church leaders. This, he learned, was new.

Seville's Archbishop Carlos Amigo Vallejo brought a smile to Ed's face. The meeting was supposed to last fifteen minutes in the Archbishop's office, which is located in a beautiful seventeenth century building facing the picturesque Plaza Virgin de los Reyes immediately behind the cathedral.

Ed noted to His Excellency that a side chapel in the cathedral had a statue of Christ that reminded him of one he had seen in New Mexico. Also, the statue had the same name, "Nuestra Padre Jesús Nazareno." Also, the statue's name was part of the formal name of the worldwide Penitentes, which is *La Fraternidad (*or Hermandad) *Piadosa de Nuestro Padre Jesús Nazareno.*

As wine was being poured, Ed explained that New Mexico had *penitentes* and that his maternal grandfather was a member of a brotherhood.

The Archbishop would not believe what he heard. "No. That is impossible." But Ed insisted that he was right.

Not convinced, the Archbishop leaned forward and said, "Look, I am the world leader of *penitentes*. We have them in the Philippines, Italy, here, and other places. But not in the United States." Now he sat upright. "Mr. Ambassador, you are mistaken."

Ed sipped some of the good red Ribera de Duero and smiled. "With all respect, Your Excellency, we have *penitentes* in New Mexico." Ed explained that he had helped travel some *penitentes* from Seville to meet their brethren in New Mexico. Ed smiled as he related the story of the Spaniards going up to Taos to meet with a group of *penitentes* at their morada, place of worship, a one story, windowless building situated next to a cemetery. They arrived after sunset and the poor Spaniards, a husband and wife were left at night outside the small L-shaped building, listening to chanting coming from inside. The wood door opened to a line of chanters, some holding candles, came out single file, circled the visitors and led them inside. The Spaniards were terrified.

At this part of the story Ed laughed. But, he assured the Archbishop that it all worked out well. The Spaniards were given a feast of food and had a great discussion about the similarities and differences between the brotherhoods in Spain and the United States.

To this the Archbishop asked what are the differences and Ed replied, "Secrecy, the product of one country being primarily Protestant and the other Catholic." He explained that the *Penitentes* in the United States went underground to avoid criticism. Even their own church tried to disband them. In Catholic Spain they are accepted.

The short meeting extended way beyond the initial fifteen minutes and into a second carafe of wine. Convinced, Archbishop Amigo told Ed about an upcoming worldwide conference of *Hermanos Mayores,* Penitente leaders, that he would be hosting. Could Ed arrange for representation from New Mexico? Ed not only could, but would. After the meeting he immediately called Archbishop Michael Sheehan, head of the Archdiocese of Santa Fe. The Archbishop made sure that New Mexico's *penitentes* were represented in Seville by sending two representatives.

Still smiling to himself Ed thought that either from his insistence or the presence of New Mexico's *penitentes* at the conference, their world leader Archbishop Amigo was convinced that there are *penitentes* in the United States. That was another link that will strengthen ties between the two countries.

The car purred as they headed back to Madrid. Cayetana shifted and distracted Ed.

He looked at her as she peacefully slept. The night's tranquility drew him to his thoughts. It wasn't but a few months ago that Ed had arrived. He thought back to the speech he gave at the airport.

He remembered starting with something like, "we have finally arrived." Ed could not help but be pleased with his initial days and weeks in Spain.

Yes, he thought, I am ready. He had been prepared by his own centuries's long heritage through the migration from Spain and Mexico of a humble ancestor who made the daunting decision to migrate to America. He wondered what his ancestors would have thought had they known.

Ed constantly sought to meet regular folk. He refused to be limited to meeting only dignitaries, which was an obvious necessity of the job and Cayetana, while still recovering from the after effects of her medical ordeal, naturally ingratiated herself with everyone. She had her own aide and the use of Ed's protocol officer. Cayetana's aide was an American who had been in Spain many years. He told her "after the King and the President, the American Ambassador is the most important person in the country." That comment impressed both Cayetana and Ed. She, as always, was a perfect complement to Ed.

Together they decorated the ambassador's residence with New Mexican art. Ed looked to benefit his home state and to share it with Spain. Taking Pueblo Indians to Corral de Almaguer or arranging for the España-Estados Unidos Foundation to hold one of its international meetings in Santa Fe, New Mexico was just the beginning. Ed arranged for Spain's Vice President, Alvarez Casco to visit New Mexico. Alvarez Casco became the key for the Spanish government's decision to establish its prestigious Instituto Cervantes in the National Hispanic Cultural Center in Albuquerque, which was about to open. Ed constantly talked about the Hispanic presence in the United States and the need to preserve the spoken language. He openly suggested that Spain could play an important and key role in preserving the Spanish language in the United States. The Spanish Vice President gladly helped.

One of the first people Ed met was, Placido Arango who was on the embassy's invite list and one of Spain's more influential individuals. He had been the president of the Premios Principe de Asturias (the Prince of Asturias Awards). The awards began and are annually presented in the city of Oviedo, the capitol of the Principality of Asturias in northern Spain.

The Prince of Asturias Foundation makes the selections of people or entities, "around the world who make notable achievements in the sciences, humanities and public affairs." The heir apparent to the King of Spain is the Prince of Asturias. At the time, Felipe, who would become King Felipe VI, was the Prince of Asturias. He started the foundation and awards in 1981. Every year the Prince presides over the proceeding that names the recipients for the prestigious award.

Ed immediately recognized that he needed to meet Placido Arango. Upon making contact, Arango invited Ed to his house. This began a friendship as well as a series of informal get-togethers, usually at Arango's house for dinner and drinks. Ed always took a little keepsake gift. One night, as they were sharing drinks and conversation, Arango put his drink down and stood up. "Ambassador, I want to show you something." He went to one of his full bookshelves and pulled out a book that he took to Ed. Holding it out to Ed he said, "This is about your New Mexico."

Ed could see that the edition being handed to him was old. Arango was not sharing a recently published book. Arango continued, "What you have in your hands is Gaspar Pérez de Villagrá's 1610 edition of *La Historia de la Nueva Mexico.*"

Ed held the book in awe. He knew of the book and, in fact, had in his own collections a bi-lingual edition recently published by the University of New Mexico Press. His friend and advisor Miguel Encinias helped edit and translate the book.

What he had in his hands was an original edition almost four hundred years old. While he could appreciate that the book was valuable, he did not know that the book he held was one of less than twenty originals known to exist. Almost fifteen years earlier, New Mexico's state history museum purchased a copy at a discounted rate of around eight thousand dollars and, he thought, the University of New Mexico's special collections had one as well. Nor did Ed realize at that moment that his direct ancestor Bartolomé Romero is mentioned more than once in the book.

Gratified for Ed's friendship and his gifts, Arango then shocked Ed. "Ed, since I know that the Prince is going to New Mexico, I am going to give this book to him to give to your National Hispanic Cultural Center. It's yours for your state."

"No, Placido, no. Thank you. This is very generous of you but I cannot accept it. My state already has a copy, maybe two. I cannot accept it. Thank you. This is a special treat for me."

Not to be deterred, Arango put his book back in it place and turned to Ed. "Bueno. Instead of the book I will give the Center a hundred thousand dollars."

During the course of their meetings Ed learned that Arango went to college in the United States. He graduated from Tufts University where, Arango noted, he paid for an endowed chair named for Felipe, the Prince of Asturias.

Ed did not have to hear more. He remembered his meeting before he left New Mexico with Bill Gordon, the acting President of the University of New Mexico, one of the university's professors, and state senator Manny Aragón where they discussed Ed's idea to establish an endowed chair. At that time Gordon stated that the cost would be a million dollars.

Ed posed the idea to Arango. Ed knew that Prince Felipe had two endowed chairs named for him in the United States. Georgetown University, where Felipe went to graduate school, has the other chair. Endesa, Spain's largest energy company sponsored the Georgetown chair. The other chair went to Tufts University.

This was a matter that Vice President Alvarez Cascos could not influence or help. Ed needed permission from the Prince and, by extension, the Royal House. Without Felipe there would be no chance. Placido Arango agreed to help. He was close to the Prince and the King. He could do something far more important and lasting than Villagrá's book. He would make arrangements for Ed to meet the Prince in Oviedo in the Principality of Asturias during the Premio de Principe de Asturias ceremony. Ed followed his friend's lead, "Of course he would be there."

The meeting took place in the Prince's suite in an Oviedo hotel. Ed and Arango met with Prince Felipe, his Chief of Staff, and the King's Chief of Staff. Ed addressed the Prince explaining his desire to create a Principe de Asturias endowed chair at the University of New Mexico.

The King's Chief of Staff cut Ed off, "Your Highness, I doubt that this is the best thing for you."

Seemingly nonplused Felipe asked, "Why?"

"Because you already have two chairs at good universities."

Ed had an answer. "The other chairs are in humanities. This one would be high tech. In New Mexico we have Los Alamos, Sandia...." Ed paused as he remembered something from his briefing, "Also, Spain invests very little in high tech. Spain could benefit."

The Chief of Staff paused. He turned to the Prince who commented, "Let me think about it."

The Chief of Staff contacted Ed the next day. "The Prince wants you to proceed."

Ed thanked the Chief of Staff and asked him to thank the Prince. Then he telephoned Bill Gordon at the University of New Mexico, who told him that the revised cost for such a chair would cost a million-and-a-half dollars. Ed had some work to do. He was a salesman after all.

He came up with a plan to seek six payments of $250,000 each from U.S. companies that did business in Spain. He would contribute to one of those parts. Within a few days he had the commitments for the total cost. Anxiously and very happily, Ed called Chief of Staff to convey the good news. Somewhat surprised, the royal official told Ed to, "come and tell the Prince!" Ed gladly obliged to this and went to meet the Prince, who upon greeting Ed seemed in a good mood. Upon hearing the news he asked, "Where did the money come from?"

Ed proudly answered, "American companies."

To this answer, the Prince's mood changed. Now he had a serious look. "Mr. Ambassador, I cannot accept it."

This caught Ed off guard. "Why?"

"Its American money. We have a tradition that Chairs in my name have to be paid by Spanish money."

Ed held out his hands and reacted. "Your Highness, money is money."

This brought a smile to the Royal's face. "I know. But Tufts was paid by Arango and Georgetown by Endesa. We have a tradition."

As it became obvious that he could not change the Prince's mind, Ed left very dismayed. He climbed into his limo and came up with another plan. He called one of his new friends, Iñigo Oriol, the President of Iberola. Iberola, a large private electric utility was expanding into the international market, including the United States. A secretary answered and Ed introduced himself and asked to speak to Iñigo. He was told to wait. Iñigo was in a meeting. After a few minutes the secretary took up the telephone, "Sorry, Iñigo is in a board meeting." This was not the answer Ed wanted. He insisted on speaking to Iñigo until finally Iñigo got on the phone.

Ed used a time-tested technique. "Iñigo, I have to see you immediately. I'm only fifteen or twenty minutes away."

"I can't. I am in a board meeting."

"Iñigo, I have to see you right now."

"I'm in a board meeting."

"Iñigo, this is important to me. I have to see you."

"Okay, the meeting is boring anyway."

Ed had his driver take him to Iberola's offices where he found Iñigo standing outside the entrance waiting for Ed with a smile on his face. "Thanks for rescuing me." They shook hands and hugged, and then went up to Iñigo's office where Iñigo settled behind his desk. "Okay, what's so important?"

Ed then told him what happened and that he needs Spanish support for the chair. Iñigo reacted nonchalantly and said, "Don't worry about it. I will put in one sixth and have a breakfast with some of the leading Spanish industrialists. I will get some commitments for the balance."

But this answer did not satisfy Ed. "Iñigo, you don't understand. I want Iberola to have the honor of endowing the entire chair."

Now Iñigo was taken aback. "The whole million-and-a-half? *Estás loco?*"

"That's right, just as Arango and Endesa had done." Ed then explained what Iberola would gain by having an endowed chair in a leading U.S. university with connections to Sandia Laboratories and the Los Alamos Laboratories. He added that he would negotiate with the university for three or four fully paid graduate student scholarships for Spanish students and that a professor would be a Spaniard and selected with an understanding between Iberola and the university.

Iñigo had no reply, nor did he want to commit without thinking about it. Ed left without an answer. The next day Iñigo telephoned. "I guess I am equally as crazy as you. We'll pay the entire amount provided that, in addition to what you told me, we can pay this in three five hundred thousand dollar increments."

Ed was ecstatic and gladly told the Prince about the good news. This time, Ed's pleasure was met by the Prince's equal satisfaction. They had created a new connection between Spain and New Mexico.

Ed's obvious interest in Penitentes and his friendship with Mayor Macheño and Father Izquierdo helped with another matter. They introduced him to José Miranda Calvo who lived in Toledo. Ed found José Miranda to be a dignified man around eighty years old. He had an aquiline face and a serious sense of humor and had been the *Hermano Mayor* of the ancient Mozarabe confraternity based in Toledo. Ed learned from José that the organization had roots extending back to before the Moorish occupation of Spain in the eighth century. He explained that the, "Illustrious Ancient Brotherhood of the Gentlemen and Ladies Mozarabes of Our Lady of Hope of the Imperial City of Toledo," originated with King Fernando III who reigned in the thirteenth century. "San Fernando," whose incorrupt body is in the altar of the Royal Chapel in Seville's cathedral, "was the first to unite the crowns of Castile and León. And then, he defeated the Moors, finally taking Seville and reaching the Mediterranean." José went on to relate that rather than continue fighting, the pious, crusading Fernando negotiated with the emirate of Granada, reducing it to a vassalage that would pay a large annual tribute.

José then walked into another room and returned holding out a blue cape with an ornate cross on it. "Blue was Fernando III's color and the cross is his as well." Today this is the cape that all Mozarabes wear. But before the Moors, the Christians practiced an ancient form of a mass, and they preserved their practice for the three plus centuries that Toledo was under Muslim rule. Today, that mass is still said under special dispensation from Rome in a designated chapel in the Cathedral.

José fascinated Ed and Cayetana. They shared with him that New Mexico had confraternities and *penitentes* but it had nothing like this. José could see that they had a special interest and appreciation for Spanish Catholicism. They became close friends, and Ed put José on the Embassy's invite list. Ed looked forward to every opportunity to share some time with José.

Ed did not have to wait long to receive a special invitation. José saw in his new friend something more than a curious and polite tourist or ambassador. He recognized that he and Ed shared similar values. José talked to his fellow Mozarabes that resulted in a telephone call from the Archbishop of Toledo, who also is the Primate of all of Spain's Catholics. Monsignor Don Francisco Alvarez had a simple question. "Would the Ambassador concede to him and his wife being named an *Hermano* (Brother) in the Mozarabe confraternity?"

Cayetana agreed with Ed that this was the pinnacle of complements. He did not hesitate to say, "yes." In fact, he was ecstatic, for here was something that spoke to his religion, history, and family. It seemed like his heritage had come full cycle in a most unexpected but immensely fulfilling way.

At 6:00 p.m. on June 18, 2000, almost a year after he took office, Ed and Cayetana were inducted as honorary members in the Mozarabe confraternity. A medal was pinned on Cayetana and Ed received a medallion. Archbishop Alvarez officiated over the ceremony in a solemn High Mass in Toledo's San Lucas church.

The Spanish newspapers went crazy with the story. The United States ambassador and his wife are Mozarabes! No previous ambassador had received such an honor. So far as anyone could tell, Ed and Cayetana were the first individuals from the United States to be inducted into the old organization. If people did not understand it before, the fact that Ed was a different kind of ambassador now became clear.

MORE WORK TO DO
Summer 2000, Madrid, Spain

As he sat in his office in front of a large, round, wall-mounted mirror framed with an American eagle, Ed could look back to his more than two years as Ambassador with some satisfaction. His message resonated, the Mozarabe induction was special, and the permission to proceed with the endowed chair was an accomplishment.

He also smiled at the thought that the Spanish government would open an Instituto Cervantes in Albuquerque, that he helped arrange for Enron to invest in wind energy installations in Spain, or that he was able to see some of the local traditions such as the Moors and Christians, or Día del Santo Niño (Holy Child Day). He even danced a *pasodoble* with the mother of the mayor in the small town of Valera de Abajo. One of Fabián's nephews arranged for him to be in Trujillo in the region of Extremadura to participate in a welcoming reception for University of New Mexico Honors students. Bill Gordon showed up as well.

The personal honors continued. In October of 1999, Ed went to the Basilica of the Royal Monastery of Escorial, the building that inspired the construction of the Versailles Palace in France, to be named a Knight of the Order of the Holy Sepulcher of Jerusalem. In the following May, he was named an "Honored Scholar of the World Academy of Science and Technology of Valencia." A month later, the International Brotherhood of Researchers under the guidance of the Church of Holy Christ of the Olive invested him as a "luminary" member. Now he belonged to an organization established to, "unite and congregate researchers in all fields of knowledge."

But now, despite all that passed, Ed was especially pleased by Iñigo Oriol's agreement to have Iberola sponsor the Prince's Chair in New Mexico. In Ed's mind, Iberola's sponsorship of the Prince's Chair could not be a more perfect match.

On Ed's recommendation, the Prince decided to travel to New Mexico. As the Honorary Chairman of the National Hispanic Cultural Center Foundation, he agreed to inaugurate the new institution with its addition of the Instituto Cervantes. At the same time, in the same city, he would dedicate his endowed chair in a ceremony at the University of New Mexico.

Of course, Ed had a third, personal reason for his pleasure. As the U.S. Ambassador from New Mexico and who had a key role in the establishment of both the National Hispanic Cultural Center and the Endowed Chair, he had to be there. He and Cayetana would be going home! Ed always believed that New Mexico was a great place to travel to, as well as from, because it was a wonderful place to return to.

Before the trip, Ed and Cayetana decided to take an unofficial visit to Zaragoza. More than one person told them that they had to visit, indeed, pay their respects to Spain's patroness, *La Virgin del Pilar* (The Virgin of the Pillar). As had become normal for him, Ed did his research. Now, as they were driven out of Madrid, he shared his newly acquired knowledge with Cayetana.

"You know, I never realized until now where the name Pilar came from."

Cayetana laughed. "It's pretty obvious."

"Did you know?"

"No. Not really."

"And? No. Never mind. But, this is what I find interesting. She appeared to Saint James, Santiago, as he was traveling through Spain. And she told him to build a church on the spot. That if he did, many people would be converted to Christianity. She appeared to him over a pillar that, I suppose, marked the spot." Here, Ed stopped, staring out the side window at the manicured countryside.

Cayetana turned toward him. "And?" She knew that he had more to say.

"Well, think about it. She appeared to Saint James, the Apostle, before her death! This is the only account of Mother Mary's bi-location! And she came to Spain. To Zaragoza or what is today Zaragoza."

Cayetana gave Ed her doubtful look. "Are you sure? I mean before her death?"

"Yes. Father Izquierdo and others assured me."

Silence followed. Both of them were lost in their thoughts as the chauffer drove them from the central flat lands into rolling hills.

Ed could never get over Spain's many magnificent churches and cathedrals.

Zaragoza's basilica did not disappoint him. The huge church is fronted by the city's main plaza and easily is the town's most prominent and main attraction. They toured the church with a guide who explained its history, the side chapels, and "Nuestra Señora" (Our Lady). As the guide pointed out all the flags arrayed above and along the main nave, Ed looked for the Stars and Stripes. He could not find it, so he turned to the guide and asked him why the United States flag is not there.

Pages from the *In Spain English Magazine* under the title "Zaragoza Pays Tribute to Old Glory." Copy in the Ed and Cayetana Romero Collection.

U.S. Flag Honored in Zaragoza

The U.S. flag was honored at a religious ceremony held in Zaragoza last month. Ambassador and Mrs. Edward Romero, accompanied by dignitaries from Madrid and Zaragoza, attended a mass offered at the Basilica of El Pilar. At the request of the ambassador, who had visited the Basilica on a previous occasion, the American flag was finally recognized along with all the other flags from Latin American countries which have Hispanic roots. At a parade, held in the city's main square, military bands played the national anthems of both countries.

October 2000, *InSpain*

The guide looked at Ed and then the flags, then shrugged. "I don't know."

Another seed had been planted in Ed's mind. He returned to Madrid decided to telephone the Reverend Elías Yanes, the Archbishop of Zaragoza. The Archbishop was not available so Ed told his personal secretary that he would like to invite the Archbishop to dinner in the ambassador's residence.

The secretary replied without hesitation. "His excellency the Archbishop will be delighted."

Then Ed shared his concern that the flag of the United States is not included among the flags in the Basilica.

This caught the secretary off-guard. "Bueno, bueno, bueno, No sé por qué." (Well, well, well. I don't know why.)

The Archbishop showed up for dinner with a couple of other Church officials. As usual, Ed oversaw an enjoyable repast. Toward the end of dinner Ed broached the issue of no United States flag in Pilar's Basilica.

Archbishop Yanes cleared his throat. He knew the question was coming. He crossed his hands before him, "Let me explain."

"Please." Ed sat back.

"We only have flags of those countries that recognize the name Pilar."

Ed was ready. "That's the reason? I have an uncle and a female cousin named Pilar! There is a town in New Mexico named Pilar!" He pulled out a map of New Mexico that he had ready for the occasion. "There," Ed's finger pointed out Pilar, New Mexico.

Ed watched the surprised reaction of the clergy arranged around the table. They had no idea. They looked dumbfounded. Ed assured them, and for good measure, told them about New Mexico's *Penitentes*.

Around a month later, Archbishop Yanes invited Ed to attend a ceremony in Zaragoza that would place the flag of the United States in the Basilica. Ed quickly answered, "Of course! When!" The news could not have pleased Ed more.

"September thirteenth"

"Of course. I will be there."

The news that the United States Ambassador would attend the ceremony resonated. Ed became involved in the itinerary leading up to the mass and blessing of the flag that marked its "placing." He arranged for a United States Marine Corp color guard to be there. They joined the "Reign of Spain Marine Infantry" color guard to present the flags of their respective countries to Zaragoza's Mayor and to Ed. This was done on the main plaza before Ed and Cayetana went to lunch in the Mayor's official house that like, the Basilica, faces the city's main plaza.

The lunch turned out to be a large luncheon where speeches were exchanged. Mayor José Atarés talked about Spain's permanent link to the entire Hispanic-American world, and that Spain wants to be a "privileged bridge between Europe and America."

Ed explained how he became curious about his country's missing flag. "I, a United States Hispanic, along with my ancestors and millions of United States Hispanics, share with the people of Spain" a common culture and language." He noted that, "many of the most sacred institutions and symbols for Spaniards, including Our Lady of the Pilar," have been a part of the "heritage of Hispanic inhabitants in the United States...throughout the centuries." So, he continued, "I was surprised that among the flags that signify the unity of five centuries of shared culture, ours was not there."

The luncheon wrapped up per the itinerary. Ed and Cayetana were escorted out the front door of the mayor's house to be confronted with a plaza full of thousands of people who applauded them as they walked to the Basilica, where Archbishop Yanes and some other Bishops waited to greet them. In effect, the civil authorities handed them over to the Church authorities, who took them into the church in a formal procession as the organ started playing the national anthems of Spain and the United States. The Basilica was packed with standing room only for the last lucky ones to get in.

The "Principe" Felipe on his 1988 visit to the historic Palace of the Governors in Santa Fe, New Mexico. The museum's director Dr. Thomas Chávez escorted His Excellency. In the background are two museum staff members Arthur Olivas and Dr. Richard Rudisill. Felipe would become Spain's King Felipe VI. Photograph by Blair Clark. Author's collection.

The people applauded as Ed and Cayetana were escorted to their places of honor. The Archbishop officiated over mass, and during the offertory he picked up a United States flag and presented it to Ed. He then escorted Ed to the altar where he blessed the flag and then directed Ed to "present the flag" to the Virgin. Ed placed the flag at the feet of the Virgin of Pilar, a small statue standing on a pillar.

After the mass Archbishop Yanes hosted a small reception for all the dignitaries. Ed thanked His Excellency and all the people of Zaragoza. He explained again how he was surprised that the U.S. flag was not included. Happily, he winked and smiled, "Not any more."

The success with the Virgin of Pilar gave Ed special satisfaction. He had achieved

Ambssador Romero presenting the United States' flag before the Virgin of Pilar in the Cathedral of Zaragoza, September 28, 2000. From *In Spain English Magazine*, October 2000. A copy in the Ed and Cayetana Romero Collection.

something that many another an ambassador had overlooked. Only someone with his background and interest in history and heritage would have noticed the oversight and, then, had the desire to correct the situation.

The next day's newspapers pleased Ed even more. The event made national news. "Ambassador Romero takes the heritage of the United States to Pilar." The headline could not be more perfect. The accompanying text reiterated Ed's ancestry, mentioning Bartolomé Romero and Corral de Almaguer, which named him an adoptive son. Then it noted that he had been invested into the Brotherhood of Mozarabe Knights. "Thanks to him, the United States participates in the Commission of Protectors of the Royal Foundation of Toledo, whose goal is the preservation of the city's patrimony." Then the media quoted Ed from his speech at the luncheon. Ed, the news reported, stated that recognition of the connections between Spain and the United States is important because in the United States, "Hispanics influence all aspects of society as they occupy more key positions in universities, the government, and the private sector," which should enrich of both Spain and the United States. He reported that within the next decade, "there will be more Spanish speakers in the United States than in Spain." This last statement rose more than a few eyebrows.

The Pilar story had been a complete success. Ed could not help but have a glass of wine to celebrate privately. A glass of wine was about all he had time for. Suddenly, or so it seemed to him, Ed realized that his tenure as United States Ambassador to Spain soon would be coming to a close. A new President of the United States would be elected in a little more than a month and will take office in January. Even given some time while the new President pondered over Ed's replacement, Ed realized that he had less than a year left. He did not have time to waste.

Besides, the Principe's pending trip to New Mexico was coming up even faster than the election. Ed needed to help with the arrangements and this meant constant contact with the Royal House as well as with key people in the United States, especially in New Mexico. The Prince would keynote ceremonies at the National Hispanic Cultural Center and the University of New Mexico.

The National Hispanic Cultural Center had completed the construction of two buildings, renovated another, and created a "plaza mayor." The staff moved in that summer. Still, the dream was a work in process. When a friend suggested that the Instituto Cervantes be housed at the Center and not in New Mexico's capital city of Santa Fe, as many sought, the idea resonated with Ed, for he already was thinking in that direction. With Vice President Alvarez Cascos's help, the Spanish government placed the Instituto Cervantes at the National Hispanic Cultural Center in Albuquerque.

Now the Prince could participate in the formal inauguration of the Center and extol the virtues of the Instituto Cervantes being established in New Mexico. As Honorary Chairman of the Center's foundation and an official representative of the government of Spain that operated the Instituto Cervantes, His Highness perfectly fit the occasion.

Then the Prince had another more recent reason for his visit to New Mexico, the fully funded Prince of Asturias Chair for Information Technology. Felipe could make the announcement at the University and Ed would be there for all of it.

Like his father King Juan Carlos I, and his mother, Queen Sofía, the Prince knew New Mexico. Queen Sofía first visited the southwestern state when she was a young teenaged Greek princess. Later, as the Queen of Spain, she joined her husband on an official state visit in 1987. The Royal Couple planted a cottonwood tree in the courtyard of the historic, almost four centuries old, Palace of the Governors in Santa Fe. The old building had become New Mexico's state history museum. The museum's staff pleasantly surprised the Queen with a framed photograph of her during her first visit.

Prince Felipe followed his parents with a subsequent visit to New Mexico. Given a tour of the same museum, he was escorted onto Santa Fe's plaza where a couple of thousand people waited to see him and hear his speech. The applause that startled him as he walked out of the museum's door is a memory he will never forget.

Ed knew of both earlier Royal visits. As a community leader he was there. Years before his ambassadorial appointment, Ed helped Arturo Ortega to successfully solicit the Prince's permission to name him Honorary Chair of the Hispanic Culture Foundation. Then, as ambassador, Ed as well as Cayetana developed a deep appreciation for the Royal Family. The Royal Family returned the same feelings for Ed and Cayetana, as well as for their New Mexico.

Ed could not help but be excited for his return to New Mexico. He could not wait to hear the Prince's words. Ed was confident that the whole visit would be triumphant for everyone involved.

Perhaps unknowingly influenced by Ed's tenure in Spain, the media gave the Prince's visit to New Mexico front-page coverage replete with photographs. It seemed as if Spain's media had become fascinated with New Mexico. The newspapers ran illustrations and photographs of the NHCC. They described its architecture in detail,

"Built in a mixture of styles, from Herrerian to Mesoamerican, with some Alhambresque details and others from the Mayan culture." The press mentioned that 56 million dollars had been spent creating the NHCC, and the media could not overlook the opening of the prestigious Instituto Cervantes. Over sixty such sites existed throughout the world and Albuquerque's opening was the third such center in the United States. The news noted that previously in the United States only New York and Chicago had an Instituto Cervantes.

The newspapers again quoted Ed and his now repeated words about the historically mutual connections between New Mexico, the United States, and Spain. He also said that the Prince of Asturias Chair would help the University of New Mexico, "remain a leader in the scientific world community."

Felipe's words made news as well. He lauded New Mexico and its people for the deep Spanish roots that he could see, for maintaining the Spanish language through the centuries, and for preserving its ties with Spain. In talking about the Chair he said that in New Mexico, "The small adobe bricks placed by those Spanish pioneers have been transformed into high technology research centers." He added that Spanish people, "should have the leading role that they deserve in the information society, Spain is prepared." As he concluded his speech, His Excellency added, "I have to say that to a large extent the Chair was born thanks to the initiative and vision of our dear friend Ambassador Ed Romero."

Perhaps more importantly, the headlines surpassed even those about the installation of the U.S. flag in Saragossa, "Don Felipe inaugurated in New Mexico the Major Center for the Dispersal of Hispanic Culture." "Prince Felipe inaugurates the Major Spanish Center in the United States." "Science and Technology Ought to Be Put to the Goal of a New Moral Conscience: Don Felipe Inaugurates a Chair in His Name at the University of New Mexico."

New Mexico's media covered the Prince's visit with the same fervor. However, the news was hardly mentioned in the national press of the United States. Ed had planted more than a seed in Spain. However, much more work needed to be done in the United States.

Spain is known for Flamenco and bullfighting. The country has exported the former—New Mexico has become a major center of flamenco starting with Ruben Romero and María Benitez in Santa Fe and then with Clarita and Eva Encinias at the University of New Mexico, which is the only university in the world that teaches both guitar and dance in the art form. On the other hand, bullfighting, considered by devotees an art form and not a sport, has been exported with mixed results. Only a couple of Latin American countries, most notably Mexico, regularly schedule *corridas* (bullfights). Bullfighting has its origins in the Mediterranean world with the Greeks and Romans, and it took root in the Iberian Peninsula.

Bullfighting had become controversial in Spain. Traditionalists and non-traditionalists divided society. Some cities and regions of the country outlawed the "art form." The *corridas* remained a tourist attraction, while the bull ranches and many subsidiary businesses benefit.

Ed had become a fan of the bullfights before he became an ambassador. In addition he liked Flamenco. For a time, his son-in-law and daughter, Christina, had a restaurant in Washington, DC that featured Flamenco. After his son-in-law died in a traffic accident, Christina kept the restaurant while her sister Ruth managed the business.

As Ambassador, Ed became a fan of Julián López, nicknamed "El Juli," one of Spain's premier *toreadores* (bullfighters). At the same time, Ed became a member of Club Amigos de la Boina (The Friends of the Beret Club), a group that informally met the last Monday of each month for good conversation.

Soon after his trip to New Mexico, Ed asked his brethren in the club if he could, "put the beret on El Juli?" Of course, there were no formalities, for the club invites all for casual conversation. Thus, on November 27, 2000, the last Monday of that month Ed inducted Julián López into the club.

On Tuesday, the next day, the Presidential results in the United States solidified Ed's fate in Spain. He would leave soon, because George W. Bush, a Republican, had won. In accordance with protocol Ed submitted his letter of resignation. At the same time he knew that it would take time for his replacement to be named and go through the required vetting process. Ed asked Senator Domenici to ask the White House to let him stay in his position until the new ambassador would be ready to assume the post. The permission was granted and Ed knew that he had a few months left and he would make the most of them.

LOVE AND TRAVEL OF THE ROUND TRIP
March 2001, Madrid

Ed had some unfinished business with the bullfighting industry. Through some negotiations, he arranged a unique event at the Embassy. The press reported that the United States Embassy opened its doors to the bullfights for the first time in its history. Ed managed to secure permission to award the "prize" to the winner of the Brihuega spring *corridas*. He would host an important and public annual event, and the recipient of last spring's *corridas* was none other than Ed's friend, El Juli.

Hosting the event was a coup. But Ed was not through, for, at the ceremony, he personally handed over the trophy and admitted that he was "a great aficionado and follower of El Juli." In exchange, the *toreador* surprised Ed by presenting him with the cape that he used the afternoon of his confirmation in Madrid's Las Ventas bullring.

Then, with Ed standing next to them, officials announced next spring's Brihuega fights. They named the three *toreadores* selected to fight, as well as the ranch (*finca*) that was chosen to provide the bulls.

The media covered the event. The papers ran photographs of Ed, the U.S. Ambassador presenting the award to El Juli, as well as a broadly smiling Ed holding the cape that El Juli had just given to him. They did not overlook Ed's stated affection for the bullfights. Meanwhile, an animal rights group protested the event off site.

The story could have been controversial, but the reaction was opposite, at least, in the press. Here was another outward demonstration of Ed's love of all things Spanish that endeared Ed to the Spanish populace. Once again, he broke new ground and from the Spanish point-of-view it was all good.

Ed would find out later that a Romero in Spain is considered the father of modern

Francisco Goya, "Portrait of the Matador (bullfighter) Pedro Romero," c. 1795-98.
Oil on canvas, unframed 84.1 x 65 cm., AP 1966.12.
Courtesy of the Kimbell Art Museum, Fort Worth, Texas.

bullfighting. In the 16th century King Felipe II, the same king who granted permission for Oñate to settle New Mexico, had a center for training horsemanship in Ronda. Bulls were used in the training at the Real Meastranza de Callaría. One day, an aristocrat fell from his horse and Francisco Romero saved the terrified man by using his hat to distract the bull.

A cape quickly replaced the hat as the tool of distraction, and bullfighting took on a new method. That was the beginning but it was Francisco's grandson, Pedro Romero, who developed all the passes and moves that to this day are used in the bullfights. Pedro fought into his eighties, and retired after killing more than five thousand six hundred bulls without ever being hurt. Today, Ronda hosts an annual Feria Goyesca de Pedro

Romero in the first week of September. Francisco de Goya is associated with Pedro Romero for a portrait that he painted of the famous bullfighter.

The news of the pending end to Ed's term became common knowledge, and the Spanish began to react. It probably began with a March 4th newspaper interview that a relaxed, maybe too relaxed, Ed gave with María Eugenia Yaqüe.

An introductory paragraph noted that Ed was leaving, and that he, "has been like a fish in water in our country." The paragraph continued that his heritage beginning in Corral de Almaguer, "helped him do his job better."

Then came a number of questions and his answers, the few of which lent them to the headline. Yaqüe asked Ed if Americans would accept a woman like Hillary Clinton in the White House?

Ed flippantly answered, "Not only Mrs. Clinton. There are very many and very strong women in the United States." Then, the relaxed Ed smiled and added in jest, "Women demand a lot, they control us."

Yaqüe quickly followed up. "Who is the boss in the Embassy?"

And Ed did not hesitate. He smiled as his face lit up and replied, "My wife, of course."

The interview ran under the headline, *"Las mujeres mandan mucho, nos controlan"* (Women command a lot, they control us). Lost in it all was Ed's thoughtful responses about the environment, his feelings for Spain, what Americans think about Spain, Spanish food, the diversity of American culture, and, "the importance of the Latino world in the United States, and the deep roots that we have in Spain."

Ed Romero being presented with the Grand Cross of Queen Isabel the Catholic from King Juan Carlos and Queen Sofia in the Spanish embassy in Washington, DC Ed and Cayetana Romero Collection.

Soon after, Ed was called to Washington, DC to attend a ceremony at the Spanish Embassy. The King and Queen, while visiting a number of cities in the United States, wanted Ed at the Spanish embassy where on March 29th they decorated him with the order of the "Grand Cross of the Order of Isabel the Catholic." Ed's friend, Father Lezama, attended the formal ceremony. Once again, Ed made history.

Ed and Cayetana returned to Spain where a month later he was named Knight of the Sacred and Military Constantinean Order of Saint George. The honors had piled up and Ed appreciated every one, but there was something left undone, a personal matter. He had gone to Corral de Almaguer many times. His connection to the town was well known. On the other hand, he had not visited Maqueda, the birthplace of Bartolomé Romero's wife, Luisa Robledo López.

Pedro Izquierdo, who was busily compiling Ed's family history as well as a history of his ambassadorship, told Ed that Maqueda had been a Jewish center. This, of course, raised questions in Ed's mind. Ed had a book that posited that it was Luisa's family that took the La Macana statue to New Mexico. Still, he wondered, could he be a distant ancestor of a Jew from Maqueda? It would not be unusual.

Cayetana and Ed had to visit Maqueda while he still was an ambassador. Such a visit would mean more to the people there. After no little effort, Ed rearranged his schedule, and on May 3, 2001, he and Cayetana once again sat in the back seat of the smooth-running embassy Cadillac as they headed south toward Maqueda in the province of Toledo.

Maqueda's mayor and parish priest welcomed them and took them to a restaurant for a traditional regional meal. Then, they were given a tour of the ancient city, parts of which the Robledos would have known before they left for the Americas. The Church of Santa María de los Alcázares is an important Middle Ages church. Maqueda's majestic rectangular castle could not help but stimulate Ed's imagination. He had to ask about Maqueda's traditional celebrations. "Yes, Maqueda has 'Moors and Christians' like New Mexico." Also, Maqueda celebrates Easter Week with a reenactment of the Living Passion of the Lord.

Ed and Cayetana had a very enjoyable day. Their only regret was that they had not done it earlier, for they could have done more, like they did with Corral de Almaguer.

This was even more evident three days later in Corral de Almaguer, as they attended a formal mass in Ed's honor presided over by the Archbishop of Valencia. Their friends, Fathers Lezama and Izquierdo, along with four parish priests, assisted with the good-bye mass. Many of Corral's residents attended because they wanted to demonstrate the affection that they had for Ed.

After mass, the attendees went to a popular restaurant for a reception. In a moving speech, Ed said good-bye to, "my Corral brothers, my friends." He spoke of how he returned to Corral, "after four hundred years." All his ancestors, he mused, must be, "smiling upon seeing another son of Corral, as he leaves for the United States a second time." But those smiles are accompanied with tears, "of sadness but also pride, knowing that they established the new life they went to establish, that the round-trip has ended. It is complete." He called himself, "a son of this land," and thanked the people of Corral for, "being a part of our lives." Both Ed and Cayetana knew that they would return.

Father Izquierdo's research had a special secondary purpose beyond compiling Ed's story. The process to bestow on Ed and his descendants a personal Heraldic Coat of Arms was completed. Pedro handed Ed a preliminary report and hinted, "we are very close."

Ed Romero's Coat of Arms. Original in the Ed and Cayetana Romero Collection.

Pedro understated the situation. Four days later at 10:00 a.m., he hurried to the offices of the Arms King Chronicler. There, as Ed's representative, he was presented with a leather folder with a gold Royal Coat of Arms on the front cover. The folder contained the King's and Minister of Justice's approval for Ed Romero's personal coat of arms. The documents were sealed with luxurious ink and paper seals as in the old days.

Pedro was as proud as Ed over this achievement. He had put together and received approval of the documentation that resulted in the award. He even had a hand in the design of the coat of arms. Pedro took the treasured folder from the Arms King Chronicler, thanked him, and rushed directly to the U.S. embassy.

Pedro handed the elegant folder to Ed, and then watched as Ed opened it to see the elegant documents, five pages with proper signatures and appropriate seals. The color rendition of Ed's new coat of arms stood out. Ed stared at the mostly gold and red image. He said nothing. He did not know what to think.

Pedro broke the silence and asked if he could explain the symbolism. Ed was anxious to learn and Pedro went ahead. He told Ed that the coat of arms reflects him and his most recent accomplishment of returning to the land of his ancestors.

Portrait of Edward Romero by Leo Neufeld done on the occasion of being named Notable New Mexican for 2003 by The Albuquerque Museum Board of Directors. Oil on linen. Collection of the Albuquerque Museum Foundation.

The colors are Spain's colors as well as those of New Mexico. The knight's helmet, which is turned to its side indicates royalty but not from the direct line of the Royal family. In this case, it refers to Ed's entitlement as a *hidalgo*, the rank of nobility that automatically was conferred upon his direct ancestor Bartolomé and all his descendants. The standing lion, "*Leon Rampante*," signifies Toledo, the province from whence his ancestors originated, and the bundle of rosemary is a direct reference to the surname Romero, which in translation means rosemary. The pilgrim's staff refers to the words on the shield's border that note Ed's personal pilgrimage. Also, another definition of "*romero*" is "pilgrim." The red border contains words in gold and they are a direct reference to Ed's story. The words read, *"Amor y Viaje de Ida y Vuelta"* (Love and Travel of the Round Trip).

Pedro told him that he thought Ed was the first person outside of Spain to be so honored, and that it only happened because King Juan Carlos I wanted it so. Ed could not be more pleased.

Three days later, when Ed received the Great Cross of Justice and was admitted in the Order of Saint Lazarus, he was still reeling from his Coat of Arms. Here was a personal accomplishment that honored both him and all his New Mexican ancestors. Moreover, it was a visual representation that Spain had accepted him as one of their own.

Now, he had nothing much left to do but prepare for his departure. It seemed like only yesterday when he changed into his blue suit and gave his first speech at Barajas Airport. Now, it all culminated with a farewell party in the embassy gardens. Ed ate barbeque, toasted, hugged, and enjoyed the music and dance performances.

Again, he thanked everyone for their care and for the wonderful experience that he, Cayetana, and his family had experienced. He added that all he really wanted to do was, "to contribute to a better understanding of Spain by Americans and then for them to love Spain as much as I love it, and for Spaniards to understand and love my country more."

Ed really meant what he said. Beyond his own experience, he reflected on what the experience had on his children, especially Steve and Adam, who spent of good deal of time with Ed and Cayetana in Spain. Then, there was a very special opportunity when Bud and his wife Jean brought Ed's mother to spend a month with him in the ambassador's residence. He smiled at the thought of her asking for, "Leroy, where's Leroy?" then insisting on interrupting whatever business he was doing or meeting he was in. She openly took credit with anyone who would listen, that "Leroy owes it all to me. I got him interested in politics." After she flew back to the States with Ed, she commented, "This is the longest train ride I have ever taken." Ed's sister, Betsy never made it to Spain, while Randy and his son Andres did visit.

There was one last official act. King Juan Carlos I and Queen Sofia invited them to their residence to say goodbye, and something unusual happened at the meeting. The Queen took Cayetana by the hand and led her away to another room, leaving the King and Ed to their own conversation. When they finally left the royal residence, Ed asked Cayetana what went on with the Queen, "What was all that about?"

Cayetana gave Ed a whimsical smile and replied, "The Queen wanted to know why the people of Spain love me so much."

El Buen Americano,
May 2003, Madrid

In early 2003, three years after Ed had left Spain, a writer for *ABC* in Madrid learned that now ex-ambassador Edward Romero had been named a "Notable New Mexican." Ed and Cayetana returned to their hometown of Albuquerque with great fanfare. Already well known in their home state, his three-year stint in the diplomatic corps in Spain added a luster to his persona that New Mexicans, many of them descendent from Spaniards of centuries past, admired with an almost surreal devotion.

The New Mexican Hispanic Culture Preservation League showered him with admiration and named him "Hidalgo," their designation for their annual award that honored an individual who demonstrated a commitment to Hispanic preservation. At the banquet, Ed played to the audience as he stood at the podium bedecked with the ribbons and medals bestowed upon him by various Spanish organizations. "This is why I like these occasions," he began, in his understated way, "I get to wear all my medals." He broke into a broad smile as the audience reacted with laughter, followed by applause. He was proud, if not still a little overwhelmed. His ambassadorship seemed like a dream, but the reality of it constantly came to the fore through his continued friendships with the many people he met in Spain.

It did not take long for the Albuquerque Museum of Art and History to join in praise of Ed. The institution's board of directors, led by Thelma Domenici, the senator's sister, named him Notable New Mexican for 2003. This, too, was another source of satisfaction for Ed. Three-time governor Bruce King, and Wilson Hurly, a famous New Mexican artist, had been named before him. One of the requirements of this honor mandated that Ed sit for an official portrait that would hang in perpetuity in the museum's main hallway.

So Ed fidgeted through two sittings in his living room. At once fascinated and bored, he patiently suffered the process. Then came the banquet, which was a black tie affair, the men in tuxedos and the women exceedingly beautiful and elegant. Some eight hundred people poured into the museum for the festivities. They milled and talked at a preliminary cocktail party before attending the sit down banquet, where they watched and applauded Ed's induction. Friends from Colorado and California attended. New Mexico Congresswoman Heather Wilson, and Congressman Ed Pastor, from Arizona, along with newly elected New Mexico governor, Bill Richardson, made sure to be there. Albuquerque's mayor, Martin Chávez, another of Ed's candidates, also attended the event.

The induction reached in faraway Madrid, where ABC's Antonio Sáenz de Miera used the occasion to write about him as, "el buen Americano."

"Ed Romero," he wrote, "breaks stereotypes of what people think about America, the United States. At a time of war in Iraq, when people are burning and desecrating the U.S. flag, people become one dimensional and prejudicial. But when confronted with attitudes and people in the flesh, such stereotypes and biases begin to dissipate."

"This," he continued, "is Ed Romero. Ed is one of those Americans that we like to consider one of 'ours' because, of his openness to the world and his freedom of thought, for his simultaneous historic and critical optimism, for his tolerance and for his pragmatic vision of life and history..."and "also because of those Hispanic roots he celebrates and has cultivated in his fruitful mission as U.S. Ambassador to Spain." Now he has taken his "tireless...construction of transatlantic relations" to reverse his efforts and "has opened a promising door for our common language via the Instituto Cervantes and the creation of the National Hispanic Cultural Center in Albuquerque. He sees the need to reinforce the Spanish language in New Mexico, a place where it has been spoken and heard for centuries."

Sáenz de Miera noted that Ed's portrait deservedly hangs on the museum walls with other illustrious New Mexicans. Praise and banquets aside, his portrait will remain: Ed Romero, bedecked in the sash of Isabel the Catholic that the King of Spain conferred upon him, with the Romero family coat of arms that he received from the same King.

The article concludes with a reference to rosemary, the plant that in Spanish is *romero*, *"Romero solo rosemary"* (Rosemary [is] only rosemary) "...a good American, one of ours, was once here in Spain, an Ambassador and the smell of rosemary remains."

The article in praise of Ed appeared in one of Spain's two largest newspapers. It was a unique and unabashed article in praise of a former U.S. ambassador, a first in the Spanish press.

LAURELS ASIDE, POLITICS ANEW
2003, Santa Fe, New Mexico

Nothing about Ed would give him leave to rest on his laurels. Even as Cayetana's health remained tenuous, her strength and admiration for him equaled his upbringing, indeed his heritage. As soon as he returned he jumped into New Mexico politics and became a key fundraiser for Bill Richardson, who was running for governor. Ed truly considered Richardson a person who would benefit his home state. So, Ed became a tireless worker for a man who was a tireless campaigner, and they succeeded.

As a result, Ed found himself an organizer and sometimes spokesman for the new administration. His influence became obvious even during the inauguration when Richardson took the oath of office inside the historic Palace of the Governors in Santa Fe. After Ed swore in the new governor, Ed took advantage of the opportunity to offer a toast. He raised his glass as the noisy multiple conversations gave way to an anticipatory silence. "Tonight we celebrate the beginning of the Bill Richardson era," he raised his glass a little higher and added, "the first governor to take an oath of office in this building since statehood." Ed knew the historic significance of the old adobe structure that was once part of the original "royal houses" built during the second decade of the seventeenth century.

In an interview at Santa Fe's El Dorado Hotel the night before, Ed was asked why this election was unique. He quickly answered that, "Diane Denish will become the first female lieutenant governor, and Richardson will be the first governor to take an oath of office in the Palace of the Governors since statehood." Ed did not miss an opportunity, even up to having one of Richardson's first "meet and greets" at the National Hispanic Cultural Center.

As much as it could, life settled back to normalcy for Ed. Later that same year, he accepted an invitation to sit on the Board of Directors for the Bank of America. Two national business magazines listed him as one of the more important Latinos in the country. He even delved into national politics again when he accepted an invitation to "head" the presidential campaign in New Mexico for Wesley Clark, a popular retired four-star general. Ed explained that he would advise Clark on veteran affairs, and lead the candidate's outreach efforts to the business community as well as to political leaders in New Mexico.

Ramona Pacheco, happy at ninety-two years old. Ed and Cayetana Romero Collection.

Richardson proved to be immensely popular during his first term. His election to a second term was a given. The governor named Ed to be a co-chair of his fifty person transitional team that split into five subgroups, one of which Ed chaired. They were charged to evaluate Richardson's administration and his second term agenda.

Even before Ed could administer the governor's second term oath of office at a private, mid-night ceremony in the governor's mansion, Ed received a call from Martin Chávez, who had started to organize a "group of mayors and other local officials to back Richardson for President." Since the Clark campaign had failed, Ed was free. However, he had one obstacle. Hillary Clinton also planned to run for president. Ed had an obvious attachment to the Clintons.

Nevertheless, in keeping with his long held attitude that home came first, he agreed to back "his governor and friend." Bill Clinton understood. Besides, Ed added, "Richardson would be very successful. He's just a popular guy."

Although not obvious at first, the governor's popularity had begun to wane, especially in New Mexico. Rumors of corruption grew into Federal investigations. The governor's methods rubbed some people wrong, even in his own party. Even, Ed, for unknown reasons, found himself on Richardson's bad side for a while.

Richardson's presidential campaign failed, never surpassing single digit support in any state primary election. Eventually, his financial support dried up and he ran out of funds.

As politicians like to say, Ed could read the tealeaves. He knew that Richardson would drop out soon, so he was not surprised when it happened. He pretended to be unaware when Martin Chávez called him to break the news. Richardson, Chávez revealed, would hold a press conference the next day.

Then, came a telephone call from Bill Clinton. "Ed, as you know," Clinton always assumed that Ed was smarter than he sometimes let on and announced, "Bill is dropping out tomorrow."

Ed could not resist. "Mr. President, don't ask me to support Hillary."

"What?"

Ed had the former President right where he wanted him. Now came the punch line. "You don't have to ask. Please permit me to fervently tell you how much I have wanted to support her since day one."

Ed always felt that he needed to endorse or back someone immediately, give a yes or no answer, or say, "I am committed." That is better than reply with, "I'll think about it. That gets you into trouble."

As it turned out, none of the three presidential candidates Ed supported won.

GRIEF IS THE PRICE OF LOVE
June 2011, Albuquerque, New Mexico

Ed kept a photograph of his mother that was taken late in her life. She is seated in an outdoor patio in the village of Chimayó. Her hands are clasped together and held up. She is looking up smiling, maybe laughing. Her round, joyous face is an image embedded in Ed's mind.

She survived Isaac by a little more than twenty-eight years, and was ninety-four years old when she died on January 8, 2000. Ed was still in Spain as ambassador at the time, but rushed back to attend her funeral and burial in Alamosa next to Isaac. Family mattered. Even after his return to New Mexico, with all the accolades and rewards, Ed remained dedicated to his family and friends. He missed his mother as well as his father.

Now he thought about himself and Cayetana. How long would they be remembered when their time came. He wondered about the research that Pedro Izquierdo was doing.

Pedro had collected newspaper clippings, researched and written historical snapshots about Oñate, Corral de Almaguer, La Macana, among other things pertinent to Ed's personal and familial history. Ed decided that he wanted something written in English, something that would be of benefit to other New Mexicans, especially the youth. So, he hired a historian to write a family history beginning with Bartolomé. Because Ed had paid for his genealogy to be done, that, along with Pedro's work, would be a strong foundation of information. The historian began to use his own resources as well. He wrote two chapters of Ed's early family history, and then stopped. He submitted a budget that was more than Ed wanted to pay. Besides the narrative, at least as written so far, leaned too heavily on genealogy. It was not what Ed envisioned, so he sought and commissioned a second historian.

Ed wanted his author to meet Pedro. Together they could compare notes, exchange information, and strike up a professional friendship. The whole idea really appealed to Ed.

Then, while driving on a clear, late-morning Albuquerque, New Mexico day in June, Ed's plans were interrupted when his cell phone buzzed.

"Hello."

"Ambassador, this is Antonio Macheño."

What a surprise! He had not spoken to the mayor of Corral de Almaguer for a while. "Antonio! *Qué tal?*"

"I have bad news," he continued without hesitating, "Pedro died."

"Oh no! When?"

"This afternoon," Ed quickly calculated that it was around 7:00 p.m. in Spain as they talked, "someone from the family probably is trying to contact you."

"Thanks for calling, Antonio. I am in my car and need to get home to tell Tanna. We'll talk later."

As Ed drove home he thought about his friend Pedro. No one visited Ed at the embassy more than Pedro. Then, after his ambassadorship ended, he and Pedro managed to get together every time Ed returned to Spain. Pedro constantly kept Ed updated on his research and on the information he was gathering. When Ed's son, Steve and his Spanish wife, Pepa, had a son Pedro baptized the infant. They named him Eduard Cayetano, to be called Cayetano.

Ed constantly invited Pedro to New Mexico, but Pedro refused, always adding that he would go after his father dies. The always conscientious and caring Pedro could not leave his ninety-five year old father under the care of anyone but himself.

During these last months, Ed knew that his friend was sick. Initially, Ed did not realize the gravity of the illness. When he talked with Pedro, the priest always insisted that he was fine, and, at least on one occasion reminded Ed that he wanted to go to New Mexico, "the day my father dies." He never mentioned that he had cancer, which he knew for at least the last two months of his life. Even toward the end, when he let himself to be committed into a convent under the care of nuns, he insisted that he was doing fine.

Ed, of course, telephoned regularly. Antonio told him, "Pedro is very sick but not fatally so." Then, Sister Ana María, who became Pedro's primary care giver, said as a matter of fact that, "Father Izquierdo is going to die." Pedro's brother, Adolfo, could only let on that, "he is really bad."

Steve, who was in Spain at the time, went to visit Pedro who mistook him for Ed. Steve reported the same dire prognosis. Things did not look good. Ed sent flowers, and Sister Ana María related that when the flowers arrived, a weakened Pedro looked at them and said, "*Mi hermano* (my brother)."

Now he was gone. Ed looked at Cayetana, who returned the look with a studied face. "I need to go there. Be there for him."

Cayetana said nothing. She let Ed continue his thought process. "I'll call Adolfo."

Ed pulled out his cell phone and speed dialed the number. Adolfo answered. Ed expressed his condolences then said that he would get there as soon as possible.

Adolfo immediately replied, "No. Do not come. He will be buried before you get here. There is no sense..."

"But we were close, I need to..."

"You were like his brother."

"We were brothers."

"We know, we know. Do not worry. Stay home. We understand. There is nothing that you can do here."

"*Bueno,* okay."

Adolfo later told Ed that he had Pedro's papers, results of his research, gathered in a couple of boxes. He would hold onto them until Ed could pick them up.

Both Ed and Cayetana felt the ache of sorrow over Pedro's death. They, too, had a renewed sense of mortality. This highlighted their realization of their own respective ages and health. Cayetana's health remained delicate. Their thoughts raced back and forth from the good memories of Pedro to wondering about themselves. Cayetana wanted to make sure that her beloved Ed would be remembered positively. With an inward sense of urgency, she quietly began to organize all of Ed's news clippings, letters, and other ephemera that she had been collecting over the years. As she became permanently attached to oxygen bottles and had to use a newly installed mechanical seat that transported her up and down their stairway, she tirelessly organized an archive of themed binders. She made sure to introduce Ed's historian to her work. Then, she wrote a short overview for any future researcher to read and use. In six single-spaced pages she wrote of her life with Ed. She referred to the different notebooks of her archive in the narrative. She gave it the title, "Ed, Love of My Life," and followed that with a quote from Robert Browning, "Come, grow old with me, the best is yet to come..."

She included a photograph of her and Ed, but not satisfied, she attached a cover page that features a casually clad Ed, and in her handwriting above that image she wrote the words, "God's Greatest Blessing to me!"

Unknown to Ed, Cayetana prepared in another way. She surveyed her possessions to determine what she wanted to hand down to each of her children. She went through her jewelry, ceramic figurines, family heirlooms, etc. Then, she photographed each item and made sheets that listed each item with its photograph, and with a letter that signified the first name of her children. She wanted the designated child to receive that item. Ed had no idea that she had done this.

He knew that her health was failing, but Cayetana kept up a positive attitude. Only once did she complain about the oxygen hose constantly attached to her. She was outside with her grandchildren who wanted to play with her, and she emotionally and sorrowfully exclaimed, "What can I do with this on me? I can't hold them." She continued to listen to music, which she loved. She also loved the Catholic mass, "All masses are beautiful, some more beautiful than others." She had the faith of her mother and, while she did not study the Bible, she liked the Beatitudes. She liked that fact that they were not negative. She had a positive personality, even as her health failed.

Her outlook could not be truer during her favorite season at Christmas. She loved nothing more than to have the whole family together, her son and her daughters and all the grandchildren. Yes, as always, they made tamales. And the house with its high ceilings, prominent fireplace, and staircase with a room-long indoor balcony (all of which Cayetana designed) lent itself to Christmas decorations to match the occasion.

For Christmas of 2012 the family gathered. They laughed and teased, listened to Christmas music, exchanged gifts, ate and drank, and loved one another. Then, the family pitched in after Christmas to take down the tree and pack all the Christmas decorations and lights for another year. This year, however, was different.

Still enjoying the interplay of her family as they put the house into order, Cayetana suddenly felt tired. She excused herself to go up to the master bedroom where she lay down to take a nap on her favorite chair, a kind of love seat with plenty of room to put her feet up.

But she did not sleep. Instead she asked Ed to call everyone up to her. Surrounded by the family, Cayetana asked to be taken to the hospital. She could tell that the time had come. The doctors confirmed her feelings. She was committed to Albuquerque's Presbyterian Hospital Hospice. Cayetana always knew more than everyone around her.

Her strength permeated the others, especially Ed. There was nothing or no one that he loved more than Tanna, his life's partner. He stood strong with his family—at least, outwardly.

He talked with long-time friends who had suffered similar losses. He told them that his Tanna was in hospice. They all talked of inner strength and faith. Sadly, Ed found out that his old friend, Fabian Chávez, was unable to talk as he too was in hospice in Santa Fe.

Cayetana did not fear death. She had been close to it before. She had prepared. When she called for a priest to receive the last rights and then wanted to confess, Ed wondered, what does she have to confess?" He knew the answer. "Nothing."

Less concerned about herself, on one occasion she asked her children, "How's dad doing."

"He's doing fine."

She gave a weak smile. "I am so proud of him."

Cayetana said her good-byes nobly. She called into her room her children and grandchildren one by one. Ed was the last to go in. "Ed, we have accomplished what God set us out to do. We have raised wonderful children and grandchildren. I want to go."

Ed had a bed moved into her room and placed it next to her's. He would not leave her. On the last night, he leaned over to her and said, "Honey, I love you." He kissed her and lay down next to her, holding her hand. Ed felt like he was asleep but he heard his daughter, Ruth, say, "Dad, mom's not breathing." He wasn't asleep and she passed with him next to her holding his hand. The sun had not risen on the morning of Saturday, January 19, 2013. Ed later learned that his friend Fabián died within hours of Cayetana's passing.

Later that week, as extended family and friends gathered and sent in condolences, Ed received a card from David Pacheco, a first cousin in Colorado, who wrote, "Ed, grief is the price of love."

NEVER TO FORGET AND ANOTHER RETURN TO SPAIN
May, 2014, Albuquerque, New Mexico

Even the idea that he could wake up for another day gave Ed pause for thought. Tanna is gone, and he must go on without her. Fortunately, his family gathered around him. Steve, who had taken a job in Texas, moved back to Albuquerque.

For the most part, Ed handled his grief very well. But, inwardly, he longed for her. He marveled at each day, that another day could dawn without Cayetana. Life continued, and Ed, who inwardly vowed never to forget her, soon realized that it would be impossible to lose her memory. She lived in him and in their children. Yes, she had raised a wonderful family and, as she wanted, Ed would enjoy them to the fullest.

Ed returned to his many activities, only now, as his historian interviewed him, or he agreed to work with the Clinton foundation, or as he attended a University of New Mexico sporting event, he sensed urgency. In short, whether he realized it or not, he devoted the rest of his life to make her proud.

Still, as he made every effort to be positive, there were memorials, correspondence, and all the well-intended words of condolences. All this reminded him of his cousin's words about the price of love.

Ironically, the death of a friend's wife helped Ed to deal with the loss of Cayetana. Ed and Joe Reyes had become friends back in the sixties. At that time they worked in the same circles.

Five months after Cayetana's death, Joe's wife passed away. Ed knew what his friend was going through. He flew to Washington, DC to attend her funeral in Bethesda, Maryland. Joe wanted to talk with Ed, and the first thing out of his mouth was the very question Ed had asked for months. "How do you deal with this?"

Ed truthfully answered, "Joe, I don't know."

Before they parted, they agreed to stay in touch and do something together. They had become soul mates. And the idea of doing something together became a key to Ed's healing. In his grief, he could not see himself traveling back to Spain without Cayetana. He had received more than a few invitations to return, not the least of which was Father Luis Lezama's desire to arrange a memorial mass for Cayetana. Ed could not make himself go to the country he loved without her. Spain and Cayetana could not be separated.

Yet, Joe provided an opening. He, too, suffered for the same reason. Then, while he was talking to a friend about Cayetana, Ed's face lit up. He stopped the conversation and picked up his phone and called Joe.

"Hey, Joe. Ed. How about you and I go to Spain?"

"Spain?"

"Yeah. We'll rent a driver and go to Semana Santa in Seville."

Joe agreed, and in April of 2014 Ed met Joe in New York and together they flew to Madrid. From there they took Spain's rapid train, the AVE, to Seville where Ed arranged for Cristóbal, his former chauffer at the embassy, to meet them. Ed knew that Cristóbal would not only drive them wherever they wanted, but he would make an excellent as well as informed companion.

Ed enjoyed showing Joe around Seville and sharing the city's famous activities of Holy Week. They stayed at the relatively recently opened Judería, a hotel that renovated a city block of old buildings in what was once a Jewish neighborhood. Now, those old buildings had been melded into one big maze of a hotel with odd passageways and hidden patios. Ed could not help but recall the first time he came to Semana Santa in Seville. The daughter of his friend, who he had hired to write his family history escorted him and Cayetana.

The three men left Seville for Portugal. While there the United States Ambassador to Spain telephoned to invite them to dinner in Madrid. Ed could not disappoint Ambassador James Costas, so they rearranged their schedule and drove directly to Madrid, where the ambassador treated them royally.

Dinners and touring aside, Ed had some business to do. He arranged a meeting with Prince Felipe. Ed wanted to update the Prince about the endowed chair at the University of New Mexico, and about the status of the National Hispanic Cultural Center. More importantly, Ed carried letters ranging from New Mexico's governor, to the president of the university, and the Mayor of Albuquerque, all of who invited the Prince for another visit to New Mexico.

On a personal matter, Ed wanted to introduce his son, Steven, to the Prince. Steve was in Madrid visiting with his wife's family. The meeting progressed as if old friends were meeting, and, of course, the Prince felt for Ed's loss. "We all loved Tanna," he said.

After the updates, Ed presented the Prince with the letters while verbally explaining what they were, adding his own request that the Prince visit New Mexico. The Prince half-heartedly thumbed through the letters and gave Ed a doleful look, "Ed, I don't know if I can respond to these." He went on to comment that he could not explain why, but, for the moment, Ed would have to accept his odd answer.

Ed nodded in agreement. The Prince had his reasons. Enough said. It did not take long to learn why. A couple of weeks later, King Juan Carlos I abdicated the Crown and his son became Felipe VI, King of Spain.

For Ed, the trip's highlight came with Father Lezama's mass for Cayetana. Three to four hundred people attended the ceremony held at Nuestra Señora La Blanca Church in Madrid.

Ed's Spanish friends Cullen and María José Bentancurt Gomez-Monche, hosted a reception for three hundred people. The trip was an obvious reminder of Ed's and Cayetana's many lasting friendships in Spain.

Ed returned to New Mexico invigorated. He knew that Cayetana was proud of him, and he knew that she wanted him to continue. He had more to do and returned ready, even anxious, to keep her proud.

Epilogue: A Legacy
2015 Albuquerque, New Mexico

The Twelfth, Thirteenth and Fourteenth Generations
(The Current Generations after Four Hundred Years)

Ambassador Edward L. Romero = Cayetana Gallegos y García

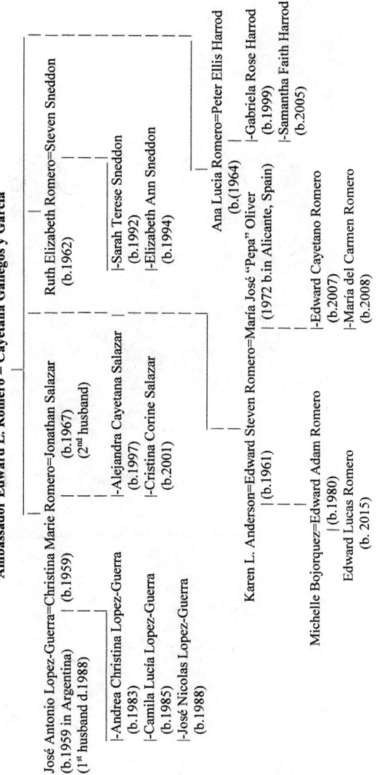

José Antonio Lopez-Guerra=Christina Marie Romero=Jonathan Salazar
(b.1959 in Argentina) (b.1959) (b.1967)
(1st husband d.1988) (2nd husband)

-Andrea Christina Lopez-Guerra
 (b.1983)
-Camila Lucía Lopez-Guerra
 (b.1985)
-José Nicolas Lopez-Guerra
 (b.1988)

-Alejandra Cayetana Salazar
 (b.1997)
-Cristina Corine Salazar
 (b.2001)

Ruth Elizabeth Romero=Steven Sneddon
 (b.1962)

-Sarah Terese Sneddon
 (b.1992)
-Elizabeth Ann Sneddon
 (b.1994)

Ana Lucia Romero=Peter Ellis Harrod
 (b.1964)

-Gabriela Rose Harrod
 (b.1999)
-Samantha Faith Harrod
 (b.2005)

Karen L. Anderson=Edward Steven Romero=María José "Pepa" Oliver
 (b.1961) (1972 b.in Alicante, Spain)

-Edward Cayetano Romero
 (b.2007)
-María del Carmen Romero
 (b.2008)

Michelle Bojorquez=Edward Adam Romero
 (b.1980)

Edward Lucas Romero
 (b. 2015)

Ed Romero and his family in a photograph taken in 2007. The family continues to grow, now to the seventeenth generation with the Romero surname, a pheonomen not unlike many New Mexican families. Standing left to right; Nicolas, Adam, Ed, Cayetana, Christina, Cayetano, Steven, Elise, Steve Sneddon, Pete Harrod, and Sarah. Seated left to right, Camila, Cristina, Andrea, Pepa, Ruth, Samantha, Anna, Gabriela, and Alexandra. Ed and Cayetana Romero Collcetion.

Ed Romero at a restaurant on the old plaza of Albuquerque, New Mexico. The mural behind him lists his direct ancestor Baltazar Romero as one of the founders of Albuquerque. Photograph by LeRoy N. Sanchez.

Ed continues, in his eighties, a product of centuries where the motifs and places, pieces of a complex history of coincidences, conflicts, and the survival of each generation after the next, and Cayetana have led him to be the person he is. He is a part of a legacy, a heritage of a people justly proud, yet still awed. He is not through. He wants to arrange for a return visit of La Macana, the statue of Mary that his ancestors first brought to New Mexico. His ancestors would be proud.

In the end, as he is always quick to remind his family that history is not different from many other New Mexican families. Nor is he the only descendent of a Hispanic New Mexican family who has served the United States as a diplomat. Lucy Jaramillo, a teacher, became the United States Ambassador to Honduras. Frank Ortiz, a veteran of World War II, became Ambassador to Argentina, Perú, Guatemala, and Barbados and Grenada over a long career in the State Department. President Reagan needed him in Argentina to deal with the aftermath of the Falklands War.

Many other multi-generational New Mexicans have gone on to honor their heritages as doctors, lawyers, judges, writers, artists, teachers, soldiers, and community as well as national leaders. Almost without exception, they too have completed the circle by going back to the birthplace of their respective ancestors, who first endured the hardships to settle in the land named in reference to Mexico City.

Ed and his equally successful brother, Isaac, continued to visit each other until Isaac's death. Isaac has three surviving children, the oldest of which is named Isaac Thomas. He has a daughter named Kathryn, and another son named Timothy. Isaac's children have given them three grandchildren and two great grandchildren. The grandson was named Lucas after his great grandfather.

Ed and Cayetana's three children have given them twelve grandchildren and one great grandchild that respectively represent the thirteenth through the fifteenth generation New Mexican Romeros.

At once normal and unique, the story of *Los Romeros* speaks to a region of the United States whose people consistently return to the homes where, in the distant past, their forefathers and foremothers left for an improved life in what was then one of the farthest reaches of the Spanish empire. It also is a story of migration into what is the United States that continues today; of caravans moving from the south to the north over centuries. The story of Ed's family, like the other old New Mexican and southwestern families from California to Texas that have produced subsequent generations who will continue to make history and contribute to the rich cultural fabric that is the United States.

[Handwritten marginalia in left margin:] sic: 21, 3, not 13 additional generations

[Handwritten marginalia in left margin:] not a proper use per Strunk

[Handwritten notes at bottom:] Restrained notes and corrections by JBC on a book loaned by Flora Sanchez 2/2022. This ambitious and important book deserves a competent bilingual editor. The historical sections are rife with errors in grammar, word choice, punctuation and syntax, undercutting the value and reputation of this otherwise impressive and valuable effort.

"Romero and Church Streets" on the corner one block north of Albuquerque's historic plaza on what was the Camino Real. Photograph by LeRoy N. Sanchez

BIBLIOGRAPHIC NOTES

A historical novel quite naturally, raises questions as to what is fiction and what is not. Or, quite frankly, how can fiction be taken as history? The answers are not definitive. As a historian, this author has read historical novels since his formative years. Those novels struck up a curiosity to delve more deeply into the true history. Historical novels, or as the academic community has come to call them, "historical or creative fiction," are an excellent way of attracting the general audience to the field of history.

However, no justification satisfies the main fact that fiction is not history. It can be based on history, but in reality, each novel must be judged on its own. How much is truth? How much research is behind the narrative, the events, and the spoken words? Is the author in any way qualified as a historian?

There are different models in New Mexico's literary and historical traditions. For example, Willa Cather's *Death Comes for the Archbishop* used fictional names for real people and played very loose with the actual history. Yet, the book generally has been so widely accepted as true history, more than a few historians have gone out of their way to demonstrate that the book has nothing to do with reality.

An example on the other extreme is Fray Angélico Chávez's *The Lady From Toledo*, which was based on a footnoted, researched article published in the *New Mexico Historical Review*. The second edition of that book actually included the original article. The reader can quickly tell fact from fiction.

To assure the reader that this story of a Hispanic American family is strongly based on fact, this bibliographic essay parallels the book's narrative. Through this method, the line between history and fiction will become clearer, and the reader can appreciate the book as an excellent introduction to one aspect of New Mexico's history.

The direct Romero genealogy beginning with Bartolomé in the 1590s and ending with Ed in the twenty-first century is primarily based on the genealogical research of Albert Gallegos, José Antonio Esquibel, and Fray Angélico Chávez. The book's genealogical charts are accurate and are placed throughout the book for the reader's convenience.

In some cases where the birth, death, or marriage dates are not available, a contextual guess was made. However, the known dates are used, and those not known are left blank on the genealogical charts. The writing of this book actually contributed to an ongoing process of updating the genealogical information. For this, the author is grateful to Albert Gallegos who always seemed to be on call to answer questions about genealogical inconsistencies.

The general historical context for the narratives of each generation is accurate. Governors, events, and expeditions are historical fact and kept in their proper place and time. Lifestyles are based on a wide range of historical information, including this author's personal experience of [working] more than two decades in the New Mexico History Museum.

The reader will note that the Romero family quickly became politically connected. As generations succeeded one another and different branches of the family took different historical paths, the direct ancestors of Ed Romero lost their political influence and became shepherds, laborers, and one became a lawman far from the center of political influence in Santa Fe. This decline in political connections ended with Ed Romero whose spectacular career brought him into the center of political influence. The zenith of his career, of course, was his appointment as United States Ambassador to Spain.

One further note: the source references in the narrative are given in full in the bibliographic list that follows the narrative.

Part I: The Return: Ambassador Romero

Most of the account of Ed Romero's return to Spain as an ambassador, as well as his earlier trips to Spain, is taken from twenty-seven interviews conducted with him from September 1, 2011 until February 10, 2015. The story of Father Izquierdo Gismero comes from the above interviews and from a personal interview with his brother, Adolfo Izquierdo, in Toracón, Spain on July 4 and 5, 2011. The story of Father Izquierdo's workplace while caring for his father, and the fact that he researched in the Archives of the Indies in Seville, and in the National Library in Madrid are all the result of the above interviews. The author also interviewed Antonio Macheño in Corral de Almaguer, Spain on July 24, 2011. Macheño was the town's mayor during Ed Romero's first and subsequent visits to Corral de Almaguer, and is another source for the Father Izquierdo story. Three interviews were conducted with Ed Romero's older brother, Isaac. The importance of the casual time spent with Ed and Cayetana cannot be overstated. Cayetana personally introduced me to her invaluable archive.

A most important source is the incomplete manuscript and the collection of sources that Father Pedro Izquierdo Gismero had begun to write and compile. He titled it "De Corral de Almaguer (Toledo) España al Estado de Nuevo México, Estados Unidos de la Mano de Don Edward Romero, Embajador de Los Estados Unidos en España." This collection is in possession of Ambassador Ed Romero.

Father's Izquierdo's research is confirmed in the above interviews along with the boxes of his papers and notes, copies of which his brother gave to me to present to Ed Romero. Izquierdo's source materials can be gleaned from his notes and from the beginning narrative of the history he was compiling. The affectionate relationship between the ambassador and the priest is confirmed throughout the documentation and interviews.

This author visited Corral de Almaguer twice. The plaza still has a tile plaque naming the plaza in honor of Ambassador Edward Romero. In addition, various Spanish newspaper sources that include photographs describe the ceremony of Ed's return to the town. The story of the Native Americans from San Juan Pueblo (as it was called then) visiting Corral de Almaguer, as well as the speeches for this occasion, are in the following accounts: *El País* and *ABC* that can be found in the Cayetana Romero scrapbooks. The trip led by New Mexico Governor Gary Johnson and his entourage also is confirmed through a telephone interview on October 26, 2011 that this author conducted with Dr. Edson Way, who was the Governor's Secretary for Cultural Affairs at the time, and was part of the delegation.

Izquierdo's manuscript/collection also is the basis for the early history of Corral de Almaguer in Part II. The collection is the source for relating the story of Father Izquierdo's research into Ed Romero's family, New Mexico, and La Macana. For Ed Romero's eventual induction into the confraternity of the Mozarabes in the Cathedral of Toledo, and the awarding of his coat of arms see the notes for section VIII.

Ed Romero's wife, Cayetana, kept and organized forty-six scrapbooks (plus ephemeral materials) of their lives together, and especially of his tenure as U. S. Ambassador to Spain, many if not all of his speeches are included along with awards and newspaper articles.

PART II: THE JOURNEY: BARTOLOMÉ

A good part of the documentation on when Bartolomé left Corral de Almaguer, the meaning of that town's name, and its history, Pedro Izquierdo Gismero's sources and research, and some additional information on Our Lady of the Macana are in the beginning of a compilation of a narrative and documents that Father Izquierdo Gismero had compiled. Among those documents are Spanish newspaper clippings. This author personally received Father Izquierdo's collection from the priest's brother. As intended, the collection was passed on to Ambassador Romero.

Anyone who would like to look further into life in the first settlement at San Juan de los Caballeros might find rich information in the site report by Florence Hawley Ellis, who oversaw the archaeological excavation of San Gabriel, the name given to the site by the Spanish. An idea of the lifestyle, the church, and the plaza are all there. The Spanish renovations of the existing native, three-story house block are described. Ellis also gives a good account of the food consumed. She provides a long discussion about the problem of whether San Juan and San Gabriel were one or two places, and mentions that, at one point, "some of the colonists had suggested that Oñate should have ordered a communal (native and Spanish) field planted."

Mentions of Bartolomé and his Robledo in-laws are found in many documents of the time that have been published in English translation. Hammond and Rey's, *Oñate: Colonizer of New Mexico,* gives the accounts of visiting the various pueblos as well as expeditions. Romero is documented for his presence on those forays, including the search for silver beyond the Hopi Pueblos. Oñate's speech beginning with "Hardships and misfortunes..." is taken from Simmons, *Last Conquistador*. The "upright in the saddle," comment comes from Kessell, *Kiva, Cross, and Crown*, in which he describes "erect" and "dark-skinned" Bartolomé as the commander of the armed escort. Gaspar Perez de Villagrá vividly describes the battle of Acoma and mentions Bartolomé's role in command of the *harquebuses*. Hammond and Rey corroborates Bartolomé's role at Acoma. The Oñate documents in Hammond and Rey clearly delineate that the "Escanjaque Indians," as the Spanish called them then, were warlike and not the same as the Quivira Indians.

France Scholes in *Church and State* documents the authoritarian reign of Fray Isidro Ordóñez and his confrontations with governor Peralta. I wrote a paper about Father Ordóñez in an early graduate seminar and concluded that the priest was a fraud.

The trip that Bartolomé and his family took to Mexico is treated in Hammond and Rey. Their return can be surmised by later accounts of their presence in New Mexico. That they had a child in Mexico, specifically Matías, is demonstrated through a number of the contemporary sources, which amount to a lot of circumstantial evidence, the only conclusion for which is that Matías was born in Mexico. The genealogical records as compiled by Chávez, Esquibel, and Gallegos, are clear that the rest of the children were born in New Mexico. The physical description of Viceroy and Archbishop García Guerra comes from an actual illustration of him. For example, see Kessell, *Kiva, Cross, and Crown*, page 117. The dire plight of many of the settlers is illustrated in the March 22, 1601 letter of Captain Luis Gasco de Velasco to the Viceroy. That letter is published in its entirety in Hammond and Rey.

Other accounts of the expedition north and settlement of New Mexico with all of its trials and tribulations can be found in Simmons' *The Last Conquistador*, Scholes article on Martínez de Montoya, in a recent multi-volume study on Villagrá by Manuel M. Martín Rodríguez, and the Martínez de Montoya Papers.

Although there is no contemporary evidence that the first Spaniards referred to the Pueblo People as Pueblo People or initially even referred to the various pueblos by the names given to them by the Spanish, this narrative does so for clarity's sake for the non-historian reader.

PART III: THE NEXT GENERATION: MATÍAS

France Scholes', *Church and State in New Mexico*, and his various articles published in volumes three through twenty of the *New Mexico Historical Review*, actually provides enough background as well as particular information for New Mexico's history from Oñate up to the Pueblo Revolt. Scholes documents the various governorships, the Rosas affair, the intricacies of the rivalry between the church and state, and the rise and fall (literally) of Juan de Mansos. Matías and Felipe as well as the episode of the poisoning of Bartolomé's wife surface in Scholes's narrative.

José Manuel Esquibel combed the Inquisitional records to masterfully add to, and occasionally correct, the record. He is the first to document and conclude that the Romeros intentionally became a powerful political and economic family during those years. This includes the documentation of their various *encomiendas* and the establishment of their Rio Abajo *haciendas*.

Ralph Emerson Twitchell's *Spanish Archives of New Mexico* is an excellent entry into the primary sources of the period. The book is a compilation and calendar of documents translated into English that are in the Spanish Archives of New Mexico. It is an invaluable tool and excellent source and reference to using the actual archives.

Fray Jerónimo de Pedraza is mentioned in various sources. His involvement in the conflict between Governor Peralta and Fray Ordóñez is documented in Scholes, *Church and State*, as is his transfer to Senecú. His relationship to Isabel de Pedraza the wife of Matías is an assumption although probably close to the truth. Isabel's marriage to Matías is in all the genealogical sources.

The use of the word "convento" for what really were the priest's dwellings can be problematic. The Spanish *convent* is used throughout New Mexico's primary sources, that is to say, actual documents to describe the place that was generally attached to the mission church and where the priest, specifically Franciscans, lived. Monasteries generally refer to off-site places housing communities of ordered priests, monks, and nuns. Adams and Chávez give a more detailed and specific definition of "convent" in their glossary in *Missions of New Mexico*.

The incident in Pecos when Governor Rosas abused the priests and, with Matías's help, took blankets off the backs of the Natives is documented in Scholes, and more so in Kessell, *Kiva, Cross, and Crown*. The conversation between Rosas and the two priests is made up, although something like that must have been said.

The execution scene is made up but the act is a fact of history. Francisco Gómez is documented to have been present. The victims are listed in the historical record but not the actual executioners, a custom generally maintained today. As a loyal captain and favorite of Rosas, it seems inconceivable that Matías was not there as a witness. However, there is no documentary record of his presence. His reaction to the executions is fictional license that makes sense for even those times.

The Inquisitional arrests and subsequent trials of Francisco Gómez and Gaspar Pérez are relatively well-known events in New Mexico's narrative history, beginning with Scholes and continuing to Hordes, *To the End of the Earth*. Bartolomé Gómez's trip south with various goods to help pay for his older brother's defense is well documented. In particular, see Angélico Chávez's *Families*. Francisco Gomez's connection with Fray Benavidez, as well as his participation in the confraternity of Our Lady of the Rosary, La Conquistadora, can be found in Angélico Chávez's *Our Lady of the Conquest*.

Matías's death is somewhat of a mystery. His cousin Gaspar Perez testified before the Inquisition that Matías died at Santa Ana Pueblo. Angélico Chávez's *Families*, and Gallegos found in the church records that he died in Santa Fe. The year of his death is not in doubt. Nor is the fact that he died suddenly and relatively young. However, how he died is not documented. That he, like his cousin Francisco Gómez, had enemies led me to add the nefarious description of his death.

PART IV: THE END OF AN EPOCH: FELIPE

The idea of the Romero/Gómez (Robledo) family ties and business empire is described in Esquibel. France Scholes in *Church and State* gives some details. These include the move of Felipe and his cousin Bartolomé Gómez to the Rio Abajo to run haciendas on the Camino Real.

The respective locations of the two haciendas are gleaned from the account of Diego de Vargas's entry into New Mexico in 1692. His chronicler wrote distances in leagues (approximately 2.7 miles), noted road conditions, and listed each known landmark. The expedition camped at the ruins of an hacienda that the journal explicitly described as once belonging to Felipe Romero. On the next day they traveled three leagues to "Las Barrancas," the abandoned "hacienda" that belonged to "Francisco Gómez." Francisco was Bartolomé's father. J. Manuel Espinosa, *First Expedition of Vargas*, first published the account of the expedition. A more complete and heavily annotated version of the journal is in Kessell and Hendricks, *By Force of Arms*.

By using the given distances from locations that are known today, it is possible to locate the estancias of both Felipe and Bartolomé. (See the appendice herein). The maps of New Mexico executed in the second half of the eighteenth century by Bernardo Miera y Pacheco confirm the site of Felipe Romero's estancia. It is located a little north of Sevilleta and close to the confluence of the Rio Grande and Rio Puerco were the trail that connected the eastern salt fields and the Jumano missions joins the Camino Real. The cartographer labeled the site Vueltas de Romero. The best source for locating sites on the Camino Real is the National Park Service, *Management Plan*.

Scholes, Simmons, and Esquibel, in *Mendoza,* published a report of the governor of New Mexico describing the February 1668 Apache raid on Felipe's hacienda, killing six Christian Indians who defended the place. They took everything "even the bed linen."

Felipe's employee, Alonso Cadimo, known as Jola, actually existed. He changed his surname to Romero out of respect for Felipe and his family. His death during the above Apache Indian raid is documented. His wife and two children, Ana María and José, survived him. See Chávez, *Families*, and Scholes, *Church and State.* That Felipe was the godfather of Jola's two children is a logical but undocumented guess. Such a move would have been normal under the circumstances. Also, documented in Chávez's *Families*, is the illegitimate birth of Bartolomé Gómez's (Barti's) son as well as Bartolomé's physical description, including the wound.

The story of the Macana statue is based on Angélico Chávez's article "Nuestra Señora de la Macana," originally published in the *New Mexico Historical Review* and subsequently included in a reprint of his novel *The Lady From Toledo* about the same subject. The genealogical record suggests María's relationship to Felipe.

Doña Ana Robledo, the granddaughter of Pedro Robledo can be confused with her daughter of the same name. Angélico Chávez identifies her as Pedro's granddaughter in his historical novel *The Lady From Toledo* and his book-length historical essay, *My Penitente Land.*

The roles of Felipe and his cousin Bartolomé Gómez in the deliberations during the Pueblo Revolt are in Hackett and Shelby, *Revolt of the Pueblo Indians ...and Otermín's Attempted Reconquest.* Their words are paraphrased but their sentiments are clear. Also clear is that Felipe was outspoken and his words were respected. The same source documents that both men left their respective *haciendas* to meet with the other Rio Abajo survivors at Isleta Pueblo. Lieutenant Governor García's activities are also well documented. The retreat and eventual meeting with the northern survivors is based on the documents.

Felipe and his son, Sebastián, participated in Otermín's wintery 1681 return to the north. They stood for the muster in which is described what weapons and horses they could provide. Sebastián is described as seventeen years old, tall and thin, with a long face and thick lips.

The instructions and complete account of the 1683 expedition downriver to the Nueces River, including Felipe Romero's participation as the third in command, is in Scholes, Simmons, and Esquibel, *Mendoza.*

What life was like in the El Paso area at that time can be gleaned from Timmons, *El Paso,* and a very revealing article edited by Ernest J. Burrus titled, "A Tragic Interlude in the Reconquest of New Mexico." Various descriptions of the mostly dire straights of the area are given in the documents of Diego De Vargas published in Kessell, and in Hackett and Shelby.

The Domínguez de Mendoza family's bad reputation is in Angélico Chávez's, *Families,* and Scholes, Simmons, and Esquibel. Also, the fact that all the Robledo men left El Paso never to return to New Mexico is in Angélico Chávez's, *Families.*

Part V: A New Beginning, Less Glory: Baltasar

The use of a plowshare will surface periodically in the narrative and is an idea made up by the author based on an actual plowshare in the collections of the New Mexico State History Museum. Not wishing to give up the story's nuance, the reasoning behind this partially fictional account will be explained in the notes for Part VI.

There are few details of what Felipe and his family did in El Paso. Judging by their muster records, they were poor and not even completely outfitted. The exact dates of the deaths of Felipe and his wife are not known. Angélico Chávez's, *Families,* states that they had died by 1685.

The words quoted for the *velorio* or funeral procession are taken from Aurelio M. Espinosa, *The Folklore of Spain in the American Southwest.* The words come from funeral songs originating in Spain. Also, the idea of the rosary comes from the same source.

The question of Baltasar's two wives has been of some concern. Chávez, in *Origins,* has him married to Francisca Góngora on January 22, 1703. Chávez has a "different" Baltasar Romero, who married a Josefa de Herrera, and they had a son named Pedro in El Paso. Kessell, in *Royal Crown Restored,* writes that Baltasar's earlier marriage was to Josefa de Herrera by whom he had a son named Pedro in El Paso. He, too, notes the second marriage in 1703. Add to this, the original Gallegos family tree has all of Baltasar's children born of his second wife, although two of them, Pedro and Jacinta, were born in 1694 and 1699, respectively. Common sense would indicate that Baltasar's first wife gave birth to those two children before she died, and Baltasar remarried in 1703. The assumption that she died is based on the fact that divorce was unheard of, and having more than one wife was not allowed. The question of the first wife's name is debatable, although this author has chosen to go with the most recent research, which is to say Gallegos, who names her María Francisca Montoya. Assumptions aside, subsequent research done by Gallegos is reflected in the family trees published in this book. My conclusion is that Baltasar first married María Francisca Montoya and had Jacinta and Tomas Ignacio by her. After her death in September of 1702 in Bernalillo, Baltasar married Francisca María de Góngora in Bernalillo and had six more children, including Pedro.

There is some mention of place names. Some come from documents of the time. Most, especially for the eighteenth century, are found in Bernardo Miera y Pacheco's maps. The assumption here is that the place names such as the Organ and Sandia Mountains existed before he made his maps. Of course, another assumption, albeit less likely, is that he arbitrarily named the places.

Baltasar's military record is published in various sources. See Kessell, *Royal Crown Restored,* which also gives the annual salary. The exact expeditions in which he participated are subject to conjecture, although Chávez's *Origins* states that in 1699, Baltasar stated he was a resident of Bernalillo. It seems he returned to El Paso, after which he returned to Bernalillo where he passed muster in 1705. The following year he, along with Fernando Durán y Chaves, was among the founders of Albuquerque. Simmons, *Albuquerque,* Sergeant and Davis, *Shining River*, and Gallegos have him among the original families, and place him as the northern-most settler, just south of the Gallegos grant, which would have placed his property around present-day Rio Grande Blvd and Griego Street, [which is] part of the current Griego neighborhood in the North Valley. Also see *Aquí Se Comienza: A Genealogical History of the Founding Families....* That neighborhood borders Los Poblanos, which, in turn, moving north, neighbored Los Ranchos. It seems that the Griego neighborhood is on what was originally Baltasar Romero's property, with the church and its plazuela possibly on the site of his original house.

A pintled doorway as defined in Taylor and Bokides, *New Mexican Furniture,* is "a door hinge formed by wooden dowels, usually extensions of the stile or vertical members of the door, protruding above and below the door and socketed into the frame so that the door swings on them."

The 1708 petition that Baltasar and Chaves wrote and presented in Santa Fe has been published in translation in Twitchell, *Spanish Archives.* The original is in the Spanish Archives of New Mexico and reproduced in this book.

The definition of a "procurator" as a self-styled legal representative can be found in Cutter, *The Legal Culture of Northern New Spain.* The Spanish word is *procurador.*

Baltasar's land transactions, including his foiled attempt to sell land to Santa Ana Pueblo, are all located in the Spanish Archives of New Mexico, as well as in Twitchell, *Spanish Archives,* a somewhat outdated calendar of the same archives. His purchase of land in Taos for his siblings is located in the same places and has been noted in Chávez, *Origins*. However, Esquibel, "Baltasar and Francisca," has discovered that the land was not given to his siblings rather than sold to some cousins, the "Cadimo" branch. If so, these were not cousins rather than the descendants of "Jola" the trusted ranch hand of Felipe Romero's. That Baltasar, who grew up knowing Jola would remember and help out the man's descendants is a story worth telling. The recipients are listed as well as the fact that Baltasar's two sons, Pedro and Felipe, witnessed the transaction. Gallegos has listed most of the land transaction documents located in the Spanish Archives of New Mexico. The fact that Gregorio is not a witness to the action, led this author to conclude that he had died, which is possibly true, but not based in fact.

Gregorio's death is surmised through circumstantial evidence. For example, the Taos land sale witnessed by his brothers, but not him. Also, absences of marriage, etc. records with his name, including his death record, raise the specter that he may have died, or have left New Mexico. I chose the former conclusion.

The story of Domingo's survival of the ambush of the Villasur expedition on August 13, 1720, is partially based on information, and partially surmised from the paucity of information. A Domingo Romero de Pedraza participated in the reconnaissance expedition of sixty-two men and around sixty Pueblo Indian allies who were attacked on the morning of August 13. Of the New Mexican soldiers and civilians, all but about twenty-two were killed. Felipe Tamaris, who was one of the survivors, included Romero as one of the fatalities. However, subsequent research has hinted at the possibility that Tamaris may have erred. First, [his] Romero's widowed wife sought to remarry, and had to bear witness before the Church that her husband had died. None of the expedition's survivors came forward. Instead, her witnesses were secondary men who had not been at the battle. Second, Romero's name and use of Pedraza definitely places him among Baltasar's clan and a descendent from his grandparents from whence the Pedraza surname originated. One of Baltasar's brothers was Domingo Mariano Romero (de Pedraza), and he is listed as still alive in 1732. He is the correct age for the Domingo who had participated in the expedition. Thus, this author took the novelist's liberty of making him the one and same person, which could be true. More likely, the Romero who died in the battle was a first cousin in a collateral branch of the family. This will require some more research. The sources for all this are: Hotz, *Segesser Paintings,* Angélico Chávez, *Origins,* Angélico Chávez, "Mission Records and Villasur," and in T. Chávez, *Moment in Time.*

Baltasar's signature on the 1737 petition from the citizens of Alburquerque to Governor Henrique Olavide y Micheleña requesting that he lift the embargo against the export of sheep and wool is printed rather than in script. The primitive signature indicates that Baltasar was barely literate with a basic, rudimentary knowledge of reading or writing. The document is in the Spanish Archives of New Mexico and is reproduced in John O. Baxter, *Las Carneradas: Sheep Trade in New Mexico, 1700–1860*, page 38.

There is no evidence as to how Baltasar died. Documentation exists for the year and his age at death. The idea that Felipe took care of him is not based in any fact. That someone did care for him seems obvious. See Chávez, *Origins* and Gallegos, "American Journey."

Chávez, in *Archives of the Archdiocese of Santa Fe*, lists all the priests and where and when they worked. Baltasar died in Alburquerque, in February of 1737, when the administering priest most likely was Fray Juan José de Oronzoro, who was stationed in Alburquerque from November of 1736 until April of 1742.

Part VI: Pedro, Two Families, and Another Move

The date of Gregoria's death and the fact that she was buried in the church in Alburqueque is in Gallegos. How she died is conjecture, as is Pedro's reaction. Pedro's residence in Albuquerque is documented through the births and marriage of his children and grandchildren. Gallegos gives the birth date of Pedro, Jr. and birth year of Cristóbal. Until recently it was assumed that Pedro had a son (Pedro II) who had a son named Juan Joseph Tomás. However, recent research by Gallegos has uncovered the following. Pedro, Sr. had two wives. After his first wife Gregoria Baca Luna died, he married Josefa Varela Jaramillo. Pedro II was one of six children born to Gregoria, the first wife. Juan Joseph Tomás was one of four children born to the second wife. Hence Pedro II and Juan Joseph Tomás were half brothers, not father and son. All the dates and discrepancies of age are in Gallegos's most recent research and are repeated in the family tree. Aside from those marriage and birth details, the only thing known about Pedro, Sr.'s later life is that he died after 1775.

The Church regularly investigated betrothed couples, and there is no reason to assume that the Romeros of this period did not go through these prenuptial investigations. The priests mentioned are listed in Angélico Chávez, *AASF*, as being stationed in Alburquerque during various times of the year. As we don't have the exact date of Pedro Romero's second marriage in 1751, any one of four priests could have officiated at the wedding. Their names are Fray Miguel Gómez Cayuela (January–March 1751), Fray José Irgoyen (May–August 1751), Fray Juan Jorge del Pino (May 1751), and Fray Manuel José Rojo (November 1751–March 1752). Fray Juan José Toledo was in Alburquerque for April of 1750. The ugly beard is a fabrication. Josepha's family background comes from the genealogical data collected by Gallegos and the connection with "Aunt Lucía" is lifted from Angélico Chávez's *New Mexico Families*. With one exception there is no particular documentation as to which expeditions Pedro II was a participant, although he assuredly did go on some, as every able-bodied man was required to do, and the fact that he became a "captain" clearly indicates this. The one exception is the 1751 expedition, for his name and date as given in the text remains prominently carved in Inscription Rock at El Morro National Monument. The inscription of Pedro, and the subsequent one of Andrés, are respectively listed as trail tour stops 7 and 8 in the Park's trail guide. Gallegos documented Pedro II's 1755 marriage in El Paso. That he became estranged

417

from his father is undocumented, although he apparently stayed in El Paso.

The change in the sheep-trade industry with the influx of Chihuahua-based merchants is vividly described in Baxter, *Las Carneradas*. That, and the background for other possible reasons why anyone would desire to move from the central valley to dangerous Abiquiu [, and, then,]What life was like there is in Alvar W. Carson, *The Spanish-American Homeland: Four Centuries in New Mexico's Río Arriba*. The dates of Josepha's death and Juan Joseph's marriage place his move within a year and some months. Josefa's death occurred at the same time that a major smallpox epidemic hit New Mexico. One fourth of the colony died from the disease, mostly in the larger population areas. Given her advanced years and that she died at the same time, the conclusion is that she was one of the casualties. Simmons, in "New Mexico's Smallpox Epidemic..." gives a graphic description of the time. Josefa's advise to Juan Joseph about "God coming to him" is lifted from a quote recorded from another person and published by Nasario García in *Fe y Tragedias*. The original quote, worded slightly differently is attributed to García's maternal grandmother.

PART VII: MIGRATION NORTH, JUAN DE JESÚS, ABRÁN, FAUSTINO, ISAAC

A 1776 description of Abiquiu and the downriver plazas can be found in Adams and Chávez, *Missions of New Mexico;* Swadish, *Pobladores;* and Carson, *Spanish American Homeland*. Those sources all mention the prominence of the Martín family in the area. The accounts for population variances are in Carson. The walls of the church at Santa Rosa de Lima still exist and can be seen from the state highway 84 that runs through what was once the village's plaza.

Locating and dating the locations of the various protagonists is based on the genealogical record. For example, birth, baptism, marriage, and death records usually give the location for such events, thus making it possible to trace the family's migration north into Colorado.

As stated earlier, the New Mexico State History Museum has in its collections an iron plowshare that was forged into a short sword blade, the ironic reference to the Biblical saying that preaches the reverse, to beat your swords into plowshares. That such a thing would happen speaks to the short supply of weapons and the desperate times. Its connection to the Romero family is fiction.

Many expeditions and punitive expeditions went through or from Abiquiu. The most famous of these is the Domínguez and Escalante expedition of 1776 that predated Juan Joseph Tomas's arrival to the area. The route to California opened in 1829 and is documented in many books. That many of the men took their whole families to California and back, see Weber, *Mexican Frontier*. With very few exceptions the people who went on that trip remain anonymous. There is no documentation that any of the Romeros made the trip, although that does not preclude their having done so. The temptation could not be avoided in Abiquiu. As a result, I took the liberty of having one of them travel the trail.

A good introduction to the Mexican War in New Mexico and its many historical implications is *Sesquicentennial Symposium Commemorating New Mexico's Year of Destiny.* Regarding Governor Armijo's decision to leave New Mexico rather than stand and fight, see T. Chávez, *Alvarez.*

Information on traveling or seasonal teachers comes from Doris Meyer, *Speaking for Themselves,* who postulates that teachers' terms generally lasted four months, and they were paid fifty cents per day. Whether or not the Romeros attended classes as described in the narrative is not known. As stated later in the book, an appreciation for education did permeate the family.

The story of Abrán's death is inspired by family legend as told by Abrán's son and people of his generation. In this case, the interviews of Ed and Isaac Romero corroborate that they were told that Abrán was a lawman who was killed for trying to help his people. To date, how he was killed is unknown. That aspect of his story is not mentioned in any New Mexican newspaper. The research continues in Colorado. The birth of his last child, coupled with his wife's remarriage provides parameters for the date of his death. The research continues in Colorado. Thus, the story of his death as given in the narrative is fiction. Also, made up is the character Michael Connel, the sheriff who recruited Abrán.

Another family story is that Faustino lost his land playing cards or gambling. This is a story that has surfaced in other New Mexican families, not the least of which is the author's. No evidence has been discovered to confirm the fact in either case. In short, the loss of land through gambling may be an apocryphal story covering what tended to happen, which was the land was lost to lawyers and land speculators who had moved to New Mexico. A perfect example of this is the history of the Santa Fe Ring.

The marriage of Abrán's widow and that the boys became shepherds is gleaned from family oral history. Ed and Isaac Romero both relate that their father, Isaac, helped his father, Faustino, herd sheep before they moved "to the city."

PART VIII: THE TWELFTH GENERATION, ED ROMERO

As in Part I, most of the biographical and family history comes from the interviews and email correspondence between the author and Ed Romero and his older brother Isaac, Jr. Some of it, like the state championship football team is corroborated in the local newspapers of the time, as well as in the City of Alamosa's current web-page, which indicates the pride of that achievement until today. Also, the author visited Alamosa and personally saw the house of Ed Romero's youth, which still exists. The author also visited the burial sites of Ed Romero's parents, as well as the Railroad's shops, photographs of which can be seen and studied on line.

The importance of Center, Colorado as a center of the Penitente movement is in Marta Weigle, *Brothers of Light, Brothers of Blood: The Penitentes of the Southwest,* and especially in Thomas J. Steele, S.J, and Rowena A. Rivera, *Penitente Self-Government: Brotherhoods and Councils, 1797–1947.* Ed Romero has in his possession his maternal grandfather's book of handwritten *alabados* (Penitente religious songs), brotherhood badge, and the *disciplina* (whip) that Lucas used on himself.

There are many books covering the government *"Bracero* Program" that began in the 1920s, although Mexican workers had been migrating north long before. The term, *surumato,* is still in use in some Hispanic New Mexican circles and its definition is given in Rubén Cobos, *A Dictionary of New Mexico and Southern Colorado Spanish.* This author once heard an elderly New Mexican refer to Governor Bill Richardson as a *surumato,* because Richardson is not from New Mexico and has Mexican ancestry through his mother.

The story of how Ed and Cayetana met is based on interviews with Ed and Cayetana and on Cayetana's notebooks, especially from a section of her recollections that she titled, "God's Greatest Blessing to Me!" The quote about Ed's pretentiousness is taken directly from this section. The quotes in reference to Ed's and Cayetana's engagement and subsequent marriage come from Ed's interviews and Cayetana's notes in her archive. In addition, Cayetana's first visit to Alamosa was recorded in Alamosa's local newspaper, a copy of which she kept in her notebooks.

Ambassador Jaramillo has a different memory of the episode when Ed visited her in Honduras after his trip to Nicaragua. She remembers that she had a reception for Ed and someone in that group got word to Carter's administration of Ed's meeting with Anastacio Somoza.

Part IX: The Return Continued, Ambassador Romero

See Part I of these bibliographic notes.

Ed's and Cayetana's induction into the Mozarabe confraternity is based on Ed's interviews, and on an interview with José Miranda Calvo, who, when Ed met him, was the Hermano Mayor of the organization. Their stories are corroborated in the newspaper clippings found in Cayetana's collection and in Father Izquierdo's papers.

Father Izquierdo's death comes from the interview of the priest's brother, Adolfo, who was interviewed on July 4, 2011. Adolfo was with Father Izquierdo when he died. Adolfo corroborates Ed's story on the telephone calls and how Ed was notified of the death of his friend.

The author personally witnessed Ed Romero's telephone call to Joe Reyes in which he arranged the trip to Spain.

Ambassador Ed Romero and the author at work on this book. November 16, 2018.
Photograph by LeRoy N. Sanchez

BIBLIOGRAPHY

Interviews

Ed Romero:

    23 August 2011,10 am to 1 pm, Albuquerque (Ed's house)
    1 September 2011, 10 am to 2 pm, Albuquerque (Ed's house)
    13 September 2011, 1 pm to 2 pm, Albuquerque (F. Star Restaurant)
    6 October 2011, 10 am to 3:30 pm, Albuquerque (Ed's house)
    26 January, 10 am to noon, Albuquerque (Ed's house)
    7 April 2012, 10 am to noon, Albuquerque (Ed's house)
    26 October 2011, 9 to 9:30 am, Albuquerque (Telephone)
    1 November 2011, Albuquerque (Ed's house)
    15 November 2013, Albuquerque (Ed's house)
    4 December 2013, Albuquerque (Ed's house)
    9 December 2013, Albuquerque (Ed's house)
    13 February 2014, Albuquerque (Ed's house)
    20 February 2014, Albuquerque (Ed's house)
    23 February 2014, Albuquerque (Ed's house)
    3 March 2014, Albuquerque (Ed's house)
    1 April 2014, Albuquerque (Ed's house)
    24 April 2014, Albuquerque (Ed's house)
    11 August 2014, Albuquerque (Ed's house)
    25 September 2014, Albuquerque (Ed's house)
    23 December 2014, Albuquerque (Ed's house)
    2 February 2015, Albuquerque (Ed's house)
    10 February 2015, Albuquerque (Ed's house)

Cayetana Romero:

    9 September 2013, Albuquerque (Ed's house)

Isaac Romero:

    4 February 2014, Glendale, California (Telephone)
    4 March 2014, Glendale, California (Telephone)
    25 February 2015, Glendale, California (Telephone)

Mari-Luci Jaramillo:

   5 September 2018, Albuquerque, New Mexico

Adolfo Izquierdo:

   4 July 2011, All afternoon, Toracón and Corral de Almaguer, Spain

Antonio Macheño:

   24 July 2011, All day, Corral de Almaguer and Toledo, Spain

José Miranda Calvo:

   24 July 2011, 4 to 5 pm, Toledo, Spain.

J. Edson Way:

   26 October 2011, Lubbock, Texas (Telephone)

Archives

Edward Romero Personal Archives, Albuquerque, New Mexico.
Cayetana García Romero Archives, Albuquerque, New Mexico.
Papers of Father Pedro Izquierdo, Cuenca, Spain and Albuquerque, New Mexico.
New State Records Center and Archives, Santa Fe, New Mexico

Unpublished Material

Ellis, Florence Hawley. "San Gabriel del Yunque: As Seen by An Archaeologist." Site Report. May 1985. (See listing for Sunstone Press book below.)
Esquibel, José (papers and unpublished material in Ed Romero Archives).
Izquierdo, Father Pedro (paper and unpublished material in Ed Romero Archives).
Gallegos, Albert (Genealogical charts and information in the Ed Romero Archives).

Documentaries

"Ed Romero." *Colores.* KNME-TV. Albuquerque, New Mexico.
"Una Noche España: Maravilla 2013." National Hispanic Cultural Center Foundation, September 7, 2013.

Books and Articles

Burrus, Ernest J., Editor. "A Tragic Interlude in the Reconquest of New Mexico," *Manuscript.* Vol. 29, November 1985. 154-65.

Carlson, Alvar W. *The Spanish-American Homeland: Four Centuries in New Mexico's Río Arriba.* Baltimore, MD: The Johns Hopkins Press, 1990.

Chávez, Fray Angélico. *But Time and Chance: The Story of Padre Martínez of Taos, 1793–1867.* Santa Fe, NM: Sunstone Press, 1981.

———. *Chávez: A Distinctive American Clan of New Mexico.* Santa Fe, NM: William Gannon, (originally)1989. New Edition, Santa Fe, NM: Sunstone Press, 2009.

———. *My Penitente Land: Reflections on Spanish New Mexico,* Santa Fe, NM: Museum of New Mexico Press, 1993 (originally 1974). New Edition, Santa Fe, NM: Sunstone Press, 2012.

———. "Nuestra Señora de la Macana," *New Mexico Historical Review.* Vol. XXXIV, no. 2, April 1959.

———. *Origins of New Mexico Families in the Spanish Colonial Period.* Santa Fe, NM: Museum of New Mexico Press, (originally 1973).

———. *Our Lady of the Conquest.* Santa Fe, NM: Historical Society of New Mexico, (originally 1948). New Edition, Santa Fe, NM: Sunstone Press, 2009.

———. *The Lady From Toledo.* Santa Fe, NM: Friends of the Palace Press, 1993.

Chávez, Nicolasa, *The Spirit of Flamenco: From Spain to New Mexico,* Santa Fe: Museum of New Mexico Press, 2015.

Chávez, Thomas E., Editor. *A Moment in Time: The Odyssey of New Mexico's Segesser Paintings.* Albuquerque, NM: Rio Grande Books, 2012.

_____. *Chasing History: Quixotic Quests for Artifacts, Art, and Heritage.* Santa Fe: Sunstone Press, 2013.

————. *Manuel Alvarez, 1794–1856: A Southwestern Biography.* Niwot, CO: University Press of Colorado, 1990.

————. *New Mexico: Past & Future.* Albuquerque, NM: University of New Mexico Press, 2006.

Cutter, Charles R. *The Legal Culture of Northern New Spain, 1700–1810.* Albuquerque, NM: The University of New Mexico Press, 1995.

Ellis, Florence Hawley. *San Gabriel del Yungue: As Seen by an Archaeologist.* Santa Fe, NM: Sunstone Press, 1989.

Esquibel, José Antonio. "Baltasar Romero and Francisca Góngora," *Aqui se Comienza: A Genealogical History of the Founding Families of La Villa de San Felipe de Alburquerque.* Albuquerque, NM: New Mexico Genealogical Society, 2007. 387-399.

Garate, Donald T. *Juan Bautista de Anza: Basque Explorer in the New World, 1693–1740.* Reno, NV: University of Nevada Press, 2003.

Garcia, Nasario. *Fe y Tragedias: Faith and Tragedies in Hispanic Villages of New Mexico.* Los Ranchos, NM: Rio Grande Books, 2010.

Greenleaf, Richard. "The Founding of Albuquerque, NM, 1706: An Historical Legal Problem," *New Mexico Historical Review.* Vol. 39, no. 1, January 1964.

Hafen, LeRoy R. and Ann Hafen. *The Old Spanish Trail: Santa Fe to Los Angeles.* Glendale, CA: Arthur H. Clark, 1965.

Hammond, George P. and Rey, Agapito, translators and editors. *Don Juan de Oñate: Colonizer of New Mexico, 1595–1628.* Vols. I & II. Albuquerque, NM: University of New Mexico Press, 1953.

Herrera, Carlos R. *Juan Bautista de Anza: The King's Governor in New Mexico.* Norman. OK: University of Oklahoma Press, 2015.

Hordes, Stanley M. *To the End of the Earth: A History of the Crypto-Jews of New Mexico.* New York: Columbia University Press, 2005.

Jaramillo, Mari-Luci, *Madame Ambassador: The Shoemaker's Daughter.* Tempe, Az: Bilingual Press, Arizona Press, 2002.

Jones, Oakah L., Jr. *Pueblo Warriors and Spanish Conquest.* Norman, OK: University of Oklahoma Press, 1966.

Kessell, John L. *Kiva, Cross, and Crown: The Pecos Indians and New Mexico, 1540–1840.* Washington, DC: National Park Service and U. S. Department of the Interior, 1979.

————, and Rick Hendricks, Editors. *By Force of Arms: The Journals of Don de Vargas, 1691–1693.* Albuquerque, NM: University of New Mexico Press, 1992.

————, Rick Hendricks, and Meredith Dodge, Editors. *The Royal Crown Restored: The Journals of Don Diego de Vargas, New Mexico, 1692–1694.* Albuquerque, NM: University of New Mexico Press, 1995.

Lucero-White, Lea. *Literary Folklore of the Hispanic Southwest.* San Antonio, TX: Naylor Co., 1953.

Martín Rodríguez, Manuel M. *Gaspar de Villagrá: Legista, Soldado y Poeta.* Leon, Spain: Universidad de León, 2009.

National Park Service/Long Distance Trails Group. *El Camino Real de Tierra Adentro National Historic Trail.* Draft. Comprehensive Management Plan/Environmental Impact Statement. Santa Fe, NM: Bureau of Land Management, 2002.

Naylor, Thomas H. and Charles W. Polzer, S.J. *Pedro de Rivera and the Military Regulations of Northern New Spain, 1724–1729.* Tucson, AZ: University of Arizona Press, 1988.

————. Editors. *The Presidio and Militia on the Northern Frontier: A Documentary History.* Vol. 1. Tucson, AZ: University of Arizona Press, 1986.

Palmer, Gabrielle G., June-el Piper and LouAnn Jacobson Editors. *El Camino Real de Tierra Adentro.* Santa Fe, NM: Bureau of Land Management, 1993.

Pérez de Villagrá, Gaspar. *Historia de la Nueva México, 1610: A Critical and Annotated Spanish/English Edition.* Miguel Encinias, Alfred Rodríquez, and Joseph P. Sánchez, Translators and editors. Albuquerque, NM: University of New Mexico Press, 1992.

Polling-Kempes, Lesly. *Valley of Shining Stone: The Story of Abiquiu.* Tucson, AZ: University of Arizona Press, 1997.

Proceedings of the Sesquicentennial Symposium, 1846–1996, Commemorating New Mexico's Year of Destiny, 1846. Las Cruces, NM: Doña Ana County Historical Society and Academy for Learning in Retirement, 1996.

Robb, J. D. *Hispanic Folk Music of New Mexico and the Hispanic Southwest: A Portrait of a People.* Norman, OK: University of Oklahoma Press, 1980.

Roybal, David. *Taking on Giants: Fabián Chávez, Jr. and New Mexico Politics.* Albuquerque: University of New Mexico Press, 2008.

Sánchez, Joseph P. and Bruce A. Erickson. *From Mexico City to Santa Fe: A Historical Guide to El Camino Real de Tierra Adentro.* Los Ranchos, NM: Rio Grande Books, 2011.

Sargeant, Kathryn and Mary Davis. *Shinning River, Precious Land: An Oral History of Albuquerque's North Valley.* Albuquerque, NM: Albuquerque Museum, 1986.

Scholes, France V., Marc Simmons and José Antonio Esquibel, editors. *Juan Domínguez De Mendoza: Soldier and Frontiersman of the Spanish Southwest, 1627–1693.* Albuquerque, NM: University of New Mexico Press, 2012.

Simmons, Marc. *Albuquerque: A Narrative History.* Albuquerque, NM: University of New Mexico Press, 1982.

———. *The Last Conquistador: Juan de Oñate and the Settling of the Far Southwest.* Norman, OK: University of Oklahoma Press, 1991.

———. "New Mexico's Smallpox Epidemic of 1780–81," *New Mexico Historical Review.* Vol. XLI, no. 4, October 1966. 319-22.

Snow, David H. *New Mexico's Frist Colonists: The 1597–1600 Enlistments for New Mexico under Juan de Oñate, Adelante & Gobernador.* Albuquerque, NM: Hispanic Genealogical Research Center of New Mexico, 1998.

Somoza, Anastasio and Cox, Jack. *Nicaragua Betrayed.* Boston: Western Islands, c. 1980.

Swadish, Frances Leon. *Los Primos Pobladores: Hispanic Americans of the Ute Frontier.* South Bend, IN: University of Notre Dame Press, 1974.

Taylor, Lonn and Dessa Bokides. *New Mexican Furniture, 1600–1940: The Origins,*

Survival, and Revival of Furniture Making in the Hispanic Southwest. Santa Fe, NM: Museum of New Mexico Press, 1987.

Thomas, Alfred Barnaby. Editor. *The Plains Indians and New Mexico, 1741–1778: A Collection of Documents Illustrative of the History of the Eastern Frontier of New Mexico.* Albuquerque, NM: University of New Mexico Press, 1940.

Twitchell, Ralph Emerson. *The Leading Facts of New Mexico History.* Two Volumes, Facsimile of 1911 edition. Santa Fe: Sunstone Press, 2007.

———. *The Military Occupation of the Territory of New Mexico from 1846 to 1851.* Facsimile of 1909 edition. Santa Fe: Sunstone Press, 2007.

———. *Old Santa Fe: The Story of New Mexico's Ancient Capital.* Facsimile of 1925 edition. Santa Fe: Sunstone Press, 2007.

———. *The Spanish Archives of New Mexico.* Two Volumes. Facsimile of 1914 edition. Santa Fe: Sunstone Press, 2008.

Weber, David J. *On the Edge of Empire: The Taos Hacienda of los Martínez.* Santa Fe, NM: Museum of New Mexico Press,1996.

———. *The Mexican Frontier, 1821–1846: The American Southwest Under Mexico.* Albuquerque, NM: University of New Mexico Press, 1982.